A HISTORY OF PSYCHOLOGY

IN AUTOBIOGRAPHY

Volume VI

THE CENTURY PSYCHOLOGY SERIES

Kenneth MacCorquodale, Gardner Lindzey, and
Kenneth E. Clark

Editors

A HISTORY OF PSYCHOLOGY IN AUTOBIOGRAPHY

Volume VI

Edited by

Gardner Lindzey

HARVARD UNIVERSITY

Prentice-Hall, Inc., Englewood Cliffs, New Jersey

Library of Congress Cataloging in Publication Data

Main entry under title:

A History of psychology in autobiography.

(The International university series in psychology)
    Vols. 1-3 edited by Carl Murchisum; v. 4 edited by
E. G. Boring and others; v. 5 edited by E. G. Boring
and G. Lindzey; v. 6 edited by G. Lindzey.
    Vol. VI , published in The Century psychology series,
has imprint: Englewood Cliffs, N.J., Prentice-Hall.
    1. Psychology—History—Collected works.
2. Psychologists—Biography—Collected works.
I. Murchilsum, Carl Allanmore, 1887-   ed.
II.   Boring, Edwin Garrigues, 1886-   ed.
[DNLM: 1. Psychology—Biography—Periodicals.
2. Psychology—History—Periodicals. W1 H186]
BF105.H5   150'.92'2 [B]   30-20129
ISBN 0-13-392274-X

Printed in the United States of America

10 9 8 7 6 5 4 3 2 1

PRENTICE-HALL INTERNATIONAL, INC., LONDON
PRENTICE-HALL OF AUSTRALIA, PTY. LTD., SYDNEY
PRENTICE-HALL OF CANADA, LTD., TORONTO
PRENTICE-HALL OF INDIA PRIVATE LIMITED, NEW DELHI
PRENTICE-HALL OF JAPAN, INC., TOKYO

to

Edwin G. Boring

CONTENTS

Preface

History can be packaged in many forms. One of the most intimate and authentic of these is the autobiography. While events transcribed in this manner may suffer from the astigmatism imposed by personal needs and too little perspective, they are enormously enriched by the background factors and events in the writer's life that could only be known directly by him. Thus, if the autobiographer is willing, he can provide the student of history with information that is otherwise virtually unattainable. The articles in this volume, as in the other volumes in the series, vary substantially in terms of how much they reveal of the subjective determinants and personal experiences surrounding the development of individual careers and psychology itself. At their best, however, they document much that could not have been recovered from the objective record.

These autobiographies have a relatively long tradition—more than four decades—within the short-term field of psychology. Psychologists, as befits their position midway between the natural sciences and the humanities, typically have been ambivalent about examining their own past. Thus, it is not surprising that the series twice has had to be rescued from oblivion (first by Edwin G. Boring and subsequently by Boring and Gardner Lindzey jointly). For the moment the future of the series seems assured, and one might even speculate that the formation of a Division of the History of Psychology of the American Psychological Association suggests some amelioration in the characteristic reluctance of psychologists to be concerned with their origins.

Initial plans for this volume began in 1966, and the following year, upon publication of Volume V, the new editorial committee was formed. It was comprised of Edwin G. Boring, Gardner Lindzey, Gardner Murphy, Kenneth MacCorquodale, Roger Russell, and Seymour Wapner. Thus, its membership included several persons from the previous committee, including one member (Boring) who had served on the editorial committee of all five previous volumes, and two members who had previously contributed their autobiographies to the series (Boring and Murphy). Invitations began to be sent out in 1968, and most of the manuscripts were in hand by 1970. At the final stage we had fifteen firm acceptances and four somewhat ambiguous commitments. As it turned out, none of the ambiguities materialized, and two of our contributors who had made firm commitments found it necessary to withdraw very late in our arrangements.

Thus, the final volume contains only thirteen autobiographies rather than the fifteen we had intended.

The members of the editorial committee based their judgments concerning who should be invited to contribute on the impact or influence of the individual on American psychology. In spite of this somewhat chauvinistic criterion, several European psychologists and several nonpsychologists were extended invitations. We are happy that one of our autobiographies is by the distinguished social anthropologist Margaret Mead, who turns out to have had more than glancing contact with psychology and psychologists.

We are very pleased that once again the series includes contributions from psychologists outside of North America, and we only regret that they are not more numerous. Based on our limited experience with this volume, it appears that Europeans and psychoanalysts are less likely to agree to prepare an autobiography than are American, academic psychologists.

We deeply regret that Professor Edwin G. Boring died while this volume was being prepared. Not only had he been an active participant in the preparation of every volume in the series, but also it was his initial letter to Carl Murchison that led to establishing the series. In view of these circumstances it seems only proper that this volume be dedicated to Professor Boring.

One unusual feature of this book is that it includes the first "autonecrology," to use Boring's term, in the form of Professor Luria's autobiography. Professor Luria found himself unable to contribute to the previous volume but at Boring's invitation began at once to prepare an autobiography for the next volume to assure that he would be represented there even if he was no longer living. Happily, Professor Luria is still very much alive. Unfortunately three of our contributors, Clarence H. Graham, Jerzy Konorski and S. S. Stevens, died during the period following preparation of their autobiographies but prior to their publication. We have followed Professor Boring's precedent and invited a small number of persons who were unable to contribute to this volume to prepare, at their early convenience, autobiographies to be included in Volume VII.

The process of selecting contributors was essentially the same as that described in the preface to the previous volume, which is reprinted on the following pages. We also provided the contributors with the same guidelines for the preparation of their bibliographies. Once again the contributors have agreed that the modest royalties earned by this volume will go to the American Psychological Foundation.

Gardner Lindzey

Preface to Volume V

Autobiography improves with age as it ripens into history. When the first volume of *A History of Psychology in Autobiography* appeared in 1930 psychologists found it interesting. Its readers for the most part were familiar with the writings of the men and women who spoke through its pages; often they knew the biographers personally or had at least listened to them, and they profited from seeing how the owner of an important name regarded his own work and what importance he assigned to events that appeared to have shaped his life. When first written, these stories lay, nevertheless, almost in the present, for—except in the speculation about how childhood forms a man—an intellectual autobiography that covers forty years does not consider that it is speaking of the past until much later. Now, however, thirty years have gone by since those first three volumes of 1930-1936 were published, and the lives described in them are now history—recent history, to be sure, but long enough ago for psychologists to send their students to sense in these accounts the attitudes of an earlier generation and the atmosphere in which it thrived, the spirit of a time when psychology was smaller, less complex, and more intimate.

How the value of present effort increases with time becomes evident when one examines the table at the end of this preface. Of the fifty-eight psychologists who contributed to the first four volumes, only five are still living. Of the forty-three who wrote for the first three volumes, only one is left—Sir Frederic Bartlett. It is necessary to get these personal records before mortality intervenes, yet not before the lives described are approaching completion. The present committee has lost Heinz Werner, who died after accepting our invitation to contribute, but we are fortunate in being able to include Kurt Goldstein, who completed his biography before he died. Three other psychologists (Heymans, Höffding, de Sanctis) died before the volume containing their contributions could be published, and three others (Calkins, Zwaardemaker, Hull) died in the year of publication.

Yet all in all the great men and women of psychology have been a hardy lot. Of the fifty-four contributors who have passed on at the date of this writing, only one, Woodworth, reached the 90's. The youngest to die was Klemm at 54, and the next youngest was Franz at 59. The median age of these autobiographers at death is at present between 77 and 79, in between Drever and Terman. Two were in their 50's, eleven in their 60's, fifteen in their 70's, twenty-five in their 80's, and one in his 90's.

At the end of the 1920's, when the new historians of the still new psychology were complaining that insufficient information was available about the lives, and thus the motivations, of the eponyms whom it was their task to describe, the present series was begun by Carl Murchison and the Clark University Press. At the time, the committee asked that the contributors tell of the motivations that guided them in their professional careers, not fully realizing in the then unformed state of motivational psychology how little a man knows correctly of his own motivations. When, after a lapse caused first by the exhaustion of the pool of sufficiently mature prominent psychologists and then by the distraction of World War II, the project was revived twenty years later, the invitation was changed to stress conscious motivation less and the events of the life more. Here follows an excerpt from the Preface of Volume IV, published in 1952:

> The reader of this volume will see how much our autobiographers differ from one another in the nature of their efforts. Perhaps they differ most in the degree with which they find unity in their lives. Presumably every one of them would like to see his intellectual history as the evolution of a single purpose, for integrity is good and simplicity is elegant. No one, of course, fully succeeds in this undertaking, for the story of every life is constrained by the exigencies of its owner's environment.
>
> Some of these accounts are more intellectualistic than others, and it may be that they show the greater unity, either because some irrelevancies are omitted from the life history or because irrelevancies are actually, at least to a certain degree, omitted from the actual living. Other accounts are more environmentalistic, because social and institutional events and accidents have figured so largely in them. The environmentalistic autobiographer may have had a chief long-term goal, have pursued it, have achieved it with some fair degree of success, yet he may feel that the unforeseeable accidents of living have determined much of his life and have perhaps even altered his goal. The intellectualist, if such we may call him, may, on the other hand, have suffered disruption of plans less than his colleague, but it is probable that he has also been less interested in the effect of external forces upon himself.
>
> No one, not even the members of this group of distinguished psychologists, can hope to deal adequately with the springs of his motivation. What he tells about himself and what he shows about his values can, however, go far toward instructing the reader as to how human motive moves to make science progress. The accidents of living do not always seem irrelevant to progress when they operate in the manner shown in the pages of this book. Psychology in autobiography cannot be complete, but it can make a contribution to the history of psychology which is unique.

Here follows an excerpt from the invitation to contributors to the present volume. It is an extension and modification of the instruction for 1952.

> The important decisions in regard to the contents of your auto-biography are yours. We hope, however, that the document will devote some attention to the historical details of your life. In connection with the *facts of life*, we hope you will identify yourself with regard to such matters as place and date of birth, significant educational and professional experiences, and family. We are, of course particularly interested in the *intellectual and professional* aspects of your life as they have influenced and been influenced by events, ideas, and persons in and out of the field of psychology. Your perception of major developments and issues within psychology during your lifetime and your relation to these events will be of special importance. We should appreciate any discussion of your *feelings, motives, and aspirations* or of significant events that would increase the reader's understanding of you and your contributions to psychology. In brief, we are interested in your intellectual life history, but at the same time we feel that it should be illuminated by as much information about your personal background and inner motives as you are ready and able to divulge.

Considerable pressure has been put upon the committee to include a complete bibliography of the contributors. Complete bibliographies for such men as these would run from 100 to more than 500 citations apiece. Psychologists look wistfully at Murchison's *Psychological Register* of 1932 and hope for its updating, but neither that nor the inclusion of bibliographies here is practicable. The committee has space for only fifteen biographies of 12,000 words each, and it would have to decrease this number to add the bibliographies. Also, there would be duplication, for complete bibliographies are often published elsewhere for distinguished psychologists. The memoirs of academies sometimes include them. There are, moreover, already available some fairly complete bibliographies of psychologists whose publications have been listed in the *Psychological Index* and in *Psychological Abstracts* from 1894 to 1958; they are in the *Author Index* to those two serials published in four volumes in 1960 by G. K. Hall and Company of Boston.

Why are only Americans included as contributors in the present volume? The early volumes were divided approximately in the proportion of eight Americans to seven Europeans. Of course psychology was then and is even more now predominantly American; the language of this book is English and its character American. Nevertheless the present committee began with the expectation that its American character would be assured by our choosing those foreigners who had made an impression upon American thought in psychology, the Europeans or others who appeared as most important in the United States even if not in their own countries. We did indeed correspond with some Europeans and quite early met with two declinations, but the crucial desideratum that fixed our decision was the great scarcity of psychologists in Europe and elsewhere who had notably influenced the thinking of American psychologists, who had not already contributed to a previous volume, and who were over 60 years old. Let the critic who suspects us of xenophobia try naming a few psychologists, foreign to America, who meet these three specifications.

On the other hand, this committee, whose authority ceases with the publication of this volume, looks forward hopefully to a Volume VI that will again be truly international. With the multiplication of psychologists on six continents it becomes more difficult to choose the outstanding names than it was when psychology seemed limited to Western Europe, Great Britain, and America, but the discrimination should not be impossible.

In the first four volumes sixty-one psychologists were invited to contribute and only three declined (Cattell, Lashley, and Köhler). For the present volume eventually we asked twenty-two psychologists. Werner died. Three would have liked to participate but had too many commitments for even our deferred deadline. They thought that if they could be asked early for a Volume VI, they could accept. Three others declined for personal reasons.

The present committee was formed by accretion. The idea of reviving the series began with Lindzey, who secured the agreement of Appleton-Century-Crofts to undertake the publication. Boring, who has been on all five of the committees and had conducted the negotiation with President Jefferson of Clark University for the transfer of the rights from Clark University to Appleton-Century-Crofts, agreed to act as chairman if Lindzey would be Executive Officer. The Committee is grateful to President Jefferson and Clark University for relinquishing these rights in the interests of this historical and scientific enterprise. MacCorquodale was included because of his long association with Lindzey and Appleton-Century-Crofts in the editing of the Century Psychology Series. Wapner was a natural continuation of the Clark ancestry for the series. Werner at Clark had been a member of the previous committee. Newbrough and Sharp had on their own initiative been conducting a poll of psychologists to assess the desirability of reviving the series. Clearly it was best to fuse the two enterprises. The American Psychological Association was asked to sponsor the undertaking, as it had Volume IV, appointing a new committee if it deemed wise, but it declined, believing that the present committee did not need its help. Nevertheless we felt that our committee could profit from more intelligence, so we added Beach and Hobbs to our membership. This committee has prepared the present volume, but it is not self-perpetuating. We believe, however, that Lindzey will be an adequate care-taker for the interests of the series between volumes. Especially must we mention the indispensable assistance of Miss Leslie Segner in the final preparation of the manuscript for publication.

We thank the contributors. They will receive no royalties but we hope they find satisfaction in this bit of immortality that it is possible for us to give them. They have now gained posterity for an audience, and long years after they are gone they can still be speaking to the strange new psychologists who will be their intellectual descendants. The small royalties that accrue from the sales of this volume quite properly go to the American Psychological Foundation.

Frank A. Beach
  University of California
Edwin G. Boring, *Chairman*
  Harvard University
Nicholas Hobbs
  *George Peabody College for
    Teachers*
Gardner Lindzey, *Executive Officer*
  University of Texas

Kenneth MacCorquodale
  University of Minnesota
J. R. Newbrough
  *National Institute of Mental
    Health*
Joseph C. Sharp
  *Walter Reed Army Institute of
    Research*
Seymour Wapner
  Clark University

January 1967

Contributors to Volumes I-VI

Volume I

1930

J. M. Baldwin
M. W. Calkins
E. Claparède
R. Dodge
P. Janet
J. Jastrow
F. Kiesow
W. McDougall
C. E. Seashore
C. Spearman
W. Stern
C. Stumpf
H. C. Warren
T. Ziehen
H. Zwaardemaker

Volume II

1932

B. Bourdon
J. Drever
K. Dunlap
G. C. Ferrari
S. I. Franz
K. Groos
G. Heymans
H. Höffding
C. H. Judd
C. L. Morgan
W. B. Pillsbury
L. M. Terman
M. F. Washburn
R. S. Woodworth
R. M. Yerkes

Volume III

1936

J. R. Angell
F. C. Bartlett
M. Bentley
H. A. Carr
S. De Sanctis
J. Fröbes
O. Klemm
K. Marbe
G. S. Myers
E. W. Scripture
E. L. Thorndike
J. B. Watson
W. Wirth

Volume IV

1952

W. V. D. Bingham
E. G. Boring
C. L. Burt
R. M. Elliott
A. Gemelli
A. Gesell
C. L. Hull
W. S. Hunter
D. Katz
A. Michotte
J. Piaget
H. Piéron
C. Thomson
L. L. Thurstone
E. C. Tolman

xvii

Volume V	Volume VI
1966	1973
G. W. Allport	F. H. Allport
L. Carmichael	F. A. Beach
K. M. Dallenbach	R. B. Cattell
J. F. Dashiell	C. H. Graham
J. J. Gibson	E. R. Hilgard
K. Goldstein	O. Klineberg
J. P. Guilford	J. Konorski
H. Helson	D. Krech
W. R. Miles	A. R. Luria
G. Murphy	M. Mead
H. A. Murray	O. H. Mowrer
S. L. Pressey	T. M. Newcomb
C. R. Rogers	S. S. Stevens
B. F. Skinner	
M. S. Viteles	

A HISTORY OF PSYCHOLOGY
IN AUTOBIOGRAPHY

Volume VI

Elsie & Roland Wolfe Studio

Floyd H. Allport

According to my mother's statement I was born on August 22, 1890, in Milwaukee, Wisconsin. Though my elder brother's birth eighteen months earlier had been duly registered in that city, no record exists of mine. My brother Gordon, whose autobiography appears in Volume V of this series, has described our early life and home environment in some detail; hence I shall add only a few personal recollections. I, too, recall our father as a man of considerable energy, engaged in many ventures besides the practice of his profession of medicine, and deeply devoted to the care of his family and the Gospel of "hard work." Upon retrospect I have felt, however, that there was usually something that was not merely prudential, but imaginative and creative, in his approach to his various enterprises.

I must have reacted differently from Gordon to what I felt to be the rather heavy religious influence in our early life. Our maternal grandmother had been one of the founders of the Free Methodist Church in Fulton, New York, and my mother had fallen heir to much of the piety of her parents. During my childhood and adolescence there were many revivals, camp meetings, and the like which we attended. Though in later years my mother became considerably more liberal, philosophical, and even critical of much of the traditional ideology, I felt, in these earlier days, a considerable intensity in her desire that I have some form of personal religious experience. I went through one or two such crises, being "converted" and then feeling much let down when the emotional fervor had passed. No doubt this experience has had some bearing on my attitudes in adult years. Later when I went to college, we would have long and friendly arguments concerning science and religion. I do not wish to exaggerate the importance of this background. On the whole, our home was a peaceful but sheltered place with kindness exhibited on every hand. To both my parents I owe a profound debt of gratitude for their fine influence upon my life. From both of them I derived a deep and lasting sense of curiosity and interest in nature.

After graduating from Glenville High School I went to Harvard College, taking my A.B. degree in 1914, but as with the class of 1913. Two or three years after graduation I returned for graduate work, obtaining for this purpose graduate fellowships or assistantships first in anthropology and then in psychology. The entrance of the United States into World War I interrupted this program. I went to Plattsburgh Training Camp and received a commission as

3

second lieutenant in Field Artillery. In October 1917, three days before our regiment and the Yankee Division were due to leave for France, I was married.

My war experience gained in two sectors of the French Front, where I served as assistant regimental adjutant, was on the whole uneventful. The following summer I was sent back to this country to serve as instructor at Camp Jackson in South Carolina. The wartime episode that stands out most vividly in my recollection was an incident that occurred during the time when I was assigned to a French observation balloon company. On my first balloon flight, with the Commandant, the balloon was attacked by German artillery fire and I jumped in a parachute, landing safely behind the lines. Though my family have tried to make something of this, there was absolutely nothing heroic about it. It was merely a matter of saving my own skin under the orders of the French Commandant, who also jumped. Though I received a Croix de Guerre and citation from the French Corps d'Armée, I soon learned that this was a routine procedure. Following a round of champagne drinking at the Officers Mess, which was the traditional ceremony after such episodes, I felt none the worse for the slight shaking up I had received. I have had a persistent fear of heights and high places all through my adult life. Friends have said that it is probably due to this balloon experience. I rather doubt this, but will concede that I was somewhat foolish to have volunteered for that assignment and that in the end it probably did me no good.

When the war was over I returned and took up my graduate studies where I had left off, wrote my doctoral thesis, and in June 1919 received the Ph.D. degree. My wartime marriage to Ethel Margaret Hudson, my first wife, had been undertaken in haste and was probably not well considered. It ended twenty years later in divorce, a fact which I attribute in no small measure to my own limitations. It would be unfair and ungrateful not to acknowledge that this marriage had some happier and rewarding moments. Among its assets were three fine children: Edward, Dorothy, and Floyd, all of whom are now married to persons of quality and ability; and I have two granddaughters, Karen and Evelyn (Edward's children), of whom I am justly proud.

In 1938 I had the rare good fortune to marry Helene Hartley (née Willey), my colleague and a professor of Education and English at Syracuse University. She was one of the national leaders in her field and a most creative teacher. Her charm and richness of personality, her deep interest and understanding of the problems in which I was engaged, and her loyalty and devotion in helping me to make those years productive have been inestimable assets. Her death in 1965 left me desolate.

A PERSONALITY APPRAISAL

In autobiographical accounts such as this, it has not been customary for the writer to begin by listing what he considers to be his salient characteristics. Since space is here so limited, however, and because I have felt that what I have to relate can best be understood only in the light of this context, I venture to begin with such an inventory. Not long ago my brother Gordon was visiting us in California. At the breakfast table my wife took the occasion to recount to him what she considered to be certain of my "fine qualities." After her lengthy eulogistic recital my brother looked up and without a moment's hesitation added: "And is he still stubborn, lazy, and procrastinating?" Aside from the fact that they were delivered by a master of the science of personality traits, what startled and dismayed me most about these words was the glibness with which he uttered them, not needing to pause for a moment's thought or recollection. Upon thinking back upon my life, and in the writing of this memoir, I have been impressed with the fact that for each of these characteristics he was probably right. However, I do have certain other attendant characteristics which my brother would undoubtedly have admitted. The trait of stubbornness referred to has shown itself in many ways. One of these has been to accept nothing on faith, but to carry forward an analysis and examination of every point to the bitter end. A critic of one of my works has referred to what he called "Allport's excruciating logic." One particularly perverse tendency was my continual effort to avoid what I called, to my wife's great amusement, a "panic of certainty." In keeping with this trait I have failed to show even a decent regard for traditional beliefs and conventions. I escaped being brought to task for these attitudes largely because of the fact that I was reclusive by nature, and did not mingle much with colleagues or associates. Combined with the foregoing traits, I have had my full share of ambition and ego-striving and, as will be later seen, a quite unrealistic aspiration level.

On the good side of the ledger (at least what I consider to be the good side), I believe I can claim a steadfast drive toward personal and intellectual honesty and, above all, an intense, almost burning, curiosity about nature. The latter trait took the form of an impelling desire to gain new truths in and for themselves, and quite apart from any humanistic presuppositions, or from any utilitarian value. This search for as complete an objectivity as it is possible for human beings to attain in questions concerning life and their own natures, a quest that has been pursued with a fervor that might seem almost fanatical, has played an undimished part in my intellectual motivation. I recall an instance in a biology course I was taking at Harvard in which the students were required to draw from dissection the anatomy of a dogfish. The professor, probably noting that some were producing rather elegant drawings, was cautioning us against putting an artistic emphasis ahead of a scrupulous fidelity to facts. "Of course," he added, "you know the fish is right." This phrase has stuck with me throughout the years. On another occasion I recall seeing a news headline at a time when an astronomical occurrence was expected. It read, "Eclipse Arrives Twenty Seconds Late." Instead of my taking this in the jocose way in which it was intended, and in which most persons would have accepted it, it seemed to me a repelling instance of human smugness and conceit. Expressions of this sort have always seemed to arouse in me the same feeling that irreverence or sacrilege might in a devoutly religious person. Perhaps such a feeling *is* my religion.

ACADEMIC BEGINNINGS

For one who, like myself, was always trying to reach answers by unfamiliar routes of his own choosing, Harvard was in my day an ideal place. The eclectic system instituted by President Eliot gave the student ample opportunity for the choice of courses and the pursuit of his special interests. But for the same reason it lacked (for me) certain necessary elements of discipline and a proper preparation for my later career. Too often I found myself studying against as well as with my professors. In my graduate work, as well as undergraduate, I suffered from an inadequacy of supervision and an excess of freedom.

The men on the Harvard faculty in psychology who influenced me most were H. S. Langfeld, E. B. Holt, and R. B. Perry. Perry I admired particularly for his clear thinking and careful organization of his lectures. At that time the philosophy and psychology departments were combined in a single division. On the whole I found the ideas of such philosophically oriented professors as Munsterberg, Hocking, and McDougall uncongenial to my line of thinking since they seemed to me to lack a suitable criterion and basis in physical reality. Santayana, also, was there for one year before his retirement. I tried his course, but found that I could not follow it. I was no doubt a thorn in the flesh of most of the members of the philosophy department with whom I was associated both as a student and later as an instructor in the division. I remember that at the close of one afternoon session (a seminar or a doctoral examination) we were discussing certain matters relating to logic and behaviorism. As the meeting was breaking up I asserted that it seemed to me that the reason why up and down were "logical" opposites was because no one had ever succeeded in moving any object (for example, his hand) up and down at the same time. Whereupon Professor Hocking, staunch idealist that he was, snorted as he strode out of the room.

I sensed considerable tension overt or covert in those days between the top floor of Emerson Hall, where psychology, and particularly E. B. Holt, were housed, and the domain of the philosophers on the first floor. I was exposed to Holt's brilliant cynicism in his course on the History of Psychology, and from him I derived the notion of circular reflexes that I incorporated in my *Social Psychology* (see Holt, 1931). In the prewar years one of my duties was to serve as assistant to Langfeld in his introductory experimental course at Harvard and Radcliffe, and in 1916 I collaborated with him in the production of a manual entitled *An Elementary Laboratory Course in Psychology*. Later, during the years 1919-1922, I had the title of instructor and taught some classes of my own.

From among the currents and undercurrents of psychology of that day, I seized onto behaviorism, which I made the basis of my textbook. Though my approach is still from that direction, I came later to see the excesses of Watsonian thinking and to realize that the notion of a stimulus and response, as then employed, was really a teleological concept in disguise. I was of course impressed by the novel findings and point of view of the gestalt psychologists, but I felt the doctrine of the whole being greater than (or even different from) the aggregate of its parts needed a much more explicit restatement and explanation. For a time I made some immature excursions into clinical psychology by way of psychoanalytic ideas. Functionalism in psychology, and philosophical pragmatism, were not to my liking.

One more personal recollection of these earlier days foreshadowing my later orientation should here be stated. I remember walking in the corridor of Emerson Hall and reflecting upon the complexities of the psychological facts which had been gained up to that time regarding memory, problem solving, perceiving, and the like. I was wondering what the underlying basis of all this could possibly be in the nervous system, cortex, or the whole physiology of the organism. Of course I was only one of many thousands who have entertained and pursued such an inquiry. Yet it seemed for me a question of the profoundest significance. It was the problem of psychology *par excellence,* capable perhaps of opening new vistas. I felt, and still feel, that relatively little progress can be made until we at least begin to solve it. The methodological doctrine of molarism, in which one stays on the outside and tries to interpret the organism by its behavior as a whole, a theory that was presently to come into full bloom in the works of Tolman and Hull and others, although it led to some useful results, has never seemed to me to hold the answers.

In 1922 the authorities at Harvard decided that a change was in order and they wanted particularly to bring Edwin G. Boring to the department. To make this possible, Langfeld was to be asked to go on half-time and I was to find a place elsewhere. McDougall was delegated to bring me the news. Langfeld rejected the suggestion and soon thereafter was appointed as Director of the Psychological Laboratory at Princeton, and I obtained a position as associate professor at the University of North Carolina. I spent two fairly pleasant years at Chapel Hill, where I profited greatly from the companionship of J. F. Dashiell, whom I always found to be both a scholar and a gentleman.

EARLIER THEORETICAL INTERESTS:
THE SOCIAL INFLUENCE—GROUP AND INDIVIDUAL

To return for a moment to my doctoral dissertation and its sequel, it was Hugo Munsterberg who had originally suggested to me as worthy of investigation the problem of the behavior of individuals acting alone versus their action together in groups. Previous studies on this problem in Germany and this country had indicated certain effects which we thought it might be well to follow up. I set up the experiment by having the subjects working at some simple psychological tasks in one set of trials alone and in separate rooms, giving them signals for timing that were needed by buzzers, and in the collective situation, in another set of trials, having them work on equivalent problems in groups. The groups ranged in number of subjects from three to seven or eight, and I gave them the time signals in person. Since I wanted to discover the effect from the basic standpoint of the mere presence of coworkers, no discussion of others or comparison of results was permitted. The subjects worked quite independently. An effort was also made to reduce any tendency toward rivalry to the very minimum. Though the controls in this experiment left something to be desired and I would perform the experiment differently today, the results seemed to show a true difference in the quantity of work done alone compared with that done together, the difference being in favor of the performance in the group. The quality of the work done in the group did not correspondingly improve, but in some instances deteriorated. Since there was a consistent increase in the amount of performance when working together, I formulated from these results the theoretical concept of "social facilitation," which was described as a tendency or *set* to perform with greater energy or intensity in the presence of others who are working at the same task. Another important finding was to the effect that in judging a series of stimuli such as, for example, the pleasantness of odors or the heaviness of weights, the subjects showed a marked tendency when working in the group to avoid the extremes at either end of the scale, thus making their judgments approach more closely, than when judging alone, to a horizontal distribution for the series. These findings were hypothetically generalized as an attitude of conformity, or "conformity-producing tendency," in the group situation. Later concepts that I introduced for theoretical purposes in my system were social projection, impression of universality, and pluralistic ignorance. These terms have now become familiar in social psychology.

By 1923 I had completed my textbook entitled *Social Psychology,* based in part upon my own findings and their interpretation as described above. In this book I strongly rejected the notion that there was some kind of "super" mental entity or "group mind" at work in such collective phenomena. I rejected also, later, the tendency to speak of groups themselves as per se entities or agencies. The effects of group or crowd influence, as well as organization, I attributed to the behavior solely of individuals. It was not, however, the behavior of individuals acting alone, but behavior that was natural to individuals when *acting under conditions that were specifically social.* Since these early experiments, the study of the effects of group conditions has become extended by others into a great range of behaviors and motivations of group members, and into a variety of circumstances of their association or affiliation. In my own work I have more recently experimented with the notion that nearly all this large, and at present somewhat formless, mass of findings that constitutes current social psychology is capable of being subsumed under a single more general formulation. Such a possibility has been implemented by an attempt to construct a tenable theory of collective structure, and has given rise in our researches at Syracuse University to what I have called a "structural dynamics" formula. This formula and the line of investigation on which it was based will be described later. I have assumed that the widespread attention which my textbook *Social Psychology* (which has been recently reprinted) has received was due mainly to two novel features. First, it was an objectively conceived and somewhat systematic presentation of the subject from the psychological rather than the sociological point of view; and second, it suggested at least by implication the possibility of a new experimental science of social psychology.

THE MAXWELL SCHOOL AND LIFE AT SYRACUSE

In the fall of 1924, through the recommendation of Franklin H. Giddings, I received an appointment to the faculty of Syracuse University as a member of the newly organized Maxwell Graduate School of Citizenship and Public Affairs. I was given the title of Professor of Social and Political Psychology. In this position I remained until my retirement in 1957. Since the Maxwell School has been principally an institution for graduate study in the social sciences and public administration, I was, in this environment, somewhat isolated from contact with experimental psychology and my psychological colleagues. I was, however, a regular member of the Psychology Department and carried on undergraduate teaching as well as the training of graduate students in social psychology along definitely psychological lines. This arrangement was in many respects a happy one. It gave me maximum freedom and considerable material assistance in pursuing my research interests, with a teaching schedule that was made increasingly light.

I believe that I was a good classroom teacher, though I am sure there were times when I would launch on some line of speculation intriguing mainly to me personally. It was said by students that there were times when "Allport goes out of the window." As a saving grace, however, it was also added that "he's worth waiting for when he comes back." I taught a seminar each year in methods and the theory of structure which I always enjoyed. Concerning my work in the coaching of graduate students in their doctoral and masters' dissertations, there is one point that should be borne in mind since it relates so closely to my own productivity. Instead of turning the students loose on the problem selected, to develop it for themselves, and then occasionally checking on their progress and the results, I worked in close touch with them continually. The spade work, of course, was left to the student, but the student was also in effect a partner in an experiment which I had helped largely to conceive and design. The result was that the dissertations produced have had to stand, in part, as a professional outlet for myself as well as for the accrediting of students for degrees. I realized that there was an element of selfishness here in that my own theoretical interests were likely to predominate over the opportunity given for the student's independent development. I am not defending this practice, which was due largely to my own eagerness to discover new facts at first hand. In extenuation, I believe it is fair to say that the students did gain something through an increased sense of the meaningfulness of the problems on which they were engaged, as well as in sharing the excitement of their solution. I did not have many graduate students at one time, otherwise such a method of working would have been impossible.

Largely because of my own tendencies, my long tenure at Syracuse University was somewhat secluded. I did not attend many scientific meetings or take many opportunities to travel and meet other psychologists, a fact which I later regretted. There was, however, a one semester's sabbatical leave abroad. On one or two occasions in my life I have suffered from spells of nervous depression, which, however, were fairly soon overcome. On the brighter side, in addition to the happiness I derived from my second marriage, two very pleasant recollections of this period stand out. One of these is the memory of summers or parts of summers spent at Mexico Point on Lake Ontario with family and friends, both academic and nonacademic. The other concerns my adventures, in the years between 1931 and 1948, in the field of watercolor painting. During this time I produced a series of colorful scenes of central New York which now decorate my apartment. I was also president, for one year, of our local art society, the Associated Artists of Syracuse. In this connection I must record my lasting gratitude to my old friend and teacher, Severin Bischof. It was he who suggested that I try to paint, and through companionship on painting trips opened up to me this whole realm of creativeness and beauty.

EARLIER RESEARCH AT SYRACUSE

In discussing my productive work at Syracuse University I would like to divide it into two parts. The first represents the period from 1925 to 1937, when a number of diverse problems were pursued. The second part, though it began in earnest about 1937, had its actual start much earlier, and constitutes what has been my major theme throughout my professional life. One of the first projects of the earlier period was the carrying out, with Daniel Katz, of a very extensive questionnaire study of the attitudes, opinions, and academic motivation of the Syracuse students. This study aroused considerable interest among those engaged in the investigation of attitudes, and parts of it have been repeated by others in other contexts. Katz, who was one of my earliest graduate students, has been a true friend to me through the years and a resource on many occasions. The work on attitudes and opinions was extended also into other fields. A rather crude technique for measuring attitudes was developed by Dale Hartman and myself, and applied to the problem of measuring tendencies toward conservativism and radicalism. These early attempts were graciously acknowledged by Thurstone as a starting point in developing his classical attitude-scaling methods. During the latter years of World War II my graduate group constituted a "Morale Seminar."

Problems investigated included the reason for belief in subversive rumors, the impact of Axis propaganda upon listeners, and the comparative effect of good and bad news headlines upon the reader's morale.

About 1930 Richard L. Schanck, then my student, was collecting opinions on various social questions in the rural community of Eaton, New York. He discovered that attitudes on these questions were by no means normally distributed on the scales employed, as we had at first expected they would be, but were often widely skewed or irregular (Schanck, 1932). It also made a difference in the distribution whether the question was asked as in a private setting or in reference to a broader community context (Schanck's "public and private attitudes"). These unexpected findings suggested an idea that led me to the development of my J-curve Hypothesis of Conforming Behavior. In this theory I attempted to describe a curve that our findings proved to be characteristic of distributions of attitudes or behaviors in situations of public opinion, practices of customs, and institutionalized performance generally. The theory went further in developing a technique for measuring the conformity exhibited in each case upon a scale, not of conformity itself, which would have amounted to a tautology, but upon a continuum representing the degree of attainment of some purpose that the "custom" or "institution" could commonly be said to sulfill. Such a construct was called a telic continuum. A "four factor" hypothesis was advanced as to the causes of such distributions in a population. Quite a range of conforming situations in various institutional practices were described, yielding such J-curve distributions. Milton Dickens, in his doctoral dissertation on traffic behavior, Basia Zambrowski, who observed church and religious observances, and others, contributed much to this study. A particularly interesting investigation was conducted considerably later by Chiang Lin Woo and myself dealing with the J-curve distribution of observed behavioral acts in seven American male custom situations. The J-curve studies, published in a number of papers, have enlisted considerable interest among social psychologists and sociologists and have been quoted in a number of texts.

I have felt that these studies have not been fully appreciated owing to the fact that the figures were sometimes construed as depictions of conformity directly. The fact that the steps of the scales in nearly all cases represented a continuum expressing degrees of fulfillment of the *purpose* of the custom or institution (from the greatest to the least fulfillment) not only exhibited the distribution of conformity and made it possible to measure it in a particular situation but (most important of all) it afforded a better understanding of its probably underlying dynamic. These facts relieved the procedure of the charge of tautology.

Another topic pursued vigorously for a time was the study of personality conceived not under the familiar concept of "traits," but pursuant to a new formulation which I called "trends." These were also called "teleonomic trends" in keeping with an earlier paper I had written. This approach differed from that of my brother in that I attempted to make a sharp distinction between characteristics as they are socially observed, or appraised in practical life, and the deeper tendencies actually representing what the individual is *characteristically trying to do* throughout his daily behavior. It was my thesis that these latter aspects, if we could identify them, and perhaps find the basis for them in the organism, would be recognized as the true individual motivating factors. The "personality" of the individual as ordinarily perceived by his associates under the "trait" concept, or "outer" social frame of reference, would then represent a partial transformation of these *trend* characteristics. The observer would perceive the expression of the trend in a different, socially relevant or normative, context. A significant piece of research designed to test this hypothesis will be described later.

It should be pointed out that my brother undoubtedly had a feeling for this aspect of personality and that the characteristics I had termed "trends" may have found a place in the revision of his textbook under the heads of personal dispositions (as distinguished from common traits), cardinal dispositions, and the unity of personality. He did not, however, make the sharp distinction of methodology which, by enlisting the change of attitude or set of the observer in describing the personality, reveals "trend descriptions" as distinct from "trait descriptions." He seemed to reject such an idea. To me it seemed important because I conceived of the "arena" for trait description or appraisal (that is, for common traits ascribed to the personality by associates) as implemental to a kind of "collective structuration" which the individual is *in* while the trend picture would be what we would see for the same individual if we should look for more intimate concerns that lie *within him.* Although some very good work on trait-trend theory was done by my students, I regret that much of it has not been published. Perhaps the fact that I have been remiss in pressing for its publication is an instance of my own trait (not trend) of procrastination.

I would like to insert, parenthetically, the fact that although I have been aiming toward a formulation of psychology and social behavior that would be more objective than such implicit notions of purposes or values by which traits or trends have been defined, there was little possibility of doing so in these earlier approaches. What I did endeavor to do was to make "teleonomic" variables more explicit in such a way that they could be quantified and used in testable hypotheses.

Let me digress for a moment to discuss some other phases of my relationship to Gordon. In addition to the interpretation of personality characteristics there were a few more points in social psychology upon which we did not see eye to eye. One of these concerned the nature of attitudes. This will be evident from an investigation to be described later. Another concerned the relation between interethnic hostility and prejudice. He was at the time writing his book *The Nature of Prejudice.* In our correspondence I suggested that the nature of "conflict," or "hostility," between ethnic groups might provide a better start, because prejudice often seems to grow out of such a conflict. He replied firmly that his book was not about conflict; it was about prejudice. A little later, after the book appeared, I questioned the importance of the scapegoat hypothesis in the light of some of our findings at Syracuse University. In her study, using careful and discriminating methods, Nancy Morse (now Mrs. Hans Samelson) had found that out of seven hypotheses the element of projection of one's own frustrations or inner conflicts upon the out-group had relatively minor significance in explaining anti-Semitism. (See Morse and Allport, F. H., 1952.) There was some interchange of correspondence between Gordon and me on this subject.

What Morse actually found was that the only one of her hypotheses which produced a substantial correlation with attitudes of anti-Semitism was national loyalty and a feeling of involvement in, or identification with, the nation. Discussing this finding in a later publication, my brother interpreted it as meaning that the kind of individual who would be this closely involved with national feeling would be likely also to be the one having an authoritative or bigoted personality. I felt that this interpretation was gratuitous and that it unfairly sabotaged my position. Although I agree that personality differences would be expected to play their part in these feelings of animosity or prejudice toward other peoples and also that they may sometimes be associated with nationalistic feelings, it has seemed to me that the phenomenon has also a deeper meaning in the involvement of individuals in a long-standing "collective structure," a structure in which they play a part and have their *modus vivendi,* and which (rightly or wrongly) they may be perceiving as potentially threatened by the members of an out-group. To infer that personality traits are the *causes* of *both* the nationalistic involvement and the ethnic hostility seems to me a long-range assumption. It overlooks the part which national involvement *per se* may be playing. For whatever else they may be, nations also consist, at least in part, of the behaviors of individuals and must somehow be related to their motivations. To neglect this fact, or to gloss over it by the assumption that the nation is a *super* individual entity to which individuals merely "belong," might be to fail to examine some of the very data which provide or constitute the phenomenon of ethnic prejudice itself. In so doing should we not be relinquishing, to that extend, our claim to being social *scientists?*

This was the challenge which, as pertaining not only to nations but to social aggregates generally, I have long been holding out to my colleagues in psychology and the social sciences.

Such instances of disagreement between Gordon and me were, however, quite unusual. I mention them only to bring out certain characteristic differences of viewpoint. Many of his intuitions, so vividly expressed, were in one way or another definitely in the direction of ideas which I had been trying to develop. This was true of his notions of personal dispositions, cardinal characteristics, and congruence in personality, and also regarding the nature of rumor and his significant treatment of "becoming." (See Allport, G. W., 1954, 1955, and 1961.) I believe that later generations of psychologists will owe him a great debt for so well establishing the consistent, autonomous, unique, and dynamically congruent nature of individual human characteristics. From a personal standpoint he helped me in many ways and stood by me in many crises. On my sixtieth birthday I received from him a warm letter of appreciation recalling what he felt that I had done for him as a younger brother in the earlier years. Unfailingly kind, he possessed a sweetness, an inner serenity, and faith in ultimates which I could not achieve; and these qualities contributed a poise and a kind of robustness to his character that were in part instrumental in his success. At his death the world lost a wise and profound scholar and a truly great person.

THE SEARCH FOR
COLLECTIVE AND INDIVIDUAL REALITY

To turn now to my research interests since 1937, which form a more or less connected story, we must go back actually before that date (and before the period we have been discussing) to my early years in Emerson Hall, my dissertation, and my textbook, of 1924. I remember that I pondered long over the experimental results I had obtained at that time. How were they to be explained? There seemed clear evidence of an increase in speed and energy of intellectual and manual activities when working in the presence of other coworking subjects. But what seemed especially remarkable was that such effects occurred when the individuals in no way communicated or took any note of what their neighbors were doing. The thought of interindividual comparisons or tendency toward rivalry had been eliminated or reduced to a minimum. Yet, under these silent and somewhat withdrawn circumstances here was clear evidence of social influence. Quite remarkable also seemed the finding that in the task of judging a series of objective stimuli when the judgments were made in a group, in spite of no communication or cognizance of how the others were reacting, the judgments ranged less widely in the extreme portions of the scale than when they were made by the subjects working alone. How were these effects to be explained? Clearly, there must have been something going on in the social context that was different from what was happening when the subjects acted alone. This was no doubt an experience of "social reality" of some sort; but common sense seemed to require that this experience had its location and operation in *individuals.*

All these effects I finally attributed to some sort of characteristic attitudes (perhaps set is a better term) which individuals adopt largely unconsciously when they perform similar activities in one another's presence. They seem to be reacting as though they were communicating with others about their work and receiving communications from others, though in fact they were not. There seemed to be a sense that "others are working so I must work too," or that "others are judging these same stimuli so I must be careful not to make atypical or extreme judgments about them." There thus appeared to be among the subjects a prevailing heightened sensitivity in regard to what the others were doing in these common acts. This sensitivity seemed to lie next door to a generalized "attitude of conformity."

I recall meeting Sherif not long after this at the International Congress of Psychology in Copenhagen. He had recently been doing his experiments on the autokinetic effect, or judgment of the extent of the imaginary movement of a point of light seen in a dark room. His subjects, however, in contrast with mine had expressed their judgments audibly; so that when they worked together they were aware of one another's reactions. Half of these subjects started in the solitary judging situation, passing in later sessions to the group condition; and half started in the group and later passed to the individual or solitary. The subjects who started alone and later moved to the group condition came closer in their judgments as soon as they were placed in the latter situation. This convergence continued or increased in later coworking situations. Those who started in the group condition were fairly close together *at the start* and remained so during ensuing sessions. In these procedures the results obtained were thus essentially similar to mine. The social influence (as we may call it) whether introduced at the start of a work program or later regularly produces an increase in the convergence or conformity of the behavior of those concerned.

Sherif assured me, however, that my interpretation of the results had been wrong. He was at that time developing his well-known theory of social norms. In this theory it is maintained that in an unstructured group or stimulus situation a "norm" of behavior or perception regularly arises with respect to whatever task is being performed. The effect of such a norm also lasts for an appreciable time. It is commonly accepted that this norm has the effect of stabilizing and unifying behavior in the group. Notwithstanding my great respect for Sherif and admiration of his brilliance in devising social experiments, in this case I preferred *my* interpretation of the conformity situation as earlier presented. The idea of a "group norm" of perception or judgment arising from and controlling the collective behavior of individuals as if from above seemed to me unrealistic. It may be objected that by social norm Sherif did not mean anything so mystical as this. That is probably so, but by the same token are we not then left with *no* explicit statement of what a social norm is—a statement that can be linked up with some definite aspects of behavior. A social norm seems to me to be a kind of statistical label. It is a designation of what is acceptable, rather than a force or determining principle governing the behavior in conforming to the norm.

The critical position I had thus taken regarding the social influence led me to a further attack upon doctrines of social causality. I was not attacking the evident truth they contain but the failure to give them more specific meaning. I was impressed by the fact that much of the terminology and conceptualization used in the social sciences was really in terms of personification or other collective metaphors. The notion of what the "government" does or of the "acts of a corporation or nation" and the like were to me merely blanket terms useful in practical life, but were they not by the same token at times confusing or concealing? The terms for agencies implied by these phrases have no explicitly denotable referents; and when we look at individuals no one of them can be described in a self-sufficient way as doing exactly the things stated. What was needed, in my view, was a science that would describe what was happening in these situations in generalized *yet explicit* terms. It will of course be objected that these myriad patternings of collective behavior of individuals are so vast, varied, and complex that they cannot be described in terms of empirical science but only in the implicit terms of collective entities and their functions or purposes. Without such group or institutional fictions, social science could not be written. To this I have replied: "How can we know that this is so until we really try?" Those interested in reviewing the trend of this controversy can follow its development in the items marked (*) in the list of References.

It should be apparent that my polemic against group fictions and "collective" agencies was not destined to enhance my popularity with my colleagues in the social sciences, including those in the Maxwell School. It was said by some that I had an "institutional complex" and was fighting a straw man. I became known as the whipping boy of the sociologists. The climax came when I was publicly denounced in an address made by the President of the American Sociological Society at their annual meeting. I was not present, but the affair was related to me by a friend who reported the speaker's statement as follows. He said that in the Middle Ages people got to quoting Aristotle so vigorously, and sometimes to so little purpose, that someone had to rise up and say "There's no truth in Aristotle." "So now," he continued, "I say there is no truth in Floyd Allport." At this point, as he made a sweeping gesture, his hand struck a glass chandelier, sending the pieces flying about the room. When I heard this I confess I was so thrilled by the company with which I had been so dramatically classed that I quite overlooked the point the speaker was trying to make.

My crusade for greater realism in the definition of social phenomena came to a head with the publication in 1933 of my *Institutional Behavior*. By this time I had come through my period of "pure individual determinism" I had espoused in my *Social Psychology*, a view which sociologists had rightly criticized as slighting the actual social reality. I had by now become fully aware of such an aspect, though I was by no means ready, nor am I ready now, to capitulate to the inadequate formulations that I had been criticizing. There was however growing on me an implicit, only dimly realized, sense of an "interstructuring" of individuals' behaviors and attitudes of which I had had an earlier inkling in connection with my group-influence studies. One must not take the term "structuring" too literally nor form for it mystical connotations that would only lead us again astray. But still there was "something there." For one thing it was manifested not only in the more subjective phases which philosophers had called "social" or "collective consciousness," but indubitably and forcibly in the type of structure that is represented by division of effort, social "roles," and the inescapable institutional nexuses of behaviors in which an individual, once these behaviors have become stabilized, is destined to live, and from which he cannot escape. Adequately to characterize and understand these situations with respect to individuals' lives now became for me the great *desideratum*.

In *Institutional Behavior* I made what was scarcely even a beginning by combining my critique of group hypostatization and the fictions connected therewith with an analysis of more substantive aspects. I called attention to the ways in which institutional behaviors, in spite of their generally conceded necessity and the benefits they had brought to mankind, were also capable of submerging individuality, reducing responsibility through "pluralistic insouciance" or impotence in the face of societal crises. They were also prone to the exclusion or alienating of many individuals or classes in the population. I carried this analysis through the current political, economic, religious, familial, and educational scenes. I was here pleading no cause nor advocating a change to any new form of institution, but was in effect questioning the efficacy of institutions as such. I offered no solutions for these problems, for I did not have any. However, I was certainly making no appeal for the elimination of such societal realities—that is, for anomie or anarchy.

Neither social students nor the public were prepared for such a book nor for the sweeping appraisal it contained. There was the additional fact that it was written at a perturbed and difficult period of my life, was at times exaggerated, one-sided, or emotional in tone, and contained some statements to which I would not now subscribe. Though the book itself met with early oblivion, I now believe that in it I had provided an inkling or forecast of much that we see today. This is indicated in the rise of an acute nationalism, in international conflicts and tensions, in rapid technological and automated expansion, in the breakdown of family relations and rise of a women's "lib" movement, in educational upheavals, and in institutional religion. What I did not foresee was that the onslaught on supposedly settled institutions (known as the "establishment") would come so soon and with such intensity from the action of the alienated segments including (tragically) many of the youth.

Not long after this book was written there came a turning point in my theoretical outlook. It was not really a turning point so much as a broadening of my inquiry. It was a pushing of my questioning back into the problems that plagued me in my earlier days in Emerson Hall, and a renewal of my persistent curiosity about the organism. One of my more thoughtful critics wrote me in substance as follows: "You'd better be careful how you attack the group concept or use the term 'group fallacy.' Is not the individual also simply an integration of many parts or processes which often cannot be explained or spelled out in detail. In your attacks on 'group fictions' you may also be selling the individual short." It struck me that this critic was absolutely right. The effect, however, was not that of making me give up my criticism of group concepts, but of leading me to include the nature of the individual also in my search for basic realities. From about 1937 on I took upon myself this almost incredible task. Since I had construed the social problem under a vague concept, "interindividual structuring," I sought to develop a general theory of "structure in nature," both individual and collective. The situation within individuals was to be explained in terms of "structures of events" within the organism, involving happenings in the nervous or neuromotor system, or throughout the body. The collective structurings, that is, the structures the individual is *in,* were conceived as lying in the outer contacts or events *between* individuals. Of course, they always *involved* the overt actions of individuals and beneath or accompanying these the complementary structurings of the first type, namely the covert nexus of neurophysiological or psychological events within the individual. The general format, or principles of structuring, was hypothetized to be the same at the two levels. This idea was not peculiar to me, but was implied both in the earlier analogies of the "social organism" and sophisticated theories such as the "general systems" view. Such a theory would of course have to embrace not only facts of the social and psychological disciplines, but would have to reach down into the biological, biochemical, and even physical levels. It must seem presumptuous and foolhardy indeed for any one person to undertake so vast a problem, let alone a psychologist who had no particular competence in some of the disciplines involved. Nevertheless, that is the course to which I set myself. As it has developed, I have called the theory by a variety of names, such as effect system, event system, event structure theory, and, more recently, enestruence.

It is only natural that with so little that was intelligible published, and with so long a time elapsing as it was developing, the nature of this ambitious program has not been well understood. Since I was now talking in terms of structures that seemed to "transcend" individuals, some of my erstwhile critics declared that I had made an about-face change. To admit any such form of social reality, it was said, was to belie my earlier statement that everything "social" could be explained wholly in terms of individuals, a change that canceled a lifetime of work under the latter concept. This statement is quite inaccurate. In the first place, after 1927, when the first three or four of my papers had appeared, I did not make any such statements implying the all-sufficiency of purely individual processes in explaining social phenomena. I soon came to see that in my book on social psychology I had not been sufficiently cognizant of the problem posed by what the sociologists were calling the "social reality," nor was I sufficiently appreciative of their efforts to solve it. All my work, both experimental and theoretical, after 1927 reflects the fact that I, too, was aware of this problem and was trying to help toward its solution. Perhaps I can best present the issue here involved by showing it in the light of the hierarchy of the sciences. It is a generally recognized fact that when a scientist approaches any given level of nature with a certain degree of fineness in his "grain of perception" or his manipulation, he will be likely to observe or encounter some kind of object appropriate to that degree of fineness of his observation. Should he refine his methods further, as by using a more powerful microscope or finer denotation, these objects will break down to smaller objects, and it is realized that it is these smaller entities whose interactions have really constituted what was seen under the coarser view. There is thus in each case an "outer" level or view and an "inner" level or view; and vice versa as we make our grain of observation coarser. This account is characteristic at all levels as we progress toward the outside view from the electron or the atom up through molecule, organelle, and organ system to the organism. When, however, we try to pass from this last level up to that of social phenomenon and seek to describe its "outside" identity, a strange thing happens. We find that the societal entity *has no outside!* Even if we should greatly coarsen our grain by observing from the viewpoint of an astronaut, we still could not identify it (or any subcollectivity within it) from an outside view. Societal phenomena are too implicit to be "encountered," too closely bound up with the meanings and actions of individuals. They consist of the interactions of such behaviors and the patternings that appear among them. But in my view, this interpretation is not tantamount to a denial of social reality; it is the realm of social reality. To this picture we should have to add the machines and modern technology, both material and semantic; but there is still no "outside" identity to what we see. What I had been criticizing was the practice of inventing for this reality an outside or molar aspect, or giving it a "body" where none exists, by the use of terms signifying collective beings and agents, thereby drawing attention away from the more denotational aspect, the action patterns or "structurings" of the individuals concerned.

THE EVENT-STRUCTURE RESEARCH PROGRAM AT SYRACUSE

As is the case of many psychological theories in their early stages, research had to proceed on a kind of "hunch" or intuition regarding the formal aspects of the theory. Our starting point lay merely in giving sufficient body to the structure concept to enable investigations to go forward. The notion of a "collective" structure seemed reasonably intelligible. The problem now was to identify and define the "organismic" structures, those within the individual. Without pretending to describe the neurophysiological details, which were of course largely unknown, it was assumed as a working construct that all fairly stable and predictable behavioral integrations within an individual, such as motives, trends, habits, percepts, and cognitions, were quasi-self-closing and self-maintaining "structures of events." As in most theories of psychology, a certain amount of subjective language was found necessary to describe them. The individual as a whole comprised many such structures and these were integrated with one another. Each of them was considered to have its own characteristic energy (density of events). Since they were so closely connected in the pattern of the organism it was conjectured that when the energies of a particular event structure (or cycle) were raised or lowered through environmental events, the energies of other, "tangent," structures would be correspondingly affected, and affected in a certain ratio to the intensities involved. This situation was considered to obtain in and between the specific structures of both the inner (organismic) and outer (collective) sort.

The intrinsic energies of each of these structures of the individual was at first called "potency of involvement" (and later "index of structurance") in the structure concerned. The relationship (a matter of probability) which any one structure had with any other was called its "relevance" to the latter (later, its "interstructurance"). Thus stated it was possible for the theory to be quantitatively tested. The work, as before, was done over a period of time by my graduate students as the basis for their doctoral dissertations. And again I worked closely with most of them. The objectivity, the devotion to their problems, the patience, and the scientific exactness displayed by these students are among my most treasured memories. Since this experimental program occupied a considerable period of my time and eventuated in some results not reported elsewhere, I would like to describe it in more detail.

At first the quantitative theorem was not systematically worked out. There has already been mentioned the study of Nancy Morse, indicating that hostility or prejudice of an individual toward an out-group was dependent upon the potency of his involvement in his own national structure to which (it was here merely conjectured) he might be regarding the members of the out-group (rightly or wrongly) as in some degree threatening (negative relevance). Another study, by Arnold Tannenbaum, investigated the morale and attitudes toward an industry in which the subjects were employed. The basic independent variables here were the strength of the various personality trends of the individuals (potency) and the relevance of these trends to certain phases of the employment program. Again the results lay in the direction of the hypothesis.

In order to test the generalizing power of the hypothesis more adequately, the following equation, known as the Structural Dynamics Formula, was devised: $\overline{S}_1 = (S_1) + S_2 i_{21} + S_3 i_{31} + \cdots + S_n i_{n1}$. In this formula S_1, the dependent variable, represents the total energy of a particular structure (for example, structure 1) that is to be appraised. Such total energy is dependent not only upon the "proper," or typical, energy of that structure, S_1, but also upon the contributions to it from all structures related to it. S_2, S_3, etc., represent the "typical" energies of the latter structures, while i_{21}, i_{31}, etc., are their degrees of interstructurance with S_1. The gamut of all relevant structures of the individual (2 to n) are to be included in the summation, and they include both the personality trend structures of the individual and the collective structures he is in. The latter can be classified as either face to face (primary group) or institutional. The interstructurances may be negative as well as positive in their contributions to S_1.

In this systematic form the theory was tested first through a monumental and meticulous research by John Valentine (1953) on the causation of attitudes. $\overline{S}_1$, the dependent variables, consisted of the strengths, or degrees of intensity, of attitudes on certain social questions. The other S's represented the strength of involvement (structurance) of the subjects in other structures. In order to obtain the identification and intensity of these base structures exhaustive questionnaires were filled out by the subjects. The i's, or degrees of interstructurances of these latter structures with the attitude (S_1), were estimated independently by qualified persons in various fields. The results of Valentine's study clearly confirmed the hypothesis. Furthermore, it was found that as more categories or types of structures were included in the independent variable ($S_2 \ldots S_n$), the higher the correlation became. In addition to this experiment, Valentine (and Reimer) conducted a similar study on learning, the results of which were again positive. I regard the work of Valentine on attitudes as a significant discovery. Attitudes have been generally supposed to be dynamic entities or motivating forces in themselves. These findings are capable, I believe, of leading to a quite new conception of attitudes. Attitudes are here seen to be not primary motivations, but variables dependent on other circumstances, namely those of a structural-involvement character. Such a finding should be borne in mind in procedures in which attitude inculcation or change is attempted.

Another important investigation, conducted by Charlotte Simon (1952), explored the predictive value of the hypothesis with respect to personality. This study employed the distinction previously made between trait and trend descriptions. Simon took as the dependent variable, $\bar{S}_1$, the degree of a trait of the subjects obtained from rating scales returned by the subjects' acquaintances. In all, three traits, ascendance, responsibility, and extroversion, were used. For the variables (S's) on the right side of the equation she used the strengths of the many separate trends of the individual which had been obtained from a separate canvas of acquaintances. The interstructurance values of each trend with respect to the trait were judged by Simon, but without any knowledge of what subject's material she was judging. This variable represented the degree of probability that that trend in the individual would be likely to lead to the appearance of such a trait as perceived by his associates (actually the covariance expected between the trend and trait). This careful study also supported the event-structure hypothesis and gave clear evidence for the "partial transformation" theory of personality appraisal previously described. Another testing of the formula was done by Theodore Vallance (1950), using methods similar to those of Valentine, in an attempt to predict the susceptibility of individuals to propaganda appeals. This study did not support the hypothesis in its main prediction; but there was a correlation between the feeling of the strength of the propaganda on the one hand and the event-structure variable on the other.

I will conclude this review with an account of a study which I like to recall. It was a little "masterpiece" of strategy and elegance—but with an unfortunate ending. It will be recalled that my Chinese student, Chiang Lin Woo, had, with most careful techniques, completed a dissertation upon J-curve distributions in custom situations (Woo, 1948). He therefore had been able to rank the eleven customs on which he had collected data according to the extent to which the individuals he observed had conformed to them. These eleven custom behaviors included such episodes as that of a man opening the door for a woman companion, the placement of knife and fork on the plate in restaurants, the acts expected of participants in a religious service, and the approved behavior when the national anthem is played. The idea occurred to me that the relative steepness of the J-distributions on the scales that Woo used to measure custom conformity might also be predicted by the structural dynamics formula. It was conjectured that in these situations the basic structural variable to which the custom behavior might be predicted to be related would be, in each case, of only one type, namely, that to which it was appropriate, as for example the boy-friend-girlfriend relationship, membership in "polite society," the church to which one belongs, and so on. An average rating of the potency of involvement that is generally obtained in a representative sample of male citizens in each of these classes of structures was obtained, for each structure, by a carefully prepared questionnaire. These self-estimates of involvement were gathered, of course, from an entirely different population from that earlier observed in Woo's study of conformity, but the type of population involved was similar. Still another, totally different but again representative set of individuals, filled out forms estimating the probable degree of importance (relevance) of the custom act for the maintenance of the structure concerned or of the individual's place in it. When all these data from different sources were assembled and computed it was found that for these eleven custom situations the degree of conformity in the particular custom act was definitely related, just as the formula had predicted, to the strength of involvement of individuals typically in the base structure concerned, times the relevance of the custom act to that structure. The Spearman rank difference correlations, obtained by computing the data in two different ways, were 0.68 (significant at the 5 percent level) and 0.82 (significant at the 1 percent level). Upon seeing this finding Woo and I shook hands. This long-armed result seemed to call into question traditional explanations of custom as based largely on social inertia or cultural lag. It appeared from our result that custom conformity was a very dynamic here-and-now phenomenon, under structuronomic influence or control. It was also thought that this finding might have value for the cultural anthropologists.

Woo, who was going back to China, was to take the data with him and work out certain computations in greater detail. He asked me if I did not wish to retain a complete copy. I cannot imagine what possessed me—it is one of those things that is hard to explain; but I said I would leave the whole matter to him and he could send me the results as soon as his computations were completed. Woo went back, first to Hong Kong and a little later to mainland China, which was undergoing an overhauling under the Communist regime. It is now twenty years since he returned to China proper, and in that time I have not heard a word from him. Because of the meagerness of my records I have not published this experiment or its finding until this moment. I must now simply ask the reader to accept my word that it was so. I regard my carelessness in not retaining a complete copy of the data as one of my worst professional errors.

To sum matters up, out of these seven investigations that were conducted under my direction at Syracuse, six supported the structural-dynamics hypothesis. A seventh, as a whole, did not, but it did give support to it in a certain part. I must report, to my great regret, that only two of the studies described above have reached publication. In view of the significance of the findings and the novelty of the approach, the reader may indeed wonder why such good material has been left, as it were, to wither on the vine. Was it in part my usual "procrastination" that was accountable for my not having published it or prodded my former students into doing so? Perhaps. But there was a further and very substantial reason: one that has a moral. This reason lay in the obscurity of the hypothesis itself, in the vagueness in my use of the term "structure," and the difficulty of stating "structural" variables in a manner that was clear enough to distinguish them from more traditional psychological constructs such as motives, values, and perceptions. In fact, this very question was raised by an editor to whom a manuscript had been sent. The moral, of course, is that, important as quantitative findings undoubtedly are in research, quantities alone, even if clearcut and decisive, cannot make a good theory. I by no means regret the time taken by me and my students to secure these very clear and definitive results, and I am certain that they will some day come into their full significance.

In my own defense I should say that I did already have a considerable backlog of theoretical structural interpretations which I was giving my classes; and many illuminating empirical charts or diagrams of organismic and collective structures had been worked out. This material, however, did not suffice to bridge the gap between theory and research. I was now as determined as ever to work toward a basic theory of the individual—probably one of a quasi-structural character—that would be both intelligible and unique. I felt that I had been on the right track; for our studies had brought to light many facts about "motivations" and "perceptions" for which the traditional use of these rubrics in psychology had afforded no basis of understanding—and the results themselves were on the whole surprisingly consistent. But it was clear that there was a drastic need of making the theory more explicit and of connecting it, if possible, not merely with overt behaviors, or attitudes and trends, but with neurophysiological and microcosmic happenings deep down within the organism. In this way, also, the findings of our Syracuse research program might perhaps be brought to their deserved fruition.

THE SEARCH CONTINUES: THEORIES OF PERCEPTION— PRESENT STATUS OF ENESTRUENCE THEORY

Work with my graduate students ended in 1953 and I was free to launch wholeheartedly into the further development of my theory—or so I thought. Being none too confident of my ability for the task, however, I at first set myself to the work of reading all the related theories of psychology I could find to obtain suggestions. In doing this I became so intrigued by the theories of perception that I did not get beyond that point. So I wrote an exposition and discussion of these theories in the light of the structure concept, planning to add an account of my own theory at the end. I had, of course, written articles on the hypothesis from time to time, but this was to be my major definitive statement.

This book, entitled *Theories of Perception and the Concept of Structure*, appeared in 1955. I have been greatly pleased by its success, and am glad of the help it seems to have given to students of perception. But it has been clear that its popularity did not rest primarily (or even remotely) on the exposition of my own theory in the last chapter. That account was still only a "preliminary" statement, and was still obscure to students and colleagues. I have sometimes wondered if writing this book had been a kind of escape, helping me to delay further the attack upon the task to which I was committed. Could this have been another example of my stubbornness and procrastination? Perhaps so, but it could hardly be called laziness. Readers who might wish to pursue the progress of my more general theory insofar as it has been published to the present day can follow its development in the items marked in the References by a double asterisk (**). These should be read in the order listed.

In 1957, after we were both retired, my wife and I moved to California, where we could be near her sister, Mrs. Mildred Mitchell. For one semester I taught a seminar at the University of California in Berkeley and later found good friends and made many helpful contacts at Stanford University. I find that my approach to the underlying structure of organisms and the implicit "epi-structure" of society has now moved, as I always knew that it must eventually, into an era of greater sophistication. The sweeping intellectual change in the life sciences has had its impact on my thinking. I am now trying to absorb some of the recent impressive findings of modern neurophysiology, biochemistry, and molecular biology. For to even approach being significant, my theory must be brought into relationship to such a context. I have also tried to keep in touch with the current mode of thinking in cybernetics, information theory, and general systems theory.

Without undervaluing the importance of any of these developments I shall mention two related respects in which they do not appear to me to be headed in the direction of my problem. The first of these applies especially to systems theory in the fields of biology and psychology, and the attempt to devise conceptual or computer models of psychobiological processes. The effort to explain or emulate the organism by designing theories or models of how it works is, I think, evading the deeper problem of what it is or how it came into being and continues. The new theorists seem merely to have assumed the existence of the organism as a prior but unexplained condition (ontological presumption). Such a point of view overlooks the very questions with which my theory is deeply concerned.

My second misgiving concerns what I regard as the subjective or teleological slanting of the new biology and biochemistry in the interpretation of biological and psychological processes. Theories seem to have emerged as *tour de force* explanations of the results of carefully performed and remarkable experiments. To one, however, who is seeking the maximum objectivity possible, such notions as "coding and uncoding" in the organism, "messenger" RNA, the "processing of information," and the organism as "recognizing and rejecting" an intruder, though familiar to us at the molar human level, seem somewhat gratuitous and anthropomorphic as applied to antibodies, cells, and genes. Their use raises problems deeper than the ones they purport to solve. In falling back on such explanations are we not somewhat like watches which, if asked to explain their origins or their running, can only reply by a further working of their springs or turning of their wheels? In the heyday of molar psychology it was said that we should not attempt to explain what is going on inside the organism, but should leave such matters until the neurologists or biologists had been able to discover the facts necessary for their explanation. It now seems that though the latter have discovered many relevant facts, the need for an objective explanation must still go begging. Just as the sociologists had failed to make explicit the nature of social reality, so the biologists seem to be unable to come cogently to grips with the elusive nature of the individual. Perhaps in addition to more powerful microscopes what we need is the ability more clearly to perceive and understand what we see. If only we could get outside the ivory tower of solipsism long enough to obtain a truly objective view!

It seems presumptuous of me to think that I might be able to throw any new light on these awesome mysteries. But I see no escape from trying if I am to continue my search; for it is apparent that the group problem will be solved only when the problem of the individual is clarified.

I feel I owe it to the reader to attempt here a brief sketch or preview of the theory of enestruence as it now stands as a result of my work for the last four years. I found it necessary to avoid some of the older pitfalls at the very start. This I did first by setting up a new criterion of physical reality and adequate objectivity. This was the criterion which I indicated by the Greek letter chi and which referred to actual, physical encounterability. By applying this criterion all around the organism or its patterns of outer and inner behavior one could delineate the organism, in reality or imagination, as a line, a surface, or a pattern of such encounters. Such a "limniation" constituted the conceptual method of the theory, and the manifold which it portrayed was called the chi-empiric.

A second major difficulty in trying to describe and generalize behavior of the individual acting alone or in groups was the inability to get away from teleology and the habit of using agency as a means of explanation. A systematic effort to escape this usage was made by rigorously employing the chi criterion. The description, therefore, was made in a quasi-geographical or topological manner which did not involve any purposive assumptions. The effort to do this, of course, parts company with almost everything that has been said about the nature of life and behavior. It is of course realized that purpose is regarded as an inalienable characteristic of life and a notion which we could not do without for a moment in practical living. My thought here is that if the suggestions put forward in my theory can be sustained, purpose can be brought back into the scene as a transconceptualization of the physicalistic account once the theory is completed. This was also conceived to be a possible step in the attempt at philosophical unity in the mind-body enigma.

Further novel postulates are called upon by the theory. It is pointed out that the physical laws of nature and thermodynamics as at present stated, although they *always hold* in both the animate and inanimate realms, are inadequate for the full description and explanation of the remarkable order in the organism. The hypothesis is here advanced that in addition to these modalities as expressed in the usual conventions of "length," "speed," and "mass" of physics, there is another modality that has been barely noticed and has been neglected in theories in both the physical and biological realms. This neglected but truly physical modality I have called *homadicity*. It is essentially a non-random property that occurs in every phenomenon *along with* the quantitative aspect (heterodicity); but it cannot in itself be defined by measurement. It occurs not in degrees, but in a "yes" or "no" (or categorical) fashion, being essentially a kind of characteristic that occurs throughout the whole phenomenal element or pattern concerned, as well as locally in each segment of such a pattern. There is, in other words, a holistic property that exists along with the measured magnitude or energy of the element or pattern. This is not however the kind of "whole property" that is postulated by gestalt psychology. Contrary to expectation it has been found possible to formulate a kind of empirical logistic for defining and stating these other-than-quantitative elements of nature.

One of the salient characteristics of life that is also found in collectivities is the presence of some *invariant* of behavior that cannot itself be completely expressed quantitatively but persists through all different circumstances and magnitudes of the surroundings until an objective is accomplished. We have, for example, the behavior of a stentor which, when disturbed by particles in its environment, performs one after another of a series of acts until one occurs which releases the animal from that situation. These several acts may be regarded as based on differences of magnitudes, or quantities, or the motion of the parts. In other words the quantitative picture may provide an infinite variety of possibilities while the other-than-quantitative (homadiac) retains its other-than-quantitative character. It is held by my theory that life and behavior in general are like this. The elementary homadiac properties are the invariants of the morphology behavior, and organismic action; and they probably exist in a finite and limited number; while the heterodiac properties give the spatial size, and in part the shape, of the phenomenon, as well as its energic density. The order that exists in nature is therefore not simple. Only part of it is the work of energy, usually defined as the capacity for work. For the remainder, or other type, of order there is the addition of this other non-energic factor we have called the homademe. The production of order is a bigeneric process requiring both these physical modalities together with their laws, which now remain to be more fully stated.

The above paragraph contains the major strategy of the theory. The operation of these two unique modalities together will, it is maintained, afford a better background for understanding the nature of physiological processes such as digestion, breathing, circulation, growth, and the nature of what are now called "mechanisms." There are therefore in the organism two arrows of time, not one. One of them is the long entropic or equilibrial process throughout the universe as formulated in the second law of thermodynamics. The other is a result of the stabilization and juncturing of the homadiac properties. This is limited in length to the life-span of the organism or the existence of a species. The two arrows can go on together in time since the types of order-disorder to which they point are not one thing but two, the order of attaining physical equilibrium on the one hand, as negative entropy passes into entropy, and the shorter term and repetitive ordering on the other, that is exhibited in the destiny of developing organisms as they grow and differentiate, or that is seen in the evolution of a species. Such bigeneric order always involves both types of properties. It brings into play the notion of energy as a distribution of (capacity for) events, which are junctures in this manifold. The existence of the organism (and we might say also the collectivity) lies between two extremes or thresholds of energic density. There is an upper threshold above which there results an "entropy of crowding," and a lower threshold below which there is an "entropy of paucity" with its characteristic fluctuations of probability. The origin of life, as well as evolutionary changes, explained by natural selection and fitness for survival in the Darwinian theory, are here revised to represent the assembly and the staying together, through shifts of the various homadiac and heterodiac elements with changes in the environment or the organism itself (enathrostarestence).

Though it is too early to know whether these ideas will contribute something toward an understanding of the enigma of the organism and organismic collectivity, it is my hope that they will. I have no desire for my ghost to return and continue to pace the corridors of Emerson Hall in an unending search for enlightenment.

I have held few offices and received few honors in my lifetime. This was as it should have been, because I wanted such recognition as I might attain to come as a result of having made this particular contribution to psychology and science, and I have felt that thus far it has not been fully made. I have been the recipient of one of the research awards of the American Psychological Association; and to my great satisfaction and pleasure I was also awarded the Gold Medal of the American Psychological Foundation for 1968. Beyond that, I have had the enduring loyalty and support of my students, colleagues, and friends. I consider that this is recognition enough. I have been fortunate in many ways and have led a sheltered and on the whole a rewarding life; though there have been times, as a result of my long commitment to such a far-reaching, and, to some, forbidding, problem, when I have felt lonely. My mother said that during my childhood she thought of me as the "seer." This was probably because I seemed to be always looking for deeper answers. She also referred to me as her "child of sorrow." Perhaps these two thoughts are in the nature of the case somehow fundamentally connected. If my brother could be classed among the Isaiahs of the present psychological scene, I, perhaps, might lay claim to being called a Jeremiah. My final word might well be a reversal of Descartes' famous dictum, changing it from *Cogito ergo sum* to *Sum ergo cogitandum est.*

REFERENCES

Selected Publications by Floyd H. Allport

The influence of the group upon association and thought. *J. exp. Psychol.,* 1920, *3*, 159-182.

Social psychology. Boston: Houghton Mifflin, 1924.

The group fallacy in relation to social science. *J. abnorm. soc. Psychol.,* 1924, *19*, 60-73.(*)

The group fallacy in relation to culture. *J. abnorm. soc. Psychol.,* 1924, *19*, 185-191. (*)

(with D. A. Hartman) The measurement and motivation of atypical opinion in a certain group. *Amer. pol. sci. Rev.,* 1925, *19*, 735-760.

The psychological nature of political structure. *Amer. pol. sci. Rev.,* 1927, *21*, 611-618. (*)

(with G. W. Allport) *The A-S reaction study: A test for measuring ascendance-submission in personality.* Boston: Houghton Mifflin, 1928.

"Group" and "institution" as concepts in a natural science of social phenomena. *Publ. Amer. soc. Soc.,* 1928, *22*, 83-99. (*)

(with D. Katz) *Students' attitudes.* Syracuse, N.Y.: Craftsman Press, 1931.

(with D. A. Hartman) The prediction of cultural change: A problem illustrated in studies by F. Stuart Chapin and A. L. Kroeber. In S. Rice (Ed.), *Methods in social science.* Chicago: Univ. Chicago Press, 1931. (*)

Institutional behavior. Chapel Hill: Univ. North Carolina Press, 1933. (*)

The J-curve hypothesis of conforming behavior. *J. soc. Psychol.,* 1934, *5*, 141-183.

Teleonomic description in the study of personality. *Character and Personality,* 1937, *5*, 202-214.

Toward a science of public opinion. *Pub. Opin. Quart.,* 1937, *1*, 7-22.

Rule and custom as individual variations of behavior distributed upon a continuum of conformity. *Amer. J. Soc.,* 1939, *44*, 897-921.

(with R. S. Solomon) Lengths of conversations: A conformity situation analyzed by the telic continuum and J-curve hypothesis. *J. abnorm. soc. Psychol.,* 1939, 34, 419-464.

An event-system theory of collective action: With illustrations from economic and political phenomena and the production of war. *J. soc. Psychol.,* 1940, *11*, 417-445. (**)

(with R. S. Musgrave) Teleonomic description in the study of behavior. *Character and Personality,* 1941, *9*, 326-343.

(with N. C. Morse) The causation of anti-Semitism: An investigation of seven hypotheses. *J. Psychol.,* 1952, *34*, 197-233. (**)

The structuring of events: Outline of a general theory with applications to psychology. *Psychol. Rev.,* 1954, *61*, 281-303. (**)

Theories of perception and the concept of structure. New York: Wiley, 1955. (**)

(with A. S. Tannenbaum) Personality structure and group structure: An interpretative study of their relationship through an event-structure hypothesis. *J. abnorm. soc. Psychol.,* 1956, *53,* 272-280. (**)

The contemporary appraisal of an old problem. *Contem. Psychol.,* 1961, *6,* 195-196. (**)

A structuronomic conception of behavior: Individual and collective. I. Structural theory and the master problem of social psychology. *J. abnorm. soc. Psychol.,* 1962, *64,* 3-30. (**)

A theory of enestruence (event-structure theory). *Amer. Psychol.,* 1967, *22,* 1, 1-24. (**)

Other Publications Cited

Allport, G. W. *The nature of prejudice.* Reading, Mass.: Addison-Wesley, 1954.

———. *Becoming.* New Haven: Yale Univ. Press, 1955.

———. *Pattern and growth in personality.* New York: Holt, Rinehart and Winston, 1961.

Holt, E. B. *Animal drive and the learning process.* New York: Holt, Rinehart and Winston, 1931.

Schanck, R. L. A study of a community and its groups and institutions conceived as behaviors of individuals. *Psychol. Monogr.,* 1932, *43,* No. 195.

Sherif, M., and C. W. Sherif. *An outline of social psychology.* New York: Harper and Brothers, 1956.

Simon, C. T. The bases of personality traits: An investigation employing a structural hypothesis and method. Unpublished doctoral dissertation, Syracuse Univ., 1952.

Thurstone, L. L., and E. J. Chave. *The measurement of attitude.* Chicago: Univ. Chicago Press, 1929.

Valentine, J. A. The structural determination of attitudes. Unpublished doctoral dissertation (two volumes), Syracuse Univ., 1953.

Vallance, T. R. An experimental study of the effects of mail propaganda and related collective and personality variables. Unpublished doctoral dissertation, Syracuse Univ., 1950.

Woo, Chiang Lin. Conformity in custom behavior. Unpublished doctoral dissertation, Syracuse Univ., 1948.

Frank A Beach

Frank A. Beach

PROLOGUE

Contributors to this series of autobiographies have adopted quite different approaches to a common assignment. Some begin with a genealogy stretching back at least two generations. Others open with the author's birth and include accounts of early childhood, relations with parents, sibling interactions, etc. My decision has been that the reader will be interested primarily in my experiences as a psychologist from my first introduction to the subject until the present. I have therefore concentrated upon my professional development and activities.

I hope I am a good enough psychologist to recognize that a man's professional life cannot logically be dissociated from other aspects of his history, but in order to emphasize facts which seem most relevant to a history of psychology I have deliberately omitted many of these "other aspects." It would be fun to write a complete autobiography, but the end product would include much that was not relevant to psychology, would be of interest only to the author and possibly to his immediate family, and would greatly exceed the page limitations necessarily imposed on contributors to this volume—limitations which have proved confining and frustrating even for the preparation of the adumbrated account that follows.

FIRST CONTACT WITH PSYCHOLOGY

My forty-year affair with "the science of mental life" began during my junior year in college (1930-1931), when I enrolled in a course in experimental psychology. At the time I had no notion that a serious relationship would develop from this chance encounter. My major subject was English and my ambition was to teach in high school. The institution I was attending was the Kansas State Teachers College at Emporia, where my father was Professor and Head of the Music Department.

In my freshman year, when I was seventeen, I enjoyed myself so much that my grades included nine hours of D's and F's. I was banished to Antioch College for the sophomore year and returned to the Teachers College as a junior full of good resolutions. My grades did improve and I was still able to participate in a wide range of extracurricular activities. These included editing the college paper, singing in the glee club and a small acapella group, playing the bass drum in the band and timpani in the orchestra, playing intramural basketball, editing the college year book as a senior, serving on the Student Council, and organizing a fraternity for men who hadn't been invited to join existing fraternities.

I can't recall why I enrolled in a psychology course but it proved to be an eventful choice. In today's jargon, experimental psychology "turned me on." Our laboratory exercises on sensation, perception, learning, memory, and emotion seemed tremendously important because they exemplified an objective, experimental approach to human experience. I could scarcely conceive of a problem more important than determination of the "true shape" of the learning curve.

Of course the most important factor in this whole experience was the personality and pedagogical skill of my first instructor. He was James B. Stroud, who had recently earned his doctorate under Harvey A. Carr at the University of Chicago. Dr. Stroud was young, enthusiastic, energetic, and sympathetic. He was the first faculty member I had known who did not "teach" science from the textbook. He showed his students where the statements in their books came from and how new knowledge comes into being. If I had to name one teacher who had the greatest effect upon my professional development it would unquestionably be Jim Stroud. Of course, some of this effect should be attributed to primacy.

My initial encounter with psychology was so stimulating and rewarding that I enrolled in enough additional courses to qualify for a major. This was at most a mild flirtation with the discipline and I had no intention whatsoever of jilting my first love and major, English. Instead she jilted me! I graduated in June, 1932, and the Depression was in full swing. There simply weren't any jobs for fledgling teachers of high school English. I couldn't even find a job pumping gas in a filling station and I was at a loss to know what to do.

Just as I was steeling myself to take a job as stock boy in a local dry goods store at thirty cents an hour Jim Stroud threw me a life line. The Psychology Department at the Teachers College had $400 to pay for a Fellowship in Clinical Psychology and I could have the job if I would go on for an M.S. in psychology. Fate obviously was conspiring to throw the two of us together. In those days clinical psychology was very primitive and I had taken the one undergraduate course in the catalog. I accepted the Fellowship with gratitude and alacrity and worked toward my Master's degree in 1932-1933. My duties as Clinical Fellow consisted of correcting and scoring Stanford-Binets and Herring Revisions that had been administered to school children by members of the undergraduate class in clinical psychology.

As a graduate student and candidate for a Master's degree I had to select a thesis problem. I will devote several pages to a description of my work on the thesis because of the light it throws on the state of graduate training in

psychology in most small colleges in the early thirties, and because it tells
something about me as an individual and nascent psychologist.

MAJOR VICISSITUDES AND MINOR TRIUMPHS
ON THE WAY TO A MASTER'S DEGREE

I cannot recall when and how I first became interested in animal psychology
but it must have come from reading because no relevant instruction was offered
at the Teachers College. Nevertheless, for my thesis I proposed to determine
whether rats had color vision. The proposal was approved and I was strictly on
my own. No one on the faculty had ever done any work with rats or even seen
an animal laboratory. In retrospect I am convinced that this enforced independence had an enduring and beneficial effect upon my intellectual and
emotional development.

The Psychology Department at the University of Kansas provided me with
enough rats to start a breeding colony but when they arrived I was afraid to
open the shipping box. With their long teeth and little red eyes rats were
obviously ferocious and dangerous creatures. Leaving the crate unopened I
hurried to buy the heaviest leather gloves I could find. Returning to my "lab"
(an unused cloakroom 6 by 10 feet) I cautiously loosened one corner of the
screen top of the shipping box, and to my surprise none of the rats sprang out to
attack me. Resolving to hold one in my gloved hand for a full three minutes, I
picked up a rat and grasped it firmly without looking at the rodent but keeping
my eyes on the sweep-second hand of my wristwatch. At the end of the third
minute I relaxed my grip and the rat fell to the floor, stone cold dead. I had
literally squeezed the life out of the poor creature.

Early fears soon were overcome and I succeeded in establishing a breeding
colony. I doubt if any rats in any laboratory ever ate as well as mine. Members
of the departmental faculty regularly brought me paper bags of table scraps to
augment those I collected at home after every meal. The regular menu included
meat, potatoes, fruit, assorted vegetables, bread, and occasionally even stale
cake. Bread and cake were served soaked in whole milk. It came as no surprise
when I read years later that *Rattus norvegicus* is omnivorous.

When it came to building my experimental apparatus I was confronted with
several difficulties, of which I shall mention only one. I wanted to reward my
subjects for each correct choice and punish them for every error. Reward was
easy enough but punishment was another matter. Moss and others had used
electric shock but in those days authors rarely bothered to publish details about
the current used. I took the position that rate of learning would be positively
related to the severity with which mistakes were punished.

The punishment grid consisted of copper strips fastened to the floor just in
front of the two doors above which the experimental stimuli were displayed. As
a source of current I fed six volts from dry cell batteries through a Ford spark

coil, an extremely useful device that disappeared with the wonderful Model T. In effect the spark coil multiplied voltage approximately 100 times. Then, just to make sure that the 600-volt shock would have real authority, I flooded the floor of the starting box in the testing cage with water 1 inch deep.

On his first trial my first subject had the misfortune to choose the incorrect doorway. When all four wet feet were on the copper strips I closed the switch, the spark coil emitted its characteristic buzzing noise and the rat jumped three feet in the air, clearing the side of the apparatus and landing on the floor five feet below. He wasn't permanently injured, but in many, many tests distributed over four or five weeks that rat steadfastly refused to emerge from the starting box. I had discovered one-trial-learning but was too naive to exploit my findings.

Eventually technical mistakes were corrected and the thesis was completed with a total N of three. Results showed conclusively that my rats were "color blind." I was very proud of the experiment and dreamed of submitting a report for publication in the *Journal of Comparative Psychology*. Fortunately for me and for animal psychology, while I was learning by doing in my converted cloakroom, Dr. Norman Munn at the University of Pittsburgh was attacking the same problem in a professional and sophisticated manner. His experiment was published just after mine was completed; but although his was much more elegant our conclusions were the same.

When the thesis was completed I was left with a number of unemployed rats and with some extra time, although not enough to undertake a second experiment. I had read a number of papers by Lashley describing the effects of neocortical lesions on maze learning in rats. The idea of performing brain surgery seemed quite exciting and I decided to try it. In this endeavor there was no lack of detailed instructions regarding procedures because Lashley's articles were most explicit. This did not mean that there were no problems, for I was entering virtually unknown territory without a guide and with a map I couldn't read very well.

First the rat is anaesthetized with ether. (How does one administer ether to a rat?) Second the hair is clipped from the top of the head. Third one or more holes are made in the skull with a trephine. (What's a trephine?) Fourth the required amount of cortical tissue is destroyed by passing an electric cautery through the trephine holes. (Electric cautery?) Finally the scalp is sutured and the sutures covered with thin collodian. (Collodian?)

Tackling these problems *a seriatim* I muddled through. I anaesthetized rats by dropping them in a large fruit jar containing ether, leaving them there until they became motionless, and then removing them before respiration stopped. Having no trephine, I made holes in the skull with a dissecting scalpel and when the opening was large enough to admit the points of a pair of cuticle clippers I broke off small bits of bone to enlarge the hole to any desired dimensions. I fashioned a primitive but serviceable cautery from two lengths of heavy copper wire (insulated with tire tape), a small loop of German silver wire, and the transformer from my younger brother's electric train. Using this makeshift equipment, with absolutely no guidance or advice but feeling my way along by trial and error, I eventually learned to make reasonably clean lesions in the neocortex without incurring an undue mortality rate. This was my only objective and its achievement gave me great satisfaction. It was not intended as research and in fact was really a kind of game, but it had the important outcome of giving me confidence that one could learn a lot without tutelage and without complicated and expensive equipment. I am sure that this remains true today in at least some areas of psychology but I suspect that few graduate students or even young faculty members would be sympathetic to such a point of view.

Despite the enjoyment I experienced doing my first full-fledged experiment in psychology and the fact that I was awarded the M.S. degree, I retained my original affection for and commitment to English. However, in the spring of 1933 there still were no high school teaching jobs to be found. Even if I had wanted to teach psychology, the subject wasn't offered at the secondary level. Nonacademic employment was equally hard to obtain. Men with families were eager to work but many of them were "on relief." Sometimes it was possible to pick up a few days' employment as a laborer or to work on a harvesting crew in the wheat fields at three dollars a day, but even in such cases family men were given preference.

AN UNSUCCESSFUL ATTEMPT
TO ESCAPE FROM PSYCHOLOGY

I had no burning desire to continue in graduate school because my most compelling hope was to get a steady job and earn a living. I believe that was generally true of all young men of my generation who had seen the effects of a major depression during their late adolescence. Financial security was of paramount importance. Nonetheless, since I couldn't get a steady job graduate study was one alternative worth exploring. I talked the problem over with Jim Stroud, asking where I should apply and what I might specialize in. I still did not realize the hold psychology had established upon me and continued to regard our relationship as a passing flirtation rather than a serious affair. Dr. Stroud recommended his own school, the University of Chicago, and, as an alternative to psychology, he suggested that I consider working for a Ph.D. in anthropology.

I had enjoyed one or two undergraduate courses in that subject and so in June 1933 I took a train for Chicago to explore the possibilities of getting a fellowship for graduate study in anthropology. It was disheartening to learn from Professor Redfield, Chairman of the Anthropology Department, that there were only two fellowships and they were reserved for advanced students with a much broader background in anthropology than I possessed. Had I been accepted in the Anthropology Department I might presently be a Professor of Anthropology in some educational institution, but fate decreed that I was not to escape so easily from the consequence of my dalliance with psychology.

Leaving Professor Redfield's office I was prepared to give up the idea of a graduate career, but as long as I was at the university I thought it would be polite to drop by the Psychology Department, introduce myself to Professor Carr and convey the regards of his former student, Jim Stroud. I don't know whether there had been any collusive correspondence between Stroud and Carr, but in any event Professor Carr received me most congenially. Our conversation somehow gravitated to possibilities for graduate training in psychology and financial support for new students. It developed that there was a Service Scholarship for which I might qualify, although nothing was assured. Professor Carr advised me to go back to Emporia, make formal application for admission and for financial aid and wait for results.

Late in the summer I received notification that I had been accepted by the Psychology Department at Chicago and was awarded a $400 Service Scholarship for the academic year 1933-1934. To earn the scholarship I was expected to work 80 hours per quarter in the departmental library. Tuition amounting to $100 per quarter was to be paid at the beginning of each quarter and my stipend would be forthcoming at the quarter's end. Obviously it was going to be essential for me to find extra sources of income.

FIRST YEAR AT THE UNIVERSITY OF CHICAGO

The first year at Chicago (1933-1934) was hectic but stimulating and in most respects enjoyable. I was used to living at home and in a small town. The freedom of independent life in a large city occasionally went to my head, with the result that the following morning the head retaliated. In the main, however, I worked very hard and for long hours both scholastically and to earn a living.

Fortunately I did not have to pay any rent for the first two quarters, during which I lived with friends of my parents whose home was about a mile from the University. Nevertheless, it was still necessary to earn enough money to pay for food, clothes, medical expenses, books, and incidentals. A partial list of jobs held at different times during my graduate student days included dish washer in a cafeteria, waiter in the University Coffee Shop, Tour Guide for the University Chapel, "Cantor" in the choir at the Chapel, grader of papers for various Extension Courses, etc., etc. The necessity to support myself didn't impress me as an undue hardship. Practically all my fellow students were in the same boat. The days of government-supported fellowships, university scholarships for which no work is required, and research assistantships paid for from faculty research grants were far, far in the future.

Memories of the first year at Chicago are a jumble of people, courses, exams, labs, frustrations, anxieties, and, occasionally, small victories. Some of my clearest and most lasting impressions are of people.

The Chairman of the Department, Harvey A. Carr, was one of the last of the Functionalists. His interests centered on learning and perception but he was a general psychologist in the best tradition and possibly the best teacher I encountered at Chicago. He had the gift of leading a student to conclusions so skillfully that the student thought he had found the way all by himself. His *Psychology: A Study of Mental Activity*, first published in 1925, went through four printings in four years and was one of the best introductory texts available.

Carr was unpretentious, rather bluff and simple, a typical Midwesterner who had probably grown up on a farm. He was quick and wise though not brilliant, possessed of a fine sense of humor, and capable of real empathy with students. Toward the end of his career he became somewhat bitter about the University. In later years he once told me that the administration had never approved any of his recommendations for new appointments or promotions. Instead, Carr claimed, the Dean always sought advice from the "stars" in the department, namely Lashley and Thurstone. I liked Carr very much and I think he liked me because, as I shall later recount, he came out of retirement to attend my thesis exam in the course of which he defended me against a young upstart assistant professor named Dael Wolfle.

Louis Thurstone was a very big man on the faculty. His method of factor analysis was at its peak of popularity and many of the best psychology students wanted to work with him. I took two courses with Thurstone and for a while was convinced that factor analysis was going to solve many of psychology's most complex problems. However, after I had learned how to rotate axes and carry out the other rituals involved in this technique only to end up with factor loadings which I had difficulty even naming, I lost confidence in the entire system. This disillusionment had lasting effects so that even today I am illogically distrustful of statistical procedures that go far beyond means, sigmas, simple correlations, and the like. At the present time computers are exerting a pernicious influence on many research areas. Some students are so impressed with the speed at which a computer can function that they forget a computer cannot do their thinking for them, and that simply because certain statistical operations are possible it does not follow automatically that they are worth carrying out.

Upon first acquaintance I thought Thurstone cold and austere but in truth he was a friendly man with enduring interest in his students. He was also a superb teacher—at least for beginning students like myself. When working at the blackboard he habitually made mistakes in addition or multiplication, and even then I was convinced that this was intentional. It gave students an opportunity to correct the teacher and this is always good for the student's morale. Thurstone was a flawless expositor, leading even the slowest student step by step through complicated mathematical arguments and never proceeding to a subsequent stage until he was sure the preceding one was completely understood.

The third faculty member I recall with any vividness was Karl Lashley. He taught physiological psychology and his course completely baffled me. By any usual standard Lashley was a poor if not an atrocious classroom lecturer. He spoke too fast and always appeared nervous. His reading assignments were impossible, frequently amounting to several hundred pages per week and often involving highly technical material far beyond the comprehension of even the brightest students. I recall that he once gave me an assignment in Russian! But "usual standards" did not apply to Lashley as far as most graduate students were concerned. They tolerated and even admired his idiosyncratic methods because of the excitement and contagious enthusiasm his lectures somehow generated. Of course, the fact that he was already a very famous psychologist did not detract from his appeal to neophytes, but his popularity was based upon much more than that. I think it rested chiefly upon his total involvement in the vast knowledge of the subject plus a charmingly unassuming and modest demeanor. He always took his research seriously but never himself.

Perhaps the strongest single influence guiding my professional development at the University of Chicago was exerted by experience gained working in the laboratory under Lashley's supervision. He was completely a self-made experimenter and he left his students strictly alone unless they asked for guidance. Even this he was sometimes slow to give. He would give counsel concerning choice of research problems and was generous in demonstrating techniques, but if the student ran into trouble he was expected to extricate himself if at all possible.

Lashley's lab always housed several senior workers whose research was exciting. While I was there Heinrich Kluver and T. S. Tsang were active. The year prior to my arrival T. C. Schneirla had been there as an N.R.C. Fellow, and while I was at Chicago Robert Leeper came to the lab in the same capacity. We all had tea every afternoon in the seminar room and usually someone talked informally about his research. There was no distinction between students and mature workers. It was a tremendously stimulating experience.

At Chicago I took courses outside the Psychology Department and thereby came in contact with several outstanding scientists representing other disciplines. Paul Weiss in physiology was a superb lecturer, and the work he was then doing on amphibian limb transplantation provoked a great deal of new thinking about organization of the nervous system. Another outstanding teacher was C. Judson Herrick, with whom I took comparative neurology. The kindest and gentlest of men, Herrick welcomed psychology students in his class and laboratory, treating them as though they were as important and as bright as medical students, who were accorded superior status by most professors in other science departments. Herrick was always ready to discuss psychological or behavioral concomitants of evolutionary changes in the central nervous system. Herrick was a good friend of Lashley and his book, *Brains of Rats and Men,* was required reading for all students of physiological psychology.

In the spring quarter I decided to move closer to the campus and therefore took an apartment with another psychology student, Hamilton Crook. "Ham" and I became close friends and apartment living suited us both, but the extra financial load began to tell on me. By the start of the summer quarter it had become clear that I could not remain in school. I had absolutely no financial reserves and the difficulty of going to school while working at several part-time jobs was getting me down. I decided to try once more for a teaching job which would pay enough so that I could save enough money to return and finish my training if I still wanted to do so.

AN INTERLUDE OF HIGH SCHOOL TEACHING

Fortunately the high school teaching situation had opened up a bit and I was able to land a job as instructor of Junior and Senior English at Yates Center, Kansas, which had a population of about 5,000. I was only twenty-one and looked younger, with the result that some members of the school board were dubious of my ability to "keep discipline." I convinced the doubters that I was really quite tough, and was given a contract extending from September 1934 to June 1935. A truly astonishing and archaic document! The school board promised to pay me $100 per month for nine months and I promised not only to perform my teaching duties but also to refrain from dancing, smoking, or playing cards in public. There were no explicit prohibitions against fornication, drunkenness, or hard drugs. Apparently the good citizens of Yates Center simply couldn't imagine a school teacher sinking that low.

The year at Yates Center was not as grim as my contract might imply. In fact, it was simply great—a fun year. I enjoyed teaching English to adolescent boys and girls. It was like dripping water on a dry sponge. The pleasure they derived from learning was obvious, and this applied to learning even such "irrelevant" subjects as Shakespeare's plays, Browning's poems, or Ruskin's essays.

I wish there were enough space to give a full account of my adventures during that stimulating year. In addition to fulfilling my regular teaching duties I initiated an optional course in journalism, and with the enthusiastic cooperation of the students inaugurated the school's first newspaper, which was an instant success. I discovered after school had started that the English teacher was also supposed to direct the Junior and Senior plays—annual events of some importance to the entire community. Having no experience along these lines I began to acquire some by putting on one-act plays for the weekly school assembly. They were so well received by the students and faculty that we offered repeat performances in the evening for parents and other interested citizens. The favorable response on the part of this admittedly prejudiced audience emboldened me to invite teachers in three neighboring high schools to send entries for a one-act play contest to be held at the Teachers College in Emporia. The judges were members of the Drama Department of the college and, mirabile dictu, Yates Center won first place! Later in the year we "produced" the two class plays and each was a resounding success—at least they received rave reviews in the Yates Center News.

Only two more items need mention in connection with my year as a high school teacher. The first is that I continued to conduct research along two separate lines. First, I had constructed at the University of Chicago a stylus maze with a pattern which duplicated that of a maze in which I had previously tested rats. I ran a number of my high school students and compared their learning scores with those of hungry rats. As I recall the results came out in favor of the students but not by much.

The second line of "research" was actually a teaching device. The students and I were anxious to find out how the student body and their parents felt about our newspaper. We constructed a questionnaire, pretested it, and circulated it to all students and parents. The results were analyzed using very simple statistics, and later the same questionnaire was sent to English teachers in four neighboring high schools. When the results were returned we had an N of 650 students and 300 parents. Simple analysis done by my pupils showed that differences between the likes and dislikes of parents and those of students were significantly different as measured by the critical ratio.

Incidentally, the entire newspaper project provided me with my first two publications. They were, "First steps in establishing the school newspaper" (*Quill & Scroll*, vol. 10, 1935, pp. 10-16), and, "Are you printing what your subscribers want?" (*Scholastic Editor*, vol. 15, 1936, pp. 4-21).

Although teaching high school was truly enjoyable I soon realized that I didn't want to make a career of it. Two years' exposure to graduate work in psychology and infection with the research virus had more or less determined my professional future. I was hooked on psychology. What began as a mild flirtation had developed into a serious affaire de coeur. Eventually this attachment threatened to result in a ménage à trois, but that can wait. It was clear that I had to return to Chicago and earn my Ph.D. Accordingly, I wrote to Professor Carr asking about chances for financial support. On April 1, 1935, I received notification that I had been awarded a University Fellowship which paid $500. Remuneration would consist of tuition vouchers of $100 per quarter, and the balance of $100 for the year would be paid by monthly check.

THE YEAR OF THE THESIS

Returning to Chicago early in the summer of 1935 I found that several changes had occurred. Lashley had accepted a Research Professorship at Harvard, and his former laboratory was occupied by one David Isadore Krechevsky (later to become David Krech), a National Research Council Fellow from Tolman's laboratory in Berkeley. He had arrived after I left in 1934 and remained as a Research Assistant in the Psychology Department. At first I was somewhat in awe of Krech but we soon became friends, and shared an apartment in the Sylvan Arms Apartment House, where many a night was devoted to the study of "applied statistics" in the form of three-card draw, plus a mind-boggling version of seven-card stud consisting of high-low with the low hole card wild. This game eventually became known as "Sylvan Arms Special" and is still played in Berkeley by a small group of elderly enthusiasts.

Prompt selection of a thesis problem was imperative because I was determined to complete my graduate work by the end of that academic year. I had done one year's work at the Teachers College in Kansas plus one at Chicago, and a total of three years seemed quite enough for a Ph.D., though even in those days many students took four and even five years. I approached Professor Carr with one brilliant plan after another, only to have each project rejected. I discussed my dilemma with Krech and one of us, I can't remember which, recalled a problem we once heard Lashley mention. This was the study of possible effects of neocortical lesions on "instinctive" behavior patterns. Without saying anything to Carr I wrote to Lashley to ask if he thought research along these lines would be important and worthwhile. He replied in the affirmative.

I prepared a proposal outlining an investigation of the effects of cortical destruction on the maternal behavior of primiparous rats and Carr snapped it up like a starving trout going after a grasshopper. On August 13, 1935, I received a note saying, "Your proposal for a Ph.D. thesis entitled The Neural Basis for Innate Behavior has been approved by the Department. H. A. Carr." It has always been my suspicion that, because of his feelings about Lashley, Carr wanted at least one thesis on brain function to come out of the department after Lashley's departure. So there I was in somewhat the same position I had occupied when I started my Master's thesis at the Teachers College. I had acquired techniques for working with rats, for making brain lesions, etc., but there were no guidelines, no previous experiments to show how to define and measure maternal behavior in the rat. Actually this made the problem much more attractive than it would have been otherwise.

I was on my own. Carr was totally unconcerned with details of the design or conduct of the experiment. In fact, when it was completed he asked me who had done the brain operations for me! My lab was in Culver Hall next door to Krech's office. I brought in an army cot and spent the night there when I expected a female to deliver her litter because I wanted to record the details of parturition. Actual experimentation took about ten months and then the hard work began.

I had to section and examine microscopically each operated brain and reconstruct the lesion by the Lashley method. I knew nothing about histological procedures but received guidance in this sphere from Krech and Dr. T. S. Tsang who was still working in Culver Hall. My knowledge of comparative neurology was too limited to permit recognition of the precise "Lashley levels" that had to be identified for reconstruction of lesions. Fortunately I had the assistance of Leon Pennington, a second N.R.C. Fellow in the lab. "Penny" taught me the finer neuroanatomy of the rat brain. So, borrowing here and begging help there, I managed to finish those parts of the thesis which had to be completed in the lab. Writing it up could be done anywhere.

In addition to completing the thesis I had to pass the Ph.D. Candidacy Examination. Technically this should have been done before the thesis was begun, but the rules were relaxed so that I could finish by June. I took the exam in May 1936. The first part consisted of half a day of objective questions. The next day I was given the five essay questions which follow.

Ph.D. Candidacy Examination
May 1936

1. What sorts of experiments have been performed to determine the relation between level of evolutionary development and efficiency in problem solving? What conclusions can be drawn from these experiments?

2. Suppose you wish to plan in detail an experiment to determine the influence of epinephrin on mental and motor efficiency. What are the important factors in the experimental setup which would have to be controlled, and how would you accomplish the controls? You are to consider this as typical for experiments on the influence of any specific condition on efficiency, and to handle it accordingly.

3. Answer all parts—
   (a) Describe four factors that may influence the size of the correlation coefficient as used in mental test work.
   (b) Describe all the factors that might influence the experimental determination of the validity of a mental test.
   (c) What are the principal sources of error in ratings of personality traits, and how can they be obviated?

4. Trace historically the sources of the main diverse concepts in current psychopathology. Explain and interpret the controversy over the functional versus the organic approach.

5. Give an analysis of the topic of "meaning" in psychology which will bring out (a) the main questions at issue, (b) the rival theories, and (c) the experimental approaches which have been attempted.

On April 24 and 25, 1936, the Midwestern Psychological Association held its eleventh annual meeting at Northwestern University and I gave my first paper, which was entitled "Effects of Cortical Lesions upon the Maternal Behavior of Rats." Other speakers at the same session were W. J. Brogdan, W. Halstead, G. Yacorzyneski, S. H. Bartley, and I. Krechevsky, who reported on "Brain Mechanisms and Behavioral Variability." Additional names on the program were R. R. Sears, P. T. Young, N. R. F. Maier, D. B. Lindsley, F. L. Ruch, R. Leeper, D. L. Wolfle, and H. H. Harlow. The major address by S. W. Ransom would be timely today. It was entitled, "The Hypothalamus: Its Role in Emotions and Sleep."

With the thesis ready for writing, employment became the next problem and I began to cast a wide net because the job market was bearish and prospective employers were few and far between. My first letter went to Jim Stroud at the Teachers College in Emporia inquiring about a teaching position there. This I considered a form of insurance because Stroud had suggested earlier that my alma mater might hire me. What I really wanted was an opportunity to continue my research, and for this reason I wrote to Lashley applying for a job as histologist with time and facilities to carry on research. I also wrote to C. W. Brown at the University of California in Berkeley. He and E. E. Ghiselli were at that time studying the effects of subcortical lesions on learning and sensory discrimination in rats. My thesis had shown that cortical lesions can disrupt maternal behavior and I thought it would be very exciting to explore the effects of subcortical injury on the same responses.

My first reply came from Stroud in January. It was so encouraging that I was sure a job at Emporia was certain and on the basis of that belief I proceeded to get married in March to Anna Beth Odenweller, a Kansas girl who was a student at the Goodman School of the Theater in the Chicago Art Institute. We had met the preceding fall while both of us were members of the choir at the University Chapel.

Lashley wrote in February saying he would be glad to have me in his lab and was applying to the N.R.C. Committee for Research on Problems of Sex for a special grant which would provide a salary of $75.00 per month, "which should be adequate." C. W. Brown's reply expressed his readiness to make room for me in his research space and his regret that the only remuneration he could offer was a readership for two semesters at $100 per semester.

The general climate of the job situation at that time is reflected in a letter sent by Carr to four of us who were, hopefully, getting our degrees that spring of 1936. Professor Carr wrote that he had suggested our names to Professor C. H. Bean of the University of Louisiana, who was looking for a new instructor. Carr's letter went on as follows. "He wishes to meet you people for an interview at the Illinois Central Railroad Station, June 5th between nine and eleven o'clock (Central Standard Time). He suggests that you inquire for him from the train announcer, and also suggests that he will sit near the Bulletin Board." Observing that Professor Bean had failed to specify A.M. or P.M. Carr advised going in the morning and returning in the evening if necessary (a two-hour round trip each time). Everybody went!

In June I received a letter from Professor Raymond H. Wheeler of the University of Kansas which I quote in part because it reveals the factionalism then still extant in psychology. Wheeler stated that he had an opening for an instructor and had been "flooded with candidates." He added, "the list has been boiled down to four, of which you are one." The salary was $1,500 a year for three years and then promotion to associate professor if performance as an instructor had been satisfactory. The most interesting part of the letter follows.

"We are looking for a young Ph.D. with experimental training who is sympathetic toward but not necessarily committed to the Gestalt point of view and who would be willing to associate with a staff, all of whom are primarily Gestalt psychologists."

I didn't follow up on that one, not because of any aversion to Gestalt psychologists but because at the time I was sure I had a teaching job cinched at Emporia. Shortly thereafter Stroud wrote that the President of the Teachers

College was dubious about hiring anyone who had only been away from the college for two years, but toward the end of June I received the following telegram: "Looks more favorable can't get decision until after July 1. Stroud." The third week in June brought a definite offer from Lashley of employment from July 1, 1936, to June 30, 1937, at a monthly salary of $75. Professor Bean wrote in August, "You are a close second to a man who has another offer," but before that time the position at Emporia had definitely fallen through, and I had accepted Lashley's offer. In fact, my wife and I were already installed in Cambridge. Professionally I was irrevocably committed to research and to psychology, although even then I didn't realize how firmly she had me in her embrace. I actually imagined that I still had some choice left.

A HALCYON YEAR AT HARVARD

When I arrived at Harvard I had three definite objectives in view: (1) to analyze the results of the thesis research and prepare them for publication, (2) to conduct an experiment aimed at identifying the sensory stimuli involved in the parturient female rat's care of her young, and (3) to learn to read German and French. The third item was important because I couldn't get my Ph.D. until I had passed my language tests. In the course of the year I accomplished the first two objectives but the opportunity to spend full time on research was so attractive that I couldn't find time for language study.

The thesis was written and sent to Carr, who approved it. The experiment on sensory control of maternal behavior was sloppy but interesting. I invented some techniques, such as the use of dummy or model young, which were then being employed by Dutch and German ethologists, although at the time I was unaware of this fact. The study of cortical lesions and maternal behavior had turned out so well that I started a similar investigation dealing with effects of brain injury on copulatory behavior in male rats. This work was about half finished by the time I left Harvard.

A number of individuals helped make the year at Harvard stimulating and enjoyable. Four postdoctoral fellows were working in Lashley's laboratory. E. E. Ghiselli with an N.R.C. fellowship had just finished his Ph.D. under Tolman at Berkeley. George Drew had recently received his degree from Cambridge University working with Barlett. André Rey was a student of Piaget and had just come from Geneva. E. E. Anderson, another N.R.C. Fellow, and his wife Sarah, also a psychologist, had recently obtained their degrees at the University of Illinois. Donald Hebb was conducting his Ph.D. thesis research.

It was a lively, congenial, and exceedingly heterogeneous group, and the regular afternoon tea in the seminar room often involved heated discussions of a wide variety of scientific issues. Lashley joined in like everyone else and the atmosphere was thoroughly democratic. Lashley behaved much as he had at Chicago. I can't recall that he ever visited my lab but I often sought him out and found him always ready to talk about any problem or theoretical issue that was bothering me at the time. As a matter of form I obtained his approval for new research projects but actually I was completely free to do anything I chose.

Earlier in this account I mentioned the fact that I became entangled in a ménage à trois involving psychology. The third party in the triangle was my wife. In connection with the experiment on mating in male rats, sexually receptive females were needed as stimulus animals. Since the species is nocturnal, females come into heat at night and that was when I ran my behavior tests. After working all day I usually returned to the lab at about 7:00 P.M. and began to screen a colony of 200 females to find five or six that were receptive. If I was lucky I might collect the required number in fifteen minutes or less, but sometimes an hour or longer elapsed before I had enough receptive females to begin testing the experimental males. By the time the evening's tests were completed it was rarely earlier than eleven o'clock and sometimes it was after midnight before I got home.

This work schedule didn't leave much time to play the role of husband in a marriage not yet a year old. How and why my wife endured it I will never understand. (We did manage to attend a movie once a week and to have a treat at an ice cream parlor after the show, but that exhausted our entertainment budget.) I wouldn't have blamed her if she had sued for divorce, but naming 200 female rats as correspondents might not have gone down so well in Boston.

During our first period in Cambridge family finances were rather tight. From the $75 monthly salary $30 was spent on rent. We ate a great deal of spaghetti and chili but actually didn't feel deprived or underprivileged. I was able to supplement our income with $20 per month earned singing in the choir at the Arlington Street Church in Boston. That extra $5.00 a week made a lot of difference!

One very important event which occurred while we were in Cambridge was the birth of our first child, a boy. When he arrived my cup ran over. I was completely content with my family and my work—a state of existence that can be achieved only by the very young and that persists for limited periods of time.

I would gladly have continued to work at Harvard for several years but I was in for a rude shock. Early in the summer of 1937 Lashley informed me that he had recommended me for a position as assistant curator in the Department of Experimental Biology at the American Museum of Natural History in New York. This was the first I had heard of the position or even of the Museum and I hinted strongly to Lashley that I would rather stay in his lab, but he was quite firm in advising me to take the job if it was offered. The handwriting on the wall was all too easy to read. I was being kicked out of the nest!

Many years later I learned that while I was at Harvard Carr asked Lashley whether he would advise hiring me as an instructor at the University of Chicago. Lashley advised against such an offer and I wasn't told about it. Lashley eventually mentioned the matter after I had been at the Museum several years. He explained that he felt I should stay in full-time research.

TEN YEARS AS A MUSEUM CURATOR

The offer from the Museum came through with the munificent annual salary of $1,800. I of course accepted and in September 1937 we moved to an apartment in Jackson Heights, which is located in Queens on Long Island. I developed an immediate and permanent dislike for New York City. Living conditions improved when we moved a year later to Englewood, N.J., but commuting to the city was tiring and tiresome. It was in Englewood in 1942 that our daughter was born and it seemed to me that I couldn't have a better planned family.

The work at the American Museum of Natural History was new and challenging. Ours was the only museum in the world with a Department of Experimental Biology and it was the creation of a highly unusual and brilliant man, Dr. Gladyn Kingsley Noble. The entire department, which was better equipped than most university biology departments, was devoted to the study of animal behavior. My only responsibility was to carry on research.

I should have been in seventh heaven, but there was a very large fly in the ointment. The fly was my boss. G. K. Noble was the only man I ever met with whom I simply could not get along. His attitude toward research was completely different from mine and the intellectual climate in his department was the exact antithesis of everything I had been accustomed to in graduate school and in Lashley's laboratory at Harvard. Noble patently disliked and distrusted me and by the end of the second year I was thinking seriously about obtaining a position in a university.

Not every aspect of the situation was unpleasant. I did have excellent research facilities and full time for research. It was possible to use some of the WPA workers assigned to me as research assistants. A number of them were well educated, intelligent, and trainable in research techniques. I had access to an excellent library in the Museum. As a result I was able to turn out a respectable number of research papers each year.

An extremely important factor was the novel and immensely stimulating experience of getting to know other young men working in areas of science which were quite new to me. I picked up a smattering of knowledge about herpetology, ornithology, entomology, ichthyology, paleontology, geology, and the new taxonomy renamed "systematics." More important than acquisition of knowledge about specific fields was the constant exposure to a scientific philosophy or point of view never encountered in the experimental laboratory. It is difficult to describe, but the central theme was closely related to the study of evolution, of adaptive characters, of factors affecting natural populations, etc. Heretofore I had equated science with experimentation and my first years at the museum broadened my horizons immeasurably.

One thing that happened during my first year in New York had an immediate and pervasive effect on my work for the next three decades. As recounted earlier, at Harvard I began a study of the effects of neocortical lesions on copulatory behavior in male rats. Before leaving Cambridge I completed the preoperative tests and carried out the brain surgery. As soon as my lab at the museum was functioning I had the rats shipped from Harvard and proceeded to carry out the postoperative tests, which revealed that some brain injured males continued to copulate whereas others failed to do so.

I worried about the possibility that loss of sexual behavior following brain operation might be due to indirect interference with the endocrine system and consequent reduction in the secretion of testis hormone. Accordingly I injected all noncopulating operates with testosterone propionate. This treatment revived mating behavior in some but not all the injected males, but these findings are not important here. What is significant is the fact that this experience with the modification of behavior by hormonal treatment stimulated me to learn more about endocrinology.

I obtained permission to audit a course in endocrinology which was taught at New York University by Dr. Robert Gaunt. The course was excellent in many ways, but it included practically nothing about behavior. When I complained, Dr. Gaunt offered to turn the class over to me for one session for a review of behavioral effects of hormones. This sent me to the library, where I soon discovered that there was no comprehensive summary of the relevant evidence, and references to hormonal effects on behavior were scattered widely through a number of different journals. As my term paper for Gaunt's course I prepared a review of some 75 to 100 studies. Later in expanded form this review became my first book, *Hormones and Behavior,* which was published in 1948.

One good thing G. K. Noble did was to keep pressure on me to complete the requirements for my Ph.D. I have never had any flair for languages and the only one I had studied in school was Latin. Nevertheless, I managed to teach myself enough German and French to pass the written exams used at the University of Chicago. Then I had to return to Chicago for an oral examination covering my thesis, which had been published three years earlier. This was in 1940 and Carr had been retired for three years, but he asked to be included as one of my examiners. Others were Kingsbury, Thurstone, and Dael Wolfle, then an assistant professor in the department. After I had distributed reprints of the thesis in its published form Professor Kingsbury, who was presiding, invited Carr to begin the questioning. Carr said, "No questions." Thurstone said, "No questions." Kingsbury said, "I have no questions." Wolfle was about to explode! He asked me a rather complex question about a recent paper by N. R. F. Maier involving effects of cortical lesions on "reasoning" in rats. I had read the paper but didn't recall the details too well. However, I assumed an air of total confidence and gave the best answer I could.

Wolfle pounced like a bobcat on a squirrel, saying I had the facts right but was wrong about Maier's interpretation. Before I could open my mouth to reply Carr interrupted saying, "No, Dr. Wolfe. Beach is right and you are wrong. I recall that particular paper very clearly." Poor Wolfle! What could an assistant professor do when contradicted by a Professor Emeritus and former Chairman?

He had to remain silent, though both he and I knew very well that Carr hadn't looked inside the covers of any psychological journal for at least fifteen years.

Although I was getting a lot of research done, my situation at the museum was becoming progressively more uncomfortable and depressing and my attempts to find another position increased in vigor. Then while I was absent attending a scientific meeting Noble died of complications accompanying a peritonsilar abscess. This occurred on December 9, 1940. The Director of the museum, Dr. Roy Chapman Andrews, called me to his office and asked how long it would take to complete research in progress so that the Department of Experimental Biology could be discontinued. Andrews had nothing against the department but simply assumed it couldn't function without its founder. As a twenty-eight-year-old assistant curator who had been at the museum only three years I didn't have impressive qualifications to head up a department. Nevertheless, I was not about to roll over and play dead.

I persuaded R. M. Yerkes, Chairman of the N.R.C. Committee for Research on Problems of Sex, to write to Director Andrews saying the department should be continued and that I was capable of running it. Lashley did the same. Then, with gusto and such political skill as I could muster I launched a campaign to win over Chairmen of other departments and Trustees, who took the position that a Department of Experimental Biology was out of place in a museum. Most of the doubters on the museum staff were anxious to gain control of the physical space occupied by our department. The complete story of that running battle would make hilariously funny reading but the upshot was that I changed the name of the department to the Department of Animal Behavior and by implication challenged anyone to claim that such a department did not belong in a great museum of natural history. The alternative, I insisted, amounted to admitting that museums dealt only with fossils, bird skins, and other dead material. The final outcome was that the Department of Animal Behavior was recognized and given equal status with other departments. In 1942 my rank was raised to full Curator and I was appointed Chairman of the Department.

If at the outset I had complied with Roy Andrews' wishes the department would certainly have been eliminated. Instead, it still survives thirty years later, and it continues as an active center of first-rate research on animal behavior. My role in preserving the department has always been a source of great satisfaction and pride to me.

When Noble died I was the only member of the permanent scientific staff. There were several research workers paid from various grants but none had curatorial rank. One of these was Lester Aronson, who had taken his Master's degree under Papez in comparative neurology. Aronson was appointed curator (I cannot remember the rank) and with his aid and advice I managed to slowly increase the permanent staff. The first addition was an experimental herpetologist, Pat Blair. Next I tried to persuade T. C. Schneirla to resign his assistant professorship in psychology at NYU and come to the museum as a full-time associate curator. Ted was unwilling to cut all ties with the university, but he did accept a half-time appointment in the Department of Animal Behavior. Several years after I left the museum he became a full-time curator and continued both research and teaching until his death in 1968.

A few years as chairman of a small department convinced me that although I could function reasonably well as an administrator it definitely wasn't something I wanted to do for a long period of time. In the beginning it was an exciting challenge, but the steady pressure of constantly having to justify the existence of the department and the petty day-to-day problems of financing, keeping staff members contented, etc., wore me down. I began once again to think about moving to a university.

I believe it was during 1944 or 1945 that Benjamin Willier, Chairman of Biology at The Johns Hopkins University, invited me to join his department. Hopkins had no Department of Psychology and Willier intimated that one could be established after I had been there a few years. The thought of moving into another administrative position wasn't at all appealing and I recommended that Willier consider a young physiological psychologist who was an instructor at Harvard. As a result C. T. Morgan went to Hopkins and eventually built up one of the best departments of psychology in the country.

I continued to wait, and one fateful day in the winter of 1946 I was visited by a very youthful psychologist from Yale. He seemed so young that we talked for quite a while before I realized that Carl Hovland was departmental Chairman at Yale. He wanted to know if I would accept a full professorship at that university. After considering the offer for a few days and discussing it with my wife I decided to accept, and in July 1946 my family and I moved to New Haven, where we were to spend the next ten years.

A DECADE AT YALE

When I arrived at Yale I had been out of graduate school ten years. I had never been an assistant or associate professor, never taught college students, and was totally ignorant of the ways of academia. Perhaps most important, for a decade I had maintained almost no contact with psychology or psychologists.

My first attempt at graduate teaching was a complete disaster. After twenty minutes of the first session I was perspiring excessively, my heart rate was accelerated, and waves of nausea threatened to overcome me. It was a classic case of stage fright. I dismissed the class, went home, and spent the entire day in bed. The situation improved with practice but the symptoms recurred in full force the first time I tried to lecture to an undergraduate class in comparative psychology. I finally solved the undergraduate teaching problem by substituting for the lecture course a small seminar for hand-picked juniors and seniors. This was a successful and rewarding endeavor and only two years later did I learn that changes of this sort simply could not be made at the whim of the instructor. A very formal and formidable Committee on Courses had to give approval in advance. Throughout the years at Yale my teaching load was quite light and completely self-determined. It consisted exclusively of small seminars plus a lot of time devoted to directing research by both graduate and advanced undergraduate students. Most of the work I enjoyed immensely.

In 1950 the President of the University and the Board of Trustees changed my title to Sterling Professor of Psychology, which was a distinct honor and very gratifying. I was also pleased at about the same time to be elected President of the Eastern Psychological Association. (Fifteen years later I became President of the Western Psychological Association, and at the time I thought how humorous it would be to be elected to the same position in the Midwestern Association, thus qualifying for the award of M.V.P.M.L., most valuable president in the minor leagues.)

At Yale I engaged in various types of "service work" for the APA and a number of national boards and committees. It has been my philosophy that the professional scientist owes a certain amount of time and energy to the support and development of his discipline, although the extent of the debt is finite so that it need not be discharged in perpetuity. During the post World War II period when the APA was being reorganized I served on various bodies, including the Publications Board and the Policy and Planning Board. I was a member of the Advisory Board of the Marine Studies and the Marine Research Laboratory at St. Augustine, Florida. I also functioned on the Board of Scientific Directors of the Roscoe B. Jackson Memorial Laboratories in Bar Harbor, Maine, and eventually became Vice President of that body. When Congress established the National Science Foundation I was a charter member of the Psychobiology Panel starting in 1951. For nearly ten years beginning in 1955 I was Chairman of a small N.R.C. committee that awarded special Senior Postdoctoral Fellowships in Physiological Psychology. The money was provided by John Gardner, then President of the Carnegie Foundation and later Secretary of Health, Education, and Welfare during Lyndon Johnson's presidency. Several of our Fellows have since risen to positions of scientific eminence. In 1955 I became a member of the N.R.C. Committee for the Study of Problems of Sex and two years later was made Chairman. This was the same committee which in 1936 gave Lashley the money to pay my salary at Harvard.

One other form of off-campus activity during the Yale period involved giving various major lectures at other universities. By far the most important and honorific of these were the William James Lectures delivered at Harvard in 1950-1951. I spent a great deal of effort on the ten lectures, which were supposed to be published eventually by the Harvard Press. Each one was carefully and completely written out, but at the time I felt they were not ready for publication. To my discredit I abrogated my "gentlemen's agreement" with Harvard, and the lectures never appeared in print. However, I'm not dead yet and still may complete that job.

When the James Lecture series was in progress I commuted between New Haven and Cambridge so that I could give a graduate seminar in the Psychology

Department at Harvard and function as a visiting faculty member of the university. The experience was enjoyable and educational and I got to know well several psychologists with whom I had previously had only a passing acquaintance. These included Boring, Beebe Center, Stevens, and Skinner.

Another extracurricular effort consisted of giving the Smith College Lecture Series for 1949. This comprised four or five lectures given over a period of two months. It was a new experience to lecture in a women's college, and I particularly enjoyed the informal discussion periods which followed dinner in the different residence halls. Much of the material covered in the Smith Lectures was later incorporated into the book *Patterns of Sexual Behavior,* which I wrote with C. S. Ford.

Two other lectures that should be mentioned were the Jake Gimbel Lectures on the Psychology of Sex. In 1952 I delivered the Gimbel Lectures at the University of California in Berkeley and Stanford, and in 1954 gave another at the University of California at Los Angeles.

In the Laboratory at Yale I continued to conduct research on the neural and hormonal control of behavior—particularly sexual behavior. Until 1948 I worked with rats, hamsters, cats, and pigeons, but in that year I instituted a research program on dogs which has continued for twenty-two years.

One particularly rewarding aspect of my years at Yale involved formation of many acquaintanceships and some friendships with other faculty members. At different times the faculty included R. M. Yerkes, A. Gesell, C. L. Hull, Carl Hovland, John Dollard, Neal Miller, Leonard Doob, Irving Child, Fred Sheffield, Seymour Sarason, and Claude Buxton.

Yerkes was on the retired list but he was in his office frequently and I got to know him fairly well. He was reputed to have been something of a martinet when he served as Director of the Yale Laboratories of Primate Biology (later changed to the Yerkes Laboratory), but when I knew him he had mellowed and was quite benign toward younger colleagues. Hull was chronically ill and came to work only long enough to check up on his research assistants. Soon after my arrival I gained the impression that although many students in the department were conducting research relating to Hullian learning theory, a substantial number of them were as interested in disproving as proving the theory.

Neal Miller taught the course in learning and was firmly committed to the notion that drive reduction is a sine qua non for all forms of learning. A master of experimental design and a lucid, highly logical expositor, Miller trained many first-rate students. At first I was almost mystified by his approach and by that of Hovland, Child, and others in the department. I was totally unfamiliar with the kind of research that is derived solely from a particular theory and aimed at testing one corollary or prediction of that theory. I recognized that this paradigm was borrowed from the physical sciences, where it worked very well, but I doubted if Hullian theory, or any psychological theory of learning, was sufficiently comprehensive and precise to justify the tremendous amount of time and energy that was then being expended on testing its various ramifications. In addition, I was distressed by the feeling that negative results produced by that approach were valueless. Very often they were interpreted as faults of the experiment rather than of the theory, and in any event if the theory was wrong, research that failed to support it represented a complete waste of time. Twenty years of additional exposure to learning theory have not dispelled my skepticism.

A list of the rewarding aspects of my years at Yale would include the following items, not necessarily in order of importance: (1) learning what it is like to live and work as a faculty member in a first-class private university; (2) gaining experience in the pleasure of teaching bright upperclassmen and graduate students, particularly in terms of guiding their research efforts; (3) having the opportunity to establish acquaintance and friendships within a group of very good psychologists and a few members of other departments; and (4) having the opportunity to carry on my own research under favorable working conditions and usually in collaboration with graduate research assistants.

At the museum I read a very interesting monograph entitled "A comparative study of human reproduction" that included a great deal of information about the sexual behavior of various societies in different parts of the world. The author, C. S. Ford, was associate professor of anthropology at Yale and his office in the Institute of Human Relations was two floors above my own. "Joe" Ford and I became good friends and in 1950 we collaborated in writing a book which was published under the title *Patterns of Sexual Behavior*. Joe wrote chapters on sexual practices in different societies and I dealt with the evidence on animals other than man as well as some material concerning physiological control of sexual behavior. We worked closely together and rewrote each other's original drafts so often that the final product seemed to be the product of a single pen. It was a very educational and emotionally rewarding venture.

During the tenth year at Yale I decided it would be a good idea to take a year off and get completely away from the lab—something I hadn't done for longer than two weeks at a time since starting my thesis twenty years earlier. This decision was stimulated by receipt of an invitation to spend a year as a Fellow at the Center for Advanced Study in the Behavioral Sciences in Stanford, California. I obtained leave from Yale and arrived at the Center with my family in June 1957.

INTERLUDE FOR CONTEMPLATION

The purpose of the Center was and is to provide up to fifty Fellows at a time with the opportunity to get away from their regular work and spend part or all of a year doing anything they feel will improve or enrich their professional lives and contributions. The Center is located on the eastern slope of the coastal hills just west of the campus of Stanford University, and the architecture and physical layout are extremely attractive. Each Fellow has a private study and there is a common dining room, rooms for seminars, a small library, plus numerous lovely patios and outdoor gathering places where Fellows can take morning and afternoon coffee with or without the company of colleagues.

Every Fellow does precisely what he chooses. There are no rules or regulations, no expectations of material evidence of accomplishment, and no provisions for doing research other than that which can be done in a library. Some Fellows spend their time organizing and conducting seminars and others just talk and exchange ideas. The range of specialties represented is very wide. The year I was there the fellowship included psychologists, lawyers, anthropologists, psychiatrists, novelists, neurophysiologists, geneticists, and one poet.

Most Fellows spend a lot of their time writing, and this was what I did. My original objectives were (1) to prepare for publication several experiments that had been carried out at Yale, and (2) to write a book based upon my William James Lectures. I accomplished the first aim but not the second. The failure was not due to lack of application. I wrote and rewrote sixteen chapters of what I hoped would serve as a textbook in comparative psychology. By the time the sixteenth chapter was finished I was thoroughly confused and disillusioned. It seemed to me that there simply was no substantive field of comparative psychology. At best there might be an "animal psychology," but that wasn't what I wanted to write about. I put the manuscript aside with a resolve to come back to it for a second try in a year or so. Thirteen years have passed and I have done no more work on that project; but I have not abandoned it forever.

Toward the end of my year at the Center I received a visit from two young men who were then assistant professors in the Psychology Department at the University of California in Berkeley. I had known both of them at Yale. Jerry McClearn had been an assistant professor and Lyman Porter had taken his Ph.D. at Yale a few years earlier. Jerry and "Port" had come to ask whether I would consider accepting a professorship at Berkeley.

This "feeler" put me in somewhat of a quandary. I was quite happy at Yale. The administration had treated me very well indeed. I liked and admired many of my fellow faculty members. Research facilities were quite good. There were no negative factors impelling me to leave Yale. There were, however, several attractive aspects of a possible move to the University of California. One of the strongest of these was the opportunity to change my academic environment.

Each move I had made in the past—Chicago to Harvard, Harvard to the Museum, and the Museum to Yale—had given me new perspectives, broadened my intellectual horizons, and in general enriched my understanding of and approach to science. At the same time experience suggested that the invigorating effects of a change in jobs dissipated gradually and was pretty well "used up" after four or five years. I was convinced that, comfortable and contented as I was at Yale, I had learned as much as I was going to learn from being there, and the opportunity to change to one of the best of the State Universities held a strong appeal. Another factor that influenced my thinking and that of my wife was the welcome possibility of escaping permanently from the sleet-swept winters and enervatingly humid summers of the northeastern seaboard. Finally, it was reassuring to realize that if we moved to Berkeley we would be joining old friends. David Krech was a professor, and so was Ed Ghiselli, whom we had known very well at Harvard.

After several weeks of deliberation and extended conferences with Leo Postman, Chairman of the Department, and Clark Kerr, then Chancellor at Berkeley, I decided to make the move. My arrangements with Kerr and Postman included agreements that I would retain the prerogatives I had enjoyed at Yale, namely determination of my own teaching assignments, if any; assignment of a full-time secretary; ample research space; and a promise I would never be asked to serve as departmental chairman.

BERKELEY: THE END OF THE ROAD?

My appointment as Professor of Psychology in the University of California began July 1, 1958, and at the time of writing I have been here fifteen years. It has been a productive stretch of time.

There are, of course, many differences from Yale, some good and some bad. The sheer size of the University has had little effect upon my situation. I have continued to teach one small seminar for undergraduates once a year and another for graduate students. The general calibre of undergraduates in the top 10 percent of each class appears comparable to a similar population at Yale. From a selfish point of view I prefer the graduate students at California over those we used to get at Yale, for only one reason. When I was at Yale the reputation of our department was based primarily on the work of Clark Hull and his associates on learning theory. Accordingly, many of the best students came to New Haven because of a prior interest in and commitment to that special area of psychology. First-year students with a primary interest in physiological or comparative psychology were few and far between. I got some very good ones and am proud of them today, but some years the pickings were pretty slim. At Berkeley, in contrast, each year's incoming class is more heterogeneous and almost always includes some young men and women who are uncommitted and can be led gently to work on research problems in the comparative and physiological areas. In the past fifteen years I have spent a great deal of time working with graduate students. In particular, many of them have first served as my apprentices in research and then gone on to develop into independent scientists. This form of teaching is the only way to train a research worker, and a number of my "final products" at Berkeley have provided me with great satisfaction and pride.

One major improvement resulting from the move to Berkeley has been the opportunity to establish a Field Station for Research in Animal Behavior. Two years after my arrival I canvassed faculty members in the departments of psychology, zoology, anthropology, and physiology to discover if there was any interest in creating a special research facility where the behavior of various species could be studied under conditions less artificial and confining than those ordinarily obtaining in the laboratory but amenable to more control than could be imposed in the natural environment of free-living animals. The response from all quarters was strongly positive and eventually a grant for approximately three hundred and fifty thousand dollars was obtained from the National Science Foundation to pay all of the costs of construction. The University provided land in the Strawberry Canyon area of the East Berkeley Hills, only ten minutes drive from the campus.

Since its opening in 1963 the Field Station has proved to be a unique and very useful research adjunct. Its use by members of various departments has gradually but steadily increased, and I feel that in getting it started I made a real contribution to the University.

EPILOGUE

In the course of nearly forty years I have seen psychology undergo many changes. The most striking of these have resulted from progressive expansion, diversification, and increasing specialization. Contemplating these phenomena I am reminded of the evolutionary history of many types of plants and animals. In the beginning there is an ancestral prototype—a population containing considerable genetic diversity, living in a variable environment containing many different ecological niches. Different segments of the original population move or are forced into various environments, and there they continue to evolve by virtue of chance mutations and differential selection pressures exerted by the different environments.

The longer they remain separated, the more distinct the descendant groups become, until eventually they are no longer interfertile and have attained the status of separate species. Some of these species may prosper, continuing their radiation and evolutionary progress. Others become static, overspecialized, resistant to the changes which may be necessitated by a varying environment and incapable of taking advantage of new opportunities offered by such changes. When a species reaches this state, it is headed for extinction.

It is clear that we already have more than one species of psychology. Clinical and industrial psychology are distinct from each other and from all other branches of specialties in the field. Social and physiological psychology have very little in common. It appears well within the bounds of possibility that in the not too distant future psychology will be completely separated into several different disciplines with totally different curricula, separate degrees, etc.

My own specialty, comparative psychology, has undergone a series of interesting changes. During the first fifteen years of this century it flourished and then fell into desuetude. In the late 1940s and early 1950s there occurred a modest resurgence of interest sparked to some degree by English translations of research conducted primarily in Germany and Holland by a small group of zoologists who called themselves ethologists. During the ensuing ten or fifteen years comparative psychology has slowly but steadily gained ground in the United States, at least so it seems to me.

I have found a career in psychology exciting and rewarding. It may seem strange to close an autobiography with plans for the future but I prefer to classify this account as a progress report rather than a terminal document. My plans are gradually to reduce by perhaps seventy-five percent the amount of time and energy I spend on research, and to devote more of my professional efforts to writing and teaching. I would like in particular to do more teaching at the undergraduate level, an obligation I have neglected almost shamefully in the past. If I live long enough and study diligently I may even acquire the wisdom needed to write a reasonably definitive textbook in my area of specialization, and this would be a very gratifying climax or consummation of my long-standing affair with psychology.

Raymond B Cattell

Raymond B. Cattell

CHILDHOOD

Psychologists have documented what wise men down the ages have always known, that light is thrown even on the most intellectual activities of man's life by his childhood experiences, his heredity, and his historical-cultural roots. What one would give to know something of the childhood of Plato, St. Paul, or Archimedes!

As far as my father and grandfather are concerned, both of whom were engineer designers running their own business in the English Midlands, I would have not the slightest difficulty in placing them in the stream of Victorian, middle-class liberalism. I grew up hearing my father talk about the virtues of Bentham, Free Trade, Darwin, Huxley, Rational Nonconformism, Gladstone, and scientific progress. The Cattells were of Scottish and, distantly, Norwegian origin (the name has been anglicized from Ketyl, meaning Cauldron). But my mother's people, the Fields, came from the Stratford-on-Avon region, and when, as Chesterton said, "Birmingham grew so big, so big, and Stratford stayed so small," they entered as a reluctant family duty into retaining the squire's status by entering the industrial game. My uncle ran the industrial plant my grandfather had set up. But Uncle Bob's heart stayed in timbered houses, thoroughbred horses, and the way of life of a conservative yeoman. I can see now his rather patrician face as he looked down his nose with gentle repugnance at my father's lively dissertations on liberalism. But I also remember the affection of his workmen when I was occasionally taken to Grandfather Field's spring and axle factory to watch the golden showers of sparks as the great steam hammers struck the white hot ingots. Although the intellectual stimulus around the family table came from my father, who loved history and literature as much as the applied science in his own work, I discovered, when I became a psychologist and ventured to test my parents' intelligence, that his IQ was only 120 against my mother's 150. This has shown up in the relative occupational records of the Fields and the Cattells, the former having in this generation five doctors (including my oldest son, a surgeon) in their offspring.

When I was six, three years before World War I, we moved to a house on the coast of Devonshire, with magnificent views. The two powerful impressions in my life between then and my going to London University, a decade later, came, on the one hand, through the carefree adventures of boyhood on that incomparably lovely seacoast, and, on the other, from the disturbing and cruel shadow which World War I threw across our lives. For a young man destined to scientific interests, 1905 was a felicitous year into which to be born. The airplane was a year old, the Curies and Rutherford in that year penetrated the heart of the atom and the mystery of its radiations, Binet launched the first intelligence test, and Einstein, the theory of relativity. But as far as an Englishman was concerned, it was also just about the year in which the British Empire and its secure and expansive way of life started downhill. The Boer War was a tremor, World War I was an earthquake, and after that the prosperous, leisurely, and disciplined way of life with its confident world leadership ended. But even as a child, I got the feel of its quality enough to mourn, with Galsworthy, over the Forsytes, and to recognize that middle-class Victorian England was in some respects a high point from which civilization was capable of falling away.

My parents were exacting on standards, but permissive about how I spent my time. I seemed to live on the beach, learned to sail at seven, and spent much of my time in boats exploring the coast in sun and rain (but never in snow, for the winters were mild). South Devon is as rich in history as it is in natural beauty. Off the beach which ran from the great stone wall at the end of our garden, Napoleon had come nearest to setting his foot on English soil—as prisoner on the *Bellerophon,* anchored just offshore. On the headland two miles away, William of Orange landed to maintain the Protestant succession. At Compton Castle, back of the woods, still lived the descendants of Sir Humphrey Gilbert, who planted the first English colony in North America. Thirty miles to the west was Plymouth and the house where the Mayflower Compact was written. At the southern edge of the "known world," as far as my boyhood, small-boat trips were concerned (seven miles to be exact!), was Dartmouth and its twin castles, whence Richard Coeur de Lion set out for the crusades.

Over all this, but with more depth of historical, emotional identification than adults are apt to think children experience, my brothers, the village boys, and I sailed, swam, fought group battles, explored caves, landed on rocky islands, and occasionally drowned or fell over cliffs. My parents were carefully shielded from knowing about the times we had nearly been blown out to sea. Many of my friends played organized games at school, too, but though I enjoyed games my closest companions were those who joined me in building our own boats, exploring Dartmoor, making gunpowder in my "chemistry shed" in the apple orchard, and so on. For us, these had more "content" than could be found in a leather ball. And I read widely. I recall particularly that at ten I "discovered" H. G. Wells, Verne, Mee's Encyclopedia, Conan Doyle, and countless others.

Then came the war, which many people thought would be over in three months, but which my father, with prophetic accuracy, said would last four or five years, adding that we would go hungry before the end of it. Sea scouts (among whom I was an underage "recruit") were deemed to have alert young eyes, useful for spotting periscopes from coast guard stations. This I enjoyed, though awestricken to see the holes as big as a house that torpedo and mine could blow in steel plates. And then came the long trainloads of wounded from Flanders (Arras, St. Quentin, Paschendael, and the whole Western front being scarcely 300 miles away), still in their bloodstained bandages. As a scout I helped at Singer's (the sewing machine Singer) mansion, half a mile from home, turned into a vast hospital. Silently there came an abiding sense of seriousness into my life, compounded of a feeling that one could not be less dedicated than these, and of a new sense, for a boy, of the brevity of life and the need to accomplish while one might. I believe one consequence of this may be the impatience with squandered research which leads me to more irascible comment than some casual recipient's of research funds nowadays think appropriate. The emotional experience of the young in those earlier times has been expressed with great fidelity and better literary grace than I can command in Vera Brittain's *Testament of Youth.*

Meanwhile, schooling went on, though the excellent teachers in our Torquay Grammar School (a scholarship, "selective secondary school") dwindled in number, and one or two returned minus hand or eye. The headmaster was a very intelligent and hard-driving man, a cousin of Kipling, whom he closely resembled. As far as I was concerned he divided his time between giving me special personal sessions in science and mathematics, and thrashing me for various original deviations from school regulations. Both really expressed a special concern for my future, as shown in other ways, too, but there were distressing moments when I found the first four lines of Kipling's "If" of help.

Our patriarchal family pattern produced, as might be expected, a fine Freudian Oedipus situation between my older brother—the first born—and father. Behind this battleline I pursued my interests screened from paternal notice, and with the warm sustenance of a mother who delighted in her three sons. My older brother had a strong and warm personality that would have made a mark on the world had his intelligence equaled it. (Over a hundred men who counted him a real friend mourned at his funeral recently.) But I constantly trod close on his heels at school (for we were promoted by ability, not age), and, with a little tactlessness on the part of teachers, this led to colossal quarrels (before my parents wisely moved him to an old public school). If I admit to scars of distrustful independence in my personality, they would come from the severe stresses of maintaining my freedom of development under a powerful brother three years older, who could be outwitted, but not overcome.

THE UNIVERSITY

At fifteen, I passed the Cambridge University entrance examination (the "Cambridge Senior" in which I was granted first-class honors), but since my scientific interests indicated London University, and my parents were loath to leave me on my own in London at that age, I did not go until sixteen. By the momentum of what were essentially boyish interests I continued in physics and chemistry, and graduated at nineteen (with first-class honors: *Magna cum laude* in American terms). It might thus seem that I had remained loyal to the physical sciences; but London is a broadening and stimulating place for a young man. People of eminence in many fields beyond the academic constantly pass through, to an extent not found in the relatively cloistered retreats of Cambridge and Oxford, nor in other provincial universities. I had browsed far outside science in my reading and attended public lectures—Bertrand Russell, H. G. Wells, Huxley, and Shaw being my favorite speakers. (The last, in a meeting at King's College, converted me to vegetarianism—for most of two years!).

A variety of circumstances conspired in my last year of work in the physical sciences to crystallize that sense of a serious concern with social problems which had been awaiting germination in the five years since the war. First there was the adolescent ferment itself. Second, there was the physical dreariness of London, and its extremes of wealth and poverty, contrasting with the self-respecting middle-class values of my Eden in the West. Compared to capitals I now know, Tokyo to Prague, or Moscow to Canberra, London is a mellow, neighborly, and "livable" city. But, in spite of the intellectual stimulus I have mentioned, it was, by contrast to what I had known, a squalid sprawl of mean streets (except, of course, for the West End, which every visitor knows). Third, there was the "intellectual" ferment or at least a ferment of discussion in the predominantly socialist groups in Bloomsbury, which we students considered "advanced."

Soon my laboratory bench began to seem small and the world's problems vast. Yet, like someone in a railroad station, watching trains depart and knowing they are not his, I declined all the standard remedies by political parties or religious affiliations. Gradually I concluded that to get beyond human irrationalities one had to study the workings of the mind itself. The task seemed enormous—dismaying, but for the optimism of youth. Yet from that moment, a few months before my science degree, I realized that psychology was to be my life interest. And like the timely flash of a bell-buoy, when one has tacked one's sloop to a new course in the dark, I had the illumination right then of hearing a lecture by Sir Cyril Burt, on the work of Sir Francis Galton. As I packed up my flasks and condensers I had to endure some good-natured chaff from my fellow chemists, since psychology was then regarded, not without grounds, as a subject for cranks. More soberly, my close friends sought to dissuade me on the grounds that with only six professorships in the country, and no such career recognized as that of a "practicing psychologist," I should starve. But, after fifteen lean years, my choice seemed to me justified. It provided exactly what I had to have—a means of contributing more fundamental solutions to social problems, along with the intellectually esthetic fascination of pursuing a science.

At that time, at University College, Spearman was in the integrating stages of his monumental studies on the structure of human abilities, and there (though registered at King's) I spend most of five years until I received my Ph.D. in February 1929. These were years which, by virtue of Spearman himself and the men from far and near gathered around, came to be lived in an atmosphere of adventure well-suited to a young man's expanding years from 19 to 23. That spirit, I gathered from friends, was very similar to what prevailed at the very same time with Rutherford at Cambridge. Great men intrigue me, with something of the feeling one gets before a lofty mountain or other magnificent natural spectacle, but with more significance. Despite a marked shyness as a young man, I have been privileged to know rather well several men in psychology and associated areas I would call great or near-great—Spearman, Sir Cyril Burt, Haldane, Sir Ronald Fisher, Sir Godfrey Thomson, Thurstone, Thorndike, Terman, Lashley— as well as all but one of the writers in the fourth and fifth volumes of these histories of psychology. It is not my purpose to try any ranking among them—their virtues are too diverse—but Spearman was uniquely great. He conveyed on the one hand, a sense of historical depth of scholarship, and on the other, an almost naive freshness of approach. He would take up a conversation as if he had just been talking to Plato, and then stagger you with a sharp experimental novelty that no contemporary psychologist had thought of. For this unworldly and absent-minded man, life was pared down to essentials: the fascinated pursuit of truth, the encountering of life's absurdities by a sanity of droll humor, and an affection for family and coworkers.

My friends proved right about the absence of positions in psychology, and, to survive in a first university position, I had to take on the protective coloration of an educationist. But already in this position at Exeter University (back in my Devon lanes, and striding across the heather of beloved Dartmoor), my mind seethed with research plans. It was plain to me, as John Stuart Mill had stated it, that the only proof of structure and causal relation lies in covariation, and that correlation and the new tool of factor analysis which Spearman had created could now be advantageously applied on a wide front—to personality structure and to the difficult problem of finding the dynamic roots of behavior. Psychoanalysis was "the rage" in English psychology at that time (it struck Britain twenty years before the peak in America); but the clinical method obviously was nothing more than a reconnaissance. The real unraveling of drive structure and the concepts of "ego," "superego," conflict, anxiety, and other dimensions of human temperament required measurement, experiment, multivariate analysis. Various futile taxonomies had been aborted, but psychology still had to have a new birth of quantitative taxonomy if it was ever to take its place among the sciences.

In a year I designed most of a strategy which, as it proved, but as I little suspected, was to take me a lifetime to execute! Of course, its tactics changed and developed, but the basic conceptions I then argued into existence with my psychologist friends have stood. Spearman was not unaware of these possibilities in the personality field, but at that time he reached retirement age and went to America. There, as some of us saw with wonder, he started a new career! Alas, however, as so often must happen in science, his remaining years were spent in lecturing, explaining, and defending (mostly against absurdly ignorant criticism) the theory of "g," for those who could not read on their own. My new proposals were therefore tried largely on Burt, who proved a sympathetic and extremely insightful commentator (my papers on temperament structure and measurement which appeared in 1933-1934 owe much to him).

CLINICAL EXPERIENCE

I think it was through Burt also that I crystallized the aim of going out of academic work into clinical work for five years. The laboratory had been my home for ten years, at school and university, but from the beginning I scented something inadequate and misdirected even in the best-intentioned brass-instrument psychology. Much of it was going through the motions and wearing the livery of a science, without any real relevance to the nature of the new problems this new science faced. Learning theory, especially sensation and perception, were at that time, it seemed to me, given over to models, e.g., the "reflex," which avoided testing against the major wholistic problems and life realities. They were in danger of developing a conventional Chinese Mandarin culture, writing more and more about less and less. Admittedly some quite fine people followed this stance of Wundt, imitating the physical sciences, and probably a "dramatic" and symbolically "brass instrumental" pose was neces-sary to emphasize that psychology needed to become a rigorous science. But I felt strongly that something more subtle was needed than a straight imitation of physics. Our problems were totally different, needing creative thought to de-velop new methodologies of our own. This I was eventually able to express, many years later, in integrated form in the *Handbook of Multivariate Experi-mental Psychology.*

Meanwhile, personality and motivation research clearly had to begin with significant personality and motivation data, and these abounded in the clinic, not, as yet, in the laboratory. By good fortune the city of Leicester was then, in advance of virtually all but London, setting up a school psychological service and clinic. In accepting its direction, I bargained for and got a division of the examination and treatment of the patient more clearly between the psycho-logical and the physical, medical side than a psychiatry-dominated tradition had previously allowed. I have written as forcefully as possible on this right of the practicing psychologist to full stature, e.g., in Berg and Pennington (Cattell, 1954), and I believe my evangelism has not been in vain. In those years I gathered just the experience I needed to balance my experimental, factor-analytic methodology with a feeling for the real issues in personality. I de-veloped projection test designs independently of Murray (published the same years, 1935-1936), differing in mine being verbal and answered selectively, for objective scoring, while his (the TAT) was pictorial and inventive in answer form. I have been asked if this was also the first use of the term "projective tests" and, not having searched the literature, I cannot say, but I described the principles, derived from psychoanalytic projection, in my 1936 book, *A Guide to Mental Testing,* and called them "projective tests" to distinguish them from other principles there described for other objective nonquestionnaire personality test devices. At Leicester I also wrote *Crooked Personalities in Childhood and After* (1938): a popular book on child guidance work, *Your Mind and Mine* (1934) (the easiest writing and reading and the best-selling book I ever wrote); and translated, from German, Kretschmer's *Psychology of Men of Genius* (1934).

Nevertheless, I must always regret that some of the potentially most vigorous research years of my life were lost in the nine-to-five administrative and clinical work of those years. I was caught in a three-cornered competition between wanting to make this first school psychological service a success, convincing to other cities, giving some steady time to continue the basic research in personality dynamics, and working on the social reform problems that had been a major component in my shift to psychology. A scholarly type of work I managed to write in the last field, *Psychology and Social Progress* (1933), received good reviews (but poor sales). Then, at this point, I saw an opportunity to combine research with social problem orientations. In daily practice I had noticed the depressing correlation of lower intelligence and larger family. It happened that I had begun to develop culture-fair intelligence tests, and the two concerns came together in a plan to test the relation of family size to culture-fair intelligence scores of children across the whole city.

In some way I do not remember (though I suspect the good offices of Sir Ronald Fisher, with whom I had discussed the plan), Leonard Darwin, the son of Charles Darwin, then President of the Eugenics Society, where I attended meetings, generously came forward with money to support a two-year investigation. I tried to write up the results in the form of an appeal to public conscience in my book, *The Fight for Our National Intelligence* (1937), the prefaces to which were better than the book, and by more distinguished men, namely, Darwin; Armitage, the very helpful Director of Education (himself a scientist); and Lord Horder, the king's physician. By virtue of these prefaces it got press notice and even a couple of leading articles, but, alas, not enough to start a chain reaction leading to a formal government investigation. (A Royal Commission *did* inquire on intelligence and birth rate some years later, with Burt and Thomson as witnesses.)

The hostile reaction of acquaintances among left-wing intellectuals (including Hogben and Laski) to my assertion of a positive correlation (0.25) between the innate component of intelligence and social status was the beginning of the end of my youthful illusion that intellectuals had a special monopoly on penetrating and unprejudiced intelligence. But it provoked me to further investigation of a matter on which there was then no information whatever in England (and only Fryer's limited data in America), namely, the actual means and sigmas of intelligence for a wide sample of occupations. First, I worked further to produce (by the "perceptual test" principle) more g-saturated and culture-fair intelligence tests. The results were published in 1934, and followed by five articles (1936, 1937a, 1937b, 1938a, 1938b) dealing with national reserves of intelligence and the theoretical analysis of the relation of intelligence distributions to sociopolitical effects.

Meanwhile I managed to squeeze some time to keep the basic personality structure investigations going by ratings, questionnaires, and objective tests (laboratory, projective, humor, etc.). In view of Sir Godfrey Thomson's "sampling theory," there began to appear grave technical doubts as to whether any factoring that yielded many factors and low communalities needed more than random structure to account for the correlations, and if this were true there would be no structural invariance from study to study. Consequently, my first studies were crucial for further advance, not so much in the particular trait conceptions they generated, as in revealing whether any stable structure whatever could be established in the personality domain by objective, multivariate analysis approaches.

The first checks across groups were encouraging. But about this time my work was interrupted. The accumulated result of years of overwork began to show in both my domestic life and in my health. As to the latter, I have ever since suffered from a functional stomach disorder (which declines to be classified as stomach ulcers) and also, curiously from a shift in sleep habits from needing seven and one-half hours a night to having to take nine. The prospects of ever being able to lead a normal professional life—to pursue psychological research in a university position without running two jobs—remained as remote as my chemist friends had predicted. Nothing new that required expenditures could develop in Britain, which had just staggered out of the depression only to fall immediately into putting all available national resources into armaments. As far as my personal life was concerned, this turn of history meant no development of psychology in Britain in the foreseeable future. Some six professors still held the same chairs as ten years earlier (all discouragingly hale and hearty); and it seemed my best years would have to be consumed by the locusts of petty routine. My wife, the daughter of an artist (who was head of a college of art) and accustomed to gracious living, was near the end of her endurance of living on a salary of $1,200 in a dark and damp basement flat. (Even allowing for inflation, it is far from what young psychologists five years after the Ph.D. are accustomed to in today's prosperous age.) Busy as I was, she had to put up with neglect as well as straightened circumstances. Our affection and compatibility were as great as in marriages that succeed in the normal ranges of stress. But I could not blame her when she finally left me, and, after two twilight years in which we exchanged letters like two people still in love and far separated, she remarried into more comfortable circumstances.

Had we known it, those years were the darkest just before the dawn. I had considered going to America, which, owing to the progressive attitude of universities there, was certainly the land of opportunity in psychology. But England was deep in my bones. In no country (except once in Djakarta, where I was taken for a Dutchman) do traveled people recognize me as anything but an Englishman. Even my American children complain of this anachronism. And this was true of my inner attachments. "In Avons of the heart her rivers run." And after a supremely fulfilled and satisfying childhood in Devonshire the thought of leaving, as it then seemed forever, the white beaches of Oddicombe, smiling like white teeth between the deep red cliffs, and the sleeping apple orchards among deep, wooded coombs, was unbearable. For those who like "travelogues," I have described the harmonies of those early years in *Under Sail Through Red Devon* (1937), telling of her rivers and estuaries, and landfalls at harbors where Elizabethans sat on the quay and talked to me.

The personal crisis, well nigh of despair, with which the social crisis of the times had faced me, tested the truth of Scawen Blunt's lines: "He who has once been happy is for aye, out of destruction's reach." The broken marriage and the bleak future could be met. But could I disloyally uproot myself from that which had created the fiber of my being? The die was cast one day when I received a persuasive letter from E. L. Thorndike, asking me to be a research associate with him for a year. Of course, I knew of Thorndike's work and it seemed to me about the most imaginative and fundamental that I knew of in America, though Hull, Thurstone, Tolman, and Lashley also strongly appealed to my scientific tastes. I was stirred by the privilege and the possibilities, and after three days of emotional struggle decided to go. After all, it was only for a year. It was characteristic of Thorndike's perspective, and independence, that he had reached out to a stranger three thousand miles away, possessing no personal "pull." He had reacted purely to what he had found in my publications. I have tried to do the same in my turn for oncoming psychologists, judging by performance, not the "old school associations."

SETTLING IN AMERICA

There was a sense in which Thorndike had taken a cuckoo into his nest, for at first I disturbed the laboratory circle of devoted followers, including Wood-yard and Lorge, by somewhat alien criticisms. Thorndike devoted the last five years of his life to social psychology, and at that time, with the three of us as research associates, he had turned to what impressed me as a more refreshingly empirical and methodologically more imaginative multivariate approach to social structure than had been thought of by pure sociologists. At Thorndike's request I read the *Encyclopedia of the Social Sciences* from end to end that year in search of any precise evidence on social motivation. I was in a minority with respect to the book—which appeared two years later as *Your City*—first because, with my doctrinaire Bloomsbury values, I thought Thorndike's definition of goodness of civic life was too bourgeois, and, second, because I had argued for using Thurstone's recent multivariate analysis instead of assuming a single dimension of goodness. Regarding the first I now realize I was caught in a typical youthful doctrinaire imbibement; but as to the second my own cross-national studies later showed the richer yield from letting values reveal their own associations.

Whether from culture shock or personal reasons of the heart I do not know, but during that year in New York I was continually depressed, and I reproached myself with not being as useful to Thorndike in that condition as I had intended to be. However, he was a sensitive man and, sensing my nostalgia, was extremely kind. Indeed, I was heartened years afterwards to hear he had reported that the years in which Lorge, Maslow, and I had been his associates had been, in diverse ways, the most stimulating high points in his research life.

I am not throwing a conventional bouquet when I say I learned a lot from Thorndike that year. It was not technical learning, but rather the beginning of a revolution in my idea of science and culture, derived initially from seeing Thorndike's informal, improvising, resourceful, pioneer style of attack. I began to see the difference between the academic scholar and the effective researcher which has since become increasingly clear. It ties up in part with a cultural difference between Mediterranean European classical learning on the one hand and the empiricism which perhaps reaches its fullest expression in the English-speaking countries. I began to be aware of a preciosity, intellectual effeminacy, and authoritarian pretentiousness in some of the European tradition to which I had been raised. For the Channel has not been wide enough to stop invasion by much wordy and subjective "theoretical concepts." The truth of Kipling's lines (which, from memory, I probably advantageously misquote):

> Oh, what avails the postulate and academic word
> Against the awkward incident that actually occurred.

became clearer to me. Of course, each has some virtues, and in living among our empiricists, I have been appalled at the lack of interest in real theory, when it actually works. In my own field I think particularly of factor analysts who think only of "condensing data" without regard to the quite beautiful personality structure model that can involve factor analysis, of the attitude to intelligence theory that "intelligence is what is measured by intelligence tests," and of the stony stare that for twenty years has greeted the exciting theories of the dynamic calculus.

A valuable year with Thorndike ended not by my returning to England but by my going to Clark University. The G. Stanley Hall Professorship seemed a plum to a young man of 34, but it was vacant primarily because most people knew Clark to be an unhappy university. Murchison and Hunter had simultaneously left the year before after six months of communicating with each other only through the departmental secretary. All the quarrels at Clark which looked personal were largely explicable on Hegelian lines—or, if ghosts are more tangible than the spirit of history, by the ghosts of Hall and Clark continuing their deadly struggle for an elite university and a poor boy's college, respectively. That is another story, but suffice it that as a newcomer I stepped in where more knowing people declined to tread. With some help from Boring, who knew the situation all too well, I soon moved from the professorship at Clark to a lectureship at Harvard. With these distractions I accomplished nothing in three years but some work on culture-fair intelligence tests, with Sarason, the findings of which, however, set me on the track of the theory of fluid intelligence which I set forth at the APA meeting in 1941. This, and my *Bulletin* article in 1943, started a valuable interaction and association with Thurstone. At the London laboratory, he and Godfrey Thomson were considered to represent two distinct kinds of heresy, and though I already admired the acumen of both of these men, it was obviously my duty to convert them when opportunity allowed. My visit to Thurstone at Chicago with this purpose resulted in my being so impressed with his fair-minded and penetrating arguments that I seem to have been defending his major positions ever since!

At Harvard, settled down and feeling the sap of creativity rising, I began once more to put out ideas and methods, and to gather data in the broad plan of personality research. At those luncheons which Boring has described, and in which he did a most skilful job of keeping conversation from splintering into triviality, I enjoyed the interaction of Allport, Beebe-Center, Lashley, Morgan, Murray, Sheldon, Stevens, and White. However, in personality theory, Allport and I spoke a different language, which circumstance, incidentally, was tough on students. (Why do we expect undergraduates to reconcile what we cannot resolve ourselves?)

Being a bachelor, I now practically lived in Emerson Hall (as also did Sheldon and Stevens, whose office lights burned with mine on Christmas Day and other unlikely times). My design for personality measurement called for correlations within each of the three basic media of observation: ratings on life behavior, questionnaire item responses, and behavior in objective test situations. In the last case, the domain of measurable behavioral responses had to be *created* in situational tests before it could be used for measurement and factoring. As to the first medium, with which there were good reasons for beginning first, I got some excellent ratings, done in a tank battalion, by men who had seen each other in many situations, and I made some progress in questionnaires. But except for polishing up tests like rigidity, cursive miniature situations, shock endurance, etc., that I had used back in London, I made no major progress in this third "T-data" medium while at Harvard.

As the second world war in my lifetime began, a difficult decision appeared. From duty, or mass excitement, most of us just beyond the upper bound of the draft age nevertheless joined in, stirred by colleagues appearing in handsome uniforms, or by talk of "important" jobs in Washington. With the precedent of Pavlov, working steadily through the clamor of the Russian revolution, before me, I chose to keep basic research going, no matter how the funds for the small back laboratory might dwindle. I was quite unable to agree with Boring that Pearl Harbor was "the last day when pure scholarship could be undertaken with a clear conscience" *(History of Psychology in Autobiography,* Vol. IV, 1952). It was a lonely time. The problem was resolved, however, when Richardson (he of the K-R formula) at the Adjutant General's Office offered me a chance to do exactly what seemed most central in the basic research area itself, namely, construct and try out objective personality tests (with officer selection as the practical goal).

The group of psychologists at the Adjutant General's Office was a highly congenial one, and the way in which basic research issues were advanced by discussion, consecutively pursued from day to day, opened my eyes to the fact that the usual university department, in which each man is relatively isolated in his own area, is far from the ideal setting for research—as distinct from teaching. When such as Richardson, Brogden, Wherry, Rundquist, and Tuddenham sat around the table, psychometric issues went briskly toward better solutions than are usually reached in any APA meeting or in departmental offices. It was this experience that was partly responsible for my working to form later the Society of Multivariate Experimental Psychology and the university-independent Institute for Research on Morality and Adjustment.

Everyone else was working on questionnaires or attitude scales and I was completely on my own with objective personality tests. For three months, borne on one of those tides of creativity which sometimes come at the right time, I worked furiously to devise all kinds of new diagnostic miniature situations. Perhaps a quarter of the four hundred or more tests that eventually appeared in *Objective Personality and Motivation Tests* (1967) were designed then, the rest coming from the Illinois period. In due course they were administered at Fort Benning—Richardson, Rundquist, and others regarding me with the friendly but amused scepticism with which square-rigged sailors watched the first steamboat. The rich harvest was gathered in for scoring and I prepared to sit down to the feast of curiosity that the first factor-analytic resolution of this area would supply. In effect, would there be a well-defined structure, and of few or many factors, and how related to known source traits? Alas, at that moment the banquet was snatched away. Peace was declared. With bewildering rapidity the organization evaporated: everyone's thoughts were reoriented, each to new personal goals. All further expenditures were stopped and my great bunch of IBM cards was conveyed officially to some dusty limbo whence only an order from the Adjutant General could release them. (My first realization of what this meant happened to come on the morning a bomber flew low over our Madison Avenue AGO offices and crashed into the Empire State Building. For the keyed-up military the sudden new demands of personal readjustments were even more disturbing than had been the call to war.)

I intended to retrieve those cards if I had to break in with a blow torch. For where would I find again, in an ordinary university setting, heavy with teaching duties and bereft of the fine computing and clerical services Richardson had accumulated, the possibility of carrying out research on such a scale? At that point, the Thorndike episode repeated itself, in that Herbert Woodrow, recently APA President, and quite unknown to me by any personal contact, got excited about something I had written, and invited me to be looked over for the new research professorship set up that year by Dean Carmichael at Illinois. Woodrow, a cousin of Woodrow Wilson, had built up a strong department, and since, along with Thurstone, he had pioneered in multivariate experimental methods, he wished to see it preeminent in that area, which through Tucker, Humphreys, Kaiser, Tatsuoka, and others it duly became.

LIFE BEGINS AT FORTY

At last, at forty, I was truly able to organize my life around research. With this ensured, I "settled down." Karen Schuettler, whom I had met at Radcliffe while at Harvard, became my wife and good companion, so that in the next decade we raised four children, whose performances (in various senses) have been a delight to us. With her mathematical assistance (she taught at Wellesley), we also brought research and test constructions into standardized and practical publications where I might not have tackled the job alone.

At this time also there began a profoundly satisfying association with a series of research assistants and associates, continuing down to the present day, which has also had the quality of a family life. I am not going to be sentimental and say that every one showed high intellectual productivity and developed into a first-class researcher, but, if I ever get to writing about personalities and the living day-to-day research process, I think I have enough insightful experiences and generalizations about the organization of a variety of men in research to be helpful wherever research teams need to be constructed. To name the more productive of those with whom I have worked and published, without invidiousness, but to provide perspective for the reader, I would mention Adcock, Baggaley, Bartlett, Barton, Bartsch, Beloff, Bjersted, Blewett, Burdsal, Bolz, Butcher, Cable, Coan, Connor, Coulter, Cross, Curran, Damarin, Das, Delhees, DeYoung, Dickman, Dielman, Digman, Dreger, Drevdahl, Dubin, Ford, Gibb, Gibbons, Gorsuch, Gruen, Hammond, Herron, Horn, Howarth, Hundleby, Klein, Ishikawa, Jaspars, Kawash, Knapp, Korth, Krug, Luborsky, Meeland, Meredith, Meschieri, Nesselroade, Nichols, Pawlik, Peterson, Pierson, Porter, Radcliffe, Rickels, Saunders, Schaie, Scheier, Schmidt, Schneewind, Schoenemann, Schuerger, Sealy, Stice, Sullivan, Sweney, Tatro, Tollefson, Tsujioka, Überla, Vaughan, Warburton, White, Williams, Winder, and Wispe—up to 1974. From among these I think we are going to see answers produced for some of the haunting questions we asked together—and others beyond my knowing.

Through such writings as those of Beveridge, Cannon, de Kruif, Drevdahl, Kretschmer, Kuhn, Rickover, Poincaré, Roe, Taylor and Barron, R. L. Thorndike, and others, we are beginning to get perspective on the personality and conditions of effective research. Had I space here and time to analyze the sum of knowledge from my thirty years of experience with the above variety of men, something could be added to that perspective. Since the university sedulously fosters its image of the teacher-researcher, we are generally unwilling to recognize how different the personalities and motivations are for optimal performance in these two distinct areas. First and foremost, the researcher does not work to a convenient timetable, but, as men from Edison to Einstein have pointed out, he is on the job night and day. And when exhausted, he may need to go right away, for say, several weeks. Moreover, he is like a pregnant woman in that he cannot risk great disturbances, lest ideas abort, and he cannot easily switch from a long-term commitment as a teacher switches from one campus to another. Consequently, he is at a tactical disadvantage in the jockeyings and competitive bickerings for position in the academic (and other) worlds. He cannot afford the luxury of battling against aggressions, because intrigue involves him in insufferable distractions from his work, nor can he threaten to leave because too much is invested in his long-term ongoing and often locally tied research material.

In terms of time alone, if I had spent the hours in "mending fences" typically spent by the ambitious academic man, half of my research would remain undone. But in terms of fertility the damage would be even greater. With his ongoing unconscious incubations in process the researcher is little adapted to the distracting hurly-burly of politics. He has to make a choice. The point has been made in famous words by Goethe, "Es entwickelt sich ein Talent in der Stille, etc. . . ." To be sure, men can be cited, like Galois to Paracelsus, who have accomplished great contributions despite political strife and insecurity, but far more frequently, as in the case of J. B. Watson, strife and occupational insecurity have ended their creativity. Newton became a wily and politically effective master of the Mint, but probably about 1 percent of his total scientific contribution stems from that administrative period.

Time and again I have seen a good research man tire of being "on sufferance" in relation to less able place seekers, and leave the field. Indeed, just as Newton was able to get "promoted" to a decent living only by undertaking administration, so, through the period I mention, a psychologist who made a name in research found the only salary promotion open to him was through shifting to administrative headships. We are not out of this difficulty yet, and in my opinion it is only to be solved either by universities creating distinguished full-time research professorships financially equal to department headships, or by setting up pure research institutions, like the Max Planck, Rockefeller, etc., centers with their own appropriate value systems. Meanwhile, let me express my gratitude to the farmers and other taxpayers of Illinois enlightened enough to surpass most other states by deciding to support a sprinkling of men in their universities dedicated to full-time research.

With Woodrow's dependable but alert and critical support I quickly organized my Illinois laboratory and soon my life hummed with the steady efficiency of a dynamo. For many years I rarely left the laboratory before 11 P.M., and then was generally so deep in thought or discussion that I could find my car only because it was the last still in the parking lot! A happy accident—it was little more—also favored my preferred multivariate approach, in that Illinois was the first university (with Harvard) to develop a powerful computer (the "Sacred Illiac," as we called it), which was exactly what my line of work needed. (Even so, Dave Saunders devised a most ingenious factoring on the IBM sorter, before Illiac was ready.)

Thus began, and continued over twenty-seven years to this time of writing, the broad sweep of the project to map out the main dimensions of human personality, in our own and other cultures, coordinated across ratings, question-naire, and objective test measures. Since no amount of statistical finesse can conjure into visibility dimensions not in the original experimental data, the main creative task before us was the invention of miniature situations (objective tests) evoking behavior covering the personality sphere concept. In my book with Warburton (1967) I have dealt with some of the fascinating problems of translating theories of personality into specific experimental situations. We have there discussed also how we kept perspective in that creation by keeping an eye on how the personality sphere had developed dimensionally and conceptually in L-data (life, rating, criterion domain) and Q-data (questionnaires), thus co-ordinating our advance across the three domains.

For many psychologists what is taken to distinguish this personality re-search at Illinois is the use of complex, factor-analytic, and allied multivariate computer methods. But among the various laboratories which competently use such techniques, e.g., ETS, Southern California, Colorado, Oregon Research Institute, Michigan, Toronto, Washington, the special emphasis of our labora-tory—which incidentally we share with Royce in his Advanced Theory Center in Alberta, Eysenck at London, Horn at Denver, and Nesselroade and Baltes at Pennsylvania—actually lies in a different direction. It is not the development of mathematical statistics as such but of mathematical-statistical advances neces-sary to test realistic models in personality and motivation theory themselves. The present adult generation of psychologists grew up when there was an almost complete mutual separation of personality and motivation theories, e.g., those of Freud, Allport, and Murray, from psychometrics. It would be no exaggeration to say that still, today, textbooks of personality theory, e.g., Bischof's scholarly work of 1964-1972, unblushingly devote nine-tenths of their space to theories with no quantitative, experimental expression, and that textbooks on scaling and psychometrics devote nine-tenths to procedures that have no relation to any developed models of personality or dynamics.

For thirty years my experience has necessarily been that of living in a no-man's land where more developed theories connected, with clinical, experi-mental, physiological, and social psychology and coordinated across three media, have been shot at on the one hand as too abstract and incomprehensible for the general undergraduate study of personality and from the other direction by psychometrists as not being always precise by conventional psychometric standards. As I write this week, a reviewer of the book by Warburton and myself (Columbia University Press textbook), setting out 400 new objective (miniature situational) tests, well-demonstrated to achieve the new ambition of spanning personality factor space, castigates us severely for presenting them without complete standardizations!

THE ATTEMPT AT GLOBAL ECONOMY IN PERSONALITY RESEARCH

One cannot pursue research for long without recognizing that as in any trial-and-error process some waste is inevitable. But surveying the discrepancy between psychology's real gains in knowledge and control on the one hand, and the endless spate of articles in innumerable journals on the other, one cannot help feeling that our subject is in need of a sense of direction and perspective more than most. In particular we seem to need (1) more sophistication in methods, (2) coordination of programmatic research among laboratories, and (3) more definite and steadily maintained strategy within each laboratory. As to the second, one quickly encounters a need for limits, for I am now convinced that the correct design is complete freedom for each of a number of leading scientists, each working with his own competent team. Committees cannot conduct inspired research, and though they can do useful surveys and advise on areas and methods, there is a constant danger that they will perpetuate the conservative consensus of their more mediocre members.

But within one laboratory—with, say, a team of three to a dozen members—some global and economic design to encircle and capture the unknown with greater strategic elegance, and a minimum expense of man-hours, is most desirable. The governing strategy of my own laboratory as regards finding the significant structures in personality was initially conceived during my first two years at Illinois, and has been stated in my 1946 and 1957 books. But it may be seen better in the present context of historical action if I briefly summarize their points here.

1. To begin without distortion of direction from *any* current prejudice as to what the main personality structures may be, and, instead, to follow the stratified "sampling" principle involved in the *personality sphere* concept of proceeding from a broad population of variables within the culture.

2. To examine the relations of these variables in coordinated studies across the three possible media of personality behavior observation—L-, Q-, and T-data.

3. To bring auxiliary methodological aids to ordinary factor-analytic techniques. Such aids are instanced by our invention of P- and dR-techniques, and remedies we introduced for certain inadequacies and indeterminisms in multivariate methods as they then existed.

4. After (hopefully) *replicating* factors in enough normal adult analyses (where administration problems are least), to make parallel cross sections at a series of lower age levels, for the sake of developmental psychology, and also in the clinical domain of abnormal behavior.

5. Similarly, to repeat analyses with the same markers across three to a dozen different national cultures, to test the degree of universality of the new concepts.

6. To move out continuously into new stimulus-response situations, created in new objective test measures, but to do so in such a programmatic way that a steady mapping of structure is ensured. This involves identifying new factors by recognizing the old, through carrying forward the best factor-marker variables from earlier studies.

7. To develop theoretical conceptions both of the individual structures and their manner of interaction in connection with an exact identifying indexing similar to the systems used in astronomy, botany, or chemistry. The primary aim here is to obtain a clear separation of the establishment of patterns from the explanation of patterns. This has involved (a) attaching only an identifying "universal index" (U.I.) number to each pattern, followed by a descriptive new title, in order not to mislead psychologists (ourselves included) by premature interpretation or use of older terms, and (b) investigating, as soon as well replicated, whether the explanation and major origin of the pattern is in genetic or environmental sources. In this way the possibility of fruitlessness in theoretical speculation is cut down at the outset.

8. To extend the methods from general personality traits to individual dynamic, motivational structure as soon as sufficient order is obtained.

To state where one thinks he is going, and how he sees the "fit" into the general movement of psychology, is, I have always believed, a duty to other psychologists. Among psychologists less trained either in mathematics or the history of science a rather common misperception has been that this whole plan is "static" and uninterested in reaching developmental, "dynamic" laws. On the contrary, our plan considered the attainment of kinetic, developmental laws so important that even twenty-five years of systematic cross-sectional work seemed little to pay for being able to reach them. Our aim has been—and there are at last many evidences of its success—to enable psychologists to enter developmental and experimental, manipulative research with valid concepts, measurable with useful psychometric validities, as in the 16 P.F., the O–A batteries, the Curran state batteries, the MAT and SMAT, etc. It aimed to do this using common reference batteries instead of an endless catalog of subjective trait terms indifferently measured.

In this pursuit we had hoped to kick the ball of theory around with a peer group of other, independent laboratories, but apparently because of the statistical skills, computer aids, and consecutive arrangement of studies needed, this cross checking in a community of laboratories has not eventuated even to this day to a degree that a seriously developing science might reasonably be expected to produce. Our traffic has been with all too few: Adcock (New Zealand), Arnold (Würzburg), Baltes, Brogden, Dermen, Eysenck, Dreger, Fahrenberg (Freiburg), Fiske, French, Goldberg, Gray (Oxford), Guilford, Hakstian, Hammond (Australia), Harman, Jackson, Kline (England), Lorr, Lushene, Meschieri (Urbino), Nesselroade, Pawlik (Hamburg), Pichot (Paris), Royce (Alberta), Norman, Rican (Prague), Schaie, Schneewind, Schmidt (Germany), Sells, Thurstone (perceptual-personality factors), Tsujioka, Tupes, Vidal (France), Wardell and Howarth (Canada),Warburton (Manchester), Wiggins, Wilde, Witkin, Wittenborn, and Vaughan, being among those who have made determined, carefully planned and interlocking studies in other universities, permitting cross comparisons (all but four, however, in questionnaires only).

This smallness of the critically interacting community (I omit from the above those given in the earlier list who worked on their own *within* the laboratory) has been a great deprivation, though perhaps inevitable in terms of the usual history of science. On the other hand, there is no excuse other than poor lines of communication within our science for the lack of a second type of interaction and feedback: that from *use* of already factored reference battery measures (such as French has worked so well to bring about) against all kinds of clinical and other criteria. Such use by psychologists in the clinical field who may themselves lack the training and/or facilities for complex systematic multivariate studies per se, but who can understand logically what the methods produce, could be immensely valuable in bringing out and shaping the personality concepts involved.

Ultimately, a solution was found for bringing about this sadly lacking scientific relationship, but in an unexpected direction. Even with only a moderate (and sometimes, perhaps, merely "idly curious") demand for the detailed objective tests, administrative instructions, etc., for the several hundreds of devices reported in our articles, our two clerical helpers lost half their time meeting requests for material. But turning to the five big and well-known test publishers did not at that time produce the least response, for [with the exception of Thurstone's (SRA)] they were not ready to believe in the future of factored tests, nor were any of them willing to face the costs, risks, and constant revisions of such new styles of tests as these (as well as those needed in developing the culture-fair intelligence tests and objective motivation measures). At a meeting of several concerned research psychologists interested in making such batteries more widely available, it was decided, in 1949, to set up the Institute for Personality and Ability Testing (IPAT). With the business impracticality of researchers, no funds and no definite organization was arranged. Some very capable people nevertheless worked on test choice, design, and development, but sporatically. The result was that for over twenty years now, IPAT has, in fact, depended for its coordination, and therefore existence, on the full-time coordinating labors of my wife! Up till 1970 anything that might have issued as a salary for her or royalties for me (and in some instances other test designers) was ploughed back into research. But this loose organization worked effectively to make available reasonably sound measures, and made possible developmental research based on unitary, meaningful personality factors—traits and states—long before any large publisher or "official" APA source took steps to do so. In the more highly organized IPAT of the last five years, under my wife, Janet Bijou, Tatsuoka, Krug, Campero, and others, these factor tests have been carried up and down the age range (in questionnaires, the 16 PF, High School Personality Questionnaire, CPQ, ESPQ, PSPQ; in objective tests the OA Battery of Hundleby and HSOA of Schuerger) into objective dynamic measurement (with the Motivation Analysis Test and the School MAT), and into culture-fair intelligence tests, extended primary abilities, and state batteries.

This experience of what could be done by a group of keen researchers, somewhat ahead of general conservative opinion, has been enlightening to one who was a socialist student in the heyday of Shavian and Wellsian socialism. One sees in communist—and some socialist—countries that in this area of test development a government bureaucracy or a professional hierarchy has already demonstrated the disadvantages of any monopoly—a lack of enterprise and an unreadiness to move ahead of the most safely conventional opinion. Factored tests were unacceptable in 1950, culture-fair intelligence tests were snidely criticized as "contradictions in terms" by conservative authorities, and objective personality tests were of course "unproven." *Large* business concerns—indeed any kind of "establishment"—can be equally uninterested, being ready only to play up to the slow moving majority.

The success of our venture in getting research results available resting on meaningful structures and defined states (anxiety, depression, regression) at least a decade earlier than might otherwise have been seen in the clinical and educational literature suggests that this solution to the lag between research and application may be the right one. It requires some effort and persuasion in organizing researchers in independent, essentially nonprofit but self-sustaining "service" groups. At any rate, both Guilford's and my own factored questionnaires were made available by small, research-oriented private concerns twenty years before large concerns, business or bureaucratic, were prepared to move into the field. The feedback in terms of obtaining standard age-growth curves, clinical meaning, and countless criterion relations important for understanding personality factors—all vital for advancing theory—has unquestionably been one or two decades earlier than it might have been. The brass-instrument experimentalist has no equivalent problem, and perhaps for this reason the "classical" academic psychologist has been slow to recognize the need for developing some machinery. However, a distinctly parallel problem exists in providing new drugs for the practice of medicine and here again the initiative of private enterprise research groups sustaining their work by their products has been the answer that has worked.

My aim as the structural findings in our laboratory began to link together was not—as is apparently sometimes thought—that of collecting "factors" in some static, taxonomic, intellectual museum. Instead, two or three alternative theories, hinging on functional concepts, were tested by re-entering factoring with carefully chosen crucial variables, as well as by the feedback from clinical and experimental associations, as just indicated. Cooperation of other laboratories in this kind of work has all too often been shipwrecked by the schism between the interest and training of clinicians and psychometrists mentioned above in relation to our own attempt at conceptual integration. Perhaps six or seven of the personality factors with which we have worked in objective tests have achieved confirmed conceptualization, but my comment of ten years ago—that we now have twenty well-confirmed behavior patterns each in search of a theory from outside our own circle—unfortunately is still literally true.

However, with the breaking into second-order and third-order structures, which began fifteen years ago and is now proceeding to sufficiency of replications, one part of the jigsaw puzzle began to fit—that of bridging from media to media. Rating and questionnaire primaries run parallel, but objective test primaries stand at the second order relative to these. It is with profound relief that I now see the rivets of confirmatory studies being driven home, enough to leave an essentially clear, overall structure which individual researchers with fewer resources can henceforth work upon in their own specific areas. To say this about the general "gestalt" as a whole is not to be under any illusion that there is no longer need to "tighten the joints," to push extensions in some areas, and to firm up the checks on the patterns in others. In spite of my explicitly set-out reasoning explaining why the nature of factor-analytic studies requires a "blocking in" of the whole picture before precisioning the parts—a precisioning that requires longer, more reliable, and valid measures than can be used in a one-hundred-subtest exploratory battery—this unreliability of some individual objective tests has repeatedly been the object of carping criticism bereft of perspective. In the development of science, as shown, for example, by the work of Pasteur, there is a time to be approximate and a time to be precise, as surely as there is a time for a low and for a high power on a microscope.

The sheer coordination during the thirty years of this strategic personality structure research has been a heavy task, quite apart from the creative work on objective test invention itself, and the statistical innovations in the factor-analytic methodological that have vastly increased its power, but to which I have not yet referred. At an organizational level it has meant concern every year over choice of able and dedicated research associates, and giving up sabbaticals over thirty years (or indeed any appreciable time away from the laboratory) lest things "go wrong" as they can with extreme ease at the cutting edge of research. And in terms of research artistry it has meant foresighted regard for sequences of experiment, the timely bringing of associates to mature familiarity with techniques, the tactful closing of perennially rediscovered culs-de-sac in the labyrinth in which new researchers wander, and the finding of dragons of appropriate magnitude for the spear length of each new young "researcher-errant" seeking challenge. Finally, descending again to mechanics, it has meant attempting steadily connected publication (over some 360 articles) when, as is well known, only a minority of Ph.D.'s write up their own good researches in a style acceptable to editors.

Since the seventh of the steps (see p. 77) in the strategically economical plan called for determining nature-nurture ratios as soon as a personality pattern could be considered well confirmed, it is appropriate to close the personality research story with a glance at a rewarding safari into genetics. (Incidentally, "confirmed" in the last sentence should be followed by "and validly measurable," for it was not unusual for a factor pattern to replicate reliably as such for five years or more—exvia-invia is a case in point—without our being able to find a set of objective subtests sufficiently loaded to yield the validities which the "consumer's digest" for everyday test users considers appropriate.)

An investigator opens up a special, new branch of his work—as we did in this study of behavioral genetics—with both fascination and trepidation. For to handle it decently, in all the branches that will open out, he may, like Ulysses, take a trip of twenty years when he intended one. Having published two twin and family heredity studies—with Malteno (Cattell and Malteno, 1940) and with Willson (Cattell and Willson, 1938)—in the late thirties, I was aware at the outset of problems and deficiencies in the standard twin method. Through discussions with Woodrow and with Saunders, who reassured me on some perhaps overbold steps I wanted to incorporate in a more global design, I ventured in a new direction of analysis, later to be called the Multiple Abstract Variance Analysis or MAVA Method (1953). Still not quite sure whether I had got hold of a vision or a nightmare, I took the opportunity on a trip back home to lay it before Sir Ronald Fisher. As usual, he turned to it with the same zest as if it had been his own baby, and to my great relief pronounced MAVA a healthy child. But it kept growing, and about three years later (1957) it got a second intensive examination by C. R. Rao, as I was visiting the Indian Statistical Institute in Calcutta. Before Nesselroade and I wrote our *Human Behavioral Genetics* (in final preparation, 1974), it had benefited again from the criticisms of Kempthorne, Norton, Loehlin, Fulker, Jinks, and others.

In 1954, Beloff, Blewett, Kristy, Stice, and I applied MAVA to factored questionnaire and objective test measures of the principal source traits. Although results were suggestive and helpful in shaping personality theory, our findings suffered the defects of most pioneer work. And perhaps, being granted reasonably generous NIMH funds at a time when behavioral genetics was not too favorably regarded, we were too eager to deliver results. Certainly we learned (one never knows error magnitudes beforehand) that much larger samples would be needed. Furthermore, through the valuable reactions thereto of Loehlin and of Jinks and Fulker, we stopped some other "leaks" in the design. Only in 1971 were we able to return to data gathering with an improved MAVA design, improved source trait measures, and a plan for adequate samples. Alas, Klein and I had barely got adequate samples (about 2000 cases) when the grant retrenchments of 1972 threatened to leave this data to gather dust upon the shelf.

As far as the investigator, if not the investigation, was concerned this ten-year sally into the neighboring science of genetics had the pleasantly bracing effect of entering a region methodologically and conceptually more rigorous than most of the other social sciences. (For let us make no mistake that in the hands of Fisher, Haldane, Malecot, and Wright, genetics *is* a social science.)

ALARMS AND EXCURSIONS

In describing the days in London when my interests moved from the physical sciences to psychology, I have pointed to two main themes: a concern with the laws governing personality—the integrating entity at the hub of all studies of process such as perception or learning—and a concern with a social science that could solve sociopolitical problems in better ways than by current rules of thumb. Little has been said about the role of the second in my life, or about a third which grew as the years progressed in the form of a positively esthetic pleasure in scientific methods and models. But of the alarms and excursions caused by the second I will now give some account.

My concern to bring social scientific research to remedy some of the irrationalities of politics and to arrest what seemed to me and many to be degenerative, e.g., dysgenic, trends in social life remain as great as ever. These remedies I saw in terms of basic research, not of so-called "action research," which is often partisan politics in disguise, and which in any case eats up research funds more voraciously than well-planned basic research. But, owing to the inexorable demands in my life of the ever-unfolding personality research design, any social research I achieved over these thirty years was sporadic. In the work I started in group dynamics, as well as in culture-pattern dynamics, I was able to present only the first act of a play. The fact that their findings made them extremely promising first acts could not conjure the time needed for the play.

Clearly, any kind of organized group, having the properties of an organism, needs to be brought first under the same taxonomic and structural analysis as personality. Sociologists had produced armchair classifications, but in 1950, despite the wave of interest in group dynamics then rearing its head, no one had attempted a naturalistic investigation of the dimensions of groups, large or small. Just how does one quantitatively describe a group? The model in which I proposed to investigate group properties and their derivation from population properties and role-and-rule structure has been set out in most final form in Geldard's book (1961). Such concepts as syntality, maintenance synergy, effective synergy, vector addition of individual attitudes, leadership defined operationally, group defined operationally, indicate how I attempted to bring together small group dynamics and cultural group dynamics. Since theory without data had for too long been a vapid and sterile feature of sociology we proceeded first to run a circus of a hundred neonate groups of ten men each at Lackland Air Base and elsewhere. The factoring of some forty variables on the surviving eighty small groups with complete records of three days' performances as well as over sixty variables on nearly a hundred modern nations, led to conceptions of dimensions both of small groups and of national syntality which were mutually enlightening. Adelson, Breul, Cogan, Gibb, Hartman, Meeland, Stice, and Wispe were my companions during those strenuous days of 1948-1954 in which we wrestled alike with the theoretical problems of generating measures for significant group behavior variables, and the organizational problems of running the "circus" of competing groups. Puzzling at first in this area was the finding of no fewer than *three* small-group morale dimensions, but the synergy concept made good sense of this. The work was well received by group dynamics' critics, but has not yet been repeated, presumably because of its formidable combination of practical and technical demands.

The dimensions of nations revealed two or three concepts—cultural pressure, morale-morality, affluence-education—both new and dynamically interpretable in interesting theoretical terms (1950, 1952). It was in connection with the next step of objectively grouping culture patterns (which yielded "civilizations" close to Toynbee's), that the pattern similarity coefficient, r_p, was invented (1949). This work was not picked up by psychologists, but instead by political scientists at Yale, Indiana, and Hawaii universities. Alker, Deutsch, Merritt, Singer, and others have since pursued it well, and Rummel with positive genius.

Regarding these "side shows" and the way they developed, I must here seem to jump like a will-o'-the-wisp, though in fact each is a continuous thread in the fabric of my thought and the connections among them have been both more logical and more cross-fertilizing than might be apparent. Recognizing that trait psychology is not enough, and that behavior is to be predicted as much from states as traits, I had begun, as early as 1935, a gradual development of what eventually became the state modulation model. Debating one day with Allport over the Harvard lunch table his objection to factors as merely "common" traits, and having the image of the covariation chart newly before me, I pointed to the possibility of what has since become P-technique (I so called it to indicate single *person* factoring). It offered at once an avenue to states and to the structure of unique traits. Allport actually rejected this conception but a percipient student, Baldwin, whose Ph.D. research he had asked me to discuss, later did an excellent study.

My wife was actually the first subject for a systematic P-technique study, since it needed someone to be tested for about two hours a day for (hopefully) a hundred days. Indeed, it has happened that the first three major experiments in the literature were by husband-wife teams. (Hence the Illinois laboratory quip that the study of the single person was done exclusively on married persons!).

These researches carried out in the late forties showed conclusively that (1) what we call traits in R-technique fluctuate enough, and in their true patterns, to appear clearly also in P-technique, and (2) that a means had been found for uniquely defining and measuring the "states" with which psychology (since Wundt) had been much concerned—states such as anxiety, depression, arousal, etc. Incidentally, in retrospect one can now recognize that my very first published research (1928) had essentially been on arousal. It gave the first demonstration (as far as I know) that states of high excitement and activation are associated with low electrical skin resistance. We now included many such likely physiological measures (as indicated by bivariate studies in the literature) along with introspective and behavioral measures and, in the course of the next fifteen years (1946-1961), put together enough P- and dR-technique researches [culminating in the work of Scheier and myself on anxiety and neuroticism (1961) and of Curran and Nesselroade with questionnaires (1970)] to define eight state patterns. These in the hands of Dimascio, Rickels, and others have opened up a new world in the precise study of psychoactive drugs.

At that time our laboratory was unfortunately alone to the point of isolation in pursuing state research with a precise model and methods (P- and dR-techniques), though the whole domain is now happily under vigorous pursuit by Baltes, Barton, Bartsch, Bolz, Cable, Corballis, Curran, De Young, Fahrenberg, Kline, Lazarus, Lebo, Sarason, Shrader, Spielberger, and pre-eminently, Nesselroade, to name a few. But investigation of the basic model as such, notably in regard to taking up modulation theory, and to separating inter- and intraindividual variance in scores, e.g., in state standardization, has been much slower than one would expect. As mentioned above and developed below in describing innovations I have almost constantly been concerned with multivariate methods as such. The rift between mathematical statisticians like Horst, or Kaiser (with his imaginative alpha analysis), or MacDonald (with his breakthrough toward non-linear analyses) on the one hand, and experimentalists on the other, has set back psychological theory. However, the modulation theory and model for states and roles is, I think, one case where close data observation and mathematical model invention have been brought together. I would predict that the next decade of study of states will develop this model in interesting ways.

The structural investigation of personality was initially for me as for many in the multivariate experimental tradition a study of *general* traits and states. The gossamer tangles of individual motivation which the psychoanalyst sought to unravel seemed at first beyond the ambitions of psychometric experiment. However, somewhere in the late forties I faced up to this problem and realized that with appropriate development of novel approaches in factor-analytic method, principally dR- and P-techniques, it should be possible to check on the number and nature of the supposed drives, as well as on much in their interaction and conflict.

What was first needed, however, was a foundation of more objective measurement of any interest or attitude in itself, and here I took a broad sweep across the manifestations of interest strength which observant psychologists have defined in learning, psychoanalysis, physiological motivation studies, perception, animal ethology, and so on. Analysis of these—in which such research associates as Maxwell, Miller, Heist, Light, Stewart, Cross, and Unger worked enthusiastically—revealed the hitherto quite unsuspected fact that motivation always expresses itself in two substantially independent factors which we called integrated and unintegrated components.

This objective measurement in turn laid the foundation for locating dynamic structures. Soon we had the excitement of finding in the latter what we called ergic patterns—for the ergs of sex, fear, hunger, assertion, exploration, etc. The patterns supported Freud and Murray relatively poorly, and the closest thing to these objective factorial findings on human drives appeared in the ethological "propensities" of McDougall and the experimental findings of Harlow. The notions of vector measurement of attitudes, of the algebraic conflict model, of the dynamic calculus, and of the dynamic lattice which developed out of this have taken what I have already deplored as an excessive amount of time to get into general motivational experiment, but perhaps this is simply inevitable with something radically new. Moreover, perhaps the *dynamic calculus*, as it came to be called, demands more statistical finesse and more immersion in the field than the typical Ph.D. student can muster, for generating the necessary theoretical precision to design crucial experiments. The logjam began to move only twenty years later, as the work of Barton, Bartsch, Burdsal, Kawash, Krug, and especially Sweney, DeYoung, Child, and Kline has shown that these measures respond to manipulative experiment in the way that bi-variate experimenters understand. Indeed, some reasonably precise equations are now being worked out in deriving ergic tension levels and changes from stimulus and deprivation conditions.

Since I have never liked to develop theory in too great advance and detachment from experiment, it was not for a dozen years that I felt it timely to develop the implications of the dynamic calculus for learning theory, which I did at the International Congress of Psychology meetings in London and Moscow in the late sixties. To what seem to me remarkable possibilities of new experiment in human learning, using the tri-vector description of behavior change, and the general position of structured learning theory, I shall return below.

Meanwhile, my experience over the years from 1944 to the present has brought home to me the vital truth in the history of science that the pursuit of substantive advance both stimulates the growth of methodology and finds such growth indispensable. Especially in convincing the doubters of these strange new developments I was forced to devise new factor-analytic designs and procedures, as well as new significance measures, sometimes demanding know-how in mathematical statistics initially far beyond my education. Space forbids me to refer to these fascinating jaunts other than by a string of names: the determination of unique oblique factor rotation by the invention of rotoplot (1963) and maxplane (1960) programs; examination of the meaning of number of factors, and reaching the scree test (1966); development of more objective factor matching (the s index; 1949, 1969) and the significance tables for congruence coefficients (1970); the pattern similarity coefficient, r_p (1949); the relational simplex theory of equal-interval and absolute scaling (1962); ipsative scoring (1944); significance of simple structure (1973); the basic data relation matrix (1946, 1966); the theory of perturbations (1964) and instrument factors (1964); trait view theory (1968); modulation (1963b, 1971); plasmodes to test factor procedures (1963c, 1967); the restructuring of validity in a three-dimensional schema (concrete-conceptual, direct-indirect, etc.; 1967); the four-component (epogenic, ecogenic, etc.) analysis of age development curves (1971); a basis for cross-cultural comparison of factors (isopodic and equipotent methods; 1972); the equations relating homogeneity and validity of items and the number of items and factors to scale validity (1973); and, especially, "real base" factor analysis (1971); and the more general solution for confactor rotational resolution (1971).

In several cases, these innovations, initially forced by a hold-up in establishing some substantive theory, or by attempts to convince critics, but often coming from sheer conceptual spontaneity, have perhaps not been as elegant as I would like from a mathematical standpoint, and remain to be polished, but they were vital to substantive progress and often helped in unforeseen ways. For example, the conceiving of the basic data relation matrix and the covariation chart (1946) revealed three further, as yet unused, possibilities of factor analysis. It led by one or two broadenings of my thinking, each taking a year or so, to the ten-dimensional basic data relation matrix or general data box (1966), comprehensively calling attention to possibilities in both factor analysis and analysis of variance. In retrospect, both in my own work and in that of other innovators, I am surprised to note how long it takes one to make the obvious next step—if that next step has no name and has never been made. Thus R-, Q-, and P-techniques were the only ones known in 1945, but today, ten minutes' reflection would seem enough looking at the BDRM (data box) to recognize that there are seventeen further possible designs (besides differential R- and similar techniques).

Since about half of these conceptual innovations appeared around the factor-analytic model and technique, I should perhaps answer at this point a question often asked by those who, apparently, regard factor analysis as a recondite and highly specialized branch of knowledge. With this perspective they naturally ask why I made it the core for so many developments. My own view is very different from these visitors from a more traditional psychological background. Factor analysis is not in any true perspective of science, recondite and specialized. It halves, with analysis of variance, the whole domain of methodology. It does so because: (1) a model accepting *multiple determination* of events is an absolute requirement in psychology, because in nothing but trivial effects of small magnitude can we "control" and "manipulate" the rest, as the physical sciences do; (2) everything that is organic has structural, trait-like attributes, and the sooner we find out what they are by objective methods the sooner we can proceed to manipulative, etc., experiments; and (3) though nonlinear relations, i.e., relations partly lost in the factor model, must ultimately be pursued, it is a merciful simplification to be able to begin in any area with linear approximations.

Returning to the substantive side—personality and motivation concepts—I believe that the pioneer years of hewing out the major human personality structures are essentially over, though those remote from the data often seem unaware of this. It is true that there has recently been a flurry of attacks, notably by Eysenck, Howarth, and Mischel, each sponsoring a different alternative regarding the concept of primary personality structures. To the doubts of Mischel about the very existence of common structures I would answer that this is an empirical question, and that countless research findings (including Eysenck's and Howarth's) show well more than half the variance of any wide array of behavior absorbed into common structures. But the criticisms and alternatives of Eysenck and certain recent factor analysts strike me as the comments of speakers who have missed the first part of the meeting. Indeed, one of the problems in getting a coordinate view of this field today is that some of the most substantial publications, in issues of sample size, reliability, uniqueness of rotation, factor matching, and significance, lie farther back in the literature than contemporaries usually go. In my recent book, *Personality and Mood by Questionnaire* (1973), I have sought to answer these doubts systematically.

Although superficial attacks on the system of twenty or more primaries and eight or more secondaries nowadays cause little concern, there were times in the first decade of this work, when methods were new and cross checks had not appeared, at which the pioneer workers had disturbing moments of misgiving. Often the methodological foundations of our world were assailed by doubts later proved false. Most workers in this field have also known exhaustion and near despair from the sheer scale of the work. I first remember experiencing something near panic over the basic concepts when Thomson showed that Spearman's results could be accounted for by a model of random factors. This passed [partly, I may say, in my case, through the reassuring findings with Dickman (1962), Jaspers (1967), and Gorsuch (1963) on plasmodes]. But the Achilles heel of factor analysis remains: that so long as we have to depend on simple structure for ultimate resolution, investigators of differing degrees of skill and persistence in finding it will continue to offer different "solutions." This kind of difficulty—which has contributed enormously to the unjustifiable doubts of onlookers about factor analysis as such—is not unknown in other sciences. Chemists with impure samples have been unable to confirm melting points and some laboratories have been unable to raise certain microbial cultures. At the risk of offending many, I have pointed out recently that more than half of the factor analyses *currently* accepted for publication by editors lack one or more of six or seven requirements for an adequate factor analysis where even one would be disabling (1973). It needs to be explicitly recognized that we are in an area of science where experience and skill, and willingness to spend much time, are essential, and that the ersatz push-button compute rotation program, for example, is not good enough.

Nevertheless, a state of affairs where subjectivity can so insinuate itself is not satisfactory, and I and my colleagues attempted to overcome the problem in two ways. First, because any one factor analytic rotation may stray we have essentially tried to "swamp error" by repeating studies on a large scale more frequently than would be considered necessary for proof in other fields. Much of what editors and others have misunderstood as merely repetitive industry has this very necessary rationale. Second, from my earliest encounters with simple structure problems—around 1935-1940—I thought my way through to a radically new approach which has been called parallel, proportional profiles or *confactor rotation*. The demonstration of the uniqueness of this solution but not the way to find it in a given case was published in 1944. Then eleven years elapsed until, with some help from my wife—a mathematician—the discovery of a definitive solution for the *orthogonal* rotation was published. However, for precision in most practical purposes, we had to have an oblique solution, and the best minds in the field who looked at it declared this impossible. Curiously, my return to this problem seemed to go in eleven-year (sunspot?) cycles, for I got my next insight, and published a tentative oblique solution therefrom, in 1966, which I read at the Oxford meeting of SMEP soon after. But this also requires special conditions, and, in fact, I am still probing into what has proved the bleakest Northwest Passage of my research life.

In summary, it is obvious that substantive findings on personality and motivation structure, integrating in higher order concepts, and issuing in objective test batteries to give concrete definition to the structures, have constituted the core of my contribution. These are my "voyages in hyperspace." I can scarcely expect to see the developmental and clinical findings that will be rendered possible, though in the last decade I have gone out of my way to illustrate by special research the potency of using structural measures in those fields. From this core the work on social psychology in group dynamic and culture patterns has been a matter of intermittent excursions, and the methodological, technical developments have been a necessary scaffolding for exact building. If I were asked which area has been most fascinating to me personally, I should say, in the early years, the creation of the 400 or more objective miniature situational tests in relation to "clinical" observation of persons, and, in the last twenty years, the development of the dynamic calculus and the structured learning theory which its concepts make possible.

These constitute the professional, scientific armature of my life, and outside that there have been delightful fields of literature—especially the poets—and history, and the love of nature, sailing, and the mountains. Yet something has bridged the two, in the sense of integrating science into life, and fortifying it by that support. These integrating threads of social concern I have already described as beginning in my switch from chemistry to psychology, and they have endured from my 1936 book, *The Fight for Our National Intelligence,* through intermittent articles and *Psychology and the Religious Quest* (1938) to my most final thoughts in *A New Morality from Science: Beyondism* (1972). This bids us go beyond the political rule of thumb of "right" and "left" or the intellectually indigestible revealed religions and enter on an evolutionary revolution from values inherent in science. The deeper problem is not that of bringing moral values into science—as, say, Oppenheimer and many other scientists have urged —but of developing new ethical values by the same scientific methods as have yielded new knowledge in all other fields.

Incidentally, it is a curious coincidence that both the research professors appointed at Illinois (myself in 1945, Mowrer in 1948) and Skinner at Harvard have come forward about the same time with attempts to integrate psychology with ethical values. It is at least refreshing, if not reassuring, to see how diverse the viewpoints are and by what different arguments they are derived from psychology.

RESEARCHERS AND THE LINE OF COMMUNICATION

For most of my life I have pursued research from intrinsic fascination with the problems. Except that I dislike waste and have some concern for social advance, I might scarcely have bothered to publish. But in the last twenty years I have become aware that even the most ardent pure researcher must—if he cares about research progress realistically—pay his tithe of help to the social and communicative processes that go with research. Had Columbus not sailed back, the New World would have remained essentially unknown. If a researcher goes too far without care for connecting links, the reinforcements for even the most profitable fields of investigation do not arrive. One must write—even in tedious oversimple terms which smooth away the truly intriguing subtleties—and one must give not one, but two or three concrete illustrative researches for every conceptual advance that is really new. Moreover, in science, as distinct from philosophy or mathematics, it is not possible to be really ahead of one's time. The factor-analytic location of basic ergs suggested a formula for ergic tension, and from these a model suggested itself for researches on second-order structure in ergic tension and its relation to anxiety. But until the validities of the integrated and unintegrated motivation component measures could be raised, the accuracy of measurement would not exist to make a real test of these further theories. And thirty man-years of research would be needed to raise those validities by, for example, trying another fifty new devices. Reinforcement depends on communication, and because men after their Ph.D. years rarely change their field and their methods, the communication has to pass down to the pages of the undergraduate textbook. Science is full of incidents of astonishing delay, readily seen in the slow percolation (or positive blocking) of the work of such well-known figures as Copernicus, Galileo, Vesalius, Harvey, Pasteur, Faraday, and Mendel.

In this matter—perhaps because my awareness of the communication problem came relatively late—I realize that I have done a very poor job. The concepts of the primary and secondary personality source traits, and the distinction of states by P-technique, get widely into textbooks, but, except for some clinicians and applied psychologists who use them every day, it is a most uncommon student who knows the meaning of the individual factors as a medical student knows anatomy. But the worst situation concerns the dynamic calculus, where I am told by teachers at the undergraduate level—where students get their ideas "for life"—that the formulae are "too difficult." Yet in fact these elementary linear action specification and conflict formulae are simple compared to concepts that are considered indispensable to the undergraduate in chemistry or physics. Some more outspoken multivariate experimentalists have said that the teacher is projecting his own deficient education. One is reminded of the answer given by Diogenes when Imperial Alexander asked how he could help the lowly philosopher—"You can keep out of my light." I firmly believe the psychology undergraduate is as bright as those in the physical sciences and awaits a challenge from teachers not content to stay in the shadow of their own upbringing. Of course, advance to a well-disciplined scientific approach to psychology is weakened at the moment by the fashion of a "humanistic," pseudo-literary psychology, but will slough off in a few years. Incidentally, a favorite defense of those who do not wish to face the real intricacies inherent in psychology, or the challenge of actual prediction, is to draw a "cordon sanitaire" around the psychonomists, the members of the Society of Multivariate Experimental Psychology, pigeon-holing them as "factor analysts" or mere psychometrists. When a two-legged man—one advancing by both multivariate and bivariate experimental methods—is considered an oddity we are indeed in a lame culture.

As to features peculiar to my own contributions within this multivariate development that might account for the lag in utilization, some critics have said that I create the need to learn a new language. It is true that many technical terms have been found convenient by my colleagues that did not exist before. And psychologists are justifiably tired of the vice of psychology which William James described as talking about things which everyone knows in language which no one understands. The charlatanry of trying to market old ideas under new names has been especially rampant in psychology. We have cried "wolf" so often that the automatic reaction is that it must be false. But for my own work I am prepared to demonstrate that I have never used a new term unless a new concept needed to be demarcated from backgrounds that were vague and not operationally defined. My *apologia pro verba sua* would begin by pointing out that factor analysis is pre-eminently a discovery technique. Such new and meaningful terms as surgency, premsia, parmia, cortertia, and exvia should surely cause psychologists no more difficulty than neologisms such as pi-mesons and anti-quarks which physicists take in their stride.

On any rational basis it is surely hard to dispute that the forty or so factors which my co-workers and I have replicated over thirty years can be precisely referred to only by abandoning the battered, changing coinage of popular language. But as to the newness of other concepts more discussion might be needed. At least in the active group of thirty or forty researchers in this area we have found a stable symbol system and language immensely helpful for precise communication in a limited time—and this circle spreads as others desire the same precision. Such terms as ipsative, data-box, P-technique, dynamic lattice, sten, procrustes rotation, behavioral index, conspect reliability, chiasms, fluid intelligence, ergic tension, aid factors, instrument factors, confluence learning, the MAVA method, modulator action, naive projection, L-, Q-, and T-data,

transferability coefficient, tri-vector learning, unintegrated motivation component, and indirect validity coefficient, which grew up in our laboratory, either
stand for entirely new but functional concepts, or have no precise equivalent in
previous circumlocutions. One could, of course, return to the circumlocutions,
as Hitler did in an attempt to purge the German of terms not of Aryan origin,
but how can a science live with xenophobia?

The research life has had for me its enormous rewards which far outweigh
the petty annoyances—annoyances which, as I have indicated, lie largely in the
area of trying to communicate findings and enlist outside research reinforcements. (For both the inventor of a better mousetrap and the prospector in a
remote gold mine are at first lonely men.) We are told that when the exhausted
remnants of Magellan's round-the-world voyage reached Portugal they were
censured for having been a day out in their celebration of saints' days. And
many another world wanderer has, like Columbus, suffered the last insult of a
petty customs inspection before being allowed to step on his native land.
Although the life of the research professor is sometimes the subject of envy, it
has problems of this kind in dealing with the mainstream of university life, and
that is one reason why I have argued the case (1973) for the organization of
research institutes administratively independent of, but symbiotic with, universities. In spite of the quite attractive traditional university ideal of the teacher-
researcher the motivation systems and daily needs of teacher and researcher are
more disparate than we are commonly willing to recognize. For example, with
regard to the former the teacher gets much of his reward in daily self-expression
and the (perhaps very muted) applause of students, but the researcher's life is a
long wrestling with difficulties alone, oriented to remote and intangible rewards.
Furthermore, there is a built-in threat of maladjustment in the research life in
that it appeals to "back-room" types who like what Pasteur called "the calm of
the laboratory," yet, when it brings some eminence or visibility, the individual
concerned is liable to those savage assassinations (here only reputation-assassina-
tions) which great eminence invites anywhere. Like the explorers mentioned
above the researcher comes back with disturbing new tales. He shatters the firm
crust of contemporary thinking and must face the resultant hostility. Even so
sound and seemingly secure a man as Newton, when he encountered the endless
heckling of Hooke and Huygens about his chromatic theories, voiced the despair-
ing note that he sometimes wished he had not published his original work. At
the very least the defense of his writings takes time that he would naturally
prefer to devote to more creative work. At times I have been urged by editors to
reply more vigorously to criticisms of my theory of the primary and secondary
structures in the questionnaire area, e.g., by Eysenck and Howarth. There are
hundreds of ways of going wrong in a complex procedure like factor analysis,
and only one that gives the truth of sound replication, and so, apart from my
recent book constructively integrating the whole questionnaire domain (1973), I
have not felt it necessary to repeat the technical pointers that I have made over
the years as to ways in which such analyses so easily go wrong. And the same has

been true of other areas of my work in which spectators would have been gratified by a fight.

On the other hand, I have felt it necessary to be more argumentative on the development of what is above briefly designated the dynamic calculus. I have done so partly for the practical reason that certain grant committees, on whose beneficence the researcher depends for permission to advance, seem unfortunately to overvalue evidence of being in the limelight. The complex science of effective distribution of research funds has not been solved either in principle or in practice in my lifetime. One would like to say that it is solved by the really original (and therefore not understood) researcher being able by his superior flair to demonstrate truths with virtually no expenditure at all—in short to get along without grants. Freud in 1890-1900 would have gotten absolutely nothing—had he proposed to investigate the superego—from such organizations as our present-day research evaluation committees—and fortunately he needed nothing. But personality and dynamics today need experiment and data gathering and not just the neat restricted experiment on a laboratory bench such as Faraday or Rutherford could do. My last experiment in behavior genetics—which one NIMH committee declined to continue—required eight hours of testing on each of over 2000 subjects to meet the statistical requirements of a worthwhile answer. And in this, as in some other areas, the statistical analyses can go on for years before the experimenter's original idea can be vindicated by results. (And few typical plodding committees are read to accept a really new idea on a basis of insight.)

A man with creative ideas in philosophy or art (except architecture) can give wings to them at once; but in science any man whose theory and mode of attack are in advance of the field can do nothing without cooperation, for extensive painstaking experiment has to be done and the development has to be constantly readjusted to findings in a way which only he can do. The superb navigational skill which Morison tells us Columbus possessed would have been useless without his ships.

Although I insist that the machinery of grant administration could be substantially improved, I cannot complain—with one exception—about the help I have received at the right places and times from NIMH, ONR, the Research Board of the University of Illinois, and such more private sources as the Foundation for Advancement of Man. However, until the age of 40 (1945), I received nothing except $1,500 from Leonard Darwin, and depended on volunteer help and midnight oil. That was the atmosphere of those times, which the fortunate young Ph.D.'s today can hardly imagine. But after World War II research became an acknowledged community obligation and I have enjoyed continuous and generous support. The exception, as I mentioned, is in the area of my research in dynamics, where as recently as last year an NIMH committee turned down a proposal on the ground that it disregarded the work of most researchers in the motivation field. Our research turned a corner there and we could no more build on old designs than workers on the early steam engine could incorporate the latest improvements in the stage coach. The problem is that men hotly engaged in research are almost invariably unwilling to serve on these committees, and the status falls to the conservative. On the applicant side, since research acquired a community prestige, the change visible in my lifetime from the man who pursued research as a devouring hobby to the professional grant applicant has been shocking. Most applications now meet well-washed, well-dressed standards of correctness in design and statistical analysis, but there is still all the difference in the world between these and inspired research that finds the pass across the mountains. Here the man is more important than the design, and we have no instruments to detect him. Research on research should be the next item of business for granting institutions.

Meanwhile, as I look at my 1959 contribution to the *Nebraska Symposium on Motivation* I realize that it has not been put out of date in the way it should have been by now through the researches indicated by its questions. Except for one grant and bits and pieces of M.A. theses this promise of superseding Freudian dynamics with a conceptually more operational and clinically more exact framework has not been implemented. During that fifteen years, for lack of what I believe might have been, e.g., in the form of a powerful P—technique for individual analysis, most clinicians tired of the elaborations of psychoanalytic subjectivities and grasped at the superficial patching job possible through behavior therapy. If someone in command of funds in the clinical research area had been capable of recognizing what the dynamic calculus might mean for clinical practise that practise could everywhere be at a different level of dependability by now. Meanwhile, in these intervening years, as opportunities passed, the words have often sprung to my mind which Shakespeare gave to Westmorland, facing the threatened defeat at Agincourt. "O! that we now had here but one ten thousand of those men in England that do no work this day." And the consolation of friends comes back in the sophistry of Henry V, "the fewer men, the greater share of honour."

What we began around 1950, as described above, in investigating objective devices measuring motivation strength, had already developed by 1959, through the discovery of the U and I components, and the ergs and the sentiment structures, into the dynamic calculus as so far defined. In the mid-sixties, although we had no resources for extension (or even consolidation) it became evident to me that the calculus had considerable relevance to learning theory, at least in the personality domain. The late great inventor Professor Pickering maintained that new developments in a field require "a certain amount of intelligent ignorance" and since I had independently reached this same conclusion I cultivated my ignorance of the more doctrinaire reflexological formulations. (I even constantly referred to Type II "conditioning" reinforcement simply as "reward.") The opening up by our research of a new capacity to measure ergic tensions and their changes enables a complete *vector* measurement of any given reward to be set down. Meanwhile the quantification of behavioral indices (loadings) and modulation indices, joined with the more exact measurement of unitary traits and tensions, has permitted a hitherto unattainable completeness of description of learning changes themselves. It led to what I have called the tri-vector principle within structured learning theory. Although I deplore that the research resources that would have given more substance to these developments were denied by a certain committee, the principles at least of the dynamic calculus are getting to younger psychologists more freely now through such alert textbook and chapter writers as Lindzey and Hall, Horn, Bischof, Delhees, Butcher, Dreger, Kline, Pervin, Sells, Semeonoff, Sahakian, Levy, Pawlik, Wiggins, and others. And the recent systematic exposition that the English psychologist, Child (1973), has carried out with me should pull many diverse researchers into perspective.

Although the avoidance of such logjams as occurred here awaits research on research I made one effort to remedy one of the main causes of holdup of much of the more sophisticated advance in behavioral science in this generation. I refer to the lack of education of psychology students concerning multivariate experimental designs and concepts. The majority of the present generation of psychologists—and virtually all outside the English-speaking countries, Germany, Scandinavia, and Japan—have missed education in, and are defensive about, concepts from multivariate experimental methods. Much as I dislike spending time in "political" activities it was the obvious root solution to the situation I complain about to organize, as I did in 1959 and 1960, the Society for Multivariate Experimental Psychology. Enthused by its relevance to current research problems, younger men, notably Eber, Howard, Sells, Cartwright, Sweney, Burdsal, Pierson, Harman, and Merrifield in the States, and Child, Pawlik, Sumner, Fahrenberg, and Warburton in Europe, have developed regional societies, and it was from the ranks of these that the truly brilliant group came together to write the *Handbook of Multivariate Experimental Psychology* (1966), and, with Cartwright and Fiske, to edit the new journal *Multivariate Behavioral Research*. Already, within a decade, one can see an exciting increase in the daring and the sophistication with which multivariate research is planned and executed. Perhaps another decade will see a corresponding increase in the psychologists who can read its relevance to personality, motivation, learning, and social psychology. Pierson's new *Journal of Multivariate Experimental Personality and Clinical Psychology* may do much to infuse personality and clinical research with more powerful methods.

It would be an incomplete story of my professional life if I did not cap it by telling of a last development which integrated my scientific interests with the thread of social-religious interest which I have indicated above has always been present in my thinking. This was the completion of my book on *Beyondism* (1972) and the formation of the non-profit *Institute for Research on Morality and Adjustment,* in Boulder, in 1973. There is an irony to be savored in the fact that the word morality is almost a bad word today, not only with the very young—for in no generation have the young liked the word—but even in some supposedly mature academics. If I am right in the above book in considering morality to be the beauty of progressive living, functioning in a complex cultural organism, its study must challenge us as offering the most intricate of the mathematico-social research areas. It is certainly destined to be the king of the sciences. Obviously as I retire from the excellent organization at Illinois to this infant Institute I am not going to be able to accomplish much, except perhaps to put it in the hands of the most brilliant young psychologists I can find. One must recognize the inevitability of the sun's arc, and yet, in the words of Tennyson's *Ulysses,* "Old age hath yet his honor and his toil," and

> The lights began to twinkle from the rocks:
> The long day wanes: the slow moon climbs: the deep
> Moans round with many voices. Come my friends,
> 'Tis not too late to seek a newer world.
> Push off, and sitting well in order smite
> The sounding furrows; . . .

What I hope I leave largely accomplished, to Telemachus, is at least a dependable framework of structured personality and motivation measurement. For when measurement is ready the real investigations of psychology as a science can begin.

REFERENCES

Selected Publications by Raymond B. Cattell

The significance of the actual resistances in psycho-galvanic experiments. *Brit. J. Psychol.,* 1928, *19,* 34-43.

The effects of alcohol and caffeine on intelligent and associative performance. *Brit. J. Med. Psychol.,* 1930, *13,* 20-33.

Psychology and social progress. London: Daniel, 1933.

Temperament tests: I. Temperament. *Brit. J. Psychol.,* 1933, *23,* 308-329.

Temperament tests: II. Tests. *Brit. J. Psychol.,* 1933, *24,* 20-49.

The psychology of men of genius. London: Kegan Paul, 1934.

Your mind and mine: A popular introduction to psychology. London: Harrap, 1934.

Occupational norms of intelligence, and the standardization of an adult intelligence test. *Brit. J. Psychol.,* 1934, *25,* 1-28.

A guide to mental testing. London: London Univ. Press, 1936.

Is national intelligence declining? *Eugen. Rev.,* 1937, *29,* 171-179.

The fight for our national intelligence. London: King, 1937.

Under sail through red Devon. London: Machehose, 1937.

Declining intelligence in the schools—Education and birth rate. *Schoolmaster,* 1937, *CXXXI,* 452. (a)

Some further relations between intelligence, fertility, and socio-economic factors. *Eugen. Rev.,* 1937, *29,* 171-179. (b)

Crooked personalities: An introduction to clinical psychology. London: Century, 1938. (a)

A study of the national reserves of intelligence. *Human Factor,* 1938, *12,* 127-136. (b)
Some changes in social life in a community with a falling intelligence quotient. *Brit. J. Psychol.,* 1938, *28,* 430-450.
Some theoretical issues in adult intelligence testing. *Psychol. Bull.,* 1941, *38,* 592.
Psychological measurement: Normative, ipsative, interactive. *Psychol. Rev.,* 1944, *51,* 292-303.
"Parallel proportional profiles" and other principles for determining the choice of factors by rotation. *Psychometrika,* 1944, *9,* 267-283.
The description and measurement of personality. New York: Harcourt Brace Jovanovich, 1946.
Concepts and methods in the measurement of group syntality. *Psychol. Rev.,* 1948, *55,* 48-63.
The dimensions of culture patterns by factorization of national characters. *J. Abnor. Soc. Psychol.,* 1949, *44,* 443-469.
r_p and other coefficients of pattern similarity. *Psychometrika,* 1949, *14,* 279-298.
A note on factor invariance and the identification of factors. *Brit. J. Psychol.,* 1949, *II,* 134-138.
Personality, a systematic theoretical and factual study. New York: McGraw-Hill, 1950.
The principal culture patterns discoverable in the syntal dimensions of existing nations. *J. Soc. Psychol.,* 1950, *32,* 215-253.
The scientific ethics of "Beyond." *J. Soc. Issues,* 1950, *6,* 21-27.
P-technique, a new method for analyzing the structure of personal motivation. *Trans. New York Acad. Sci.,* Ser. II, 1951, *14,* 29-34.
On the theory of group learning. *J. Soc. Psychol.,* 1953, *37,* 27-52.
Research designs in psychological genetics with special reference to the multiple variance method. *Amer. J. Human Genet.,* 1953, *5,* 76-93.
The meaning of clinical psychology. In L. A. Pennington and I. A. Berg (Eds.), *An introduction to clinical psychology.* New York: Ronald Press, 1954, 3-25.
Personality and motivation structure and measurement. New York: World Book, 1957.
A universal index for psychological factors. *Psychologia,* 1957, *1,* 74-85.
The dynamic calculus: A system of concepts derived from objective motivation measurement. In G. Lindzey (Ed.), *Assessment of human motives.* New York: Holt, Rinehart and Winston, 1958, 197-238.
The dynamic calculus: Concepts and crucial experiments. In M. R. Jones (Ed.), *The Nebraska symposium on motivation.* Lincoln, Nebr.: Univ. Nebraska Press, 1959, 84-134.
Personality theory growing from multivariate quantitative research. In S. Koch (Ed.), *Psychology: A study of a science.* New York: McGraw-Hill, 1959, 257-327.
The multiple abstract variance analysis equations and solutions: For nature-nurture research on continuous variables. *Psychol. Rev.,* 1960, *67,* 353-372.
Group theory, personality, and role: A model for experimental researches. In *Defence psychology.* Elmsford, N. Y.: Pergamon Press, 1961, 209-258.

Theory of situational, instrument, second order, and refraction factors in personality structure research. *Psychol. Bull.*, 1961, *58*, 160-174.

Psychological measurement of anxiety and depression: A quantitative approach. *Canad. Psychiat. Assoc. J.*, 1962, 7, 11-23.

The relational simplex theory of equal interval and absolute scaling. *Acta Psychol.*, 1962, *20*, 139-158.

The structuring of change of P-technique and incremental R-technique. In C. W. Harris (Ed.), *Problems in measuring change.* Madison, Wisc.: Univ. Wisconsin Press, 1963.

Personality, role, mood, and situation-perception: A unifying theory of modulators. *Psychol. Rev.*, 1963, *70*, 1-18.

Validity and reliability: A proposed more basic set of concepts. *J. Educ. Psychol.*, 1964, *55*, 1-22.

The parental early repressiveness hypothesis for the authoritarian personality factor, U. I. 28. *J. Genet. Psychol.*, 1964, *106*, 333-349.

The scientific analysis of personality. Baltimore: Penguin Books, 1965.

Handbook of multivariate experimental psychology. Skokie, Ill.: Rand McNally, 1966.

Anxiety and motivation: Theory and crucial experiments. In C. B. Spielberger (Ed.), *Anxiety and behavior.* New York: Academic Press, 1966, 23-62.

Multivariate behavioral research and the integrative challenge. *Multivar. Behav. Res.*, 1966, *1*, 1, 4-23.

The scree test for the number of factors. *Multivar. Behav. Res.*, 1966, *1*, 2, 140-161.

Trait-view theory of perturbations in ratings and self-ratings (L(BR)- and Q-data): Its application to obtaining pure trait score estimates in questionnaires. *Psychol. Rev.*, 1968, *75*, 2, 96-113.

Progress in clinical psychology through multivariate experimental designs. *Multivar. Behav. Res.*, special issue, 1968, 4-8.

The isopodic and equipotent principles for comparing factor scores across different populations. *Brit. J. Math. Statist. Psychol.*, 1970, *23*, No. 1, 23-41.

Separating endogenous, exogenous, ecogenic, and epogenic component curves in developmental data. *Develop. Psychol.*, 1970, *3*, No. 2, 151-162.

Abilities: Their structure, growth, and action. Boston: Houghton Mifflin, 1971.

Real base factor analysis. *Multivar. Behav. Res. Monogr.*, 1971, *8*.

Estimating modulator indices and state liabilities. *Multivar. Behav. Res.*, 1971, *6*, 7-33.

A new morality from science: beyondism. New York: Pergamon, 1972.

The nature and genesis of mood states: A theoretical model with experimental measurements concerning anxiety, depression, arousal, and other mood states. In C. B. Spielberger (Ed.), *Current trends in theory and research,* Vol. 1. New York: Academic Press, 1972.

Key issues in motivational theory (with special reference to structured learning and the dynamic calculus). In J. R. Royce (Ed.), *Studies in multivariate psychology.*

The 16 P.F. and basic personality structure: a reply to Eysenck. *J. Behav. Sci.,* Durban, South Africa, 1972, *2*, 1-30.

Personality and mood by questionnaire. San Francisco: Jossey-Bass, 1973.

Unravelling maturational and learning developments by the comparative MAVA and structured learning approaches. In J. R. Nesselroade and H. W. Reese, (Eds.), *Life span developmental psychology.* New York and London: Academic Press, 1973.

The rotation problem in factor analysis. In Enslein (Ed.), *Computer procedures in the social sciences.* 1973.

The organization of independent basic research institutes symbiotic with universities. *Higher Education,* 1973, *2,* 1-14.

(with Karel R. Balcar, J. L. Horn, and J. R. Nesselroade) Factor matching procedures: An improvement of the s index; with tables. *Educ. Psychol. Measure.,* 1969, *29,* 4, 781-792.

K. Barton. Real and perceived similarities in personality between spouses: Test of "likeness" versus "completeness" theories. Psychological Reports, 1972, *31,* 15-18.

(with D. B. Blewett and J. R. Beloff) The inheritance of personality. A multiple variance analysis determination of approximate nature-nurture ratios for primary personality factors in Q-data. *Amer. J. Human Genet.,* 1955, 7, 122-146.

(with H. Breul and H. P. Hartman) An attempt at more refined definition of the cultural dimensions of syntality in modern nations. *Amer. Soc. Rev.,* 1952, *17,* 408-421.

(with A. K. S. Cattell) Factor rotation for proportional profiles: Analytical solution and an example. *Brit. J. Statist. Psychol.,* 1955, *8,* 83-92.

(with A. K. S. Cattell and R. M. Rhymer) P—technique demonstrated in determining psycho-physiological source traits in a normal individual. *Psychometrika,* 1947, *12,* 267-288.

(with D. Child) *Principles of motivation and dynamic structure.* London and New York: Holt Rinehart and Winston (In press, 1973).

(with G. E. DeYoung) Confactor resolution. *Multivar. Behav. Res. Monogr.,* 1971, *9.*

(with K. Dickman) A dynamic model of physical influences demonstrating the necessity of oblique simple structure. *Psychol. Bull.,* 1962, *59,* 389-400.

(with J. M. Digman) A theory of the structure of perturbations in observer ratings and questionnaire data in personality research. *Behav. Sci.,* 1964, *9,* 4, 341-358.

(with M. J. Foster) The rotoplot program for multiple, single-plane, visually-guided rotation. *Behav. Sci.,* 1963, *8,* 156-165.

(with R. L. Gorsuch) The uniqueness and significance of simple structure demonstrated by contrasting organic "natural structure" and "random structure" data. *Psychometrika,* 1963, *28,* 55-67.

(with M. Adelson) The dimensions of social change in the U.S.A. as determined by P-technique. *Soc. Forces,* 1951, *30,* 190-201.

(with A. B. Heist, P. A. Heist, and R. G. Stewart) The objective measurement of dynamic traits. *Educ. Psychol. Measure.,* 1950, *10,* 224-248.

(with J. Jaspers) A general plasmode (No. 30-10-5-2) for factor analytic exercises and research. *Multivar. Behav. Res. Monogr.,* 1967, *67,* 3, 1-212.

(with G. F. Kawash and G. E. Deyoung) Validation of objective measures of ergic tension: Response of the sex erg to visual stimulation. *Journal of Experimental Research in Personality,* 1972, *6* 1, 76-83.

(with G. W. Kawash and T. E. Dielman) Changes in objective measures of fear motivation as a function of laboratory-controlled manipulation. *Psychological Reports*, 1972, *30*, 59-63.

(with E. F. Maxwell, B. H. Light, and M. P. Unger) The objective measurement of attitudes. *Brit. J. Psychol.*, 1949, *40*, 81-90.

(with E. V. Molteno) Contributions concerning mental inheritance: II. Temperament. *J. Genet. Psychol.*, 1940, *57*, 31-47.

(with J. L. Muerle) The "maxplane" program for factor rotation to oblique simple structure. *Educ. Psychol. Measure,* 1960, *20* 569-590.

(with J. R. Nesselroade) Likeness and completeness theories examined by 16 P.F. measures on stably and unstably married couples. *J. Pers. Soc. Psychol.*, 1967, 7, 4, 351-361.

(with J. R. Nesselroade) *Human Behav. Genet.*, In preparation, 1973.

(with K. E. Nichols) An improved definition, from 10 researches, of second order personality factors in Q data (with cross-cultural checks). *Journal of Social Psychology*, 1972, *86*, 187-203.

(with J. A. Radcliffe) Reliabilities and validities of simple and extended weighted and buffered unifactor scales. *Brit. J. Statist. Psychol.*, 1962, *15*, 113-128.

(with I. H. Scheier) Clinical validities by analyzing the psychiatrist exemplified in relation to anxiety diagnoses. *Amer. J. Orthopsychiat.*, 1958, *28*, 699-713.

(with I. H. Scheier) *The meaning and measurement of neuroticism and anxiety.* New York: Ronald Press, 1961.

(with G. Schroder and A. Wagner) Verification of the structure of the 16 P.F. Questionnaire in German. *Psychol. Forsch.*, 1969, *32*, 369-386.

(with G. F. Stice) Four formulae for selecting leaders on the basis of personality. *Human Relations*, 1954, 7, 493-507.

(with G. F. Stice) *The dimensions of groups and their relation to the behavior of members.* Champaign, Ill.: Institute for Personality and Ability Testing, 1960.

(with G. F. Stice and N. F. Kristy) A first approximation to nature-nurture ratios for eleven primary personality factors in objective tests. *J. Abnor. Soc. Psychol.*, 1957, *54*, 143-159.

(with W. Sullivan) The scientific nature of factors: A demonstration by cups of coffee. *Behav. Sci.*, 1962, 7, 184-193.

(with B. Tsujioka) The importance of factor-trueness and validity, versus homogeneity and orthogonality, in test scales. *Educ. Psychol. Measure.*, 1964, *24*, 3-30.

(with F. W. Warburton) *Objective personality and motivation tests. A theoretical introduction and practical compendium.* Champaign, Ill.: Univ. Illinois Press, 1967.

(with J. L. Willson) Contributions concerning mental inheritance. I. Of intelligence, *Brit. J. Educ. Psychol.*, 1938, *8*, 129-149.

Gorsuch, Richard L., and R. B. Cattell. Second stratum personality factors defined in the questionnaire realm by the 16 P.F. *Multivar. Behav. Res.*, 1967, *2*, 211-224.

Horn, J. L., and R. B. Cattell. Refinement and test of the theory of fluid and crystallized general intelligences. *J. Educ. Psychol.*, 1966, *57*, 5, 253-270.

Hundleby, J. D., K. Pawlik, and R. B. Cattell. *Personality factors in objective test devices.* San Diego, Calif.: R. R. Knapp & Co., 1965.

Pawlik, K., and R. B. Cattell. The relationship between certain personality factors and measure of cortical arousal. *Neuropsychologia,* 1965, *3,* 129-151.

Rickels, K., and R. B. Cattell. The clinical factor validity and trueness of the IPAT verbal and objective batteries for anxiety and regression. *J. Clin. Psychol.,* 1965, *21,* 257-264.

Schneewind, K. A., and R. B. Cattell. Zum problem der faktoridentifikation: Verteilungen und Vertrauensintervalle von Kongruenzkoeffizienten fur Personlichkeitsfaktoren im Bereich objektiv-analytischer Tests. *Psychol. Beitr.,* 1970, *XII,* 2, 214-226.

The 71 articles, 22 books, and 11 chapters in books by others, above, are selected from 330 articles, 36 books, and 43 chapters in books by others, by the present writer, an appreciable fraction in coauthorship with 102 jointly publishing research associates.

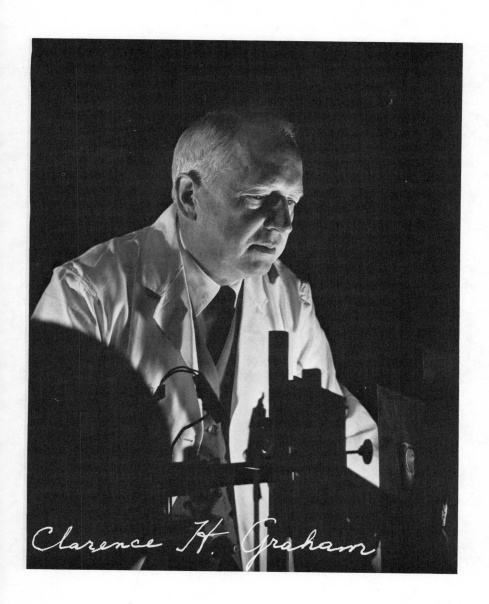

Clarence H. Graham

Clarence H. Graham

EARLY LIFE AND EDUCATION

I was born in Worcester, Massachusetts, on January 6, 1906, the oldest of four children, three boys and a girl. My parents were Irish Protestants from County Donegal. They first met in the United States and were married three years before my birth. My mother had been "sent for" by her aunt, a strong-willed woman who pretty well dominated her small group of relatives in this country until her death at almost the same hour as Franklin D. Roosevelt's in 1945. This grand-aunt of mine had an important influence on my life. She had no children of her own, and I sometimes thought she asserted an unwarranted claim upon my affections. Still, I now recognize that this strong woman did indeed shape me in a way that modulated some influences derived from my quite permissive parents.

When I was five I went to kindergarten in the Cambridge Street School of the Worcester School System. My introduction to school was marred by the fact that, having just suffered a quite severe childhood illness, I was more than usually emotional in my response to my first school experiences. The period of adjustment soon passed, and from then on I became a well-habituated pupil in a way that probably had implications for my total life pattern.

My most memorable days in grammar school were in the later grades during World War I. The pupils were, in the days after America's entry into the war, in a chronic state of excitement. The usual topics of the curriculum were taken up, but there was in addition a great deal of singing of patriotic and popular songs. Various circumstances caused uncertainty in the time and place of parts of the school program, and many changes were made in the school sessions, aimed for one thing at saving fuel. What with rationing, Liberty bonds, war gardens, and the countless other things out of the ordinary, the period of World War I was an exhilerating time for the pupils of the Cambridge Street School, before it was finally capped by Armistice Day in 1918. I was awakened by bells and whistles at 2 o'clock on the morning of November 11 with my mother bending over me and announcing that the war was over. I remember that I dressed as fast as I could and hurried to the center of Worcester where the beginning of the celebration was taking place with many bonfires and much milling about. A

103

parade was arranged for the afternoon, in which SATC (Students Army Training Corps) contingents at Worcester Tech, Clark, and Holy Cross Colleges took part, as well as other military groups. Students commandeered the trolley cars, and excitement permeated the crowd as feelings of comraderie and good fellowship prevailed. My memories of V-E and V-J days in 1945 are dim by comparison with those of Armistice Day of 1918 when I was a twelve-year-old boy. I remember thinking that now at last all nations would be saved for democracy, even those wicked ones that didn't want to be.

I was graduated from grammar school in 1919 and went to South High School in Worcester. I think of high school days as a time when learning was easy and my teachers in general were very good. I did not spend much time on homework, and in fact I worked in a grocery store during most of my afternoons. Some nights, I spent several hours in the Y.M.C.A. gym and swimming pool. I realize now that I may have been busier during this period than I ever was in my life, before or since. My experiences in the public schools of Worcester, grammar and high school, provide a generally happy memory. As I look back I feel that I was lucky to have been taught by such a dedicated group of teachers.

In 1923 I was graduated from high school and spent the vacation months working in the spring mill of the American Steel and Wire Company, thereby adding to my financial backlog at the rate of 40 cents an hour for 48 hours a week, quite respectable wages at the time.

My mother's aunt, whom I called Aunt Maggie, was aware of Clark University from nearly the time of its founding and, as a person meagerly educated herself, was respectful of the aura of knowledge and scholarship that existed in its early days under G. Stanley Hall and an initially brilliant faculty. At any rate, she early determined that I should go to Clark. Backed by my own savings and her support, I entered Clark in September of 1923 and spent three years trying to decide what schedule I should follow and what my "major" should be. I changed from chemistry to literature, sampled some other topics, and in my third year took my first psychology course with John Paul Nafe shortly after he had received his degree with Titchener. I cannot say that the substance of Nafe's course was memorable, but somehow or other Nafe had a way, not of instructing students, but of treating them as personalities who could be interesting in their own right. That they were worthwhile was further demonstrated to a fortunate few by the fact that Nafe paid considerable attention to them, even becoming their friend. This magic seems to have touched many students, graduate and undergraduate, who later became well-known psychologists.

I finally became of student of psychology and took experimental psychology with Nafe in my senior year. Frank Geldard, two years my senior, was starting work on his doctor's thesis and beginning to recruit subjects and, as it turned out, an experimenter (myself) for his work on light adaptation. I remember that I experienced an almost joyful feeling as I sat in the dim ambient illumination of the dark room, timing the stimulus presentation, hearing the accompanying clicks and later, seeing the data take shape under Geldard's computations. That year's activity surely bent the growing branch in a way that has persisted.

In 1927 I started graduate work at Clark. The staff, in addition to Nafe, consisted of Carl Murchison, Vernon Jones, and most especially, Walter Hunter. Raymond Willoughby, associate editor of *Psychological Abstracts,* also was an influential force among the students, especially in such areas as developmental and abnormal, which would otherwise have had little representation. Of course, the two main influences on me were Nafe and Hunter. I soon came under Hunter's influence through his seminars, Animal Behavior and Principles of Psychology. The former course developed in me an appreciation of objective psychology, especially certain criteria of experimentation and careful analysis of problems. Although I responded positively to Hunter's statements, I remember that on one matter I made a choice of systematic approach that neither he nor the other students of the class supported. In our study of the points of view represented by Jennings and Loeb, I favored Loeb. I have since recognized, of course, that in fact Jenning's approach would probably be favored by many or most students of behavior, but even then I had the feeling that for me an account of behavior would require some more explicitly analytic and testable variables as objectives of study. And so, it is probably not surprising that my interests in sensation and perception have been along the paths laid out by such workers as Helmholtz, Maxwell, Hering, Mach, and, to repeat, Loeb.

In my last year of graduate work I took Hunter's *Principles of Psychology,* a course that reflected Hunter's early training in philosophy. By this time, 1929, Hunter had become stabilized in his systematic orientation: he was a behaviorist and I believe he had thought his position through, perhaps not to the degree of subtlety exhibited more recently by J. R. Kantor, but he surely provided meaty fare for students. He never aimed at indoctrination for the sake of personal support; that is not to say that he would not argue for his point of view. With him, one had to know not only wherein one disagreed, but also why. I particularly remember a discussion of a paper of his own that he had assigned, "The Subject's Report" (Hunter, 1925). I was of the opinion that the subject's report is a response to be treated from the point of view of psychology like any other response. Hunter disagreed, probably, as I recall, on the basis that the manner of specifying criteria in the two cases would be greatly different.

I did my thesis with Nafe, but unfortunately he was absent on sabbatical leave in Europe during my final semester. Nevertheless, I finished the thesis, a study of binocular summation at threshold (Graham, 1930). I found little or none. Years later, Leonard Matin, my colleague and former student at Columbia, studied the same problem by an improved technique and was able to show the existence of a very small effect over a small portion of the relevant psychophysical functions (Matin, 1962).

During my graduate student days at Clark I found myself in able company. Other students who were there for various periods at that time were Frank Geldard, Luberta Harden, Dorothea Johanssen, Harry Ewert, Wayne Dennis,

Norman Munn, Louis Gellermann, Mason Crook, and Robert Leeper, the last five of whom received their degrees when I did in 1930.

TEMPLE, PENNSYLVANIA, AND THE JOHNSON FOUNDATION

Nineteen-thirty was a hard year for academic jobs (it was the first year of the Depression). I applied without success for a National Research Fellowship early in the year (Louis Gellermann of my group did receive one), and Robert Leeper, Mason Crook, and I tried by various devices to get in touch with persons who might have or at least know about an opening for a young psychologist. Finally, Crook received an appointment at Dartmouth, and Leeper received one at Arkansas. The summer dragged on, and near its end Leeper received a letter (in reply to about one hundred he had written) telling him of an opening at Temple. Would he be interested in applying? Since he had already agreed to go to Arkansas, he wrote that he had a colleague by the name of Graham whom he would like to nominate. Shortly thereafter, I met Thaddeus L. Bolton, chairman of the department at Temple, and in September 1930 I was appointed to a one-year term at Temple to take the place of a staff member who was completing his Ph.D. work at Ohio State.

I liked Bolton very much, a feeling that was enhanced by the fact that I knew something about some of his early papers and also that he had been at Clark in the early days. He was one of the very early behaviorists before Watson, and dealt, I think, in an insightful way with an objective version of perception. He was an outstanding scholar, but his interests turned in the 1920s to administration during tenures at Nebraska and Temple. For a short while he was president of the latter.

Of the staff members at Temple, I had more in common with Hughbert Hamilton than the others; he was an experimentalist from Columbia and, until recently, has guided the experimental program at Temple. He has been succeeded by Philip Bersh, with whom I have had many stimulating discussions when he was a graduate student at Columbia.

At the beginning of the academic year, I went with James Leach, a Temple biologist, to visit some biology laboratories in which Leach was working for his degree at the University of Pennsylvania. During that visit, I went to the physiology department, where I met H. C. Bazett. Bazett and I had a long talk during which he told me about some of his recent work on touch spots and then about some related work by Dallenbach. He was extremely cordial and seemed happy to discuss sensory research with a kindred soul. In the course of the discussion, he suggested that I meet a young Finnish-Swede from Helsingfors named Ragnar Granit, who had come the year before to work in the Johnson Foundation for Medical Physics. (I later learned that Granit had worked in psychology with Gelb before he received his medical degree.) The Johnson

Foundation was then headed and directed by Detlev W. Bronk, who only recently has retired as President of The Rockefeller University and a few years earlier as President of the National Academy of Sciences.

At any rate, I soon met Granit and Bronk, and both seemed happy to have me work in the Johnson Foundation when my fifteen-hour-a-week teaching schedule at Temple would allow. I'm afraid that I often spent more time at the Johnson Foundation than I did at Temple. This was possible since my teaching took place between 9 and noon five days a week. My teaching of four courses in general psychology and one in educational psychology may have suffered during this regime, but Bolton did not seem to think it was totally lamentable. At midyear he told me that he would support me for an additional year despite the fact that the man I had replaced would be returning. By this time, however, I had made up my mind to apply again for a National Research Fellowship so that I could spend full time on research at the Johnson Foundation. I was supported in my application by Granit, Bronk, and Bazett. I heard that I received the fellowship in February 1931 and thereupon told Bolton that I would not be at Temple after June.

At just about that time John Paul Nafe was offered the chairmanship of the psychology department at Washington University, St. Louis. The department at Clark tried at first to replace him with some well-established psychologists but soon gave up the search in the face of a shortage of funds that developed as the Depression progressed; they instead decided to find a junior staff member and offered me the position. I was, of course, unable to accept the Clark appointment for 1931-1932, having already accepted the NRC Fellowship as of July 1, 1931. The problem was resolved by making my appointment start as of July 1932. Very importantly, it turned out that some of the funds saved by this arrangement could be used to refurbish and supply the Clark laboratory during 1931-1932 in preparation for my arrival.

During the entire academic year 1930-1931, I taught at Temple and worked with Granit at the Johnson Foundation. The main result of our research was a joint paper involving a determination of critical flicker frequency under various conditions (Graham and Granit, 1931). We found that each of two adjacent semicircles equal in area and luminance gives, in the presence of the other, a critical frequency that is higher than either one alone. The effect was interpreted to represent a process of retinal summation. On the other hand, when the luminance of either of the two is reduced (while the other remains the same), the critical frequency of the dimmer semicircle is essentially unchanged from its value alone. The absence of change in critical frequency under conditions of different luminances was interpreted to mean removal of summation by inhibition of the dim semicircle by the brighter. This type of finding was later expanded by Granit and myself (individually and with students) in experiments on inhibition.

Late in my second semester at the Johnson Foundation, Keffer Hartline returned from a three-year study of physics at Baltimore and Munich following his medical degree at Hopkins. Thus were Granit and Hartline, two future Nobel Laureates, brought together in the same laboratory. Hartline had done a number of studies of electroretinograms in the vertebrate eye and (a foretaste of his future research) the eye of *Limulus*, the horseshoe crab, which existed in profusion at Woods Hole. I spent the summer of 1931 there with Hartline, during which time he, with some help from me, succeeded in recording impulses from single fibers of the *Limulus* optic nerve, there establishing it as the almost perfect preparation on which to test simplified models of photoreceptor activity (Hartline and Graham, 1932).

In September 1931 we went back to Philadelphia, and I spent the time until June largely in learning some experimental techniques and principles of equipment design. I also did more work on flicker, along the lines of the earlier work with Granit. This work was not published.

During this time things were progressing with the refurbishing of the laboratory at Clark. Carl Murchison, the chairman, took a personal interest in my plans, and spent a great deal of effort supervising the construction of two large dark rooms, a photographic dark room, the installation of a direct current generator, and the purchase of optical and electrical recording equipment that I had ordered.

CLARK

I returned to Clark in July 1932 and spent a leisurely summer preparing the laboratory and developing some new equipment for work on flicker and threshold stimulation. My work began in earnest in September with the teaching of a number of courses, including General Psychology, Experimental Psychology, Sensory Psychology, Selected Advanced Topics, and a new course (based on work I had had with Professor H. M. Jacobs, the general physiologist at Pennsylvania), Quantitative Treatment. This course was concerned with curve fitting, rates, and integrals in problems with physiological and psychological applications.

I soon became engrossed in the work of my students, who in those days were expected to start work on their M.A. theses well before the Christmas after their arrival. I began working with Robert Beitel, J. Roy Smith (both of whom later became physicians), Robert R. Brown, Harry Karn, and Elaine Foraker. In the approximately nine months of their first year these people had to carry out a short experiment, learn how to develop equipment, run subjects, and write an acceptable essay. The benefits of this procedure would become clear in their third year when they worked on their Ph.D. theses, and even in their second year in time left over from Hudson Hoagland's comprehensive course in physiology, which all of them took.

In September 1932, Carl Murchison asked me to write a chapter for his *Handbook of General Experimental Psychology* in the hope that I might produce a manuscript that would take the place of the one by L. T. Troland, who had recently died. As it turned out, Troland's chapter was completed before his death, and I wrote one that did not repeat any of his material. My chapter, entitled "Vision: Some Neural Correlations" (1934b), gave an early statement of a topic, interaction, which has assumed new vitality in the last twenty years, and which has been shown to play a particularly important role in almost all types of visual processes, including adaptation. This chapter and my interest in this topic probably influenced my students, as three of them at this time did theses on interaction.

Lorrin Riggs entered Clark as a student in 1933 and soon showed interests in line with my own. We put together an amplifier and string galvanometer (the original used by Lillie for his iron wire model experiments and lent to us by Hudson Hoagland) with which we determined the white rat's rod luminosity curve (Graham and Riggs, 1935), and later, with Edward Kemp, a postdoctoral student, the rod curve for the pigeon (Graham, Kemp, and Riggs, 1935). Later, Riggs used the amplifier-string galvanometer equipment to study the effect of preadaptation in the frog electroretinogram (1937). This work showed that Kohlrausch's electroretinograms of various shapes, which he attributed to color vision processes, could be reproduced by changes in intensity. In the same year, Keffer Hartline and I completed research on the luminosity curve of *Limulus* (Graham and Hartline, 1935). I commuted at irregular intervals between Worcester and Philadelphia in order to do this.

BROWN

In 1936 Walter Hunter was invited to Brown University to become chairman of psychology after Leonard Carmichael moved to Rochester. Edward Kemp, who had spent the year 1935-1936 on an NRC Fellowship with Hallowell Davis, had already been hired by Carmichael and was at Brown in September when Hunter arrived, accompanied by J. McV. Hunt, who had just completed an NRC Fellowship at Worcester State Hospital and thus was well known to us at Clark. With Hunter from Clark went Raymond Willoughby, in his role as associate editor of the *Abstracts,* and myself, newly appointed Assistant Professor at Brown. Harold Schlosberg and Herbert Jasper welcomed us on our arrival in Providence. After the inevitable short period of adjustment, we found ourselves at home in Providence. As compared to Clark, the greatest difference lay in the size of the undergraduate program, which at Clark has been quite small. The program at Brown had been developed by Carmichael and was quite popular. As I remember it, the first year course contained about 630 students, approximately 130 Pembroke women and 500 Brown men. I taught sections of about 150, some semesters men, others women. A good deal of care was given to this course, and I found that I had to pay attention to my teaching in a way that I never had to before. The other courses I gave at Brown were seminars, mainly on topics similar to those I had given at Clark, with the addition of a course of a systematic and theoretical sort.

Once the instructional program was under way, we were ready to organize our research. Kemp and I (Graham and Kemp, 1938) began some work along lines developed at Clark in an earlier study of acuity. The investigation was concerned with the influence of duration (τ) of the intensity increment (ΔI) in brightness discrimination. The durations used extended from 2 to 500 msec. The general findings may be symbolized by the relation $\Delta I \cdot \tau = cf(I)$ for a value of τ smaller than a critical duration τc and by the relation $\Delta I \cdot \tau c = f(I)$ for values of τ equal to or greater than τc. In these equations I represents prevailing intensity and the term $f(I)$ may be taken as equal to an expression in Hecht's brightness discrimination equation.

This study was important because it proposed a theoretical formulation of two effects, brightness discrimination and its dependence on the duration of flash increment as described by the Bunsen-Roscoe law of photochemistry.

During these early years at Brown, I had the pleasure of working with or knowing many students who later became well-known psychologists: Robert Gagné, Neil Bartlett, Fred Mote, William Verplanck, Margaret Keller, Charles Cofer, Frank Finger, and Parker Johnson. With Gagné, I experimented on latencies in the running behavior of the white rat (Graham and Gagné, 1940), a project on which I had made preliminary observations before leaving Clark.

With Fred Mote and Bob Brown (who came for a summer from Clark) I worked on the area-intensity problem in vision (Graham, Brown, and Mote, 1939). Our formulation attempted to show why the intensity threshold in both the fovea and periphery decreases as stimulus area increases according to rule involving the integration of elemental excitatory processes. The experiment accounts for the manner in which photochemical and interaction processes combine to predict the observed trade-off relation existing between area and intensity at threshold.

The years at Brown from 1936 to 1940 were some of the happiest of my life. The members of the staff included, in addition to those previously mentioned, Donald Lindsley, who came in 1938 to succeed Herbert Jasper after the latter went to Montreal; Carl Pfaffman, who came from the Johnson Foundation in 1940; and Lorrin Riggs, who took a year's leave of absence from the University of Vermont in 1938. During that year Riggs and I worked on *Limulus*. In 1941 he came back to Brown for further experiments on *Limulus* and stayed there on NDRC work until his appointment in 1945 to succeed me. The Brown psychologists were an unusually compatible group. Each member showed interest not only in his own area, but also in other fields, thereby producing a broad spectrum of scientific tastes.

The 1930s passed into the 1940s and brought with them World War II, first signaled by Munich, and then the Fall of France and the Battle of Britain. By this time America started to bestir herself and among the first activities that took place was the emergence of the National Defense Research Committee

(NDRC) organized as part of the Office of Scientific Research and Development (OSRD) under Vannevar Bush to mobilize the scientific talent of the United States for work on projects related to defense. Psychology was late in being represented. In 1942 the Committee on Service Personnel-Selection and Training was formed under the Psychology Section of the National Research Council, of which Leonard Carmichael was then chairman. John Stalmaker became the Committee chairman, and projects were developed in branches of the armed services. The Committee soon gave way to the Applied Psychology Panel of NDRC. The organization and work of the early Committee has been summarized by Bray (1948) in his account of the work of the Applied Psychology Panel as the latter developed with enlarged membership under Walter Hunter as Chief. The members of the Panel served as supervisors, administrators, and research personnel. My role on the Panel was mainly in programs relating to the control of gunfire, in which I was ably aided by several other psychologists, in particular, W. E. Kappauf, W. G. Brogden, William Biel, and Douglas Ellson. In addition to the work on gunfire control, I supervised the development of a Personal Inventory, set up with Walter Shipley, as a device for selecting emotionally unstable personnel in various types of military activities. The inventory was used to expedite the work of psychiatrists in selecting recruits at Newport Naval Training Station and elsewhere as well as submariners at New London.

The work on the Personal Inventory may owe something to my experience in psychoanalysis for a number of years following 1936. I shall not attempt to evaluate in detail the effect of psychoanalysis on me. I suppose that a major effect was that I became less obsessed with it as I progressed in the program. In any case, it is of interest that I, a psychophysiologist, should feel that the problem of emotional stability should be at least minimally examined at a time when psychologists in the area of selection and psychometrics felt that this approach promised little. In fact, it turned out better in the military situation than had been expected, probably because men could express their affects more freely than usual and might gain secondary benefits by so doing.

My first experience with work under NDRC sponsorship had begun earlier in the spring of 1941 when I began research under Division 7, the fire control division, on problems of height finder and binocular range finder operations. I continued work on problems of the binocular range finder until 1945, although after 1942 this instrument assumed a largely standby role for radar. Nevertheless, Division 7 felt that work on it should continue.

My experience with war research acquainted me with several new areas of activity. Mainly, I learned about a larger than usual research organization and the problems arising therein. For a period at Brown I administered a program that had about 150 psychologists and technicians in projects at about twelve widely separated establishments.

A number of graduate students at Brown participated in NDRC work. Among them were Richard Berry, Richard Blackwell, Conrad Mueller, Richard Solomon, Eliot Stellar, and some of those mentioned earlier who had by this time received their degrees: Bartlett, Mote, and Verplanck. Most of these participated for one, two, or three years. They were eventually taken into the Armed Forces or moved to other projects as needs for experimental personnel developed. Finally, in 1945 V-E day arrived and then in August came V-J day following the explosion of the atomic bomb.

In January 1945 I had been approached by Henry Garrett of Columbia who sounded me out on the possibility of my going to New York in September. I discussed the prospect with Walter Hunter, and he and I finally agreed that I should probably move. I very much regretted leaving Brown, but it seemed that a move would be for me, as for many other psychologists, an inevitable consequence of the demand for new personnel after the war. Hunter knew what was going to happen. Within a year following the end of hostilities, he saw the department which he had built after 1936 dispersed. Donald Lindsley, J. McV. Hunt, and I moved to other posts, as did Stanley Williams, who had been at Brown for a short time early in the war. I was happy to know that Lorrin Riggs would continue at Brown after his NDRC work. Today only he remains from the group that was at Brown in the 1930s and 1940s. Hunter liked to say that he never regretted seeing a good man leave him to take on a job with greater responsibility. He felt that both psychology and the man would benefit from the change; and as for himself, while he might have personal regrets, his major concern was the welfare of science. Several of us who had left Brown at that time were reunited at the dedication of the Walter S. Hunter Laboratory of Psychology in 1958 when honorary degrees were awarded to Hunt, Lindsley, and myself.

COLUMBIA

When I arrived at Columbia, Woodworth had just retired, and I began teaching the Advanced Experimental course that he had been associated with for many years. My emphases were largely on the topics of sensation and perception together with excursions into such systematic, theoretical, and historical treatments as centered around them. In a word, the topics that interested me as a graduate student still interested me. I also dealt for a short time with some aspects of learning, but because this topic was covered extensively by Fred Keller and Nat Schoenfeld, I felt there was little need for it in my course.

In September 1945 the members of the staff consisted of Garrett as chairman, Pffenberger, Landis, Warden, Keller, Klineberg (who was on leave of absence in Brazil), and Schoenfeld. Others were on appointment in General Studies, including Woodworth, who continued to lecture to large classes in his two famous courses, Contemporary Schools of Psychology and Dynamic Psychology.

There were very few graduate students at Columbia in 1945, but the postwar influx started with a vengeance in 1946. Thereafter, for about five years, I had what I thought was a large number of students, as many as eight or ten working on doctoral theses at any given time. Other members of the staff also had more than the usual number. The number of students per staff member has decreased since those days because of fewer entering students and larger staffs.

My own and my student's research was well supported. At the time of Selig Hecht's death in 1947 (the end of the year in which he and I enjoyed giving a seminar together), the University allowed me to transfer the equipment of Hecht's laboratory to psychology. And so we came into possession of some historically important as well as useful equipment (the Hecht-Shlaer-Pirenne monochromator used in the research on quantum requirements at threshold, the Shlaer acuity apparatus, the Hecht-Shlaer adaptometer, and other valuable equipment). The Office of Naval Research has supported my activities from 1947 to the present. I shall not say that our funds were ever large. For example, until 1968 ONR funds never exceeded $26,000 a year, and this figure included part of Yun Hsia's salary, an amount that was supplemented by a Lectureship in General Studies. Hsia, a Woodworth Ph.D. who had done postdoctoral work with Hecht, was my colleague for 21 years, from 1947 until his death in 1968. When it came to color vision, his contribution to students and collaborators was great. He has been greatly missed at Columbia.

Starting about 1948, Hsia and I performed a number of experiments on normal and color blind individuals. These studies we believed established some new facts, particularly as related to luminosity (i.e., spectral brightness) functions. The first of the series involving determinations of quantal energies was performed on several normal subjects (Hsia and Graham, 1952). The results showed that luminosity is at a maximum near 560 nm with the data showing decreasing values into the extremes of the spectrum along curves that showed variations in structure. In particular, they showed a well-marked depression near 460 nm and a smaller one near 600 nm. These depressions were taken to represent processes attributable to color fundamentals.

Another series of experiments (Hsia and Graham, 1958) was performed on color blind subjects under conditions identical with those used on the normal subjects. The color blind group consisted of two classes of dichromats, protanopes and deuteranopes, individuals who can match any spectral color by a mixture of two primaries. As compared with the normal subjects, the protanopes showed a loss of luminosity in the red. In contrast with some previous interpretations but in conformity with earlier estimates by Hecht and Hsia, five or six deuteranopes showed a loss of luminosity in the green. The implications of this finding are important and will be discussed in connection with our work on a unilateral dichromat.

A young woman at Barnard College (Graham, Sperling, Hsia, and Coulson, 1961) was found to have trichromatic, probably normal, vision in one eye, and dichromatic vision in the other. Such a subject, referred to as unilaterally dichromatic, is very rare. Although about ten have been studied with some profit in the last hundred years, the technical methods and equipment used have not made possible dependable classifications in most cases. In addition, the fact that the subjects could not be observed over sufficient periods of time precluded extensive analyses. Analysis of unilateral cases of color blindness is important to color theory, because it is only in the case of the unilaterally color blind person that one can infer what colors a color blind person may see in terms of normal vision.

Hsia and I (Graham and Hsia, 1958) examined absolute luminosity for this subject who had trichromatic vision in her right eye and dichromatic vision in her left, and found that her right eye was considerably more sensitive in the blue and green than the color blind eye; both eyes seemed to be equally sensitive to the red.

Another matter of theoretical importance concerned the colors seen by this subject in her dichromatic as contrasted with her trichromatic eye. An experiment on binocular colormatching was performed and the results indicated that the subject saw only two hues in her dichromatic eye. She matched all wavelengths greater than her neutral point (the wavelength seen as white at about 502 nm) by a yellow of about 570 nm seen in the trichromatic eye. She matched wavelengths shorter than the neutral point by a blue of about 470 nm seen in the trichromatic eye.

The facts so far described raise an important theoretical problem for dichromatic theory; how can that eye see yellow if sensitivity to green is lost, either totally or to a major extent? In addition, one might ask about the mechanism by which a single hue of blue is seen for all wavelengths shorter than the neutral point. Nothing will be said about the latter question, but the problem of yellow must be considered.

Let it be supposed that in deuteranopia, for example, the subject's usual red receptors become attached to cells that signal central yellow, while the green receptors signal a similar yellow. The net result of this arrangement is that either red or green wavelength stimulation will be seen as yellow. The precise modifications in the absorption spectra of receptors that are required for appropriate losses are readily specifiable. Further work on spectral brightness matching and flicker was performed by Eda Berger in collaboration with Hsia and me (Berger, Graham, and Hsia, 1958).

About ten years after the work on dichromats and the unilaterally dichromatic subject, Hsia and I participated in an experiment with Harris Ripps and Irwin Siegel (Siegel, Graham, Ripps, and Hsia, 1966), two former Columbia students who are now research scientists in the Laboratory of Ophthamology at New York University Medical Center. The young woman on whom we made determinations had been previously studied by William Rushton of Cambridge University while he was in the United States at NIH. Rushton demonstrated that the subject was totally color blind at low photopic luminances; thus it was presumed that she exhibited exclusively rod-type vision. In fact, Rushton demonstrated a single type of dark-adaptation curve representing rod function.

Our examination of the subject showed that although her vision was totally color blind at low photopic luminances, her results on the Fransworth test showed that she had a tritan defect ("blue blindness") which was superimposed on a generalized reduction of cone sensitivity. This investigation was important in showing how an almost totally color blind subject may show some degree of dichromatic effect (in this case, a tritan defect) against a background of reduced cone sensitivity.

The last study on which Hsia and I collaborated (Graham and Hsia, 1969) was one on the foveal achromatic interval, the difference between the logarithms of the foveal chromatic and achromatic thresholds. We found that the curve for the chormatic threshold has the form of a curve of colorimetric purity as a function of wavelength; that is, it is the reciprocal of a saturation curve and does not have the form of a luminosity function. The curve for the achromatic threshold is below and shaped differently from the curve for the chromatic threshold.

It is pointed out that colorimetric-purity thresholds and chromatic thresholds seem both to be reciprocal measures of saturation. Chromatic thresholds may have an advantage in estimating saturation because they do not involve a physical mixture of color with white. This is not to say that an achromatic component (white) is not involved; the chromatic and achromatic components are intrinsic.

Since doctoral theses of graduate students often mirror the interests of the sponsor, it is probably not surprising that several of my students have performed experiments in color. Among these are Shakantala Balaraman, who collaborated with Hsia and me (Balaraman, Graham, and Hsia, 1962) on some experiments and wrote an historical account of color blindness (1962); Aleeza Beare (1963), who performed some important experiments on color naming; and Joan Pollock (1968), who determined human luminosity curves by means of a reaction-time study that was cosponsored by W. J. McGill. Gerald Howett and Gary Yonemura have continued their interest in vision by working for many years in color at the National Bureau of Standards.

These experiments on color by students may be taken to illustrate a principle that I have adhered to in guiding students during the initial stages of a doctoral project. So far as I could direct the choice of thesis subject, I tried to come to some agreement with the student on a topic that might be an introduction to a program of research in which one segment would lead to another. I have found that most students soon get interested in their topic and very often follow it intensively with useful, sometimes important, results.

I have sometimes thought that I have not followed my precepts in my own research. It is true that I have concerned myself with vision and visual perception, but it is clear that within my chosen field I have taken part in a considerable variety of experiments, ranging from electrical recording to work on perception of the Ames window. The work with Yun Hsia on color vision took place at Columbia from 1948 to 1968, and a different set of studies took place following the paths laid down in my work with Granit and in the work by myself and students at Clark and Brown. The latter experiments involved primarily such topics as interaction and various psychophysical parameters of visual discrimination. I have in mind such experiments as the one at Clark with Carolyn Cook (Graham and Cook, 1937) on intensity-time parameters of acuity and the study with Kemp at Brown on intensity-time relations in brightness discrimination (Graham and Kemp, 1938). An experiment of the same sort is the one by Graham, Brown, and Mote (1939) on the area-intensity relation, also done at Brown. Such experiments are important because they deal with essential variables that theory should account for. At Columbia, I participated in two experiments that had some of the characterists of the studies at Clark and Brown, the first a study in dark adaptation with John L. Brown, Howard Ranken, and Herschel Leibowitz (Brown, Graham, Leibowitz, and Ranken, 1953).

Luminance thresholds for the visual resolution of various widths of alternating light and dark lines were determined at various times in the dark. The finest gratings, representing high degrees of visual acuity, showed only a single cone curve that dropped quickly from a high luminance threshold during the first moments of dark adaptation to a final steady level. Coarse gratings produced a duplex curve that showed an initial cone portion and a delayed rod portion. The higher the criterion for degree of resolution, the higher the dark-adaptation threshold.

An interesting experrmiment on parameters of brightness discrimination with particular reference to interaction was performed by Philburn Ratoosh and me (Ratoosh and Graham, 1951). The experiment antedates studies on the excitatory and inhibitory interactions of adaptation stimuli, a problem that has received considerable attention in recent electrical recording work on lower animals as well as in recent psychophysical experiments.

We studied the effect on foveal brightness discrimination of changes in the diameters of the test (ΔI) and adapting (I) fields. With respect to the effects of area, two findings emerged from the results: (1) for a given brightness and constant test-field size, brightness discrimination improves as the size of the adapting area increases; and (2) for a given brightness and constant adapting-field area, brightness discrimination improves as the size of the test field increases until an optimal size of test field is attained; beyond this size, an increase in the size of the test field may result in higher values of Weber's fraction, $\Delta I/I$. An interaction hypothesis was advanced that seemed to account for the effects of area and luminance in this experiment.

MORE ABOUT COLUMBIA

My graduate students performed a considerable number of experiments on psychophysical parameters. Among the group were Leonard Diamond (1953), who worked on contrast; Celeste McCollough (1955) on Mach bands; Howard Baker (1949) on light adaptation; Robert Herrick (1956) on intensity discrimination; John Coulson on Fechner's Paradox (unpublished); Joel Pokorny (1968) on acuity; Munehira Akita (1964) with Hsia and me on color contrast; and several others. Conrad Mueller (1951) independently examined some implications of Poisson distributions of increments in luminances for brightness discrimination. An experiment by Florence Veniar (1948) on the just discriminable distortion of rectangular figures gave the unusual result that, for this sort of shape discrimination, Weber's law holds over the total large range of prevailing stimulus dimensions investigated.

Another area of interest was investigated by Elaine Hammer (1949), to whom I have been happily married since 1949. Her thesis on temporal influences on figural after-effects studied their development as a function of exposure duration of an inspection figure and their decay as a function of the time interval between the presentation of inspection and test figures.

I first became interested in movement discrimination after World War II, when I felt that data on thresholds for monocular movement parallax were badly needed. Monocular movement parallax is a strong and basic cue for depth. When a human being who is moving through space fixates an object that is not moving, a changing difference angle exists between the lines of sight to the fixated object and another object. If objects in the environment move while the observer's eye remains motionless, a comparable condition of changing difference angle exists to the principal line of sight.

We determined the threshold monocular movement parallax (i.e., differential angular velocity) as a function of the prevailing rate of stimulus movement in the subject's frontal plane (Graham, Baker, Hecht, and Lloyd, 1948). The subject was instructed, except under certain conditions, to follow with one eye the movements of the stimuli (e.g., two vertical needles) and to fixate the small region of separation between them. With his eye following the movement of the needles, he adjusted the lower needle until the two needles appeared to be in the same frontal plane.

The threshold differential angular velocity varied with background luminance, with the rate of the prevailing standard needle movement, and with the visual axis of movement. It is surely true that small differences in angular velocity may be discriminated; thresholds are of the order of 30 to 60 seconds of arc/second. It is of great interest that discrimination of space by monocular movement parallax can be made in any axis of vision, whereas stereoscopic vision occurs only for conditions of disparity in the horizontal axis. Similar results were obtained by a method directed toward another objective by Aubert (1886) and by my former student Father Richard Zegers (1948).

The circumstances in nature to which differential movement discrimination apply are, of course, manifold. A differential angular velocity exists, for example, between any pair of arbitrarily selected points on a moving object every time that object changes its orientation in space. A striking manifestation of the effect is exemplified in Ames's rotating trapezoid window. The trapezoid window consists of a flat surface cut out of wood or metal, painted to resemble a window with its panes of glass and other characteristic features. One side of the window is larger in the vertical dimension than the other. The window rotates at a constant rate about a point that is nearer the short end than the long end. As the subject looks at the window he observes that instead of seeming to rotate in a circle about the center of rotation, the window appears to oscillate back and forth, centering about the perpendicular to the frontal plane.

The stimulus conditions providing this type of apparent movement have been discussed by me (1963) in terms of an analysis based on two types of cues: (1) the differential angular velocities subtended at the eye of the subject by selected points on the surface of the window, and (2) linear perspective provided by the long and short vertical sides. It has been shown that the angular differential velocity $d\Delta\theta/dt$ at the eye is, for counterclockwise rotation, negative for certain positions of the points behind the frontal plane and positive for appropriately disposed points in front of the frontal plane. In consequence of these conditions, the subject cannot tell whether the points on the window are approaching him in front of the frontal plane or moving away from him behind it. Under these circumstances, how does the subject see the movement of the window? The answer is that he resolves the ambiguity of movement parallax cues by depending on perspective cues. The short side seems to move alternately toward and away from the subject behind the frontal plane with a periodic oscillating motion over an angular range averaging 180° behind the frontal plane. The long end seems to move in a comparable manner in front of the frontal plane. Thus the oscillation seems to be a movement through nearly half a circle and a return at a rate which is the rate of physical rotation.

In a recent study, my colleague Barbara Gillam and I (Graham and Gillam, 1970) tested the theory that reversals in the Ames window are the outcome of a resolution of ambiguous differential angular velocity cues by linear perspective cues. A parallel projection of the window on an opal glass screen was used as the stimulus. Our subjects almost always reported *two* apparent reversals per rotation. The short vertical side of the figure was always apparently in front of the long vertical side. These results were interpreted to be in line with theoretical expectations.

Other work on various aspects of space and movement has been carried out by my former students: Alfred Lit (1949), who studied the Pulfrich effect extensively starting with his doctor's thesis; Vivianne Smith (1969), who studied fusion perception for parts of a small area; John Foley (1964), who worked on the Luneberg theory of space discrimination; and David Henderson (1970), who performed a dimensional analysis of the threshold stimulus for motion discrimination.

Visual movement is a discrimination which, if one is to judge by the results of electrical recording studies, exhibits elaborate and complex types of neural interaction phenomena, especially of an inhibitory nature. This type of mechanism seems to provide the basis for the directional sensitivity shown by certain cells of the retina (Barlow and Hill, 1963).

Barbara Mates, a former student, and I have reported (Mates and Graham, 1970) new data on the velocity threshold for real movement. As the length of a narrow stimulus object increased, width remaining constant, we found that the velocity threshold also increased. These findings were discussed in relation to some psychophysical experiments by Diamond on brightness contrast, where it was shown that the dimming by contrast (with an inducing field of higher luminance) of a test field was a function of length of an inducing field of constant width.

The effect of stimulus length on threshold is analogous to the findings of Barlow and Levick (1965) on the effect of size on motion. They say, "If the image of a moving object spreads outside the receptive field onto its surround there are fewer impulses than when it is confined to the receptive field alone. This must be the inhibitory mechanism that elevates the threshold for large compared with small spots and it is presumably different from the inhibition responsible for sequence discrimination." From this point of view, then, the longer stimulus line should provide a higher threshold than does the short stimulus line. One possibility concerning this relationship was suggested in my Tillyer Medal address at the Optical Society in 1963: "Increasing the size of a bright object on a darker background at prevailing low rates increases ... the rate threshold. This may mean that an increase in length of the moving stimulus provides, over its length and in adjacent unstimulated areas (particularly at the leading and trailing edges), a change (in interaction effects). The effect at a given (contour) point is, presumably, increased (or decreased, depending on contrast relations) by virtue of the greater number of converging units that exist with longer lengths of stimuli than with shorter."

THEORETICAL FORMULATIONS

From my days as a graduate student, theoretical and systematic problems have played an important role in my thoughts about psychology. The article, "Psychophysics and Behavior" (1934a), published while I was at Clark (but first formulated in 1932 while I was at the Johnson Foundation), served as the introduction to a number of articles concerning the field of perception and its specification as an area of objective psychology. At Columbia I published the second article of this sort, entitled "Behavior, Perception, and the Psychophysical Methods" (1950). After the latter came out, I gave an invited paper at an APA symposium in which I attempted to interpret the systematic status of some recent experiments in terms of formulations given in the two papers (1952). I chose to discuss Kohler's experiments on figural after-effects, Bruner's experiments on estimates of the value of coins, and Luneberg's theory of non-Euclidean space. In my treatment I revised some terms that often implied a phenomenological context and attempted to recast them in an objective formulation. It became clear to me after reviewing the papers mentioned that a more elaborate account of these (and the systematic discussion that appeared in short form in my chapter in Stevens' *Handbook*, 1951) would be required to do even approximate justice to a formulation of perception in an objective psychology. I took advantage of my presidential address at the Eastern Psychological Association meeting in 1956 to discuss the topic, "Sensation and Perception in an Objective Psychology" (1958b). In this paper I tried to give a broadened account of the psychophysical experiment, discussing it in wider terms than the usual methods of constant stimuli, limits, and adjustment. I considered, for example, an experiment on color naming classifiable as a psychophysical investigation. I also tried to give a treatment of introspection as it contrasts with the usual psychophysical experiment. Other aspects of the discussion concerned specifiable differences that underlie sensation as contrasted with perception. Surely, I decided, no operational difference exists between the natures of the two. As for differences which concern matters of definition and specification, that may be another story. It would seem that elements may be included in either class on the basis of whatever criteria are justifiable; however, some empirical basis must underlie the cataloging.

It is probable that little more need now be said concerning my thoughts about perception in an objective psychology. A number of additional treatments have been offered on other aspects of this topic, but they will not be summarized here. It is sufficient to say, I think, that the field of perception may become coextensive with psychology, and the field of objective psychology can, at least symbolically, become coextensive with perception, in terms of the stimulus-response formulation $R = f(a, b,...,n,...,t,...,x,y,z)$, where R is response, the first letters of the alphabet refer to stimulus variables, the last letters to conditions of the organism, and n and t refer to number and time, respectively.

JAPAN

My two most noteworthy travel experiences in connection with psychology began in the same year, 1952. In the summer of that year, I was invited by the University of Illinois to participate in its Program in American Studies at the University of Kyoto, sponsored by the Rockefeller Foundation. Five of us left San Francisco for Kyoto in early August and returned seven weeks later having participated in a project designed to present examples of American programs in various fields: political science, American literature, education, economics, and experimental psychology. I was very fortunate to conduct a seminar with a group of young psychologists who varied in academic rank from instructor to associate professor and were assembled from the major universities of Japan. Senior professors also attended frequently. We took up mainly topics of vision, visual perception, and conditioning. I soon found out that my main contribution was in discussions of sensation. In other areas, particularly perception, the Japanese participants, with their extensive acquaintance with the German literature, exhibited a very clear and knowledgeable background. They were well versed in conditioning and our sessions consisted of lively exchanges of views. The seminars provided a warm and pleasant interlude on both sides and the feeling of mutual good fellowship has lasted to the present time. I have greeted a number of Japanese professors at Columbia for stays of two days up to a year. I particularly remember the visit of Professor Motokawa of Tohoku University for a month. I have a warm place in my heart for some younger men: Professors Indow of Keio, Oyama of Chiba, and Akita of Kyoto Technical University. I was glad to introduce Professor Indow to Professor Stevens at Harvard, and they had a profitable and pleasant three years together. Professor Oyama's work is known in the American literature, and he spent a year at Columbia, where the elegance of his experiments impressed us all. Professor Akita spent four years as a student and postgraduate fellow at Columbia (he received his Ph.D. at Columbia).

Eight years after my first visit, I had the opportunity to make another trip, accompanied by my wife. This time I did not spend my time mainly in one place. On this trip, which was sponsored jointly by the State Department and the National Science Foundation, I visited the twelve most active and generally prestigious psychological laboratories. They included (from south to north) Kyushu, Hiroshima, Kwansei Gakuin, Nagoya, Osaka, Tokyo, Tokyo University of Education, Waseda, Keio, Tohoku, and Hokkaido. About seven weeks were spent in visiting the laboratories and lecturing. The visits to the laboratories involved talking to the research people and instructional staffs, and taking extensive notes on the experiments, personnel, and laboratory equipment. Sometimes this program took part of a day and sometimes two or three days, particularly when I was called on to lecture or conduct a seminar. Usually, after visiting each laboratory I would return to my hotel and dictate my notes. The tapes were sent back to Columbia and I finally completed a report in November after my return to New York in late September.

My experience at Professor Motokawa's physiology laboratory is one I remember well. Shortly after arriving by plane from Tokyo, my wife and I went with Professor Motokawa to his laboratory and viewed some experiments for about half an hour. Thereafter, totally unprepared, I faced about twenty graduate students. When Professor Motokawa introduced me and said, "Now Professor Graham will discuss our work with us," I was more than a little surprised. In one way or another, we participated in some sort of discussion, the Japanese in a sometimes imperfect English, and I in terms of an imperfectly understood experimental context. At any rate, we were able to discuss certain matters of vision relating to the experiments I had seen, and we completed the discussion without serious misunderstanding, or so it seemed to me. Of course, in this and similar experiences in other laboratories, the success of the visits depended on members who spoke English, many very well and others only understandably.

OFFICE OF NAVAL RESEARCH, LONDON

The academic year 1952-1953 was my first sabbatical year. Although I had been officially a member of several academic staffs after 1930, the fact remains that sabbaticals had, except in possibly one or two universities, ceased after the Depression and during World War II. They were renewed after the war and my turn came in 1952. Before I left for Japan in August, I had made arrangements to spend my leave working as a scientific liaison officer with the Office of Naval Research, London, and my wife and I went there in October 1952.

The duties of a scientific liaison officer involved visits to psychology and related laboratories in various countries of Europe, and writing informative accounts of the work being done in the laboratories, the people doing the work, and a generally descriptive version of the backgrounds of research. These reports were subsequently distributed to American colleagues and other interested or officially designated persons. The liaison officer, through his visits to laboratories and associated activities, such as giving a paper on some topic of interest to members of a particular laboratory, provided an important source of scientific intercommunication.

An important part of this activity involved the distribution of reprints and reports from American laboratories. The liaison officers in the life sciences (biology, medicine, psychology) had little contact with classified research (I don't remember that I ever reported or transmitted any classified material), but the representatives of other sciences, mainly physics, did deal to some extent with classified documents.

The contacts between the liaison officer and his European colleagues resulted in many friendly relationships. I believe the overall effects of the interchanges that took place were useful to all the scientists involved. For me, the experience was personally satisfying. I visited about twenty-five laboratories and discussed many matters. I also attended a number of professional meetings. I met many active and well-known scientists, including major figures in psychology as well as in related fields. I remember some valuable discussions, particularly with my old friend Granit in Stockhold at the Karoline Institute, and with Professor Toraldo at the Institute of Optics in Florence. Having some months before reviewed work on Mach bands, I discussed this topic with Professor Toraldo, whose work in the area has since been outstanding. His interest in it developed because as a physicist he first thought of it as a peculiarly recalcitrant topic in diffraction optics.

A highlight of my experience in Europe was my visit to Professor Michotte's laboratory in Louvain. I spent a total of three days there viewing the experiments on causality and discussing psychology with Professors Knops, Nuttin, and Montpellier, as well as Michotte. I was particularly happy to see Professor Montpellier again, for we had spent months together in the early 1930s when he was a postdoctoral fellow working with Hunter and I was a young assistant professor.

A BOOK: VISION AND VISUAL PERCEPTION

In 1948 I had a number of conversations with representatives of John Wiley & Sons, including most importantly Professor Langfeld of Princeton, who was advisory editor for psychology. We discussed the possibility of my writing a book on vision and, although I knew that the project would be long and arduous, I finally agreed to do it. It was soon obvious that the book was more than should be undertaken by one man, and I therefore decided to interest a group of former students and colleagues to contribute various chapters to a large volume of which I should be editor and an author. If we had foreseen the problems and difficulties which were to face us until the publication of the volume, *Vision and Visual Perception*, in 1965, I suspect that we would have been even more hesitant to write it than we were in the beginning. The coauthors were John Lott Brown, Neil R. Bartlett, Yun Hsia, Conrad G. Mueller, Lorrin A. Riggs, and myself. The book was generally well received by many reviewers, especially by some in Europe.

AN APA PROJECT

As a member of the APA Policy and Planning Board that in 1948 formulated a plan that developed as Projects A and B, I served on the steering committee. Project A was concerned with psychology as a scientific discipline and was directed by Sigmund Koch, then of Duke University. Project B was concerned with problems of personnel and their training; its director was Kenneth E. Clark, then of the University of Minnesota. My contribution was mainly to Project A, and then as a contributor to the Koch volumes. I saw a great deal of Koch in London in 1952-1953 while he was a Fulbright Fellow at University College. I wrote a rather long manuscript on color vision, its data, and systematic nature for Volume 1 (1958a) and, with Philburn Ratoosh, an article for Volume 4 (1962). The latter article contained some aspects of discussions from other theoretical papers of mine plus contributions made by Ratoosh and some new material of my own. The article on color vision in Volume 1 may be regarded as a first version of chapters in *Vision and Visual Perception;* in fact, in some details it is more exhaustive.

FINAL THOUGHTS

My main work in psychology has been concerned with research and the training of graduate students. Except for a short interval devoted to the running behavior of the white rat and some wartime experiences with selection and training procedures, my investigations have involved problems of vision and visual perception. Of nearly equal importance from my point of view has been my interest in theoretical and systematic problems, particularly the formulation of psychophysical and perceptual behavior in an objective psychology.

These endeavors have been honored by my election to the National Academy of Sciences, the American Philosophical Society, the American Adademy of Arts and Sciences, and by my being awarded the Warren Medal of the Society of Experimental Psychologists, the Tillyer Medal of the Optical Society of America, the Distinguished Scientific Contribution Award of the American Psychological Association, the President's Certificate of Merit, and a Guggenheim Fellowship.

It is surely true that the area which has claimed my attention has not been the most popular in psychology, but it has, nevertheless, for me been a most intellectually stimulating and enticing one. It has no doubt satisfied needs which have dominated my development as a scientist. I am happy that my activities have allowed me to participate not only in the nominal area of psychology, but also in related scientific areas such as physiology. For a certain kind of person a feeling of enhanced scientific scope is additionally rewarding. However, I am glad to report that after taking the Strong Vocational Interest Inventory three times over a period of thirty-three years (in 1935, 1948, and 1968), my highest score with great reliability was in psychology. I like to think that I may be forgiven if I take this finding as a happy confirmation of my choice of profession.

REFERENCES

Akita, M., C. H. Graham, and Y. Hsia. Maintaining an absolute test hue in the presence of different background colors. *Vision Res.,* 1964, *4,* 539-556.

Ames, A. Visual perception and the rotating trapezoidal window. *Psychol. Monogr.,* 1951, No. 324.

Aubert, H. Die Bewegungsempfindung. *Arch. ges. Physiol.,* 1886, *39,* 347-370.

Baker, H. The course of foveal light adaptation measured by the threshold intensity increment. *J. Opt. Soc. Amer.,* 1949, *39,* 172-179.

Balaraman, S. Color vision research and the trichromatic theory: A historical review. *Psychol. Bull.,* 1962, *59,* 434-448.

———. C. H. Graham, and Y. Hsia. The wave length discrimination of some color-blind persons. *J. Gen. Psychol.,* 1962, *66,* 185-201.

Barlow, H. B., and R. M. Hill. Selective sensitivity to direction of motion in ganglion cells of the rabbit's retina. *Science,* 1963, *139,* 412-414.

———. and W. R. Levick. Mechanism of directionally selective units in rabbit's retina. *J. Physiol.,* 1965, *178,* 477-504.

Beare, A. Color-name as a function of wavelength. *Amer. J. Psychol.,* 1963, *76,* 248-256.

Berger, E., C. H. Graham, and Y. Hsia. Some visual functions of a unilaterally color-blind person. I. Critical fusion frequency at various spectral regions. *J. Opt. Soc. Amer.,* 1958, *48,* 614-622.

Bray, C. W. *Psychology and military proficiency: A history of the Applied Psychology Panel of the National Defense Research Committee*, Princeton: Princeton University Press, 1948.

Brown, J. L., C. H. Graham, H. Leibowitz, and H. B. Ranken. Luminance thresholds for the resolution of visual detail during dark adaptation. *J. Opt. Soc. Amer.*, 1953, *43*, 197-202.

Diamond, A. L. Foveal simultaneous brightness contrast as a function of inducing- and test-field luminance. *J. exp. Psychol.*, 1953, *45*, 304-314.

Foley, J. M. Desarguesian property in visual space. *J. Opt. Soc. Amer.*, 1964, *54*, 684-692.

Graham, C. H. An investigation of binocular summation: I. The fovea. *J. Gen. Psychol.*, 1930, *3*, 494-510.

———. Psychophysics and behavior. *J. gen. Psychol.*, 1934, *10*, 299-310. (a)

———. Vision: III. Some neural correlations: In C. Murchison (Ed.), *A handbook of general experimental psychology*, Worcester, Mass.: Clark University Press, 1934, pp. 829-879. (b)

———. Behavior, perception, and the psychophysical methods. *Psychol. Rev.*, 1950, *57*, 108-120.

———. Visual perception. In S. S. Stevens (Ed.), *Handbook of experimental psychology*, New York: Wiley, 1951, pp. 868-920.

———. Behavior and the psychophysical methods: An analysis of some recent experiments. *Psychol. Rev.*, 1952, *59*, 62-70.

———. Color theory. In S. Koch (Ed.), *Psychology: A study of a science*. Vol. 1. *Sensory, perceptual, and physiological formulation*. New York: McGraw-Hill, 1958, pp. 145-287. (a)

———. Sensation and perception in an objective psychology. *Psychol. Rev.*, 1958, *65*, 65-76. (b)

———. On some aspects of real and apparent visual movement. *J. Opt. Soc. Amer.*, 1963, *53*, 1015-1025.

———. (Ed.) *Vision and visual perception*. New York: Wiley, 1965.

(with K. E. Baker, M. Hecht, and V. V. Lloyd) Factors influencing thresholds for monocular movement parallax. *J. exp. Psychol.*, 1948, *38*, 205-223.

(with N. R. Bartlett) The relation of size of stimulus and intensity in the human eye: II. Intensity thresholds for red and violet light. *J. exp. Psychol.*, 1939, *24*, 574-587.

(with R. H. Brown and F. A. Mote) The relation of size of stimulus and intensity in the human eye. I: Intensity thresholds for white light. *J. exp. Psychol.*, 1939, *24*, 555-573.

(with C. Cook) Visual acuity as a function of intensity and exposure time. *Amer. J. Psychol.*, 1937, *49*, 654-661.

(with R. M. Gagné) The acquisition, extinction, and spontaneous recovery of a conditioned operant response. *J. exp. Psychol.*, 1940, *26*, 251-280.

(with B. J. Gilliam) Occurrences of theoretically correct responses during rotation of the Ames window. *Percept. Psychophys.*, 1970, *8*, 257-260.

(with R. Granit) Comparative studies on the peripheral and central retina: VI. Inhibition, summation, and synchronization of impulses in the retina. *Amer. J. Physiol.*, 1931, *89*, 664-673.

(with H. K. Hartline) The response of single visual sense cells to lights of different wave lengths. *J. gen. Physiol.*, 1935, *18*, 917-931.

(with Y. Hsia) Luminosity curves for normal and dichromatic subjects. *Proceedings of the Fourteenth International Congress of Psychology*, 1954, 114.

(with Y. Hsia) Color defect and color theory: Studies on normal and color-blind persons including a unilaterally dichromatic subject. *Science*, 1958, *127*, 675-682.

(with Y. Hsia) Saturation and the foveal achromatic threshold. *J. Opt. Soc. Amer.*, 1969, *59*, 993-997.

(with E. H. Kemp) Brightness discrimination as a function of the duration of the increment in intensity. *J. gen. Physiol.*, 1938, *21*, 635-650.

(with E. H. Kemp and L. A. Riggs) An analysis of the electrical retinal responses of a color-discriminating eye to lights of different wave lengths. *J. gen. Psychol.*, 1935, *13*, 275-296.

(with P. Ratoosh) Notes on some interrelations of sensory psychology, perception, and behavior. In S. Koch (Ed.), *Psychology: A study of a science*, Vol. 4, New York: McGraw-Hill, 1962, pp. 483-514.

(with L. A. Riggs) The visibility curve of the white rat as determined by the electrical retinal response to lights of different wave lengths. *J. gen. Psychol.*, 1935, *12*, 279-295.

(with H. G. Sperling, Y. Hsia, and A. H. Coulson) The determination of some visual functions of a unilaterally color-blind subject: Methods and results. *J. Psychol.*, 1961, *51*, 3-32.

Hammer, E. Temporal factors in figural after-effects. *Amer. J. Psychol.*, 1949, *62*, 337-354.

Hartline, H. K., and C. H. Graham. Nerve impulses from single receptors in the eye. *J. Cellular Comp. Physiol.*, 1932, *1*, 277-295.

Henderson, D. The relationships among time, distance, and intensity as determinants of motion discrimination. *Percept. Psychophys.*, 1971, *10*, 313-320.

Herrick, R. M. Foveal luminance discrimination as a function of the duration of the decrement or increment in luminance. *J. Comp. Physiol. Psychol.*, 1956, *49*, 437-443.

Hsia, Y., and C. H. Graham. Spectral sensitivity of the cones in the dark adapted human eye. *Proc. Nat. Acad. Sci.*, 1952, *38*, 80-85.

———. and C. H. Graham. Spectral luminosity curves for protanopic, deuteranopic, and normal subjects. *Proc. Nat. Acad. Sci.*, 1958, *43*, 1011-1019.

Hunter, W. S. The subject's report. *Psychol. Rev.*, 1925, *32*, 153-170.

Lit, A. The magnitude of the Pulfrich stereophenomenon as a function of binocular differences of intensity at various levels of illumination. *Amer. J. Psychol.*, 1949, *62*, 159-181.

Mates, B., and C. H. Graham. Effect of rectangle length on velocity thresholds for real movement. *Proc. Nat. Acad. Sci.* 1970, *65*, 516-520.

Matin, L. Binocular summation at the absolute threshold of perceptual vision. *J. Opt. Soc. Amer.*, 1962, *52*, 1276-1286.

McCollough, C. The variation in width and position of Mach bands as a function of luminance. *J. exp. Psychol.*, 1955, *49*, 141-152.

Mueller, C. Frequency of seeing functions for intensity discrimination at various levels of adapting intensity. *J. Gen. Physiol.*, 1951, *34*, 463-474.

Pokorny, J. The effect of target area on grating acuity. *Vision Res.*, 1968, *8*, 543-554.

Pollack, J. Reaction time as a function of wavelength in the human fovea. *Perception Psychophys.*, 1968, *3*, 18-24.

Ratoosh, P., and C. H. Graham. Areal effects in foveal brightness discrimination. *J. exp. Psychol.*, 1951, *42*, 367-375.

Riggs, L. A. Dark adaptation in the frog eye as determined by the electrical response of the retina. *J. Cellular Comp. Physiol.*, 1937, *9*, 491-510.

———. and C. H. Graham. Some aspects of light adaptation in a single photo-receptor unit. *J. Cellular Comp. Physiol.*, 1940, *16*, 15-23.

Siegel, I. M., C. H. Graham, H. Ripps, and Y. Hsia. Analysis of photopic and scotopic function in an incomplete achromat. *J. Opt. Soc. Amer.*, 1966, *56*, 699-704.

Smith, V. Scotopic and photopic functions for visual band movement. *Vision Res.*, 1969, *9*, 293-304.

Veniar, F. Difference thresholds for shape distortion of geometrical squares. *J. Psychol.*, 1948, *26*, 461-476.

Zegers, R. Monocular movement parallax thresholds as functions of field size, field position, and speed of stimulus movement. *J. Psychol.*, 1948, *26*, 477-498.

Stanford University

Ernest Ropiequet Hilgard

My graduate study in psychology did not begin until two years after I had earned a bachelor's degree in chemical engineering, and I had thought little of becoming a psychologist at that time. I had taken a one-semester course offered to seniors at the University of Illinois by a popular teacher, Coleman R. Griffith, but I remember at the time wondering who the graduate assistants were who would commit themselves to a career in psychology.

CHILDHOOD AND PRE-PSYCHOLOGICAL LIFE

My early childhood in Belleville, Illinois, where I was born on July 25, 1904, was relatively uneventful. This was the year of the World's Fair in St. Louis, where Cattell had a booth in which psychological testing went on; my home was near there, but I attended the fair only *in utero*. My father was a practicing physician. We were in very moderate circumstances, and I well remember the lame horse my father drove to make his house calls before he shared a new Buick with his banker brother. Still, we had a confident pride of being well born, partly because of some family attainments in the past. The house we lived in was one in which Abraham Lincoln had been a house guest of my great-grandfather on my father's side, and as we played there we liked to fantasize about the speech Lincoln had given to the local citizens from our second floor balcony. My grandfather Ropiequet, on my mother's side, from whom my middle name derives, had been the city's mayor. I believe that there is an influence upon career motivation that comes from growing up within a "saga" that encourages expectations. My parents clearly expected something of me, enhanced perhaps because I was an only son, between two daughters, with all the favoritism that is likely to engender.

I was too young to have thought very much about vocational plans when my father, in a patriotic gesture, volunteered to become a medical officer in World War I, although he was already 40 years of age and had served in the Spanish-American War. I had vaguely expected to follow in my father's footsteps as a physician, for having a father in practice gave a son an advanced start, and most of the doctors' sons I knew planned to become doctors; the only professions known to us in our small town were those of doctor or lawyer. But my father died in France early in 1918; somehow I never again thought seriously about going into medicine. When the time came to enter the university and choose a major I stumbled about, but selected chemical engineering because I liked and had done well in science in high school.

Being young in high school, owing to double promotions in grade school that put me two years ahead, was more of an interference with full participation than later on being young in college, for the boys who had matured ahead of me in high school were much taller and more developed than I. Hence, what opportunities for leadership I could show were somewhat limited, though, with a couple of friends, we kept a Boy Scout troop going, managing all the programs and camping trips, after a scoutmaster resigned and we could not find a replacement. Also I began a little public speaking, as I came to be called upon to encourage the public to purchase Liberty Bonds and War Savings Stamps through talks at intermissions in the local motion picture theater.

At the university I soon plunged into extracurricular activities. I was the freshman member of an Open House Committee of the chemistry department as my first committee assignment; as a sophomore I began to work on the college annual, and became its managing editor as a junior. About this time I began active participation in the Y.M.C.A., and was sent as a delegate to the national convention at Atlantic City, where I first met the Rev. Harry Emerson Fosdick. This also gave me the opportunity for my first trip to New York City, where I visited my distant cousin, Oswald Garrison Villard, editor of The *Nation*, and his mother, Fanny Garrison Villard, the widow of Henry Villard (who in his youth had changed his name from Hilgard), and the daughter of William Lloyd Garrison, the abolitionist. She treated me to tea and loaded me with peace literature to take home to my mother, thus reinforcing such liberal views as were already developing within me. The next year I was elected to the presidency of the Y.M.C.A., became also vice-president of the Student Council, and was elected to the senior activity honor society. At the time, I valued this election more highly than the academic honors that had come to me.

The broadened activities and interests diverted me from a career in chemistry. For reasons that I do not fully understand, I refused to accept a generous fellowship that was offered me to do graduate work in chemistry. Instead, I tried somewhat half-heartedly to find an industrial position with my bachelor's degree. I received several supporting letters in reply to my applications, but all urged me to favor a better career by doing graduate study. Then an opportunity was offered me to remain a year as one of the secretaries of the student Y.M.C.A., with special responsibilities for discussion-group planning and for managing the university student employment office. This gave me the promise of a kind of "moratorium" year, so well described by Erik Erikson, a year during which I might find out what I wanted to do, so I accepted the offer. My duties were not heavy, I had enough to live on without being a further burden to my widowed mother, and there was free time to explore new avenues.

The invitation to take on the discussion group project arose out of an opportunity that had come my way the preceding year. A large Student Volunteer Convention had taken place in Indianapolis over the Christmas holidays in 1923, during my senior year. I had been invited to be one of the discussion group leaders there. My discussion group took up the problems of racial injustice, and I remember putting on the blackboard overlapping probability curves to show that even if there might be average differences between the races it would be impossible to assert anything about an individual on the basis of racial membership alone. This was a time when the Ku Klux Klan was prominent in Indiana, and the issues of prejudice and injustice seemed of as high priority as they do today.

During that year, Dr. Fosdick, the distinguished clergyman I had met at Atlantic City, made a several day visit to the university, and, having been prodded by my Y.M.C.A. superior, he told me about the new Kent Fellowships which gave an opportunity to do graduate work in religion. They were intended for those who were heading for teaching rather than for preaching. I applied, was accepted, and so made a rather abrupt shift to the Yale Divinity School for a year's full course of study. That was a good year, in some sense continuing the "moratorium," for I made lasting friendships, engaged in endless discussions, learned more philosophy, a little Greek, biblical criticism, and some social ethics. Among friends met there whose friendship has meant a great deal to me over the ensuing years were Eugene Adams, later a dean at Colgate: Howard Jefferson, who became president of Clark University; John Nason, successively president of Swarthmore and Carleton College; and Henry Sprinkle, editor of The *World Outlook*.

The social ethics program was under the direction of Jerome Davis, by temperament a radical, at the same time a deeply religious and humane person. He had raised funds for a small cottage on the edge of Long Island Sound, known as the Henry Wright Cottage named after an earlier Yale evangelist; here, in an attractive setting, students from the Divinity School could bring their friends and invited guests for discussions of pertinent social issues. A devoted hostess served food and coffee as required. I recall many pleasant times there, with those who were becoming my lifelong friends, and listening to zealous reformers of society. Professor Davis had also arranged for an opportunity for a number of us to study American industry first-hand the following summer by working as laborers in the Ford plant (and other automotive factories) in the Detroit area. My assignment took me to the Ford plant in Fordson, Michigan, where I worked at various jobs—on the assembly line, in the glass plant, in the employment office, in the power plant, with both day and night shifts as the summer wore on. (We were making Model T Fords, but there were already rumors of a new car, which later came out as Model A.) Then the whole group of us, perhaps a dozen or so, would meet at nights for a continuing seminar on our experiences, with invited speakers such as Harry Laidler from the League for Industrial Democracy. The mood was definitely liberal, but this could scarcely be thought of as radical from the present vantage point; we were mostly arguing in favor of trade unions, in an industry which was then fighting hard to keep them out. There was an essay contest at the end of the summer, with Henry Ford listed as one of the panel of judges, though I doubt that he read the essays; I shared the first prize for my essay revealing (and disapproving of) Henry Ford's methods for preventing the unionization of his factories. Professor Davis was later fired from Yale, ostensibly for neglect of his duties; I came to his defense as best I could, and had long letters from Yale's president, James Rowland Angell, assuring me that he had done his best to be just.

The shift to psychology came about through a combination of factors. Although I had done well in the course work of the Divinity School (actually having an award assigned because of leading my class), I still felt more comfortable with the exactness and objectivity of work in science and mathematics, and I was ready now to return to more scientific studies after gaining the confidence that I could handle other intellectual problems if occasion demanded. Psychology may be thought of as an Hegelian synthesis for me between the scientific thesis (chemistry) and the nonscientific antithesis (religion). I found part-time employment in the personnel office at Yale, where A. B. Crawford, then director of the Bureau of Appointments, was very kind to me. Building upon my employment responsibilities in my postgraduate year at Illinois, vocational psychology appeared to balance my scientific and human-social interests.

Before deciding how to proceed with my study in psychology, I went to Harvard as a guest of Ross McFarland, whom I had met as a Kent Fellow, and who was completing his graduate study there under Professor Boring. He introduced me to Boring, Troland, and McDougall. I also met Gordon Allport, then a young staff member in a new program in social ethics, associated with the physician Richard Cabot, but I did not seriously think of entering upon that unconventional venture. When I proposed that I might follow my interest in vocational psychology, perhaps through a study of human motivation, I received a cool reception from Professor Boring, who thought I had better turn to education, and from Professor Troland, who said his interest in motivation was essentially philosophical and not practical. Only Professor McDougall extended an invitation, saying you could study anything you wished "provided you can find a method." I decided to take my chances back at Yale, where the department head, Professor Roswell P. Angier, was offering a course on motivation and personality. A new Institute of Psychology (the forerunner of the Institute of Human Relations) had just come into being, with a prominent staff of Raymond Dodge, Arnold Gesell, Clark Wissler, and Robert Yerkes—all with the blessings of Yale's psychologist-president, Angell. Thus, in the autumn of 1926, I enrolled as a bona fide graduate student in experimental psychology, and my career as a psychologist was launched.

The Kent Fellowship continued to support me in my graduate study in psychology. A little later, while still in study, I did some fund raising to support the fellowships, and the experience I had then with foundations and philanthropically minded individuals taught me some things I needed to know when I later held administrative positions within the university. I also became well acquainted with C. Ray Carpenter, another Kent Fellow, who participated with me in the money-raising ventures, prior to his later joining us at Yale.

THE YALE YEARS

During my first year as a psychology graduate student I had a little catching up to do, but Yale's psychology department has never placed much emphasis on the number of hours in class. I did the introductory laboratory exercises, a small rat-learning project on the side (unpublished), a course in abnormal psychology, one in educational psychology, and dissected dogfish and human brains in the Anatomy Department under Harold Burr, who welcomed us to afternoon tea at the end of the day's class. By the end of the year, I felt pretty well oriented, and abreast of the other graduate students.

During the following summer I participated in a summer conference on student counseling at Teachers College, Columbia University, planning to further my interest in vocational psychology by taking courses in vocational guidance under Professor Harry D. Kitson, and on student personnel problems generally under Professor Ben D. Wood, with whom I was later to enjoy a number of years when both of us were on the Board of Stephens College. Richard H. Edwards, who was in charge of the Kent Fellowship program, had planned the summer conference on counseling, and together we edited the report. Thus I became a psychology "author" for the first time when the report appeared in 1928 (Edwards and Hilgard, 1928). A fringe benefit of the summer was meeting Professor John Dewey socially, because he was an old friend of the Edwards family with whom I was living, Mrs. Anna Camp Edwards having been one of his teachers in the original Dewey School at the University of Chicago.

By the fall of 1928 I became a teaching assistant in introductory psychology. The following fall, owing to the departure of L. T. Spencer to become a stock broker (unfortunately for him, just before the October stock market crash), the department needed an instructor to handle the laboratory courses as well as to participate in the introductory course, so I became a regular instructor, although I had not yet completed my dissertation.

I reported back early in the fall of 1929 in order to assist in arrangements for the International Congress of Psychology to be held in New Haven, with my adviser Dodge in charge of the program. This was a great opportunity for me to meet distinguished psychologists from all over the world, and to come to feel a part of this larger enterprise. Those who attended represented so much of psychology's early history. From abroad there was Pavlov as the great luminary, but also Claparède, Piéron, Spearman, Michotte, Piaget, Rubin, Köhler, Lewin, and many others; from all over the United States came Lashley (the APA president then), Cattell, Ladd-Franklin, McDougall, Thorndike, Woodworth, and hundreds more. I did a good many service tasks in connection with a complex meeting of this sort; the most pleasurable was being invited by President Angell to present the guests to him one at a time at the reception he offered to them as president of the host university. His instructions to me were meticulous, written in the fine hand then common among scholars; among other things, I had to be aware of his one bad ear, and I was to call all foreign visitors "Mister" in order not to mix up appropriate titles; he had no doctor's degree himself, and always wished to be called "Mister Angell." He was, however, quite astute at knowing when to say "Herr Geheimrat Professor," after which I would get a dirty look from the visitor for having said "Mister." Professor Woodworth came over to me, with his characteristic smile, and said people were trying to guess who I was; he added, with a twinkle, that some thought maybe I was Robert Hutchins, who was making a stir as Yale's bright young man, just elected to the presidency of the University of Chicago.

By the fall of 1929 I had completed my preliminary examinations, and I look back on these as providing an excellent educational opportunity. The course program at Yale was not systematic, and some of us looked longingly at Harvard, where Boring gave a two-year sequence of highly factual and systematic psychological science. The most systematic course we had was a two-year seminar conducted by Angier on the history of psychology, with the time occupied very largely by student papers, each on some ancient philosopher-psychologist or some movement, prepared prominently from Brett's several-volume history of psychology. I still have a paper I prepared on the psychology of St. Augustine. Because of some dissatisfaction with the course work, as graduate students we organized our own Colloquium as a kind of "journal club" and discussion forum, and took positions on problems such as insight, instinct, and phenomenology, which never seemed to come up in any exciting way in classes. Ring leaders in the first Colloquium were Donald K. Adams, Junius F. Brown, C. M. Louttit, and Carleton N. Scofield, a little ahead of me in their Ph.D. preparation, though I was with them from the start. The Colloquium continues to this day, but serving new purposes. Because we were not prepared for our preliminary examinations by our course work, we had to do a good deal of independent preparation. I sometimes think that the paucity of teaching was the best kind of teaching we could have had.

The preliminary examinations included an examination on "special authors," whom we had individually chosen in advance: one living, one dead. I had selected William James and William McDougall. The presumption was that we had read most of their works, at least the psychologically important ones, and hence were prepared to discuss their views in detail. I have never regretted my choices, for these men were good at what I call "psychologizing," that is, making pertinent psychological observations which set the problems for psychology, rather than confining themselves to "experimentally established facts," which often make psychology seem a frail and starved science of man.

I completed the dissertation and obtained the Ph.D. degree in 1930. The dissertation, on conditioned responses, had been supervised by Professor Dodge, and was published in the monograph series that he then edited (Hilgard, 1931).

The teaching opportunities as an instructor at Yale were very fruitful ones for me. I had interesting undergraduate students—among them, Robert Wagner, later mayor of New York City; and Winthrop Rockefeller, later governor of Arkansas—and my required course in experimental psychology brought all the new graduate students into my class.

For a time we divided up the introductory courses into several with differing emphasis, such as social psychology (taught by E. S. Robinson), and comparative psychology, which I taught. Because I lacked very much experience in this area at the time I planned to teach it, I arranged with Professor Yerkes to spend the summer of 1931 at Orange Park, Florida, where the Yale Laboratories of Primate Biology (as they were then called) were in the early years of operation. Dr. and Mrs. Yerkes invited me to live with them and their son David, who also worked with us at the station. Mrs. Helen S. Morford, Dr. Yerkes' faithful secretary, completed the household. Hence, a very important social opportunity was opened up for me, in addition to the professional one.

The W. N. Kelloggs were there, with their attentions being divided between their young son Donald and their "adopted" chimpanzee daughter, Gua; the Carlyle F. Jacobsens were also there, having made a study of the first colony-born infant, Alpha. The summer was a valuable one for me, permitting a first-hand acquaintance with primate behavior under more naturalistic conditions as well as in the laboratory, and establishing a continuing friendship with the Yerkes family, both important and satisfying to me in the years to follow. The first bonus was that they offered their Franklin, New Hampshire, summer home to Josephine and me as the place to spend our honeymoon after our September wedding. Josephine Rohrs had come to Yale for graduate study after Smith College, and obtained her master's degree in 1930, when I received the Ph.D. After our marriage she continued toward the Ph.D., and had it awarded in 1933, with a dissertation under Arnold Gesell, just before we left for Stanford.

The Yale teaching years covered the time of moving from the old quarters in Kent Hall on the Yale campus to the new institute of Human Relations building, near the medical school. I experienced the efforts to achieve some sensible integration among the diverse interests represented there. We did manage some interdisciplinary work across departmental lines with psychiatry, with neurophysiology, and neuroanatomy, but the separatism even within the department itself was difficult to manage, Gesell having essentially his own program, Yerkes his, Dodge and Miles theirs, and Hull his; the unifying factor was chiefly that the graduate students wanted psychology degrees, so that the departmental examinations had to be met, and dissertation requirements fulfilled. Stanley Lindley and I cooperated with the psychiatry department by curing a case of hysterical paralysis by conditioning methods, although the only report is a paragraph in the later book with Marquis (Hilgard and Marquis, 1940, pp. 297-298). A study of hysterical blindness was carried on in cooperation with a psychiatrist, L. H. Cohen (Cohen, Hilgard, and Wendt, 1933). Some cooperative work was done with brain surgeons and neurologists, in connection with a disturbance caused by a unilateral lobectomy (German, Fox, and others, 1932). But, on the whole, the hope that bringing sociologists, psychologists, psychiatrists, and others together would bring into being a new science of human relations was not fulfilled. Later, Clark Hull and Mark May did their best to meet these goals, but such success as they achieved was after I left.

It was common for young instructors to try to supplement their incomes in one way or another during their years of beginning salaries, and I did some night school teaching as the opportunities presented themselves. I taught chemistry and physics briefly in a private high school, and industrial and applied psychology in New Haven College, a night school run under Y.M.C.A. auspices. I remember talking about this once with President Angell, who was still bitter about the many nights he had to take the Illinois Central to the Loop from the University of Chicago campus in order to make enough to live on when he had been a young professor at the University of Chicago. Some opportunities for public lecturing also arose, about which I shall say more later.

The opportunity to go to Stanford seemed to have been in the making for some time. From Stanford had come my good friends Ray Carpenter, L. P. Herrington, Stanley Lindley, Donald Marquis, and Robert Sears. Walter Miles, who had worked with my adviser Dodge at Wesleyan, and with him in the Carnegie Nutrition Laboratory in Boston, was leaving Stanford for Yale, and a Dodge disciple would be a very natural replacement. Furthermore, Yerkes, who by this time was an ally, was a personal friend of Lewis Terman, head of the Stanford Department, they having worked together during World War I on the Army intelligence tests. It was Yerkes who introduced me to Terman at the Toronto meetings of the APA in 1931; I met Mrs. Terman at the meetings in Ithaca the next year, and the offer came to me the following year. Assistant professorships were not so plentiful in those Depression years, and appointments were made with circumspection. Both Josephine and I were very happy in New Haven, and she had the offer of an opportunity to continue to work with Dr. Gesell beyond her degree. Neither of us had ever been to California, and, in those days of train travel, it seemed very far away. It took us some time to decide to take the plunge. Yale was prepared to meet the offer, and promote me to assistant professor, but Professor Angier couldn't see how anyone would wish to stay at Yale if he didn't have private means. President Angell warned that he found his Stanford friends seemed to spend as much time on the East Coast as they could; Hull couldn't see how I would give an offer away from Yale a hearing at all; Mark May thought I ought to get Stanford to raise the ante. In any case, the offer was finally accepted, and I became an assistant professor at Stanford in the fall of 1933, to spend the rest of my career there, except for wartime interruptions.

A PROFESSOR AT STANFORD

We drove across the country in a new Essex Terraplane, seeing the sights as we went. At Stanford the Termans gave us a warm welcome, and invited us to stay with them until we found a house. We were a little slow in this, and I am sure that the Termans wondered if we would ever leave, but they gave no sign of it. Josephine decided to separate her career from mine by taking up medicine, fulfilling a vague wish in any case, for she was the only child of a physician. This meant that she had to squeeze into one year the then requirements for medical school—physics, inorganic and organic chemistry, quantitative analysis, embryology, microbiology. It was a tough year for a young faculty wife making her adjustment to a new university in a new part of the world, having thought her studies over when she finished the Ph.D. Still, we were both young and in good health; she did well, and got admitted to medical school, and was elected to Alpha Omega Alpha, the medical honor society, by the time she graduated.

I had brought from Yale the Dodge pendulum photochronograph upon which I had done my dissertation, and subsequent research, and was soon set up to go, with the able assistance of Albert Walton, who had just finished his dissertation but was staying on as a kind of combination instructor and laboratory assistant. (Not only that; he also lent us enough money to get through our first year!)

Promotion, as it turned out, moved more rapidly at Stanford than it had at Yale, and by 1938 I was a full professor, accelerated promotion having no doubt been aided by attractive offers elsewhere. Following in the footsteps of Professors Terman and McNemar, I accepted a joint appointment in the School of Education (although psychology was then, as today, in the liberal arts part of the university, at first in the School of Social Sciences, now part of the School of Humanities and Sciences). Hence, through the years I have been officially a professor in both psychology and education.

TEMPORARILY AWAY FROM STANFORD

My first sabbatical year was spent at the University of Chicago, 1940-1941. I was invited to participate as a collaborator in a program in child development in relation to education, sponsored by the American Council on Education, and conducted under the leadership of Daniel Prescott, with headquarters in Judd Hall, the education building. The book on *Conditioning and Learning* had appeared, Josephine had completed her M.D. degree, and it was a good time to broaden out a little. She was able to undertake her psychoanalytic training at the Chicago Psychoanalytic Institute, while also working at the Institute of Juvenile

Research; I became familiar with all manner of physiological and psychological measurements of children, and learned about projective tests from people like Nevitt Sanford, who came to talk to our group. The group included those of diverse views, such as Theodore Perkins, whose organismic psychology (developed in collaboration with Raymond H. Wheeler) was still popular among educators, and Horace B. English, a man of wide interests as represented in part by his dictionary writing. I was welcomed in Thurstone's seminar, engaged in some socially activist work under the direction of Arthur Kornhauser, got better acquainted with Harold Gulliksen, Samuel Stouffer, Ralph Tyler, and Dael Wolfle, and on the whole had a year in which my psychological horizons were expanded; those named all meant a good deal to me in later years as friends and colleagues.

I returned to Stanford in the fall of 1941, leaving Josephine and our young son Henry in Chicago, because her analysis would require a little more time. Then came Pearl Harbor, and early in 1942 I went to Washington at the invitation of my old friend Rensis Likert, to serve in a program of civilian surveys in connection with the war effort. Josephine and Henry joined me soon thereafter, and she was able to continue her psychoanalytic work at Chestnut Lodge and the Washington School of Psychiatry. I remained with Likert until some administrative changes sent me temporarily to New York to work with Elmo C. Wilson, also with the Domestic Branch of the Office of War Information. Then I returned to serve with Eugene Katz in the Bureau of Overseas Intelligence of the Office of War Information. A final move took me to the Division of Consumer Surveys of the Office of Civilian Requirements, where Charles E. Noyes, the son of my old chemistry professor at Illinois, and whom I had known as an undergraduate, felt I could be useful. My psychologist friends Helen Peak and Ruth Tolman soon joined us. Apart from learning the techniques of sampling, interviewing, coding, and the rest that goes into survey research, the experiences were enormously valuable for the wide acquaintance provided with people from many disciplines. In the survey field I was soon acquainted with George Gallup, Paul Lazarsfeld, Frank Stanton, Elmo Roper, and others whose experiences covered a wide area heretofore unknown to me. In the international area our offices were adjacent to the group under Goodwin Watson, monitoring foreign broadcasts. I had come to know Goodwin Watson in the summer at Teachers College many years before, and my old friends Theodore Newcomb and John Gardner were there; new acquaintances with whom I was to be frequently associated later included Hans Speier, Nathan Leites, and Bernard Berelson. Our own staff included anthropologists Ruth Benedict and Geoffrey Gorer, sociologists McQuilken DeGrange and Herbert Blumer, as well as psychologists Leonard Doob and Helen Peak (prior to her move, with me, to the office of Civilian Requirements). The later consumer studies brought me in touch with economists, of whom the best known is Simon Kuznets. I had also participated most congenially in a study of smaller war plants with the then young economist Howard R. Bowen, later the president of the University of Iowa. The willingness of so many people of varying backgrounds to work together on common problems during the war shows that such cooperation is intellectually possible when the motivation is there.

A pleasant social and intellectual experience was provided by a small discussion group meeting occasionally for dinner in a private room in a small Washington hotel. The members, as I recall them, were Lyman Bryson, Lawrence K. Frank, Rensis Likert, Margaret Mead, and Goodwin Watson. The kind of discussion carried on by this warm-hearted and enthusiastic group was prophetic of those in which I participated twenty-five years later as chairman of the Behavioral and Social Science Survey Committee.

THE DEPARTMENT HEADSHIP

With the war folding up in Europe, I was eager to return to Stanford, where, following Terman's retirement in 1942, I had been made department head in absentia, and duty called. I had no sooner returned than I had a telephone call from Robert Oppenheimer from Los Alamos, inviting me to come and do a study of a very interesting illustration of the cooperation of many scientists in solving a problem; we had often discussed such matters (without the details of content) during his wartime visits to Washington, in the home of Ruth and Richard Tolman. I felt that I had my duties before me, and thus missed the opportunity to be associated in this way with the drama of the atomic bomb.

Professor Terman had been department head at Stanford from 1923 to 1942, and the department, although small, had gained national distinction under his leadership. Of the staff members he attracted, five became presidents of the American Psychological Association, and many of those with Stanford Ph.D's had gone on to distinction. I believe that the departmental chairmanship at Stanford gives more opportunities for leadership because it is not a position that rotates according to a fixed term, as it does in many universities. A rotating chairmanship is often accepted as a distasteful chore, rather than as an opportunity for constructive initiative and planning; furthermore, enough genuine leaders are not always present in a department to keep up the rotation. I found the usual problems of a department head facing me: money, space, staff, and programs of instruction and research. The influx of undergraduate and graduate majors, as a consequence of returning veterans supported under the GI Bill, was almost more than we could handle with our small staff; our lack of scholarships and assistantships no longer kept things in equilibrium, so the students came, but there was little money for staff. The classes became larger, we taught more of them, and relied to some extent on part-time help until a new phase of increasing support for faculty gradually came about. I shall not detail the course of my departmental administration, except to indicate that it included a move to new and more adequate quarters in the Education Building (soon to be outgrown), and a large program in clinical psychology, aided by the Veterans

Administration, which provided almost everything: laboratories and equipment, and stipends for students and staff. Howard F. Hunt gave it vigorous leadership, until he left for Chicago. At the same time I was eager to see child psychology established on a sound basis, with a nursery school under departmental control, to function also as a laboratory of child development, Roger Barker, who had been here during the war, had developed a small cooperative nursery school, so the climate was proper; with the aid of a local women's organization known as Peninsula Volunteers, and eventual support from the National Institute of Mental Health, the program soon became a reality under the devoted (if part-time) services of Lois Meek Stolz, who had previously headed the work at Teachers College, Columbia. The intellectual flavor of the department was broadened by bringing in a research project on the psychological consequences of visible physical injuries under Tamara Dembo and Beatrice Wright, who were Kurt Lewin associates, and Helen Jennings, who had worked in sociometry under Moreno. Accretions to the staff were very few during my regime, with Donald W. Taylor and Douglas Lawrence coming as assistant professors in the general and experimental areas, and others mostly coming and going in the other areas, except for the more permanent staff of Maud Merrill James, Calvin P. Stone, Edward K. Strong, Jr., Quinn McNemar, and Paul R. Farnsworth, present when I returned from the war absence.

THE GRADUATE DEANSHIP

When President Sterling invited me in 1951 to accept the position of Dean of the Graduate Division, I saw it as a good opportunity. It would provide a chance for the department to bring in a senior person, which I sensed would be a good thing for the department, though I had been unable to find the money for it; and the time was ripe for the university to surge forward in the social sciences, where I felt my experience could be of service. Hence, after getting some agreements for including in the responsibilities of the dean's office the monitoring of requests for research funds, and a special responsibility for review of the budgets of the various institutes and laboratories not connected with departments, I accepted the position. The first objective, of strengthening the Department of Psychology, resulted in bringing Robert R. Sears from Harvard to the headship, a move which through his energetic leadership strengthened the department as I had hoped it would. The second objective, of building up social sciences through my office, also worked out well, in part because of the favorable timing of support of the social sciences through the Behavioral Sciences Division of the Ford Foundation, which, in its initiation, had been strongly influenced by my friend and collaborator, Donald Marquis, and was soon under the direction of Bernard Berelson, one of my wartime associates. Stanford received a free grant of $100,000 to strengthen the behavioral sciences. I was instrumental in setting up a committee chaired by Albert Bowker, then head of our statistics department, to see to the utilization of this money. A small institute for Social Research was set up, under Alfred de Grazia, and a survey facility headed by Wendell Bell. The economics department began to consider research in economic development, and brought Simon Kuznets (whom I had known in Washington) to conduct an interdepartmental seminar. Thus some new excitement was generated; the money was intended to catalyze other projects, which indeed it did. Then there was another grant for a self-study of present activities and prospects in the behavioral sciences, headed by Stuart Hughes. This resulted in an appeal to the Ford Foundation for some $500,000, chiefly for "temporary" professorships that were much needed. That is, these professorships would be supported for about five years, at which time it was hoped that through retirements or in other ways the university could finance them. This permitted an immediate strengthening of the university through adding people such as Leon Festinger, Wilbur Schramm, Samuel Karlin, and Sanford Dornbusch.

I had a small part, also, in bringing the Center for Advanced Study in the Behavioral Sciences to Stanford. This is not a part of Stanford, but an attractive professional and scientific neighbor located on a hill within the Stanford lands. I had been serving as a consultant to the Ford Foundation in making plans for such a Center, and I was also on the Land Development Committee at Stanford, so that I knew of the availability of this attractive site. My only role was to take visitors from the Foundation to see the site; in the end, through some accidental happenings, such as the burning down of a building that had been selected as the preferred site, the Stanford site was chosen, much to the advantage of the behavioral sciences at Stanford and other West Coast universities.

My effectiveness as graduate dean was weakened by the most unpleasant series of experiences of my career, when doubts were raised about my loyalty to the United States, and I had to call upon my friends to defend my loyalty. The happy side of this is the extent to which they rallied to my support. The difficulty first arose during the war, when Alvin Eurich, then a Commander in the Navy, with personnel responsibilities, invited me to accept a commission and join his staff. I went through all the processing, including a final physical examination, when suddenly I had a handwritten note from Dr. Eurich indicating that the admiral had called it off. I found out later that the admiral had heard of my liberal views and was afraid that I might push for black officers in the Navy—a change in practice that did indeed come about later under Dr. Eurich's direction, but without my help. A turndown of this sort gets into the record and is hard to overcome when small things are piled upon it: membership in the League Against War and Fascism, petitions to give the Communist Party its rightful place on the ballot, small contributions to the California Labor School. I eventually had a hearing in Washington, and made the mistake of indicating that I had done nothing of which I was ashamed; I had never been a Communist, which seemed what they were worried about, but I had been a liberal and a defender of the underdog. The review board reached an unfavorable decision, and I was never thereafter asked to serve on any Department of Defense committees, although I was not directly "fired" from any on which I served (though one of them never met again). This naturally affected my security clearance, so that I could no longer review classified projects in my capacity as graduate dean. The administration was very supporting, arranged other channels for the classified research applications, and left me alone to go about my business.

The clearance problem soon caught up with me as a member of the National Advisory Mental Health Council, the policy board within the National Institute of Mental Health, and the charges were made all over again, in about the same form. This time, with additional legal advice, I modified my answers somewhat, admitting that even if I felt as I did perhaps I was unwise to have taken some of these ways of expressing my position. This time, with the help of a sympathetic reviewer in the form of Nelson Rockefeller, who then had this responsibility within the Department of Health, Education, and Welfare, I was cleared and permitted to resume my duties on the Council. I found out only much later, from a newspaper reporter, that I had been placed on a confidential blacklist so that I was not invited back for any policy purposes within the Department of Health, Education, and Welfare. I should add, however, that my research has been generously supported in recent years by this same agency, and I feel that my career has not been seriously handicapped.

I did come to feel, however, that it would be better to leave the deanship and return to the department (which I would have done shortly in any case), and I requested this change of President Sterling. I had done much of what I had planned to do in four years as dean; much remained to be done, but others could serve as well as I.

A EUROPEAN TRIP

A pleasant interlude between the graduate deanship and the return to the professor's role was provided by an invitation from Jerome Bruner to join a small conference on cognitive processes to be held at St. John's College, Cambridge, to be chaired jointly by him and Sir Frederick Bartlett. At the same time, Bernard Berelson invited me to represent the mental health program of the Ford Foundation in visiting some people in England who might wish financial assistance. In 1955 the new interest in cognition was just emerging (actually pre-Sputnik, which later accelerated it). This rather intimate conference permitted easy acquaintance, including punting on the Cam, with colleagues from England such as Broadbent, Mackworth, Oldfield, Magdalen Vernon, Zangwill, and others, Joseph Nuttin from Belgium, and better mutual understanding with some American colleagues such as Roger Brown, George Miller, Karl Pribram, and Heinz Werner. The mental health mission brought me in touch with Anna Freud, who was most cordial to us; a visit with her included seeing her father's study as he had left it. It meant also meeting Bowlby and Trist, at Tavistock, and Sir Geoffrey Vickers, a public-spirited coal chemist (like myself!) with strong mental health interests. Because of Lady Adrian's mental health interests I was invited to a very pleasant dinner at the high table at Trinity College by its master, Lord Adrian (the distinguished physiologist), without her, of course; but we retired to their private quarters for a very pleasant visit with her after the dinner, with Sir Isaac Newton's clock still ticking away near the door.

The timing was good for the visit for two other reasons. The first was the International Congress of Psychoanalysis which was meeting in Geneva, and we there met Ernest Jones, who proudly carried about the second volume of his biography of Freud, we saw Anna Freud again, along with Melanie Klein, though they refused to be on the platform together. The second was a family occasion, a reunion of the Hilgard and Engelmann families at Bacharach, Germany, on the Rhine, where the two families first intermarried many years ago. (My father was named George Engelmann Hilgard because of an Engelmann grandmother, and after a distinguished St. Louis cousin, founder of the famous Shaw's Botanical Gardens.)

This, our first visit to Europe, in which my wife and both children accompanied me, was a refreshing experience for us all, as I returned to academic life in the fall.

THE RETURN TO TEACHING AND RESEARCH

While as graduate dean I had continued to teach—including lecturing in the introductory course for at least one term each year—I had had to give up research, so I had some retooling to do.

The Behavioral Sciences Division of the Ford Foundation had made a grant to the Social Science Research Council early in 1953 so that a working staff, in cooperation with an advisory committee, might prepare a planning proposal to assist the Ford Foundation in initiating support of mental health research. I served as chairman of the working staff, and three of us (Merton Gill, David Shakow, and I) spent the month of July at Stanford working out a draft of the proposal, following some planning meetings earlier in the year with the advisory group, which was chaired by John Romano, and included psychiatrists, psychologists, sociologists, and political scientists. My former student, M. Brewster Smith, served as the S.S.R.C. staff representative. The report was mailed out to the advisory committee, and, following suggestions discussed at a meeting in New York in October, it was reedited by the working staff members and submitted to the Ford Foundation. During the fiscal year 1952 the National Institute of Mental Health was devoting approximately $1,400,000 to mental health research; when, therefore, our committee recommended that the Ford Foundation spend $3,000,000 per year over a ten-year period, the suggestion seemed particularly daring, although by later standards of research expenditures it now seems modest. The Foundation received the report, allocated $15,000,000 instead of $30,000,000. and a new committee was appointed, within the Foundation, to allocate the money. Despite some embarrassment over conflict of interest (because I was on this committee also), some $500,000 of the total was eventually assigned to Stanford for a Laboratory of Human Development, with programs within it to be operated by the Sears and the Hilgards. This made it somewhat easier for me to plan what to do when I returned to the department from the deanship.

In its discussion of needed research in the areas of psychodynamics, the proposal at various points recommended the study of hypnosis, a field in which both Gill and Shakow were experienced, and in which I (with little experience) had become interested. It was to this general domain that I had directed my portion of the Stanford research proposal, and with the funds now promised, I had to prepare to do the research. I took one year after the deanship to get back into the department, and to complete revisions of two books, and then spent a year as a Fellow at the Center for Advanced Study in the Behavioral Sciences.

I made another decision, in addition to that of entering upon hypnosis research. That was that I would throw away all my old lecture notes, start over again, and, apart from the introductory course, teach only courses I had not taught before. Hence, I began to teach abnormal psychology, dynamic psychology (a course on Freud and other related views), and a new graduate course on human motivation. I found this new tack an exhilarating experience, and it carried me into my emeritus years with a feeling of freshness instead of boredom. I became an emeritus professor in July, 1969, and as I write now (late in 1970) I am in my second emeritus year. Thanks to the generosity of Stanford University and the Department of Psychology, I continue to have facilities for research, and I do some teaching on my own initiative.

Activities Outside Teaching and Research

Most professors in leading universities have very light teaching schedules but live very busy lives. It is often stated that they spend about half their time in teaching and related duties and about half time in research. For many of us this is a very distorted picture. While we may divide some time about equally between teaching and research (if supervising graduate students is counted as teaching), we do a great many other things, so that, in my case at least, it might be a truer picture to assign about 25 percent to teaching, 25 percent to research, and 50 percent to other more or less legitimate demands upon time. If these autobiographies are to serve as description of careers as they are lived, I believe it is worthwhile to try to give an accurate picture of what actually happens.

Writing

There are at least two major classes of scholarly writing: research reports, which are part of the total research enterprise, and all other professional writing, such as essays, literature reviews, textbooks, or the preparation of reports of various kinds.

Bookwriting has taken a great deal of my professional time, first the review of conditioning with Marquis (Hilgard and Marquis, 1940), then the book on learning theories (Hilgard, 1948), and the introductory textbook (Hilgard, 1953). *Conditioning and Learning* was revised by Gregory Kimble in 1961; neither Marquis nor I had anything to do with the revision; instead, we became part of the book's title! The revisions of the other books were, however, in each case major tasks: the theories of learning in two subsequent editions, and the introductory textbook now in the fifth edition. A book on hypnotic suscepti- bility (Hilgard, 1965) relied more on my own research than had any of the earlier books. In addition, there were chapters in several other books, and an edited yearbook for the National Society for the Study of Education (Hilgard, 1964). Both the *Theories of Learning* and the *Introduction to Psychology* were widely adopted as textbooks, with sales of the former totaling some 150,000 copies and of the latter some 1,500,000, not counting their translations into other languages. Thus the influence of such textbooks may be far greater than the influence of one's research reports.

Lecturing

A university faculty is a favored source for lecturers invited to appear before many different groups: luncheon clubs, teachers' institutes, alumni conferences, businessmen's conventions, or welfare agencies. My invitations began to come when I was an instructor at Yale.

One early opportunity to try my hand at a series of popular lectures came after a Community Forum of Meriden, Connecticut, had permitted an agency interested in adult education to conduct a survey of adult interests. To see if their survey had been realistic, they derived a series of topics from their questionnaire replies, and invited me to lecture on their topics: if the attendance was good, they would feel their survey validated. The lecture topics given me were (1) What makes a personality; (2) Getting along with other people; (3) Influencing others; (4) Psychology of career building; (5) Fear, worry, and mental health; and (6) How to live successfully. I gave these lectures in the spring of 1931; they were so well received that I gave another series in the fall. I was urged to publish the lectures but felt it was not the thing to do. The next year Dale Carnegie gave the lectures under the same auspices and on similar topics and his best-seller, *How to Win Friends and Influence People,* was the result (Carnegie, 1936).

I have in my files well over 100 unpublished lectures given on various occasions; they were usually written out, in order to be of appropriate length, although I preferred to speak from notes when the lectures were popular rather than scientific. I have taken particular pleasure in some of the invitations, such as that at the dedication of the new psychology building at the University of

California in Los Angeles in 1940 (where I shared the platform with the venerable George M. Stratton), and, a number of years later, a corresponding invitation to give the dedicatory remarks at the dedication of Tolman Hall for psychology and education at the University of California at Berkeley.

Committee Duties within the University

Before I became a dean, and after I left that post, I continued to do the kinds of things faculty members are called upon to do within the university outside their teaching and research. Because of my vocational guidance background, I was early appointed chairman of the vocational guidance committee at Stanford, as the faculty committee on student personnel problems was then called. Later in my career I served in succession as chairman of the two major elective committees of the faculty, and was president of the Faculty Club while a new building was under construction. I also served as chairman of the faculty advisory committee in connection with the university's major fund-raising campaign, and was a member of a number of ad hoc committees to select new deans or other university officers. I mention these activities merely to point out that time spent in such duties does conflict with recognizable scholarly work; yet it is work that someone must do for the common good and the work is not without its satisfactions.

Professional Service to Psychology

I early became active in the work of the American Psychological Association, serving as a member of the Council of Directors, representing it at the National Research Council and also at the Social Science Research Council, eventually becoming its president, and serving repeatedly in one capacity or another.

Among the more interesting of these services was that in connection with the revision of the by-laws of the American Psychological Association during World War II. A rift had been growing between the APA and the AAAP (the American Association of Applied Psychology). The applied psychologists, who had formed the new organization in 1937, felt that the APA was too much under control of academics, and threatened to withdraw. The steps that led to a healing of the breach are worth recounting here, because they are of importance to the growth of psychology as a science and as a profession, and because I was deeply involved.

A Subcommittee on Survey and Planning of the Emergency Committee had been established early in 1942 under the chairmanship of Robert M. Yerkes. Its initial members included, in addition to the chairman, Edwin G. Boring, Alice I. Bryan, Edgar A. Doll, Richard M. Elliott, Calvin P. Stone, and me. The initial meeting of the Subcommittee was as guests of the Vineland Training School,

Vineland, N.J., June 14 to June 20, 1942. Carl Rogers and Rensis Likert were added later. At the recommendation of this group, an Intersociety Constitutional Convention was called in May, 1943, under the chairmanship of Professor Boring. I scarcely won the right to attend—only through activating a paper organization known as the National Institute of Psychology did I become a delegate. It turned out that Leonard Carmichael and I did most of the writing of the new by-laws, alternately dictating and writing, with our associates looking over our shoulders; this put something concrete before the convention and converted into understandable form the agreements that the convention reached. It was decided that the preferred option was to revise the by-laws of the existing APA rather than to create a new organization, an option that had been left open to the convention. The main new direction was that of the divisional structure, whereby all interests could be represented, and the Council of Representatives would become just that—representatives of the divisions. So two activating committees were created, and somehow I became chairman of both of them: a Continuation Committee on the Constitution, consisting, in addition to the chairman, of John E. Anderson, Alice I. Bryan, C. M. Louttit, Sidney L. Pressey, and Willard L. Valentine. This was balanced between those with prestige in APA and in AAAP circles. The other committee, called the Division Organization Committee, had as its function the proposing of temporary chairmen and secretaries for each of the new divisions, to help them come into being, organize themselves, and elect regular officers. The members of the committee, in addition to the chairman, were Horace B. English, Alvin C. Eurich, David Shakow, and Robert M. Yerkes. It took a good deal of negotiating and mailing of ballots, to say nothing of consulting with attorneys, but eventually the new by-laws were adopted, became operative, and the way was opened for establishing a Central Office and becoming prepared for the enormous expansion of psychology when the war ended.

Nothing of this sort is done once and for all; now that 25 years have passed, a different kind of rift has occurred, as the Psychonomic Society asserts its autonomy from the APA for a reason symmetrical to, but opposite from, the reason for the creation of the AAAP: the members of the Psychonomic Society believe that the APA, instead of being too academic, as earlier charged, is now not academic enough!

Public and Community Service

Even though one often participates in public and community service because he is a psychologist, the roles in which he is asked to serve may be only in part psychological. I do not think it pertinent here to attempt to recount in detail these extra activities, not particularly appropriate for a psychological audience, though I shall cite a few to give something of the flavor of my life outside classroom teaching, research, and professional services to psychology.

Some of the calls upon me have been because of my social welfare interests, while others have derived from my interest in the broader problems of education.

Just after returning from World War II I helped plan and manage, with I. James Quillen, later the Dean of Education, the Stanford Workshop on Community Leadership, held in August 1945. This was designed to help board members (rather than the professional staffs) to sense their responsibilities in the readjustments to be made after the war. The main speaker was the sociologist Louis Wirth, of the University of Chicago, and the whole was successful enough to be repeated again. A report was issued on the first workshop under the title *Community Planning for Peacetime Living* (Wirth, Hilgard, and Quillen, 1946).

Over the years I have served on a number of policy advisory bodies, such as the U.S. Education Mission to Japan in 1946, the National Advisory Mental Health Council in the early 1950s, and more recently on the President's Medal of Science Committee. I have had the opportunity to serve as a consultant and advisor to a number of universities at home and abroad, most recently to the Hebrew University of Jerusalem.

During the years 1967 through 1969 my major commitment away from the university was as chairman of the Behavioral and Social Sciences Survey Committee appointed jointly by the National Academy of Sciences and the Social Science Research Council. The National Academy of Sciences, through its Committee on Science and Public Policy, had been issuing a series of reports on various fields of science, reviewing their present status, level of support, and needs for the future. Carl Pfaffmann, a psychologist member of the committee, felt that the behavioral and social sciences should participate in this self-evaluation, so he enlisted my help and a national committee was eventually constituted of the chairmen and co-chairmen who had agreed to prepare panel reports in the various social science disciplines, and a few others. I was designated as general chairman; my co-chairman, Henry W. Riecken, and our executive officer, Stephen Viederman, constituted an executive staff that managed a fairly complex survey of the field, and guided the products of the panels through to publication. It was a very satisfying, and I believe fruitful, collaboration. In the end we issued a central report (National Academy of Sciences/Social Science Research Council, 1969) and nine panel reports in the various fields of specialization, including one in psychology edited by Kenneth E. Clark and George A. Miller (1970). It is hoped that these may serve as planning documents within the universities and within government; there are already signs that attention has been paid to them.

My concern for problems of information retrieval led me to accept board membership many years ago (and the continuing presidency) of Annual Reviews, Inc., a nonprofit publishing firm that, as its name implies, publishes critical reviews of the recent literature in many scientific fields, including an *Annual Review of Psychology,* now published continuously for more than 20 years.

My liberal philosophy led me to participate in some organizations seeking to improve the quality of our common life in one way or another. The Consumers'

Cooperative movement was an attractive one in the early Depression years, and I helped organize a local society, and had my turn as an early president of it. It continues to this day, with several large retail stores in our community. For a number of years I was a board member of the Northern California branch of the American Civil Liberties Union, associated congenially with Bishop Parsons, Alexander Meiklejohn, Robert Oppenheimer, and Kathleen Tolman. For a time I was active also in various teachers' unions and associations.

Other obligations have included membership on the Board of Curators of Stephens College, Missouri. In recent years I have been serving as president of the Board of Trustees of the Neuva Day School, a small private school located in a neighboring community devoted to the education of children of high potential, hopefully providing a testing ground for new teaching methods stressing creativity.

The question may naturally be asked whether or not, as one devoted to advancing psychology as a science, my time has been well spent in so much involvement in matters taking me away from my desk and laboratory. All I can say is that nobody forced me to do these things, and what I did, I enjoyed doing.

RESEARCH

If one commits himself to a scientific career in a major university, he tends to give high priority to what he contributes through his research. He hopes that he may discover something in the way of new facts or relationships, he hopes to formulate some kinds of laws or theories that are recognizably his, or perhaps open up new and significant lines of investigation. Not many scientists satisfy their goals in this respect; it is easier to find experimentable problems than solvable ones, and it is easier to do precise and satisfactory investigations than inventive and revolutionary ones. I have indeed felt some disappointment in the limitations within my own scientific contributions.

My research reports are of course a matter of public record, and little purpose would be served in reviewing them in any detail. There was a decade devoted to studying eyelid conditioning in dog, monkey, and man, including a number of dissertations in this area, and culminating in the book with Marquis. There were other studies of human learning, chiefly on motor skills, and several on verbal learning. Then there were some studies on level of aspiration, including group effects. World War II meant a detour into social surveys. Then there was a beginning of a research program on problem solving, but that was interrupted by my taking on the graduate deanship. The final phase, leading up to the present, has been directing a laboratory devoted to hypnosis research, now in its fourteenth year. This is by all odds the most extensive and coherent research program in which I have been involved.

Despite the seeming range and diversity of my research there is a core running through it all, not always evident to others, but of which I have all along been aware. This core is a concern for aspects of human motivation bearing on planning and choice. I entered psychology with an applied interest in how vocational dilemmas are resolved. I soon turned to the relations among reflex, conditioned, and voluntary action; the later work on conditioned discrimination set voluntary action in conflict with involuntary conditioned responses. The level-of-aspiration experiments had to do with goal setting by the person himself. Even during World War II I did a survey to detect attitudes toward voluntary participation (as in War Bond purchases) and involuntary or coerced participation (as in taxation or rationing). Finally, the very essence of hypnosis lies in achieving or relinquishing control. Hence, while there have been detours around the central problem, there is more unity to the research than meets the eye.

REFLECTIONS

As I look back on my career, as sketched in this account thus far, I ask myself: What kind of a person am I? What do I stand for as a psychologist? These questions are essentially unanswerable by a person himself, but in an autobiography something ought to be said to supplement the more objective catalog of the events of a life.

If a person is what other people think of him (his social stimulus value, as Mark May once put it), then I have had my share of recognition. I was early elected to membership in the Society of Experimental Psychologists, which got me off to a good start, enhanced by receiving their Warren Medal in 1940; I was honored by election to the presidency of the American Psychological Association (as well as to the presidencies of the Western and California Associations), and of the Society for the Psychological Study of Social Issues; made an Honorary Fellow of the British Psychological Society; then the academy elections, including the National Academy of Sciences, the National Academy of Education, the American Philosophical Society, the American Academy of Arts and Sciences; late in my career I received the Distinguished Scientific Contribution Award of the American Psychological Association. Yale, at its 1971 commencement, gave me the Wilbur Cross Award, which goes to those with advanced degrees from Yale who have achieved some measure of distinction. Earlier I received an honorary Doctor of Science degree from Kenyon College. My colleagues have accepted me and honored me on various occasions, and this is satisfying.

But it is more important to know what a person thinks of himself, for his private image may differ markedly from the public one. I recognize a number of limitations in myself which I would have preferred to overcome. I am afraid that my pleasure at being actively in the midst of things distracted me somewhat from the patient pursuit of scientific problems in greater depth; time is after all the commodity that is scarcest of all, and time spent in action cannot be spent in ratiocination. Perhaps I was a little misled by my own facility, for I can design a workable experiment readily, I read rapidly, and I write with ease; as I went along I did not realize that I was missing a certain profundity that I might otherwise have attained.

I believe that I have a certain clarity of mind that is valuable; I understand rather easily what others propose, and I can relate one idea to another. Despite these abilities, somehow I have held back from bold, ingenious, and exciting departures from what is known. Perhaps I have been afraid of the "creative instability" which leads to the kinds of originality I admire in others. I early adopted an intellectual style that mediated between the views of others rather than one that represented commitment to any one position, or that proposed a new view of my own that I was prepared to defend.

My limitations have in some ways been turned to advantage. I may be better at expository writing because I can see the other fellow's position, and can cut through muddy writing to some kind of clarity, without an interference from a fixed position of my own. My most influential work is doubtless of this expository kind, as in *Conditioning and Learning, Theories of Learning,* and *Introduction to Psychology.*

My psychological style is not, however, simply expository as this suggests. I see some positive virtues in eclecticism. Let me come to its defense.

Before I start my defense, however, I wish to point out that I have a dislike for eclecticism that is shared by most of us with some penchant for theorizing. Like others, I see an elegant theory as comprehensive, internally consistent, parsimonious, and esthetically satisfying. By contrast, eclectic theories, although they cover a wide range of topics, do so in a diffuse manner, and they are not parsimonious. Like a crazy-quilt, they lack something in providing esthetic satisfaction. Why then do I choose to support a position that I find distasteful?

There are some things to be said against the alternative, that is against "finished" systems at this stage of science:

1. If we are guided by what we know, and what we do not know, we are on more solid ground if we do not demand consistency among all our formulations. That is, some empirical generalizations can be soundly established, using concepts that are largely ad hoc. A collection of such generalizations is then eclectic, or, in the sense of system, pluralistic. To insist that established systematic concepts be used to integrate all facts into a finished system is likely to lead to enforcing scientific laws instead of discovering them.

2. A sense of wonder before the unknown appeals to me more than the confidence that comes from always having something to say that dissolves the mystery. To say: "It couldn't have been otherwise," does not itself move us very far along. Guthrie once said, in his inimitable way, "A philosopher is a person who has one noise to make appropriate to all occasions." He could have said this about the committed monoeidic theorist.

Perhaps because of my varied background, and the kinds of people, such as the facile Robinson and the humane Dodge, who did so much to set my intellectual style, and the varied views of those who came as graduate students and postdoctoral fellows to Yale in my student days, I have always tried to learn from anyone who was seriously trying to understand human behavior and experience. At the same time, my very breadth made me wary of exaggerations; hence, while receptive, I have also been critical and argumentative.

Perhaps in comparison with other psychologists as to style (not implying equal distinction), I find myself in many ways like Woodworth or Boring, rather than like Hull, Lewin, Piaget, or Tolman. Woodworth and Boring wrote on a wide variety of topics, including social ones, but were strongly identified with experimental psychology, even though their experimental contributions were not dramatic. They are remembered more as generalists and as wise and states-manlike psychologists than for their specific experimental discoveries or their theoretical systems. The others mentioned (Hull, Lewin, Piaget, Tolman) were, by contrast, above all ingenious and inventive, and perhaps systematic to a fault. In retrospect, I would rather have been like them. So much for my "reflections."

SOME POSSIBLY PROVOCATIVE IDEAS

I would like, in closing, to indicate a few ideas that were generated along the way, always in interaction with students or colleagues. They entered the stream of psychological thought in some small way, and in this way kept it flowing.

1. *Reminiscence over short intervals.* Reminiscence refers to a rise in the curve of retention before it begins to fall. Lewis Ward had begun his research on reminiscence with me at Yale, with the hypothesis that this effect would be found. The reasoning was very simple, and characteristic of the "functionalist" approach. If, with moderate time between trials, the subject gains from one trial to the next, there must be an appreciable time interval after the previous trial before forgetting sets in. Ebbinghaus had tested first at 20 minutes, by which time the forgetting was already prominent. Hence, at some time within the 20 minutes, the curve must both rise and fall. When I left Yale, Ward turned to Hull as his adviser, and found that Hull, in one of his notebooks, had predicted the same thing, but in a different manner, as the interference between spontaneous recovery and forgetting. Ward's dissertation (Ward, 1937) is a model study of nonsense syllable learning and retention; it showed also a curve on "learning to learn," in a way anticipating some of Harlow's later work, and placing some limitations on the cumulative proactive inhibition through practice that Under-wood later reported.

2. *The partial reinforcement effect.* Lloyd Humphreys' dissertation on greater resistance to extinction following partial reinforcement (Humphreys, 1939a) was the beginning of a whole series of studies on PRE ("partial reinforcement effect"), and his verbal analog, in which subjects had to guess whether a second light would come on following a first light (Humphreys,

1929b), not only was significant in introducing the notion of "expectancy" into human conditioning, but had something to do with the later work on probability matching.

3. *"Classical" vs. "instrumental" conditioning.* The book with Marquis brought conditioning and other kinds of learning together into a sensible synthesis. The terms "classical" and "instrumental" conditioning were introduced, as alternative to Skinner's "respondent" and "operant," to indicate that the chief differences were in experimental arrangements rather than in underlying processes. I had first proposed that this was the case in a review of conditioning literature, before Skinner's book came out (Hilgard, 1937). The view was sound, as is now being amply demonstrated by Neal Miller under the general slogan "Anything that can be done by classical conditioning can be done by operant conditioning." We made a small contribution (for which Marquis deserves the credit) in introducing the bibliography as an author index, a practice widely followed in subsequent texts: a great nuisance to the author but a great convenience to the reader.

4. *The Snoddy growth hypothesis.* Several tests of the Snoddy hypothesis that the effects of distributed practice in motor learning could be accounted for by a growth process over time that was relatively independent of specific practice showed promise (e.g., Hilgard and Smith, 1942), but the results proved not sufficiently general. This illustrates the kind of "luck" that is involved in scientific success: it might have been true that the problems of distributed practice would have been solved in this way. Had they been, many other implications would have followed.

5. *Ideas in "Theories of Learning."* Some ideas, introduced into books that are largely expository, tend not to enter into controversial discussion as much as if they were published as theoretical articles. I wish to note some of the ideas in *Theories of Learning* (1948) that seem to me to have been a bit ahead of their time:

(a) *A proposed reversal of Lloyd Morgan's canon.* "A peculiar twist is sometimes given to psychological thinking which takes the form that a process, in order to be scientifically reputable, must be demonstrated to occur in lower animals. If it occurs only in man, it is excused away because man possesses verbal or related abilities. It would be better to reverse this viewpoint: *Only if a process demonstrable in human learning can also be demonstrated in lower animals is the comparative method useful in studying it"* (Hilgard, 1948, p. 329).

(b) *The provisional try.* "The alternative [to Thorndike's conception of trial and error] is that the original behavior is not the running off of earlier habits in the new situation, but is a genuine attempt at discovering the route to the goal. Such an interpretation makes the original adjustment a provisional try, to be confirmed or denied by its success or failure" (Hilgard, 1948, p. 336). At this time the notion of feedback had not yet come into prominence, but the provisional try was obviously based on a feedback concept as an explanation of the "law of effect." Other writers picked up the concept of the provisional try, but I backed away from it as not being sufficiently original to justify a new name for it.

(c) *Stimulus-response concepts not essential.* "It is a carryover from the prestige of Sherrington and Pavlov that stimulus-response concepts are bandied about as they are. Yet the whole history of stimulus and response has been one of compromise and amendment" (Hilgard, 1948, p. 349). Such criticisms mounted in the years that followed (e.g., Miller, Galanter, and Pribram, 1960).

(d) *Recommended return to naturalistic observations.* A feeling that something was wrong with learning theory that could be corrected by its enrichment through a return to naturalistic observations (Hilgard, 1948, p. 351) has gained indirect support not only through the ecological studies of Barker (1968), but through a greater concern for the natural setting as in Head Start programs, and, in the laboratory, an awareness of the linguistic "code books" that the learner brings to the experiment, and the reintroduction of imaginal mnemonic aids. The whole impact of ethology was something else, unforeseen at the time.

6. *Ideas in "Introduction to Psychology."* In each of its editions, the *Introduction to Psychology* has had within it kinds of "psychologizing" that have gone beyond an effort to write paragraphs digesting the recent psychological literature. Introductory textbooks tend not to be taken as serious contributions to the literature of psychology. Book reviewers discuss them as pedagogical aids, and seldom note the new insights that they may contain. A serious textbook writer takes responsibility not only for presenting psychology but for broadening and advancing it.

Without further characterization of the textbook in its successive editions, I will mention merely two illustrations of the kind of "psychologizing" which seem to me to represent some degree of originality.

The first has to do with the attempt to integrate emotion and motivation. The triangle theme of love and jealousy, the tragic themes of ambition and unfulfilled hopes, are surely both emotional and motivational, and it seemed to me that psychologists had missed something in their preoccupation with emotional expression. I therefore proposed that one could think of emotions, in the then current language of motivation, as (a) drives or (b) incentives, but a third category was needed also: (c) by-products of motivated activity, as for example, in the pleasure found in striving, before the goal is attained. I presented a summarizing diagram in the third edition (1962, p. 162), which expressed these relationships in a form that I would defend today as a contribution to our understanding of emotion and motivation.

As a second illustration, some unity was achieved in the later editions through a recognition of how much of behavior is analyzed according to a developmental mode (sequential, historical), and how much according to an interactive mode (contemporary, dynamic, ahistorical). I summarized these relationships also in a diagram to show how they accounted for divergent approaches to the understanding and appraisal of personality (1962, p. 487).

Although such contributions in textbooks seldom find their way into the professional literature, they are read by a great number of students, and through them, whatever contribution there is gets a hearing.

7. *The nature of hypnosis.* This is an unfinished story, for I am actively engaged in research with able graduate students and colleagues. Some of the things we now know about hypnosis, about which we were much less sure 10 or 15 years ago, can be asserted as follows: hypnotic susceptibility is a relatively stable and enduring characteristic, about as stable (and modifiable) as IQ; there are no important sex differences; the height of susceptibility is in the pre-adolescent years, with gradual decline thereafter; the skill (or sex) of the hypnotist in bringing about hypnotic behavior is relatively unimportant, compared with the subject's ability to be hypnotized; there are resting EEG-alpha differences between the more and less hypnotizable, prior to hypnosis; a possible hereditary link is suggested by the high correlation between identical twin pairs in susceptibility, compared with other twins or ordinary siblings; susceptible subjects can reduce what would otherwise be severe pain, with supporting evidence of lack of pain through failure to raise their blood pressure under the usually painful stress; what the highly susceptible subject brings to hypnosis is a capacity for imaginative involvement, and in many cases, a history of severe discipline in childhood with a tendency to use imagination to defend against it. Hypnotic therapy can be highly useful, but care has to be exercised to distinguish between what belongs to the hypnosis and what to the therapy, for a wide range of psychotherapy can use hypnosis as an adjuvant. Our laboratory has not been alone in arriving at these conclusions, but each of them has been supported by published work from our laboratory. A new direction of theorizing (neo-dissociation theory) is just beginning to emerge.

Oddly enough, one visible contribution to the field of hypnosis has come about through my entering it. Many graduate students from other universities have written me that their supervisors have permitted them to work on hypnosis because I have helped to make it respectable. I aided in establishing a Division of Psychological Hypnosis within the American Psychological Association, and was its president during my first emeritus year. I have also served (and now serve) on the American Board of Examiners in Psychological Hypnosis, which is seeking to upgrade the work in the hypnotic domain by recognizing those who are competent and serious. The Society for Clinical and Experimental Hypnosis has seen fit to give me its Morton Prince Award. Entering the field was timely, because the new interest in consciousness expansion, the puzzlements of the drug culture, the control of conscious states through biofeedback, have all made the kinds of experiments we do relevant to the interests of our day.

SATISFACTION THROUGH STUDENTS

The pleasure of knowing former students and visiting with them as occasions arise is one of the satisfactions of an academic career, along with observing the progress of their careers. A price of an eclectic position such as mine is that students diverge widely in what they do subsequently, so that there is no clear "master-disciple" pattern. The first student to complete a dissertation under my direction, Angus Campbell (who worked on conditioning), is now the director of the Institute of Social Research at the University of Michigan. Only David A. Grant, of those who did dissertations on eyelid conditioning, followed up the experiments of his dissertation and extended the findings through his own excellent research and that of his students.

Perhaps my pattern of accepting social responsibility may have influenced my students as much as my research style. While I hesitate to assign any causal relationship, it is of interest that a number of students who worked with me in the early years, such as Hugh M. Bell, John W. Gardner, John S. Helmick, Lloyd G. Humphreys, Sylvan J. Kaplan, Arthur A. Lumsdaine, M. Brewster Smith, and John T. Wilson, turned prominently to administrative positions in universities, government, or other agencies.

The number of those who have written their dissertations under my direction has greatly increased since the hypnosis research began. They are early in their careers, however, and I shall not attempt to list them, though I am already deriving satisfaction from them and their work.

CONCLUDING REMARKS

I have said very little about my personal life with my family, our personal friends, our travels, our recreational interests. My wife I have mentioned from time to time as a professional colleague and ally; she has an office next to mine, and works now in the same general area, but with a freshness and vitality all her own (e.g., J. R. Hilgard, 1970). But she has been a devoted wife and mother to our children; to mention only her professional side would be to give a very false picture of our happy life together. Our son Henry, with both the M.D. and Ph.D., is launched on an academic and scientific career, and finding in his research on immunology results that strike sparks as my research never did. Our daughter Lisby, without advanced degrees, in her love of her family and her animals may have found a style of life fully as satisfying as that of the rest of us. We are delighted with our children's spouses, and with the grandchildren they have given us.

If I had it all to do over again, would I do the same? That is a rhetorical question; if I wish to be different now, it is up to me, for there are still some years ahead.

REFERENCES

Selected Publications by Ernest R. Hilgard

For more complete bibliography see APA Committee on Scientific Awards, Distinguished scientific contribution awards, 1967. *Amer. Psychologist*, 1967, *22*, 1131-1135.

(with Donald G. Marquis) *Conditioning and learning.* New York: Appleton-Century-Crofts, 1940.

Theories of learning. New York: Appleton-Century-Crofts, 1948. [2nd ed., 1956; 3rd ed. (with Gordon H. Bower), 1966.]

(with Lawrence S. Kubie and Eugene Pumpian-Mindlin) *Psychoanalysis as science.* Stanford, Calif.: Stanford Univ. Press, 1952.

Introduction to psychology. New York: Harcourt Brace Jovanovich, 1953. [2nd ed., 1956; 3rd ed., 1962; 4th ed. (with Richard C. Atkinson), 1967; 5th ed. (with Richard C. Atkinson and Rita L. Atkinson), 1971.]

(Ed.) *Theories of learning and instruction.* Sixty-third Yearbook of the National Society for the Study of Education. Chicago: Univ. Chicago Press, 1964. (Author of Chapters 3, 8, 17, and postscript.)

Hypnotic susceptibility. New York: Harcourt Brace Jovanovich, 1965. (Shortened paper version under title *The experience of hypnosis,* 1968).

Other Publications Cited

Barker, R. G. *Ecological psychology,* Stanford, Calif.: Stanford Univ. Press, 1968.

Carnegie, D. *How to win friends and influence people.* New York: Simon and Schuster, 1936.

Clark, K. E., and G. A. Miller (Eds.). *Psychology (The Behavioral and Social Sciences Survey).* Englewood Cliffs, N.J.: Prentice-Hall, 1970.

Cohen, L. H., E. R. Hilgard, and G. R. Wendt. Sensitivity to light in a case of hysterical blindness studied by reinforcement-inhibition and conditioning methods. *Yale J. Biol. Med.,* 1933, *6*, 61-67.

Edwards, R. H., and E. R. Hilgard. *Student counseling.* Ithaca, N.Y.: The National Council on Religion in Higher Education, Bulletin VII, 1928.

German, W. J., J. C. Fox, and others. Observations following unilateral lobectomies. *Proc. Assoc. Res. Nerv. Ment. Dis.,* 1932, *18*, 378-434.

Hilgard, E. R. Conditioned eyelid reactions to a light stimulus based on the reflex wink to sound. *Psychol. Monogr.,* 1931, *41*, No. 184.

Hilgard, E. R. The relationship between the conditioned response and conventional learning experiments. *Psychol. Bull.,* 1937, *34*, 61-102.

Hilgard, E. R., and M. B. Smith. Distributed practice in motor learning: Score changes within and between daily sessions. *J. Exp. Psychol.,* 1942, *30*, 136-146.

Hilgard, Josephine R. *Personality and hypnosis: A study of imaginative involvement*. Chicago: Univ. Chicago Press, 1970.

Humphreys, L. G. The effect of random alternation of reinforcement on the acquisition and extinction of conditioned eyelid reactions. *J. Exp. Psychol.,* 1939, *25*, 141-158 (a).

Humphreys, L. G. Acquisition and extinction of verbal expectations in a situation analogous to conditioning. *J. Exp. Psychol.,* 1939, *25*, 294-301 (b).

Miller, G. A., E. Galanter, and K. H. Pribram. *Plans and the structure of behavior*. New York: Holt, Rinehart and Winston, 1960.

National Academy of Sciences/Social Science Research Council. *The behavioral and social sciences: Outlook and needs*. Englewood Cliffs, N.J.: Prentice-Hall, 1969.

Ward, L. B., Reminiscence and rote learning. *Psychol. Monogr.,* 1937, *49*, No. 220.

Wirth, L., E. R. Hilgard, and I. J. Quillen. *Community planning for peacetime living*. Stanford, Calif.: Stanford Univ. Press, 1946.

Jean Lattes

Otto Klineberg

During my student days I wrote for the college literary magazine some verses which I entitled "The Ballad of the Misplaced Highbrow." I still remember one stanza, which went as follows:

> I was meant to be as other people are,
> I was meant to go where other people go,
>   But by some miscalculation
>   I forsook my destination,
> I'm a Highbrow when I should have been a Low.

This is not an entirely adequate summary of my life, but it does have a certain relevance. I have combined a continuing interest in psychology with a tendency to spend a lot of time in directions which might reasonably be considered trivial. I often wonder what I might have done with all the hours I have lost reading detective stories, doing crossword puzzles, watching baseball games and old films on television, listening to light as well as serious music, playing tennis and chamber music, and in purely social or sociable activities.

This combination of the serious and just plain amusing in my life has made me something of an enigma, especially to my European friends. I remember that long ago two young Italians with whom I was exploring Turin found it hard to believe that I was a doctor of philosophy, since I was having so much fun dancing.

Of course I can argue that "nihil humanum" is really alien to psychology. All these extracurricular activities have certainly added to my enjoyment of life. In any case, I have always found it difficult to make a real distinction between work and play. Teaching psychology I never regarded as merely a job to be done; it has given me so much satisfaction that I have occasionally felt that I should be paying for the privilege of teaching rather than using it as a means of earning a living. I developed very early in life a strong and abiding curiosity as to why human beings behave the way they do. I have enjoyed talking in public, which made teaching easy and pleasant. I have also the ability to write clearly and quickly, so that my first draft has always approximated closely the final, published version. This has helped me to produce a substantial number of books and articles in spite of the fact that my interests have been so varied.

163

BECOMING A PSYCHOLOGIST

I was born on November 2, 1899, in Quebec City, but my family moved to Montreal when I was about five, and it was there that I attended public school, then the Montreal High School and McGill University. My parents both had a very modest education; they were born in different parts of the old Austro-Hungarian Empire and brought to Canada as children. We were eight children, brought up in a friendly and warm atmosphere and conservative Jewish tradition, with a strong emphasis on education and scholarship. We did not have much money, but all of us attended the university and four went on to graduate school. I perhaps abused the privilege resulting from my parents' permissive attitude, since I continued my studies for what must have seemed to them an unconscionably long time, and I shall always be grateful to them for their patience and understanding.

I was a good student and was graduated from McGill with a Bachelor of Arts degree before I was twenty. Canada was at war when I entered in 1915, and the only psychologist then on the staff (W. D. Tait) was in the army. My honors course was in philosophy and psychology, but all the courses were taught by a philosopher, and J. W. A. Hickson, a brilliant teacher, was my professor in psychology. His knowledge in this field was limited; he read long passages from William James in the introductory course and from Margaret Washburn in the course on comparative psychology. In the field of philosophy, however, he was a real scholar, who wrote very little but read a great deal, and he was the first to acquaint me with what a life of scholarship might have to offer. I was the only student enrolled in his seminar on Kant, and as a consequence had the privilege of having a private tutor of the highest competence.

I was graduated with First Class Honours and the Prince of Wales Gold Medal, and with Hickson's help I obtained a Tuition Scholarship at Harvard. That was a wonderful year (1919-1920), the first time I was really on my own, with all the riches of Harvard and Boston suddenly made available—many new friends, excellent lectures, and the Boston Symphony. Most of my courses were in philosophy, but I sat in on Floyd Allport's lectures in social psychology and took a seminar with H. S. Langfeld. Both of these were eye-openers in comparison with the psychology I had previously studied, and gave me some insight into the potential riches in the field. Langfeld, who later became a friend and a close associate in the activities of the International Union of Psychological Science, was most helpful and encouraging. Toward the end of term he asked me why I didn't leave philosophy and specialize in psychology. For the first time I thought seriously about an academic career in psychology.

I went back to Montreal with my Master's degree, and everybody I met, including my former professors, discouraged me from going on to the Ph.D. It was just too difficult and dangerous to plan for an academic career, they felt.

There were then three English-language universities in Canada (McGill, Toronto, and Queens), and jobs were almost impossible to obtain. I should add that at that time my horizon was limited to Canada; it simply did not occur to me that I could go to the States to teach. I was urged strongly to get a professional degree; then I would not be likely to starve while waiting for an academic opening.

I followed their advice. If I could not be a psychologist, I would do the next best thing and become a psychiatrist. After summer courses at the University of Chicago to catch up on prerequisites, I enrolled in the Medical School of McGill in the fall of 1920. It was a five-year course, the last year being more or less equivalent to an internship. About halfway through, however, I decided that this was not for me. The only part of medicine that interested me was psychiatry, and it practically didn't exist then at McGill. There was only a half-year course at the hospital, with patients being subjected to hydrotherapy and various forms of restraint. Freud wasn't even mentioned. I finished my medical course in 1925, but I had long since decided that I wanted to teach psychology.

I had not forgotten all the negative counsel, but I was now determined. Perhaps I would starve for awhile. Perhaps I would live in a garret and have to burn my manuscripts(?) and furniture in order to keep warm as in "La Vie de Bohème." Nothing would stop me. I felt that the only thing I wanted to do was teach. Research and writing were far from my thoughts—it was the teaching aspect of academic life that attracted me. As soon as I got out of McGill, I enrolled in the Psychology Department at Columbia, starting with summer school.

I have often been asked whether it was worthwhile to study medicine on the way to becoming a psychologist. In many parts of Latin America, as well as in Italy and Spain, a large proportion of psychologists are M.D.'s, apparently on the assumption that a medical training is highly desirable if not essential. In my own case it was exceedingly helpful in many ways. When I wrote *Race Differences* I made considerable use of material from the medical and physiological literature, which I would have been unlikely to discover and unable to evaluate properly without medical training. It was, however, a high price (five years) to pay, even though the M.D. was an advantage when later I became involved in the World Federation for Mental Health. Besides, doctors were willing to talk to me! If students ask me whether they should follow my example, my advice is that they would be better served by taking a number of selected courses (physiology, neuroanatomy, psychiatry, for example), rather than spend the time necessary to complete medical school.

I could of course have profited financially from my medical degree. When I became friendly with René Spitz and other distinguished psychiatrists and psychoanalysts, they urged me to do some part-time practice, offering to send me some patients to get me started. But by that time, my interests had moved too far away from psychiatry and psychopathology; and besides, the relative freedom of a teacher as compared with that of a practitioner, plus my keen interest in travel, made me turn down their generous offers. I have never regretted that decision.

COLUMBIA UNIVERSITY: THE PH.D.

The two years of graduate work at Columbia University (1925-1927) had a definitive influence on the rest of my academic life, in part accidentally. The first year was rich in new personal contacts and a growing awareness of the content of psychology. R. S. Woodworth (Woody) was not the greatest orator in the world, but he was an excellent teacher, and his courses (including one in social psychology) gave me an insight into his eclectic approach, which I continue to find palatable even today. He and A. T. Poffenberger (Poff) were a constant source of help and encouragement. I frequently crossed 120th street (the widest street in the world?) to listen to E. L. Thorndike, who was also kindness personified. That year was marked by my first contact with Gardner Murphy. Very much later, when he presented me for the Kurt Lewin Memorial Award of the Society for the Psychological Study of Social Issues, I said in response to his generous introduction that in 1925 I sat at his feet and never got up. I could never adequately express what our friendship (which later included our wives) has meant to me.

That year at Columbia was important also for my discovery of anthropology. My curiosity about all kinds of human beings led me to take a summer course on Culture and Personality with Edward Sapir, and I found him and his material fascinating. During the regular academic year, in addition to my work for "credit" in psychology, I sat in on as many courses in anthropology as I possibly could, even the departmental seminar directed by the great Franz Boas, which was attended by Ruth Benedict and other members of the staff. My contact with anthropology affected me somewhat like a religious conversion. How could psychologists speak of *human* attributes and *human* behavior when they knew only one kind of human being? How did we know that "instincts" functioned the same way all over the world, in spite of the variations in background and cultural experience? Was there any such thing as "general" psychology? What would our field be like if the books had been written by Hottentots or Eskimos rather than by Europeans and Americans?

I became as deeply involved in anthropology as in psychology and it was my great good fortune to be accepted by students and faculty in both disciplines. Boas was also *my* "Papa Franz," and I was included in the delightful evenings at his home where I met Margaret Mead on her return from Samoa. It was my close friendship with the graduate students in anthropology which resulted in the "accident" that changed the whole pattern of my work.

When I moved from medical school to psychology, it was with the intention of making use of my medical training by concentrating on psychopathology, beginning with a doctoral thesis in that field. In spite of my growing interest in anthropology, that was still my idea at the end of the first year at Columbia. The accident was that a graduate student in anthropology, the late Melville Jacobs (for many years professor at the University of Washington in Seattle), was driving out to the West Coast in an old Ford to do field work in linguistics, and asked me to come along. Possibly I could do something among the Indians; give tests, perhaps? I jumped at the idea, partly because I was curious about the Indians, but mostly because I wanted to drive across the continent. I asked Woodworth and Boas whether any research money might be available. It was Woodworth who said he could get me a modest amount if I would use my research among the Indians as the basis, at least in part, of my doctoral dissertation. Quickly I made the mental shift from abnormal psychology to "race," and agreed. That changed my life.

I would suppose that, judging by the reactions of the public as well as of my colleagues, my work in the field of race, in particular my position that psychological research gives no justification for the belief in a racial hierarchy of abilities, constitutes a reasonable claim to recognition. It began with my application of performance tests to Yakima Indian children and to whites in the town of Toppenish, Washington. Until that time I had no special interest in race or race problems, except to the extent that I had been influenced by the position of Boas and other anthropologists. On the contrary, before coming to Columbia I had read William McDougall's *Is America Safe for Democracy?*, and I thought he had made a pretty good case for qualitative genetic differences between ethnic groups.

This first research experience gave a result I had not expected, namely that the Indian children appeared almost completely indifferent to the amount of time required to complete the tasks. No matter how often I repeated or emphasized the words "as quickly as possible," they paid no attention. On the other hand, they made fewer mistakes. This led me to concentrate in my research on the factor of speed in group comparisons and gave me a lasting interest in the problem of cultural versus genetic factors in such comparisons.

During the second year at Columbia I completed my dissertation and was also assistant to Henry Garrett in his course in advanced experimental psychology. I think I was probably prouder of being asked to be an Assistant, actually in the employ of the University ($1,000 a year), than when I was appointed full professor at a slightly larger salary many years later. Garrett and I were on very friendly terms at the time, but our contrasting views on race finally brought about a permanent divergence.

FIRST INTERNATIONAL EXPERIENCES

I had always had a strong urge to travel, and during my second year at Columbia I obtained a National Research Council Fellowship for research in Europe. Before the award came through, I was offered an instructorship at the City College of New York. Jobs were very scarce at that time, and all my friends and fellow students advised me to accept. However, I felt that if I were offered a full professorship at Columbia or Harvard (who could aspire higher than that?) and the Fellowship, I would go to Europe. That started me on an "international" career which gave me so much opportunity to travel as later to cause one immigration inspector at the New York airport to say as he examined my passport: "You're quite a commuter, aren't you, Professor?"

The first trip abroad brought me into contact with a number of European psychologists, principally Henri Piéron in Paris and William Stern in Hamburg, who both became good friends of mine. My research dealt mainly with the comparison, again by means of performance tests, of children in France, Germany, and Italy, who showed the physical characteristics of Nordics, Alpines, and Mediterraneans, respectively, and I obtained essentially negative results. When on my return to the United States I attended my first International Psychological Congress at Yale in 1929, I met C. C. Brigham there. I told him how happy I was to meet him, because I had some data related to his conclusions in *A Study of American Intelligence*. "Oh," he said, "I don't stand by a word in that book!" I did not know at the time that he had published a full and courageous withdrawal from his original position. His remark was a bit of a letdown from one point of view, but of course I was pleased that he had arrived at the position of skepticism with regard to innate racial differences that had become my own.

While I was still in Europe I received from Boas an invitation to return to Columbia as a Research Associate in Anthropology to continue my work on race differences, and I accepted with enthusiasm.

TEACHING AND RESEARCH AT COLUMBIA, 1929-1962

I spent the next two years with Boas, consolidating my relations with anthropology, but also giving two courses in the psychology department, one on race differences, and the other on psychology and ethnology. At the same time I collected the material which led to my first publication in hard covers, a little book on *Negro Intelligence and Selective Migration*, which appeared in 1935. Since there was considerable evidence to the effect that northern Negroes (perhaps I should say "blacks," but at that time everyone said Negroes) obtained higher scores on intelligence tests than those from the South, I tried to discover why. One theory was that there had been a selective migration of Blacks from the South to the North such that the most intelligent ones had left; hence the better scores. The other explanation of course was that the superior northern environment was responsible for the difference. My results supported the second view. Since at that time many psychologists still believed in a genetic explanation of ethnic differences in achievement, my book aroused considerable interest. One reviewer referred to it as "concealed dynamite."

In 1931 Poffenberger offered me an instructorship in psychology (no vie de Bohème for me, after all!), and I remained a member of the department until

1961, slowly moving up the various levels until I became full professor in 1950. During the early part of this period I worked closely with Gardner Murphy in teaching and in directing student research in social psychology, and after he left, I continued for some time as the sole social psychologist in the department. For a portion of this period, I also taught anthropology on a part-time basis at Sarah Lawrence College in Bronxville.

My interest in teaching, which was the prime motivation for my entering academic life, has never left me. After forty years I still enjoy the contact with young people, as well as with those not quite so young among professional and lay groups who have asked me to speak to them. I remember once hearing Gordon Allport, whose friendship I enjoyed for many years, urge psychologists to bring their knowledge into the marketplace; I think he felt that I did not neglect that aspect of a psychologist's task.

At Columbia I had the great satisfaction of being able to play a part in the careers in social psychology of a large number of excellent students. At the college level I had in my classes Herbert Hyman and Robert Chin, both of whom went on to their PH.D.'s at least partly under my direction. Kenneth B. Clark, a recent president of the American Psychological Association, did his research with me, as did H. N. Schoenfeld and many others who have had distinguished careers. Muzafer Sherif, S. E. Asch, Irving Janis, Joseph Stone, Eugene Hartley, Charles Wagley, G. M. Gilbert, and Oscar Lewis are among those who took courses with me. I have had no greater pleasure as a teacher than the knowledge that all of these and many others turned out so well. (My apologies to those whose names are not mentioned.)

There was, however, one serious frustration. With social psychology developing rapidly and effectively in places like Michigan, Harvard, Yale, and California (Berkeley), I felt that the training given by the Department of Psychology at Columbia was incomplete. My colleagues, although for the most part cooperative and friendly, had other research and teaching interests. Students planning careers in social psychology complained that they had to fulfill too many requirements which were alien to their special field of interest: a number of good potential candidates decided to study elsewhere. It was clear, however, that there was enough talent around Columbia to supply first-class training in social psychology if it were possible to call on colleagues in other departments. Goodwin Watson, who was then at Teachers College, and I became co-chairmen of an Interdepartmental Committee in Social Psychology, which was authorized to direct research toward the Ph.D., the degree to be granted not through a department, but directly by the University on our recommendation. We were joined by Richard Christie, at that time with the Bureau of Applied Social Research; Paul Lazarsfeld and Herbert Hyman from Sociology; Conrad Arensberg from Anthropology; and the late Irving Lorge from Teachers College. We began the program in 1953 and soon found that our interdisciplinary training appealed to a number of excellent students. We were so successful that we soon needed more staff directly in the field of social psychology. As a consequence, a separate Department of Social Psychology was set up by the University in 1961, including Stanley Schachter and William McGuire in addition to Christie and myself; I served as the first chairman until I left for Paris in 1962. When I gave up my teaching at Columbia several years before retirement age, I was the Robert Johnston Niven Professor Emeritus of Social Psychology. The University later decided to reintegrate social psychology with psychology in general, but as a much more important subdivision than in the past. From this point of view I would consider our experiment to have been a success.

Some Publications during This Period

In addition to the little book on Negro migration, to which reference has already been made, my *Race Differences* appeared in the same year (1935). This volume was suggested by Gardner Murphy, then editor of a psychological series for Harper & Row. I attempted to gather together the relevant theoretical and empirical material from medicine and physiology as well as from psychology, sociology, and physical and cultural anthropology. This was followed by my *Social Psychology* (1940 and 1954), which the publishers asked me to write at Woodworth's suggestion. I used this opportunity to bring to the attention of psychology students the tremendous potential contribution of cultural anthropology to a better understanding of human behavior. This textbook, particularly in its second edition, was quite successful and was translated into a number of languages, including Persian and Arabic. The book is out of date in the United States, where so many more modern treatments of the subject have appeared, but it still sells in French and other languages in which the competition is not so keen.

I must mention my wife at this point. We met in 1931 at the summer Institute for Politics at Williamstown, where she was a weekend guest, and were married in 1933. She is a Vassar graduate with a doctorate in French history from the University of Paris, and is not only one of the most intelligent persons I have known, but also a delightful companion who has added to the joy of living all these years. We share many interests, including a love of travel, and we have had lots of fun together in many different ways. My work really became *our* work. Even before we were married I dictated to her the text of the selective migration book, and she criticized and improved the writing as we went along. I dedicated that book to her. As for *Race Differences,* she sat in on my course on this topic at Columbia and took it all down in shorthand, so that we had a first draft all ready for revision. In the preface I wrote: "I would express my thanks to my wife, if this book were not hers as well as mine." The same comment would apply to nearly everything I have written. When I mentioned earlier that I saved a lot of time because my first draft was usually close to the final published version, I should have said *our* first draft. There are no words adequately to express gratitude for this kind of partnership.

THE WAR YEARS, 1941-1943

Although I was able to continue with a certain amount of teaching during most of the war period, I also was associated with three different federal agencies in which psychologists could play a part. The first was in Washington with the Analysis Division of the Foreign Broadcast Intelligence Service of the Federal Communications Commission. This division was directed by Goodwin Watson and included such distinguished colleagues as T. M. Newcomb (whose friendship I have valued ever since), John Gardner, Hans Speier, Nathan Leites, Don McGranahan, and many others. Our major task was the application of the techniques of content analysis to incoming radio broadcasts, from both friend and foe, in the attempt to assess morale, to make predictions as to future developments and in general to interpret the local situation. I cannot refrain from reporting on one amusing occurrence during those difficult times. For one period I was in charge of the analysis of broadcasts from our allies; these would usually be monitored during the night, and the transcripts placed on my desk in the morning. One such transcript was of the Australian radio's report of a speech made by the Foreign Minister, Mr. Evatt, addressed to Britain after the French surrender in 1940, when the general war picture was very bleak indeed. Mr. Evatt spoke some encouraging words and ended with a brief poem, which was transcribed for me as follows:

> And we shall say to all the world
> That kinship conquers spice,
> And he who fights the British oils
> Must fight the British rice.

Since I had learned to speak English in Canada, I was able to translate this for my puzzled American colleagues. Anyone who has trouble may be helped by the reminder that many Australians pronounce the word "basin" as if it were written "bison."

I left Washington after a year or so to work in the New York branch of the Office of War Information. Here my task was as a member of the "control" division, which was responsible for making sure that our outgoing broadcasts followed the directives laid down by headquarters in Washington. I was especially, although not exclusively, concerned with broadcasts in the German language, and for a time even made a short weekly broadcast in German myself; my colleagues wanted someone who could speak German, but not so well that he would be taken for a German refugee. I was never certain whether my previous training in psychology was relevant to my activities in O.W.I., unless it helped me to get along on friendly terms with writers who might otherwise have resented having their texts "controlled."

Third and last, I spent several months with the Morale Division of the United States Strategic Bombing Survey, conducted by what was then called the War Department. This division was under the direction of another old friend, Rensis Likert, and included Ted Newcomb once again, Richard Crutchfield, Herbert Hyman, Alfred Metraux, David Krech, Gabriel Almond, Henry David, and a number of others who are also well known. One of my first tasks was to interview and engage a number of interviewers who could speak German, and among my "employees" was W. H. Auden, for whom an exceptional security clearance was obtained in spite of his British nationality. I was in uniform as an assimilated colonel (I forgot to mention that I had become an American citizen in 1938) and spent some time in London, where I became acquainted with the Tavistock group, particularly Henry Dicks, A. T. M. Wilson, and the late Ronald Hargreaves, before going on to Germany. The work on German morale in relation to strategic bombing *was* social psychological, since it involved careful interviewing of representative samples of respondents in a number of communities systematically varied with regard to their experience of bombing.

BECOMING AN INTERNATIONAL PSYCHOLOGIST

My first two years of travel in Europe (1927-1929) had whetted my appetite for getting to know more places and different peoples. The next opportunity came when Ruth Benedict arranged for an ethnological field trip to the Huichol Indians in Mexico during the summer of 1933. Even though I was already teaching in the department of psychology, I was at least as close to the anthropologists; there was even a question in my mind as to which of the two disciplines would constitute my definitive academic identity. In addition, Benedict was herself deeply interested in the psychological aspects of culture and wanted to give me the opportunity to take what might be called a "psychological" look at the Huichol. I did not stay with them long enough to do a thorough job, but at least she thought well enough of my report to have my "Notes on the Huichol" published in the *American Anthropologist*. Selma and I were married that April, and both Boas and Benedict were very doubtful about my taking a new wife on that kind of expedition. Since I suspected that she was marrying me partly in order to share the trip to Mexico, I held out, and in spite of what were really tough living conditions, we found the experience exciting. We had so little to eat that Selma would divide the available food into what she thought were two equal parts, and then let me have my choice—which really insured a 50-50 division. Only later did it dawn on me that this was unfair since I normally ate more, but by that time it was too late.

Before we were married, Selma and I had independently drawn up identical lists of the countries we wanted most to visit—China, Brazil, and the Soviet Union. As I had become greatly interested in the question of cultural factors in emotional expression, nothing seemed to us more suitable (and more fun) than to do research on what was alleged to be Chinese inscrutability. Do we find the Chinese inscrutable because their faces show so little, or because what they do show, they show differently? Is there less expression, or a different kind of expression? A Guggenheim Fellowship for 1935-1936 gave us the opportunity for which we were looking. On the research side, what I discovered was that both explanations were true, at least in part. The Chinese showed some emotions less, and some emotions differently. On the personal side we had a wonderful year and a trip around the world. We liked China and the Chinese so much that we planned I would retire at the age of fifty(!) so that we could then settle down for the rest of our old age in Peking. We should have liked another year for the study, but we returned home as planned when the Sino-Japanese situation grew too tense toward the end of our visit. Since we had learned to speak and even to read Chinese well enough to enjoy our personal contacts, we greatly regretted leaving, but were thankful for the year we had had.

Next, Brazil. Late in 1944 the famous Columbia geneticist Theodosius Dobzhansky asked me to come to his office to meet a former student, André Dreyfus, who had become Dean of the Faculty of Philosophy, Science and Letters of the University of São Paulo in Brazil. Dreyfus was looking for an American psychologist to join his faculty for at least two years to help create a department of psychology. He said it had to be someone who could lecture in Portuguese or another Latin language—French, Spanish, or Italian. He himself spoke very little English, and we had been conversing in French. He asked me whether I could suggest somebody. I played the game and mentioned the names of a number of colleagues who I thought might be suitable. Then came the crucial question: "Would you be interested in coming yourself?" I answered with the equivalent of "And how!" and thus became the first professor of psychology at São Paulo University.

We spent two happy, satisfying years in São Paulo and are still in close touch with many good friends there. By this time we had three children, ranging in age from five to eight, and of course they came with us. This was the first time, but not the last, that Selma had to set up a new home for the five of us, but her interest in travel more than made up for the inconvenience as far as she was concerned. We all learned to speak Portuguese almost as well as English, and we had friends not only among my university colleagues, but also among artists, musicians, architects, and even businessmen. Originally I planned to give my lectures in French, but Selma thought it hardly made sense for me to speak in a language foreign to me and to my students alike, so I decided to try speaking Portuguese. The first two or three months I wrote out my lectures and had them translated; then I switched to lecturing directly in Portuguese and was soon able to manage comfortably. One of the consequences of my visit was to bring together in São Paulo a group of psychologists who customarily saw little of each other, but who all attended an advanced seminar which I had introduced. Out of these contacts came a book, *Modern Psychology*, in Portuguese, with each person writing on his own field of specialization. We started this book in

1946, but it was not published until 1953, which led one impatient collaborator to suggest that we change the title to *Ancient Psychology*.

After a summer of travel which took us through a large part of South America, we returned home to Scarsdale in the fall of 1947, and I to Columbia. We then had every intention of staying put for at least a few years. Shortly before, however, UNESCO had opened its headquarters in Paris and included in its program a number of social science topics (such as national characteristics, stereotypes, etc.) under the general heading of Tensions Affecting International Understanding (the "Tensions Project"). On the occasion of a visit to New York of Arvid Brodersen, the Norwegian sociologist who was then Acting Director of the Social Sciences Department of UNESCO, the Carnegie Endowment for International Peace brought together a number of social scientists to suggest some of the directions which this project might take.

I had been interested for some time in the possible applications of the social sciences, in particular social psychology, to international affairs. In the summer of 1931 I had served as the secretary of a Round Table on Psychology and International Relations, directed by G. M. Stratton at the Institute of Politics at Williams College. In 1943 I gave my presidential address to SPSSI on the subject *A Science of National Character*. As a consequence I did have some background for the discussions with Brodersen, and the Carnegie Endowment sent my name to UNESCO as their recommendation for Director of the Tensions Project. In the meantime, UNESCO headquarters had invited the late Hadley Cantril to fill that post; he had accepted, but on the understanding that he could stay only a few months. I was asked to replace him, beginning in the spring of 1948. We had not yet unpacked all our cartons of books and bric-a-brac; we began instead to refill the empty ones. As was to be expected, the authorities at Columbia took a rather dim view of my request for leave so soon after the return from Brazil, but they did grant the necessary permission. I shall always be grateful for the understanding shown by the University in making possible my exciting and (I hope) useful years abroad. I happen to know that other universities have not always been so generous in this respect.

This first job at UNESCO in Paris lasted approximately fifteen months, from May 1948 to September 1949. Fortunately for me Cantril stayed on a couple of months after my arrival, and we worked harmoniously together, planning further social science research in the field of international relations. In the meantime the Carnegie Endowment and the Social Science Research Council had asked me to prepare a critical survey of available materials in this field. I completed the job in Paris, and it was published by the Council in 1950 under the title *Tensions Affecting International Understanding: A Survey of Research*. A translation into French was later published by UNESCO. This monograph resulted in the award of the Butler Medal by Columbia University the same year largely (I believe) at the suggestion of my good friend Poffenberger. I felt that this year in Paris had been most rewarding, even though neither my colleague nor I could claim that international tensions had been greatly reduced as a consequence. One of the more successful enterprises in my judgment was in response to a request from the Economic and Social Council of the United Nations which led to the preparation of the project on race and science. This resulted in a series of publications which were among UNESCO's "best sellers," as well as a number of statements by social and biological scientists summarizing their position on the race question. The fact that Julian Huxley was then Director-General was a great boon: he was friendly and accessible, and contact with his brilliant mind was a delightful experience. A few months before I returned to Columbia Arvid Brodersen resigned, and I became the Acting Director of the Social Science Department.

The period at UNESCO had intensified my interest in what the social sciences, particularly psychology, could contribute to better understanding of international affairs. When I received the Kurt Lewin Award from SPSSI in 1956, I spoke on "The role of the psychologist in international affairs." Later I wrote a small book on *The Human Dimension in International Affairs,* which was published in 1964. I had hoped that I might thereby have some slight influence on public opinion, but in this I was disappointed, since it has been read mostly by students, and only rarely by individuals outside the university. It has, however, been translated into several languages, including Norwegian, German, and Japanese. I have also participated in a number of Conferences for Diplomats held under Quaker auspices at Clarens in Switzerland, renewing my earlier connections with the Friends as director of several institutes on race relations in the United States.

The UNESCO period also added two important new dimensions to my international activities. The World Federation for Mental Health was about to be founded, and UNESCO sent me as an observer to the planning meeting at Roffey Park, outside of London, of the Interprofessional Advisory Committee. This group had been brought together by the late John R. Rees, the first President and Director of the Federation, and included, among others, Harry Stack Sullivan, Margaret Mead, Lawrence K. Frank, Henry Dicks, John Cohen, and others well known to the psychological fraternity. Brock Chisholm, then Director-General of the World Health Organization, spent some time with the group, and I was privileged to become a friend of this truly great man, whose recent death was a blow to all who knew him.

As a consequence of this contact, I became a member of the Committee, and later successively member and Chairman of the Executive Board, President, and (now) Honorary President of the Federation. For me this whole experience has meant a partial return to my very early interest in the field of mental health, my own emphasis being mainly on its social and cultural aspects. My presidential address, delivered in Lima in 1967, was called "An international view of mental health."

The other new activity resulting from the UNESCO experience was my growing identification with the "international family" of psychologists. There had for a long time been an international committee, whose major function was to prepare the ground for international congresses. When I was in Paris in 1948-1949, Piéron was chairman of this committee and Langfeld its secretary; at Piéron's invitation I became a member. Largely under the stimulus of UNESCO's Social Science Department, which had been instrumental in setting up international associations in sociology, economics, and political science, the psychologists also decided to organize. The International Union of Psychological Science was founded in Stockholm in 1951; the occasion was, however, the *thirteenth* international congress. Piéron was elected president, and Langfeld, secretary-general. Three years later Piaget became president and I replaced Langfeld, remaining as secretary during the following three years under Michotte's presidency, then becoming president myself from 1960 to 1963. Of course this activity (I remained on the Executive Board until 1969, when Piaget and I both retired to make room for younger colleagues) meant meeting and knowing psychologists from all over the world, and many of the friendships that resulted have been important to me. I am the proud possessor of honorary membership or fellowship in the Belgian, British, Canadian, French, Philippine, Spanish, and Swedish psychological associations. I am proudest of all that my colleagues on the Executive Board unanimously recommended me for the Human Rights Award of the United Nations. (I didn't get it, but just the same. . . .)

To go back a little in time, I had a second period of membership in the UNESCO Secretariat from 1953 to 1955, as Director of the Division of Applied Social Sciences, at the invitation of Alva Myrdal, then Director of the Department. I had met the Myrdals when Gunnar was working on his classic *An American Dilemma* years before. I helped him in the collection of background materials and edited a volume in the same series, *Characteristics of the American Negro* (1944). The two years in Paris passed pleasantly and too fast; in my paper on "The role of the psychologist in international affairs," I have described many of the activities in which our department was involved, as well as some of our difficulties. This was during the McCarthy period, and obtaining the cooperation of American social scientists when "clearance" was required sometimes represented an insuperable obstacle. Conditions have of course greatly improved since then, but the shadow cast by McCarthy has not entirely vanished.

As far as research at UNESCO is concerned, I once referred to my role as that of a midwife rather than a mother. As long as I was a member of the Secretariat working at headquarters, I could read and write (a little), but I never had the time to go out and collect new data. There were, however, at least two such "midwiferies" which gave me considerable satisfaction. I was involved in sending Gardner and Lois Murphy to India, which resulted not only in the publication of Gardner's book, *In the Minds of Men* (1953), but in a great deal of additional research by Indian colleagues to whom Gardner and Lois gave the necessary training. I also helped to send Jean Stoetzel to Japan, and to make possible his publication *Without the Chrysanthemum and the Sword* (1955). These successes made up a little for the frustrations due to the paper work and bureaucracy which seem to be unavoidable in large organizations.

After the UNESCO interlude, the next move was to the University of Hawaii in Honolulu as Carnegie Visiting Professor for one semester in 1958. This hardly counts as foreign travel, but the atmosphere was different enough to make us feel we were not quite in the United States. Then in 1960, just before the International Congress in Bonn, my wife and I were invited by the American Psychological Association to visit the third country on our priority list, the Soviet Union. We have returned twice since, once to attend the International Congress in 1966, and again the following year to participate in a seminar under the auspices of UNICEF. In brief I would say that we liked the people (we visited Leonitiev, Luria, and other old friends), but found the atmosphere too restrictive. The last trip took us to such romantic-sounding places as Tashkent, Samarkand, and Tiflis; we could admire the progress made in raising the general standard of living, but there was very little romance left.

I cannot leave this international section without adding a word about foreign languages. There are few things that have given greater satisfaction to my wife and to me than the ability to communicate directly with people in a number of different countries. I have taught or lectured in French, Portuguese, German, Italian, and Spanish—not always well, by any means, but well enough to be understood. My wife speaks all of these languages, in several cases better than I; we both can get along in Chinese and Russian (hers is much better), and she manages also with Norwegian and Finnish. My friend Wallace Lambert of McGill says that people are successful in learning foreign languages when they are interested in the human beings and the cultures involved, not usually because they have a "gift" for languages. Certainly we have both had that interest and we are grateful for the dimension which languages have added to our experience. If there is one piece of advice I feel capable of giving to young psychologists, particularly if they want to work abroad, it is that there is no substitute for being able to talk with people.

THE PARIS YEARS

In 1960 I was invited by Jean Stoetzel to join him in the teaching of social psychology at the University of Paris, the Sorbonne. (Incidentally, the Sorbonne is a building, not an institution; it would be reasonable to say that one teaches *at* the University of Paris *in* the Sorbonne, if that happens to be where the lectures are given.) The French system does not, however, allow the appointment of a full professor who is not French and who has not obtained the "big" doctorate (doctorat d'état) from a French university. Everything is now in the process of change, but at the time of my invitation it was possible to appoint a foreigner only as *professeur associé* (best translated as visiting professor) for a period limited to two years. In spite of this we decided to accept, being optimistic enough to believe that two years later something else would turn up. I should add that I did not leave on account of any dissatisfaction with Columbia, quite the contrary. I was motivated partly by the thought that it would be interesting to start out on a new career in a new environment, but also because we had both fallen in love with Paris long ago. It was impossible to say "no" to Paris and the Sorbonne. In 1961 we bought a little house in Neuilly not far from the Etoile and we moved there in the summer of 1962.

Although I have for a long time fought against the tendency to think in terms of national stereotypes, something happened toward the end of our second year to reinforce *my* particular stereotype of the French. I was in the Sorbonne one day when the Dean of the Faculty asked me to come into his office for a moment. When I was seated opposite him he said: "You're not thinking of leaving us next year, are you?" My answer was that of course I would like to stay on, but I had been told that no more than two years would be possible. I shall never forget his response. "Oh, you know," he said, *"on s'arrange."* It is this ability to "arrange" things in spite of rules to the contrary that I would venture to describe as typically and endearingly French.

As it happened, I stayed only one additional year at the Sorbonne, moving in 1965 to the Ecole des Hautes Etudes, an institution directly under the Ministry of Education, and concentrating on research training. I am still there having started my ninth year last October. My "chair" (Direction d'études) is ethnic psychology, which gives me and the students in my seminar a chance to deal with race problems, minorities, immigrants, national characteristics, and any other problems within the general framework of "culture and personality." All the teaching is in relatively small seminars, as distinct from the large lecture courses I had given at the Sorbonne, and in which on one occasion I had more than a thousand students. Largely for this reason, the Ecole escaped the crisis in the University usually referred to as the May events (*les évènements de mai*) of 1968.

Most of the students working with me have prepared or are preparing their "doctorat troisième cycle," which is about the equivalent of an American Ph.D.; or the "diplôme," which more or less corresponds to a Master's thesis. I have frequently been asked how my French students compare with those whose research I directed at Columbia. In general, though with many exceptions, my American students usually knew more about the content of social psychology, but my French students express more elegantly what they do know. In any case, I have already had the satisfaction of seeing some of my former students in Paris move on to positions of research and teaching, not only in France, but also in other countries, particularly in French-speaking Africa.

Starting in 1962 and continuing until 1970 when the money ran out, I went to Rome once a month to lecture on intergroup relations at the Università Internazionale degli Studi Sociali Pro Deo; most of my students there were young priests or seminarians. This invitation came as the result of the "dialogue" opened up in the Catholic Church in the period leading to Vatican Council II. Since the University is close to the Vatican in many ways, the rumor spread among some friends and colleagues in the United States that I was lecturing in (if not to) the Vatican. During the last few years I gave my lectures in Italian, but an Italian so contaminated by other Latin languages that students would often tell me they were sure I must speak a good Spanish or Portuguese. Since 1963 I have also been giving a course at the Institute of American Studies, originally set up by the American Embassy and the United States Information Service, but now an overseas division of the State University of New York. These courses are given in English for French students and deal with various aspects of American life. I have been lecturing mostly on the applications of the social sciences in the United States. During the past three years I have also been the adviser to Columbia and Barnard students spending their Junior Year in Paris.

At the time that I moved to the Ecole des Hautes Etudes, we organized, under the joint auspices of the Ecole and the International Social Science Council, an International Center for the Study of Intergroup Relations, which has been generously supported by the Aquinas Fund. I am still the Director, with Marisa Zavalloni [Italian by birth with a French "license" (M.A.) and a Columbia Ph.D. in social psychology] as Associate Director. Together, we have published a volume, *Nationalism and Tribalism Among African Students* (1969), in which we reported on the basis of an investigation commissioned by UNESCO the results of the application of questionnaires in six African universities, designed mainly to determine the relative salience and importance of tribal as compared with national identity. Another study, with a Moroccan research associate, Jeanne Ben Brika, on the adaptation of students from the developing countries attending universities in four European countries was published in Paris in 1972. Research in progress under the auspices of our Center is concerned with student attitudes in thirteen different countries, mainly to discover to what extent one may speak of a universal "youth culture," and what variations are found from one country to another. Another study under the auspices of an international committee of university presidents, with Chancellor Vernon Cheadle of the University of California at Santa Barbara as chairman, deals with the evaluation of international exchange programs, of faculty as well as of students, in seven countries. My job here is to coordinate the various studies being carried out by the local investigators. With my colleagues at Pro Deo in Rome I have published a volume in Italian, *Religion and Prejudice* (1968), which reports the results of a content analysis of Catholic school texts in Spanish and Italian, designed to discover the treatment accorded to other religious and ethnic groups.

This brings me fairly up to date with regard to activities in and out of Paris. I should add that living here has made it possible for me to accept a number of interesting and pleasant engagements relatively nearby. I gave the invited address at the annual meeting of the British Psychological Society in Belfast, and of the British Sociological Society in London; I took part in a symposium at Amerika Haus in Nuremberg and in meetings of the European League for Mental Hygiene in Palma de Mallorca and in Helsinki; I have spoken to the Mental Health Associations of Sweden, Norway, Finland, and Denmark. In connection with my research project on international university exchanges, Selma and I visited Delhi, Tokyo, and California. Through my activities as Vice-President of the International Federation for Parent Education (founded by André Isambert), I have attended meetings in Caracas, Llubljana, Neuchâtel, Tunis, and Brussels, and for the World Federation for Mental Health I have been in Bangkok and Jerusalem, Lima and Sydney. The USIS invited me to give some lectures in French-speaking Africa, and that took us to Kinshasa in Zaire, Dakar in Senegal, the Ivory Coast, Mali, Madagascar, Mauritius, twice to Morocco, and three times to Tunisia. The Government of the Ivory Coast was host to a psychological meeting in Abidjan, and I was one of three French (!) psychologists who were invited to participate. I have also attended meetings in Ghana and Nigeria, and have recently lectured in Montreal, Palermo, Cardiff, São Paulo, and Stockholm.

This is far from a complete list of recent travels, but it gives an idea of my international activities in the field of psychology. We are often asked whether all this traveling does not exhaust us, but most fortunately we have both been extremely healthy, and adapt easily to changes in climate, food, and time. We continue to enjoy being in our own way part of the "jet set."

One of the rewards has been that we have good friends in many parts of the world whom we see again when they visit Paris; we are at home in a number of different countries. We appreciate this extension to our experience, which has given us a sense of wider international and human identity. For someone who has always wanted to travel, I have not done too badly.

A PERSONAL NOTE

It is not easy to evaluate a life, particularly one's own. As I look back, I can claim no significant contribution to psychological theory, and no discovery of new research methods. At the same time I have received my fair share of honors. I have four honorary degrees, which mean a great deal to me, since one came from the University of Brazil, where I helped in the development of psychology; one from Howard following my role in connection with the Supreme Court decision against school segregation; one from my old university, McGill, almost fifty years to the day after my graduation as Bachelor of Arts; and one from Drew University mainly (I think) because the president, Robert Oxnam, is a good friend of mine.

What I feel I can claim, however, is that I have been successful as an *entrepreneur* for psychology, particularly at the international level; as a teacher; as an early advocate of the importance of anthropology as well as of sociology in the training of social psychologists; and as one among those who have tried to make psychology relevant, to use a term which has recently become popular, to current social problems, particularly race, international affairs, and mental health. I have recently given expression to my philosophy with regard to race in a paper, "Black and White in International Perspective," which I presented at the

APA convention in Miami as the invited guest of the President, Kenneth B. Clark. I have tried to bring the importance of cross-cultural comparisons to the attention of psychologists; it is certainly encouraging to note the tremendous development of psychological research now carried on in far-off places. Conversely, I have urged anthropologists, with some success, to be more concerned with individual variations rather than concentrating almost entirely on cultural norms or patterns. It has all added up to challenge and enjoyment.

On the personal side, I am one of the fortunate ones. My "family of orientation" was probably responsible for an early development of an attitude of security and optimism. I may possibly already have mentioned my wife; I owe so much to her that I cannot "count the ways." We have three children in the United States, a daughter, Rosemary, and two sons, John and Stephen, all happily married, all with graduate degrees, enjoying useful and productive lives. Although we live far from them and our six grandchildren, we manage frequent visits, and they have all come to spend vacations with us. We are the best of friends and get a great deal of enjoyment out of being together.

I have always liked hearing and telling a good story. This has had certain slight disadvantages; occasionally I run into someone who has heard me lecture and remembers only my stories. I shall take that risk now, in order to tell an old favorite. It is about a French boy in a small village, who was christened "Formidable." As can be imagined, he suffered a lot of teasing as a consequence and hated the name all his life. After sixty years of a happy marriage, he asked his wife on his deathbed not to put the name "Formidable" on his tombstone; he wanted that forgotten. She promised, and had engraved on his stone, "Here lies a man whose wife remained faithful to him for sixty years." And all the passersby remark, "Ah, c'est Formidable!"

That is how I feel about what life has given me. As I say, I am one of the lucky ones.

REFERENCES

Selected Publications by Otto Klineberg

An experimental study of speed and other factors in "racial" differences. *Arch. Psychol.*, No. 93, 1928.

A study of psychological differences between "racial" and national groups in Europe, *Arch. Psychol.*, No. 132, 1931.

Notes on the Huichol. *Amer. Anthropologist*, 1934, *36*, 446-460.

Negro intelligence and selective migration. New York: Columbia Univ. Press, 1935.

Race differences. New York: Harper & Row, 1935.

Social psychology. New York: Holt, Rinehart and Winston, 1940, 1954.

Characteristics of the American Negro (Ed.). New York: Harper & Row, 1944.

A science of national character, *J. Soc. Psychol.*, 1944, *19*, 147-162.

Tensions affecting international understanding: a survey of research. New York: Social Science Research Council, 1950.

Psicologia moderna (Ed.). Rio de Janeiro: Agir, 1953 (in Portuguese).

The role of the psychologist in international affairs. *J. Soc. Issues,* Suppl. series, No. 9, 1956.

The human dimension in international relations. New York: Holt, Rinehart and Winston, 1964.

(with R. Christie, Eds.) *Perspectives in social psychology.* New York: Holt, Rinehart and Winston, 1965.

(with W. E. Lambert) *Children's views of foreign peoples.* New York: Appleton-Century-Crofts, 1967.

(with T. Tentori, F. Crespi, and V. Filippone) *Religione e pregiudizio.* Rome: Cappelli, 1968 (in Italian).

(with M. Zavalloni) *Nationalism and tribalism among African students.* Paris: Mouton, 1969.

Alternatives to violence, in Nobel Symposium, 14, *The place of values in a world of facts.* New York: Wiley, 1970, 229-240.

Black and white in international perspective. *Amer. Psychologist,* 1971, *26,* 119-128.

(with J. Ben Brika) *Etudiants du tiers-monde en Europe,* Paris: Mouton, 1972.

Other Publications Cited

Boas, F. *The mind of primitive man.* New York: Macmillan, 1911, 1938.

Brigham, C. C. *A study of American intelligence.* Princeton, N.J.: Princeton Univ. Press, 1923.

Brigham, C. C. Intelligence tests of immigrant groups. *Psychol. Rev.,* 1930, *137,* 158-165.

McDougall, W. *Is America safe for democracy?* New York: Scribner's, 1921.

Murphy, G. *In the minds of men.* New York: Basic Books, 1953.

Myrdal, G. et al. *An American dilemma.* New York: Harper & Row, 1944.

Stoetzel, J. *Without the chrysanthemum and the sword.* Paris: UNESCO, 1955.

UNESCO series on the race question in modern science, first published in 1951.

Zakład Fotograpiczn
Leonard Siemaszko

183

Jerzy Konorski

This work is dedicated to the memory of Stefan Miller, whose close cooperation in the remote past was decisive for the accomplishments described in these pages, and to all my friends in America, to whom I owe much gratitude, in particular: Robert Livingston, Neal Miller, Mortimer Mishkin, Hal Rosvold, Richard Solomon, Eliot Stellar, and Lucille Turner.

FIRST STEPS (1927-1931)

A reader who is for some reason interested in the biography of a scientist would want to know where and when he was born and how it happened that he became a scientist. To satisfy this curiosity, I shall mention that I was born on December 1, 1903, in Łódź, an industrial Polish city with a population of half a million, which at that time belonged to Czarist Russia. My father was a lawyer, I was the youngest of his four children. In 1910 I went to a Polish gymasium, which was a combination of elementary and high school. At that time there were in Polish cities either governmental Russian gymnasia or Polish gymnasia, which were private or semiprivate. It was, however, considered utterly unpatriotic to send one's children to Russian schools, which were under social boycott.

I finished the gymnasium in 1921, after Poland had attained independence. As far as I remember, I already wished to become a scientist, although my interests were broad and undefined. While still in school I studied books in sociology, and since I was also interested in mathematics I dreamed of combining these two disciplines in some way.

Because of this lack of determination of which speciality to choose, I began to study mathematics at Warsaw State University, but I soon realized that I was not gifted in this field. Then I became interested in how the human brain works and thought that if I studied psychology I would be able to find answers to all the questions which bothered me at that time. Unfortunately, after one year of this study I became completely bored and disappointed, since I found no answers either in the classical textbooks of psychology or in the courses of human psychology taught in the University. I did gain, however, one great benefit during this year: not in the faculty of psychology but in the faculty of

185

law, where there were lectures by a famous professor of the theory of law, Ignacy Petrazycki, who had come to Poland from Petersburg. He had developed his own system of psychology, which was at that time completely original. According to his views, the essential processes of mental life were the emotions: fear, hunger, thirst, curiosity, and many others. He considered these processes to be at the same time afferent and efferent; that is, they were thought to contain both the receptive experiences and the urge to react in a particular way. He considered that the perceptions and feelings, on the one hand, and volitional acts, on the other, derived from emotions. His book *The Foundations of Emotional Psychology,* published originally in Russian (Petrażycki, 1908) and then translated into Polish (Petrażycki, 1959), is now in total oblivion, although his ideas were very progressive and, as a matter of fact, most of them can be still considered quite modern. This was perhaps the first scientific book which influenced my thinking and helped to shape my ideas. I finally decided to study medicine, hoping that neurology and psychiatry would teach me how the brain works. I knew nothing about the physiology of the brain, except the meager facts presented in Polish textbooks of physiology.

My study of medicine was another string of disappointments. The study of anatomy contained a great number of data which had to be learned by heart and which were of no use to me. In particular, the anatomy of the skull and the brain contained innumerable details difficult to memorize, but completely devoid of any functional meaning. It was very frustrating for me that, being obliged to learn an extensive bulk of facts concerning human anatomy, physiology, and pathology, I still could not learn anything about how the brain works.

Rescue from this troublesome and seemingly hopeless situation came quite unexpectedly. This happened in 1927 during my third year of medical studies. I was then on very friendly terms with a colleague, Stefan Miller, whose scientific interests were exactly the same as mine. We both came quite incidentally across two of Pavlov's books on conditioned reflexes, which had just been published (Pavlov, 1925, 1926). The books were written in Russian, but Miller had spent his childhood in Russia and knew the language quite well. From these books we learned for the first time about conditioned reflexes, and we immediately realized that this was exactly the field of science we were looking for.

The extent of our excitement brought about by this discovery is difficult to describe. We became entirely involved in studying Pavlov, and only by some miracle, not quite clear to me yet, did we succeed in being graduated in medicine. We assigned to the obligatory courses in medicine a strict minimum of time and went to our exams after a few weeks of hasty learning. This is why my knowledge of the clinical disciplines is now almost nil. It was purely a matter of my short-term memory, and I completely forgot everything I had learned as soon as the exam was over. Instead of medicine, we read and reread Pavlov and discussed every detail of the experimental work of his coworkers. Moreover, we found in the library of the Nencki Institute of Experimental Biology the Russian journals in which the papers on conditioned reflexes were published.

After some time spent on these studies, we began to realize that Pavlovian conditioned reflexes are not sufficient to explain the whole acquired behavior of animals and men, as Pavlov had claimed. In particular, we became aware that the motor behavior established by way of reward and punishment could not be reduced to the paradigm of these reflexes. Accordingly, we began to ponder how it would be possible to incorporate the experiments involving motor behavior into the general scheme of Pavlovian experimentation.

After some consideration we came to the conclusion that the proper paradigm of experiments fulfilling this purpose should run as follows: If a given neutral stimulus, say the sound of a metronome, is combined with a given movement, say raising the leg, and it is then reinforced by food, whereas the same stimulus presented separately is not reinforced (in other words, when the movement is the necessary condition for obtaining food), then the animal should perform that movement in the presence of the stimulus. On the contrary, when the movement following a given stimulus is reinforced by a noxious agent, whereas the stimulus alone is not, then the animal should resist performing that movement. Since we considered that such conditioned reflexes differ essentially from those of Pavlov, we decided to call them conditioned reflexes of the second type, whereas the Pavlovian conditioned reflexes we denoted as first type.

After settling on this project of experimental work, we began to look for a laboratory where the experiments could be performed. Accordingly, we approached several professors of medicine, asking them to provide us with a room and facilities to start our experiments. Our inquiries were, however, completely unsuccessful. The reason for our failures was obvious, and I don't think these professors should be blamed. After all, here were two young students trying to persuade a distinguished professor that they planned to perform experiments constituting an essential complementation of Pavlov's research work, and the professor (not being acquainted with the area concerned) was rather suspicious of the supplicants and anxious to get rid of them. Therefore, we went from one distinguished man to another, telling them about our plans, and were always politely refused.

I don't remember who suggested that we approach Professor Jacob Segal, who had a chair of psychology in the Free Polish University, an institution somewhat analogous to the Collège de France in Paris. Unexpectedly, Professor Segal fully understood our ideas, became interested in them, and offered us a small room in his department, located on the third floor of what was actually an apartment house. We had no financial support, but we were allowed to utilize the meager equipment of the department, which was mainly concerned with education. The introduction into our first laboratory took place on February 1, 1928, the day which thereafter we celebrated as our anniversary day.

The first thing we had to do was to buy a dog. For this purpose we went to the marketplace, found the area where people sold dogs, and after long deliberations, chose a young and nice bulldog, which cost ten zlotys (about one dollar). We called him Bobek. He immediately became friendly with us and we brought him to our "laboratory." The housekeeper agreed to let him stay in her apartment.

Our next task was to organize a conditioned reflex laboratory in the room which was assigned to us. Putting together two square stools we made a "Pavlovian stand" and used cardboards for a screen. The bowl was made of tin and was fixed to the front part of the stand. Pieces of food were thrown from the small aperture in the screen by the experimenter. I do not remember how the horizontal bar above the stand was fixed in order to keep the animal in the harness during the experimental sessions. Since in the department of psychology there was a kimograph with a long tape, we utilized this for recording the dog's movements. For a long time we used a strip of toilet paper, which was both cheap and convenient, provided that it was relatively smooth and did not have transversal perforations. You can imagine the comical picture presented by two serious young men going to a paper store and asking to be shown all the possible varieties of toilet paper, scrutinizing them thoroughly, and choosing the one which fulfilled both conditions. Recording of movements was accomplished by a very primitive and crude arrangement made mainly out of pieces of wire.

The first experiment was performed in the following way. A band with electrodes connected with the induction coil was attached to the dog's left hind paw. We presented a tone from a harmonium (luckily found in our lab), and after a few seconds a light electric shock was applied to the paw. When the dog lifted his leg, immediately a piece of sausage was thrown into the bowl. Occasionally the tone was presented without the shock and without reinforcement.

We considered it a great triumph when after a few days of such procedure, Bobek began to lift his left hind leg without the electric shock, turning immediately to the bowl and expecting food. At the beginning he did so both to the tone and in the intervals, but very soon the intertrial movements disappeared. Thus, we succeeded for the first time in establishing the type II conditioned reflex under experimental conditions.

The next step in our experimentation was an attempt to establish the type II conditioned reflex by using the passive lifting of the leg. The rationale of this experiment was the assumption that the indispensable condition for the formation of the type II conditioned reflex was that the proprioception of the movement should become the type I conditioned stimulus, that is, a signal of presentation of food. We turned on an electric lamp placed in front of the stand, and then we raised Bobek's left foreleg by pulling a string attached to the wrist; this compound was reinforced by food, whereas the lighting of the lamp without the passive movement was not reinforced. After a short time Bobek began to actively raise his foreleg; at the beginning he did it throughout the experimental session, and then only in response to light.

Then by mere accident we discovered the following fact. When the band for recording was attached to the left hind leg, Bobek performed the movement of that leg in response to both the tone and the lamp; when the band was attached to the left foreleg, he raised that leg to both the conditioned stimuli. When the band was attached to one of the right legs, no movement was performed. We called this phenomenon "motor generalization" and were very much impressed by this unexpected finding.

I shall not describe all the experiments we performed during the first few months of our experimental work. We were very lucky with the dog, who was amazingly intelligent and learned very quickly all the conditioned reflex tasks with which he was presented.

In order to hasten our experimental work we decided to train the dog in two tasks simultaneously, one task involving alimentary conditioned reflexes being trained in the morning, and the other involving defensive conditioned reflexes being trained in the afternoon. The dog put up with all the difficulties presented to him and seemed quite happy. Only once, when we attempted to teach him to extend the hind leg in response to one stimulus in order to avoid the electric shock, and to raise the same leg in response to another stimulus in order to get food, did he refuse to work. Concurrently he developed an interesting experimental neurosis: when placed on the stand, he took a catatonic position, with his hind leg lifted continuously and his eyes half closed. However, when we stopped this type of experiment, he soon returned to normal.

Since at that time we did not consider it necessary to use more dogs—in fact, the results obtained on Bobek were most reliable and were repeated many times—we were able within a few months to make many interesting discoveries concerning the properties of particular varieties of type II conditioned reflexes. We were much impressed when we came across a phenomenon now called "avoidance conditioning." In accordance with our ideas we applied the following procedure: An auditory stimulus alone (a whistle) was followed by a puff of air into the ear (provoking a very strong defensive response), whereas this stimulus accompanied by a passive movement of the right foreleg was not followed by the air puff. Bobek began to raise the foreleg to the sound of the whistle and continued to do so consistently in spite of nonreinforcement.

After having obtained these first results we decided to do two things: one was to present a report before the Warsaw Branch of the French Biological Society in Paris, and the second was to write a letter to Pavlov presenting him with our achievements.

The first two papers, concerning the elaboration of the type II conditioned reflexes and their transfer, were delivered to the Society in the summer of 1928. As I remember it, the reaction of the audience was quite favorable, and after a few months these papers were published in *Comptes Rendus de la Société de Biologie et de ses Filiales* (Miller and Konorski, 1928a, 1928b).

More or less at the same time, to our great joy, we received an answer from Pavlov. He congratulated us on our results, took them to be important, and asked for details. Thus we considered our first experimental season, which had lasted only five months, to be fully successful. This was just at the end of our fourth year of medical studies, and, to our great annoyance, we had before us still one full year at the University.

When the new academic year began, our position was much strengthened. We boasted of the letter received from Pavlov, and we also proudly displayed the reprints of our papers to everyone. As a result, Professor Czubalski, head of the chair of human physiology in the Medical Faculty of the Warsaw University, allowed us to continue our work in his laboratory. This was, of course, a great step forward. The physiological laboratory was equipped with all necessary instruments and there was, therefore, no difficulty in making salivary fistulas and recording not only motor acts but also salivation. Moreover, all the expenses connected with our work, which had previously weighed on our pockets, were now covered by the University. We repeated the experiments performed on Bobek on new dogs with salivary fistulas, calling our technique the "salivo-motor method." Moreover, we became engaged in a study of the relations between type I and type II conditioned reflexes, and we discovered that the classical positive conditioned stimulus inhibits type II responding, whereas the negative conditioned stimulus does not. At that time this finding was quite unexpected. As a result, two new papers were published in the *Comptes Rendus de la Société de Biologie et de ses Filiales* (Konorski and Miller 1930a, 1930b).

Since everything follows the rule of coming to its end, in the fall of 1929 we graduated in medicine and had to face the problem of finding jobs. This was, at that time, far from easy in Poland, because the positions in the universities were very scarce and we were ready to take only such jobs as would enable us to continue our work. As there were no vacancies in Professor Czubalski's Department of Physiology, we decided to work in psychiatry, judging that this specialty was not very remote from our main field of interest. Accordingly, we applied to Professor Łuniewski, director of the big State Psychiatric Hospital situated in Pruszków, near Warsaw. Professor Łuniewski's reaction was most positive. He had already heard about us and favored our project of establishing a small laboratory of conditioned reflexes in his hospital.

In this way our practical problems were solved. We both received rather decent salaries and apartments inside the hospital. We were allowed to build and indeed were assisted in building, the laboratory of conditioned reflexes (the third so far in our brief careers).

However, our work in this field did not progress, because we were at that time so much concerned with psychiatry—a field quite new to us—that it was practically impossible to perform systematic experiments on conditioned reflexes. Even so, the knowledge of psychiatry which I acquired during that time has remained with me and has occasionally been of great help to me with regard to both my livelihood and my scientific work.

During our stay in Pruszków we prepared a monograph written in Polish in which we presented all our experimental results on type II conditioned reflexes (Konorski and Miller, 1933). We claimed that these reflexes represent the physiological model of voluntary behavior and we considered that they possess a quite different mechanism from the Pavlovian (type I) conditioned reflexes.

In the meantime our contact with Pavlov was not broken and in one of his letters he proposed that we should come to Leningrad to discuss our results and perhaps perform some work. Now that we had graduated, this was possible.

At that time there was a true "iron curtain" between Poland and Soviet Russia, and contacts between the two countries were practically nonexistent. Therefore, the idea of our going to Leningrad seemed quite exotic to a number of our colleagues. The success of our enterprise was entirely due to Pavlov, whose authority in both Russia and Poland was so high that both Professor Czubalski and Professor Łuniewski assisted us in obtaining passports to Soviet Russia, and we were easily granted the Soviet visa.

Late in 1931 on a foggy November morning we boarded the train going to the Soviet frontier, and then by a Soviet train we arrived in Moscow and from there the next day went to Leningrad. So it was that our big adventure began.

IN LENINGRAD (1931-1933)

It would be both unreasonable and impossible to depict chronologically my stay in Leningrad, telling how I gradually adapted myself to the difficult and unusual conditions of life, how I began to understand and master the Russian language and became familiar with the city and the people around me. The period of my stay in Leningrad resides in my memory as a compact entity with quite definite spatial dimensions but with no temporal coordinate. I cannot recollect just what was the sequence of events as my own experiences were developing. Therefore, I shall rather describe the atmosphere of the Institute in which I was working, my own work, and, perhaps most important, I shall tell about Pavlov as I remember him in those days.

When Miller and I arrived in Leningrad we didn't know how long we would stay. Miller had been married just before our journey and therefore he could stay in Leningrad for only a few months. As far as I was concerned, I was single and completely free to do whatever I wished, having no precise plans for the future. Just at the beginning of our sojourn, after a few discussions with Pavlov, it became clear that it would be most profitable if I remained in Leningrad and performed some systematic experimental work. Consequently, I was accepted by Pavlov as a member of his laboratory and thus became one of "Pavlov's pupils," with all the privileges of this little clan and with all its advantages and short-comings.

Pavlov headed at that time two big laboratories situated in separate districts of Leningrad. One was the Department of Physiology of the Institute of Experimental Medicine. The Institute was founded mainly for Pavlov at the end of the nineteenth century and was situated in the outskirts of the city. In this department the famous studies of Pavlov on the physiology of the digestive glands had been performed, the studies rewarded by the Nobel prize. In 1910 a Moscow businessman provided Pavlov with funds that enabled him to erect for the study of conditioned reflexes a special laboratory with soundproof chambers, the famous Tower of Silence. This was a building with very thick walls, which could not be penetrated by noises or vibrations from the outside world. During my stay in Leningrad, one of the soundproof chambers in the Tower of Silence was allotted to me to share with a colleague. The second laboratory, situated near the center of the city, belonged to the Academy of Sciences of USSR. Although the two laboratories were administratively separate, they were united in respect to the scientists and the scientific work performed in them. About forty scientific workers worked in both of them.

Pavlov spent alternate days in the two laboratories. Wednesdays were free from experimental work, because before noon there were meetings of all scientific workers of both laboratories to discuss the current experimental work, and in the afternoons there were meetings in either psychoneurological or psychiatric clinics directed by two of Pavlov's coworkers; here the particularly interesting neurotic or psychiatric cases were analyzed and discussed from the point of view of Pavlov's ideas about brain pathophysiology.

During the morning meetings Pavlov was usually the only speaker. He was perfectly acquainted with the work of every one of his coworkers and presented the material from memory without the use of notes. Indeed, his excellent memory was famous and at the time that I was there—he was 82 years old—it had not deteriorated. Usually, after talking for about 20 minutes he would ask whether there were any questions or comments. Most often the discussion was rather limited and only occasionally would an argument develop.

Rarely was Pavlov opposed. The criticism, which was very feeble, would be circumlocuted by such phrases as: "How do you explain, Ivan Petrovitch, this or that fact?" Generally speaking, to openly criticize Pavlov was rather a shocking act and required some courage. First, Pavlov himself was a very strong debater, quite aggressive and not quite fair in discussion. Besides, if anybody dared to criticize Pavlov, the entire group would side against the critic. In such a situation, it was no wonder that Pavlov always prevailed. However, in spite of this, Pavlov truly esteemed those people who did oppose him and he highly respected the independence of one's views, as long as he did not consider them to be nonsense. After arguing strongly and defending his own viewpoint, and after cooling down, Pavlov would often accept the view of his opponent and would openly admit that he had been wrong.

Every morning, after arriving in the laboratory, Pavlov would sit down in a large open room, where everybody was free to join him. Most often people came to him to report their new experimental results. Pavlov listened attentively, then gave his comments and explanations of the data obtained. Here people were much more free to take part in the discussions than they were at the Wednesday meetings, and time and again a hot argument about some problem broke out. These discussions were, of course, exceedingly interesting, because of their informal character, and therefore I always attended them when I had finished my daily experiments.

In general, Pavlov was the "spiritus movens" of the work going on in his two laboratories. He assigned the problems to be worked out to each of his co-workers and he controlled all the stages of their research. Only in exceptional cases did a student follow his own line of research, but then it was rather difficult to win Pavlov's attention and appreciation.

From this description it is clear that scientific and intellectual life in the Pavlovian laboratories was very vigorous and that it was fully concentrated around Pavlov. In the absence of Pavlov we usually talked about him, quoted what he said, how he behaved, etc. Moreover, there was clear jealousy among Pavlov's pupils about who was the closest to him. People boasted when Pavlov spoke to them at some length, and, as a matter of fact, the attitude of Pavlov toward an individual was the main factor determining the hierarchy within the group. Another characteristic of "Pavlov's pupils" was that, although squabbling among themselves, they were united with regard to other scientific groups, having a feeling of superiority and self-importance. Of course, I fully shared this feeling. To sum up, the atmosphere reigning in the group reminded one of that usually encountered in royal courts, with Pavlov being the indisputable king.

Since the general character of the experimental work carried out in the Pavlovian laboratories is not well known by American psychologists, I shall briefly describe it:

Each member of the laboratory had several dogs (from 3 to 8) on which he performed his experiments. Usually the dogs remained in the laboratory for many years and they were trained in a great number of experimental tasks, all of them in classical salivary conditioned reflexes.

The routine of the experimental procedure was very rigid and essentially the same in the whole laboratory. Every day, except Sundays and Wednesdays, the animals were brought to the chambers from the animal house at exactly the same hour. All the dogs had fistulas of one parotic gland, which enabled measurement of salivary responses. Usually, when a dog was brought to the chamber, he jumped immediately on the stand and a small glass capsule was sealed to his cheek by the experimenter at the place of the fistula with a special sealing wax (whose formula was given by the great Mendeleev). The capsule was connected with a thin horizontal glass tube situated in front of the experimenter and filled with colored fluid. When the dog salivated, the meniscus of the fluid moved and thus salivation, in response both to the conditioned stimuli and to the unconditioned stimulus, was recorded. The reinforcement used in all experiments was prepared for the whole laboratory. It consisted of a powder made from minced crackers and minced boiled meat. Before a session the experimenter mixed the two powders in equal proportion and added a given portion of water. In this way, the powder had a consistency of moist sand and was easily chewed and swallowed by the animal, producing copious salivation. The constant portions of this cracker-meat powder were distributed in even quantities to the bowls, situated along the round disc mounted in the feeder and with one aperture just in front of the dog. By pneumatic control, the experimenter put a bowl with food into position so that the food was available to the animal. The act of eating lasted about 20 to 30 seconds.

Experimental sessions consisted of 6-10 trials separated by intertrial intervals of about 5 minutes each. In most experiments performed at this time the intertrial intervals were always the same in the given series of experiments.

The conditioned stimuli were auditory (the sound of a metronome, tones, the sound of bubbling water, whistles, buzzing, etc.), visual (continuous or rhythmic light, rotating or oscillating objects, etc.), and tactile (a small gadget was attached to the skin in such a way that by pneumatic control the experimenter was able to produce tactile stimuli). In well-trained animals the operation of a conditioned stimulus preceded the presentation of food by 20-30 seconds, so that the experimenter could record the rate of conditioned salivation over a relatively long time span. Besides the positive conditioned stimuli, negative conditioned stimuli were also used. These were similar to the positive stimuli but presented without food reinforcement: for instance, the sound of a metronome of different frequency, the tactile stimulus applied to another place of the body, and light of another intensity were among those used as negative stimuli. The training, consisting of the presentation of positive (reinforced) and negative (nonreinforced) stimuli, was called differentiation. Usually in experiments with each dog various conditioned stimuli, both positive and negative, were used. It should be noted that according to the habits of the laboratory, the negative stimuli were presented only once or twice per session, because it was found that if they were presented too often, the magnitudes of the positive conditioned reflexes became less regular.

Each experimental session usually lasted 30-45 minutes. At the end of the session a boy came to the chamber, took the animal out, and brought in the next one. In the animal house the dogs were fed at definite hours with fixed portions of cereal with bones. This highly stereotyped way of conducting experiments resulted in amazingly constant and stable responses to each of the conditioned stimuli and amazingly stereotyped behavior of the animals during the sessions.

When Miller and I began our work on type II conditioned reflexes in Pavlov's laboratory, we had to modify the stable routine. A number of arrangements had to be made to teach the animals to lift their legs in response to conditioned stimuli, to register their motor responses, and so forth.

We got five dogs, which had previously served for many experimental studies. We received their entire biographies, their age, the dates of their coming to the laboratory, the whole story of their conditioned reflex careers, and the lists of all positive and negative conditioned stimuli used in their training. Accordingly, what we had to do was to introduce some new stimuli and train the animals in type II conditioning.

The work in the Pavlovian laboratory was of utmost importance for me and certainly determined my entire future. Whereas our work on conditioning performed in Warsaw had been somewhat amateurish, here we could profit from the tradition and experience of this big scientific center. Moreover, since we received dogs with firmly established positive and negative classical conditioned reflexes, we were provided an excellent background for introducing type II conditioned reflexes and studying the interrelations between the two types. Finally, only in the Pavlovian laboratory were the methods of salivary conditioned reflexes well developed, and accordingly the relations between salivary and instrumental responses could be studied.

Beside this, I had the opportunity to get thoroughly acquainted with the whole bulk of the past and the present work on conditioned reflexes and thus to become a well-trained specialist in this field.

What were the main achievements during my stay in Leningrad? First, confirmation under more rigorous experimental conditions of the results we had found in Warsaw, to the effect that positive type I (classical) alimentary conditioned stimuli completely inhibit type II response, whereas negative type I conditioned stimuli may even increase this response. Second, we performed important experiments in which a given stimulus was reinforced by food, but this stimulus accompanied by passive flexion of the leg was not. As a result, the dog learned to extend his leg in response to the conditioned stimulus, in this way resisting passive flexion. Third, by applying as an unconditioned stimulus introduction of acid into the dog's mouth, we established avoidance conditioned reflexes and could study the relations between motor and salivary responses in these rather unusual conditions. All these results were presented in an extensive paper published in *Transaction's of Pavlov's Laboratories* (Konorski and Miller, 1936), and they laid the foundations for the further development of my ideas concerning the mechanisms of type II conditioning.

To end this description of my almost two years' stay in Leningrad, I would like to say a few words about my relations with Pavlov. As a matter of fact, they were far from being simple. There was no doubt that Pavlov highly appreciated the importance of our contribution to the field of conditioned reflexes, which, according to his own words, led to "physiological understanding of volitional movements." However, he strongly opposed our thesis claiming the existence of two types of conditioning and failed to see any difference between them. He was so sensitive about this point that when writing the above-mentioned paper for his journal we simply did not dare to use our own terminology and called type II conditioned reflexes "motor conditioned reflexes" or "conditioned reflexes of the motor analyser." Both of these terms were misleading.

It should be noted that this negative attitude of Pavlov toward the specificity of type II conditioned reflexes had a detrimental effect on the development of the study of these reflexes in Russia. In fact, had Pavlov accepted this specificity, the situation would have been clear and the experimental work on this type of conditioning would certainly have developed in Russia as it did develop, quite independently of our work, in the United States, where type II conditioned reflexes were called "instrumental" or "operant" responses. However, when the greatest authority in this field stated that type II conditioned reflexes simply do not exist, this was decisive and meant special investigations along this line, with insignificant exceptions, were not undertaken in Russia. Moreover, when in 1949 the orthodox Pavlovism was introduced in the Soviet Union, the term "type II conditioning" was denounced as a manifestation of my revisionistic tendencies and disapproved of.

BACK IN WARSAW (1933-1939)

In June 1933, there came a day when I packed all my luggage, consisting mainly of books, journals, and experimental materials, and returned to Warsaw. The first problem I was confronted with was how I should organize my future life. It was, of course, quite easy for me to return to the psychiatric hospital in Pruszków, where Stefan Miller continued to work and where I had many friends; but I firmly decided to devote myself entirely to scientific work and knew already that this could not be combined with working in the hospital.

Strangely enough, the problem of my future was decided the second day after my arrival in Warsaw. Since the date of my return had been known in advance, Professor Jan Dembowski, one of the leading biologists in Poland, had arranged for me to give a lecture concerning my work with Pavlov. Among the audience there was a young woman who after the lecture asked me a number of competent questions concerning the views of Pavlov on the problem of inhibition and the relation between Sherringtonian and Pavlovian ideas in this matter. This was Dr. Liliana Lubińska; six months before my returning from Leningrad, she had returned from Paris, where she had spent eight years. She had studied biology at the Sorbonne, obtained a doctoral degree there, and was a pupil of a famous French neurophysiologist, Louis Lapicque. At that time there were very few neurophysiologists in Warsaw, and therefore we were very lucky to have met each other, even more so that while I was mainly trained in the higher nervous activity, she was competent in the lower parts of the nervous system.

From our first talk I learned that after returning from Paris she had obtained a position as a scientific worker in the Nencki Institute of Experimental Biology, in the Department of Physiology, whose head was Professor Kazimierz Białaszewicz. Although his specialty was physiology and biochemistry of insects, he very willingly accepted Dr. Lubińska as a scientific worker in the department and encouraged her to continue her work in neurophysiology. In this way he considerably helped the opening up of research work in this discipline in Warsaw.

A few days later, Lubińska brought Miller and me to Białaszewicz and we discussed with him the possibility of establishing a small laboratory of conditioned reflexes in his department. He gave his consent and offered us a room suitable for our experiments. Thus, in the fall of 1933 two important events occurred in my life. I established the laboratory on conditioned reflexes in the Nencki Institute, and Dr. Lubińska became my wife.

From the scientific point of view my collaboration with Lubińska was for me extremely valuable. As a matter of fact, from the very beginning of my scientific career I had engaged myself in the study of conditioned reflexes. However, my general knowledge of neurophysiology was very poor. On the other hand, Lubińska had an excellent knowledge in this field, having worked for a number of years in one of the best known centers of neurophysiology in Europe. Accordingly, she taught me a great deal about neurophysiology, with regard both to methods and to the theories.

This circumstance was decisive for the further development of my scientific ideas. During the time I worked in Pavlov's laboratory I was under the spell of his ideas and personality. In spite of my argument with him about type II conditioned reflexes, in all other respects I supported his views and was strongly convinced of the soundness of his ideas concerning the activity of the cerebral cortex. After my return to Warsaw I propagated these ideas very broadly in numerous lectures, seminars, and articles.

However, as I had learned more about Sherringtonian neurophysiology, I realized that the views of these two scientists were completely incompatible. According to Pavlov the general picture of the activity of the cerebral cortex was roughly the following: Excitatory and inhibitory processes are assumed to arise in particular "points" of the cortex as the effects of excitatory and inhibitory conditioned stimuli. Both these processes spread in a wavelike manner over the cortex, affecting larger or smaller areas, and mutually restrict each other. The greater the areas of the excitatory processes, the stronger the predominance of excitation over inhibition; the larger the areas of the inhibitory processes, the stronger the dominance of inhibition. If the inhibitory process spreads all over the cortex and subcortical centers, it gives rise to sleep. Often the excitatory area is surrounded by the inhibitory area, the phenomenon called by Pavlov negative induction; or vice versa, the inhibitory focus is surrounded by excitatory fields, the phenomenon denoted as positive induction. Pavlov imagined that the perpetual interplay between the excitatory and inhibitory processes was the essence of the normal activity of the brain—in other words, of the mental processes occurring in a subject. If there is a conflict between excitatory and inhibitory processes tending to occupy the same place in the cortex, then the pathological state called neurosis issues. All the experimental results obtained in Pavlov's laboratories on dogs, as well as observations of human patients in psychoneurological and psychiatric clinics controlled by Pavlov, were explained by reference to the above theory.

The Sherringtonian idea concerning the functioning of the nervous processes was entirely different. It was based on the neuronal theory of the structure of the central nervous system advanced by Ramon y Cajal in his monumental work. According to this theory, the conveyance of nervous processes is always unidirectional, leading from the cell body through the axon to other neurons. Sherrington has shown that the nervous impulses arriving along an axon to a given neuron can either activate the neuron and cause it to discharge, or inhibit it, that is, block energy brought to it through other axons. Accordingly, each neuron is a convergence point of both excitatory and inhibitory influences, which determine the intensity of discharges produced by this neuron and which in turn are conveyed by axons to other neurons.

It was quite clear to me that the Pavlovian and Sherringtonian concepts of the functioning of the nervous system could not be reconciled with each other, and it was even impossible to find a "dictionary" which would translate one set of notions into the other. Simply, one of the two theories should be rejected in toto, and the facts so far explained by the rejected theory should be reinterpreted in the framework of the other theory.

By that time I already had no doubt that it was Pavlov's theory that should be rejected. The more I pondered Pavlovian explanations of various facts in the field of conditioned reflexes and tried to analyze the explanations, the more I discovered inconsistencies and contradictions in the Pavlovian interpretation of the facts. Thus, the idea grew in my mind to try to explain the whole bulk of experimental work collected by Pavlov's school by the Sherringtonian principles of functioning of the central nervous system.

Besides this theoretical work undertaken during that period, I was intensely involved in experimental work on conditioned reflexes carried out in collaboration with Lubińska and Miller. Unfortunately, most of this work was performed before the war and the experimental material was lost. Perhaps the most important published work was that concerned with the problem of interrelations between alimentary and defensive type II conditioned reflexes. The procedure of these experiments was that, using dogs, type II conditioned reflexes, both alimentary and defensive, were established. Raising the foreleg was the alimentary type II response, and raising the hindleg was the type II defensive response (active avoidance). It was shown that the animals never exchange the defensive response for the alimentary one, and vice versa. On the other hand, when the animal was trained to perform two different movements in response to two different stimuli, *both* under food reinforcement, exchange of these responses occurred quite often. This work was published in Polish just before the war in a practically unknown scientific journal (Konorski, 1939).

It should perhaps be noted that during this time Miller and I became involved in an interesting discussion with Skinner. In 1935 Skinner published a paper entitled "Two Types of Conditioned Reflex and a Pseudo-type" (Skinner, 1935). In this paper he developed ideas somewhat similar to ours, showing the existence of two types of conditioned responses. Skinner called these type I and type II, but his type I was what we called type II, and vice versa. (Only later did he introduce the terms "respondent behavior" and "operant behavior," which are now in common usage.) It was because we did not agree with his approach to the problem of distinguishing between the two types of responses that this discussion developed (Konorski and Miller, 1937b; Skinner, 1937; Konorski and Miller, 1937a).

This discussion seems to me to be not quite obsolete. Skinner performed experiments based on his now well-known experimental procedure (the "Skinner box"). A rat was introduced into a box with a lever; time and again among his other activities the animal pressed the lever, and this was followed by presentation of food. As a result the animal learned to perform lever pressings with maximal frequency. Accordingly, Skinner considered that the formation of the operant responses consisted in the increase of *probability* of the performance of that movement. Since Miller and I worked with a quite different technique, in which we evoked a given movement either by passive flexion or by electrical stimulation of the paw, we argued that Skinner's explanation could not hold, because the probability of the performance of the movement of the animal before it was trained is in our experimental situation simply zero.

These were my main scientific activities in the thirties. They were abruptly cut short on September 1, 1939, when Germany invaded Poland. In a few weeks our country was defeated, which led to a complete change in our way of life and to a long period of insecurity and hardship.

THE WAR (1939-1945)

I don't think it would be sensible to attempt to describe the days of the beginning of the War, which I remember very vividly and in great detail. The panic of the population, the smell and sight of the fires, the rapid advance of the German Army toward Warsaw—in five days they were already at the outskirts of the city—the bombardment by artillery of the Nencki Institute, which was situated on the western outskirts of Warsaw and which the Germans wrongly took for the military building situated in the vicinity, the gradual deterioration of Warsaw when the water supply, the electric power, the transport and finally the telephone contacts were extinguished—all this is beyond the scope of this narrative, which is supposed to be a scientific autobiography. Our only scientific occupation during that time was directed to carrying scientific books, reprints, experimental materials from one place to another, according to which place seemed to us for some reason most secure.

After a three-week siege of Warsaw, during which a heroic resistance was maintained in spite of the complete dominance of the Germans in the air and on land, the municipal authority decided that further resistance was absurd and the city surrendered. In the first months of occupation our main task was to put our scientific materials in order. In particular, since I had already written a few chapters of my prospective book on conditioned reflexes, we tried to type them in several copies in order to save them from destruction. The days in October and November were already short, and since there was no electricity we brought home accumulators from the laboratory; and this was the source of our light, which had, of course, to be maximally economized.

In October or November we received information from England through Belgium (which was not yet in the war) that a friend of ours in Cambridge had transferred a sum of money to Riga (the capital of Latvia) in order to help us come to London via Scandinavia. Many people used that route, which was not particularly difficult. Because of the great chaos on the frontiers, travel between the countries was not very dangerous then. Therefore, we decided to go east in order to reach Riga. However, a few days after our arrival Białystok (a Polish city which was then in the hands of the Soviet Army) the frontier between Russia and Latvia was closed and there was no possibility, except with great danger, of crossing it.

Since we had to remain in Białystok, I began to work in the large psychiatric hospital near the city. I got in touch with my colleagues at Pavlov's laboratory in Leningrad, and they lent us a helping hand. I obtained a formal invitation to come to Leningrad to attend a scientific session concerned with conditioned reflexes and to present a paper there. This invitation obliged the Soviet authorities to facilitate our journey, and so, in May 1940, I arrived with my wife in Leningrad, where we received good care and help on the part of my Pavlovian colleagues. By the way, this shows the great solidarity among scientific workers all over the world. The efforts of our colleagues in England to bring us to that country, for one, and the concern extended to us by people from the Pavlovian laboratories, for another, are excellent examples of this solidarity.

The helpfulness of my colleagues in Russia went even further, for they proposed that I be made head of the Department of Physiology in the Subtropical Biological Station in Sukhumi, Caucasus, a famous Primate Research Center. This was arranged so quickly that in the beginning of June 1940, we found ourselves in a most beautiful submontane place, situated on the shore of the Black Sea. The war was so remote from this place that one could almost forget about it, which was of course quite unthinkable in our situation. Dr. Lubińska and I obtained a very nice laboratory (whose previous head went to another place), and we had full freedom to develop scientific work according to our own plans.

The chief aim of the Primate Biological Station in Sukhumi was to breed monkeys and either to utilize them for scientific purposes in the laboratories of the station or to send them to other institutes concerned with experimentation on animals. In accord with the first purpose, the Station had laboratories of primate biology, psychology, physiology, higher nervous activity, immunology, and cancer research.

I decided to continue my work on type II conditioned reflexes, now utilizing monkeys instead of dogs. I had two good soundproof chambers and I equipped them with several instruments which played the role of manipulanda. There were levers to be pressed, chains to be pulled, buttons to be pushed. The animals were trained to perform various responses to various conditioned stimuli, or to establish chain conditioned reflexes, in which the responses had to be performed in a definite sequence.

Our relatively quiet life, disturbed only by our worrying about the fate of our friends, came abruptly to an end on June 22, 1941, when it was announced by radio that the German Army had entered Soviet Russia and that war was declared.

We understood at once that the continuation of our work along the same line would be completely inappropriate and we decided to work in the field, which might be of some value for practical war medicine. Accordingly, some quite new projects were begun, namely studies of traumatic neuroses and their treatment, and of nerve regeneration after the cutting of nerves, performed on dogs and monkeys. On the last topic we discovered that nerve regeneration occurs much faster than had so far been supposed (3 to 4 mm/day, not 1 mm), and that it is easy to find the tips of the regenerating fibers because of their strongly increased mechanical excitability (responses to very light hitting).

Although there were no apparent changes in our life at the beginning of the War, gradually the situation became more and more distressing. The swift victories of the German Blitzkrieg were most depressing, many young men from the Station were mobilized, and the economic situation went rapidly from bad to worse. There was a period when the German Army was quite near Sukhumi, and it was decided that the Institute should be evacuated partly to middle Asia and partly to Tbilisi, the capital of Georgia. Because of this I stayed for a number of months in Tbilisi, where I worked in the neurological wards of an army hospital. Since the front was very near at that time, there were many cases of traumatic concussion of the brain, and I studied their symptomatology in great detail.

Again I shall leave out the description of my most variegated experiences during this difficult time, when the fate of Soviet Russia and the whole world was at stake. I would only like to emphasize the most admirable attitude of the Soviet population and the Soviet Army during this difficult period. There was no tendency to panic in spite of the most dangerous situation, and the people's patience was infinite. I heard many stories about the extraordinary endurance of the Soviet soldiers, and I could confirm these from my contacts with them in the hospital. It was most amazing to see how the Soviet nation, which seemed to be on the verge of disaster, found enough moral strength to transform the impending defeat into victory. I think that only those who witnessed this transformation can properly appreciate it and give it full credit.

The first spark of hope was when, quite unexpectedly for all of us, in the middle of defeats the Soviet Army began a tremendous offensive at Stalingrad, which after a few months of bitter fighting ended with a smashing victory. However, at that time, the beginning of 1943, the situation was far from being clear and the outcome was still uncertain. Only in the summer of 1943, when the German offensive on Moscow was crushed and the Soviet armies began their magnificent advance, did it become clear that the war was won and that final victory was not very remote. The time was exceedingly hard. There was hunger all over Russia, but it was now certain that this hardship would eventually come to an end.

In the spring of 1945 we decided to end our stay in Sukhumi and go to Moscow, in order to return as quickly as possible to Poland. We already began to think about the new life in our country and about restoration of Polish universities and Polish science. In Moscow we met our good friend Professor

Dembowski, one of the previous directors of the Nencki Institute. After much deliberation we decided to restore the Institute. At the end of August we returned by Soviet train through Brest to Warsaw.

FIRST POSTWAR PERIOD (1945-1955): IN ŁÓDŹ

The return to Warsaw after six years of peregrinations was full of excitement, joy, sadness, and hope. Only then did we learn how many of our closest friends had perished during the War. Among them were Stefan Miller and his wife, both of whom had committed suicide during the extermination of Jews by the Nazis.

Warsaw was in ruins. Only the suburb of Warsaw, Praga, situated on the right side of the Vistula, was not completely destroyed, because it had been liberated earlier by the Russians. Therefore, almost all the people lived then in Praga and the government had its seat there. It was most impressive and encouraging to see how quickly the authorities and offices came into being and how energetically they began to work.

The first people whom we met were Dr. and Mrs. Niemierko, our old friends who before the war had worked in the Nencki Institute. Again we discussed together the problem of our future and decided that the Nencki Institute should be reestablished. With this project we went to the Ministry of Education, where we saw the director of the newly created Department of Science, Professor Arnold, a well-known Polish historian, and presented our plan to him. In half an hour the plan was accepted and two friendly couples, my wife and I and Dr. Niemierko and his wife, formed the organizational committee of the Nencki Institute. We chose Dr. Niemierko as chairman of the committee. Our decision was immediately accepted by the Minister of Education, Mr. Wycech, who signed the appropriate certificates. It is curious to note how quickly every new idea could be materialized at that time, because there existed no bureaucracy which could delay and hamper any new project, at best, or cancel it, at worst.

Since Warsaw was totally in ruins after the War and our prewar Institute was almost completely demolished, it was clear that we should place the Institute in another city, at least temporarily. After some hesitation we decided to settle in Łódź, which was still intact because the Germans withdrew from it very quickly, without a battle. Among other motives which determined our decision was that the new University was being organized in Łódź and Professor Kotarbiński, our very close friend and famous philosopher, was nominated its President. Again a problem was solved in five minutes; Professor Kotarbiński offered the chairs of animal physiology and neurophysiology to Professor Niemierko and to me, respectively. It was decided that we should have two positions, one in the University and the other in the Nencki Institute.

Soon we visited the city governor, who was very pleased to know that a well-known scientific institute would be placed in Łódź. It should be noted that before the War Łódź was only an industrial city; and it was a sort of Cinderella with regard to cultural life. The new authorities of Łódź had very high cultural ambitions and set out to establish several higher schools, including the University, a higher technical school, and others.

The governor of Łódź offered us temporarily a small building where the Niemierkos, my wife, and I could have very modest apartments and where the germ of the Institute could be established. In one year the city authorities kept their promise and offered us a much more suitable building where regular laboratories could be arranged.

In 1947 the Institute was ready to begin experimental work. It consisted of three main departments: the Department of Biology, whose head was Professor Dembowski following his return from Moscow; the Department of Biochemistry, whose head was Professor Niemierko; and the Department of Neurophysiology, headed by me. Professor Dembowski became Director of the Institute.

I shall leave out a description of the seemingly insurmountable difficulties connected with the organization of our Institute. We had to work in a complete vacuum, having no equipment, no trained staff, and even no furniture. Still, however extraordinary our deed seems to me now, this was quite typical and usual for that time; everybody was confronted with the same situation. One cannot imagine the enthusiasm which at that time animated the Polish intelligentsia. There were no bureaucratic obstacles and limitations, and through energy and dedication one could bring every project into existence.

The difficulty of our situation was that between our generation (people from 45 to 60) and very young people (about 20 years of age) there was a generation gap, because most of the people who would then have been about 30 had been killed during the war or in the Warsaw uprising. Accordingly, when assembling the scientific staff, we simply took people who were in their first year of university studies. We were their teachers in the University and their bosses in the Institute. It was not usual that they were starting their scientific career so early, but there was no other choice. We were so anxious to begin our work that we had to expose our young colleagues to a not quite correct order of education.

It should be added that these people did overcome successfully these disadvantages and became highly competent scientific workers. Most of them have remained in the Institute and are working in it at present. After a short time a few previous workers of the Institute joined us, and this group came to constitute the core of its staff.

Returning now to my own history, it ran as follows: After I returned from Russia in 1945, my idea of writing a book that would present the whole field of conditioned reflexes "translated" into the language of modern neurophysiology grew completely ripe. Since in early 1946 there was still not very much to do in the Institute—the work began only in 1947—I decided to devote my time mainly to writing the book. During my stay in Moscow I had spent all my days in the Lenin Library, where I studied all the experimental works on conditioned reflexes. Having these materials now at hand and having my ideas completely ripe, there was no great difficulty for me in organizing them, and in less than one year the Polish manuscript of the book was ready. I entered into correspondence with Dr. Waddington in England, who was editor of the Cambridge Biological Series, and explained the project to him. He readily accepted it and proposed that I find a competent translator in England with whom I would cooperate. I received from our Ministry of Education a modest fund to go to England, my travel expenses having been covered by the British Council. So in the early summer of 1946 I went to London, where I met a great number of my old friends, among them my elder brother, who had emigrated from Poland in 1939. He helped me considerably in my accommodation, and I was very lucky to find an excellent translator, Mr. Stephen Garry.

Since Mr. Garry was not a specialist in the field concerned, all of the technical translation rested with me, while his duty was to shape the sentences and phrases properly. Accordingly I spend most of my time in the libraries to learn technical English expressions from the books on conditioned reflexes. During that time I became so thoroughly acquainted with the terminology and idioms used in this field that since then I have been able to write all my publications directly in English, perhaps not quite correctly, but without special difficulty.

After four months of hard work, the translation was completed and submitted to Dr. Waddington. It appeared that it was indeed quite good, and only a few corrections were made by scientists who kindly read the typescript.

The book was published in 1948 by the Cambridge University Press. Its title was *Conditioned Reflexes and Neuron Organization* (Konorski, 1948). Its reviews were generally favorable, although living in Poland and having no relations with Western scientists I had no feedback about how it was accepted. My feeling was that while in England the book became quite popular and well known, in America it passed almost unnoticed, judging from the very sparse references to it in papers and monographs concerned with the problems of conditioning. My explanation of this fact is that at that time (1948) experimental psychology was strongly Skinnerian or Hullian, and physiological explanations of the mechanisms of conditioned reflexes were utterly unpopular. I suspect that either people did not read the book at all, not being attracted by its title, which to me seemed highly attractive, or else, if they had it in their hand, they rejected it.

Quite different was the attitude toward my book in Soviet Russia. After a big conference in Moscow in 1949, at which were present all of Russia's prominent scientists engaged in research on higher nervous activity, Pavlov's concepts were announced to be obligatory, and no deviations from them were to be tolerated. As a result, a number of first-class scientists, such as Orbeli, Beritoff, and Anochin, were denounced as revisionists and strongly criticized. Therefore it was no wonder that when my book became known in Russia it also drew bitter criticism and disapproval, which considerably reflected on my position in my own country. In spite of the difficult situation for our laboratory produced by this circumstance, our research work developed normally and we did not yield to any demands we were asked to fulfill.

While we were in Łódź there were a dozen scientific workers in our laboratory who began as undergraduates and only after several years received their degrees. During that time my chief aim was to perform experimental studies directly related to the hypotheses put forward in my book. The other objective was to resume the work on type II conditioned reflexes which was interrupted during the War.

Perhaps the most important accomplishment in the former field of investigation was a radical change of my views on internal inhibition, caused by completely unexpected results of our experiments (Konorski and Szwejkowska, 1950, 1956). The concept, put forward in my monograph of 1948, asserted that internal inhibition arising in the course of extinction of differentiation of conditioned reflexes was a synaptic process, and that inhibitory conditioned reflexes are due to the inhibitory synapses being formed between the center of the conditioned stimulus and the center of the unconditioned stimulus. These inhibitory synapses were supposed to grow side by side with excitatory synapses, so the inhibitory reflex was considered to be in essence an excitatory-inhibitory reflex, because the connections between the two centers were considered to be both excitatory and inhibitory. It was further assumed that inhibitory connections develop because of the prior existence of excitatory connections; accordingly, the strength of the inhibitory conditioned reflex was thought to be positively correlated with the strength of the excitatory reflex from which it was formed. However, to my great amazement, the results of our new experiments were just the reverse: it turned out that the stronger was the original excitatory reflex to a given conditioned stimulus, the weaker was the inhibitory reflex produced by that stimulus when it was not reinforced. In other words, the inhibitory connections were not enhanced, but prevented, from growing, when the excitatory connections were already there. Conversely, the strongest inhibitory conditioned reflex as judged by the difficulty of its transformation to the excitatory reflex, was established when a given stimulus from the very beginning of its presentation was not reinforced by the unconditioned stimulus. Of course, this finding compelled me to change radically my view on internal inhibition.

The second line of research, no less important than the first, was the study of the mechanism of instrumental (type II) conditioning. The first achievement in this study was the new paradigm of this conditioning proposed by Wyrwicka (1952). On the basis of her experiments she came to the conclusion that there are double connections linking the "center" of the conditioned stimulus with the "center" of the instrumental motor act. On the one hand, there are indirect connections running through the center of the unconditioned stimulus—in the case of alimentary conditioning, through the food center. On the other hand, there are direct connections linking the two centers. Both kinds of connections must work together in order that the instrumental conditioned reflex be produced. It has been shown that many experimental facts from the field of instrumental conditioning can be explained well by reference to this model.

In this period a new field of investigation was also opened up in our laboratory. I felt very strongly that we should broaden our research work by studying the functional organization of the cerebral cortex, using ablation techniques on animals trained in various types of conditioning. Unfortunately, I had never had the opportunity to learn neurosurgery. But again we were lucky, because a prominent Polish neurosurgeon, Dr. Lucjan Stępień, became strongly interested in our scientific work, and joined us. As a matter of fact, he taught brain surgery to the entire group, and he raised this important technique to a high level of performance in our laboratory.

The first study performed in this field was concerned with ablations of the prefrontal area of the cortex. The main reason for entering on this problem proved to be quite erroneous. I was disappointed by the fact that our dogs were too "clever" and would not behave like conditioned reflex machines, responding automatically to our stimuli, in a regular and predictable manner. On the contrary, quite often they reacted inappropriately or not at all to a given conditioned stimulus, according to its actual significance. Instead they responded to more sophisticated cues, based on the whole stereotype of the conditioned reflex sessions, which enabled them to determine whether the next stimulus would be positive or negative. Therefore, I thought that the prefrontal area might just be responsible for this higher order of behavior and that, when we removed this area, the animal would become a conditioned reflex automaton similar to the spinal reflex automaton obtained after decerebration in Sherringtonian experiments.

This hypothesis was not confirmed; instead, we discovered the important fact that after prefrontal lesions, the inhibitory conditioned reflexes are strongly disinhibited while the excitatory reflexes remain unchanged. This finding was afterward examined in great detail and many experimental studies were performed to elucidate the mechanism of this phenomenon (Brutkowski et al., 1956).

Another project developed during this period was concerned with the role of the motor area in instrumental responding. The working hypothesis was that this area was a "site" of instrumental responses and that after its ablation these responses should be abolished.

This prediction again appeared to be wrong, because although the instrumental responses *were* usually impaired, or even absent after the operation, they were always recovered after some period of time without any additional training. Since we thought that this spontaneous recovery was due to the small extent of the lesions. We performed several operations on one subject in succession. All these operations, in general, did impair to a greater or lesser degree the *performance* of the movement, but failed to abolish the movement as a behavioral act. In plain language, the animal *knew* what he had to do, in spite of the fact that the execution of the movement was deficient (Stępień et al., 1961).

In this period I also became interested in the effects of lesions of the cerebral cortex in humans. Here the cooperation with Professor Stępień appeared to be extraordinarily fruitful. We became particularly interested in the problem of aphasia and we made an attempt to establish a classification of speech disorders on the basis of localization of lesions in the cerebral cortex. This work was further developed and extended after we moved back to Warsaw.

SECOND POSTWAR PERIOD (1956-1970): BACK IN WARSAW

There are at least two reasons why I can divide my postwar life into two distinct periods, with the demarcation point being 1955. First, 1955 was the year in which, two years after Stalin's death, the "thaw" began, when Khrushchev came into power in the USSR and dissociated himself sharply from the Stalinist period, denouncing it somewhat euphemistically as "the cult of personality." This was immediately reflected in all fields of cultural life in the USSR and even more so in Poland. In my own field the pseudo-Pavlovian indoctrination vanished completely, and I stopped being a revisionist and a servant of capitalism. On the contrary, I became even more popular than before, because my earlier protagonists were now able to openly take my side, whereas my antagonists were simply ashamed of their previous conduct and tried to apologize. The sign of this radical change of attitude came when Professor Dembowski, the President of the Polish Academy of Sciences, charged me with the task of organizing a symposium on brain and behavior, of which I was to be the main speaker. A big lecture hall at the Palace of Culture was fully attended by an audience which greeted me with an enthusiastic ovation. I was elected a member of the Polish Academy of Sciences, an honor which had been refused me, ostensibly as "punishment" for my sin.

By the way, the change which occurred then turned out to be permanent; we were no longer taught and instructed by incompetent persons as to what was and what was not correct in our thinking, and the atmosphere in science became quite normal. Whereas in the Stalinist period we were completely cut off from Western scientists, this barrier was now removed.

The second big change which occurred in 1955 lay in the fact that in that year our Institute was transferred from Łodź to Warsaw, where a new special building had been erected. After the war the Institute was established in Łodź because the prewar building had been destroyed by Nazis, but the appropriateness of moving back to Warsaw seemed self-evident to all of us. The decision of the government to this effect was certainly due to the fact that our Director, Professor Dembowski, played an important role in the organization of science in

Poland after the war and was first President of the Polish Academy of Sciences. Besides this, the high scientific reputation of the Institute and its long-time existence was an important factor facilitating this decision at the time, when a strong tendency to restore the past and revert to old traditions was predominant in all fields of culture, except, of course, politics.

Although it was because of Dembowski that the Institute was moved back to Warsaw, the main burden of making detailed plans for the transfer fell again to the Niemierkos, my wife, and myself. The difficulty of the job was that the type of building best suited to our needs was relatively new in postwar Warsaw and the engineers were completely incompetent to design and construct it properly. Moreover, since the work on erecting the Institute had begun during the Stalinist period, and we were not allowed to go abroad to see how such edifices were built we had to rely on our own rather meager and obsolete experience.

Generally speaking, the Institute was in many respects first class. Among other things, my Department possessed ten soundproof chambers for the experiments on conditioning in dogs, operation rooms for neurosurgery (planned by Professor Stępień), and a large animal house for animals subjected to recurrent experiments. I consider all these details to be a part of my autobiography, because truly every detail was planned or accepted by me. I can boast that the Department of Neurophysiology, with all its virtues and defects, is my own child.

Another important event, both for me and for our Department, was that very soon I was sent forth by the Polish Academy of Sciences to visit the United States for several months to become acquainted with scientific centers concerned with brain research. My visit came into being at the end of 1957 and was successful owing to one man, to whom I will remain grateful all my life. This man was Robert (Bob) Livingston. I don't remember how I got in touch with him, but I do remember that he sponsored my visit and organized it in an excellent way. He was at that time Director of Basic Research on Neurological Sciences and Psychiatry, National Institutes of Health, and the headquarters for arranging my visit were in Bethesda. He had planned all my itinerary, choosing those places which he thought would be particularly interesting for me. Since I had given him a list of the titles of ten lectures concerning our work in the Department, one or a few lectures were scheduled in each place I was to visit.

I left Warsaw in December 1957 and remained in America for three months. First, I visited Bethesda and explored all the laboratories I was interested in. Thereafter, I made a great tour around the United States, visiting all the important centers concerned with physiological psychology. I visited both the east coast (Bethesda, New York, New Haven) and the west coast (Los Angeles, Stanford, Berkeley), as well as Middle America (Ann Arbor, Bloomington, Chicago, Madison, Rochester, Urbana).

Although from that time on I was a very frequent visitor in America, I do remember most clearly my impressions from that initial visit.

My first impression was that of a most efficient organization of my trip and the great hospitality of my hosts. In each place I had a host who met me at the airport and took care of me during the period of my stay. As a matter of fact, I was the first scientist concerned with brain research to visit this country from Poland after the war, and probably the first from Eastern Europe, because during the previous era this had been practically impossible. Perhaps this was the cause of the curiosity which I aroused wherever I went. But everywhere I encountered a most friendly reception.

Second, to my great amazement and pleasure I learned that I was not unknown in the United States. Since so far almost all my papers had been published in Polish or Russian (except my monograph of 1948), I thought that people would not even have heard of my existence. Sometimes it was true, but not often.

Third, what I had expected was that most people whom I had to meet would be Skinnerian, and that consequently I would not find a common scientific language with them. I expected that people would argue bitterly with me and would not acknowledge the physiological approach to behavioral phenomena, the approach I represented. This again was not true. I had not realized what a great change had occurred in America in the preceding years and how much my approach was welcome. It was quite clear that a new era had already begun in America, an era of increasingly close cooperation between brain physiology and behavioral sciences. Consequently, instead of finding scientific adversaries and antagonists, I found in almost every place I visited scientific friends.

This being so, it was not surprising that my visits in various places immediately led to establishing close friendly relations with the people I met, at first scientific and then also personal. These relations turned out to be long-lasting, since they have remained up to the present time and have become even closer.

I was also happy to learn that in spite of the great distance between America and Poland, and the lack of direct relations, I was quite well acquainted with new American achievements: wherever I went, I had known in advance the research that was going on. This was due to the fact that we had established an excellent library in the Nencki Institute, and had all the important journals in the field.

This first visit of mine to America had very great significance for the further development of our scientific work and its relation to the work going on in the United States. Owing to my connections with American scientists, almost every member of our laboratory was able to visit the United States for one or two years, which gave him (or her) the opportunity to become acquainted directly with the American investigations; this significantly enlarged their scientific horizons. Consequently, our work became much better known by American scientists than it was before.

If the exchange of scientific information can be regarded as some sort of "intellectual market" in which the intellectual goods representing the results of research are sold and purchased, our laboratory—to my great satisfaction—was included in this market, and thus the long period of isolation came to an end.

Of course, the new political period, which began in 1956 and was characterized by the end of the Cold War, enabled the establishment of scientific relations not only with the United States but also with most countries of Western Europe.

There was also great improvement in the relations between our group and the scientists of the Eastern countries. In the previous period, these relations had been practically nonexistent, because of their boycott of me, which extended to my whole laboratory. Truly, the boycott was rather advantageous for me, because I could avoid pseudo-scientific discussions, which were characteristic for that period and had a rather negative effect on the development of the younger generation.

Now the attitude of Soviet scientists toward me changed almost overnight. They became friendly and began to invite an improvement in our relations, feeling that bygones should be bygones.

As a result of this change of atmosphere, three laboratories dealing with the physiology of the central nervous system—the Institute of Higher Nervous Activity and Neurophysiology of the Soviet Academy of Sciences, headed by Professor Asratian; the Institut of Physiology of the Czechoslovak Academy of Sciences, represented by Dr. Gutmann, and our laboratory—decided to arrange a common symposium, which was held in Poland in 1959.

This symposium was a great success, both scientifically and socially. We learned that there are in these other two institutes very nice and valuable workers in science. Friendship between the laboratories became stable, and we arranged similar symposia thereafter every three or four years.

Returning to our relations with America, the closest bonds were established between our laboratory and the Section on Neuropsychology of NIMH headed by Dr. H. E. Rosvold. At that time a very wise idea was proposed that the Polish debts to America, which were to be paid in zlotys, should be utilized for scientific purposes. This was done in such a way that certain Polish scientific projects in which American science was interested could be supported from these funds, according to Public Law 480. In 1962 we signed an agreement with the Section on Neuropsychology of NIMH. It was extremely valuable for us for financial reasons, and also led to very close contacts, both scientific and personal, between the scientists of the two groups. This agreement is in operation now and its range has even been enlarged.

The reason I say so much about the life of our laboratory is that all these things are a part of my autobiography and inseparable from it.

Owing to my frequent visits to the United States and to the visits to Warsaw, of many American students of brain research, I became increasingly popular in the United States. People realized that we (Stefan Miller and myself) were the first investigators to introduce instrumental responses into conditioning experiments. Perhaps this is the main reason why in 1965 I was elected foreign associate of the National Academy of Sciences. Of course, from an objective point of view, it does not matter at all who has made a given discovery; still it does matter to the person who made it. Although for a scientist the esteem and recognition of his colleagues do not play a decisive role in his endeavors, nevertheless they cannot be ignored. Accordingly, if somebody makes a discovery which he considers important but which is overlooked by other specialists, he feels frustrated. But he is even more unhappy if *he* was the first who did it, yet the discovery is ascribed to someone else. I think that these feelings are deeply rooted in all of us, and I would be astonished to find anyone lacking them. When Stefan Miller and I discovered that our conditioned reflexes of the second type were different phenomena from Pavlovian conditioned reflexes, we fully realized that this was an important discovery and clearly saw the vast perspectives which were opened up by the introduction of these phenomena into conditioned reflex studies. Since we were not in the center of the scientific market but on its periphery, and since we had published only a few papers in the prewar period in French or English, we considered it quite natural that we were unknown. Then the war broke out and our original work would have been even more forgotten. The fact that it was not, and that my monograph *Conditioned Reflexes and Neuron Organization* did find appreciation among American scientists, gave me great satisfaction. The only regret was that Stefan Miller died prematurely and did not live to see this appreciation.

Since the transfer of our Institute from Łodź to Warsaw, our scientific facilities have grown immensely. As I said above, there are in the new building in Warsaw excellent soundproof conditioned reflex chambers, the dogs are kept under excellent conditions, and the surgery is on a high level. The prewar journal of the Nencki Institute, *Acta Biologiae Experimentalis,* was taken over by our Department and has been devoted to studies on the brain and behavior. The journal is published in English and its title is now *Acta Neurobiologiae Experimentalis,* to define the scope of the problems with which it is concerned.

The scope of research dealt with in our department has been considerably extended in comparison with the preceding period. I shall present here briefly only those lines of research in which I was directly involved and which have contributed to the further development of my own ideas.

In the studies concerning the mechanisms of instrumental conditioning, the important discovery was made by Górska and Jankowska (1961) to the effect that deafferentation of the limb involved in a previously trained response does not abolish that response; this means that the proprioceptive feedback of the limb performing a given acquired movement is not indispensable for the execution of that movement. This result clearly contradicts the theory of type II conditioning, originally advanced by Miller and myself, according to which this type of conditioning if fully dependent on the proprioceptive feedback.

Another important result was obtained by Tarnecki (1962), who has shown that a movement of the hind leg elicited by stimulation of the motor cortex, followed by food reinforcement, cannot be transformed into an instrumental response, whereas a movement elicited by the sensory cortex can. The analysis of this fact, together with some other data, has led to the conclusion that only movements elicited by the afferent input (including stimulation of the sensory cortex) can be instrumentally conditioned.

Finally, the experiments of Ellison and Konorski (1965) have shown that the alimentary instrumental response (or rather its kinesthesis) does not necessarily elicit the salivary response as was postulated by our original theory of instrumental conditioning.

These facts have considerably clarified my ideas concerning the mechanisms of instrumental responding. Another group of findings helped me to better understand the organization of central mechanisms of conditioned reflexes in general. Here belong the results of the experiments on the hypothalamus and the amygdala performed by Wyrwicka (Wyrwicka et al., 1960) and Fonberg (1967, 1969), which allowed me to distinguish two parallel systems determining the animal's behavior: the thalamo-cortical system on the one hand and the hypothalamo-amygdalar system on the other.

All these facts—combined with the most daring idea advanced by Sołtysik, claiming that consummatory food conditioned responses (mediated by the thalamo-cortical system) inhibit instrumental responses produced by the hunger drive and mediated by the hypothalamo-amygdalar system—led to a new view of the mechanisms of conditioning. This view is much different both from my previous concepts and from the concepts advanced by other investigators.

The other line of inquiry begun in the preceding period, namely the study of the functional organization of various regions of the cerebral cortex, also gained new impetus. The most important task consisted in the analysis of the effects of partial prefrontal lesions upon animal behavior. It was found that disinhibition of negative conditioned reflexes and impairment of delayed responses (which was studied in our laboratory in great detail by Ławicka on dogs and cats) depend on different prefrontal areas (Brutkowski and Dąbrowska, 1966; Ławicka et al., 1966).

To conclude this very short report on the development of some of our investigations over the last fifteen years, I should mention the continuation of our studies on the effects of focal cerebral lesions on the behavior of patients, undertaken with Professor Lucjan Stępień and his group in the neurosurgical hospital. We concentrated on the problem of speech disorders and came to definite conclusions concerning the pathophysiology of various forms of aphasia. The reader interested in this problem should consult my recent paper on this subject (Konorski, 1970).

From all these bits of evidence a coherent picture of integrative cerebral activity began to crystallize, a picture which allowed me to understand a great number of data both in the field of behavioral studies of animals and in the field of human psychology. The principle cementing this knowledge and providing the foundation for the architecture of cortical activity was deduced or rather extrapolated, from the important discoveries made in recent years in the physiology of perceptual processes. Here belong in the first place the studies of Hubel and Wiesel concerning visual perception. According to these studies, visual stimulus patterns are represented in the cerebral cortex, not by complex assemblies of neurons, as postulated earlier by Hebb, but by individual neurons which react selectively to a given pattern. This selectivity is achieved by the principle of convergence, by which the elements of the given pattern are addressed to a given neuron, and lateral inhibition, by which the foreign elements of the pattern are filtered out. One step from these findings leads to the hypothesis that all "unitary perceptions" of the natural stimulus objects of various modalities (known visual objects, sounds, smells, etc.) are represented by separate units in the "associative" or "gnostic" cortical fields. In this way we obtain a general model for perceptual processes, while the interconnections between the units of various gnostic fields provide a basis for associations between various experiences.

After having arrived at all these ideas I felt that it would be reasonable to present them systematically in a special monograph. The decision whether to undertake this task or not was far from easy. On the one hand, I had a strong temptation to do so, according to a general shortcoming of human nature, so well expressed by Bernard Shaw, who said: "When a man has anything to tell in this world, the difficulty is not to make him tell it, but to prevent him from telling it too often" (Caesar and Cleopatra). On the other hand, since I was already over sixty, I was simply afraid I might not be able to fulfill such a difficult task, requiring a tremendous mental effort, a good memory (which was clearly deteriorating in me), and great powers of concentration. The decision was made even more difficult by taking into account my numerous duties, both scientific and administrative, connected with the running of the Nencki Institute and my own laboratory.

In the midst of these hesitations I received unexpectedly a letter from the University of Chicago Press asking me whether I had in mind writing a monograph in my field, and if so, proposing they publish it. How they came to this idea I do not know, but it was a strong catalyzer facilitating my positive decision. In the summer of 1963 during the International Congress of Psychology in Washington, I met Mr. Richter, the assistant director of the University of Chicago Press, and after a thorough discussion the matter was settled.

I worked on this book for three and a half years, having many ups and downs, many moments when I was elated and full of enthusiasm, and other moments when I was completely broken and strongly blamed myself for having decided to undertake this job. Certainly, the work *was* too difficult for me, and there were periods when I was completely exhausted. The difficulty was even greater because the book was written directly in English, and time and again the proper formulation of my ideas presented great difficulties. But I clearly realized that writing in Polish and then translating into English would be even more difficult and unsatisfactory, because of the great differences in the idioms of these two languages.

Finally, in the summer of 1966, the book was completed, and the typescript was submitted to the Press. In about one year the book was published (Konorski, 1967).

Contrary to my expectations the reaction to the book was rather poor. I had a feeling that many of my friends and colleagues simply disliked it, or had not read it, or even did not know about it, because its advertising was inadequate. I had an impression that with a few manifest exceptions, the book was received coldly or even in an unfriendly way.

What I think about the book now is this. I consider, just as I considered when I was writing it, that the book is good and important. Some of my hypotheses have proved to be either inadequate or wrong, but this shows that they were good starting points for further experimentation. This was, for instance, the fate of my hypothesis concerning the mechanism of the cerebellar function as presented in the book. Starting from this hypothesis I began with Tarnecki experiments on the cerebellum which showed that my previous concept was wrong, but these experiments did lead us to a solution of the problem which seems to be correct (see Konorski and Tarnecki, 1970). On the other hand, other hypotheses which were quite daring when I proposed them seem now to be confirmed. This would apply to my idea on the gnostic units (Charles Gross, personal communication), or my idea about two types of units in the lateral hypothalamus responsible for hunger and the taste of food, respectively (Gallistel et al., 1969).

The great drawback of the book is that it is too concise, since within one volume I have condensed material which should be presented in two separate volumes. This makes the book difficult and requires very attentive reading and rereading. I was also told by my colleagues that some paragraphs are not sufficiently clear.

I am very curious to know what will be the final fate of the book: will it eventually win general recognition, which I think it deserves in spite of its shortcomings, or will it have no important impact on the further development of behavioral sciences. I am rather afraid that the latter fate may prevail because the investigations concerning the mechanisms of conditioning are still in the hands of experimental psychologists, who simply do not care about the physiological interpretation of the phenomena of animal behavior and have quite different frames of reference from those applied in my book.

I am now approaching the end of my scientific biography. You have seen that it began almost fifty years ago, when I first asked myself the question: How does the brain work? The question was general, because my knowledge was nil, but it was not naive, because I knew very well what I had in mind.

At first I was completely in the dark, because I failed to come across those sources in which this question had already been coped with. The first beam of light came to me from Pavlov's work, which stimulated me to begin studies on this subject myself, in close cooperation with Stefan Miller. We thought at that time that by specifying and defining *all types* of conditioned reflexes, the answer to our question would be found. That is why we called the conditioned reflexes we studied type II, hoping that afterward we should discover conditioned reflexes type III, type IV, and so on.

When through Lubińska I came across the Sherringtonian physiology of the nervous system based on Ramon y Cajal's notion of its anatomical organization, it was possible to project the studies on conditioned reflexes upon the actual network of the brain. I accomplished this task by writing my earlier monograph (Konorski, 1948). Thereafter came twenty-five years of investigation in our postwar laboratory, during which time the scope of our work grew immensely, and I became acquainted with the effects of cerebral lesions not only in animals but also in men. This allowed me to make a new step forward in understanding the functions of the brain, since I was able to broaden the foundations of my ideas by including perceptions, associations, skilled movements, behavioral acts, and drives. In consequence, I was able to present a new synthesis of the integrative activity of the brain (Konorski, 1967) based on new facts and new concepts. Since, in my experience, the full cycle of renewal of my scientific ideas requires about two decades, this is probably the last version of my thoughts about the functioning of the brain. Therefore, my scientific biography seems really to have come to an end.

REFERENCES

Selected Publications by Jerzy Konorski

[On the variability of the motor conditioned responses. The principles of cortical switching.] *Przegl. Fizjol. Ruchu,* 1939, *9,* 1-51.
Conditioned Reflexes and Neuron Organization. London: Cambridge Univ. Press, 1948.
Integrative Activity of the Brain. Chicago: Univ. Chicago Press, 1967.
Pathophysiological mechanisms of speech on the basis of studies on aphasia. *Acta Neurobiol. Exp.,* 1970, *30,* 189-210.
(with S. Miller) L'influence des excitateurs absolus et conditionnels sur les salivomotrices. *C. R. Séanc. Soc. Biol.,* 1930(b), *104,* 907-910.
(with S. Miller. L'influenc des excitateurs absolus et conditionnels sur les réflexes conditionnels de l'analysateur moteur. *C. R. Séanc. Soc. Biol.,* 1930(a), *104,* 911-914.
(with S. Miller) *The foundations of physiological theory of acquired movements, motor conditioned reflexes* (in Polish). Warsaw, 1933.
(with S. Miller) [Conditioned reflexes of the motor analyzer] *Tr. Fiziol. Lab. I. P. Pavlova,* 1936, No. 1, 119-278 (in Russian).
(with S. Miller) Further remarks on two types of conditioned reflexes. *J. Gen. Psychol.,* 1937(a), *17,* 405.
(with S. Miller) On two types of conditioned reflexes. *J. Gen. Psychol.,* 1937(b) *16,* 264-272.
(with G. Szwejkowska) Chronic extinction and restoration of conditioned reflexes I. Extinction against the excitatory background. *Acta Biol. Exp. (Warsaw),* 1950, *15,* 155-170.

(with G. Szwejkowska) Chronic extinction and restoration of conditioned reflexes II. The dependence of the course of extinction and restoration of conditioned reflexes on the "history" of the conditioned stimulus (the principle of the primacy of the first training). *Acta Biol. Exp. (Warsaw)*, 1956, *16*, 95-113.

(with R. Tarnecki) Purkinje cells in the cerebellum: Their responses to postural stimuli in cats. *Proc. Nat. Acad. Sci.*, 1970, *65*, 892-897.

Other Publications Cited

Brutkowski, S., and J. Dąbrowska. Prefrontal cortex control of differentiation behavior in dogs. *Acta Biol. Exp. (Warsaw)*, 1966, *26*, 425-439.

Brutkowski, S., J. Konorski, W. Ławicka. and L. Stępień. The effect of removal of frontal lobes of the cerebral cortex on motor conditioned reflexes. *Acta Biol. Exp. (Warsaw)*, 1956, *17*, 167-188.

Ellison, G., and J. Konorski. An investigation of the relations between salivary and motor responses during instrumental performance. *Acta Biol. Exp. (Warsaw)*, 1965, *25*, 297-315.

Fonberg, E. The motivational role of the hypothalamus in animal behavior. *Acta. Biol. Exp. (Warsaw)*, 1967, *27*, 303-318.

Fonberg, E. The role of the amygdaloid nucleus in animal behavior. *Progr. Brain Res.*, 1969, *22*, 273-281.

Gallistel, C. R., E. Rolls, and D. Greene. Neuron function inferred from behavioral and electrophysiological estimates of refractory period. *Science*, 1969, *166*, 1028-1030.

Górska, T., and E. Jankowska. The effect of deafferentation on instrumental (type II) conditioned reflexes in dogs. *Acta Biol. Exp. (Warsaw)*, 1961, *21*, 219-234.

Ławicka, W., M. Mishkin, J. Kreiner, and S. Brutkowski. Delayed response deficit in dogs after selective ablation of proreal gyrus. *Acta Biol. Exp. (Warsaw)*, 1966, *26*, 309-322.

Miller, S., and J. Konorski. Le phénomène de la généralisation motrice. *C. R. Séanc. Soc. Biol.*, 1928(a), *99*, 1158.

Miller, S., and J. Konorski. Sur une forme particullière des réflexes conditionnels. *C. R. Séanc. Soc. Biol.*, 1928(b), *99*, 1155-1158. (There is an English translation).

Pavlov, I. R. [Twenty years of the objective studies of higher nervous activity behavior of animals] (in Russian), 3rd ed., 1925. (There is an English translation).

Pavlov, I. P. [Lectures on the function of the cerebral hemispheres] (in Russian), 1926. (There is an English translation).

Petrażycki, I. [*Introduction into the studies on law and morals*. The foundation of emotional psychology] in Russian, 1908; in Polish, Warsaw: PWN, 1959.

Skinner, B. F. Two types of conditioned reflex and a pseudo-type. *J. Gen. Psychol.*, 1935, *12*, 66-77.

Skinner, B. F. Two types of conditioned reflex: A reply to Konorski and Miller. *J. Gen. Psychol.*, 1937, *16*, 264-272.

Stępień, I., L. Stępień, and J. Konorski. The effects of unilateral and bilateral ablations of sensori-motor cortex on the instrumental (type II) alimentary conditioned reflexes in dogs. *Acta Biol. Exp. (Warsaw)*, 1961, *21*, 121-140.

Tarnecki, R. The formation of instrumental conditioned reflexes by direct stimulation of sensory-motor cortex in cats. *Acta Biol. Exp. (Warsaw)*, 1962, *22*, 114-124.

Wyrwicka, W. Studies on motor conditioned reflexes. V. On the mechanism of the motor conditioned reaction. *Acta Biol. Exp. (Warsaw)*, 1952, *18*, 175-193.

Wyrwicka, W., C. Dobrzecka, and R. Tarnecki. The effect of electrical stimulations of the hypothalamic feeding center in satiated goats on alimentary conditioned reflexes type II. *Acta Biol. Exp. (Warsaw)*, 1960, *20*, 121-136.

David Krech

David Krech

I have been, in my time, a prelaw student; psychologist; editor of a neo-Marxist four-page biweekly newspaper; political "functionary" of New America (an "Indigenous American Revolutionary Force"); Chief Economic Analyst in the U.S. Department of Agriculture; M/Sgt., A.U.S.; and now, I write this biographical essay as psychologist again. As psychologist I have worked on animal learning, effects of brain lesions on memory and learning, brain chemistry and behavior, social psychological theory, self-perceptions of the American poor, and the attitudes of the war-bombed in Germany and Japan. Nor have I been constant in my psychological faiths. I have professed Watsonian Uncompromising Behaviorism, Tolmanian Purposive Behaviorism, Crypto-Gestaltism, Cognitive Psychology, and Reductionism (of sorts).

What I have believed and said and done as psychologist have been peculiarly susceptible to the scientific and social winds which have blown every which way during my life. To trace in any conprehensible manner the development of my psychological notions, I must interlard the telling of that tale with discussions of anti-Semitism in academia, the Great Depression of the 1930s, my expulsion from American university life for political reasons, World War II, and that slum of a decade, the 1960s.

FAMILY

According to the only documentary evidence available (my father's notation on the flyleaf of Yitzhok-Eizik Haver's *The Foundations of the World,* a treatise written by my mother's great grandfather, and whose namesake I was to become, I was born on the fifth day of the month of Nissan, in the year 5669 (March 27, 1909) in Swiencianke, a small *shtetl* "three stations distance from Wilno" on the border between what are now the Byelorrussian and Lithuanian states of the Soviet Union. I was the eighth child in a family of nine children, of whom one did not live to maturity. My memories of the family scene, both in Russia and in America, are those of a full but uncrowded household; of grown-up brothers and sisters (some of whom had already left for homes of their own), and of others who were just the age which older and younger brothers and sisters should be. I recall no problems of sibling rivalry with either brothers or sisters, except trivial and intermittent ones. (This can be read, I suppose, as: Sibling rivalry there was, but so profound and omnipresent as to have been repressed beyond recall.)

While I cannot detect in me any pronounced sibling effect, I find it easy to recognize the influence of my parents. Indeed I fancy that I see in myself a mosaic pattern of parental influences: a number of nonblending, contradictory traits and propensities inherited intact from each of my parents.

My father was the descendant of a long line of successful (small-scale, I would gather) Jewish merchants in White Russia. One of my forebears (whose family name was "Epstein"), to spare his children the brutalizing twenty-year conscription in the Czar's army, forgave "his" Polish nobleman, Krechevsky, a sizable debt on condition that Krechevsky adopt the Epstein sons, since as the legal children of a nobleman they would be exempt from conscription. And thus through terror of conscription and for an outrageous price did we acquire the noble name "Krechevsky."

My grandfather was rich enough to be able to indulge my father's taste for learning and scholarship, and throughout my father's youth and early married life he remained a scholar, living in his father's house and fully supported by him. Later my father took over the management of a turpentine extraction and exporting business inherited from his father, but I have the impression that his business activities were somewhat extracurricular. His major concern was studying the Talmud; and throughout his life, he reserved his highest regard for men of learning. He seemed constitutionally incapable of suffering fools and ignoramuses gladly—especially those in high places.

My father had a definite set of beliefs as to what was dignified and honest in dealing with his fellowman, and he sought forever to live up to these standards. This would often result in lost opportunities to make money, and the patronizing pity of his more successful brothers. When my father gave in and violated his own standards, this would bring on a bitter lashing out against American business (and everything else American), and a retreat to his books.

My father was a proud man, easily given to enduring anger when he perceived insult to his dignity. Within the family he was sentimental and tolerant. His children's lapses from dignity and honesty, their preference for Business over the Book, and their nonchalant attitude toward religion were always forgiven with, I thought, a resigned sadness. For our part, we all took pride in his learning, in his honesty, and even in his pride. We all respected him greatly and loved him deeply.

My mother (Sarah Rabinowitz) was of "royal family," a daughter of a long line of rabbis and Talmudic scholars. Her great grandfather was but the most recent luminary of a line which could be traced back to the Gaon Reb Judah ben Eliezer Mintz (c. 1408-1508) head of the Yeshiva of Padua in Italy.

Like many a child born to the purple, my mother was completely relaxed about the noble virtues. She approved of honesty, learning, piety, and family pride but thought it silly to make a fetish of any of these. Certainly they were not to be permitted to interfere with the health, education, or welfare of her children. And sometimes, when my father's attenuated income threatened to do this, she would berate him for his "exaggerated" honesty and the time spent on his books. This would be followed by tears and day-long headaches. I well remember the many silent oaths I took to become a most wealthy millionaire when I grew up and never, never to be responsible for such pain and bitterness.

My mother was a knowledgeable practitioner of her religion, but she preferred the company of the witty, the clever, and the joyous to the pious. What I remember most about my mother was her laughter, her jokes, her wit, her teasings, and her love of lively music.

It was my mother who yearned for America, the land where children were not snatched away by the Czar's army; the land of opportunity where Jewish students were not subjected to the *numerus clausus* of Russian universities, and where everyone, with perserverance, could do well. And it was my mother who nagged and nagged until my father, quite unwillingly, gave up his life as Talmudic scholar and sometimes businessman, and emigrated to gentile, money-grubbing America. His first emigration did not take. He could not abide this country. But my mother would not let him rest at home (especially since the second son was now approaching conscription age—the eldest boy having already fled to America) and in May 1913, we all emigrated, and this time for good.

We settled in New Britain, Connecticut, where my father's brother had established himself in the wholesale grocery business. My father first worked as a salesman for my uncle, and later became a managing partner of a coal company, and then of a paper supply house.

The New Britain in which I grew up was a middling-sized (population ca. 50,000) New England mill town, dominated by massive, ugly, smoke-blackened factories which manufactured knives and forks and locks and bolts and small tools during peacetime, and during World War I, bayonets "with which to stick the Kaiser." Its working population was mostly Polish, Italian, Irish; its professional life, in the hands of the "Americans"; its merchant enterprises, almost a Jewish monopoly; its school system, controlled by the few remaining resident "Yankees"; and its industry and wealth, almost entirely in absentee ownership. All of this made for an extraordinarily varied group of playmates (I could almost truthfully say that none of my best friends were Jews), and an excellent school system.

EARLY SCHOOLING

I was almost always a good boy in school, was almost always first in grades (at least through junior high school), and very early became a most happy and enthusiastic reader. I also wrote Yiddish and English poetry, an adventure novel ("inspired by" a Clarence Buddington Kelland story in *The American Boy),* and humorous articles for the junior high school magazine.

My scholarly and literary work was duly noted and highly regarded by my family. None of my other brothers or sisters having received an academic schooling, and my parents having remained forever as strangers to the American culture, I soon became the most "educated American" in our family. And thus, from the age of twelve on, by default and by necessity, I took full responsibility for all decisions about my schooling. My father intervened only to send me to Hebrew School, where for six years, five days a week, and for one hour each day I learned to read and write Yiddish and some Hebrew, studied the Old Testament ("in the original"), and picked up a romanticized history of the Jewish people. My father, having a nascent hope that I might yet become a Talmudic scholar, arranged for private lessons with the town's rabbi. After a summer of Talmudic law, I announced that the rigors of my high school work would not permit me to continue. That was the end of my Hebrew education and my father's hopes for a rabbi in his family.

In actual fact, I found my high school work easy, partly because, with none to say me nay, I had begun to choose the easier courses. Finding Latin and French both difficult and dull, I took (and barely passed) the minimum required number of these courses. I liked and did well in English, history, and mathematics.

As graduation day approached I began to think about a college of my own choosing. There were several obvious constraints upon my freedom of choice. I would have to live inexpensively; there would be parental resistance to far-off places; the college would have to be liberal enough to admit an Isadore (my Americanized version of "Yitzhok-Eizik") Krechevsky, since by that time I knew that even in America the Czar's *numerus clausus* held; and, finally, I did want to live in New York City, where one of my best friends had recently moved. On the advice of my friend who suggested that Washington Square College of New York University met all of my specifications, I chose NYU.

On the matter of *why* I was going to college, there was a bit more vacillation. Both my family and I agreed that I was to be a college graduate. That was an end in itself. I also considered two career possibilities. Inspired by Sinclair Lewis's *Arrowsmith,* I thought that a scientist would be a noble thing to be. My major reservation stemmed from my uncertainty whether I could become a *great* scientist. The one science course (physics) I had had in high school, and in which I received an easy "A" was kid stuff, but I suspected that science courses at the University would be "hard," and I had grown wary of difficult courses which required interminable memorizing. My second choice was law. Supreme Court Justice Louis Brandeis was then the hero of almost every American Jewish family, and I thought that being a Supreme Court Justice would not only permit me to do well (I remembered my mother's distress), but also to do good (I had interiorized my father's teachings). In addition, I was certain that I could easily handle the law curriculum, which I vaguely thought of as a combination of Talmudic studies, history, and English composition. I therefore decided that I would enroll in the prelaw curriculum with the view of becoming a Supreme Court Justice.

NYU AND INTRODUCTION TO PSYCHOLOGY

My uncle's $500 college loan paid a semester's tuition and bought my books and supplies. I looked for work. My first job was teaching English to newly arrived immigrants. Over the next four years, I worked as errand boy, "grease monkey" in gasoline stations, busboy in summer resorts, and in other unskilled jobs.

My first two years at Washington Square College reinforced some of the notions with which I came, changed some of my self-evaluations, shattered my illusions about law, and set the stage for psychology.

I found that in college, as at high school, I could do well in history and English. I also found that the nearest thing to a law school course, English Legal and Constitutional History, was indeed a mixture of Talmudic studies and history (I shone in that course). I tried out for and made the Freshman Debating Team. (My father was shocked that we were taught to uphold, with vigor and "sincerity," either side of every issue on our schedule!) But I also had several comeuppances. At high school my forte had been geometry; now I was faced with advanced algebra and calculus, and I did poorly in both. In biology I was overrun by the frenetically competitive premeds in class, and since as a prelaw student I did not "need" biology, I expended just enough energy (although my interest *was* engaged) to earn a respectable grade.

My greatest disillusionment was law. I very quickly, of course, was disabused of my notions that one could become a Supreme Court Justice soon after graduation from Law School. This bothered me little, since I was prepared to wait the requisite number of years, but what troubled me exceedingly was the way those waiting years were to be filled. Very few of the Law School students or young lawyers whom I got to know seemed to be the kind of person I imagined a college graduate to be. Almost none of them was interested in scholarship or in doing good; they appeared to be single-mindedly dedicated to doing well. And most of the ways of doing well seemed either boring, shady, or cynical. By the middle of my sophomore year I had lost all zest for the study or practice of law. But in that same year, as required by the prelaw curriculum, I enrolled in Introductory Psychology and became almost at once enmeshed in it.

Our professor was William Darby Glenn, newly come from Dashiell's laboratory at Chapel Hill. We used Woodworth's text but Glenn found it not quite behavioristic enough and not quite physiological enough. I remember filling several notebooks with lecture material on the anatomy of the nervous system. What sold me on psychology were two wondrous discoveries. Somehow it finally got through to me that Glenn was asserting that through psychology *man himself could be examined objectively and scientifically*. This revolutionary (for me) idea made it a science more noble than all the rest. In the light of this, my second insight was a most welcome and reassuring one: *Psychology was an easy science*. It seemed clear that one did not have to be technically trained, mathematically adept, or stuffed full of memorized details, in order to do the kinds of experiments described in our textbook (Glenn's neural anatomy seemed to have nothing to do with these). I, too, could become a scientist—and without tears.

While these two discoveries predisposed me strongly toward psychology, Glenn's personal influence was the determining factor. He became my companion and friend. Precisely when I needed it most, when I later sought entrance into the then almost entirely gentile world of academia, his encouragement and his faith gave me the necessary reassurance.

Without consulting or even telling my parents, I gave up all thought of Law School and enrolled in all the "scientific" psychology courses I could. I had become a Convinced Behaviorist and was no longer interested in either doing good *or* in doing well; I was only interested in Doing Science. And therefore I avoided almost any course that had to do with people, for after my first course with T. C. Schneirla (where John B. Watson's 1914 *Behavior: An Introduction to Comparative Psychology* was our text) it was clear to me that only through the ant and the rat would we achieve a truly scientific understanding of man.

By my senior year I was completely involved in psychology. I helped organize the undergraduate *Psychological Association;* I read every past and current issue of the *Journal of Comparative Psychology* and many other journals; and held down my first appointment in psychology, laboratory assistant to Schneirla (caring for his rats and army ants). But the two most significant things that happened that year were Frances Holden's decision to become my patron, and my falling ill with the flu.

Ever since my first course in experimental psychology with Frances Holden, I had been a great admirer of hers. At the beginning of my senior year she suggested that if I wished, she would help make it possible for me to do my own animal research. Of course "I wished"! Her help was absolute. She (with a very feeble assist from me) designed and built what later became known as "my" Hypothesis Box. Actually, the box was a Gestaltoid-Lashleyan variant of a discrimination apparatus first described by C. P. Stone in the *Journal of Genetic Psychology* in 1928. In very short order I was running rats in several fanciful test discrimination problems. By the end of the year I was well on my way to becoming a seasoned rat-runner—and I had learned to love it all.

During that winter I fell ill with the flu, was paid a visit by "my girl," who came bearing a sick-bed gift, and I was then and there launched on my "hypotheses-in-rats" phase—a phase which was to last almost ten years. The gift was Lashley's *Brain Mechanisms and Intelligence*, which had just been published (1929). Being in bed with the flu I could do nothing but read, and so I read Lashley most carefully—much more carefully than was (or is) my wont. I read the book so carefully that I found therein a crucial incidental passage, unnoticed by all reviewers, which almost got me out of bed shouting "Eureka!" This was the passage (I have quoted it frequently in my publications) in which Lashley, faced with some divergent findings from his brain-lesion experiments, proposed that all could be understood (post hoc) if one assumed that " . . . in the discrimination box, responses to position, to alternation, or to cues from the experimenters' movements usually precede the reaction to the light and represent attempted solutions." However, Lashley was quick to point out that "there is no present way to record such behavior objectively, and I can present the description only as an impression from the training of several hundred animals in these problems." Well, I also had trained several (not hundreds) animals in discrimination problems, and I experienced a delightful shock of recognition, for now that Lashley had expressed it that way, this was precisely my impression also! But—and this is what made me burn with something more than the flu—I thought I saw a clear and simple way "to record such behavior objectively." And, further, I thought I saw that if my hunch turned out to be correct, my data would necessitate a radical reexamination of some of the most firmly held notions and assumptions of contemporary (1930) learning theory. It was with difficult impatience that I waited out my flu to get to my box, my rats, my data. When I finally did, my hunch turned out to be bountifully correct. My method of analysis and the resulting data were eventually to lead to the opening of the Continuity-Noncontinuity controversy in learning theory (which even now surfaces occasionally), and to bring to me the enthusiastic support of Tolman, the saddened disapproval of Schneirla, the benign approval of Lashley, the vigorous wrath of Spence, and the unforgiving suspicion of all professing Behavorists—Watsonians in their time, then Hullians, and finally Skinnerians.

But all of this was still in the future. At the moment my senior year was drawing to an end, and I was faced with some immediately pressing problems of survival. This was 1930; the Great Depression had just settled in for a long gruesome run; money was scarce and jobs almost nonexistent. I *had* to go to graduate school, but the Graduate Assistantship which I could expect paid only $200 a semester. Frances Holden guessed my problem, and one day Professor P. D. Stout, the Chairman of the Department, called me in to tell me that through Professor Holden a new Departmental stipend of $300 had become available for me. I accepted her gift, and the next year I appeared at NYU as candidate for a Master's degree, Graduate Assistant in Psychology, and the one and only (ever) holder of "the Frances Holden Fellowship in Psychology."

My first year as a graduate student was a most happy one. Much of it was spent stooped over my box running wonderful rat after wonderful rat. I was oblivious to the major revolutionary economic and political forces which were being let loose in the country. I was Doing Science, and, I thought, preparing for a revolution of my own making in learning theory. When I came to the writing up of my research I found, just as I had anticipated, that to accommodate my data comfortably, I had to move over somewhat from the extreme Behaviorist position I had been occupying.

I made my move with what I thought was the right mix of the revolutionary pronouncement and the apt citation suggesting that I was really in the scientific mainstream after all. I first described my "compelling" data, and then announced with something of a flourish that "helter-skelter, trial and error learning is going by the boards." Then, preparing to ascribe to the rat's behavior such dangerously mentalistic attributes as "attention," I first called upon authority, pointing out that N. R. F. Maier "in a recent study concludes that he has isolated errors which 'seem to be due to the attention or lack of attention to the stimulus light'. . . ." Finally, after more justification for my unorthodoxy I summarized and concluded: "The characteristic form of the learning curve obtained in . . . discrimination problems was investigated . . . and it is shown quite definitely that [prior to solution] the animal is engaged in bringing to perfection various attempted solutions. After each 'wrong' solution is discarded in turn, the animal attempts another until he finally hits upon the 'correct' one . . . . Attention plays an important part in animal learning as well as in human learning."

I did not realize it at that time, but I had made my first significant step toward becoming a convert to Tolman's Purposive Behaviorism.

Believing that five years at NYU was enough, I applied for admission and fellowship aid to several other graduate schools and received and accepted an invitation from Berkeley. Its teaching fellowship carried with it more money than did North Carolina's (the only other school to offer me aid); Frances Holden (a summer neighbor of Tolman's) spoke enthusiastically of Tolman and glowingly about Berkeley; and I had never been west of New Jersey and here was my opportunity to travel.

In August 1931 I left for Berkeley with a Master's degree, a copy of my precious thesis, and a small case of alcohol-filled specimen bottles in which I was to embalm California ants to be shipped back to Schneirla. I felt happy and fulfilled. The University and New York had been good places in which to grow up. Not only had I been under the tuition and care of excellent and supportive professors, but I had gotten within knowing distance of some of the other NYU greats, such as Thomas Wolfe and Eda Lou Walton. I had also nibbled a bit at Bohemian life in Greenwich Village (where I had lived for one semester); had become a knowing aficionado of the *New York World* with its FPA, Heywood Broun, Alexander Woolcott, and the other giants; and, by courtesy of the cut-rate ticket counter in Gray's Drug Store, I considered myself a patron of the Broadway theatre. I left New York feeling a full sophisticate, and competent to hold my own at a "foreign" university.

BERKELEY

The campus in Berkeley with its strange eucalyptus and live-oak trees, its massive white buildings, its Campanile and Sather Gate, and its unobstructed view of San Francisco; the Bay and her ferry boats and sea gulls; the Golden Gate (unspanned as yet by a bridge) leading directly to China; and the many browned and still "undeveloped" Berkeley Hills to the east—and all, all illuminated by dazzling sunlight (at least during the first few days of my arrival) was indeed a foreign land to me. I knew I was far away from Swiencianke, New Britain, and New York. Yet, I did not long feel like a stranger in this strange land. Not only was I greeted at the railroad station by Frances Holden, but the very next day I met Edward Tolman and Robert Tryon—and almost immediately I was at home.

I remember well my first meeting with Tolman. He found me wandering in the corridors of the then new Life Sciences Building into which the Department had recently moved. Tolman ushered me into his office and immediately imprinted me on him by asking me to tell him about my Master's research. I told him, but not at length, for I had no sooner given a bare outline of my findings than he caught fire and jumped out of his seat and practically shouted out "Hypotheses in rats!" And from then on we jabbered and talked and plotted experiments. Years later (perhaps twenty or more) when I reminded Tolman of this, he insisted that the word "hypothesis" was my own. I know full well it was his, although I quickly accepted his suggestion and it soon did become my own—but this was not the only time I caught Tolman out in trying to hoodwink his students into believing that they had themselves arrived at ideas which were essentially Tolman's own.

This first session with him serves me as a template for all my memories of Tolman as teacher. He was just completing the final draft of his *Purposive Behavior in Animals and Men,* and his weekly seminars were superb educational *happenings.* The seminar would start in a civil enough manner, with a student's critique of a recent journal article, or with a research report of his own. Before the student had gone very far, however, Tolman would be at it—interrupting with comments, reinterpretations, or excitingly new hypotheses suddenly arrived at. And sometimes he would have to shout to be heard, for after Tolman had started, we would all go to it, spouting and talking and planning new experiments. I took no other courses from Tolman, only his seminar for four consecutive semesters.

Neither did I take any other courses from anyone else at Berkeley except a one-semester statistics course with Tryon. But from Tryon I learned more from talks with him at illicit gin parties (we were in the era of prohibition) and from lab talks than from any formal courses.

I can still recapture my excitement when Tryon first demonstrated to me his selectively bred Bright and Dull rats. The animals which were being tested were placed in cubicles around the circumference of a revolving delivery apparatus, such that descendants of Bright and Dull parents could be delivered into the automatically recording maze in alternate sequence. The animal's progress through the maze was recorded by an electrically triggered stylus which marked up an error on the moving strip of paper whenever the animal entered a cul-de-sac. Tryon was then working on the eighth or ninth generation, and these particular animals had already had several days of training in the maze. "Now watch, Professor" (for Tryon we were all "Professors"), he whispered to me "the next character (for Tryon every animal was either a "kid" or a "character"; it was never a depersonalized "subject") is a Dull. Watch, watch!" And as the apparatus turned and the Dull "character" was admitted to the maze, the electrical stylus soon began to write a record of error after error. The rat finally did reach the end of the maze, entered his goal box, the turntable moved into the next position, and a Bright rat entered—and started to scoot through the maze. Now the stylus remained quiet. This continued for rat after rat: Bright, silence; Dull, chattering stylus.

I could not shake the conceit that I was seeing the very genes themselves writing out the story of each animal's inheritance on the moving paper. I don't think I have ever been as excited before or since by any scientific demonstration. What I was seeing, of course, was one of psychology's classic experiments, *the* experiment which established behavior genetics as an experimental science. And my Behaviorist's faith with its strong environmentalist bias took another blow. After I had had my fill of this heady demonstration, Tryon took me into the adjoining room and we talked. I cannot now recall what he said (the forces of pro-active inhibition were undoubtedly powerful), but this was only the first of many such lab talks. Above all, I learned from him to be alert to the differences between the psychological study of the robustly idiosyncratic individual, and that of the group, that pale abstraction which spawns so many phantom theories in psychology.

Training for a Ph.D. in the Department at Berkeley was indeed an unstructured enterprise. I can remember no course requirements. There were examinations to take, but how you overcame them was your own affair; you could take courses, audit courses, read on your own, or do none of the above and flunk out. Thanks to the excellent training I had had at NYU, I passed my first (and most difficult) set of examinations during my first semester at Berkeley, failing only in Professor George M. Stratton's examination in social psychology—and social psychology, as everyone seemed to realize, was of little consequence.

Tolman's seminar students made up an elite group. Among this company I can remember Egerton L. Ballachey, Jack Buel, Edwin E. Ghiselli, Calvin Hall, James A. Hamilton, Charles Honzik, John Horowitz, and Esther Robinson. We comprised a "nuclear educational group." We not only studied and talked psychology together, but above all we worked together. I have never since seen so much and so promiscuous scientific collaboration in any laboratory. During my two years at Berkeley, I collaborated on three publishable experiments with three different partners (Ballachey, Hamilton, and Honzik) besides a number of pilot (i.e., unsuccessful) experiments. These experiments were formulated jointly, jointly done, and jointly written and rewritten. We did indeed teach each other. Whether as a result of that experience, or whether as a reflection of a strong gregarious (or is it really "dependency"?) character trait, I have been a very active collaborator throughout my subsequent scientific life. Of the approximately 125 articles and books I can list in my scientific bibliography, at least 75 are joint publications, involving over 30 different coauthors, and as of this date I am engaged in four collaborative writing projects. Fortune has been most generous in providing me with compatible partners; only once have I had a falling out with a collaborator.

Early in my second year at Berkeley it became evident that I would be able to take my Ph.D. that year. I had passed most of the examinations and I had already published, or had in press, ten journal articles. (Clearly, I had spent no time in the world outside; I was still an encapsulated, apolitical scientist.) The problem of a doctoral thesis was solved by collecting my various "hypotheses in rats" reprints (six of my ten articles), binding them together, and adding a one-paragraph introduction. Essentially my doctoral work was a replication, elaboration, and systematization of my Master thesis's thesis. Much of this was summarized in *Psychological Review* (1932) and *Journal of Comparative Psychology* (1933) articles.

I began to think about a job, and Tolman began to work on the problem. But the year was 1933, the very depth of the Depression. We did not even get a nibble. Just how many letters he wrote and what the responses were I do not know, except in one instance. A Professor Douglas Fryer of University Heights College of NYU (not to be confused with Washington Square College) had written to Tolman that he needed a man in animal psychology. Tolman had replied, naming three people: Charles Honzik, John Horowitz, and me. Fryer answered with a letter which so upset Tolman that he came raging down the hall to my office and showed it to me. Fryer had written that the only man he could even consider was Charles Honzik, since he was the only non-Jew among the three. Then Fryer went on with something to the effect that it was interesting how the "Children of Israel" yearned to return to New York, the "new Jerusalem." Tolman was absolutely infuriated, both at Fryer's blatant anti-Semitism and the boorishness of the man. For my part, I was terribly saddened and hurt that such ugly things could happen in my beloved psychology, but I was not altogether surprised (I doubt that any Jew is ever genuinely surprised by anti-Semitism). It soon became clear that we had better look elsewhere than the academic job market to place "Isadore Krechevsky."

There was only one place to look, and that was to the National Research Council (NRC), which provided a few postdoctoral fellowships in psychology. I decided that I would "go for broke" and seek my fellowship with Lashley, at Chicago. Lashley was not only the top American experimental psychologist, but I let myself believe that he might even approve of my research. There was another reason. Watson, in his fear of the "mind," had cast out the brain from psychological study because of his suspicion that the brain might harbor the mind. Tolman fought valiantly to return "mind" to learning theory, and happily did I follow his banner, with experiment and with polemic. But when Tolman, accepting (indeed, overaccepting) Watson's other dictum, sought to build a psychology without any reference to physiology, I balked. This violated my conception of psychology as a science among sciences. (This remains true today; I find little merit in the mindless, brainless learning theories of the contemporary neo-Behaviorists.) To become a neurological psychologist, therefore, would be a good thing, and in 1933 everyone who was, hoped to be, or pretended to be anyone in neurological psychology had to do lesion experiments. And how better to learn this art and this science than with Lashley?

I had finished all my work at Berkeley. I was completely without funds, and there was little reason for me to stay on. After getting permission to take my degree *in absentia*, I prepared to leave for New York before even hearing from Washington about the NRC Fellowship. (I had made arrangements with "Major," the Departmental secretary, to have her telegraph me as soon as the answer came from Washington.) Although by any objective assessment my future looked bleak indeed, I could not feel anything but happy, and the world was bright and shiny. I had achieved much, by anyone's reckoning: I was a Ph.D.; I had become well known among experimental psychologists, receiving reprint requests even from abroad; and I was certain that I could achieve more. I had established enduring friendships among my fellow graduate students, some of which are only now being cut off by death. I had found in Tolman a great teacher, a great scientist, and a man to love. His attachment to me ended in 1959 with his death; my attachment to him persists. And much the same was true of Tryon. And, finally, I knew (although she did not) that I had met the girl who was going to be my wife—or at least who *should* be my wife.

Hilda Sidney Gruenberg had come to Berkeley to study psychology during her junior year's leave from Swarthmore College. When I met her and discovered that she was enrolling in Tolman's course I arranged with Major to have Hilda assigned to my section. I soon proposed to her, she turned me down; and that was the beginning of a campaign that lasted until Friday, September 17, 1943, when we were married in Washington, D.C., at which time I was a Corporal, A.U.S. And what can I write, in such a tome as this, of Hildy and me? Let me write only that we have loved each other much, and strengthened each other much, and needed each other much, and cherished each other much.

CHICAGO

I boarded the *Overland Limited* out of Berkeley convinced that not only would I somehow manage to remain in psychology, but that one day I would return to Berkeley as a Professor. Two days out my first conviction was realized. The Pullman conductor came through with Major's telegram: I had been awarded the Fellowship! I was delighted beyond mortal joy. The Fellowship (I knew the terms by heart) was for 12 months and paid $1,620—an eon in time perspective and a fortune in income for a 24-year-old who just a very little moment ago had nothing at all. I was going to be in Lashley's laboratory. I had broken the anti-Semitic barriers and was an accepted, established, and well-paid scientist. (I was not again to earn as much as that, or be appointed to as acceptable a position as that in psychology until 1945—twelve very long years later.)

When the *Overland Limited* reached Chicago, I took a several-hour layover before continuing east. I wanted to see "my" new laboratory, meet Lashley, and announce the good news to him(!). I knew that Lashley's laboratory was in Culver Hall, and when I found it I was directed to the third floor. It was a hot Chicago day, and through the open door of a large barnlike room filled with rat cages I saw Lashley (I somehow knew it was he) in his shirt sleeves, standing at a "Lashley Jumping Stand" *whipping* (with a small leather thong tied to the end of a pencil) the tail of a rat which was reluctant to jump from its platform! Lashley looked up, continued to whip away at the rat, and bade me come in and wait until the animal had made its jump. I entered the room, the rat jumped, and Lashley looked up at me again. I told him my name, and that I had just learned about my NRC Fellowship award. He asked me to wait until the animal had completed its run of trials and then we would talk. I watched with astonishment as Lashley ran his rat: Never, in describing his already famous apparatus, had he specified that he whipped his rats to make them jump. Certainly this was not quite proper science.

When the rat finished its allotted number of jumps and had been returned to its cage, Lashley ushered me into his office, welcomed me, assured me that he would be glad to teach me what he could, that his histologist would also be available to guide me, but that I would be expected to learn and do my own brain operations and histology. He was making it clear to me that we were to interfere minimally with each other. I assured Lashley that maximum independence was what I also wished, and during the two years we were together, we kept our bargain faithfully, parting with enduring respect for each other, a respect which grew over the succeeding years. Actually during those two years we did get in considerable lab talk together, and Lashley would hold forth scathingly about the pretentiously formulated learning theories which were just then becoming the vogue. We did not know enough, Lashley would insist, for anything more formal or stringent than a descriptive approach to the problem.

After a visit with my parents, I returned to Chicago, earlier than necessary, to attend the APA meetings being held that year at the University of Chicago. It was a glorious meeting. With Tolman as my guide I met all the greats, men who had heretofore been only journal names, and I went to almost every session and heard almost every paper. Just as Tolman had me in tow, so did Clark Hull have Neal Miller in tow. Those were the days when each Great Man had his own system and his own disciples who believed and experimented loyally within that system. In 1933 Clark Hull was beginning to come to the front as Edward Tolman's adversary, and Neal Miller and I were their chosen and loyal disciples. About the second day of the meetings Neal came to me with an invitation to attend a very select "bull session" with Hull. I was immediately put on guard but was flattered and I accepted.

The meeting was held at the Quadrangle Club. Clark Hull spoke to the assembled multitude (about fifty). We were, he told us, among the most promising young experimentalists in psychology. Unfortunately, he went on, the country was in an economic depression and many of us, he warned, would find ourselves in small colleges with even smaller budgets which would make the building of research apparatus impossible. However, he, Clark Hull, had access to some research money which he could make available to the deserving poor experimentalist. And as he continued it became clear that a deserving experimentalist was one who worked within Hull's principles of behaviorism. Indeed, Hull concluded, he was thinking of establishing a new journal, to be called something like the "Journal of Neo-Behaviorism," and thus provide us all with a platform for this new and truly scientific psychology.

I was flabbergasted. Hull was trying to buy disciples. No sooner was the meeting over than I sought out Tolman and with wrath and indignation told him what had happened. Tolman thought the whole thing funny, calmed me down, and assured me (without convincing me) that I had probably misinterpreted Hull's intent.

The excitement of my first APA meeting was followed almost immediately by the excitement of my first (and last) lesson in performing brain operations. Early the next week Lashley took me and about half a dozen rats to the operating room. He operated on a rat, running through and talking out each step at his characteristic nervously rapid pace. He did the same with a second rat. Then he told me to operate on the next rat while he watched. Somehow I went ahead, and somehow I finished the job, and somehow the rat survived. Lashley then suggested that I do several more operations by myself that day, and that I continue doing about six rats a day until I had reduced the mortality rate to something less than 10 percent. And then he left. My next three rats died before I could complete the operations, but by the end of the week, I had operated on about thirty rats, had met Lashley's mortality criterion, and I was now a technically trained physiological psychologist. Such was the state of our science and our art ca. 1933. Of course, I still had some neuroanatomy and some histology to learn, but having become a qualified brain surgeon, I was now prepared to start on my own lesion experiments.

During my Fellowship year I completed one fairly extensive experiment, involving 100 animals of whom 76 were subjected to brain operations. I did not find the usual Lashley-type results. I found that cortical lesions did diminish the number, complexity, plasticity, and kind of hypotheses, but these effects instead of being correlated with the amount of cortical tissue destroyed, appeared to be a complex function of at least two anatomically delimited cortical areas which I labeled "S" and "V." I thought it was an important experiment because it not only proposed a way of reconciling the traditional brain localization notions with the Lashleyan "Equipotentiality" hypothesis but also suggested a new "dynamic" theory of brain action. Lashley read it and gave his *nihil obstat;* the *Journal of Comparative Psychology* let me take 46 pages to tell the story (1935); and no one was impressed. I do not recall anyone (besides myself) ever referring to this paper; some of its findings had to wait for about 20 years when Bennett,

Rosenzweig, and I used them for our initial guiding hypothesis of our brain chemistry work.

Toward the end of my Fellowship year it again appeared that, I was not going to be able to continue in psychology, and again I was given a last-moment reprieve. Lashley offered me a research assistantship (at $100 per month) for the next year. I grasped at that offer, not only because I had no alternative, but because my year at Chicago had proved to be a most rewarding one, and the next year promised to be even better. I was now a published brain researcher; I liked this new kind of research; I was affluent enough to live grandly and even to send some money home (my father was now ill and could work no longer); and the people around Lashley's laboratory were a most stimulating group.

During 1933-1935 my colleagues included C. W. Luh, on sabbatical leave from his posts as Professor of Psychology and President of Yenching University; Robert Leeper and L. A. Pennington, who were also there as NRC Fellows; Y. C. Tsang, who was completing his doctoral work and whose exquisite brain operation on hour-old rats were the wonder of the laboratory; and Donald Hebb and Frank Beach, who came as graduate students. The laboratory hummed with people until Lashley left Chicago for Harvard.

When Lashley left for Harvard, at his suggestion I was offered the job of supervising the laboratory in Culver Hall (at $1,000 per year) until a "proper" replacement could be made. Again, I did not take long to make my decision. The money was inadequate and the appointment was belittling (the other Ph.D.'s in the laboratory were starting their climbs on the academic ladder at various institutions, and I was being offered a temporary caretaker's job), but I would be maintaining a foothold in psychology, I would have the time and facilities to continue research, and finally and compellingly, I had no other offer.

I stayed on for two more years. I completed an additional half dozen experiments, one of which measured "Lewinischen tension" in the rat and which was reported by me at the 1935 topological meeting at Bryn Mawr. In what turned out to be my last Chicago experiment, I proposed the noncontinuity hypothesis of problem solving *(Psychol. Rev.,* 1938). My term for this hypothesis proved to have a significant metaphorical meaning, for during the last Chicago year the seeds were sown for noncontinuity of my own story.

Immersed though I was in my rats, I was becoming increasingly aware that things outside were not getting better and that my failure to get an academic job was not only a reflection of bad economic times, but also of a bad society. I was becoming disaffected.

About that time I joined New America. New America, with headquarters in Chicago and the bulk of its (small) membership in the Midwest, was an avowed Marxist revolutionary organization. It was self-consciously indigenous, taking its style from the American scene, and wearing its Marxism lightly. While it assiduously avoided Communist-baiting, most of its members took an exceedingly dim view of the Communist Party and of the USSR. It was completely and compulsively democratic in its public idealogy and in its internal activities. New America attracted a number of intellectuals, scientists, students, and writers; a scattering of labor, educational, and religious leaders; and even some steel and automobile workers (of whom we were inordinately proud). I learned a great deal about the outside world through New America, and I had a great deal to learn.

Inspired by New America's objectives, I conceived the idea of stimulating more psychologists to direct their efforts toward the making of a new and better America. Together with two fellow New Americans, Ward Halstead (then an instructor at the medical school) and Lorenz Meyer (a graduate student), we arranged with Oscar Ameringer, editor of *The American Guardian* of Oklahoma City (a feisty, homespun, independent socialist paper) to run a special front-page "Box" announcing our objective. We paid $14.26 to have copies of that issue sent to a selected list of 712 psychologists. To circularize all the 1,800 APA members would have cost $36.00 and we could not quite make that.

This was in January 1936, and by early February we had received enough replies to know that we were well on our way. From among those who responded we formed a "National Organizing Committee" and prepared for the 1936 APA meetings, where we hoped to launch the new society. On the evening of September 1, 1936, in McNutt Hall on the Dartmouth campus, the Society for the Psychological Study of Social Issues (SPSSI) was formally organized. We agreed, *inter alia*, to promote "psychological research on controversial topics, especially those related to the central fields of economics and politics, and the encouragement of the applications of the findings of psychology to the problems of society." It was, for its time and for a group of academicians, a "way-out" radical statement.

As of January 1, 1937 (when charter membership was closed), the SPSSI had 333 members, an irregularly issued *Bulletin,* and its activities were underway. Today the Society (Division 9 of the APA) is an accepted member of the Establishment and has a membership of over three thousand. How its present ethos compares with that of 1936 I do not know. I should point out, to reassure its present membership, that there was never any attempt by New America to "use" the SPSSI. This would have been as foreign to my thinking and that of my New American colleagues as it would have been futile.

My last two years at Chicago were not encapsulated ones. While I continued to spend the major portion of my waking time with my rats, considerable energy went into SPSSI and New American work. It was also early during that period that I met Wolfgang Köhler, who had come to Chicago on a Visiting Professorship. I was soon so captivated by Köhler's intellect and his way of formulating exciting and novel psychological problems that I frequently sought him out for discussion. After he returned to Swarthmore College, I received an offer from Robert MacLeod of a $1,000 Research Associateship. The opportunity to work with Köhler was most appealing, but MacLeod's offer was again a stopgap, and I had begun to hope that my Chicago four-year cliff-hanger might turn into a permanent job. I did not, however, have much time to ponder the problem, for in May of that year occurred an event which forced my decision and which, within two years, was to force me out of psychology altogether.

In 1937 as part of the steel workers' unionization drive, the "Little Steel" strike was called in the Chicago area. On Memorial Day the strikers, in holiday dress and accompanied by their wives and children, attempted to establish a symbolic picket line before the Republic Steel Corporation plant in Gary. They were met by point-blank fire from a force of Chicago Police. Ten people were killed, and about eighty wounded. The "Memorial Day Massacre" was witnessed by approximately a thousand labor sympathizers, newspaper men, students, and others. I was there with several New American friends, including the novelist Meyer Levin.

Meyer Levin drew up a *J'Accuse,* a few phrases of which must evoke in the contemporary reader a gruesome shock of recognition: "We feel that the people of Chicago can no longer permit this lawless, murderous use of their agencies of government. The suppression of civil rights in Chicago must be stopped. Police violence and brutality in Chicago must be stopped. . . ." Together with Levin and three other witnesses I signed the document. We sought additional signers to the protest, and we found them: Paul Douglas (later U.S. Senator), Clarence Darrow, Harold Lasswell, Carl Sandburg, and about 50 other eminent Chicagoans.

As soon as the protest (with my name attached) was published, Dean Taliaferro, under whose jurisdiction the Psychology Department operated, immediately dispatched a letter of alarm to Harvey Carr, the Chairman of our Department. Carr replied that what I did off campus should not be Taliaferro's concern, and then sent copies of this correspondence to me. I am certain that Carr would have behaved this forthrightly in any case, but he had special reasons for being annoyed with Taliaferro. Carr was due to retire in June, and for over a year he had wrangled with Taliaferro on the choice of a successor. The Dean wanted a physiological psychologist, while Carr wanted the Chicago functionalist tradition carried on by one of his own Ph.D.'s (and Thurstone muddied the waters by insisting upon a factor analyst). The result was that no successor had been appointed, the morale of the Department had declined precipitously, and Carr foresaw for his beloved Department what, in fact, did happen: a leaderless Department which was to deteriorate rapidly over the next several years.

I was aware of all of this, and when I received Carr's packet of letters, I realized that my tenure at Chicago was now at an end. Carr advised me to accept MacLeod's offer; Taliaferro informed me that I had "no future at the University of Chicago"; I wrote to MacLeod accepting the Research Associateship.

I left Chicago without the euphoria which had characterized my previous comings and goings across the continent. I was now four years, an NRC Fellowship, a Lashley Research Assistantship, and nineteen publications beyond my Ph.D., yet here I was on my way to still another one-year, one-thousand dollar, stopgap appointment. Nor did I feel that things would soon get better. I had lost my innocence in Chicago and knew too much about the inherent ills of our society to be sanguine. And, finally, I had again experienced what I considered unfair treatment within the groves of academe.

SWARTHMORE AND COLORADO

Swarthmore's Psychology Department in 1937 was a unique and improbable site on the American Psychological scene. On the campus of a small undergraduate Quaker college, Robert MacLeod (the most knowledgeable, creative, supportive, and effective leader of a scientific department I was ever to know) had assembled an outstanding graduate faculty, established the American headquarters for Gestalt psychology, and had created an altogether excellent intellectual, scientific, and teaching enterprise in psychology.

When I arrived, the faculty consisted of MacLeod, Köhler, Edwin B. Newman, and Hans Wallach, with Mason Haire as the (unofficial) "graduate student." We were soon joined by Karl Duncker and Donald A. Adams (on leave from Duke University). A frequent visitor was Max Wertheimer (from The New School in New York), and together with Harry Helson and Donald W. MacKinnon (both then at Bryn Mawr), we held joint seminars, sometimes at Swarthmore, sometimes at Bryn Mawr, and once, I remember, at Princeton, where Albert Einstein joined us.

I had gone to Swarthmore to initiate an animal laboratory and to do research. My visible achievements that year were rather modest: Mason Haire published one rat experiment, and so did I, and together with Karl Duncker I had published a theoretical article. But I had been busy becoming acquainted with new (to me) experimental research in perception, and novel methods of inquiry and analysis. My Gestaltoid tendencies, initiated under Tolman, flourished in Swarthmore's rich Gestalt ambience, and I became a sort of Crypto-Gestaltist *cum* would-be phenomenologist, the latter under MacLeod's influences. I have never recovered from either.

I could have been entirely happy in this sheltered enclave (for that is what it was; it definitely was not in the mainstream of American psychology), except that my Jewish background, and my New American and SPSSI work constantly reminded me of an outside world made hideous by a Hitler in Germany, Mussolini in Italy, and Franco in Spain. However, what took me away from Swarthmore was not a call for social action, but a call from the University of Colorado.

Late in 1938 Karl Muenzinger asked me whether I would come to Boulder as a half-time Assistant Professor at (the inevitable, it seemed) $1,000. This was, by any criterion, a very modest offer, but I saw it as a smashing breakthrough. It was the first invitation I had ever received to enter academia through the front door. I wired back "Happy to accept offer," packed my bags, and set off for Columbus, Ohio (where the APA meetings were being held that year). This time I was shuttling back across the continent to an Assistant Professorship!

When I arrived at my hotel I found, forwarded there, the official letter of appointment from Colorado's President George Norlin to a half-time *instructorship*. I was utterly bewildered at this new instance of dirty pool in academia. Muenzinger urged me to come to Boulder anyway, and assured me that everything would be set to rights next year. I swallowed hard, and again, having no alternative, I accepted the instructorship.

What had happened? I later learned that when my appointment had come before the Board of Regents at Boulder, they were hesitant to take action because (and from here on I will quote from a document prepared by Norlin when the AAUP intervened in my case a year later) "one of them [Regents] had received confidential information to the effect that Dr. Krechevsky was a difficult person—a trouble maker. The matter of appointment was deferred until further investigation could be made.

> Then I myself wrote to Professors Tolman . . . Lashley . . . Carr . . . President Aydelotte of Swarthmore and Dean Taliaferro. . . .
>
> Dean Taliaferro . . . wrote: "While at Chicago he showed a decided tendency toward the extreme left and was active in several labor demonstrations [the only possible referent here was the signing of the "Memorial Day Massacre" protest]. Besides this, I understand that he is secretary of a society of younger psychologists who have rather radical tendencies.
>
> The other letters, however, were very reassuring . . . . On the basis of the evidence before me, I then recommended Dr. Krechevsky's appointment to a half-time instructorship.[!]

Despite this unpropitious beginning I had a good year at Boulder. I leaped into teaching eagerly, as though I had suddenly broken away from a restraining leash. I discovered that I liked teaching and that I sought and enjoyed the students' approval. I became a popular lecturer. But I also discovered that I spent hours preparing for each easily flowing, effortless lecture. Much later I was to find that it would ever be thus.

We had no active animal laboratory that year at Boulder, so Muenzinger and I turned to writing. We set out on an ambitious undertaking, a book on the psychology of learning which would encompass within one systematic set of principles all kinds of learning, from conditioning in dogs to syllogistic reasoning in man. Our system turned out to be Tolmanian Purposive Behaviorism, undergirded by principles generalized from the Gestaltists' laws of perceptual organization, and adorned with Lashleyan and field-theoretical neurology (our outline called for three chapters of brain-behavior research). We also planned to explore the implications of our system for educational practice, since neither Muenzinger nor I sought to be purer-than-thou in our science, nor indeed have I ever aspired to that form of grace. I suppose that if I have sinned in that area, it is in my overreadiness to speculate publicly on the social implications of laboratory findings.

Muenzinger and I spent several months talking out the project, convinced ourselves of its feasibility, and even made palpable progress. I still have in my library a nine-page detailed outline of the projected book and some 40,000 words I had written for four of the chapters. But the book was never to be finished.

PARADISE LOST

Toward the end of the year, Muenzinger, Harold Benjamin (Dean of Education within which psychology operated), Dean Van Ek of the College, together with President Norlin unanimously recommended to the Regents that I be promoted to an Assistant Professorship at $2,000. Early in June, Norlin called me to his office. The Regents, he regretted to inform me, were still uneasy about my "Memorial Day Massacre" past, and had therefore modified the recommendation to an instructorship, and at a lower salary. He understood my distress, Norlin assured me, but he counseled me to accept the Regents' offer because, he told me, everyone from whom he had inquired agreed that I had a promising future as a scientist and teacher, and he would not want to see me jeopardize that future. For surely, he went on, I must realize that it was not easy for a Jew to get an appointment at a University. An instructorship was, at the very least, a foothold and in these parlous times I should be grateful for that.

I was utterly crushed. These were indeed parlous times. This was June 1939—in three months Hitler was to start World War II—and here in beautiful Boulder, far away from Hitler's Germany, I had just been told by the President of the University, and a Classics scholar of note, that because I was a Jew I should gratefully accept what the Regents, in violation of academic propriety and justice and motivated by political bias, had deigned to toss my way!

The rest of the story is quickly told. The next morning I wrote a letter to Norlin in which I summarized (for the record, and to give him an opportunity to correct anything I might have mistakenly ascribed to him) what he had said to me, and then concluded: "After considering the implications of the Board's action and the information which you gave me . . . I have decided that I cannot possibly accept the appointment and I hereby respectfully request that you urge the Board to reconsider the entire question."

The matter soon became public knowledge. Muenzinger led a faculty protest, the American Federation of Teachers as well as the SPSSI issued "strong statements," the AAUP prepared to make an investigation, Tolman canceled a summer conference engagement at Boulder, and Dean Benjamin (who was the noblest soul of all in this sorry mess) resigned in protest. All of this, of course, was to no avail. I learned from others that my refusal to take Norlin's advice had convinced him that I was indeed a troublemaker and, as he wrote in his report, "The Regents voted supporting the *recommendation of the President* [italics my own] that in view of Dr. Krechevsky's refusal to accept the appointment as made by the Regents . . . the offer of the appointment is hereby withdrawn."

And thus on June 10, 1939, I was fired from the University of Colorado and expelled from academia.

I now made a decision of my own: With all my heart and with all my strength I would work for a new and better America. After attending my "last" APA meetings in September (at Berkeley that year), meetings which were high-lighted by an on-the-scene radio broadcast describing Hitler's invasion of Poland, I reported to Chicago for full-time New American work.

I worked for New America from September 1939 to July 1941. During those two years I served as Managing Editor of our two publications (a biweekly paper, *The New American*, and a quarterly magazine, *Social Change*), and also (for a brief period) as District Director for New York. But despite my many activities the world continued to go to hell. Very few people had time to think about building a better America; the overriding concern was to defeat Hitler. In July 1941 under the title, *Our Objective Still Lives,* the New American officers sent a special recommendation to the membership that the organization be dissolved. By a mailed ballot vote (democratic to the end) of 2:1 the membership approved, and New America as a formal organization officially and forever disappeared. Our objective, of course, still lives.

I now sought other ways and, through the good offices of some Swarthmore friends, I was given an appointment in the food-stamp agency in the U.S. Department of Agriculture. My assignment was to probe the attitudes of the urban poor who, although eligible for food-stamp subsidies, were not taking full advantage of that program. I found among other things that poor people had pride and they refrained from using stamps which publicly proclaimed them to be on charity, but their pride also prevented them from telling me this. I wrote long and confused reports. This was my introduction to field work in social psychology and some of the complexities of opinion research.

After a year I transferred to Rensis Likert's Division of Program Surveys (in the War Office), where I learned a great deal about attitude research. My three months work there brought about a profound and lasting change in my appraisal of this research field. Never again was I to harbor the supercilious attitude toward attitude research which was (and still is) affected by many "hard-nosed" scientists. I learned to respect the scientific integrity, methodological sophistication, psychological thinking, and social utility of what Likert and his people were doing.

I left Likert only because the food-stamp agency, its personnel having been decimated by the draft (because of my myopia I had been rejected by the Army), appealed to me to come and help run the Washington office, which was still trying to feed the poor. After I had served four months as "Chief Economic Analyst" for the food-stamp agency, the Army decided that neither my myopia nor my age (33) were disqualifying now, and on December 5, 1942, I became Private Isadore Krechevsky, of the Army of the United States.

My activities in and out of the Army for the duration of the war were varied and curious and completed by field training in social psychology. I begged off from an army office job and a commission; I wanted to get overseas as quickly as possible. However, it soon became clear to me and to the Army that I was not a combat soldier, and so when Tryon, who was now in Washington as civilian head of an OSS office, wrote and asked whether I would want to be transferred to the OSS for "important but secret work," I agreed.

In Washington I was first assigned to the Morale Division to concoct rumors which were to be planted by OSS agents in occupied countries, and which were designed to harass and discomfit the German forces and their collaborators. Apparently my Colonel thought well of my rumors because not only was I soon promoted to be M/Sgt., but he proposed that I join him after the war to help him regain control of a huge corporate business he had lost to "unethical" competitors. My job (for which I would be generously paid) would be to invent and plant psychologically effective rumors to discredit his unethical competitors.

Through Tryon's intercession I was quickly transferred from that Colonel's Office to the OSS Assessment Station just outside Washington. There I found many old Berkeley friends and other psychologists and psychiatrists testing the moral and emotional stamina of men who had volunteered for OSS work (sabotage, assassinations, espionage, etc.) in enemy-occupied territory. The assessment work was under the overall command of (Colonel) Henry Murray and under the immediate supervision of Donald MacKinnon. No one will ever know, I suppose, whether we did an effective job. It was almost impossible to validate our psychological prognoses of men who were sent off to kill and be killed in secrecy and in far-off places. But we believed that we were creating a novel and valuable psychological testing program. Indeed, like my Colonel in the Morale Division, we wanted to salvage our experience for peacetime use. And after the war we were delighted when Donald MacKinnon was able to do just that by setting up, in Berkeley, the Institute of Personality and Assessment Research.

I was with the OSS for two years, during which time I helped establish a station (under the command of John Gardner, who was then a lieutenant in the Marine Corps) on the West Coast to assess agents destined for the Pacific Theater of War. Also, during that time Hildy and I were married and I changed my name. These last two events were not unrelated. I had suffered too many indignities because of the name "Krechevsky" to have it continued with my son, should I ever have one (I did). It was a name which seemed to alert and energize every American xenophobe. I would not deny my Jewishness, but neither was it incumbent upon me to perpetuate the name of a bygone dissolute Polish nobleman who had ruled over my forebears in the Diaspora. We therefore took for our last name the diminutive by which all my friends had known me since Berkeley graduate days, "Krech," and for my first name, we took "David," a name we both liked and which, incidentally, was the name of an ancient Hebrew nobleman (also somewhat dissolute).

Early in 1945 Rensis Likert invited me to join his projected USSBS (United States Strategic Bombing Survey) study. The plan was for Likert's group to follow the American invading army through Germany and do depth interviews with German civilians to determine what effects the allied bombings had upon their war morale. (The findings were to be used in shaping policy on the Japanese front.) Civilian researchers were wanted for this, and so on March 20, 1945, I received my army discharge ("for the convenience of the government") and I prepared to invade Germany, with questionnaire at the ready.

Likert's USSBS study seemed to be wholly an SPSSI operation. Among those present in Germany were Dorwin Cartwright, Daniel Katz, Herbert Hyman, Richard Crutchfield—every one an officer (then or later) of SPSSI. Many an evening was spent in Darmstadt and Bad Nauheim plotting and planning the postwar future of social psychology in America and the role SPSSI could play.

My four-month's tour of duty in Germany provided me with intensive field training in survey methods, and convinced me that academia with its psychologists was the place for me after all; I would scarcely be happy elsewhere.

PARADISE REGAINED

Again MacLeod came to the rescue and, for the first time ever, I was offered an Assistant Professorship. Of course, I accepted gladly. My two Swarthmore years were spent in supervising (from a distance) the work of a USSBS group in Japan; in teaching; and in writing. My first four social psychological publications mark this period, three of them appearing in 1946. In the *Psychological Review* (1946) appeared my first paper after a publication hiatus of seven years. Signed by "David Krech" with references to articles by "Krechevsky" which were described as "previous work by the present writer," that paper informed the psychological community that I was back in business, but under a different name, and at a different stand. I was now professing social psychology and suggesting that if we were to apply the same techniques I had used in my work on "hypotheses in rats" to the study of the formation of attitudes in man, we might find that *all* attitudes (like my rats' wrong hypotheses) were functional, and that even "irrational" man (like the supposed "helter-skelter" rat) was rational after all.

In my second paper (in *The American Psychologist*) I urged the experimentalist to consider using subjects of social value even when working on his "pure" problems. My third publication effort was editing SPSSI's tenth anniversary number (November 1964) of the *Journal of Social Issues,* titled "The Challenge and the Promise." Here the thesis was that social scientists must immediately set to, in cooperation with government and civic leaders, on research *and action* on social problems because, I wrote apocalyptically, "the time is short, the task is tremendous, but the stakes are high."

All of this was preparatory and ancillary to the major objective on which I had set my sights: a book which would provide social psychology with a comprehensive theoretical treatment, and direct its specific attention to the problems of war and peace, racial prejudice, and labor conflict. Both MacLeod and Crutchfield (who was now on the Swarthmore faculty) showed an interest in such an enterprise, and for several weeks we met regularly to discuss this problem. We soon began to formulate a set of "Propositions" based on Gestalt laws of organization and Tolmanian learning principles (Crutchfield, too, had taken his Ph.D. with Tolman) and reflecting a strong MacLeodian phenomenological cast. These Propositions sought to encompass much of what we knew about social psychology from the field and laboratory, and to suggest further work. MacLeod had taken the lead in our discussions, but for various reasons he decided not to continue with the project. Crutchfield and I went ahead without him, although his help was sought (and given) throughout. The final product, *Theory and Problems of Social Psychology,* was published in 1948. I have already indicated the nature of the "theory" part of the book. It remains the most extensive theoretical work in which I have had any part, and here I owe a great deal to Crutchfield, who seemed to thrive on confrontations with theoretical issues, confrontations which I watched admiringly and with profit. The "problems" part of the book reflected both my personal concerns and experiences, as well as Crutchfield's extensive field research and technical psychometric skills. (Of the writing of books there is no end to Crutchfield's and my collaboration: as of the moment we are working together on three more.)

Both Crutchfield and I were pleased with what we had written. We were therefore as surprised as we were delighted when the book was widely adopted as a text. We had done well by doing good.

In 1947 I was invited to come to Berkeley as an Associate Professor. The wish I had wished for myself when I left Berkeley on the *Overland Limited* in 1933 had come true, and I was outrageously happy. My appointment at Berkeley was to teach social psychology, and that is what I did for several years. I also published a number of papers in the field, and at the 1948 Boston APA meetings at a special session called by Jerome Bruner I participated in the launching of the "New Look" movement in perception (I adopted that term from the then popular mode in women's fashions). It might be said that this movement sought to bring about the socialization of perceptual theory. Out of this meeting eventually came a collection of papers, *Perception and Personality,* edited by Bruner and me, and published by the Duke University Press in 1950.

It soon became apparent, however, that my zest for social psychology was waning, and I began, tentatively, to return to my rats. Even now I know not why. Partly, my social psychological "tensions" may have relaxed upon the completion of our *Theory and Problems.* Partly, it may be that my ancestral memories were responding to the call of the rat as I again returned to the Life Sciences Building where once I had held communion with M.N.A., and where I was again daily surrounded by Tolman and his rat-running graduate students.

Despite all of this, in 1949, after but two short years in long-yearned-for Berkeley, Hildy and I picked up our three-year-old son, left our newly bought house on the hill, and set out for far-off and unknown Norway to do missionary work for social psychology! The call to Norway came from Vilhelm Aubert, a student of social science at Oslo University, who had a most romantic tale to tell. During the German occupation an Oslo philosophy student, active in the underground movement, had escaped to England to be trained and returned (via airplane drop) for espionage work. His comrades assembled at the secret rendez-vous to receive him; the man jumped from the plane, but his parachute failed to open and he was killed. Aubert was in the party sent to retrieve his gear, and among the dead man's radio-sending equipment, etc., was George Lundberg's *Social Research*. This book became, as Aubert expressed it, "some kind of bible for me." Aubert and his group were fired by this book and other readings with a vision of a science of man which would forever eradicate war and its horrors from the world. They determined that after the war (they were certain that Hitler would not prevail) they would make Norway a major center for this new discipline of man. (The fateful book eventually found its way to the dead man's girlfriend, who later became a sociologist in Sweden.) In fulfillment of their vow, the Oslo social science and philosophy students had sent Aubert to scout out the American social scientists and to seek help of those who would most likely promote their objective. Unknown to me Aubert had been auditing my classes in social psychology, and he now came with this tale and an invitation to spend a year at Oslo. They had arranged with the University of Oslo to have me appointed a Visiting Professor there. Neither Hildy nor I had it in us to deny such a plea.

The Oslo year was most productive. I lectured in social psychology, helped with several survey projects which had been started during a previous visit by Paul Lazarsfeld, and made the initial plans with Erik Rinde for the institution which became, under his leadership, the highly regarded Institute of Social Research.

But as at Berkeley, my activities were not altogether social psychological. I also lectured on learning theory and research in experimental psychology. One of the students initiated a (short lived) rat laboratory, and another, Per Saugstad, followed through with his interest and is now Professor of Experimental Psy-chology at Oslo. I also laid the foundations for my later work in brain chemis-try: first by completing work on a series of papers which brought my thinking back to physiology and even earned me the reproach of being a "reductionist" (see especially my two papers in the *Psychol. Rev.,* 1950), and second, through a serendipitous meeting with a Berkeley colleague.

In the spring of that year Professor Melvin Calvin of Berkeley visited Oslo as a guest lecturer. Bare acquaintances in Berkeley, we fell into each other's arms far away from home. It was then that I first discussed with Calvin the possibility of a chemical approach to brain-behavior research. I had always been of the opinion that the anatomical approach of the lesion technique could at best help us write the statics of brain mechanisms; what I wanted was a way to understand the dynamics. This had been my objective in the very first paper I had written from Lashley's laboratory in 1935. And perhaps, I now proposed to Calvin, a chemical approach to brain-behavior research would do just that.

I found in Calvin a sympathetic listener with a quick and lively interest which almost immediately made him the ball carrier. He was, obviously, a Chemical Imperialist Adventurer: Any scientific problem, he seemed to believe, could best be handled by the chemist, and he was particularly intrigued by new scientific territory where no chemist had trod before. We left each other with the vague promise to explore the possibilities of using chemistry for brain research when I got back to my laboratory.

I was not, however, to get back to my laboratory on schedule, for this was the "Year of the Oath." Just a week or so before we had left Berkeley, Edward Tolman had risen in the meeting of the Academic Senate and announced that he would not sign the political loyalty oath newly created by the Regents and which they insisted must be signed before a man could teach at the University. But the Regents were adamant and were prepared to dismiss (as indeed they did) any nonsigner, no matter what his rank. Tolman's principled refusal to sign had clearly defined an important academic freedom issue, and the University was now in deepest travail. I dreaded going back to Berkeley, for I saw this sorry action of the Regents almost paranoically. I had thought that with an Associate Professorship at *my* Berkeley I was quit forever from playing out once more my dreary role in what I had begun to see as a recurrent nightmare of Academia vs. Me. But "they" were after me again, and I knew I could but lose again.

It was at that very point in my inner turmoil that Bruner telephoned from Cambridge and asked me to come to Harvard as a visitor for the next year. I remember the state of excited relief induced by this trans-Atlantic telephonic *deus ex machina* solution to my problem. Turning to Hildy I told her that I had been invited to Harvard, and her response was "Any port in a storm!" I accepted, and I spent the academic year 1950-1951 at Harvard as Berkeley Refugee, Visiting Lecturer on Social Psychology, and Research Associate in the Laboratory of Social Relations.

This port, however, did not provide the complete shelter for which I had hoped. I had filled out my form requesting a leave of absence from Berkeley, after scratching out the loyalty oath. President Sproul wired back that the Regents had ruled that my failure to sign the loyalty oath would mean dismissal from the University. I signed.

The year at Harvard was a lonely and unhappy but a very busy one. Aside from scurrying around soliciting money to help carry on the fight at Berkeley (which Tolman and the other nonsigners eventually did win for us), I had a new course to teach, "Cognitive Processes," jointly with Bruner; I collaborated with George Klein (who was also a visitor, and to me a very welcome colleague, at Harvard that year) on experiments with brain-injured people, on theoretical papers, and in editing another "New Look" volume for the Duke University Press, *Theoretical Models and Personality Theory;* and with Kenneth Clark I brought forth social psychological testimony to confound the "separate but equal" doctrine in the 1951 suit brought by the NAACP on behalf of parents of Negro children in Clarendon County, South Carolina. According to our attorney,

Thurgood Marshall, this was the first time a Federal Court allowed social psychologists to testify as expert witnesses.

When I returned to Berkeley the "Loyalty Oath" fight was over, most of the faculty who had been dismissed were returned (some did not want to come back), and everybody seemed relieved that somehow the University had not been altogether destroyed. I turned to experimental psychology. From now on, except for a long writing stretch with Ballachey and Crutchfield when we revised our *Theory and Problems of Social Psychology* into *Individual in Society* (1962), I was no longer to do any sustained work as a social psychologist.

BRAIN CHEMISTRY

Within a year or so after my return I was back on the fifth floor of the Life Sciences Building running rats in my hypothesis box in the very same laboratory where I had worked as a graduate student. But this was not quite full circle. I was, in fact, starting out on a completely new tack. I had finally gotten around to following up my Oslo conversations with Calvin; he was still interested and introduced me to his Research Associate, Edward L. Bennett, a biochemist. Bennett agreed to join forces for an attack on brain chemistry and behavior and I also enlisted the help of Mark R. Rosenzweig, who had recently come to the Berkeley faculty and had been trained in physiological psychology. Later we were joined by Dr. Marian Diamond, whose neuroanatomical work has contributed so significantly to the group's research.

We first set out to test the hypothesis that the two anatomically delimited cortical areas ("V" and "S") which I had isolated and described in Lashley's laboratory as the controlling areas of visual and spatial hypotheses behavior, respectively, also differed correspondingly in cholinesterase (ChE) activity levels. (The ChE suggestion came from Bennett.) That is, we predicted that the spatial hypotheses animals would show relatively high ChE levels in the "S" areas; the visuals, in the "V" areas. We were wrong. *But* we did find a consistent and statistically significant higher cortical ChE activity level for our spatial than for our visual rats. A *post hoc* explanation of this unexpected but striking relation between brain chemistry and behavior was easily concocted, and our first paper was published in *Science*, December 1954.

This was the start of a collaborative research project which lasted for over fifteen years, and from which I withdrew after a falling out with one of my colleagues on a question of scientific manners. During these fifteen years the project grew in number of laboratory rooms occupied, in hundreds of thousands of dollars received and expended, in papers published, in foreign junkets attended, and in recognitions achieved. And throughout, Calvin has liberally supported (and indeed made possible) our work. When we started our research I doubt that there existed more than two or three laboratories anywhere in the world which did serious and systematic work on brain chemistry and behavior.

Today, I doubt that there is any serious biological or psychological laboratory in the world that is not doing such work. The *Zeitgeist* was with us.

It must have been the *Zeitgeist,* for it is clear that today's widespread research work in brain chemistry and behavior does *not* derive from our research. Our work was characterized by a relatively molar level of analysis; had pretty much restricted itself to the study of the acetylcholine-acetyl-cholinesterase system; and had been primarily interested in examining normally occurring physiological events in the cortex. We had intervened experimentally only by manipulating the animal's "psychological" environment. On the other hand, most of the work in almost every other laboratory (including the work of our own students after they left "the nest," and of some, such as McGaugh and Petrinovich, even before leaving) is more concerned with a molecular analysis; has examined a wide variety of chemical compounds; and typically involves experimental intervention, e.g., injecting, or feeding, nonphysiological doses of drugs and then noting effects on behavior.

I think it safe to say that both approaches are complementary and we may soon see a merging of the two. Certainly, in my opinion, our approach has already paid off. We have brought forth substantial evidence to support two propositions which, stated generally, are: (1) Differences in specified chemical and anatomical characteristics of the cortex are, in part, determinants of differences in adaptive behavior; and (2) differences in environments are, in part, determinants of specified chemical and anatomical changes in the cortex. In biology what is cause is effect, and what is effect is cause. Perhaps the one paper whose publication gave me the most satisfaction is the paper (1960) in which we first announced the second of those findings (in a journal, which had also changed *its* name since I first appeared in it. It was now the "Journal of Comparative *and Physiological* Psychology"). To be sure, we have evidence for these two propositions only for the rat, and only for a few strains of the rat. I believe, however, that these propositions have wide generality, and I have often taken to the public forum during the past several years to alert the public to the potential social dangers and promises of these findings.

Where am I now? I left our brain chemistry project about five years ago. Except for some experiments on chemical transfer (done jointly with Bennett) I spent several years teaching (as a stay-at-home and as a peripatetic lecturer), a year or two as a somewhat active "radical Berkeley professor" specializing on the issue of the Vietnam War ("active" in the sense of doing much worrying-out-loud about the evil which is abroad in the land, comforting and trying to send supportive signals to the genuinely active students, signing petitions, and making occasional speeches), and writing psychology (I find that I still have much that I want to say about this discipline which can yet become the noblest of all sciences). Two years ago, at the age of 62, I requested early retirement and have finally achieved incontestable permanent tenure in Academia: I am, now, Professor Emeritus.

ENVOI

Let me say a first and last word about myself, and sandwiched between them a few hyperbolically stated beliefs I have about psychology. The perceptive reader will see in this 1973 catechism of beliefs all that has gone before; failing that, let all that has gone before serve as *caveat*.

1. About 1947, for reasons beyond recall, I took the Strong Vocational Interest Test. I received "A" ratings on the following occupations: Artist, Psychologist, Physician, Chemist, Advertising Man, Lawyer, Author-Journalist, and President of Manufacturing Concern.

2. I believe that what we have learned about learning in the rat (or of the pigeon, dog, monkey, etc.) is of only trivial value in helping us to understand the mental life of people. And this is true for the emotional, social, and motivational life. I believe this because the human brain is different from the bird brain, which is different from the rat brain, etc., etc., and because language, which only people have makes human mental and emotional life unique in the animal world.

3. I believe that what we have learned about the brain physiology of the rat (or of the pigeon, dog, monkey, etc.) is of absolute value in helping us to understand human brain functioning. I believe this because the same kinds of proteins and enzymes operate pretty much in the same way in the cell body, or the dendritic, axonic, and synaptic zones of a bird's neuron as they do in a person's. My guiding principle can be stated as follows: The smaller (or simpler, or "more basic") the unit of analysis, the greater the generality of the findings across species.

4. I detect no beginnings of a unified theory of learning, and general laws thereof. If and when we do arrive at a reasonably respectable theory and reasonably general laws, they will encompass both behavioral *and* physiological variables, with different weights for each variable and for each species and perhaps for each individual. (If the reader is interested in a more reasoned statement of my—and William James's—position, I refer him to my discussion on pages 1-11 in *Williams James: Unfinished Business.*)

5. I subscribe to the "separate but equal" doctrine for the various psychological sciences and arts and professions, to the end that each may prosper. As a researcher, I see no merit in the "well-rounded psychologist," nor heavenly grace in the "generalist." A sophisticated discipline needs specialists specially trained. (The province of teaching may require quite different men.)

6. In my forty-odd years of wandering in and out of academia and psychology I have found ill will, nastiness, and fraud; I have also found warmth, companionship, friendship, integrity, excitement, intellectual wonder, and fulfillment. On balance, I am satisfied.

REFERENCES

Selected Publications by David Krech

Krechevsky, I. "Hypotheses" in rats. *Psychol. Rev.*, 1932, *39*, 516-532.

Krechevsky, I. Hereditary nature of "hypotheses." *J. Comp. Psychol.*, 1933, *16*, 96-116.

Krechevsky, I. Brain mechanisms and "hypotheses." *J. Comp. Psychol.*, 1935, *19*, 425-462, vi.

Krechevsky, I. A study of the continuity of the problem-solving process. *Psychol. Rev.*, 1938, *45*, 107-133.

Krech, D. Attitudes and learning. *Psychol. Rev.*, 1946, *53*, 290-293.

Krech, D., and R. S. Crutchfield. *Theory and problems of social psychology.* New York: McGraw-Hill, 1948.

Krech, D. Dynamic systems, psychological fields, and hypothetical constructs. *Psychol. Rev.*, 1950, *57*, 283-290.

Krech, D. Dynamic systems as open neurological systems. *Psychol. Rev.*, 1950, *57*, 345-361.

Krech, D., M. R. Rosenzweig, E. L. Bennett, and B. Krueckel. Enzyme concentrations in brain and adjustive behavior patterns. *Science*, 1954, *120*, 994-996.

Krech, D., M. R. Rosenzweig, and E. L. Bennett. Effects of environmental complexity and training on brain chemistry. *J. Comp. Physiol. Psychol.*, 1960, *53*, 509-519.

Krech, D. Does behavior really need a brain? In R. B. MacLeod (Ed.), *William James: Unfinished business.* Washington, D.C.: American Psychological Association, 1969.

251

A. R. Luria

The work presented here was preceded by an interesting correspondence which explains its appearance. In 1963 Professor E. Boring proposed that I participate in the preparation of *A History of Psychology in Autobiography*. I questioned the appropriateness of only one Russian autobiography when Soviet science should be represented by, at least, a few investigators and Professor Boring proposed that I and colleagues whom I named submit our written material to be held until 1970. "If you live to 1970," wrote Professor Boring, "the material you have written will go in the next volume of *A History of Psychology in Autobiography*. If you die before then, it will be published as an autonecrology."

Professor Boring's invitation seemed more than a superfluous diversion. In fact, retrospective analysis of the road one has traveled is always useful. Therefore, I have responded to the proposition with complete seriousness and I have prepared the present material in order that it might be useful in one or the other of the forms proposed by Professor Boring.

INTRODUCTION

It certainly does not seem essential that a participant in the volume *A History of Psychology in Autobiography* write autobiographical notes on the assumption that he must recount all the events of his life. This would be not only insufficiently modest but also beside the point. A series of such autobiographical sketches would not be likely to result in a true picture of the history of science.

Individual people come and go, contributing some, to them insufficiently distinctive, bits of knowledge to the general enterprise. The real interest lies in the conditions in which they lived, the ideas which made up the scientific atmosphere of their time, and the influence of those important people whose experience they incorporated into themselves.

Translated by Michael Cole, The Rockefeller University.

That is why these pages will be least of all an attempt at an autobiography; rather, they will be much more occupied with a description of· the period in which the author lived and a biography of the people who were decisive influences in the development of the psychological science of which he was a part.

The following *vita* should be sufficient for the purpose of summarizing biographical data. I was born in 1902, in Kazan, one of the oldest cultural centers of the Eastern part of European Russia, into a doctor's family. My father was a well-known and talented therapist who, after the Revolution, became one of the leading figures in Soviet medicine and who headed the Department of Therapy first in Kazan and then in Moscow. I graduated from Kazan University in 1921 with a degree in the humanities and immediately began to work in psychology. Recognizing the significance which natural science preparation has for the study of psychology, I entered the medical faculty of Kazan University. However, I did not complete my medical education until 1936, at the First Medical Institute in Moscow.

In 1923 I moved to Moscow and began to work in the Institute of Psychology of Moscow University, which was then directed by Professor K. N. Kornilov. It was here that I met L. S. Vygotsky, who was to become a decisive influence in all of my later life.

In the first years I devoted my work to the objective investigation of emotional processes with the aid of the combined motor method which I invented for this purpose. At the same time I taught and did research in the Department of Psychology of the N. K. Krupskaya Academy of Communist Education.

In 1931, I, along with L. S. Vygotsky and A. N. Leont'ev, founded the Center of Psychology of the Ukrainian Psychoneurological Academy, where I worked for three years in addition to carrying on my work in Moscow.

In the period 1934 to 1936 I began to work on developmental psychology at the Moscow Medical Institute of Genetics, where I headed the section on psychology and carried out a series of experiments on the analysis of psychological processes in identical twins with the purpose of clarifying how the relation between genetic and environmental factors changes during the course of the child's development.

In 1936 I switched into the area of neuropsychology. I created the Laboratory of Neuropsychology in the Institute of Neurosurgery (later the N. N. Burdenko Institute of Neurosurgery) and began to develop neuropsychological methods for the investigation of localized brain damage.

At the time of World War II I continued this work, heading the Neurosurgical Restoration Hospital in the Urals and then, returning to Moscow, I continued to carry on this work in the Institute of Neurosurgery. The only departure from this course was in the period 1953-1959, when I carried our psychophysiological investigations of anoma-

lous children in the Institute of Defectology of the Academy of Pedagogical Sciences.

Throughout all this time I combined research and teaching as
Professor of the Department of Psychology of Moscow University,
where for many years I taught the basic course on psychology and
directed a large number of students and graduate students. At the
present time I head the Department of Neuropsychology in the Faculty
of Psychology at Moscow University.

In 1936 I defended my dissertation for the degree of Doctor of
Pedagogical Sciences (in Psychology) and in 1943 a dissertation for the
degree of Doctor of Medical Sciences. In 1967 I received the Honorary
Degree of Doctor of Science at Leicester University (England) and at
Nigmegen University (The Netherlands). I was chosen in 1945 as a
corresponding member and in 1947 a full Member of the Academy of
Pedagogical Sciences of the RSFSR (then of the USSR). I became a
foreign member of the American Academy of Arts and Sciences in
1966, of the American Pedagogical Academy in 1967, and of the
National Academy of Sciences of the United States in 1968.

As one of the organizers of the Soviet Society of Psychologists I
headed for many years its section on psychophysiology and medical
psychology. In 1960 I was made an honorary member of the British
Psychological Association and later an honorary member of the
Switzerland Psychological Society, Columbian Psychological Society,
and the French Neurological Society. I have for many years been a
member of the editorial board of *Problems in Psychology* and in recent
years have been coeditor of the journals *Neuropsychology, Cortex,
Cognition,* et al. In 1966 I served as a Chairman of the Program
Committee of the XVIII International Psychological Congress in
Moscow, and 1969-1972 as Vice-President of the International Union
of Psychological Sciences.

ATMOSPHERE

The scientific atmosphere of Soviet Russia in the twentieth century, as
many authors have noted, was very unusual, not to say unique. The greatest
social revolution ever to take place had just occurred. It had occurred in an
economically backward country but one which possessed strong intellectual
traditions.

Certain of these traditions, having their roots in Czarist Russia, represented
a barrier to the development of scientific thought. One such was the tradition of
idealistic philosophy, which isolated the discipline of psychology from other
scientific disciplines by maintaining the position that it should not be a subject
of natural science, of cause-effect analysis.

The introduction of the techniques of exact psychological experimentation
(laboratories of experimental psychology were opened in some Russian universi-

ties in the last decade of the nineteenth century, and the Institute of Psychology was founded in Moscow in 1911) did not defeat these agnostic positions of official philosophy but rather served to strengthen them. The blind alley into which this approach would have led psychology is obvious.

However, in prerevolutionary Russia there existed another, revolutionary tradition, that of the Russian revolutionary democrats of the middle of the nineteenth century, the humanistic tradition of Herzen, Chernishevskii, Dobrolyubov, and Pissarev. Theirs was the tradition of the natural science approach to the mental life of man. It attempted to understand man, his social existence, and his inner world by using those objective methods which had been applied in other sciences.

In the second half of the nineteenth century the latter tradition influenced the formation of I. M. Sechenov's approaches. Sechenov can be considered in equal measure the father of Russian physiology and of scientific psychology. He began with the publication in 1861 of *Reflexes of the Brain,* in which he defended the idea that reflex structures underlie all psychological processes and that it was possible to study them using objective methods. His later works defined psychology as "the science of the formation of mental activities," and in one of his last works, *Physiology of Nerve Centers,* published in the last decade of the nineteenth century, he proposed that science should study complex processes in the development of mental activity, in the course of which "sensations become motives and purposes and movements become actions." Sechenov's appeal to study mental processes objectively and to view them as the product of development became a strong tradition of Soviet psychology.

The studies of I. P. Pavlov and his school, and to some extent the works of V. M. Bekhterev, developed objective methods for the study of the behavior of the whole organism. They marked the beginning of that physiological analysis of the mechanisms of complex mental activity which in many respects defined the general line of development of Soviet psychology in the first half of this century.

However, the work of Pavlov and Bekhterev, which made the physiological analysis of mental phenomena the subject of objective scientific investigation, contained certain limitations. It had not provided an adequate method for the analysis of more complex forms of man's conscious activity—his active behavior, voluntary attention, deliberate remembering, and abstract thinking. Young psychologists of that time were not attracted by the simplified attempts to interpret mechanistically the more complex phenomena of mental life as systems of food or sex reflexes, although this approach received wide attention and popularity in the literature of the 1920s. They doubted the perspectives of a scientific approach which dealt only with elementary psychophysiological processes and left the higher forms of man's conscious activity to the subjective analysis of philosophical idealists or to phenomenological description. Psychology became divided into "explanatory" (the application of scientific criteria to the analysis of elementary forms of mental activity with a consequent neglect of its higher forms) and "descriptive" (the description of higher forms of consciousness, which, however, rejected approaching them from a natural-scientific, causal point of view). This division, current at the beginning of the twentieth century, did not appeal at all to the young Soviet psychologists in the first decade after the Revolution.

It was necessary to overcome "the crisis in psychology," to try to establish the most complex forms of conscious activity of man as the subject matter of psychology while preserving the objective scientific approach to its analysis and producing a scientific explanation of the appearance and course of the higher forms of mental activity.

The solution of this "crisis" was found in an historical approach to the higher mental functions of man which would attempt to show that the processes of conscious life, interpreted by the idealistic philosophers as a special "world of the mind," were in fact the product of a long social-historical development of the social life of man. It was also held that a scientific approach to understanding the origin and history of higher mental functions could be carried out only by going beyond the limits of a naturalistic analysis of mental phenomena and interpreting them as forms of activity evoked by the social experience of people, their interactions with each other, and their mastery of objectively laid down forms of social life.

The development of new paths in scientific psychology emphasizing the social-historical nature of mental functions, which while reflex in structure were consciously and voluntarily directed in their functional aspects and of social-historical origin, became the undertaking of a group of young investigators led by the great Soviet psychologist L. S. Vygotsky. Without for a minute abandoning the position of an objective approach to mental phenomena, Vygotsky initiated the study of the higher mental functioning of man, and through his students and friends (A. N. Leont'ev, D. B. Elkonin, A. V. Zaporozhets, and others) defined the path of development of Soviet psychology.

THE 1920s AND EXPERIMENTAL PSYCHOPATHOLOGY

Out of the problems described above was created the scientific atmosphere of the 1920s—the period when the world view of the first generation of Soviet psychologists was established. All these psychologists had experienced dissatisfaction with the academic psychology created prior to the Revolution: its detailed study of separate elementary psychological processes and completely useless approach to any scientific study of the most complex phenomena of mental life. They were all prepared to apply objective methods to the investigation of complex mental activity and implicitly accepted the idea of the reflex nature of mental processes; and they all attempted to find new ways to produce effective analyses of the complex forms of mental life. Certain of them (including myself) who had not come under the influence of any of the existing psychological schools, at one time believed that a scientific approach to the wholeness of personality was best represented by the new field of psycho-analysis. It was believed that the psychoanalytic approach to the concrete mental life of the individual had found the true path between the extremes of the nomothetic sciences (which interpret general laws but lose their individual features) and the idiographic sciences (which describe the individual features but cannot combine them into general laws). Many thought that the concept of individual lawfulness, the "concrete psychology" studied by Freud and Adler, created the pathway for the scientific approach. This was the subject of a youthful study by the author, "The Foundations of Realistic Psychology" (1922), which remains unpublished and is only of historical interest. However, these young psychologists repudiated the kind of arbitrary interpretation which was already characteristic of psychoanalysis. They did accept the necessity of using objective methods for the analysis of affective states, actual and repressed affective complexes, and for approaching the concrete dynamics of mental life from an objective, physiological position. Thus began the first serious experi-ments by the author, which were to continue for almost ten years and which culminated in the publication of a series of investigations on the "combined motor method" in *The Nature of Human Conflicts* (1932).

It is well known that the associative processes sometimes occur correctly and quietly, but at other times are accompanied by stress phenomena which disrupt their quiet course. In the inner life of man there can occur affective disturbances leading to the disorganization of human behavior and to neurosis. How can one objectively study these phenomena? How can one establish their symptomology, discover the mechanisms which produce them, and study the means to overcome them?

The attempts of psychoanalysis were fantastic and led it beyond the borders of an exact science. Psychoanalysis did not afford an opportunity to discover a means of determining the "objective symptomology" of the emotional con-ditions—breathing, pulse rate, and electrophysiological changes—which were only then being discovered. The findings of psychoanalysis were insufficiently re-liable, resting on nonessential and unstable indicators of deep processes oc-curring below consciousness. The development of Soviet objective psychology benefited from the idea of uniting inner (verbal-associative) processes, which can be used to merge affective states into a single functional system, with their outer, motor manifestations, to create a *single dynamic contour* in which the inner changes are necessarily reflected in the outwardly observable motor pro-cesses. This is how the "combined motor method" came to be invented. This method, described in a series of reports (Luria, 1928, 1932, etc.), served as the beginning of a widely used approach for the objective study of affective processes. The collection of a large amount of comparative material concerning natural emotional processes, the investigation of criminals (later, in a simplified form modified from the initial method, this work was applied to the construc-tion of "lie detectors"), and studies of neurotics permitted a wide application of objective methods to study affective processes. The application of the technology to artificially evoked conflicts, including even those in hypnotic states, proved useful for the analysis of certain mechanisms underlying the origin of affective states (Luria, 1932).

Investigations carried out at that time permitted us to replicate with human beings the experiments in which Pavlov had observed "conflicts" and "breaks" in animals. This analysis of experimentally evoked conflicts as a source of intense affective states can be viewed as a contribution to the objective study of the mechanisms of the disorganization of human behavior, even though it was carried out by a group of young psychologists who were just beginning their research careers.

An important fact concerning this work is that the research did not long dwell on the study of the objective symptoms of affective complexes and the physiological conditions which evoke a disorganization of behavior. These investigations very soon began (partly as a result of Vygotsky's influence) to reflect new motifs which were not to be fully developed in Soviet psychology until much later and which became the center of investigation only in the 1950s.

These early researchers came more and more to interest themselves in ways of overcoming affective states, in discovering the means that could be used to gain control of disorganized behavior, to control the affective flareups and reduce conflict.

Now, looking back on these investigations of 40-50 years ago, it is clear that these young scientists took the right path when they decided to study the role played by verbal generalizations in the control of affect. They conducted an extensive series of experiments which represented an approach to the objective mechanisms for the willful control of disorganized behavior. Thus *The Nature of Human Conflicts* was subtitled "Emotion, Conflict and Will," and was devoted to an attempt to demonstrate the role that compensatory mechanisms can play in the organization of human behavior, and the significance of meaningful restructuring of the situation (today we would say re-coding) with the aid of verbal generalizations for the control of conflict and the affective states which conflict evokes. A whole series of studies showed how verbal reorganization of mental processes may lead to the liquidation of "conflicts of inadequacy" or "conflicts of contradiction"; how verbal reorganization of psychological processes leads to the liquidation of stress; and how in the process of the child's development the increasingly complex influence of verbal reorganization of psychological activity leads to the formation of complex, organized forms of "voluntary activity" which takes the place of primitive affects.

It is possible that certain of these studies, although straightforward and not devoid of naivete, retain their significance to the present time. They certainly represent some of the first attempts to study experimentally the role of speech in the organization of behavior. They were early searches for the physiological basis of psychotherapy and the physiological mechanisms of voluntary activity. And even now, nearly fifty years after the beginning of these experiments, I remember with a feeling of gratitude the attention my friend and teacher, L. S.

Vygotsky, paid to the attempts to lay the foundations of psychological investigation into what Vygotsky called "higher motorics."

THE 1930s AND DEVELOPMENTAL PSYCHOLOGY

Investigation of the complex psychological forms of reorganization of physiological processes, which I termed "psychological physiology" (incidentally, a term I have not previously used in print), made it necessary to study more closely the processes by which behavior becomes organized. In other words, the study of developmental psychology was indicated.

It would be incorrect to conclude, by the way, that this change in the direction of my interests came from the inner logic of my research. The fundamental factor influencing the change was the impact of Vygotsky's ideas. From the end of the 1920s until his death in 1934, I and my colleague A. N. Leont'ev were closely tied to Vygotsky and his work, which for many years defined the course of development of Soviet psychology.

L. S. Vygotsky was born in Gomel in 1896. Having obtained an excellent philological education, Vygotsky wrote a series of works on the psychology of art [which was published only recently (1968)], published his early work, *Pedagogical Psychology* (1926), and in 1924, on my initiative, moved to Moscow. This is when he began his research on a wide number of theoretical problems of general and developmental psychology; it was then that he began his fundamental studies and taught courses. At this time he set forth the directions which became central for Soviet psychology.

Vygotsky decisively discarded the subjective, introspective approach of phenomenological description of the complex conditions of consciousness, typical of the idealistic psychology of that time. Acknowledging the reflex basis of all, even the most complex, psychological processes, he held that any attempt to reduce mental activity to a system of reflexes is incorrect. To believe that mental processes can be reduced to simple reflex acts, he said, means a failure to analyze psychological activity separating those units, each of which retains the quality of the whole, and to break it into elements, which may in the last analysis constitute all psychological processes but which still do not include their specific peculiarities. Such "analysis into elements" would lead to elevation of the observed process to the level of the general—this general level would be characteristic of the psychological as well as the more elementary physiological processes, but would still not reflect the fundamental properties of psychological activity. There is no doubt that water consists of hydrogen and oxygen atoms; however, to think the quality "water" reduces to the qualities of hydrogen and oxygen, losing thereby the peculiarities of the molecule H_2O, results in excluding from study the special properties of water.

What constitutes a "unit" of the psychological activity of man which retains all its fundamental properties? How are these "units" formed and how do they function? Is it possible to construct a simple model of a unit that would possess a reflex structure but would acquire new properties characteristic only of the psychological processes of man?

Vygotsky saw such an elementary unit, characteristic of human consciousness, in the process of mediation, which arose in human society because of the use of tools directed at mastery of the environment and the use of signs directed at the control of man's behavior.

Man is not able to exceed the limits of natural laws and by "force of will" move even a single molecule of the external world; he is not able, "by free will," to master his own behavior, inhibiting his reflexes or making himself move his hand so much as a millimeter. He can do all this only in accordance with the objective laws of nature, only having used objectively existing reflex processes, creating from them the means of organizing his own behavior. *"Natura parendo vincitur"*—this is the position presented in Roger Bacon's motto to his early work, *Essays in the History of Behavior* (Vygotsky and Luria, 1930), uniting to this idea another: *Nec manus nuda, nisi intellectus sibi permissus, multum valent. Instrumentis et auxilibus res perfictur.*

How are these "instruments" and "means," which are the characteristic traits of the psychological life of man, created? The study of these concepts occupied so central a place in Vygotsky's work that at one time he proposed to name his system "instrumental psychology."

It is well known that the behavior of animals and man possesses a reflex structure which may be represented by the symbol S-R. However, man not being in a position to overcome his dependence directly may get around it by an indirect mediated path: introducing changes into the external world, man subsequently subordinates himself to the changed conditions he created; acting on nature, man all the same acts on himself; mastering nature, he masters himself. In this act, reflex processes, constituting the essence of the behavior of animals, both remain and change. The S-R scheme is replaced by the more complex $S_X R$ scheme. The simple reflex is replaced by a complex reflex system; the application of a tool directed toward the outer world becomes used as a sign directed toward oneself. The determinism of the reflex scheme remains, adding to itself the traits characteristic of complex forms of "voluntary," organized behavior.

Vygotsky's model of these processes robbed the mental world of its "spiritual essence" and made the processes accessible to objective investigation. Moreover, his position forced a rejection of oversimplified methods of investigation. In place of simple stimulus-response methods, which can as easily be used in studies of animals, Vygotsky established another method, which he called the "instrumental method" or the "method of double stimuli." Presenting the subject a certain task (S) he also gave him a certain means or sign (X) by which he could master the task and adquire the appropriate response (R). In accordance with the fundamental model of complex psychological processes, such a method manifested the necessary form ($S \rightarrow X \rightarrow R$), and the objective of investigation became the way in which the subject forms the auxiliary means (X) and the degree to which he is capable of using it. The study of "significative" activity (which forms and uses signs) became the central task of the objective study of higher mental functions. It underlies the work of Vygotsky, carried out with his young pupil L. S. Sakharov (who died prematurely), which investigated the role of the word or sign in the formation of concepts. This work was published posthumously (1934). It constituted the theoretical foundation of A. N. Leont'ev's *The Development of Memory* (1930), a work which introduced the "method of mediated memory" and which was the first to objectively study the fundamental paths of development of the higher forms of active human memory. The Vygotsky and Sakharov study was the basis for a series of studies of signifying activity using the "pictogram" method (in which a picture serves as a memory aid), which, under the direction of Vygotsky, were conducted by myself and a group of young researchers (A. V. Zaporozhets, L. I. Bozhovich, N. G. Morozova, and others) who later became the nucleus of psychologists working to develop Vygotsky's ideas.

The concepts developed by Vygotsky in the 1920s and 1930s had a double significance. By providing a new approach to the essence of complex psychological processes, his conception provided an escape from the crisis of psychology which, according to him (1927), consisted in the fact that psychology, deterministically approaching the analysis of elementary psychophysiological processes, continued to view the higher psychological functions as a phenomenon of "spiritual life" which could not be explained. The investigators now had a way of approaching the most complex phenomena of mental life, analyzing it in adequate "units" and reproducing in experimental models its most complex forms.

Second, this conception convincingly demonstrated that a scientific approach to the analysis of man's consciousness requires us to discard not only spiritualistic but also naturalistic approaches to mental phenomena, and to seek the kernel of higher forms of psychological activities in social history, in those objective factors which led the most ancient societies of men to the use of tools and to the development of language, which in turn became the most important factors in the formation of man's mental processes. The views of Marx and Engels concerning the social foundations of productive forms of object-activity ("Tätigkeit") and their role in the formation of human consciousness underlay the reorganization of psychology which began to take shape in the work of young Soviet psychologists.

The conception of man's higher mental processes as a product of social development did not remain merely a general theoretical position with Vygotsky and his colleagues. It became the foundation of a series of investigations on developmental psychology which were begun at that time.

If such phenomena of man's social life as voluntary movement and active attention, meaningful memory and abstract thought, are not inherent forms of mental life which can only be described, then should it not be possible to make a cause-effect analysis of them, to indicate how they are formed and what stages they manifest? The question of "the formation of mental activity" had been posed 50 years previously by Sechenov but it became for Vygotsky and his coworkers the subject of concrete investigation.

Observing the early ontogenesis of the child's behavior, Vygotsky concluded that voluntary direction of one's own behavior is not a product of natural development. Initially guided by the command of an adult, the child moves his hand to the command "Give me the cup" or changes the direction of his gaze in response to the question "Where is the cup?" But at a certain stage the child includes his own directive sign in his speech as a result of which it becomes possible for him to regulate his own behavior. *"Functions which are initially shared by two people tend to become turned upon themselves or shortened and thus become an inner form of the organization of the psychological functions of the individual himself."* In this conversion of interpsychic processes into intrapsychic organization of functions, Vygotsky saw the social genesis of the higher forms of individual mental activity. The investigation of the genesis of higher mental functions and the stages of their further development were the subject of a series of concrete studies of the formation of active attention, mediative memory, abstract thought, and voluntary movement which were developed within a close-knit circle of coworkers and students of Vygotsky, and which later were incorporated into his own works (1934, 1956, 1960) as well as the work of his coworker (Leont'ev, 1959; Zaporozhets, 1960; Gal'perin, 1959; et al.).

These studies made it possible to trace the decisive role of language in the formation of higher mental functions in the child. Language first reflects isolated aspects of the perceived world but then isolates and generalizes fundamental attributes and creates the conceptual forms of the reflection of reality which allow the individual to subordinate his activity not according to surface characteristics but to much deeper connections and relations between the things of the perceived world. These investigations showed that in the process of the child's psychological development not only the structure of mental acts changes but there are also changes in the underlying "interfunctional relations" of mental acts. This is what was meant by changes in the "meaningful and systemic structure of consciousness," the study of which Vygotsky (1960) considered one of the most important tasks of psychological investigation. Finally, in a series of special investigations carried out in the same context, I and my collaborators succeeded in establishing that in the process of psychological development the child not only changes the internal structure of his psychological activity (Luria and Yudovich, 1956) but also experiences a radical reconstruction of the relations among his complex mental functions (Luria, 1936). The latter series of studies, which investigated changes in the relations among mental functions in twins, and which evoked considerable interest in Vygotsky, made a convincing case for the generalization that while in the early stages of mental development the changeability of such factors as memory is in large degree determined by genotypic factors, in later stages of development the changeability of processes such as memory becomes restructured under the influence of speech, loses its direct tie with the genotype, and begins to depend closely on paratypic factors connected with the influence of the environment. The discovery that in the process of mental development the child substantially changes not only its structure but also, to a certain degree, the *nature* of his psychological functions logically led to that cycle of investigations on the genesis of higher mental processes which was begun by Vygotsky toward the end of the 1920s and beginning of the 1930s, and in large measure defined the interest of Soviet psychologists in the succeeding years.

The position that the most complex psychological processes are a product of social-historical development and that they are connected with mastery of general human experience, the philosophical significance of which has been fully evaluated only recently by A. N. Leont'ev (1959), naturally directed interest toward an analysis of the concrete facts which indicated that the most important psychological factors change their structures in the process of social-historical development. This position also held that the fundamental categories of such psychological processes as the structure of perception, meaningful memory, and abstract thought are a product of historical conditions in the process of which everyday experience is more and more permeated by abstract speech, and that this process produces a decisive influence on the restructuring of the fundamental psychological processes which change not only in their content but also in their structure.

The position of Levi-Bruhl, according to which the qualitative changes in consciousness which are evoked in the processes of social history are connected with a change from magical to realistic thinking, seemed to Vygotsky and his coworkers incorrect from the very beginning. The findings which were derived from the conception discussed above made us think that the process of historical formation of higher psychological functions is completely different. It is necessary to represent qualitative change in consciousness as a change from a concrete form of mental activity, in which the leading role is played by immediate forms of practice, to complex forms of abstracted and generalized types of behavior, generalized forms of knowledge based on language.

These ideas, developed in cooperation with Vygotsky, led me to a whole series of works devoted to concrete manifestation of the historical formation of the fundamental psychological categories. The great strides made under the influence of the rapid economic, social, and cultural transformations were especially noticeable in those years in the Soviet countryside, where there was a rapid transformation from backward to contemporary technology and progressive social relations. These circumstances led us to turn our attention to the question of how, under the influence of social-historical advances, not only the content but the structure of processes such as meaningful perception and abstract thought changed. It was in these years that we collected unique experimental material which permitted us in concrete form to trace the changes in the structure of psychological processes which occurred under the influence of changing social-historical conditions.

This material, obtained by the writer and a large number of colleagues, indicated the correctness of this conception of historical development of psychological processes. Unfortunately this material was not readied for publication until 1970. It first appeared in a paper in the *International Journal of Psychology* in 1971; a more complete account will be found in my latest book *On the Historical Formation of Cognitive Processes*, published only in 1973.

THE 1940s AND THE ANALYSIS OF THE BRAIN MECHANISMS OF HIGHER MENTAL FUNCTIONS

While developing the theory of the formation of higher mental processes, Vygotsky, toward the end of the 1920s, began a new line of investigation which more and more began to occupy him and which in the future was to become one of the fundamental spheres of interest of his coworkers.

Studying the structure of higher mental functions, Vygotsky began to turn his attention to an analysis of their brain mechanisms. This enterprise would provide an underpinnig for the theory of higher mental functions in the form of a material foundation and thus introduce the new psychology into the circle of the natural science disciplines.

If the higher mental functions are a product of social-historical development, why is it necessary to represent their brain mechanisms in strictly localized and preestablished "cortical centra"? The idea of narrow localization of brain functions, which held that each psychological function possesses its own "brain center" serving as its material substratum, was not acceptable to this new theory. Functions which have their beginnings in the process of prenatal development, which are mediated by the use of language and which represent complex *functional systems,* could not possess as their material base limited groups of nerve cells which fulfill a constant function. The new psychological theory was just as dissatisfied with the equipotentiality theory proposed by Lashley and subscribed to in some degree by the Gestalt psychologists, such as K. Goldstein.

Observations of the behavior of patients with aphasia convinced Vygotsky that disturbances of speech evoke a much wider range of effects on behavior than one would suppose at first glance and that the patient who has lost his central speech mechanisms may suffer substantial disturbances of perception, thought, and the organization of his own behavior. Observations of aphasics during this period gave us a way to view those interfunctional systemic changes which evoked the seemingly specific disturbance of aphasia and which strengthened our belief in the systemic organization of higher mental processes.

At the same time another series of observations began which was destined to become the touchstone for further important investigations. It was in the 1920s that scientists first began to study diseases such as encephalitis and disturbances of subcortical structures which produce the symptoms of Parkinsonism. Vygotsky made the behavior of Parkinsonian patients the subject of special investigations which led to quite unexpected results.

It is well known that Parkinsonian patients manifest gross disturbances of automatic movements; they may take two to three steps, after which the disturbed tonus of the muscles and the characteristic palsy make further movement impossible. However, the same patient may easily walk up or down stairs and if a number of paper cartons, for example, are strewn on the floor he may easily walk among them without experiencing noticeable difficulties. The stimulation to perform any motor act and the substitution of a series of isolated movements carried out at the cortical level for the subcortical automatism makes it possible to reconstruct the entire functional system and to carry out the given motor act on a new, safe basis.

A focal brain lesion, which leads to aphasia, also leads to disruption of more complexly organized forms of mental activity and often shifts the entire range of behavior toward a more narrow functional level. Lesions of subcortical structures lead to a condition where the elementary forms of motor acts become impossible while at the same time the complex, mediated forms of their organization are maintained. I published observations on the restructuring of functional schemes in both groups of patients (especially Parkinsonian patients) in one of my early works (1932). These observations not only permitted us to determine the basic forms of brain disturbance, but also opened a wide range of possibilities for the systematic, dynamic analysis of complex forms of brain activity in man. It was these investigations which permitted Vygotsky to begin a systemic conception of the work of the brain, which he presented in an address shortly before his death (1934), and to formulate an exceptionally bold hypothesis concerning those changes in the intercentral relations which are manifested by the brain in the latter stages of its development.

This important hypothesis, formulated in Vygotsky's article "Psychology and Localization of Functions" (1934) was published only after his death. (It appeared in the journal *Neuropsychologia* in Vol. 3, 1965.) It can be summarized by saying that if a child has a focal lesion disturbing a certain "center" of the brain which hinders further development of higher overlying formations and thus leads to malfunctioning of a higher, more developed fundamental "center," then a focal lesion in the same "center" in an adult will affect the more elementary functions which depend on it and will lead to the disturbance of centers which lie below it. This hypothesis gave us the first concrete possibility of producing a "chronogenic localization of functions" and opened up new perspectives for the investigation of functional organization of brain activity in the later stages of mental development. One can only regret that the fundamental significance of this hypothesis remains insufficiently valued and that it has not had the influence on the further development of the science of the function of the brain which it deserves.

Investigation of systemic changes of mental functions during aphasia, begun together with Vygotsky and then continued after his death, led me to a closer analysis of the brain function and speech processes and consequently to a more systematic set of clinically oriented psychological investigations. Having obtained additional medical training (which until then had been virtually absent) I undertook a new program of clinical investigations of aphasia in Kharkov at the Ukrainian Psychoneurological Academy and later in Moscow.

Studies conducted at the Neuro-Surgical Clinic carried out at that time with considerable success permitted us to analyze those changes in higher mental functions which occurred as the result of focal brain lesions. Close analysis of verified instances of brain lesions which passed through the Neuro-Surgical treatment indicated the many and complex forms that disturbances in higher mental functions could take. It became possible to approach more analytically the question of the specific cortical mechanisms underlying different forms of speech disturbances. Through investigation of these cortical mechanisms, disturbances of which lead to different forms of speech disturbance, we were able to give a detailed description of the factors underlying the brain organization of speech activity. These studies opened a new, neuropsychological path for analysis of the structure of higher cortical functions.

This work, begun in the second half of the 1930s in the Institute of Neuro-Surgery (later called the Burdenko Institute of Neuro-Surgery), was continued during World War II in a special branch for nervous diseases of the All-Union Institute of Experimental Medicine (later called the Institute of Neurology of the Academy of Medical Sciences) which it fell to me to direct. Occupying more than 30 years, this work culminated in the analysis of two problems which, in equal degree, were of great significance for the development of scientific psychology.

The first of these problems, which is partially described in two unpublished monographs by the author (1940a, 1940b) and comprehensively in the book *Traumatic Aphasia* (1947a; published in English in 1970) was concerned with an analysis of the brain foundations of higher (systemic) mental functions and speech processes in particular. The second problem, dealt with in the book *The Restoration of Functions Following War-caused Trauma of the Brain* (1948; published in English in 1963), was concerned with the closely related problem of the restructuring of higher mental functions disturbed by brain lesions. Both these books, although dealing with neurological material, were further developments of those psychological problems whose investigation was begun by Vygotsky.

The systemic representation of the physiological structure of higher cortical functions found in this work eliminated all kinds of searches for special "centers" in the brain and led us to propose that the higher cortical functions (including speech) are carried out by means of the interactions of complex zones of the cortex, each of which carries more general functions but the ties among which are formed in the process of concrete activity and the mastery of objective systematic language. This meant that the investigator of the cortical foundations of mental activity and, most of all, of speech processes, had to carefully study the nonspeech functions of the basic zones of the cortex in order then, with a better foundation, to study the role each of these zones plays in the organization of complex speech activity.

Careful study indicated that the separate zones of the cortex which support the work of one or another of the "analyzers" (auditory, visual, tactile, motor) also present certain more general properties. For example, the areas located within the limits of the occipital-parietal area of the cortex may be viewed as the apparatus supporting synthesis of separate (let us suppose successively arriving) stimuli in separate simultaneously (spatial) organized groups. But the areas which are included in the temporal and precentral areas of the cortex carry out a different function, guaranteeing the synthesis of stimuli arriving in sequential (successive) *series*. I. M. Sechenov's idea of two basic types of synthesis, which are of decisive significance for the reflection of the influence of the environment, found its concrete support in this work. Our views concerning the two types of synthetical activity in the cortex formulated during that period and published in a volume on the jubilee of the great physiologist (Grashenkov and Luria, 1945) represented a substantial advance in the understanding of the spe-specific roles of separate zones of the cortex in carrying out higher forms of mental activity.

Conceptualizing the nonspeech functions of the separate zones of the cortex allowed us to separate factors composing the speech processes and to describe the fundamental symptoms characteristic of focal brain lesions. The fundamental symptom of disturbance of the cortex of the left temporal area turned out to be a disturbance in phonematic hearing leading to a disturbance of auditory language codes and to sensory aphasia. The fundamental symptom of a lesion in the parietal-occipital areas of the cortex was found in the disturbance in those complex codes, the fulfillment of which was impossible without simultaneous synthesis. The physiological foundation of such phenomena as the disturbance of operations of grammatical and numerical understanding, which occurred with lesions in the parietal-occipital areas of the left hemisphere, was also explained.

However, analysis of the brain organization of complex mental (and in particular speech) functions was only one side of the investigations occupying the years following World War II. Another, equally important problem was the investigation of how to restore brain functions disturbed as the result of focal lesions. Our studies had indicated that such processes as reading, writing, counting, and other intellectual operations, not to mention speech itself, all of which can be disturbed by focal brain lesions, can also to a certain degree be restored if the investigator finds the unimpaired links in the functional systems which may substitute for the disturbed components. We found that rational use of these methods of substitution may lead to the restoration of processes which had seemed irrevocably lost. These investigations once again convincingly indicated that "higher psychological functions" are in fact complex functional systems* and made it possible to follow the fundamental stages in their formation. Perhaps the most important attainment of this series of investigations was that they verified our hypothesis that the formation of complex functional systems proceeds "from the outside to the inside." At first the functional system is based on the use of external supporting means and only later, and under certain conditions, does it change over to a restructuring of the inner organization of psychological activity. This method of reconstituting functional systems was successful not only in the restoration of speech but in the restoration of such complex processes as active thinking.

Looking ahead, I continue to consider these experiments on the restructuring of intellectual activity and the restoration of active thought disturbed after injury to the frontal areas of the brain among the most interesting experiments which I have been able to carry out in the many years of work on the study of the brain organization of psychological processes.

Studies of the means by which brain functions disturbed as the result of focal lesions could be restored once again returned investigators to theoretical considerations relevant to the development of higher psychological processes and experimental attempts at their analysis which occupied a central place in the first steps made by Vygotsky and his coworkers. The result of the study of the formation of complex types of psychological activity, expecially the study of appropriate "models" for their analysis, later led to that wide circle of studies on the psychological investigation of "programmed mastery of knowledge" which occupied a central place in Soviet psychological science for almost twenty years and which was excellently described in the latest book of my coworker L. S. Tsvetkova, *Rehabilitative Training in Local Brain Lesions* (1972; the English version to be published by Mouton, The Hague).

THE 1950s AND THE INVESTIGATION OF THE REGULATING FUNCTIONS OF SPEECH

In the preceding section I discussed the investigations of certain brain mechanisms underlying cognitive processes and the organization of speech. These mechanisms constitute an important section of neuropsychology, but still do not include those substantial aspects of man's activity which distinguish it from the activity of other animals and which, in the early stages of the development of Soviet psychological science, were at the center of attention.

We have already indicated that the young Soviet psychologists who worked with Vygotsky in the 1920s were most interested in an objective study of the higher psychological functions of man which were social-historical in their

---

*The idea of "functional systems" was broadly elaborated by the outstanding Soviet physiologist P. K. Anokhin.

origin, took place by means of mediated participation of speech as their fundamental structural component, and which were capable of voluntary direction as their functional characteristic. It is natural that the mechanisms of voluntary regulation of higher psychological processes, which were comparatively poorly studied in the investigations just described, should again become the center of attention and that the regulating function of speech, which attracted such great interest in the first decade of the development of Soviet psychology, should again become the center of investigation, but this time on a new level.

The beginning of the 1950s saw in Soviet science an upsurge of interest in the physiological mechanisms of higher nervous processes studied by Pavlov and his coworkers. It was natural that special attention should be devoted to Pavlov's views on the "second signal system" since these not only opened the way for the physiological analysis of speech processes but also coincided with the central problem of the regulating function of speech which was emphasized by Vygotsky. Therefore, the efforts of several Soviet psychologists were directed to a more detailed description of these processes. The problem of the mechanisms by which speech regulates the course of psychological processes came to occupy a leading role in their investigations.

Although the auditory and the motor structure of speech as well as its lexical, grammatic, and syntactic structure had been studied for many years, the regulating influences of speech on the course of behavior—its "pragmatic" side—long remained without attention. Nevertheless, it is exactly through the influence which speech exercises on the formation and course of all psychological processes that one can study the fundamental features of human consciousness. Therefore, there was every reason to assume that the formation of the highest level of human behavior might be tied to the regulating role acquired by speech, and that the origin of a whole series of anomalies of development and pathological conditions might be found in the loss of speech and its regulating influence. We began a series of studies in order to clarify these important questions. With the assistance of several younger colleagues I succeeded in making a series of important findings on the development and pathology of the regulating function of speech, which are described in a number of special publications (1956, 1958, 1959, 1961).

It is well known, for example, that the phonetic side of speech is laid down during the third and fourth years, and that at this time the nominative and semantic functions of speech go through a series of levels of development. But how does the regulating aspect of the child's speech look at these ages?

Experiments carried out by myself and coworkers showed that the speech command of the adult, which is capable of starting the movement of a child 1½ to 2 years old, still cannot establish the stopping of this same movement nor can it create the preparatory program for the completion of a complex movement or overcome the inertia of an act already begun. The 1½- to 2-year-old child who is asked to complete one or another simple task (show a cup, point out a fish, and so on) still is not completely under the control of adult speech; his movement still continues to be regulated by factors outside the realm of speech, such as immediate perception, the direct orienting reflex, or inert traces of the previous act. Consequently, in cases where, in response to the command "give me the fish," the 1½-year-old child looks at the fish but turns to a brighter, more interesting, or closer chicken, we can conclude that the choice has been evoked by the unmediated orienting reflex, which dominates in the behavior of children of this age. Only gradually, as the child approaches the third year, does the regulating influence of the adult's speech begin to dominate over the non-mediated impressions; the *new functional system,* in which the speech traces strongly lead to the creation of the child's act and attain a dominating significance (1956, 1958, 1959, 1961), begins to form.

What psychological characteristics must the speech of the child have in order to become "the highest regulator" of behavior? It seems natural that the psychological processes underlying speech activity must possess sufficient persistence, concentration, and lability. Without this, speech traces could not be preserved and the speech system could not enter into that flexible connection with the motor system which would be necessary to guarantee its regulating influence. Does the speech system of a young child possess these properties? Do the relations or associations which he has formulated enter into a sufficiently strong connection with the motor acts and attain a strong and flexible regulating influence?

An experimental answer to this question required new experimental methods; these were suggested by E. D. Homskaya (Khomskaya) and were incorporated into a series of investigations devoted to the systematic analysis of the formation of the regulating influence of speech at successive stages of the child's life and in the presence of different forms of anomalous development. Superficially these methods were similar to the "combined motor method" I had used in the 1920s but they were distinguished in a fundamental way from this earlier method.

The child was asked to squeeze a bulb in response to each conditional signal (in more complex experiments, to refrain from pressing during the appearance of another, inhibitory signal). These experiments, carried out together with S. V. Yakovleva and O. K. Tikhomirov (1956, 1958), showed that children 2½ to 3 years old could not fulfill this task with sufficient control: the excitation evoked in the experiment remained too diffuse, and as a result the child, once having pressed on the bulb, was not able to wait quietly for the following signal without giving additional motor reactions during the preintervals.

How can one overcome this initial diffuseness of the stimulating processes? Is it possible to use the child's own speech for this purpose? Has the child reached a stage where his speech can fulfill this role?

For an answer to this question we substituted the child's speech reaction for his motor reaction; when the positive signal appeared he had to say "go!" and when the inhibitory signal appeared he had to say "no!", still not giving any kind of motor reaction. This experiment showed that the speech system of the

2½-year-old still does not possess the needed flexibility, for the speech responses were just as delayed and just as diffuse as the motor reactions. Only toward the third year does the child begin to give speech responses with sufficient rapidity, easily changing over when necessary from positive responses ("go!") to negative responses ("no!").

The observations of S. V. Yakovleva (Luria, 1956, 1958) showed that the diffuse and rigid (according to its neurodynamic specifics) speech of the child 2 to 2½ years old cannot be combined in one functional system with the motor response, and that the child responding "go!" concentrates his whole attention on this response and either does not give the necessary squeeze or gives it after considerable delay, because he is not able to coordinate the two components into one act. It is clear that the development of the child at this stage has not reached a point where we can ascribe a regulating function of speech.

Only toward the third year does this diffuseness and sluggishness of the neurodynamics of the speech process begin to wane; as the experiments of O.K. Tikhomirov have shown, the 3-year-old child makes adequate speech responses quite easily to signals presented to him and even combines his speech responses with motor responses. However, and this is the important point, the combination of speech and motor responses into one synchronous system still does not mean that the speech of the child has completely attained its regulating role and that complex speech mediated functional systems have been formed.

These experiments produced rather striking results. The integration of positive speech responses like "go!" with a motor reaction introduced a certain orderliness into the motor behavior of the child at this stage. Reinforced by the child's own speech commands, the motor responses became faster, they became organized, the indication of superfluous motor excitation and inadequate inter-signal reactions disappear. However, while the excitatory ("impulse") function of the child's speech at this age seemed sufficiently established, the inhibitory function still remained unformed. For upon pronouncing the words "no!" in response to a negative signal, the 3-year-old child simultaneously gave a strengthened motor response which had been disinhibited rather than inhibited by this command. At this stage the child is under the influence, not of the semantic content of the speech command, but its nonmediated "impulse" effect. This separation of regulatory influences into "impulse" and "semantic" dimensions was an important discovery permitting us to describe a new and, up until that time, poorly understood stage in speech development. Only in the 4- to 4½-year-old child does the association of nonmediated ("impulse") and semantic influences of speech appear. The child begins to subordinate his acts to the regulating influence of the semantic aspect of speech; the inner speech of the child begins to develop, there is an accumulation of those functional systems of mediated, linguistic, and psychological processes which constitute the essence of the higher psychological functions of man.

These findings also permitted us to approach from a new point of view important problems of anomalous development and abnormal psychology which had remained intransigent to scientific investigations.

In the clinic, diverse forms of anomalous development and pathological changes in psychological processes had been described repeatedly. Following up these descriptions investigators have sought to identify general laws of pathological deviation and, where possible, to discover the fundamental physiological processes which, it was hoped, would permit the grouping of various pathological conditions and serve as the starting point for their rational classification. Certain Soviet investigators, having studied the features of higher nervous activity accompanying different types of pathological conditions, came to believe that it would be possible to differentiate pathological conditions by an analysis of the characteristic changes in strength, concentration, and lability of the nervous processes and to build, on this basis, a pathophysiology of abnormal behavior. However, such attempts to reduce these pathological conditions to general changes in the excitatory and inhibitory processes inevitably shared those inadequacies of excessive generality which Vygotsky had criticized. This position closes off any possibility of reflecting the real, rich, and many-faceted aspects which distinguish pathological changes in the forms of psychological life.

We took a different approach: would it not be possible, using observations on the formation of higher psychological processes in normal development, to propose a new approach to the analysis of pathological conditions and to express them in units more adequate to their complexity?

The observations on normal development led us to propose that an adequate and rich indicator of the anomalous development of the child or of the pathological condition of psychological processes might be the different forms of the loss of those complex functional systems which are laid down during childhood.

It is well known that among all the forms of anomalous psychological development two can be distinguished as being in many respects the opposites of each other. One is often characterized as an "asthenic" condition which occurs as a result of trauma or some kind of general infection. For the most part it leaves the intellect preserved but results in a weakening of the neural processes which manifests itself in the heightening of excitatory or inhibitory tendencies in the child, in his inappropriate persistence or distractability as a result of disruption of the lability of fundamental nervous processes. The other form of anomalous development is oligophrenia, in which the intellectual functions are primarily disturbed but underlying which *there is always a gross disturbance of the neurodynamics which is evenly distributed among all types of nervous processes* (Luria, 1956, 1958). Would it be possible using these two "models" to verify the new approach to the psychophysiological analysis of pathological conditions which we had just formulated? Experiments carried out by E. D. Homskaya, E. N. Martsinovskaya. A. I. Meshcheryakov, V. I. Lubovski, and others (Luria, 1956, 1958) provide an answer to this question.

Children with the "cerebral asthenic syndrome" studied by Homskaya (Luria, 1956, 1958-1959, 1961) manifested a gross disturbance of the balance between excitatory and inhibitory processes; however, these pathological features of the neurodynamics, while clearly manifested in their motor reactions, were much less apparent in their speech processes. It was sufficient to use the method of combining motor and speech processes described above to see that the regulating role of speech remains essentially preserved and that the complex functional systems of activity in which speech controls the flow of psychological processes is disturbed in this case only in a secondary way.

By contrast, in oligophrenic children the pathology of the neurodynamic processes was manifested in the more elementary levels of behavior, but even more markedly in speech activity, giving speech a more sluggish and unstable character. With these children, all attempts to combine speech and movement in a single system preserving the regulative role of speech failed. The experiments objectively indicated the great depth of the loss which had occurred for the complex psychological systems in these children. These forms of pathological condition have thereby received a very clear characterization.

THE 1960s AND 1970s AND NEUROPSYCHOLOGY

The work carried out in the previous years led to the necessity for the next, synthetic stage in the formation of a new psychological science, neuropsychology. A great deal of my work during the 1960s was devoted to this subject, and this work continues to the present time.

This work included the preparation of a series of publications which generalize the research carried out earlier and with which I hope to make a contribution to a firm foundation to the science of the brain foundations of man's psychological activity, the application of the methods of experimental-psychological investigations to the diagnosis of focal brain lesions, and the restoration of disrupted brain functions. It also includes a series of later investigations of the brain mechanisms of psychological activity which were prepared during the earlier stages of my work. During this entire period, as in the preceding years, my research was closely tied with my work at the faculty of psychology at Moscow University and in the Burdenko Institute of Neurosurgery, where the research was concentrated.

After a long period of investigation, during the 1930s, 1940s, and part of the 1950s I had collected a great deal of material which suggested a general conception of the systemic structure of higher cortical functions, I began to evolve a special neuropsychological method, the "syndrome analysis" of focal brain lesions, which permitted us not only to describe changes in psychological activity produced by focal brain lesions but also made it possible to distinguish the *factors* underlying the disturbance of higher cortical functions in these situations. This approach permitted us to substitute for the disturbed behavior which occurs in focal brain lesions because we had completed an analysis of the mechanisms which underlie the disturbances. At the same time we could approach a series of important questions concerning the internal structure of the psychological processes themselves. It is easy to understand the importance for general psychology of knowing the role played by separate systems of the brain in the construction of different forms of psychological activity and the factors leading to each of them in the course of concrete psychological processes.

As early as the 1940s I had made attempts to arrive at a general conception of the systemic structure of higher cortical functions and to find a new approach to the analysis of changes in psychological activity resulting from focal brain lesions. In 1947 I published *Traumatic Aphasia* (Luria, 1947a), based on voluminous data collected during World War II; in 1948, *The Restoration of Functions Following War-Caused Trauma of the Brain* appeared; to the same period belongs the paper published jointly with Professor N. I. Grashchenkov, *The Systemic Localization of Functions in the Cerebral Cortex* (1945), which first gave a synopsis of my views on the systemic localization of higher psychological processes and their disturbance due to focal brain lesions.

As a result of new investigations in the 1960s, earlier findings on the disturbances in higher cortical functions caused by bullet wounds were supplemented by a great deal of material on the psychological analysis of behavior changes resulting from brain tumors. Successes in neurosurgery made it possible to obtain clear and verified data concerning localization of functions. Neuropsychological investigation of patients with tumors of the brain, which had as their task more exact topical diagnosis of lesions, was introduced into the neurosurgical clinic. The restoration of psychological processes disturbed as a result of focal brain lesions became an important applied problem. All this made it possible to collect significant material on the psychological analysis of focal brain lesions. The general conception of *neuropsychology,* that new area of science falling on the border between psychology and the neurological clinic, was the result of this activity.

In 1962 the first edition of the author's book *Higher Cortical Functions in Man* (1962; published in English in 1966) appeared, and in 1963 his book *The Human Brain and Psychological Processes* (published in English in 1966). A revised and significantly widened variation of the book *Traumatic Aphasia* was published in English in 1970. Continuing, intensive investigation created the necessity for preparing a second, significantly expanded edition of my basic work *Higher Cortical Functions of Man,* which was published by Moscow University in 1969, translations of which were published in Italian 1964, in German in 1970, and a French translation was begun at the same time as the Russian edition. At the same time a second volume of *The Human Brain and Psychological Processes* was published (Luria, 1970c) in which I discussed the problem of the neuropsychological analysis of conscious activity and which included both theoretical articles and neuropsychological investigations of patients with lesions of the frontal lobes and disturbances of complex forms of conscious activity. At about the same time our laboratory produced a large volume, *The Frontal Cortex and the Regulation of Psychological Processes,* edited in collaboration with my closest coworker, E. D. Homskaya, and another book, coauthored by L. S. Tsvetkova, *Neuro-psychological Analysis of the Solution of Problems* (1966; published in French in 1967).

Publication of these works permitted me to summarize the fundamental positions concerning neuropsychology as a science and its separate areas. Specific articles devoted to the general principles of neuropsychology include "Factors and Forms of Aphasia" (1964a), "Problems and Facts of Neuro-linguistics" (1967b), "Complex Mechanisms of Psychological Processes" read at the IBRO-UNESEO meetings on the investigation of the brain and man's behavior in Paris in 1968 (1968a), "Neuro-psychology as a Science," which was read at the 16th International Congress of Applied Psychology in Amsterdam in 1968 (1968b), and also "The Origin and Brain Organization of Conscious Activity," being an evening lecture to the 19th International Congress of Applied Psychology in London in 1969. Also, certain most important investigations concerning neuropsychology were two volumes, *Basic Problems of Neuropsychology*, which is being prepared for Harvard University Press, and *Basic Problems of Neurolinguistics*, which will be published by Mouton (The Hague), while a series of works related to the neuropsychological analysis of the functions of the frontal cortex was included in a volume *Behavioral Psychophysiology of the Frontal Lobes*, edited by K. H. Pribram and myself and published by Academic Press. Finally, a comprehensive volume on neuropsychology "The Working Brain" was published by Penguin Psychological Series, Allan Lane, and Basic Books in 1973, and a comprehensive review "Psychological Studies in the USSR" appeared in the Proceedings of the National Academy of Sciences of the USA in 1973.

What is the fundamental position underlying publications identified above and the fundamental lines of work to which it is related? The answer to this question is not too difficult: the scientific investigation, which occupied a lengthy period of time, takes its logic and much of its structure from the work that had already been described in the preceding pages. Important in this regard was Vygotsky's statement of the 1920s that psychology was really divided into two sciences, one of which described the most complex phenomena of the spiritual life of man but refused causal analysis, while a second branch explained the physiological mechanisms of elementary processes excluding from its spheres of interest the complex spheres of conscious activity. Vygotsky saw the way out of this crisis in the creation of a psychological science which studied the origin and laws of the organization of the most complex forms of conscious activity, while not denying the deterministic approach to its causal explanation.

Other Soviet psychologists (A. N. Leont'ev, P. Y. Gal'perin, A. V. Zaporozhets, and D. B. Elkonin) continued the line begun by L. S. Vygotsky, the investigation of the development of psychological processes in ontogenesis and the construction of a theory of psychology beginning with these principles. I took as my task an attempt to develop the same position with relation to the brain mechanisms of complex psychological activity and to develop a path to its neuropsychological analysis. To this task I devoted approximately 40 years of my life.

My approach to neuropsychology can be summarized by saying that the higher psychological processes represent complex functional systems, social in their genesis, mediated in their structure, and carried out by whole complexes of jointly working zones of the brain with certain applications of social ("extra-cerebral") tool and sign using mechanisms. Of the most fundamental importance is the fact that each area of the brain, including the cortex, enters into functional systems in terms of its own *particular role* and makes its own *specific contribution* to the work of the whole functional system. Therefore, disturbance of any of the areas of the brain may lead to a loss of the entire functional system, but each disturbed center excludes a special factor from a given functional system. As a result, brain lesions in different locations affect the system in a different way. It is this fact which permitted us to use the disturbance of the higher psychological processes resulting from focal brain lesions for a topical diagnosis of the locus of the lesion.

In later publications (1968b, 1969, 1973) I described attempts to distinguish three fundamental areas of the brain which necessarily participate in any, even the least complex, psychological activity, each of which exerts a special influence in the organization of psychological processes. The first general part, including the apparatus of the upper brain stem and limbic cortex, was conditionally designated as the area of tonus or the energy area (for the past decade the function of this area has been especially carefully studied in the worldwide physiological literature). The second part, which includes the posterior areas of the cortex (occipital, parietal, temporal), was designated the area for reception, processing, and storage of information. The third part, which includes the frontal cortex, was designated the area for programming, regulation, and control of movements and activity. Detailed analysis of the functions fulfilled by each of these general areas in the organization of psychological activity were the subject of research which I began in the 1930s and which continued for about 40 years.

The role of the brain formations which comprise the structure of the second of the three general areas was the subject of my first period of investigation on this topic, which began even before World War II and continued in the following years. The analysis of the temporal area of the brain and its role in carrying out phonematic hearing, and the analysis of the parietal-occipital areas of the brain and their significance for simultaneous spatial synthesis of incoming information, was reflected in several publications (1940b, 1945a, 1947a, 1948, 1962, 1969, 1970a, 1973a, and others). The disturbance of gnosis and praxis—counting, writing, reading, and complex intellectual operations—which occurs as a result of lesions in these zones permitted us to discover important factors in the organization of these complex psychological activities. I am inclined to consider particularly important the disruption of the role of phonematic hearing in the construction of speech and writing, which was discovered during analysis of instances of focal lesions of the left temporal area, and disturbances of those simultaneous spatial schemes involved in the construction of complex symbolic processes, which were discovered during detailed analysis of parietal-occipital lesions of the left hemisphere.

It was these investigations which permitted me to propose that neuropsychological analysis makes it possible to uncover significant differences in processes which at first glance may seem identical (for instance, musical and phonematic hearing), and to find an inner similarity among processes which at first glance seem to be quite different (for instance, orientation to spatial relationships and certain logical-grammatical structures, the process of counting, and so on). I am certain that future use of neuropsychology for the analysis of the structure of higher psychological processes will turn out to be highly productive in aiding the construction of future scientific psychophysiology (see 1964b, 1967a, 1968b, 1968c, 1970c, 1973a, et al.).

In the 1960s the core of my research and the research of my coworkers has moved from an analysis of areas processing information from sensory input to an analysis of the functions of the *frontal lobes of the brain*. The question of the role of the frontal lobes in the organization of man's behavior had long remained without an adequate solution and investigators had wavered between viewing the frontal lobes as the "higher organ of the brain" and a complete denial of any special function for these areas. The disagreements were in significant measure tied to the fact that the function of the frontal lobes, the latest and highest product of evolution, could not be expressed in the classical terminology of the reflex arc. The absence of any disturbance of sensitivity, or of associative or motor processes, gave some reason to believe that the frontal lobes were a "luxury of nature," whose role in the organization of behavior remained unclear.

Matters changed considerably when people began to apply the conception of self-regulating systems which had developed in recent decades in cybernetics to the organization of behavior. In neurophysiology this movement, among other things, led to a closer investigation of the connection between the frontal lobes and the brain stem formations which support the necessary tonus of the cortex.

Investigations in these directions became the center of attention of physiologists and neuropsychologists of various countries. N. A. Bernstein, in the USSR, put forth the idea of a reflex circle, the mechanisms of which underlie the regulation of motor acts, and studied the organization of motor processes on different neural levels. P. K. Anokhin, one of the leading physiologists in the USSR, proposed the concept of "the acceptor of action," an apparatus which permitted evaluation of the relation between the effect of an act and the initial intention. With good reason he associated the acceptor of action with the functions of the frontal lobes. A very similar position was put forth by K. Pribram, who studied the role of the function of the frontal lobes in the programming and regulation of behavior.

This same theme underlies the work of myself and my coworkers which has been in progress for many years, beginning in the 1930s and continuing almost without interruption up to the present time. It was widely known in the clinic that patients who had suffered massive damage (bullet wounds or brain tumors) in the frontal lobes suffered from a disturbance of voluntary behavior and an inability to recognize their own difficulties. However, the number of detailed experimental-psychological and physiological investigations of these disturbances was very limited and there was no sufficiently well-based hypothesis concerning the neurophysiological factors underlying the disturbances themselves.

The present context permits only a résumé of the most fundamental results of our investigations on frontal lobe functions, presented not in chronological but in logical order. Using a large number of response measures (plethysmographic and GSR components of the orienting reflex, frequency analysis of the alpha rhythm and its changes, changes in the dynamic waves of asymmetrically increasing and decreasing of the fronts of alpha rhythm potentials, and evoked potentials), E.D. Homskaya and her coworkers (E. Yu. Artem'eva, O. P. Baranovskaya, A. Ioshpa, and E. G. Simernitskaya as well as N. A. Filippycheva) showed that disturbances of the frontal lobe do not eliminate involuntarily evoked indicators of the orienting reflex. In all normal subjects and in all patients with disturbances of the posterior areas of the brain, the presentation of a stimulus with signal significance ("count the signals," "look for changes in the signals," etc.) leads to stabilization of all the orienting response indicators and delays their disappearance which ordinarily occurs as a function of adaptation. The patients with disturbances of the frontal lobes (especially the medial areas of the frontal lobes) manifested a completely different behavior pattern. Experiments showed that *in patients with disturbances of the frontal lobes it was impossible to evoke stable increases in the tonus of the cortex by using speech instructions, and that the stabilization of the vegetative and electrophysiological indicators of the orienting reflex* (which were preserved in patients with disturbances of the rear areas of the brain and which had been established in normal subjects as well) *was completely absent in these patients or appeared in them only in a very reduced and unstable form.*

These findings, which before Homskaya's investigations were unknown in the literature, placed the frontal lobes in a completely special position with respect to other areas of the cortex. As a result of these investigations we can view frontal lobes as an apparatus which participates very directly in the regulation of the tonus of the cortex, so necessary for its alert working condition. It is of particular import that the frontal lobes are connected with lower-lying formations, particularly with the extensive incoming and outgoing signals of the reticular formation, the apparatus guaranteeing the regulation of the conditions of activity which is carried out with the close participation of the speech system. (All these findings are discussed in the recent book of E. D. Homskaya, *Brain and Activation*, Moscow University Press, 1972 as well as in a volume edited by K. H. Pribram and myself, 1973.)

Even our investigations begun in the 1940s had shown that in patients with massive disturbances of the frontal lobes the elementary motor reflexes are preserved; but while there are no manifestations of paresis or paralysis the ability to bring these movements under the control of speech instructions is quite disturbed. These investigations, which were only partially published later (Luria,

1962, 1966, 1969, 1970a, 1973a, etc.) showed that even in the case of simple motor reactions according to speech instructions ("When there is a bell lift your hand") patients with massive disturbances of the frontal lobes can make the response only with great difficulty, and the response turns out to be very unstable. Patients with massive frontal lesions, particularly those with a clearly expressed "frontal syndrome," easily remembered the instruction and were able to repeat it even after a considerable lapse in time; yet after only a few motor responses they would stop performing the task, repeating "Yes, yes, I have to raise my hand!" and not making any movement at all. The regulating function of speech instructions disappeared although the semantic side of the instructions was preserved (A. I. Meshcheryakov). Experiments on *choice reactions* manifested even more clearly the disturbance of the regulating function of speech. Patients in this group readily learned the instruction "In response to a red light press the right key, in response to a green light press the left key" or "In response to one tap lift your right hand, in response to two taps lift your left hand" and could easily repeat such an instruction. However, it was necessary only to change the stereotyped order of presenting the signals for the performance of the given program to be disturbed; the patient would repeat the previous action, complete the alternating movement of the hand regardless of which signal was given to him, or continue to respond to any signal with one and the same hand (M. P. Ivanova).

These defects appear with particular clarity in those situations where the action of an immediately perceived signal is in conflict with its conditional significance (for instance, when the patient is asked to respond to one signal by making two responses and to two signals with one response, or to answer to a long signal quickly and to a rapid signal with a slow movement). Experiments carried out under these conditions by Homskaya and M. Maruszevskii (Luria and Homskaya, 1966) showed that patients with massive disturbances of the frontal lobes very quickly stopped regulating their movements to the speech instructions and instead responded with elementary echopractic repetition of the signal.

It is easy to see that disturbances of the regulating function of speech caused by disturbances of the frontal lobes destroy those functional systems which, as our early experiments showed, are formed in the 3- to 4-year-old child during the period of maximal growth of the frontal lobe system, and the loss of which may be observed clearly only in the clinic, where disturbances of these areas of the brain are treated.

Analysis of the disturbance of behavior during massive disruption of the frontal lobes has not been restricted to these relatively simple forms of motor reactions. In the 1940s we had carried out investigations showing that frontal lobe patients lost the ability to independently formulate plans and programs of complex constructive activity. This was shown initially in the work of S. G. Gadzhiev (Luria and Homskaya, 1966) with Link Cube and then in the work of L. S. Tsvetkova (Luria and Homskaya, 1966) with Koh's blocks. In both instances patients were clearly unable to construct a plan of action, and their behavior was sharply distinguishable from that of patients with disruption of the posterior (parieto-occipital) areas of the brain, who manifested the optical-spatial defects characteristic of these disruptions.

Similar findings were obtained during a detailed analysis of the perceptual capability of patients with disturbances of the frontal lobes. They showed clear defects in the perceptual orienting-investigatory activity, which allows man to collect the information he needs and which makes meaningful perception an active, directed process. These data were obtained in my laboratory by O. K. Tikhomirov (Luria and Homskaya, 1964) and were closely studied in experiments which recorded eye movements during the perception of complex pictures (V. A. Karpov, A. R. Luria, and A. L. Yarbuss, 1968).

This cycle of experiments was completed by investigations of changes which occur in frontal lobe patients in respect to complicated forms of cognitive activity—for example, understanding complex oral fragments and solving problems. In these experiments carried out by Tsvetkova and myself (Luria and Homskaya, 1966; Luria and Tsvetkova, 1966), we clearly showed how the frontal lobes play an important role in the regulation of such complex intellectual processes. The experiments permitted us to contrast the insufficiently convincing and overgeneralized notions concerning disturbance of "abstract sets" with a significantly more reliable conception of the role of the frontal lobes in the programming, regulation, and control of psychological activity.

As in much of our work, the research on frontal lobe functions has been concerned with the application of neuropsychology to the restoration of functions disturbed as the result of focal brain lesions. Our experience during the war, when I and my coworkers found it necessary to work in neurosurgical hospitals specializing in restoration, permitted us to formulate theoretical assumptions concerning the restoration of brain functions after war trauma (Luria, 1948). In the course of later years my principles were verified and extended in a series of studies on the programming of restorative training, the basis of which was developed in collaboration with Tsvetkova (1964) and summarized in the latest book of L. S. Tsvetkova, *Re-habilitative Training in Local Brain Lesions* (1972).

I have dwelt in detail on those aspects of neuropsychology which were developed in the course of many years and have a relatively completed character. I shall only briefly mention one area of this large section of psychology which is the subject of current investigation and whose completion is a matter of the future. This concerns the role played in the organization of complex forms of psychological activity by the deep structures of the brain, in particular those sections which enter into the structure of the first of the three "fundamental areas" which I noted above and which support the tonus and activation level of the cortex.

The whole history of science of recent decades shows the great attention that has been given by physiologists to the detailed study of the functions of the brain stem, the reticular formation, and limbic areas. As a consequence it is completely indefensible to continue not paying attention to the vertical organization of the brain apparatus. Therefore, I have been faced with the question: What significance do these deep structures of the brain have for the structure of the higher forms of psychological activity of man?

Investigation of patients with lesions of the upper area of the brain stem (the hypothalamic and thalamic areas and the limbic system) using the usual methods for the study of gnosis, praxis, speech, and thinking, produced no substantial results; consequently, I was forced to search for new ways to evaluate the contributions which these brain formations make in complex forms of psychological activity. Various attempts carried out in the course of several years led to substantial results, indicating the path for future investigations. It turns out that lesions of the deep structures, along with disturbing the general tonus of the cortex, lead to substantial disruption of *memory,* as many leading investigators have pointed out, and this fact led me and my coworkers to devote recent years to the study of the nature of the changes in memory which are produced by such lesions.

In 1967 I published the results of a study carried out jointly with E. D. Homskaya, S. M. Blinkov, and MacDonald Critchley on a patient with a tumor in the medial area of the frontal lobe. These observations showed that lesions of these areas of the brain do not lead to much noticeable disturbance of gnosis, praxis, and speech but do evoke lowered cortical tonus, a condition which makes careful selective psychological processes impossible; old and irrelevant ties begin, under these conditions, to disturb behavior and to occur as readily as the substantial and needed ties. This change in the selective structure of the psychological processes turns out to be characteristic for patients in this group.

Further investigations have verified that this was the proper way to view the role of the deep brain formation in the flow of complex forms of psychological activity. It turned out that whenever there was a lesion of the upper brain stem and its ties with the limbic cortex (including the hippocampus), there was an increase in the extent to which interfering factors inhibited traces. It is because of this phenomenon that the primary disturbance of memory, which is characteristic for this type of brain pathology, occurs. It was also found that disturbances of memory such as appear in these cases do not manifest any modal specificity, appearing alike in all types of activity (visual, auditory, motor, speech). Finally, we found that while a limited lesion of the upper brain stem might appear symptomatically only as increased inhibition of the traces, in cases of massive disturbances in this area (a tumor of the deep structures, distributed along the midline) there was not only the heightened inhibition of traces but also the disturbances of selectivity which we noted above and which apparently evoke the phenomenon of "equality of excitation of traces" characteristic for weakly functioning cortexes. When, along with the disturbances of this zone, there are lesions leading to a dysfunction of the medial areas of the frontal cortex (as the result of a tumor or arterial spasms), the symptoms are manifested in a particularly sharp form and neuropsychology is in a position to study the mechanisms underlying the altered conditions of consciousness and the confusions which are components of Korsakow's syndrome. These findings are published in a series of works of my collaborators (L. T. Popova, M. Klimkowski, N. K. Kyascenko, Pham Ming Hac, and N. A. Akbarova) and in a monograph by A. R. Luria, A. N. Konovalov, and A. Ya. Podgornaya (1970), in a forthcoming book by N. K. Kyascenko, L. Moskovichute, T. O. Faller, et al., and in my two-volume monographs *Neuropsychology of Memory* (in press). They show that neuropsychological analysis may be productive in evaluating the contributions which the deep structures of the brain make in the flow of complex forms of higher psychological activity. In addition, they open up new perspectives for analysis of the inner mechanisms of activation and consciousness which, until now, have not been accessible.

The neuropsychological analysis of memory disturbances was only one topic of my work during the early 1970s. The second was a series of research leading to a new branch of science—that of *neurolinguistics*.

The analysis of basic cortical processes underlying language and speech was the starting point of our early studies of aphasia, which started in the 1930s, which was summarized in the volume *Traumatic Aphasia* in 1947, and which was followed by a series of special papers on aphasia. That brought me to the necessity to return to the basic problems of language disorders and the description of the cortical organization of speech from a new standpoint.

During the last two decades significant changes in linguistic sciences occurred and a new branch of science, psycholinguistics, was created. A series of outstanding authors turned to the description of basic problems of phonemic and lexical, syntactical, and semantic descriptions of linguistic structures. It became impossible to ignore these achievements and to continue the study of language disorders without a good knowledge of this new and important branch of science.

That is why starting from the late 1960s and during the early 1970s we returned anew to the problems of aphasia, trying to reconsider our former concepts of language disorders in local brain lesions. We started a revision of the problems of verbal communication, of basic laws of encoding and decoding of verbal processes, and we came to a reconsideration of the basic forms of aphasic syndromes. We had to try to formulate some new concepts of the psychophysiological mechanisms of speech disorders, and to formulate once more our concepts of aphasia, adding some important considerations to the revision of the concepts of complex forms of aphasia—"conduction aphasia," "transcortical aphasia," and "amnestic aphasia." The result of these observations were given in a series of papers such as "Factors and forms of aphasia" (1964), "Problems and facts of neurolinguistics" (1967), "Aphasia reconsidered" (1971), "On two basic forms of aphasia" (1973), and so forth. New vistas in neuropsychological analysis of the processes of verbal communication became clear, and I felt a necessity to summarize these new approaches in a volume *Basic Problems of Neurolinguistics*, which was ready toward the end of 1973 and which had to be published in Russian and English as one of my last books. To come to this decision I had both to study very carefully the most important achievements of modern linguistics and to reconsider my former approaches to the disturbances of speech and language in local brain lesions. I still have the feeling that this step of my work will be of a significance for the developing of this new branch of science and that together with my coworkers and friends I could contribute to this new step in the development of our knowledge.

Neuropsychological investigations, which have been a large part of my scientific life, have helped to clarify one position with which I would like to conclude these pages.

The study of the phenomena under consideration began with a "complex syndrome" investigation of psychological processes and convinced me of the productivity of that path, which unfortunately is still not part of contemporary psychology.

It is well known that the psychologist always concentrates his investigation on one or another interesting process, constructs hypotheses, and develops adequate methods for the investigation of this process. The reliability of the data he obtains is demonstrated by statistical analysis and replication. Lack of attention to the remaining processes of psychological life, and the narrowing of his interest to the study of the single process he has decided to focus on, represents a necessary condition for the logic of his investigation.

A completely different logic characterizes clinical (including neuropsychological) investigations. The neuropsychologist, studying the role which one or another system of the brain plays in the flow of complex psychological processes, finds himself in quite a different situation. As a rule the number of cases (patients) with focal brain lesions on whom he can investigate his hypotheses is very limited, and the reliability obtained as a result of the investigation cannot be determined by statistical methods. As a result the neuropsychologist must choose another method. This method is widely used in clinical studies under the name "syndrome analysis." Its essence, well formulated by the leading neurologist Kurt Goldstein, consists in the following. The investigator chooses a fundamental symptom which usually appears following a focal brain lesion and then hypothesizes some factor the inclusion of which must have led to the manifestation of this syndrome (for instance, disturbances of simultaneous spatial synthesis resulting from lesions of the parietal-occipital lobes of the brain, disturbances of successive motor synthesis resulting from lesions of the premotor area of the brain, etc.). In order to verify the correctness of this hypothesis, the investigator turns to a detailed analysis of other psychological processes the study of which is not a primary part of his task. These should be psychological processes which are included in his "factor" as being the result of a focal brain lesion and which must necessarily manifest themselves in the form of a disturbance. The opposite is also required:

psychological processes which do not enter into this factor must remain intact. As a result of such an analysis one obtains a whole complex of interrelated symptoms or "a syndrome," and the more correlated attributes it includes, the more certain we are of our hypothesis.

The method of "syndrome analysis," which is the fundamental method of neuropsychology, permits one to carry out a unique kind of "factor analysis" on one individual and has established itself as a general method for clinical psychology. However, its significance extends far beyond the confines of the clinic. It is one of the most promising methods for one of the most difficult areas of general psychology—the *psychology of personality,* which usually is of a descriptive character.

I have attempted to apply such a "syndrome analysis" to an instance of extraordinary memory, published in a small book *The Mind of a Mnemonist* (1968d). In this book I attempted to analyze the structure of the personality of a man who possessed an exceptional (in practice, unlimited) synesthetic memory. I concentrated not so much on the special features of his memory as on the consequences that this extraordinary memory had for the structure of the entire personality. I followed the same way in another book, where a single person with a lesion of the parieto-occipital part of the brain and a disturbance of spatial relations and complex memory was studied. It appeared in Russian in 1971 under the title *The World Lost and Re-gained* and in English in 1972 under the title *A Man with a Shattered World* (Luria, 1972c).

I would hope that this initial attempt would represent a small "kick-off" which may initiate neuropsychological investigations relevant to the exploration of important problems of psychology as a whole.

UNSOLVED PROBLEMS AND PERSPECTIVES

This summary of the path I have followed over a span of almost 50 years of work has of necessity been long. Certain thoughts concerning the problems which remain unsolved and *future perspectives* can of course be significantly shorter. This is understandable because it is natural to think that a summary of the past is based on much richer information than are glimpses of the future, and because the time which remains for me for future work is incomparably shorter than the time already spent in traveling the path I have described.

As often happens with investigators when they are contemplating unsolved problems, I experience real feelings of dissatisfaction and I well understand the extent to which the "mountain of the unknown" is greater than the small bit that is already known. But as always occurs in such instances, I try to take comfort from the thought that the little bit which each man may accomplish, especially in cases where the man is of moderate talents, is only a component part of the work of a group as well as of that system of studies carried out in a given area of science. This thought can serve as support for the idea that this chapter from *A History of Psychology in Autobiography* should be concluded with some reflections about the perspectives of future research.

In all my work, which basically has been devoted to the development and loss of higher cortical functions and the neuropsychological analysis of brain functions in man, I have consciously assumed the validity of three kinds of abstractions. We abstracted the phenomena we studied from the whole of the rich material of the clinic; we did not go into the neurodynamic analysis of pathophysiological data; we were too isolated from some neighbor fields of science, especially from the progress of modern linguistics; finally, we abstracted the psychological processes that we have studied from a probabilistic matrix of events.

This tripartite abstraction, which is inescapable at our level of development, will not be permissible in the future. Before us lies the holistic task of going beyond the limits of those schemes which have guided our work up to now and which, although they are correct as basic models, are inadequate for a closer analysis of the entire range of phenomena.

There is little that I can add in the way of describing the basic functions of the separate systems of the brain of man, particularly with respect to the frontal lobes, which were the primary subject of our analysis. However, the richness of these functions and the differences among them are so great (as are the effects of different lesions) that what actually occurs goes far beyond what I have been able to describe here.

Close analysis has shown that none of the fundamental areas of the cortex, least of all the frontal lobes, represents a unitary whole. Clinical experience convinces us that lesions of the basal, medial, prefrontal, and frontal lobes, as well as lesions of the right and left hemispheres, all lead to completely different syndromes, and that the underlying function of each of these areas is apparently different. The same can be said for the different brain systems. If we add that lesions of each of these systems take place under different subcortical and cortical conditions, and that the psychological significance relating to the areas of the left (dominant) and right (subdominant) hemispheres is quite different as between the two, we can see that neuropsychological investigation faces a huge task. I have undertaken only the first steps in such work by having begun, together with my closest coworker E. K. Homskaya, to think about the "varieties of the frontal syndrome," and with other coworkers (in particular E. G. Simernitskaya, T. O. Faller, N. K. Kyascenko, et al.) to discuss the problem of the neuropsychological analysis of deep lesions of the brain and the syndromes of lesions of the right hemisphere. And if, which is more than probable, I am unable to significantly progress on this problem, others will certainly do so.

In previous years we consciously neglected to make a physiological (neurodynamic) analysis of the phenomena we observed. Now such neglect is becoming a hindrance for future work. It is well known that a pathological focus not only disturbs one or another factor in a given part of the brain; it changes the normal course of neural processes and the change represents sometimes general and sometimes specific effects.

Now we are beginning to find out that pathological changes in the cortex change tonus and disturb the normal "law of strength" according to which the strength of a response is a linear function of the strength of the stimulus (or stimulus trace). It is well known, also, that the pathological changes caused by a brain lesion change the lability of neural processes and thus lead to a condition wherein the evoked system of excitation acquires a pathologically inert character which must necessarily influence the normal course of psychological activity.

Before us lies the task of reviewing the facts established earlier and of passing their analysis through the prism of the laws of pathological change of neurodynamics. It is hardly necessary to state that this work, which has become central to the future progress of neuropsychology, will require years and will have to be the fundamental concern of future investigators.

In the flow of the last decades when I was busy with the construction of basic concepts of neuropsychology, I was very separated from the significant achievements of a series of neighbor sciences and, first of all, from modern linguistics and psycholinguistics. That branch of science made a tremendous success during the last decades, and it would be unwise to ignore the progress of this field. That is why a necessity arose—to incorporate the richness of new ideas of linguistics and psycholinguistics in our knowledge, to construct some new approaches to the problem of verbal communication and speech pathology which would include new concepts of linguistics as well as new neurodynamic approaches toward the brain mechanisms of language. That required a construction of a new field—that of *neurolinguistics*, and a revision of basic approaches to aphasia.

It is easy to understand that this became one of the most powerful motives of my work during the last years; the results of this work were reflected in a series of my latest publication on aphasia and will be reviewed in my next book, *Basic Problems of Neurolinguistics*, which will appear in 1974 in the Moscow University Press and the English version in Mouton (The Hague).

In the course of many years I have investigated the formation and disturbance of psychological processes, the structure of which was accepted in contemporary psychology, and more or less ignored the probabilistic structure of these processes. This abstraction, which was unavoidable at that level of research, limits the perspectives of future research.

Investigations carried out by many researchers convincingly demonstrate that such processes as recall of words and decision making can never be reduced to a simple linear association between the sound and the significance, or the intention and the movement, as was accepted previously. Now it is quite clear that all these processes possess a probabilistic character such that when a word is remembered, or a solution is chosen from among a set of alternatives, and either of these processes occurs with differing probabilities, then both the choice of the word and the final problem solution are the result of a choice among alternatives.

These conceptions of the structure of any complex psychological process must be used in psychological investigations. Problem solving is based on an organized and selective flow of higher nervous processes, and whether the pathological focus changes the normal condition of the cortex only within the limit of a single system or throughout the entire brain, the organized process of "problem solving" may be substantially disturbed. An approach from this point of view to the phenomena of agnosia or apraxia, of disturbed speech or conscious activity, would uncover a much deeper set of intimate mechanisms related to the flow of psychological processes than does the idea of a linear succession of phenomena which underlie many of our earlier studies. This leads me to think that analysis of the course of normal and pathologically changed psychological processes which evaluates the probabilistic nature of their structure will throw substantially new light on the data collected in previous investigations.

It is obvious that a rational statistical approach to all these phenomena has to be elaborated; but it is clear as well that the existing mathematical apparatus for elaboration of the reliability of the symptoms we describe in patients with local brain lesions is insufficient, and that a new mathematical apparatus adjusted for a syndrome analysis in a relatively small number of cases has to be elaborated. We tried to express some ideas concerning such an apparatus in my paper with E. Yu. Artemieva (1971), and we hope to continue this search.

And here I find myself convinced that the facts already obtained by our own research must be reviewed from this new viewpoint, and that a new perspective will thus be afforded for the reconstruction of the research carried out earlier. There is no doubt that this reconstruction, toward which I have only begun to move, will occupy many years and will be substantially advanced only by future investigators. A life lived in the context of scientific search is, after all, very short, and each investigator who travels a seemingly long path must have the willingness to conclude a retrospective review of his work by indicating the perspective which will be followed without his participation.

But I began these notes with the thought that while people come and go, the solid work remains, and that the work which has been accomplished through the efforts of the individual investigator will be continued in the future by virtue of its own internal logic. I can only hope that this will be the result in my own case.

REFERENCES

Selected Publications by A. R. Luria

The foundations of realistic psychology. Kazan (unpublished manuscript), 1922.

The combined motor method and its application for the investigation of afferent processes, 1928. (Also in the journal, *Psychol. Forsch., 12,* No. 2-3, 1929.)

The nature of human conflicts. New York: H. Liveright, 1932.

The development of mental functions in twins. *Charac. & Pers.,* 1936, *5,* 35-47.

The study of aphasia in the light of brain pathology. Part 1. Temporal aphasia (doctoral dissertation); Part 2. Parietal (semañtic) aphasia (unpublished study), 1940.

The disturbance of set and behavior by brain lesions. *Works of the Institute of Psychology.* Georgian SSR: Academy of Science, 1945. Volume in honor of D. N. Uznadze. (a)

The pre-motor syndrome and disturbances of movements. *Uch. Zap. Mosk. Univ.,* 1945, No. 90. (b)

Traumatic aphasia. Moscow: Izd-vo. Akad. Med. Nauk, 1947. (English edition, *Traumatic aphasia.* The Hague: Mouton, 1970.) (a)

Two kinds of synthetic activity of the cerebral cortex. *Trud. Odess. Univ.,* 1947, No. 147 (later published in *The human brain and psychological processes).* (English edition, New York: Harper & Row, 1966.) (b)

The restoration of functions following war-caused trauma of the brain. Moscow: Izd-vo. Akad. Med. Nauk., 1948. (English edition, Elmsford, N.Y.: Pergamon Press, 1963.)

The motor analyzer and the cortical structure of movements. *Vopr. Psichol.* 1957, No. 2.

Essays in psychophysiology of writing. Moscow: Acad. Pedag. Sci. Publ. House, 1950.

Problems of the higher nervous activity of normal and anomalous children, Vol. 1. Moscow: Izd-vo. Akad. Pedag. Nauk, 1956.

Problems of the higher nervous activity of normal and anomalous children, Vol. 2. Moscow: Izd-vo. Akad. Pedag. Nauk, 1958.

Dynamic approach to the mental development of the abnormal child. In *Experimental study of the higher nervous activity of the abnormal child,* Vol. 2, 1958, 3. Moscow: Acad. Pedag. Sci. Publ. House.

The directive function of speech in development and dissolution. *Word,* 1959, *15,* Nos. 2-3.

The mentally retarded child. Moscow: Izd-vo. Akad. Pedag. Nauk, 1960. (English edition, *The feeble-minded child.* Elmsford, N.Y.: Pergamon Press, 1963.)

The role of speech in the regulation of normal and abnormal behavior. Elmsford, N.Y.: Pergamon Press, 1961.

Higher cortical functions of man. Moscow: Izd-vo. Mosk. Univ., 1962, 2nd revised edition, 1969. (English edition, New York: Basic Books, 1966.)

Psychological analysis of the pre-motor syndrome. In *The human brain and psychological processes,* Vol. I. Moscow: Izd-vo. Akad. Pedag. Nauk, 1963.

Factors and forms of aphasia. In *Disorders of language.* London: CIBA Symposium, 1964, 143-161. (a)

Neuropsychology in the local diagnosis of brain lesions. *Cortex,* 1964, *I,* 3-16. (b)

Neuropsychological analysis of focal brain lesions. In B. B. Wolman (Ed.), *Handbook of clinical psychology.* New York: McGraw-Hill, 1965, 687-754.

Neuropsychology and its significance for behavioral science. *Psychologia (Intern. J. Psychol. Orient),* 1967, *X,* 1-6. (a)

Problems and facts of neuro-linguistics. *Intern. Soc. Sci. J.,* 1967, *19,* 36-51. (b)

Complex mechanisms of psychological processes. *Impact of science on society.* IBRO, 1968, XVIII, No. 3. (a)

Neuropsychology as a science. Evening lecture to the 16th International Congress of Applied Psychology, Amsterdam, 1968. (b)

Risultati e perspettive delle richerche neuropsicologiche. Rome: *Il Pension Scientifico,* 1968, 345-356. (c)

The mind of a mnemonist. New York: Basic Books, 1968. (d)

Origin and brain organization of conscious activity. Evening lecture to the 19th International Congress of Psychologists, London, 1969.

The human brain and psychological processes, Vol. II. *Neuro-psychological analysis of conscious activity.* Moscow: Izd-vo. Prosveshchenie, 1970. (a)

The frontal syndromes. In P. J. Vinken and G. W. Bruyn (Eds.), *Handbook of clinical neurology,* Vol. III. Amsterdam: North-Holland, 1970. (c)

The functional organization of the brain. *Scientific American,* 1970, *222.* (b)

Memory disturbances in local brain lesions. *Neuropsychologia,* 1971, *9.* (a)

Towards the problem of the historical nature of psychological processes. *Intern. J. Psychol.,* 1971, *6.* (b)

The world lost and re-gained. Moscow: Moscow Univ. Press, 1971. (English edition, *The man with a shattered world.* New York: Basic Books, 1972.) (c)

Aphasia reconsidered. *Cortex,* 1972. (d)

The working brain. London: Penguin Psychological Series, 1973; New York: Basic Books, 1973. (a)

Neuropsychological studies in the USSR. Proceedings of the National Academy of Sciences of the USA, Vol. 70, Nos. 3 and 4, 1973. (b)

Two basic kinds of aphasia. *Linguistics,* No. 134, 1973. (c)

On the historical development of cognitive processes. Nauka Publishing House, 1973 (the English version to be published by Harvard University Press). (d)

Basic problems of neurolinguistics. In *Current trends in linguistics,* Vol. XII, in press.

Neuropsychology of memory, Vols. I and II. Moscow: Pedagogica Publishing House, Vol. I, 1973; Vol. II, in press (the English version to be published by Winston & Sons Publishers). (e)

Basic problems of neurolinguistics to be published by Moscow University Press (the English version to be published by Mouton, The Hague).

(with E. D. Homskaya, A. M. Blinkov, and M. Critchley) Impaired selectivity of mental processes in association with a lesion of the frontal lobe. *Neuropsychologia,* 1967, *5,* 105-117.

(with A. N. Konovalov and A. Ya. Podgornaya) *Derangement of memory in the clinical syndrome of the aneurism of the anterior communicans artery.* Moscow Univ. Press, 1970.

(with E. Yu. Artemieva) Two ways of providing the reliability of psychological data. *Questions on Psychology,* 1971.

(with V. D. Naydin, L. S. Tsvetkova, and E. N. Vinarskaya) Restoration of higher cortical functions following local brain damage. In P. J. Vinken and G. W. Bruyn (Eds.), *Handbook of clinical neurology,* Vol. IV. Amsterdam: North-Holland, 1970.

(edited with K. H. Pribram) *The behavioral psychophysiology of the frontal lobes.* New York: Academic Press, 1973.

(with K. H. Pribram and E. D. Homskaya) An experimental analysis of the behavioral disturbances produced by a left frontal arachnoidal endothelioma (meningioma). *Neuropsychologia,* 1964, *2,* 257-280.

(with T. A. Karasseva) Disturbances of auditory-speech memory in the deep lesions of the left temporal lobe. *Neuropsychologia,* 1968, *6.*

(with M. Klimnowski and E. N. Sokolov) Towards a neurodynamic analysis of memory disturbances with lesions of the left temporal lobe. *Neuropsychologia,* 1967, *5.*

(with E. G. Simernitskaya and B. Tybulevich) The structure of psychological processes in relation to cerebral organization. *Neuropsychologia,* 1970, *8.*

(with L. S. Tsvetkova) The mechanisms of dynamic aphasia. In M. Biczwisch and K. Heidolph (Eds.), *Progress in linguistics.* The Hague: Mouton, 1970.

(with L. S. Tsvetkova) *Neuro-psychological analysis of the solution of problems.* Moscow: Izd-vo. Prosveshchenie, 1966. (French translation, *Les troubles de solution des problémes.* Paris: Gautier-Villar, 1967.)

(with L. S. Tsvetkova) The programming of constructive activity in local brain lesions. *Neuropsychologia,* 1964, *2,* 95-107.

(with O. S. Vinogradova) The objective investigation of the dynamics of semantic systems. *Brit. J. Psychol.,* 1959, *50.*

(with F. Y. Yudovich) *Speech and the development of psychological processes.* Moscow: Izd-vo. Akad. Pedag. Nauk, 1956. (English edition, London: Staples Press, 1959, and Baltimore: Penguin Books, 1971.)

Other Publications Cited

N. I. Grashenkov and A. R. Luria. The systemic localization of functions in the cerebral cortex. *Zh. Nevropat i psikh.,* 1945, No. 1.

V. A. Karpov, A. R. Luria, and A. L. Yarbuss. Disturbances of the structure of active perception in lesions of the posterior and anterior regions of the brain. *Neuropsychologia,* 1968, *6,* 157-166.

L. S. Vygotsky and A. R. Luria. *Essays in the history of behavior.* Moscow: State Publishing House, 1930.

P. Y. Gal'perin. The development of studies concerning the formation of intellectual acts. *Psychological science in the USSR,* Vol. 2. Moscow: Izd-vo. Akad. Pedag. Nauk, 1959.

E. D. Homskaya. *Brain and activation.* Moscow Univ. Press, 1973.

A. N. Leont'ev. *The development of memory.* Moscow: Izd-vo. Akad. Komm. Vospit. im. Krupskoi, 1930.

A. N. Leont'ev. *Problems in the development of mind.* Moscow: Izd-vo. Akad. Pedag. Nauk, 1959.

L. S. Tsvetkova. *Re-habilitative training in local brain lesions.* Moscow: Moscow Univ. Press, 1973.

L. S. Vygotsky. *Pedagogical psychology.* Moscow: 1926.

L. S. Vygotsky. The historical crisis of psychology (unpublished manuscript), 1927.

L. S. Vygotsky. *Thought and language.* Moscow: Sotsekgiz, 1934. (English version, Cambridge, Mass.: M.I.T. Press, 1962)

L. S. Vygotsky. *Selected psychological investigations.* Moscow: Izd-vo. Akad. Pedag. Nauk, 1956.

L. S. Vygotsky. Psychology and the localization of functions. In *The development of higher psychological functions.* Moscow: Izd-vo. Akad. Pedag. Nauk, 1960. (English text, Psychology and the localization of functions, *Neuropsychologia,* 1965, *3,* 381-386.) (c)

L. S. Vygotsky. *The development of higher psychological functions.* Moscow: Izd-vo. Akad. Pedag. Nauk, 1960. (b)

L. S. Vygotsky. The development and loss of higher psychological functions. In *The development of higher mental functions.* Moscow: Izd-vo. Akad. Pedag. Nauk, 1960. (a)

L. S. Vygotsky. *The psychology of art.* Moscow: Izd-vo. Iskusstvo, 1968.

A. V. Zaporozhets. *The development of voluntary movements.* Moscow: Izd-vo. Akad. Pedag. Nauk, 1960.

Reo Fortune, 1929

293

Margaret Mead

As the Irish speak of a "spoiled priest," I might be counted as a spoiled psychologist. I left the fold officially in 1924, after taking my M.A. at Columbia University, to go into anthropology. Anthropological research seemed to me to be more urgently in need of being done. Also, it dealt with human beings in real life, rather than with the accounts of experiments which other psychologists had done within a laboratory setting. But I left psychology to live, in many ways, always within its precincts, working with psychologists and concerning myself with psychological problems. On the whole my professional life has been a responsive one. In the field I took a problem area with me and then surrendered to the material the culture provided, and eventually developed theories generated by these particular sets of observations. And as far as theoretical papers are concerned, I have written those that I was asked to write, for a specific purpose, a symposium on adolescence (1930a), a handbook of child psychology (1931b, 1946d) a discussion of the exceptional child (1954a). My early exposure to academic psychology provided a background for the continuing resort to psychological methods and psychological findings, and the later invitations from psychologists evoked responses that would not otherwise have been made.

I am convinced that today we need to pay far more attention to the early development of cognitive style, to the way in which vocation is related to the vocation and cognitive style of both parents, and the sense of ease or discomfort which accompanies vocational choice. So I have altered the prescribed order to place first the familial setting in which I was reared.

CONTEXTS OF CHILDHOOD LEARNING

I did my first drawing on galley proofs, glazed paper that only took a pencil mark if you pressed till it scratched—all the mechanics of bookmaking were familiar to me before I could read or write. I don't think I ever had any doubts that making books was what adults did. I learned to say in one long difficult utterance: "My-father-majored-in-economics-and-minored-in-sociology-and-my-mother-majored-in-sociology-and-minored-in-economics" long before I had a clue as to what the words meant. I learned the lines of poetry which my mother was fond of quoting, like: "Have-you-seen-with-flash-incessant-bubbles-bursting-under-ice," a line that came back to me fifty years later when I had a delightful hour being given an interpretation of my mother's Rorschach test. My first toys came from a magnificent string of animals, including a snake and a monkey, a joke present given to Professor Simon N. Patton of the University of Pennsylvania, to commemorate his lectures on the descent of man. I was the first baby in that faculty and so inherited a playful version of the whole of evolutionary theory. Mother's mortar board hung on the wall of her small study where she clipped and filed innumerable papers and I fitted that together with the tragedy of a parchment B.A. in which everything had been eaten away by mice except President Harper's signature, and, I had gathered, that was no precious momento because he had once preached a sermon over a student who had died of starvation. There was a beautifully illustrated copy of the Rubaiyat with majestic lions and ignoble lizards, which father and mother had given to each other with Greek inscriptions, but I knew that my grandmother—my father's mother who lived with us always—only knew Latin and had no Greek.

Later, when my brother was studying Latin in college and Grandma was over seventy, she picked up his Sallust—which she had never read—to read for fun on the fourth of July. Both my father and mother had tremendous rote memories, and the long quotations from Macaulay and Gibbon and Burke, Wordsworth and Browning, and Veblen, who had taught both my father and mother, meant that I learned the way thought was organized and expressed, painlessly, in great unanalyzed lumps. When I was ten, and visiting school with a neighbor's child, I wrote a book review of my favorite book, *Castle Blair,* which the teacher pronounced as the most remarkable paragraph to be written by a child my age she had ever seen. Years later I found that I had reproduced verbatim a review by John Ruskin which had been printed in my copy of the book. At about the same time, my cousin was threatened with expulsion from Bryn Mawr for cheating because she had the same kind of memory. So I learned that such reproduction was dangerous, but I did not learn it hard enough to prevent an explosion in school during World War I when in response to a request for a definition of patriotism I gave one by Veblen (1919) that my father was fond of quoting: "Patriotism is a sentiment of partisan solidarity in respect to national prestige that is never so active as when bound upon some work of concerted malevolence." (This was a condensation of two separate sentences in *The Nature of Peace.*) But I was also learning to tamper with the written lines when I recited, to change an end rhyme, throw the prompter into fits, and alter the next verse to fit. But I tried not to play such games if my father was in the audience, firmly teaching me to avoid what he called "the lawn sprinkler effect"—spraying your words over an audience instead of looking one or two people in the eye. He sat there and saw that I looked him in the eye. If I was also to alter the words of the poet, and look at him, I had to keep my head. This was the beginning of the extempore speaking which has made my life so much easier.

During the period when I wrote out class speech assignments and "memorized" them, they were criticized, acutely, rigorously, but not unkindly, as when at thirteen I wrote—for a speech entitled "If Germany had . . .": "Unless the setting star of Germany rose sufficiently above the horizon to enable her to extend a helping hand to Austria, the consequences are too terrible to contemplate." Father said, "Well you've got a prize mixed metaphor there, sister, but we'll let it go." These various abilities, a very good rote memory, memory for nonsense syllables and for sensible material, a facility for innovating in the midst of a poem; and constructing situations which were plausible and more acceptable than the actual happening—such as the claim that the cut on my nose came from my baby sister's fingernails rather than from a penknife which I was forbidden to use, and, as I was only to find out much later, a facility in dreaming plausible, detailed dreams, dreams which no bizarre detail proclaimed to be dreams—taken together made me cautious.

We were the kind of family who argued about historical facts and quotations at meals, so that the invocation of encyclopedias and dictionaries was continuous. There were no metaphysical doubts as to what a fact was, and my father regarded as the most valuable activity in the world "the addition to the store of knowledge of exact facts." I could almost memorize anything, I could twist it around in ways that were undetectable, but actual facts, verified, indisputable, untampered with by imagination or veniality, were the most important thing in the world.

I found very early that it was necessary to write things down, lists of dates and names, and sequences of events. As we moved four times a year, there was abundant material to work with, addresses, telephone numbers, neighbors, as well as dates when we all had the measles, or the names of all the children on the block.

My grandmother, who was my formal teacher for the years that I did not attend school, had a disciplined mind with a great respect for observation and inductive thinking. She would read me the description of a class of plants from Gray's botany and then turn me loose in the meadows and woodlots to find three examples of them as a lesson for the day. She had done a great deal of thinking about education—the house rang with the names of Pestalozzi and Froebel and Montessori and Spencer. She had concluded that algebra was a more suitable beginning for mathematical training than arithmetic. But she did not, to my mother's sorrow, believe in drill.

I learned to respect books. My paternal grandfather, who died when my father was six, was a bookish man. We still had his great bookcase, with doors that could be screwed on for shipment, because he was a crusading superintendent of schools who each year was asked to move on—with the highest recommendations—by an exhausted school board. Grandfather, I was told, couldn't bear to see a book abused by such practices as laying an open book face down, or turning down corners to mark a place. Book marks had to be paper or flowers. I was sixteen before I came across a book that had been marked up. It was Shaw's *Quintessence of Ibsenism,* and in the margin my hostess had written "Bosh." I was delighted and fascinated by the idea that one could talk back to a book. Today I like reading books that identified people have marked up, but I myself put my notes in the back of the book. Books belonged to people, were written by people you knew, were of all kinds and shapes, and some of them were forbidden, like the Horatio Alger books, not for their content, but because they were poorly written. So I read them secretly and studied what was wrong with the style. Once I heard Mother comment that her family were the kind of people who read Emerson, so I sought for Emerson on her bookshelves, and finding his poems instead of his essays, read them through and noted that this was a point about family tastes that I did not understand.

Remarking on things that I did not understand and that I couldn't put in a form that was likely to get answers was established early. Most of them were behavior points—the blind woman, a pillar of society, revered by everyone, who had done nothing—so it was said—while the hired man raped the hired girl within her hearing. The obese middle-aged man who had beaten his wife with his son's train of cars when he found she was pregnant by a riproaring young bachelor, and later when the baby was born had given away cigars in the country store. Complex events like these were stored away, and when I was a college student I tried to write short stories that would explain them. Later I found that an understanding of the culture in which they occurred provided a more satisfying understanding than fictional reconstructions of character. I stopped writing fiction after my first field trip, and I have never been tempted to resume it. I know that I lack the imagination to construct anything as satisfyingly intricate and as improbable as a cultural tradition, shaped by thousands of imaginations through the centuries. If one can learn enough about such a culture, record it in enough detail, then one has kept it for all mankind, including that particular people who, as they encounter the modern world, lose their own distinctive unique culture, a culture that is a work of art, multisensory and multidimensional in multimedia, as the current phrase has it. But it is only very slowly that we have acquired the technical aids to do this, and when I began my field work, I was entirely dependent on script, script to put down what I observed, and print to put "into words" what I had learned, so that it would be intelligible to other people.

I learned about observation and about the senses early. My mother had kept a very careful record of my infancy, including her intentions for her child, and she had written out carefully a quotation from William James about the importance of educating all the senses. She also noted the encyclopedia article on which she had been working on the days immediately before my birth. I knew that there were thirteen fat notebooks about me, fewer for the brother and sister next in line, and none at all for the youngest. Being observed seemed to be an act of love, the kind of love and attention that parents were only free to give fully to a first child. As a result, I have never felt that to observe others was other than a friendly act, one that enhanced rather than diminished their uniqueness and identity.

We moved and moved and moved when I was a child, living in rented houses in the winter, near the University of Pennsylvania, in the house we owned in Hammonton, a small New Jersey town where we had gone to live so Mother could make a study of the Italian immigrants there, in the spring and fall, and going away to some resort for the summer (Meade, 1907). New houses, new landscapes, new playmates, new cooks and housemaids—an endless procession, as Mother struggled with high principles and the shifting availability of immigrant groups, Germans, Irish, Poles, Northern Negroes, descendants from the days when the farm to which we moved when I was ten had been a part of the underground railroad—and a few runaway slaves had stayed behind. The wife of one of them worked for us intermittently, and mother insisted that we call her Mrs. All of this, the ever-changing kitchen scene, the new playmates and new neighbors, new neighborhood stores, provided me with a constant stream of experience, all against the continuity of a household of father, mother, grandmother, brother and younger sisters, and the periodic return to a familiar house, with a familiar landscape first at Hammonton, and later in the Buckingham Valley in Bucks County, Pennsylvania. These are valuable experiences for an anthropologist, who must, if he is to do good work, have a pretty firm grasp of his own cultural identity and a lively sense of the relativity of cultural forms.

As I was used to active discussion of the meaning and implications of everything around me, the adaptation of immigrants, the effects of education, the defects of education, the importance of kindergarten in giving a child a command of many manual and group skills, the fact that what appeared to be racial differences were only cultural—the word wasn't used then, of course, but my mother and grandmother were clear about the point. And not only had I been observed myself, but I was taught early to observe, for example, plants in great detail; my grandmother saw to it that I made a properly labeled collection whenever we went to a new place for the summer. She taught me how to study my two young sisters, seven and one-half and nine years younger than I, to record the development of their speech and watch the differences in their emerging personalities. Both were left-handed, and Grandma, who had a firm belief in the authority of expert knowledge, took them into the psychology department of the University of Pennsylvania, saying that she felt children might mature better if their natural left handedness were to be developed. She was firmly disabused of such ideas, it was absolutely necessary for children's social development that they be changed. Grandma changed them; one became a state spelling champion and wrote a copperplate hand, the other mispelled three words out of five, became an artist, and when she was in her twenties and started to study architecture, began to stutter. By that time I had learned something about strephosymbolia and its various consequences and I changed her back to her left hand and stopped the stuttering.

I used to visit Ira Wile's clinic, and have lived through the fashion of explaining everything by handedness and dominance, to the total disregard of the whole subject. It has been one of my most vivid experiences of the faddism and lack of continuity in the behavioral sciences, of the way excellent, well-supported work will be overapplied, and then reactively dropped. In graduate school I did a paper on "The Will," only to learn that the subject was going out of style—and hasn't come back yet—and that William James in his vast encyclopedic imagination had anticipated everything that later writers had to say. Some of the most useful tools in my research tool kit have been concepts which have gone temporarily out of style, like "freedom from load," which perfectly describes the Balinese, "allopsychic disorientation," which I rescued in the form of "allopsychic orientation" when the National Institute of Mental Health insisted on a title which contained only a limited number of letters. As I was not classified in the official categorizations as a psychologist I was not constrained to be fashionable, nor did I have the burden of deciding whether experiments on rats or human beings paid off better "careerwise."

But at home all such matters were discussed, as each child brought some new insights, or new ideas reached the literate world. My first encounter with Freud was in a set of magazine articles luridly titled "The man who was married by a marble hand," in which the overriding importance of early experiences was driven home. At the time that I was just learning formally about early man, my youngest sister was carrying around a small pamphlet entitled "Self Contradictions in the Bible," and invoking paleontology.

Comparative mythology was also a part of my early education, and we were read the Greek myths, with the explicitly labeled Latin versions, and then Norse mythology, also with a discussion of the parallelism between the Norse gods and the Greek gods. Mother read me the story of the Incarnation in the German version where the concrete improbabilities would be more evident. But by the time I was ten I had acquired, through a series of sorties into different religious settings, an interest in religion, and my room was meticulously divided into a pagan and a Christian half; the pagan half held the Aurora by Guido Reni and a small replica of the Venus de Milo for which I had saved my allowance for a whole winter; the Christian half, madonnas, a beautiful carved old prie dieux, bought by accident at an auction, and a small clay jar made from earth from the Holy Land. Around the top were rotogravure reproductions of the murals in the State Capitol depicting the religious sects of Pennsylvania.

A mixed tradition from William Morris—I slept as a baby in a Morris chair—and John Ruskin and the early German and Swiss educators kept the importance of education in the arts and crafts before my parents. They worked as citizens to introduce manual training and home economics into the public schools. Wherever we were living, Mother looked for someone with skills to teach us pottery, basketry, carpentry, weaving. All of this stood me in good stead later when I had to study and record the arts of primitive peoples. I had built a loom and made clay models for bas reliefs to be carved by the time I was eight.

All the experiences that Mother and Grandma devised for us were discussed as they did them, with each other, with us, and with friends. We had one neighbor in Philadelphia who was a child psychologist and who let his children read *Little Black Sambo,* and another, wife of a lecturer and patron of the arts, who was a friend of Raymond and Isadora Duncan, and who decided in advance what her children were to be. I read the books of my grandmother's childhood, and those that my mother and father had read, and then the books explicitly written for children of my generation. The technological and cultural differences in the three sets of books, the moralizing of the Rollo books by Jacob Abbott, the sentimentalizing of the Elsie Dinsmore books, the explicit discussion of caste and poverty in the Little Colonel Books, were all there to be thought about.

There was a set of stories in a child education journal about "Mother and Father Gypsy," who gave up nomadism when their babies were born, and Kipling's "The Cat That Walked by Itself"—someone sent us that as a clipping from a newspaper—and Jack London's *Before Adam,* all of which gave different versions of the life of early man.

Mother bought the first Victrola records with comparative music. I was fascinated by a "Hymn to Apollo," which had an accompanying note saying that no one really knew whether it was right or not. Everything we did was related comparatively to the past, vigorously and ethically to the present, and hopefully to the future that was in the making. In a sense we were like a family of refugees, always a little at odds with and well in advance of the local customs, proud of our heritage, busily preparing ourselves for a new and unknown land. No one knew where we would be living next, but I always made certain that when we arrived in the next house, I would have the most remote room at the top of the house, a room which combined the charms of godmothers and wicked fairies and was far enough away so that I could hear an adult coming and pretend to be asleep.

Very early I began making small-scale cultural comparisons myself, collecting "counting-out" rhymes and different versions of the way in which games were played, and later, beginning a bit of "culture building," inventing new games, consciously using elements from the old. This in a sense prefigures later stages in the things I tried to do with anthropological research, first to collect and record valuable and contrasting materials, then to try to make something of the contrasts, which would generate greater understanding, and then to begin the task of culture building, of devising new institutions needed for a changing world.

Most of the experiences which young people meet for the first time in college, I had had by the time I was five. They were part of my whole self, as the child of my parents and grandparents, not a new self discovered in an academic setting, for I had always been within an academic setting. All the things that the first generation in a new occupational style have to struggle with, the essential tools of the new trade, whether it is banking, painting, programming, or being a psychologist capable of *thinking* about psychological processes, I learned not as student but as a child. A language one needed for a purpose had to be learned, and learned fast. My father had learned the French needed for his doctoral examinations in ten days. An article that had to be written, had to be written on time. As the galley proofs of *The Railway World* littered the floor, and Mother came in to tell Father that he needed two more lines in a textbook revision and he replied, "Well write them." I wrote my doctor's dissertation in a winter while finishing my course work and holding a half-time job and keeping house, because a dissertation held no mysteries or terrors for me; it was something you finished and so concluded the apprenticeship which the academic world demanded. Social scientists, writers, college professors were people who came to breakfast on Sunday morning, some of whom talked sense and some nonsense and some of whom kissed me when I didn't want them to. Because both my mother and my grandmother were professionally educated women, I never had to struggle with the problems of identity which bedevil most first-generation professional women. Women had brains; I knew that I had my father's mind and he had his mother's, and my brother and youngest sister had my mother's kind of mind, and my other sister had a kind of artist's imagination for which there were no immediate precedents. Women both used their brains and married and had children. Unless, of course, they were nuns, a career that appealed to me at ten . . . active, energetic nuns who became saints. Grandma thought boys were more vulnerable as little children than girls, and this was borne out by my brother's endless frightening illnesses. Father thought it was easier for girls to get high marks than boys, so I had to make 2½ points higher grades than my brother for the same financial bonus. Father would remark occasionally that it was a pity I wasn't a boy, but I understood that to be a necessary consequence of being a wife, mother of a large family, and having a profession also. Mother, it is true, was a suffragist—the anti's called them suffragettes—but grandma, a professional woman a generation earlier, shared none of her rhetoric and rancour about women being classified with the feebleminded and criminals. Obviously it was necessary to get the vote, and I learned to typewrite at eleven, doing seven carbon copies for the local county newspapers because mother was press chairman. But in a household which was alive to change and to the necessity for change, working for changes in the position of women seemed reasonable, necessary, but did not in anyway disturb my sense of myself. I never wanted to be a boy, and I still feel that getting one of those obscure masculinizing diseases would be a fate worse than death.

I have emphasized this childhood preparation for my later career because I believe that it is vitally necessary, as we cope with the generation gap which exists today, to recognize that it is the children who have followed a given vocation to which their parents belonged, who provide the necessary bridge between young and old. I have worked for thirty years to try to get younger people involved in all sorts of deliberations, committees, faculties, international meetings, interdisciplinary symposia, and conferences. On the whole it has been a discouraging task that had to be done over and over again. In ongoing groups, the young I brought in got three or four years older and they kept younger people out. Organizers would promise to include young people, but in the end I would find there were none there; so many important older people had agreed to come. And meanwhile in the late 1960s the demands of youth for inclusion were pushed with anger and intemperance. Organizers began to include young people, but then I found that the youngest members could only speak out in the presence of their distinguished seniors by being totally ignorant and abominably rude. I began to see that we were asking too much to expect a promising and aspiring young scientist to stand up and contradict a Nobel Laureate, however much the Nobel Laureate was talking nonsense. The anger and the insistent ignorance were the only armor they could wear when asked to do something intrinsically impossible for them. I also found there were exceptions, and these were the students whose fathers and mothers had been distinguished in the same field in which they were working. They were neither ignorant nor overwhelmed nor afraid, and they did not need to be angry in order to speak.

This is a period in which we have such tremendous changes to bridge rapidly and where the sciences, especially the social sciences, are under such attack by the impatient and perceptive young, so I believe we need to understand far more about the way in which novices enter their chosen professions, in which decade of life they find their true vocation—and here we have William James with his late entry and extraordinary inclusiveness—and how much they learned, at a deep level, in childhood. Each profession, psychology not the least, is made up of those who entered from very different backgrounds and for very different emotional reasons. The psychological roots of vocational choice have been belabored in the literature of biography and autobiography, but I keep remembering Phyllis Greenacre's experience with psychoanalyzing authors who wrote books they didn't mention in their analysis. Or Marie Bonaparte's (1949) analysis of the roots of the purple passages in Edgar Allen Poe's work, which were quite clearly based on early childhood traumas and were failures. We have done too little with the predisposing conditions for felicitous vocation and much too little with the question of when, where, and how the basic vocational style is first encountered.

ANCESTRY

There are adequate geneologies in existence, so I feel no obligation to present the objective facts of my ancestors, only those which were presented to me and so shaped my sense of a relationship to the past. All my forebears came to this country before the Revolutionary War, and seven of the eight lines can be traced to ancestors who fought in the Revolution; the eighth were Tories from upper New York State who migrated to Canada; Mother always said that the Tories were probably some of the best people, but she classified all marriages with later immigrants, whether they were McMasters from Canada or the descendants of Polish Jewish pipe-organ designers, as "marrying a foreigner." Three of my grandparents were born west of Pittsburgh, the fourth, my maternal grandfather, in Old Deerfield, Massachusetts. Father always said that civilization stopped at Pittsburgh, and mother, born in Chicago just before "the fire," never tired of comparing the backward schools of Pennsylvania, supported by a false pride in a late immigration—Pennsylvania was not settled until almost the *end* of the seventeenth century—with her Chicago high school, where every child had a microscope. My mother's family were merchants; the difference between wholesale and retail was crucial, and my maternal Grandfather Fogg failed in his wholesale seed business when my mother was a sophomore at Wellesley; she had to go home to help, and finally graduated from the University of Chicago, where she met my father. My mother's mother was born in Prairie de Chien, Wisconsin, of a sturdy family line who lived into their nineties.

I knew that we were of mixed English, Scotch, Irish, and Welsh stock, and was told that my ancestors had all suffered in the cause of religious liberty, as pilgrims, puritans, and covenanters who had to hide in caves to escape persecution. They had traveled in great hardship across the seas and across the prairies, up from Kentucky into Ohio, where two of my great-great-grandfathers founded the little town of Winchester, where my paternal grandmother was born. There great-grandfather Ramsay had been a sort of squire in his tiny town, a cabinet maker, owning a number of farms, serving a term in the legislature, a local preacher. The minutely concrete tales my grandmother told me of that little town, which I did not see until sixty years later, provided me with one certain knowledge of community, while my mother's urban and urbane background—"it cost Cousin Frank $1,500 to send Polly on that camping trip where she finally got engaged—contrasted strongly and gave me a sense of alternative life styles, all legitimately available to me. Once a wagon train, in my mother's line but unspecified, had been attacked by Indians, and only a blue-eyed young mother and her blue-eyed baby had been spared. One of my great uncles had been a great Methodist preacher in his day and a great-great-grandfather had been read out of the Unitarian Church for heresy—and of course refused to leave. Another great uncle had been a convert to Islam.

There were disappointingly few villains; an unknown uncle on my paternal grandfather's side—who went places that my mother didn't like to have my father seen—in Philadelphia, who died before I was born; a few rapscallion cousins, who told me tales of lives with which I would never have come in intimate contact otherwise.

Aside from my grandmother, who lived with us, we never lived very long or very close to our relations, but they came and went, and I got a sense of family resemblance, its charms and its apprehensions, as I discriminated between relatives I loved and relatives I liked, and speculated on which traits I would like my children to inherit. Mother pointed out how much one disliked the relatives of a spouse who had the same traits as the spouse, traits with which one had to put up all one's life.

Then there were father's and mother's friends, who were called uncle and aunt, whose children we invariably disliked, and who came to visit in surreyfuls on holidays. These adults attached us firmly to the wide world, in which they played all sorts of different roles, teaching at every college I thought of going to, and ranging in politics and religion from high Episcopalians to a family who went to the Soviet Union to find the new Utopia in the 1920s. Mother's friends, from Wellesley and Bryn Mawr where she was a fellow, were "fine women," and Father's friends, from Oberlin, DePauw, Chicago, Pennsylvania,—were "the kind of people who would lend you money without interest." Father, who became Professor of Finance at the Wharton School of the University of Pennsylvania, expressed all values in monetary terms; Mother in the idealistic, mildly socialist, agnostic mood of her period. She danced with joy at the news of the Russian Revolution in 1917, and died saddened by the Cold War in 1950.

I have one brother, Richard, two years younger, who is presently, after retiring from the University of Southern California, teaching at the State University at Fresno; three sisters, one of whom, Katherine, died at the age of nine months, and Elizabeth, seven years younger than I, now Professor of Art at Leslie College, and Priscilla, wife of Leo Rosten, who died in 1959. The death of Katherine split the family into two groups, and the "the babies" became objects of study and solicitude. When my sister Elizabeth was born, I found her an almost perfect restitution for the lost little sister and to this I trace a good deal of my optimism and tendency to put "Acts of God" in the best light possible. But the lost baby sister also merged with a lost imaginary twin sister, who had been stolen by gypsies or pirates, for whom I sometimes searched, while at other times I daydreamed of being stolen myself, given time to learn a great many foreign languages and other skills, such as portrait painting, after which I would return and be recognized as "myself" by my previously sorrowing relations. When I fell and cut my wrist at five, I rejoiced that now I could never be permanently lost or mislaid, I was irrevocably identifiable as me. Like so many of the problems that plagued my contemporaries later, I got my major identity crisis settled before I was six.

My father and mother married as graduate students at the University of Pennsylvania, where my father taught all his life. He helped found the evening school and the extension courses up into the coal regions, and for many years he traveled upstate two or three nights a week to teach. As a young man he had been working on the quantity theory of money; then he became fascinated with the technical processes that produced gold, wrote a small book on gold (E. S. Mead, 1908), and gradually moved more and more into technical fields—corporation and trust finance (E. S. Mead, 1903, 1914, 1923), on the one hand, and on the other changing technology, the implications of the new commercial agriculture (E. S. Mead and Ostrolenk, 1928, 1933), problems of changing types of transportation—in which my brother later specialized, the relationship of investment to rising and declining industries (E. S. Mead and

Grodinsky, 1939), problems of resource retrieval, processes of temperature resistance, and water recycling.

When he died at the age of eighty-three my father was working on an analysis of what went wrong at the University of Pennsylvania when a dean lost the confidence of his faculty. His students each did massive first-hand research, usually on their own family businesses, and he used to say there wasn't a bank in the Northeast where he wouldn't find a former student behind a management desk. He was impatient with Utopianism, distrusted planning, and was in his late sixties before he came to full emotional terms with Negroes as members of the human race, and with the validity of social security and socialized medicine. But he was still learning when he died, and when he attended seminars that I gave, however avant garde the students and I thought we were, his comments and questions were always the most acute. He became forgetful about small material things, in which he had never taken much interest, frugal where he had been prodigal—his motto had always been "if you need more money, make it," but although he often served his former students as a consultant, he always managed to consult only with businesses that were failing so badly that there was no profit in it for him. My grandmother, his mother, was completely in possession of her senses when she died suddenly of pneumonia; my mother had a stroke in her late seventies and a period of aphasia, from which she fully recovered. Her sister, now ninety-nine, still reads books I haven't heard of. And her mother was making dates with other old people to meet them in Florida or Hawaii two or three years hence when she was ninety. I have as part of my heritage a sense of the kind of old age which I would not mind experiencing, but also I am sure that together with most of my generation I learned, as a child who fought my way through all the childhood diseases, to keep on living, under any circumstances. If we do not fear old age, we are also—unless we take special precautions and leave "Living Wills" forbidding artificial maintenance of life after consciousness has gone—likely to keep stubbornly alive, when, given the choice, we would not have chosen to do so.

My own ancestors, my adopted aunts and uncles, formed a part of the vanguard of my predecessors, about whom I wrote:

> On your shoulders falls their mantle
> Settling light as a caress
> Will you answer, heirs of ages,
> Saints and sages, we say Yes.

This was in a class poem which I wrote for the high school class ahead of my class, because they had no poets.

I had the unusual and strengthening experience of being told, always, that I was a "thoroughly satisfactory child," the child who had received the best from each parent. My father firmly resisted attempts of those who sought to get at him in terms of his daughter's reputation, and my mother never grudged for a moment, but instead delighted in the fact that I was able to live fully the life she would have liked to have lived. Grandma, with her humorous little moral stories, kept my feet on the ground. I also experienced only horizontal mobility, that most satisfying form of success in which one goes on in one's parents' field but to a larger or wider version of the same kind of work. Both my father and my mother had obituaries in *The New York Times*, my mother for her many years, contribution as a citizen of Philadelphia, where, to the end of her life she was counted as a stranger, while I, who have not lived there since childhood, am addressed with respect as a native. My own success came very young, and sometimes I was the youngest by twenty years in a symposium; but this was a natural state to me, as was the experience of being intellectually the most active in any group I was in. My constant daydream was to find a group of contemporaries all of whom were my intellectual equals or superiors, and I remember with delight the first conference, in 1948, where the most exciting people there were twenty years my junior.

FORMAL EDUCATION

As the child of educational enthusiasts, my own formal education reflected their preferences and prejudices. My grandmother had been a teacher of small children and was legally qualified to teach us at home. So I was sent to kindergarten—this was the wave of the future—but not to the first three grades of elementary school. My grandmother gave me lessons about an hour a day, and the rest of the time I was free to read and explore the woods and fields near us. When I was eight, we moved to Swarthmore, which had pretty good schools; while we were there we helped introduce the "Gary system," and it was arranged that I would attend school half days, a special privilege disliked by the teacher and my classmates, two of whom are still my close friends. The first month I made twenty in arithmetic, which was discouraging, but I worked up to ninety finally. I had an allowance of ten cents a week and began buying lemon sticks at a penny each every day, until I became badly frightened for fear I had become addicted, and slowly, by careful stages, broke the habit, without telling anybody. My grandmother taught my brother and three other small children of neighbors at home. I loved school and had little sympathy with my parents' notion that sitting all those hours was unnecessary and bad for children. Also I wore bloomers and all the other little girls wore petticoats and pants, although I had successfully rebelled the year before and been allowed to wear a hat instead of a tailored beret.

The next year, in a different house, we all had whooping cough, and were taught at home, and spent the winter playing with the children next door—reading exhaustively, the rest of Dickens, Charlotte M. Young, any historical novel I could find. At the end of the whooping cough, we sold our house in Hammonton and bought a farm in Bucks County in a small rural community which has been a ready model for thinking about communities ever since. The next year I was again taught at home, and yearned for the company of other children. Then there were two years in a one-room schoolhouse—eighth grade and two years of high school, where I studied from the same texts from which my grandmother had studied, and came to delight in English grammar as taught by parsing and diagramming, already out of style in contemporary schools, learned Latin from a teacher who had never passed Virgil, and whom I tried to have a crush on because I knew this was the appropriate and rewarding attitude toward one's teachers, and learned a lot about the relationships of eighteen-year-olds—sent out from the city as foster children—and to small determined eleven-year olds who tried to resist their bullying, born of dullness, retardation, and boredom.

The third year, we went to a three-year high school, two miles in the other direction, and with the same teacher, studied L'Allegro and Il Penserosa for the second time (of three), agriculture out of a book, and were exposed to buying high school pins, rings, and pennants by a small-souled, aspiring principal. I used to study my lessons with gloves on in the early morning, before the heat was turned on, and then I was able to escape from school for most of the day; I had a parental letter permitting me to leave whenever I liked. The new school had a good library and I read everything in it, including the "trash," which like grade "B" films is so much closer to the core culture. Then we moved to the neighboring county seat, Doylestown, and I had two more years of high school, L'Allegro again, Virgil with a Latin teacher who gave me high marks because I understood that Virgil was poetry. It was the middle of World War I, so after my second year of German, German was discontinued. Graduating at sixteen, two years younger than the rest of the class, I was unprepared for Wellesley, and so the family moved to New Hope, the artist colony six miles the other side of our farm. We all attended the Holmquist school, a frightfully idealistic, expensive, little private school, where for the first time I encountered teachers whose standards began to compare with the standards I experienced daily at home. Everything that went on at school had come under constant review at home, and the idea of parents who were humble before their children's teachers was so unfamiliar to me that I was shocked when I encountered it in Bronxville parents in the 1940s.

At the Holmquist school I had three years of French from a magnificent old grand dame, trigonometry in the ornate room which had been converted from the pig pen. I felt myself somewhat set apart from the other girls, none of whom were yet destined for college; I was also privately engaged to be married. It was still wartime—the armistice came that fall—and I kept house for the family—mother didn't learn to cook until she was sixty—and plunged delightedly into amateur theatricals. Then came a crisis. Father began picking at Wellesley, saying it was full of the old maids who had taught mother, and anyway what did I need a college education for if I planned to get married. Mother resorted to strategy and began discussing how interesting it would be for me to go to

DePauw, where Father had graduated after being expelled, or about to be expelled, from Oberlin for playing cards. Father began to daydream about which of his old classmates were still there: of course I would be a Theta, it would be amusing. It was a great deal cheaper than Wellesley, even with the train fare for 800 miles, and so I went to experience the best teaching I ever had—and the worst social ostracism, as an Easterner, an Episcopalian, unfit even for the Y.W.C.A., someone who dressed for dinner, didn't own the proper kind of collegiate clothes, read books, had pictures and a tea set in my room, and no female forbear who had been a member of a Greek letter sorority. The teachers were good; few of them had ever published a "paper"; teaching was what they had been asked to do. But I sat in the library and read *The New York Times,* which I had never read before, and as I read the play reviews, I longed to be in New York.

I learned about minorities; I worked out what the possibilities were for success for a nonsorority social outcast and set about them, making the honorary English society, writing the play for the dormitory, writing the year's pageant, and observing how the minority group of girls—who all hoped to be chosen someday—were unwilling to work together or be friends with each other. I had put the sororities into a position where they couldn't afford to ignore me. I would have been asked to join the next year, and that would have been intolerable. But attempting to lead a group of people, each of whom was willing to betray her roommate, if necessary, to get a bid—this was also intolerable. There was no way in which it could be made tolerable. The system of sororities and fraternities obviously had to go, just as the system of "integration," picking off acceptable Negroes one by one and grudgingly offering them a place in the system, has had to go today. (This experience made it much easier for me to give up integration as a major social mechanism for justice and to see where Black Power is going.)

DePauw was also my sole experience in real politics; I engineered the election of the first nonsorority vice-president DePauw had ever had.

At DePauw I was introduced to the whole religious excitement about the social message of the Old Testament prophets and an interpretation of both the prophets and the Gospels that served me very happily until ecumenism again engaged my interest in theology. History as past ethics, taught by a crusading, fiery-eyed enthusiast who was later Dean, emphasized that no man was under any obligation to tell *all* the truth at once.

By the end of the year, my father's fortunes had improved and I persuaded him to both increase my allowance and send me to Barnard, which had the added attraction that my fiancé was at the General Theological Seminary. The perennial worry about dating or not dating would be solved, and there would be plenty of time to study.

Up to the time that I went to Barnard my formal education had been out of step with my education at home, more an exploration of social styles than an opening of new vistas. I expected to be a writer—after giving up painting at sixteen because I was told I would have to go to art school instead of college—and my success with the DePauw pageant suggested community pageantry as the kind of supplementary and movable career that would go with being a minister's wife. I had declared my major to be English. At Barnard I encountered the best kind of education available in the women's colleges of the day; first-class people of both sexes as teachers. I took "baby psych," so as to have also a semester of "baby philosophy," and was completely bored. The next year I took experimental psychology and discovered that I found no stimulation whatsoever in repeating experiments to which the answers were already known. This is, of course, an essential function of a beginning science course; only those who are going to make science teaching a career can bear it, and perhaps even they should not. I learned about experimentation rather than learning anything interesting about human beings. Then I took Hollingworth's developmental psychology, which I found interesting because I already knew something about children. We never saw a child, we never made an observation, and there were no films from which one could learn. The text was based on what other people had observed, systematically or unsystematically, about children. Yet Hollingworth had an ingenious and wondering mind. I liked his discussion of reintegration, of apperceptive mass, and of how the shape of our notebooks fitted our choice among rectangles of different proportions. Leta Hollingworth was studying adolescence at the same time and we got the reflections of her work. I was beginning to feel that writing was not, after all, my metier, and that in making a choice among the arts, science, and politics—I had a flair for public speaking and organization—I would choose science, which within the context of my education meant social science, and I declared a second major in psychology. My senior year I did a special methods course in which we were allowed a good deal of freedom in experimenting with different kinds of tests. I tested definitely insane on the Kent Rosanoff association test which had been standardized on the general population and made no allowance for literary literacy, and it interested me to find out why. At the same time I took William Fielding Ogburn's magnificent course in Psychological Factors in Culture, where we read the whole of Freud and his coworkers and began to see real relationships between the way the minds of human beings worked and the cultures within which they were reared. Ogburn cautioned us against ever advancing a psychological explanation of a piece of behavior until we had exhausted the cultural and historical antecedents.

My senior year I took anthropology with Franz Boas. I had read *The Mind of Primitive Man* (1911) for "baby psych" and got nothing out of it at all. The context was wrong. By the middle of my senior year, I began auditing every course Boas gave—there was a rumor that he would retire the next year. I was enchanted with the opportunity to study under a man who had built a science. I also—because at this time I thought I would be a school psychologist—made the mistake of taking a course in Teachers College in Educational Psychology, The Psychology of the Elementary School Subjects, filled with men who hoped some day to be—or already were—elementary school principals.

The contrast with what I was learning in anthropology, where the world was opening up, and in Ogburn's course, where man's unconscious was being laid bare, was devastating. Additionally, anthropology presented a chance to see the very stuff of creation in the making. And also, both Boas and Ruth Benedict, who was in her first year of teaching, were able to convey a sense of urgency, of the need to record those unique primitive cultures which once gone could never be recovered. The loss of each culture, each unique record of a language and a way of life, constituted an irreparable loss to mankind. An old preference for using one's talents—I originally misread the Gospel story—was vigorously revived. Not only must I do what I could do well—science rather than art in which genius was demanded—but also what needed to be done now. It was clear enough that there would be cohorts of college students on whom psychological experiments could be repeated on and on into a future when all the primitive peoples of the world would have died, or been assimilated into some great tradition.

By the spring, after lying awake all night in the excitement of genuine vocational choice, I decided to become an anthropologist. But I went on to take an M.A. in psychology, as I had already planned my master's essay, a study of Italian children in the town my mother had studied a generation before, to measure the effect on intelligence test scores of the language spoken in the home (Mead, 1926, 1927). A review of the literature which accompanied that essay reveals how little real progress has been made since, for all the paraphernalia of chatter about identical twins by Garrett (1965) and Jensen (1969).

But I had never met Woodworth. He was on leave my senior year and I believe that if I had had him—how odd that idiom is—I would have remained in psychology. When I took his psychophysical methods, a subject in which I had little specific interest, we all sat transfixed as he made new discoveries with his back to the class, talking delightedly to himself. Later he was to ask me a question which set my feet on a path from which they have never strayed: "When does an Indian become an Indian?" Most of the behavioral science world still does not understand that a day-old baby is a perfect day-old sample of the culture within which it is born. I learned, too, from the way he carried the smallest detail along to find an error fifty pages later in a thesis, how to read a student's work.

In Hollingworth's abnormal psychology, we read Jung (and I *drew* my term paper—the miserable introverted half of the personality rolling down a steep flight of stairs to roll up in a schizophrenic ball) and in improving my understanding of Jung, I arrived also at the formulation that "if you can't draw or diagram (I would now add, "model") an idea you don't understand it."

I finished my thesis, took my M.A., and became a candidate for a Ph.D. in anthropology. At my orals, Hollingworth, still part of my committee because of my previous commitment to psychology, asked me what relationship my thesis—on the relative stability of different elements of culture in Polynesia (Mead, 1928c)—had to the normal curve of relativity. I said none, and he walked out of the exam, in excessive disapproval. Later, there was an interval of some ten years during which my courses were not listed at Teachers College because I had said, publicly and explicitly, that I would not mark a class of 200, varying in age from twenty to sixty, in experience from nurses' training to a Harvard graduate school, and in expectation from a third-grade teacher to a research linguist or kinesicist, on "a normal curve." I had each student make out an autobiographical card with a picture and I marked each examination in relation to that student's past and future. But after all, I had learned about individual differences in psychology, too. An even later onslaught against grading on the curve, and refusing to treat Yale undergraduates as if they were a "normal population," helped along the acceptance of the pass-fail convention in the 1960s.

PSYCHOLOGICAL INTERESTS IN LATER PROFESSIONAL LIFE

So this is indeed an odd autobiography of a psychologist from someone who concluded a major commitment to academic psychology at the age of twenty-two. It can be, I think, a useful measure of what that kind of academic training can give a student who later decides for one of the other human sciences. I wish to discuss first what I learned then and carried forward, and second what cooperation with individual psychologists and with various psychological enterprises gave me.

I learned the testing field well enough so that I have been able to follow and absorb the long development of testing, the appearance of projective tests, of objective tests, of Piaget-type cognitive tests, of the work of Sherif and Witkin. I knew enough about tests so that I could make my own in the field; I constructed my own opposites tests and "picture interpretation tests" in Samoa, and ink blot tests and other tests for animistic thinking in Manus. The original work of Goodenough on "Draw a Man" has provided an impetus to my use of children's drawings, a series of 3,500 in Manus and selected comparative series in many other cultures. Maze tests prepared the way for the understanding of culture-free tests, like the Stewart ring puzzle test, and the understanding of the subtler problems of the relationship between cognition and culture. At the same time Witkin tests have provided me with an excellent training device for field workers, for in anthropology we need field workers who don't see a pattern too soon, but, after a struggle, can see it in the end. My original interest in tests led to an interest in David Levy's type of testing; he gave me a Rorschach in 1932, and I took a doll to Arapesh that year as well as the Rorschach. It was fifteen years later that Klopfer had enough experience with cross-cultural testing to be able to read an Arapesh Rorschach, which he initially scorned, so that we have only the one which I worked up initially. The others—done in the native language—were too cold to put into perfect form after I had placed four other cultures between the Arapesh and 1947.

Theodora Mead Abel and I sat next to each other in Woodworth's class and our work has enlivened each other's ever since, through her extensive work in analyzing cross-cultural Rorschachs and other projective tests, to the initiative she took in 1954 to have us (Mead and Metraux, 1954e) prepare a comparative exhibit of projective tests in different cultures for the American Psychological Association meetings.

The use of toys and children's drawings formed a perfect introduction to later enlightenment from Erik Erikson's play configurations of children (Erikson, 1951), which in turn was an introduction to Henry Murray's work in the 1930s (Murray and others, 1938) on the use of the Thematic Apperception Tests. In the 1953 American Museum of Natural History Admiralty Island Expedition we used three of the Murray cards, three of the cards developed specifically for anthropological studies in Micronesia, and three painted from the old photographs of the Manus' abandoned primitive way of life. From the early and continuing interest in tests, I have also been able to work with Margaret Lowenfeld's great body of insights, and the tests that illuminate it—Mosaics, Kaleidobloc, Poloidoblocs, and the World Game, which in turn has contributed to distinguishing between a child's response to the system of human relationships around him and to his own body (Lowenfeld, 1939, 1950, 1954).

Preliminary reading in Gestalt psychology prepared me for the use of the idea of pattern—as Ruth Benedict, Sapir, and I all learned from the works of Koehler and Kofka—and later integration of the analysis of cultural configurations, ritual, and the significance of carefully recorded crucial instances—as in the theatrical sibling rivalry behavior of the Balinese mother—as keys to culture, with Roheim's (1934) psychoanalytically derived notion of basic cultural traumas. Early familiarity with Gestalt also formed a natural prelude to work with Kurt Lewin, and with Gardner Murphy's formulations about cognition in personality structure (Murphy, 1947).

A dose of the law of exercise and the law of effect provided a road to the later work of Hull, to the integration of cultural, psychoanalytical, and learning theory, exemplified in John Dollard's *Criteria for the Life History* (1935), in Gregory Bateson's theory of deutero learning (1942), in Geoffrey Gorer's integration of psychoanalytic and learning theory, when he was working at Yale. In 1939 a conversation with Woodger (1939), fresh from his experiences in working with Hull, helped Gregory Bateson and myself carry forward the search for units in cultural analysis, begun in *Naven* (Bateson, 1936), which I was able to use in systematizing the study of food habits, and later in identifying the more complex unit of cultural change. (It is one of the tragedies of transdisciplinary history that Malinowski, who learned from good students, did not find the illumination of psychological theory which he hoped to find at Yale.)

The very simple experiments in the recognition of emotions in photographs, to which we were exposed, was a precursor to the work of Klineberg, and Boas' initiation of the work of Efron (1941), and a preparation for the use of photography, still and film, as a research tool. This combined with the early work of Myrtle McGraw (1935), which I followed actively, and the later integration of cross-cultural analysis of the Gesell-Ilg type of analysis with Balinese records (Gesell and Ilg, 1943).

From the Gesell groups' response to photographs came my determination to pick up somatotyping at once, so that we now have records of Manus somatotypes over a fifteen-year period, which do not demonstrate, as I had thought they would, the impositions of a constitutionally originated cultural style on a wide range of constitutional types, but a narrow correspondence between a distinctive and narrow constitutional type and the type of behavior which Ilg had been able to deduce from a miscellaneous set of photographs (Heath and Carter, 1971). But the continuing thread of interest in temperament which lead through my use of Ruth Benedict's interest in culture as "personality writ large" which took its clues from temperament (Benedict, 1934), to Bateson's discussion in *Naven* (1936), to *Sex and Temperament* (Mead, 1935) with the hypothesis that much that we attribute to sex is actually an attribute of temperament, and finally to the Manus somatotyping, goes back to Hollingworth's class, Jung's *Psychological Types* (1923), and the fact that I was prepared to discuss them with Sapir and Goldenweiser at the Toronto meeting of the British Association for the Advancement of Science in 1924.

Gardner Murphy's interest in ESP prepared me to take a long look at Manus trance as a possible locus of ESP; and so trance and ESP became a research cluster, punctuated by my serving on the research committee of the American Society for Psychical Research, to back up Gardner, who had been heavily penalized for an unorthodox research interest. In the meantime Jane Belo had brought back a set of Balinese trance films, in a hurried trip to New York in 1938, and met Abraham Maslow, who introduced her to Milton Erickson, with whom both Gregory Bateson and I have worked closely ever since on hypnosis and trance (Erickson, 1967); on the relationship between the kinds of perception involved in many ESP performances and trance. Trance and hypnosis met again in the encounter with Merton Gill and Margaret Brenman (1959). The perception of nonverbal cues was later extended from the original impetus from Darwin to the elaboration of the whole field of semiotics and the use of audio visual recordings of behavior.

I met Kurt Lewin in 1935 at a conference at Bryn Mawr and this started a long and active collaboration which ended only with his death, involving also his students, Bavelas, Lippit, and Zander, as my interest developed in group processes as a subject of study and as a mode of research and interdisciplinary behavior. During World War II, when I was made executive secretary of the Committee on Food Habits in the Division of Anthropology and Psychology of the National Research Council, Kurt Lewin's group at the University of Iowa provided an ongoing laboratory, and it was in those years that many of the principles and procedures of group dynamics were born. My vignettes of cultural styles and Bavelas' accounts of his experiments have provided a continuing source of ideas, since we first began to elaborate them, during my visits to Iowa City during the War. Ronald Lippitt, in another set of contexts of the study of larger groups, has provided stimulating materials, especially with the advisory group of Irving Milgate's Zycom projects.

I have left out here the specific lines of stimulation from psychiatry when the psychiatrists were not also at least in some sense psychologists. However, the enterprises which Lawrence K. Frank initiated over the years between 1934 and 1968, when he died (Mead, 1969b), all interdisciplinary in character, all fed upon the insights of Gardner Murphy, Kurt Lewin, Mary Fisher, Lois Barclay Murphy, Gotthard Booth, Arnold Gesell, Eugene Lerner, among many others, and so can be said to have psychological roots, which made them the perfect place for me, bred originally in a psychological tradition, to work: in the Hanover Seminar of 1934, in initial explorations of the field of psychoanalysis, in cooperation with the Macy Foundation projects at Vassar and Sarah Lawrence, in the development of the field of food habits into living habits and then into technical change, and finally into efforts to build institutions which can monitor, assess, and modify headlong culture change.

Ronald Hargreaves played a comparable but briefer role in the 1950s, in bringing together a unique group of those interested in psychology, electro-encephalography, ethology, and child development (Tanner and Inhelder, 1957-1960). Here my original work in Manus in 1928 (Mead, 1930c) on Piaget's assumptions was finally brought together, with all that Erikson and Bowlby and I had to offer, with Piaget himself, in combination with the new fields of brain research and comparative animal behavior.

My early exposure to theories adumbrated from the behavior of rats prepared me to use with moderation the results of such experiments, to greet with pleasure the inclusion of the idea of species—specific characteristics in experimental animals—to welcome the wealth of material on ethology, to use such experiments as Calhoun's on response to crowding, to relate studies of infancy to the biologically given in maternal and infant behavior, and to deal with the presently popular subject of aggression, from a long history of naive hypotheses about frustration and aggression (Mead, 1964b).

Throughout my professional life, my original brief psychological education, my continuing friendship and collaboration with psychologists, and my willing-ness, even eagerness, to include the work of psychologists as part of the core of theory building have meant that I have received many invitations to collaborate in undertakings which were specifically psychological. These have ranged from the original Murchison *A Handbook of Child Psychology* (Mead, 1931a), when my article on the primitive child was only a program of research: through the Carmichael *Manuals* (Mead, 1946d), in which I had to carry the burden of the now excluded psychoanalytical approach, and where I inaugurated the custom of surveying unpublished research: to participation in Macy conferences on con-sciousness (Abramson, 1951-1955) and on maternal behavior; the UNESCO evaluation of the tensions study; the WHO study group in child development (Tanner and Inhelder, 1957-1960); the Macy Conference on Group Processes; the Conference on the Expression of the Emotions in Man (Mead, 1963f); to the invitation to contribute to this volume. As my work depends to an enormous degree on face-to-face close work with collaborators—among whom I number my friends, my scientist former husbands, and my students—these continuing invitations to work with psychologists and in psychological contexts have been extraordinarily valuable.

It is also hard to place exactly the whole line of research which culminated in the study of national character during the War. From the time that the psychological committee of the Social Science Research Committee asked me to develop a series of cultural studies of cooperative and competitive habits (Mead, 1937)—and, said Gardner Murphy "none of that anthropological insistence on whole cultures,"—we had been aware of the relationships between sociocultural forms and character, a position strengthened by John Dollard's *Criteria for the Life History* (1935), written for the same project, by Gregory Bateson's, Geoffrey Gorer's, and Ruth Benedict's interest in that project. Psychoanalytic forays into the field of cultural character had interested me since Sapir's comments on Seligman's (1932) original article. Larry Frank had inaugurated a seminar in the field in the 1920s. When we began these studies in the early 1940s, combining them with a study of the enemy's probable tactics, problems of cooperation with our allies, and problems of national morale, we added several other important collaborators: Martha Wolfenstein, a psychoanalytically trained clinical psychologist; Rhoda Metraux, an anthropologist originally trained in literature; and Nathan Leites, whose work stemmed from Harold Lasswells' integration of psychology, psychiatry, and political science. In addition to the specific studies from those projects, Martha Wolfenstein and I have continued to cooperate on studies of the relationship between psychological development and specific cultural settings. A later project which included the cross-cultural work of Margaret Lowenfeld, a National Institute of Mental Health project in allopsychic orientation, has resulted in my present formulation of the generation gap, in *Culture and Commitment* (1970b), as well as a continuing attempt to treat mothers and infants as a single transactional system, biologically, psychologically, culturally, and situationally defined. A recent venture for Stephen Richardson's book on childbearing has been a joint article with the psychologist Niles Newton, a former student who is specializing in perinatal psychology (Mead and Newton, 1967).

Of another sort were my intermittent but enjoyable contacts with Gordon Allport, first as one of those of us who worked together on the Cooperation and Competition Project, where John Dollard suggested we all write life histories showing how our own lives had displayed these themes, and Gordon and I did. Later, during World War II, in the Committee for National Morale, a group of us were trying to organize the contributions to be made by the human sciences to the foreseeable involvement of the United States in World War II (Mead and Metraux, 1965). Later again, we worked together on a project where the Hazen Foundation had textbooks scanned for their treatment of religion, only to find that such activities as prayer and religious vocation were completely omitted from the psychology textbooks of the day; this was 1946. Finally, I am indebted to Gordon Allport for his immortal description of liberals as aggrieved anti-bigots.

I notice, as I approach the end of this account, that I have not discussed my field test of psychological theories of adolescence—*Coming of Age in Samoa* (1928a)—and subsequent discussions of these findings in a psychological context. I believe this is not accidental. Psychology and psychiatry have continued to treat such cultural studies as unassimilatable objects. With a bow to "except of course in cultures like Samoa," they have remained culturebound, treating "culture" as a "dimension" or an "intervening variable" so abstracted and disassociated from human beings with bodies that the concept has been relatively useless, sometimes even harmful. John Dollard taught his students to interpolate I.O.C.—in our culture"—but it didn't get them out of their culture-bound categories. *Coming of Age* is ubiquitous on reading lists on adolescence; it often affects those who do not become psychologists or sociologists, but the hopeless fragmentation of our present-day teaching makes pretty sure that it doesn't affect those who do. And so, in studies of national character, we have the spectacle of Angus Campbell—at an American Psychological Association meeting where I presented some of the material on national character—accusing me of racism; of Jensen (1969) getting a hearing, when he understands neither race nor culture; and of such reviews of the field as that by the two Dutch psychologists for UNESCO (Duijker and Frijda, 1960); and finally—in unhappy reactivity, British social anthropologists solemnly discussing whether—as they are not "psychologists"—they have a right to discuss children or child development within the cultures which they have studied (Mayer, 1970). It is truly a parlous state of affairs.

It has been said that any one of the human sciences, which now pursue their separate ways in narrow and specialized scorn and indifference to one another, could have evolved into a single human science, in which we could then take the place, so ardently desired by some of us, among the sciences. We are outcasts, or at best adjuncts, not because we do not command methods appropriate to our complex subject matter; these methods are being sharpened every day, with techniques for objective recording and computers for the analysis of a large number of variables. But our stubborn exclusion of whole fields or whole approaches, our parochial preference for some methods over others whether they are appropriate or not, our overinflated bodies of trivialities, under the "publish or perish" rule, have divided us and rendered us relatively impotent in a time when the insights of the human sciences are grievously needed. I left psychology because psychology itself was ignoring basic insights about the human psyche, about the human child, about human culture, and about human social groups. Through the clumsy methods of first specializing and then attempting to reunite the discipline, we have been able to make some progress. I would like to ask those psychologists who recently have been educated and who are educating others whether what they teach their students today is preparing them at least to go out among other disciplines—as the generation of Gardner and Lois Murphy, Kurt Lewin, Henry Murray, and Otto Klineberg did—and find what they need?

REFERENCES

Selected Publications by Margaret Mead

The Methodology of Racial Testing: Its Significance for Sociology, *American Journal of Sociology, 31,* No. 5 (March, 1926), 657-667.

Group Intelligence Tests and Linguistic Disability among Italian Children, *School and Society, 25,* No. 642 (April 16, 1927), 465-468.

Coming of Age in Samoa: A Psychological Study of Primitive Youth for Western Civilization. New York: Morrow, 1928.(a)

A Lapse of Animism among a Primitive People, *Psyche, 9,* No. 1 (July, 1928), 72-77. (b)

An Inquiry into the Question of Cultural Stability in Polynesia. ("Columbia University Contributions to Anthropology," Vol. 9.) New York: Columbia University Press, 1928; reprinted 1969. New York: AMS Press. (c)

Adolescence in Primitive and Modern Society. In *The New Generation: The Intimate Problems of Modern Parents and Children,* V. F. Calverton and S. D. Schmalhausen, Eds. New York: Macaulay, 1930, 169-188. (a)

An Ethnologist's Footnote to *Totem and Taboo, Psychoanalytic Review, 17,* No. 3 (July, 1930), 297-304. (b)

Growing Up in New Guinea: A Comparative Study of Primitive Education. New York: Morrow, 1930. (c)

The Meaning of Freedom in Education, *Progressive Education, 8,* No. 2 (February, 1931), 107-111. (a)

The Primitive Child. In *A Handbook of Child Psychology,* Ed. Carl Murchison. Worcester, Mass.: Clark University Press, 1931, 669-686. (b)

Two South Sea Educational Experiments and Their American Implications. In Eighteenth Annual Schoolmen's Week Proceedings, March 18-21, 1931, *University of Pennsylvania School of Education Bulletin, 31,* No. 36 (June 20, 1931), 493-497. (c)

Contrasts and Comparisons from Primitive Society, *Annals of the American Academy of Political and Social Science, 160,* No. 2409 (March, 1932), 23-28.

Sex and Temperament in Three Primitive Societies. New York: Morrow, 1935.

On the Institutionalized Role of Women and Character Formation, *Zeitschrift für Sozialforschung, 5,* No. 1 (1936), 69-75.

(Ed.). *Cooperation and Competition among Primitive Peoples.* New York: McGraw-Hill, 1937.

Social Change and Cultural Surrogates, *Journal of Educational Sociology, 14,* No. 2 (October, 1940), 92-109.

Administrative Contributions to Democratic Character Formation at the Adolescent Level, *Journal of the National Association of Deans of Women, 4,* No. 2 (January, 1941), 51-57. (a)

Bateson, Gregory, and Margaret Mead. Principles of Morale Building, *Journal of Educational Sociology, 15,* No. 4 (December, 1941), 206-220. (b)

And Keep Your Powder Dry: An Anthropologist Looks at America. New York: Morrow, 1942, 1971. (a)

The Comparative Study of Culture and the Purposive Cultivation of Democratic Values. In *Science, Philosophy and Religion, Second Symposium,* Lyman Bryson and Louis Finkelstein, Eds. New York: Conference on Science, Philosophy and Religion in Their Relation to the Democratic Way of Life, 1942, 56-69. (b)

Educative Effects of Social Environment as Disclosed by Studies of Primitive Societies. In *Environment and Education,* Ed. E. W. Burgess. (Human Development Series, I. Supplementary Educational Monographs, 54.) Chicago: University of Chicago Press, 1942, 48-61. (c)

Anthropological Data on the Problem of Instinct. In Symposium—Second Colloquia on Psychodynamics and Experimental Medicine, *Psychosomatic Medicine, 4,* No. 4 (October, 1942), 396-397. (Abstract.) (d)

Bateson, Gregory, and Margaret Mead. *Balinese Character: A Photographic Analysis.* (Special Publications of The New York Academy of Sciences, 2.) New York: New York Academy of Sciences, 1942. Reissued 1962. (e)

The Committee on Food Habits, *Psychological Bulletin, 40,* No. 4 (April, 1943), 290-293.

Training of Regional Specialists in Psychology—In the War and After (VII), by Gregory Bateson, Margaret Mead, and Walter Miles. *Junior College Journal, 14,* No. 7 (March, 1944), 311-312.

Human Differences and World Order. In *World Order: Its Intellectual and Cultural Foundations,* Ed. F. Ernest Johnson. New York: Harper, 1945, 40-51.

Cultural Aspects of Women's Vocational Problems in Post World War II, *Journal of Consulting Psychology, 10,* No. 1 (January-February, 1946), 23-28. (a)

Personality, the Cultural Approach to. In *The Encyclopedia of Psychology,* Ed. Philip Lawrence Harriman. New York: Philosophical Library, 1946, 477-488. (b)

Professional Problems of Education in Dependent Countries, *Journal of Negro Education, 40,* No. 3 (Summer, 1946), 346-357. (c)

Research on Primitive Children. In *Manual of Child Psychology,* Ed. Leonard Carmichael. New York: Wiley, 1946, 667-706; reprinted 1954, New York: Wiley. (d)

Age Patterning in Personality Development, *American Journal of Orthopsychiatry, 17,* No. 2 (April, 1947), 231-240. (a)

The Application of Anthropological Techniques to Cross-National Communication, *Transactions of The New York Academy of Sciences,* Ser. 2, *9,* No. 4 (February, 1947), 133-152. (b)

The Concept of Culture and the Psychosomatic Approach, *Psychiatry, 10,* No. 1 (February, 1947), 57-76. (c)

The Implications of Culture Change for Personality Development, *American Journal of Orthopsychiatry, 17,* No. 4 (October, 1947), 633-646. (d)

On the Implications for Anthropology of the Gesell-Ilg Approach to Maturation, *American Anthropologist, 49,* No. 1 (January-March, 1947), 69-77. (e)

A Case History in Cross-National Communications. In *The Communication of Ideas,* Ed. Lyman Bryson. New York: Institute for Religious and Social Studies, 1948, 209-229.

Character Formation and Diachronic Theory. In *Social Structure: Studies Presented to A. R. Radcliffe-Brown,* Ed. Meyer Fortes. Oxford: Clarendon Press, 1949, 18-34. (a)

Collective Guilt. In *International Congress on Mental Health, London, 1948, Ill: Proceedings of the International Conference on Medical Psychotherapy, August 11-14,* J. C. Flugel and others, Eds. London: H. K. Lewis; New York: Columbia University Press, 1949, 57-66. (b)

Male and Female: A Study of the Sexes in a Changing World. New York: Morrow, 1949. (c)

Psychologic Weaning: Childhood and Adolescence. In *Psychosexual Development in Health and Disease,* Ed. Paul Hoch. New York: Grune & Stratton, 1949, 124-135. (d)

Some Anthropological Considerations Concerning Guilt. In *Feelings and Emotions: The Mooseheart Symposium,* Ed. Martin L. Reymert. New York: McGraw-Hill, 1950, 362-373. (a)

The Comparative Study of Cultures and the Purposive Cultivation of Democratic Values, 1941-1949. In *Perspectives on a Troubled Decade: Science, Philosophy and Religion, 1939-1949,* Lynan Bryson, Louis Finkelstein, and R. M. MacIver, Eds. New York: Harper, 1950, 87-108. (b)

Experience in Learning Primitive Languages through the Use of Learning High Level Linguistic Abstractions. In *Cybernetics: Circular Causal and Feedback Mechanisms in Biological and Social Systems, Transactions of the Seventh Conference, March 23-24, 1950,* Ed. Heinz von Foerster. New York: Josiah Macy, Jr., Foundation, 1951. 159-185. (a)

Research in Contemporary Cultures. In *Groups, Leadership and Men,* Ed. Harold Guetzkow. Pittsburgh: Carnegie Institute of Technology, 1951, 106-117. (b)

The School in American Culture. (The Inglis Lecture, 1950.) Cambridge: Harvard University Press, 1951. (c)

Soviet Attitudes toward Authority. New York: McGraw-Hill, 1951. (d)

Mead, Margaret, and Frances Cooke Macgregor with photographs by Gregory Bateson. *Growth and Culture: A Photographic Study of Balinese Childhood.* New York: Putnam, 1951. (e)

Some Relationships between Social Anthropology and Psychiatry. In *Dynamic Psychiatry,* Franz Alexander and Helen Ross, Eds. Chicago: University of Chicago Press, 1952, 401-448.

(Ed.). *Cultural Patterns and Technical Change: A Manual Prepared by the World Federation for Mental Health.* Tensions and Technology Series. Paris: UNESCO, 1953. (a)

National Character. In *Anthropology Today: An Encyclopedic Inventory,* Ed. A. L. Kroeber. Chicago: University of Chicago Press, 1953, 642-667. (b)

Mead, Margaret, and Rhoda Metraux, Eds. *The Study of Culture at a Distance.* Chicago: Univ. Chicago Press, 1953. (c)

The Gifted Child in the American Culture of Today, *Journal of Teacher Education*, 5, No. 3 (September, 1954), 211-214. (a)

Cultural Discontinuities and Personality Transformation, *Journal of Social Issues,* Supplement Series, No. 8 (1954), 3-16. (b)

Some Theoretical Considerations on the Problem of Mother-Child Separation, *American Journal of Orthopsychiatry, 24,* No. 3 (July, 1954), 471-483. (c)

The Swaddling Hypothesis: Its Reception, *American Anthropologist, 56,* No. 3 (June, 1954), 395-409. (d)

Mead, Margaret, and Rhoda Metraux. *Themes in French Culture: A Preface to a Study of French Community.* (Hoover Institute Studies, Ser. D, Communities No. 1.) Stanford: Standord University Press, 1954. (e)

Effects of Anthropological Field Work Models on Interdisciplinary Communication in the Study of National Character, *Journal of Social Issues, 11,* No. 2 (May, 1955), 3-11. (a)

Mead, Margaret and Martha Wolfenstein, Eds. *Childhood in Contemporary Cultures.* Chicago: Univ. Chicago Press, 1955. (b)

Applied Anthropology, 1955. In *Some Uses of Anthropology: Theoretical and Applied,* Joseph B. Casagrande and Thomas Gladwin, Eds. Washington, D. C.: The Anthropological Society of Washington, 1956, 94-108. (a)

The Cross-Cultural Approach to the Study of Personality. In *Psychology of Personality: Six Modern Approaches,* Ed. J. L. McCary. New York: Logos Press, 1956, 201-252. (b)

Some Uses of Still Photography in Culture and Personality Studies. In *Personal Character and Cultural Milieu,* Ed. Douglas G. Haring, 3rd rev. ed. Syracuse: Syracuse Univ. Press, 1956, 79-105. (c)

Changing Patterns of Parent-Child Relations in an Urban Culture, *International Journal of Psycho-Analysis, 38,* Part 6 (1957), 369-378. (a)

Illness as a Psychological Defence. In *Personal Problems and Psychological Frontiers,* Ed. Johnson E. Fairchild. New York: Sheridan House, 1957, 60-78. (b)

Towards More Vivid Utopias, *Science, 126,* No. 3280 (November 8, 1957), 957-961. (c)

Mead, Margaret, and Rhoda Metraux. Image of the Scientist among High-School Students: A Pilot Study, *Science, 126,* No. 3270 (August 30, 1957), 384-390. (d)

Cultural Determinants of Behavior. In *Behavior and Evolution.* Ann Roe and George Gaylord Simpson, Eds. New Haven: Yale Univ. Press, 1958, 480-503.

An Anthropologist at Work: Writings of Ruth Benedict. Boston: Houghton Mifflin, 1959. (a)

Apprenticeship under Boas. In *The Anthropology of Franz Boas,* Ed. Walter Goldschmidt. (Memoirs of the American Anthropological Association, 89.) *American Anthropologist, 61,* No. 5, Part 2 (October, 1959), 29-45. (b)

Creativity in Cross-Cultural Perspective. In *Creativity and Its Cultivation,* Ed. Harold H. Anderson. New York: Harper & Row, 1959, 222-235. (c)

Cultural Factors in Community-Education Programs. In *Community Education:*

Principles and Practices from World-Wide Experience. (Fifty-eighth Yearbook of the National Society for the Study of Education, Part 1.) Chicago: University of Chicago Press, 1959, 66-96. (d)

Feral Children and Autistic Children, *American Journal of Sociology, 65,* No. 1 (July, 1959), 75. (e)

A New Framework for Studies of Folklore and Survivals. In *Men and Cultures: Selected Papers of the Fifth International Congress of Anthropological and Ethnological Sciences, Philadelphia, September 1-9, 1956,* Ed. Anthony F. C. Wallace. Philadelphia: University of Pennsylvania Press, 1960, 168-174. (a)

Problems of the Late Adolescent and Young Adult. In *Children and Youth in the 1960s: Survey Papers Prepared for the 1960 White House Conference on Children and Youth.* Washington, D.C.: Golden Anniversary White House Conference on Children and Youth, 1960, 3-12. (b)

Mead, Margaret, and Theodore Schwartz. The Cult as a Condensed Social Process. In *Group Processes: Transactions of the Fifth Conference, October 12-15, 1958,* Ed. Bertram Schaffner. New York: Josiah Macy, Jr. Foundation, 1960, 85-187. (c)

Anthropology among the Sciences, *American Anthropologist, 63,* No. 3 (June, 1961), 475-482. (a)

Cultural Determinants of Sexual Behavior. In *Sex and Internal Secretions,* 2 vols., 3rd ed., Ed. William C. Young, Baltimore: Williams & Wilkins, 1961, II, 1433-1479. (b)

National Character and the Science of Anthropology. In *Culture and Social Character: The Work of David Riesman Reviewed,* Seymour M. Lipset and Leo Lowenthal, Eds. New York: Free Press of Glencoe, 1961, 15-26. (c)

Psychiatry and Ethnology. In *Psychiatrie der Gegenwart: Forschung und Praxis, III: Soziale und Angewandte Psychiatrie,* H. W. Gruhle and others, Eds. Berlin: Springer, 1961, 452-470. (d)

Schwartz, Theodore, and Margaret Mead. Micro—and Macro—Cultural Models for Cultural Evolution, *Anthropological Linguistics, 3,* No. 1 (January, 1961), 1-7. (e)

A Cultural Anthropologist's Approach to Maternal Deprivation. In *Deprivation of Maternal Care: A Reassessment of Its Effects.* (Public Health Papers, 14.) Geneva: World Health Organization, 1962, 45-62. (a)

Retrospects and Prospects. In *Anthropology and Human Behavior,* Thomas Gladwin and William C. Sturtevant, Eds. Washington, D.C.: The Anthropological Society of Washington, 1962, 115-149. (b)

The Social Responsibility of the Anthropologist, *Journal of Higher Education, 33,* No. 1 (January, 1962), 1-12. (c)

Culture and Personality. In *The Encyclopedia of Mental Health,* 6 vols., Albert Deutsch and Helen Fishman, Eds. New York: Watts, 1963, II, 415-426. (a)

The Factor of Culture. In *The Selection of Personnel for International Service,* Ed. Mottram Torre. Geneva and New York: World Federation for Mental Health, 1963, 3-22. (b)

Patterns of Worldwide Cultural Change in the 1960's. In *Social Problems of Development and Urbanization,* Vol. VII. *Science, Technology, and Development: United States Papers Prepared for the United Nations Conference on the Application of Science and Technology for the Benefit of the Less Developed Areas.* Washington, D.C.: Government Printing Office, 1963, 1-15. (c)

The Psychology of Warless Man. In *A Warless World,* Ed. Arthur Larson. New York: McGraw-Hill, 1963, 131-142. Preprinted as Recapturing the Future, *Saturday Review* (June 1, 1963), 10-13. (d)

Socialization and Enculturation, in "Papers in Honor of Melville J. Herskovits," *Current Anthropology, 4,* No. 2 (April, 1963), 184-188. (e)

Some General Considerations. In *Expression of the Emotions in Man,* Ed. Peter H. Knapp. New York: International Universities Press, 1963, 318-324. (f)

Totem and Taboo Reconsidered with Respect, *Bulletin of the Menninger Clinic, 27,* No. 4 (July, 1963), 185-199 (g)

Violence in the Perspective of Culture History. In *Violence and War,* Ed. Jules Masserman. New York: Grune & Stratton, 1963, 93-106. (h)

Continuities in Cultural Evolution. New Haven: Yale Univ. Press, 1964. (a)

Cultural Factors in the Cause and Prevention of Pathological Homicide. *Bulletin of the Menninger Clinic, 28,* No. 1 (January, 1964), 11-22 (b)

Food Habits Research: Problems of the 1960's. Publication 1225. Washington, D.C.: National Academy of Sciences-National Research Council, 1964. (c)

Vicissitudes of the Study of the Total Communication Process. In *Approaches to Semiotics,* Thomas A. Sebeok, Alfred S. Hayes, and Mary Catherine Bateson, Eds. The Hague: Mouton, 1964, pp. 277-287. (d)

The Future as the Basis for Establishing a Shared Culture, *Daedalus* (Winter, 1965), 135-555. (a)

Mead, Margaret, and Rhoda Metraux. The Anthropology of Human Conflict. In *The Nature of Human Conflict,* Ed. Elton B. McNeil. Englewood Cliffs, N.J.: Prentice-Hall, 1965, 116-138. (b)

Alternatives to War. In "War: The Anthropology of Armed Conflict and Aggression," *Natural History, 76,* No. 10 (December, 1967), 65-69. (a)

Ethnological Aspects of Aging, *Psychosomatics, 8,* Sect. 2 (July-August, 1967), 33-37. (b)

The Life Cycle and Its Variations: The Division of Roles *Daedalus* (Summer, 1967), 871-875. (c)

Mead, Margaret, and Niles Newton. Cultural Patterning of Perinatal Behavior. In *Childbearing—Its Social and Psychological Aspects,* Stephen A. Richardson and Alan F. Guttmacher, Eds. Baltimore: Williams & Wilkins, 1967, 142-244. (d)

Conferences. In *International Encyclopedia of the Social Sciences,* 17 vols., Ed. David L. Sills. New York: Macmillan and Free Press, 1968, *3,* 215-220. (a)

Cybernetics of Cybernetics. In *Pusposive Systems: Proceedings of the First Annual Symposium of the American Society for Cybernetics,* H. von Foerster and others, Eds. New York: Spartan Books, 1968, 1-11. (b)

Incest. In *International Encyclopedia of the Social Sciences,* 17 vols., Ed. David L. Sills. New York: Macmillan and Free Press, 1968, *7,* 115-122. (c)

Problems and Progress in the Study of Personality. In *The Study of Personality,* Edward Norbeck and others, Eds. New York: Holt, Rinehart and Winston, 1968, 373-381. (d)

Wolf Children. In *Encyclopaedia Britannica,* Warren E. Preece and others, Eds. Chicago: Benton, 1968, 507. (e)

Mead, Margaret, and Paul Byers. *The Small Conference: An Innovation in Communication.* (Publications of the International Social Science Council, 9.) The Hague: Mouton, 1968. (f)

From Intuition to Analysis in Communication Research, *Semiotica, 1* (1969), 13-25. (a)

Lawrence Kelso Frank 1890-1968, *American Sociologist, 4,* No. 1 (February, 1969), 57-58. (b)

Violence and Its Regulation: How Do Children Learn To Govern Their Own Violent Impulses? *American Journal of Orthopsychiatry, 39,* No. 2 (March, 1969), 227-229. (c)

The Changing Significance of Food, *American Scientist, 58,* No. 2 (March, 1970), 176-181. (a)

Culture and Commitment: A Study of the Generation Gap. Garden City, N.Y.: Natural History Press/Doubleday, 1970. (b)

Golde, Peggy, Ed. Margaret Mead: Field Work in the Pacific Islands, 1925-1967. In *Women in the Field.* Chicago: Aldine, 1970, 293-331. (c)

Mead, Margaret, and Rhoda Metraux. *A Way of Seeing.* New York: McCall, 1970. (d)

Other Publications Cited

Abramson, Harold A., Ed. *Problems of Consciousness,* 5 vols. New York: Josiah Macy, Jr. Foundation, 1951-1955.

Bateson, Gregory. *Naven.* Cambridge, England: Cambridge Univ. Press, 1936; 2nd ed., Stanford, Calif.: Stanford Univ. Press, 1958.

Bateson, Gregory. Social Planning and the Concept of 'Deutero-Learning.' In *Conference on Science, Philosophy and Religion in Their Relation to the Democratic Way of Life,* second symposium. New York: Science, Philosophy and Religion, 1942, 81-97.

Benedict, Ruth. *Patterns of Culture.* Boston: Houghton Mifflin, 1934; reprinted 1961, Sentry edition SE 8. Boston: Houghton Mifflin.

Bonaparte, Marie. *The Life and Works of Edgar Allen Poe.* London: Image, 1949.

Boaz, Franz. *The Mind of Primitive Man.* New York: Macmillan, 1911.

Dollard, John. *Criteria for the Life History.* New York: Peter Smith, 1935.

Duijker, H. C. J., and N. H. Frijda. *National Character and National Stereotypes: A Trend Report Prepared for the International Union of Scientific Philosophy.* Amsterdam: North-Holland, 1960; New York: Humanities Press, 1961.

Efron, David. *Gesture and Environment.* New York: King's Crown Press, 1941.

Erikson, E. H. Sex Differences in the Play Configurations of Preadolescents, *American Journal of Orthopsychiatry,* 21, No. 4 (October, 1951), 667-692.

Garrett, Henry E. *How Classroom Desegregation Will Work.* Richmond, Va.: Patrick Henry Press, 1965.

Gesell, Arnold, and Frances Ilg. *Infant and Child in the Culture of Today.* New York: Harper, 1943.

Gill Merton, and Margaret Brenman. *Hypnosis and Related States.* New York: International Universities Press, 1959.

Gill, Merton, and Margaret Brenman. *Hypnosis and Related States.* New York: International Universities Press, 1959.

Heath, Barbara H., and J. E. Lindsay Carter. Growth and Somatotype Patterns of Manus Children, Territory of Papua and New Guinea: Application of a Modified Somatotype Method to the Study of Growth Patterns, *American Journal of Physical Anthropology, 35,* No. 1 (July, 1971), 49-67.

Jensen, Arthur R. How Much Can We Boost IQ and Scholastic Achievement, *Harvard Educational Review, 39,* No. 1 (Winter, 1969), 1-123.

Jung, C. G. *Psychological Types.* New York: Harcourt, Brace, 1923.

Lowenfeld, Margaret. The World Pictures of Children: A Method of Recording and Studying Them, *British Journal of Medical Psychology, 18,* Pt. 1 (1939), 68-101.

Lowenfeld, Margaret. The Nature and Use of the Lowenfeld Method Technique in Work with Children and Adults, *Journal of Psychology, 30* (1950), 325-331.

Lowenfeld, Margaret. *The Lowenfeld Mosaic Test.* London: Newman Neame, 1954.

McGraw, M. B. *Growth: A Study of Johnny and Jimmy.* New York: Appleton-Century, 1935.

Mayer, Philip, Ed. *Socialization: The Approach from Social Anthropology.* London, New York: Tavistock, 1970.

Mead, Edward S. *Trust Finance.* New York: Appleton, 1903.

Mead (Meade), Edward S. *The Story of Gold.* New York: Appleton, 1908.

Mead, Edward S. *Careful Investor.* Philadelphia: Lippincott, 1914.

Mead, Edward S. *Corporation Finance,* 5th edition rev. and enlarged. New York: Appleton, 1923.

Mead, Edward S., and Bernard Ostrolenk. *Harvey Baum: A Study of the Agricultural Revolution.* Philadelphia: Univ. Pennsylvania Press, 1928.

Mead, Edward S., and Bernard Ostrolenk. *Voluntary Allotment: Planned Production in American Agriculture.* Philadelphia: Univ. Pennsylvania Press, 1933.

Mead, Edward S., and Julius Grodinsky. *Ebb and Flow of Investment Values.* New York: Appleton-Century, 1939.

Meade, Emily Fogg. Italian on the Land: A Study in Immigration, *U.S. Bureau Labor Bulletin, 14* (May, 1907), 473-533.

Murphy, Gardner. *Personality.* New York: Harper, 1947.

Murray, Henry A., and others. *Explorations in Personality.* New York: Oxford Univ. Press, 1938.

Róheim, Géza. *The Riddle of the Sphinx.* London: Hogarth, 1934.

Seligman, C. G. Anthropological Perspective and Psychological Theory, *Journal of the Royal Anthropological Institute, 62* (1932), 193-228.

Schaffner, Bertram, Ed. *Group Processes,* 5 vols. New York: Josiah Macy, Jr. Foundation, 1955-1960.

Tanner, J. M., and Barbel Inhelder, Eds. *Discussions on Child Development,* 4 vols. London: Tavistock, 1956-1960; New York: International Universities Press, 1957-1960.

Woodger, Joseph H. *Technique of Theory Construction.* Chicago: Univ. Chicago Press, 1939.

Veblen, Thorstein. *An Inquiry into the Nature of Peace and the Terms of Its Perpetuation.* New York: Huebsch, 1919.

327

O. Hobart Mowrer

Although Sigmund Freud is today not one of my favorite authors, there was a time when I read his works fervently and *in extenso*. And as I begin the task of writing this account of my life, I recall a rather striking illustration he uses to clarify the concept of sublimation. An inhibited, neurotic young man discovers that he has some artistic ability, and through it he is able to give expression to certain universal unconscious human aspirations, which brings him fame, money, and "the love of women" (Freud, 1920, p. 328). In this way the man achieved not only indirect (sublimated) satisfaction of his repressed impulses but, in the end, a partial "undoing" of his repressions and at least a modicum of the direct impulse gratification which was initially denied him.

Sublimation has not proved to be one of Freud's most substantial concepts, either in the eyes of his critics or his friends; but the illustration he employed in this connection nevertheless has more than passing relevance to the course of my own personal experience. As a youth, for reasons which I shall explore later, I was badly "out of touch" with both my own emotions and with other people. It was therefore scarcely an accident that I became an "intellectual." The cognitive sphere was the only one in which I functioned with any degree of facility, and my functioning even there had a definitely compulsive, driven quality.

But eventually, my work, compulsive and driven though it was, brought me around to the areas of my own incapacity. Today, my main personal and professional interest is in "Integrity Groups," whose objective is to provide a social setting in which people can learn, among other things, to get in better touch with each other and with their own emotional life. Now in the middle of my seventh decade, I still have both constitutional and characterological peculiarities which will probably prevent me from ever being what might be called a "psychologically robust" person. But I have found people and I have found feeling; and I shall always know what the Good Life is, even though at times I may not be able to experience it. I have achieved some degree of "visibility" in my profession (Myers, 1970; *Who's Who in the World*, 1971-1972 edition), made a good living, have a devoted family, and today enjoy not just "the love of women" but rather an expanded capicity for loving and receiving the love of both men and women. And not only has the nature of my work changed; it is also less compulsive and driven.

If the chapters of this book had formal titles, I think I would therefore choose for mine a fragment from one of Rod McKuen's poems, "From Torment into Love." By this I do not mean to say that my life is today entirely free of pain or that I have fully achieved the kind of interpersonal relations to which I earnestly aspire; but, over the course of four decades, this is the direction in which I have slowly but definitely moved—a fact for which I am deeply grateful.

For a long time, from adolescence on, I led what might be called a Double Life: my external, visible, public, (and later) professional life; and a very subjective, secretive, and tortured private life. I think I can do no better in this autobiography than to describe these two "existences" separately, and then indicate how they have come together—how my life has achieved a degree of integration or integrity which, for all too long a time, it sadly lacked. This, then, will provide the organizing principle for this account, and one which I trust will permit me to write with maximal economy and also fidelity.

EXTERNAL CIRCUMSTANCES AND EVENTS

Perhaps the outstanding and most determinative feature of my birth and childhood can be suggested by a deliberately enigmatic statement: I was my father's grandson. I was born in 1907, when my father was 45 years old and my mother 39. There was an older sister, then aged 19, and a brother of 15. About a year after my birth, my sister married; and although she and her husband for a time lived something over a hundred miles away, my mother and I were often in their home and they in ours. Later, in 1917, they returned to our community; and, psychologically speaking, my sister and her husband were more like parents to me than were my actual father and mother, and my sister's children were nearer my own age than she and my brother. My brother, who married when I was six, was like a young uncle rather than a sibling. My mother's mother sometimes was in our household, and my father had (along with several other siblings who had left our part of the country) two brothers, both older than himself, who with their families lived nearby. They, too, were from my point of view "grandfatherly," and the children of one of their sons (my cousin) were, like my sister's children, my own age and playmates. These, then, were the people who constituted my "extended," if somewhat anomalous, family and my immediate world of kinship.

All of us were "farmers," at least in terms of origin. My father's two brothers, David and Edwin, moved from the country into "town" (our county seat of some 2,000 souls—Unionville, Missouri) when I was very small; and the summer I was six, my father sold our farm and followed suit, although at that time he was only 51 years old, and the move was not exactly one of "retirement." It was by then already apparent to my father that I probably would "never make a farmer" (since I seemed to have a constitutional aversion to physical labor) and was instead "talkative" and bookish; and since he had completed only three or four short winter terms of country school, back in the 1870s, and had always wished he could have been a lawyer, he evidently saw some prospect that I might, with proper encouragement, become the professional man he had always wanted to be. We, along with my father's two brothers, lived in rather imposing houses out on the west (the "good") end of Main Street; and my cousin, Claude, and his numerous brood lived nearby.

Those were idyllic years for me, 1913-1920, which I have described in detail elsewhere (Mowrer, 1966). Although my immediate family and I were not a part of what we termed the "social uppercrust" of our community, there was not a more privileged youngster in town from the standpoint of home, play space, and natural facilities to delight a boy's soul. But this world suddenly crumbled for me with the death of my father on March 20, 1920, when I had just turned 13. In about a year and a half, our home was sold, my mother went to live with my sister in the country, and I started high school living in a small boarding house in a rather shabby part of town. During my last three years in high school, however, the situation was somewhat improved by the fact that my mother and I lived together in modest quarters in town. I was a good student and received a number of class honors; but my classmates properly "pegged" me when, in our Senior Yearbook, they wrote under my picture: "He thinks quite a lot of Hobart." As I shall later indicate, I was actually very lonely and my self-esteem extremely low; but I wasn't a good "mixer" and am sure I gave the impression of being aloof and conceited.

College and Graduate School

It was more or less a foregone conclusion that, upon graduation from high school, I would attend the University of Missouri, at Columbia. This I did from the fall of 1925 to the spring of 1929. Those were rich and eventful years for me; but since I have already spoken at length about them in the other autobiography already cited, I shall here limit myself to the description given in that document of what was easily the most spectacular, if not exactly illustrious, episode in which I was involved during my sojourn at the University.

The three facts about my Senior year which warrant special notice are these: (a) I became "pinned" to a talented student-pianist, (b) took part in an oratorical contest and placed third despite the fact that I "forgot" my memorized speech and had to leave the stage (there were only three of us in the contest!) and (c) precipitated the University of Missouri "sex-questionnaire scandal" of 1929. The latter has been written-up in detail elsewhere (Esper, 1964) and needs only cursory mention here. The second semester I was taking a sociology course on "The Family," and as part of the work of the course students were required to do a little research project of some sort in pairs. In the late 1920's there was a lot of talk (as there is today) about "changing sex standards"; together with a classmate I decided it would be interesting to have a random group of University students and their parents fill out the same questionnaire in order to see what the trends in this area actually were. The questionnaire, in draft form, was approved by the Sociology instructor, the head of my department, Dr. Max F. Meyer, and was seen by two or three other members of the faculty. We then had it printed and put the student copies in the mail. Immediately there was a veritable explosion of criticism of the University, as a result of which the Sociology professor was dismissed, Professor Meyer was suspended, and I lost my laboratory assistantship in Psychology, although allowed to continue as a student. As a gesture of protest, but also because of the unpleasant notoriety involved, I petitioned out of the University.

I will not attempt to indicate all the personal and political factors that went into the making of this "fracus," but there was shortly an an investigation by the American Association of University Professors which resulted in the resignation of the President of the University. He had been in the forefront of those who instigated the original disciplinary actions. The questionnaire, as I now see it, was poorly constructed scientifically and involved bad judgment, but the reaction that occurred was all out of proportion to the facts of the case.

Rarely has a university alumnus left his alma mater with less honor than I did in June of 1929. To the credit of the University, let me say that I was eventually *given* enough class hours to permit me to get the A.B. degree. In addition, perhaps not wisely but very generously, in 1956 the University awarded me one of the first three "Certificates of Merit" it now gives each year to distinguished alumni. Life has involved many strange quirks of fate for me, and this was certainly one of them (p. 13).

There was, as I have indicated, little or no question about where I would go to college. But the choice of The Johns Hopkins University, in Baltimore, for graduate study in psychology was very much of a happenstance. During my senior year at the University of Missouri, I had taken a course in social psychology with Professor Meyer; the textbook in this course was by Knight Dunlap, then head of the Hopkins department. I had minored in sociology, and here was the first attempt I had seen to "integrate" sociology and psychology. I liked the substance of the book, and I also liked the author's clean-cut, lucid style of writing. So, perhaps it was in April 1929, after I had somewhat vaingloriously "resigned" from the University of Missouri, I wrote to Dunlap, explained my circumstances, and asked if there was any way in which I could begin graduate work at Hopkins without a bachelor's degree. As it happened, Hopkins was then experimenting with what it called "The New Plan," which permitted students to enter Graduate School at the end of the undergraduate sophomore year and then required them to complete four years of graduate work for the Ph.D. degree, instead of the usual three. Dunlap admitted me to Hopkins under this plan, but I was not required to spend the fourth year as a graduate student. As Dunlap put it, somewhat wryly, in a letter to the President of the University, I already had the "equivalent" of a college degree and should be permitted to complete my graduate work in three years. Quite unexpectedly, in 1931 the University of Missouri granted me full credit for the courses I was taking when I left school in the spring of 1929 and awarded me an A.B. degree as of the later date. To avoid confusion, I usually list the date of my University of Missouri A.B. as 1929, but actually the official date of its award was 1931. Without explanation, it would otherwise appear that I got my Ph.D. degree in one year, 1931-1932.

As I now review the period of my actual graduate study, 1929-1932, two developments stand out as most noteworthy: my initiation into research and my marriage. And the direction which my research took was again determined quite fortuitously. Upon arriving by train in Baltimore in June 1929, I soon discovered that I was "turned around"; and during my subsequent years of residence there, I was never able to correct this faulty directional orientation. Despite full conscious knowledge that, for example, Charles Street runs North and South, it always seemed to run East and West, and no amount of intellectual effort on my part would alter this stubborn misperception. That fall, in a seminar with Dunlap, I happened to mention these circumstances; and since Dunlap himself, during World War I, had been connected with a program at Mineola, L.I., for the testing of directional orientation in Army aviators, my remarks interested him, and he encouraged me to start some independent research and also to collaborate with him on a project he then had under way.

Although a hardworking man, Dunlap was usually in good spirits, often witty in conversation, and enjoyed interaction with his staff and graduate students. There were frequent parties at his home and at a cottage, on a tributary of the Chesapeake Bay. These gatherings often had some professional aspect, and our regular classes and research also commonly had an element of joviality and "play" about them. It was therefore not difficult for graduate students to get interested in their "studies," and Dunlap was especially delighted when they began to do research. I can, for example, remember him once shouting for joy when we first viewed together a 16-mm motion-picture research film which clearly showed the phenomenon which we were investigating.

Under this benign and stimulating tutelage as a graduate student, I completed four research projects, in addition to my Ph.D. dissertation, in the area of vestibular and visual functions having to do with spatial orientation and thus laid the basis for a line of research in which I continued to be interested for several years thereafter.

Perhaps it will be of some interest to report one episode which occurred in connection with my research on spatial orientation as a function of visual and vestibular sensations and reflexes. During the summer of 1933, there was a World's Fair in Chicago; and since, during the academic year 1932-1933, I was at Northwestern University (see next section), I visited the Fair on a number of occasions. During the course of these visits, I discovered a "motordrome," a large cylindrical structure, perhaps 40 feet in diameter, made of heavy wooden planks held in place vertically by steel cables encircling them on the outside. This cylinder had a wooden floor and also what was called a "slant-wall," made of boards (perhaps 30 inches in length) extending, at an angle of 45°, from the floor to the inside of the cylinder proper or "straight-wall."

The purpose of this structure was to provide an opportunity for the performance of special feats with a motorcycle. A rider would start moving around on the floor of the cylinder and then, when he had gained a little speed, he would go up on the slant-wall; and when he had gathered still greater momentum, he would go up on the straight-wall; and there, if he were a "star," would perform such feats as standing on the seat of his motorcycle as it sped around the inside of the motordrome in a virtually horizontal position. On the outside of the drome there was an elevated circular platform with a railing so that spectators could look over the edge and view the activities within.

Normally the pull of gravity is in the vertical direction, congruent with the visual cues provided by trees, telephone poles, houses, etc., and perpendicular to the horizon. But a motorcycle traveling on the straight-wall of a motordrome (at approximately 35 miles per hour) is subject to centrifugal force approximately four times as strong as gravity. When this force combines with natural gravity it produces a resultant vector only 17° from the horizontal. Vestibular and visual cues are thus thrown into violent conflict; and I found myself wondering how, with continued experience, a conflict of this kind would be resolved: would visual cues eventually predominate so that the rider would perceive the large cylinder as vertical and he and his motorcycle as perpendicular to it or would the combined gravitational and centrifugal forces (amounting to about 4 g) overpower the visual cues and give the rider the impression that the cylinder was lying on its side revolving around him as he rode along in a seemingly vertical, "level" position? I questioned a number of the riders who were associated with the motordrome, and they all reported that it was the latter perceptual phenomenon that occurred. Later I made arrangements to be taken up on the straight-wall by one of the most expert riders. In a paper by Gibson and Mowrer (1938) I have reported my experiences, as follows:

> On the first occasion when the writer accompanied a professional rider in the motordrome, the only describable experience was one of complete spatial disorientation. Movement was clearly perceptible but it was impossible to give it any definite directional reference. It was as if a complexly integrated perceptual mechanism had completely broken down; and this, we conjecture, is precisely what had happened. Visual and postural factors were thrown into such violent conflict that no stable perceptual organization could emerge. However, on the occasion of the second ride (which occurred only a few minutes after the first), this confusion disappeared, and the spatial illusion reported by veteran riders was vividly experienced (pp. 317-318).

In recounting these experiences orally, I have sometimes mentioned that one of the "acts" in the motordrome involved a young woman going up on the straight-wall on a motorcycle with a sidecar in which she took, as a fellow passenger, a rather unkempt, dejected-looking lion. The rumor has occasionally circulated that in my "experiments" I took the place of the lion in the sidecar. For all persons now living and for all posterity, I would like it understood that this was not the case: I had my two rides in the motordrome with the "head man" on a regular motorcycle, sitting sideways on the gas tank directly in front of him!

Although, within limits, illusions with respect to verticality can be produced by manipulating visual cues (as in another carnival contraption known as the "magic swing"), it is easy, in retrospect, to see how, in a situation such as that provided by a motordrome, gravitational forces eventually dominate perceptually: if one gets "out of line" as far as the latter are concerned, one may fall and be injured or even killed, whereas discrepancies between visual cues and one's bodily orientation may be of no great importance, provided a correct gravitational alignment is maintained.

I have previously mentioned that in addition to my introduction to research, the other major event that occurred while I was in graduate school was my marriage, to another graduate student, Willie Mae Cook, of Athens, Georgia. We entered graduate school together, in the fall of 1929; and because of her unfailing friendliness, gaiety, thoughtfulness, and personal attractiveness, she was soon much respected and liked by faculty and fellow-students alike. As the months passed, I was aware of a growing fondness for this young woman, but was quite sure she had no special interest in me, so refrained from making any attempt to "keep company" with her. But then one Saturday afternoon—I think it was in January 1931—a very remarkable thing happened. There were only a few of us students in the Psychology Building, and I was working in the carpenter shop on a piece of apparatus; Willie Mae, I had noticed earlier, was studying in the departmental library. Presently, to my astonishment but immense delight, she strolled into the carpenter shop, went to one of the windows, and remarked on the beauty of the snow (a rarity in her part of Georgia) that had just started to fall. At that moment, I realized, for the first time, how deeply in love I was with this girl; and today, more than 40 years later, I love her even more dearly and devotedly. On March 26, 1931, we were "secretly" married, in the presence of a few close friends, in Alexandria, Virginia; and the following fall, on September 9, our marriage was publicly solemnized at Willie Mae's home in Georgia.

For nine years after she completed (in June 1931) the work for her doctorate degree in psychology (she already had a Master's degree when she came to Hopkins), Willie Mae—or "Molly" as she was now often called—was professionally active. We then had three wonderful children—Linda, Katie, and Todd—and for 17 years, while they were growing up, Molly was professionally inactive; but then, in 1957, she had an unexpected opportunity to start teaching child development and family relations here at the University of Illinois; and for the past several years she and I have, in addition, collaborated closely, and with deepening satisfaction, in the Integrity Groups program, which will be discussed later.

My marriage to and years with Molly have been the most meaningful experience of my life, and I am grateful beyond measure for the good fortune that has been mine. This is perhaps the main reason I requested and graciously received permission from the editor of this volume to reproduce, at the outset of this chapter, a family rather than individual photograph. Although we have had our share of troubles and difficulties, my wife and three children have for most of my adult life been a precious and intrinsic part of "me"; and the picture here reproduced is especially meaningful in that it was taken Wednesday, September 8, at the Statler Hotel in New York City during the annual meeting of the American Psychological Association the year I was president (1953-1954). From left to right in the photograph, the children are Linda, Todd, and Kathryn. Today our family is happily enlarged by the addition of Linda's husband, Peter K. Carlston, and their son Randy, and Katie's two children, Amber and Paul Toliuszis, and her husband William M. Leach, Jr.

Postdoctoral Fellowships and the Years at Yale (1932-1940)

Although my wife was able to remain on as an instructor in child development at John Hopkins, I could not get a teaching position in the spring of 1932 (the Great Depression was then at its worst) and considered myself lucky to obtain a National Research Council Post-Doctoral Fellowship for the year 1932-1933. This I spent in the laboratories of Professor Franklin Fearing, of the Department of Psychology at Northwestern University. Fearing and his students were at that time primarily concerned with the effects of surgical assault on various parts of the vestibular mechanism (semicircular canals and otoliths) in the pigeon; and so the line of research I had started as a graduate student at Hopkins fitted in well with ongoing activities in Fearing's laboratories.

I was fortunate enough to be reappointed as an N.R.C. Fellow for a second year, and this I spent at Princeton University. My main reason for wishing to go there was the access I would have to the apparatus which Weaver and Bray had developed for studying the electrical activity of the auditory branch of the eighth cranial nerve during aural stimulation (for a bibliography of their work, see Woodworth, 1938); and I wanted to make a similar study of the activities of the vestibular branch of this nerve, to see if the protracted aftereffects of continuous bodily rotation ("postrotational nystagmus") were due to ongoing receptor stimulation or to neural reverberation in the vestibular ganglia. It turned out that the latter was the case (see O. Lowenstein's work as reviewed by Wendt, 1960).

In the spring of 1934 teaching positions were still very hard to obtain, so I made application for a Sterling Post-Doctoral Fellowship at Yale University, which I obtained and held for two years, under the sponsorship of Professor Raymond Dodge, some of whose research was related to the line of investigation I was then pursuing. During those two years, I, so to say, "rounded out" my study of vestibular and visual functions and became increasingly intrigued with the "core" activities going on in the Yale Institute of Human Relations, which had been established in 1929. The Institute had been conceived and founded by James Rolland Angel, then President of Yale, Acting Dean Robert Maynord Hutchins of the School of Law, and Dean M. C. Winternitz of the School of Medicine and had been funded, for an initial ten-year period, by the Rockefeller Foundation. The underlying idea was that by bringing psychology, psychoanalysis, and the social sciences together, in a combined teaching and research context, new and powerful "integrations" or scientific "breakthroughs" might be achieved. In addition to Raymond Dodge, whom I have already mentioned, the senior psychologists then connected with the Institute were Clark L. Hull, Robert M. Yerkes, Walter R. Miles, Mark A. May, R. P. Angier, and Arnold Gesell; and there were correspondingly prominent persons representing the other disciplines comprising the Institute program. During that period, there were also many very gifted younger men and women in psychology, both at the lower academic ranks and as graduate students, no fewer than six of whom were later to become presidents of the American Psychological Association. (My position at Yale University, between 1936 and 1940, was Instructor in Psychology and Research Associate in the Institute of Human Relations.)

In short, the Yale Institute of Human Relations was at that time probably the most exciting, stimulating, and productive enterprise of its kind in the world. And it was here that my own interests and research activities began to move in new directions. As a result of contact with and stimulation from Clark Hull, Neal Miller, Don Marquis, Shirley Sprague, and Kenneth Spence, I became involved in the psychology of learning; and through the influence of John Dollard and Earl Zinn, I also became actively interested in Freudian psychoanalysis, and since one of the main objectives of the Institute program was to effect "cross fertilization" between disciplines, I joined with Dollard, Miller, Robert Sears, and others in attempting to "integrate" psychoanalysis and learning theory, to "translate" psychoanalytic concepts into learning theory, and, whenever possible, to produce laboratory analogues (see, for example, Dollard et al., 1939).

Because most of the papers which I published as a result of the work done along these lines at Yale (and continued for several years after I had moved to another university) have been reissued and are readily accessible in the form of a book entitled *Learning Theory and Personality Dynamics* (1950), they need not be individually cited here. However, I should say that I was now involved in a very "hot" area of psychology and social science; and my work soon began to receive generous, and generally favorable, attention (see Kanfer and Phillips, 1970, especially pp. 78-79). One of the first papers I published after I began working on the interrelation between learning and psychoanalysis was entitled "A Stimulus-Response Analysis of Anxiety and Its Role as a Reinforcing Agent"

(1939), which has been extensively cited, has stimulated considerable research, and has been reproduced in at least half a dozen collections of readings (including the 1950 volume cited above).

In 1935 my wife resigned her position at The Johns Hopkins University and joined me in New Haven, where she was employed as a psychologist at the New Haven Children's Community Center, a residential facility for disturbed and neglected children. Here we conducted a number of minor studies, and jointly published one major paper entitled "Enuresis—A Method for Its Study and Treatment" (1938), which is now often cited as one of the first strikingly successful applications of learning theory to a "clinical" problem. As such, it was a forerunner of what has since become known as "Behavior Therapy" (see Ullmann and Krasner, 1969, pp. 538-540).

Because of failure of continued funding, the Yale Institute of Human Relations has, I believe, now been officially dissolved; but a photograph of the Oak Street entrance to the building, where it was housed, today hangs above my desk as a reminder of bygone splendor and delights. It was my great good fortune and privilege to have been associated, during those halcyon days, with this bold, if not fully consummated, venture.

A Detour through the
Harvard Graduate School of Education (1940-1948)

On Monday, May 10, 1940, the Nazis invaded the Lowlands—and I went from New Haven to Cambridge, Massachusetts, to be interviewed for a possible job in the Harvard Graduate School of Education. President Conant had recently appointed Frances Spaulding as Dean, with a mandate to modernize the School and convert it from a rather pedestrian "teacher-training" institution into a more creative and research-oriented part of the University. One of Spaulding's strategies in this connection was to appoint, whenever feasible, persons trained in psychology and the social, biological, or physical sciences rather than in education. My credentials proved acceptable, and I assumed my duties in the Graduate School as Assistant Professor of Education the following September, with a courtesy appointment, and office, in the Department of Psychology (then housed in Emerson Hall).

I don't know how much I was myself able to contribute to the revitalization of the Harvard School of Education; but I am sorry to say I found it a rather dull place and was never very challenged or stimulated by it. For the first and only time in my professional career, I carried—acceptably, I believe—a regular teaching load (in educational psychology, learning, and personality theory); but my main concerns continued to center on research problems which had been generated during the stimulating years at Yale (see the 1950 book already cited). I remember, with much pleasure, student collaboration at Harvard in a number of these researches. But I never became really "plugged in" as far as the School of Education itself was concerned; and, programmatically, it never "got off the ground" during my sojourn there. (It has since apparently developed, from the impetus it received from Frances Kepple, a real "dynamic.")

I had cordial but not close relations with many of the members of the Department of Psychology (which was tensely polarized into two feuding factions); but I did find a friendly and congenial haven at the Psychological Clinic, then under the direction of Henry A. Murray, who, from the outset, was extremely gracious and helpful to me. Through him I came to know (and collaborated with) the anthropologist Clyde Kluckhohn, and also met Talcott Parsons, in sociology. Eventually we formed a little club—called, for some reason which was never entirely clear to any of us, "The Levelers"—which also included Gordon Allport and Bernard DeVoto (formerly of the Department of English but now a highly successful writer of historical novels and *Harper's* Editor of "The Easy Chair"). This group eventually formed the nucleus of the new Department of Social Relations at Harvard, which came into being partly because of the success of the Institute of Human Relations at Yale, but also because of the restive and unhappy situation prevailing in the Harvard Department of Psychology.

Only two other developments need be mentioned in connection with the eight years I spent at Harvard. In the spring of 1944 I accepted an appointment, in Washington, D.C., with the Office of Strategic Services, where I served for approximately a year (until sometime after V-Day in Europe). As a result of my work in OSS, my hitherto largely academic knowledge of human personality was put to the acid test of practice (in the assessment of men and women for "special hazardous overseas assignments"). Through a number of other psychologists and psychiatrists who were in our "shop," I came to know Frieda Fromm-Reichmann and Harry Stack Sullivan; and in the spring semester of 1945, I took a seminar with Dr. Sullivan at the Washington School of Psychiatry. As a result of these combined circumstances, my "clinical" interests were piqued and given a radical new turn, which I shall describe in some detail later.

The other development I should mention here is that, just as I was leaving Yale to go to Harvard, I found myself becoming interested in the psychology of language, with special reference to the use of learning theory as the conceptual underpinning. The basic idea which I developed in my 1954 presidential address to the American Psychological Association was conceived during my stay at Harvard, as were many of the ideas which went into my 1960 book, *Learning Theory and the Symbolic Processes*.

Although I came to have a very warm and reverent feeling toward Harvard University as a whole (and we loved the old Victorian house in which we lived at 88 Washington Avenue, on "Gallows Hill," in Cambridge), I must say I left with little regret when, in 1948, I was offered a Research Professorship at the University of Illinois. The basic difficulty at Harvard was not that I was a "man without a country," but rather a man without a department with which I felt strongly identified. In more ways than one, I always had a sense of "marginality" at Harvard, which was in marked contrast to the deep sense of identification and involvement I had enjoyed at Yale.

Professional Activities and Events (1948-1960)

After it had become generally known that I had resigned at Harvard to accept a position at the University of Illinois, a fellow psychologist expressed his astonishment that I should do such a thing: How much closer to Academic Heaven could you get than Harvard? I replied that I certainly was not making the change because of either geography or climate but that there were financial advantages and that the position I had been offered was a Research Professorship, with no teaching responsibilities, and for the first two years I probably would not be doing much research. My friend's laconic reply was: "I guess you better take that job!" A little earlier, Illinois had offered me, first a professorship in the College of Education and then one in the Department of Psychology, both of which I had declined. But Research Professors could be appointed directly by the University Administration, through the Graduate College; and it was informally understood that between 1948 and 1950, if I accepted such an appointment, I would have some minor administrative responsibilities, in grooming for the headship of the Department of Psychology at the end of this time, if I wished it.

What I did not know in the beginning but soon learned, to my dismay, was that the University was then embroiled in fierce intramural administrative conflicts, which first resulted in a series of "resignations" on the part of highly placed officials and culminated in the "ouster" of the president himself, in the summer of 1953. As a member of the University Research Board and Acting Director of the Psychological Clinic, I had found myself caught in, what was to me, a quite unintelligible "cross fire" from various directions and soon decided on a continuing career in research rather than a change to administration. I have never regretted that decision—nor did it deprive the academic world of any special administrative talents.

During the period under review, my research, writing, and lecturing moved along two occasionally coalescing but usually distinct channels: clinical psychology (discussion of which will come later) and learning theory. My 1953 book, *Psychotherapy: Theory and Research* (written in collaboration with others), was an expression of the former interest; and *Learning Theory and Behavior* and *Learning Theory and the Symbolic Processes,* which appeared simultaneously in 1960, reflect—and, to all intents and purposes, ended—some 25 years of work in the latter field. Since I have now neither researched nor written on the psychology of learning per se for a full decade and have no intention of returning to this field, it is possible, at this point in time, to begin to separate the "wheat from the chaff" in respect to my contributions in this area.

My first experimental studies in this field had been initiated while I was still at Yale and were largely concerned with what was then known as "avoidance learning" but is today (under the influence of the technical vocabulary of B. F. Skinner) commonly called "aversive conditioning." Here an initially neutral stimulus of some sort is presented to a laboratory animal and shortly followed by a noxious stimulus (e.g., an electric shock), which can be terminated by the subject only by performing a specific response of some sort, such as leaping into the air. Presently, after a few paired presentations of these two stimuli, the subject will be observed to leap into the air in response to the first stimulus, or "signal," before the noxious stimulus occurs—and which, by the design of the experiment, now does not occur (i.e., is avoided)—hence the term "avoidance learning."

From the outset it seemed clear to me that neither Thorndike's famous Law of Effect nor Pavlov's classical principle of conditioning, at least as traditionally formulated, could account for this phenomenon. Thorndike had been almost exclusively concerned with the development of habits through the use of "reward" and with their elimination through the use of "punishment." In avoidance learning no reward (in Thorndike's sense) was involved; and since a response was developed rather than inhibited, one could likewise not speak of "punishment." Superficially, it looked as if Pavlov's principle of conditioning or "stimulus substitution" would explain avoidance learning. But in 1938 Brogden, Lipman, and Culler had reported an experiment which cast serious doubt on this assumption; and in an experiment which R. R. Lamoreaux and I reported in 1946, we showed that it is possible to set up an avoidance response to a conditioned stimulus which is totally unlike the "unconditioned" response (i.e., the response which the subject has to make to escape from the noxious stimulus). Obviously the principle of simple stimulus substitution or "classical conditioning" could not handle this phenomenon.

For a long time, I had suspected that avoidance learning involved not one but two kinds—very different kinds—of learning. It seemed to me that in avoidance learning the subject has to learn three things: (1) what to do as a means of excaping from the noxious unconditioned stimulus; (2) to be afraid when the conditioned stimulus, which betokens danger, occurs; and (3) what to do as a means of reducing or escaping from the fear thus generated, which involves avoiding the noxious unconditioned stimulus. By a slight extension of Thorndike's conception of reward (to include drive reduction of any kind), one could thus explain the learning that occurs under (1) and (3), and Pavlovian conditioning adequately accounts for the learning that occurs under (2). On the basis of this kind of evidence, I published (in 1947) a paper entitled, "On the Dual Nature of Learning—A Reinterpretation of 'Conditioning' and 'Problem-Solving'," the central thesis of which soon became known as "two-factor learning theory." (For an evaluation of my work up to this juncture, see Rescorla and Solomon, 1967, and Herrnstein, 1969.)

Thorndike had largely ignored the phenomenon of conditioning and took the position that if it actually occurs, it is of only trivial importance, Clark Hull (1943), who was in many respects a follower of Thorndike, tried to show that conditioning, while real and important, could, however, be derived from his modified version of Thorndike's Law of Effect. And in a paper published in 1932, Pavlov had made the reverse attempt, not too successfully, to show that habit formation could be explained in terms of conditioning. In contrast to these "monistic" interpretations, my position, as of the 1947 paper and for a number of years thereafter, was that conditioning (sign learning) and habit formation (solution learning) are two separate and distinct but complementary processes (see Konorski and Miller, 1937; Skinner, 1938). Paradoxically, by the time the two learning books were published in 1960, I had come back around to a "monistic" interpretation and was taking the position that, in the final analysis, all learning can be reduced to Pavlovian conditioning or "sign learning" (as Tolman, 1932, had long maintained; also see the recently published English version, 1969, of Miller and Konorski's 1928 paper, with a Foreword by B. F. Skinner and a Postscript by Konorski).

I continued to argue that there are, however, two types of reinforcement, that is, two circumstances under which conditioning takes place: (1) that which occurs with the sudden onset of a drive (punishment), and (2) that which occurs when a drive terminates (reward). And I further held that stimuli associated with drive onset acquire the capacity to produce fear and that stimuli associated with drive termination acquire the capacity to produce hope. From these two types of conditioning, I argued (with Konorski, 1948) that one could derive (1) avoidance learning, (2) approach learning, (3) habits, and (4) inhibitions. The details of this argument are somewhat involved and will not be repeated here. Suffice it to say that, as of the present date, the argument still stands up surprisingly well.

That stimuli, both independent and response-correlated, which are temporally associated with the onset of strong noxious drives acquire the capacity to arouse fear is easily demonstrated empirically and has never been seriously questioned. There has, however, been some doubt about the capacity of stimuli associated with drive termination to arouse the emotion of hope (positive secondary reinforcement). Beginning with his Ph.D. thesis, which was completed in 1957, Robert C. Beck of Wake Forest University has devoted a great deal of attention to this problem (see Beck and Brooks, 1967, and Segundo et al., 1961); and recently Beck sent me an as yet unpublished manuscript entitled "Human Responses to Stimuli Associated with Shock Onset and Termination" (Sutterer and Beck, 1969), accompanied by a letter, the last sentence of which reads: "If you were writing *Learning Theory and Behavior* today, you'd find more evidence [on this score] than you could shake a stick at" (see also Gray, 1971).

The conception of learning, or behavior modification, set forth in the 1960 books posited that approach behavior develops when hope is conditioned to an external, independent stimulus (or "signal"), that avoidance behavior develops (given the proper circumstances—see above) when fear is conditioned to an external, independent stimulus, that habits are formed by the conditioning of "hope" to the proprioceptive and other sensory feedback from responses which are rewarded, and that habits are inhibited when such stimuli are conditioned to the emotion of fear. Although the contradictory evidence is still somewhat equivocal, it is today by no means certain that response-produced stimuli are involved in precisely this way in habit formation and habit elimination. For some of the most pertinent negative evidence on this score, the reader should consult Greenwald (1968) and Konorski (1969).

The specific and only difficulty involved here is the contention that the "feedback" conception of habit sketched above can account well enough for the inhibition of a previously punished response and for the facilitation of a previously rewarded response once such responses start to occur but that it cannot explain why *one* rather than any of innumerable *other* responses is selected and initiated in the first place. I was not unaware of this problem in the 1960 books (see particularly a section entitled "Response Initiation and Related Problems," pp. 283-288, Mowrer, 1960b). I offered two conceivable but frankly speculative solutions. In 1962 Ishihara published a critique of the 1960 books in which he took the position that this problem had not been adequately recognized and resolved and that the resulting inadequacy undermined the whole approach. McCall and Hart (1962) quickly published what seemed to me a well-reasoned and persuasive reply; and McMahon (1973) has just published an article in which his stance is much more congruent with that taken by McCall and Hart than with that of Ishihara (see also Sheehan, 1972). It may be that here, in the line of reasoning pursued and elaborated by McCall and Hart and Bugelski, there is a solution to the difficulties raised by Konorski and by Greenwald. In other words, as of this writing, the overall theoretical position espoused in the 1960 books accounts rather beautifully for a broad range of behavioral data, and the apparently contradictory evidence is still tenuous and controversial. Ultimately, a better conceptual scheme may be developed; but, after more than a decade of logical and empirical testing, the theory just discussed still seems to have substantial merit—and, on the whole, I "feel good" about it. Even Konorski, in a paper based on some very careful and sophisticated new research (1970) has come back to a position which considerably softens his erstwhile repudiation of his 1948 hypothesis (which was basic to my 1960 books). In this paper Konorski sums up the situation as he presently sees it in the following three sentences:

> After deafferentation of a limb, the animal is still able to perform instrumental responses with this limb, if these responses are either very simple or well trained. On the other hand, if the response requires precision, it cannot be performed by the deafferented limb. *Probably training of skilled movements in the young also requires afferent input from the limbs concerned* (p. 49, italics added).

For an indication of the way the two 1960 volumes were "officially" received by my profession (i.e., reviewed in *Contemporary Psychology*), see Amsel (1961) and Jeffrey (1961); for some later evaluations, see Bugelski (1964), Sahakian (1970), and D'Amato (1970).

During the time I was at the Yale Institute of Human Relations, I published, as already indicated, some laboratory (animal) paradigms of psychoanalytic "dynamisms." During the sojourn at Harvard, with the aid of students in psychology and education, I made several attempts to show how "persistent non adjustive behavior" (see Shaffer, 1930) could be derived from, and indeed experimentally produced from, learning principles as such. In concluding this evaluation of my work in the field of learning, I should perhaps briefly allude to these studies and some of the further work they have stimulated. In 1945 A. D. Ullman and I published a paper entitled "Time as a Determinant in Integrative Learning," in which we showed that if a given action has both rewarding and punishing consequences, it may persist indefinitely (even though the punishment is inherently more potent than the reward), if the reward comes first and the punishment is somewhat delayed, and that, conversely, such a response will be inhibited, even though the reward is greater than the punishment, if the punishment comes first and the reward is delayed. This research has stimulated a long series of confirmative and elaborative studies by K. E. Renner (see, for example, Renner, 1964, 1972).

Three years later, Peter Viek and I published a paper entitled "An Experimental Analogue of Fear from a Sense of Helplessness," which demonstrated that rats fear an electric shock which they themselves can terminate less than a shock of the same duration over which they have no control. For follow-up studies on this line of investigation, see, for example, Seligman, Maier, and Geer (1968). Barbara Lynden (Mowrer, 1960a) and Whiteis (1956), working on an informal laboratory observation at Yale reported to me by J. S. Brown, showed that, given the right circumstances, a punishment can be used to keep a habit alive rather than inhibit it (the "vicious-circle" phenomenon). Brown himself (1969) has just published an excellent review of subsequent research in this area, the objective of which he characterizes as follows:

> It is the purpose of this review to examine in detail the procedures associated with these contradictory outcomes with the aim of increasing our understanding of conditions essential to obtain the vicious-circle effect. In order to keep the task within manageable limits, it has been necessary to exclude studies involving the punishment of wheel-turning and lever-pressing avoidance and escape. An excellent summary of much of this material has been provided recently by Azrin and Holtz (1966).

Manifestly the studies just cited are pertinent to the growing field of behavior therapy, but as yet they have been given only peripheral recognition.

Space permitting, it would be possible to cite and discuss a few more studies which were published prior to my coming to the University of Illinois, or afterward, which have stimulated a modicum of interest and experimental follow-up: e.g., "Preparatory Set (Expectancy)—A Determinant in Motivation and Learning" (1938); "Animal Studies in the Genesis of Personality" (1939b); "Extinction and Behavior Variability as Functions of Effortfulness of Task" (with Helen Jones, 1943—there have been a number of replications of our findings but also some negative results; Fischer et al., 1968, have, however, recently reported what appears to be definitive empirical confirmation and explained the prior failures to replicate our results); "A Method of Measuring Tension in Written Documents" (1947, with John Dollard); and "How Are Intertrial 'Avoidance' Responses Reinforced?" (1958, with J. D. Keehn). This list could be extended, but the preceding discussion should suffice to indicate both the scope and the substance (or lack of it) in what I have done in the general field of learning and by way of trying not only to recast certain psychoanalytic "dynamisms" in the vernacular of learning theory, but also to use that theory to devise independent models of "persistent non-adjustive behavior" (Shaffer, 1930) or "identity crises" (Erikson, 1968).

THE SUBJECTIVE SIDE OF MY LIFE STORY

A psychiatrist friend recently repeated to me an "in" quip which circulates among his colleagues: "Psychiatry is not a profession, it is a diagnosis." Equivalent observations have often been made about and reported by psychologists, and they have special pertinence to my own life and choice of a profession. Thus far I have had eight more or less incapacitating depressions (1921, 1929, 1933, 1935, 1940, 1944, 1953, and 1966). I wish with all my heart that I might have been spared this affliction; but at the same time I realize that it was the force behind the choice of my profession and provided much of the motivation for the work I have done.

In the autobiography already cited (1966), I have written in considerable detail about my struggles with psychopathology and shall here be relatively synoptic. Let me begin by saying that I now regard six factors as having been contributory to my depressive tendencies: (1) a genetic predisposition, on my mother's side of the family, to depression; (2) the death of my father when I was 13 years old, with many unresolved attitudes toward him; (3) the presence of a powerful, although not fully conscious, personal ambition; (4) the inhibition of the free and full expression of emotion on my part by my father, who came from stern, humorless Germanic stock; (5) the loss of highly important privileges and status symbols following my father's death; and (6) the presence, for many years of my life, of guilty secrets with which I did not know how to deal at all adequately.

The Sequence and Apparent
Significance of Recurring Depressions

My first depression occurred when I was a freshman in high school (1921) and was fourteen years old, about a year and a half after my father's death and almost immedeately after the breakup of our family and the sale of our home, to which I alluded near the beginning of this account. This depression was characterized mainly by feelings of depersonalization and unreality and lasted upward of two years. We consulted a number of physicians about my difficulties, one of whom thought that I had a "focal infection" in my slightly enlarged tonsils and forthwith removed them, and another who detected a slight trace of albumin in my urine and prescribed bedrest and a special diet. My own private surmise at the time was that the trouble came from sexual conflicts, but I never dared discuss them with anyone. School counselors were unknown in those days, and I grew up in a church where our ministers often proclaimed, as a great virtue, that we Protestants, unlike those foolish Catholics, did not confess our sins to "another human being" but rather took our troubles "to God in silent prayer." Under this ideology I prayed, without effect—and remained silent! It was this experience, more than anything else, that made me decide to go into psychology as a profession. I was looking for an "answer" which apparently did not exist in the "culture" in which I grew up.

Depression number two (1929) came eight years later, just after I had left Columbia, Missouri, and entered Graduate School in Baltimore. This move had meant leaving old friends, a familiar environment, and a young woman to whom I was engaged, and entering a totally new and strange situation. With the onset of this depression, I consulted a physician, who prescribed the Weir Mitchell treatment, which involved complete bedrest for a couple of weeks and some sedation. After I was released from the general hospital where I had been, I tried psychoanalysis briefly. Here, for the first time, I admitted the guilty secrets in the sexual area, which the analyst dismissed as inconsequential; but I experienced no relief from this or the other discussions we had. I usually felt worse, rather than better, after an analytic hour, and so, after two or three months, I discontinued the analysis.

The only possible reason I could find for the third depression (1933), which occurred toward the end of my postdoctoral fellowship year at Northwestern was that I had been "working too hard." I did nothing about this period of distress, which gradually lifted over the course of the next few months. (I should add that by this time I was married and that, because of circumstances already described, my wife and I had had to be apart during the academic year. However, the depression "hit" me during the summer, when my wife and I were living happily together.)

Depression number four (1935) likewise occurred without ostensible precipitating cause, a few months after I took up my work at Yale. The following fall my wife was able to join me permanently in New Haven, and soon thereafter I embarked upon three years of classical Freudian psychoanalysis, five days a week, with a seemingly favorable outcome. The premise on which my analyst and I worked was that my tendency toward anxiety and depression came from "repressed sexuality and aggression," which we tried to release. However, about a year and a half after the termination of the analysis, when my wife and I had left New Haven and moved to Cambridge, Massachusetts, depression struck again (1940). Naturally, both she and I were dismayed to find that I was not "cured" after all; but we decided that perhaps my earlier analysis had, in some obscure but crucial way, been "incomplete" and that I should try analysis again. This time I was able to obtain the services of a very gracious, intelligent, and kindly man, Hanns Sachs, who had been one of Freud's closest associates and friends and who was a devoted and assiduous student of Freud's ideas and methods. Here, at last, I would surely find the solution to my difficulties! Over the course of some months, the depression lifted and the analysis was terminated. However, I again became depressed shortly after my family and I moved to Washington, in the spring of 1944, and I obtained a leave of absence from my position there to go back to Boston to work intensively with Dr. Sachs for a month, followed by a long series of weekend trips from Washington to Boston for one or two interviews with him.

However, as the months passed, there seemed to be little change in my state of mind; and I finally became so discouraged, not merely with the work I was doing with my particular analyst but with psychoanalysis generally, that I decided to abandon it, once and for all. It was shortly after this that I had an opportunity to take the seminar with Harry Stack Sullivan, which, as I have remarked earlier, was a turning point in my life, both personally and professionally. Later I shall trace in some detail how this all came about; but here I should first complete the account of my later "bouts" with depression.

It was nine years after the depression of 1944 until I was again afflicted in this manner (1953); and this attack (number seven) was the most severe I had ever experienced. It came at a time when my personal and professional life were both proceeding in an extremely satisfactory way and was thus particularly inexplicable from the standpoint of any external circumstances. This time I was extremely agitated, eventually found myself thinking much too seriously about suicide, and admitted myself to the small psychiatric hospital conducted by our own University of Illinois Department of Psychiatry, in Chicago. This meant considerable "loss of face" for me professionally, for it occurred at a time when I was not only President-Elect of the American Psychological Association as a whole but was also President of two divisions of the Association and scheduled to give a presidential address to each, which I was now unable to do. It seemed that all I had worked for, professionally, for more than 20 years, was irreparably lost; and the torture I went through for several weeks can properly be described by only one word: hellish!

Eventually, however, my anguish began to subside, and after three and a half months of hospitalization, I returned home, although I continued for many months more to make regular trips to Chicago to see the psychiatrist who had mercifully seen me through the acute phase of my crisis. This was before the days of antidepressant medication (which date from 1958, when imipramine hydrochloride was discovered); and I did not want, and my psychiatrist did not urge, electroconvulsive shock treatment. The therapy I received was thus largely supportive, supplemented by medication for insomnia.

Further Discussion of the Causes of My Psychopathology and of Depression in General

For reasons I shall discuss presently—or perhaps it was purely fortuitous, I do not really know—I did not have another depression until 1966, 13 years after the one just described. Because of the length of this interval, I had come to believe that I had found the psychosocial cause and cure for my own difficulties and perhaps those of many others; and although I am still persuaded that I did find something, it is obviously not, however, a panacea. It is today generally conceded that serious personality disorders are multiply caused (i.e., a resultant of the interaction of two or more relevant variables commonly referred to as the "diathesis-stress hypothesis"; see, for example, Shields, 1968, p. 119); and in my own situation, I can identify six circumstances (see p. 23) which seem to have been of greater or lesser pertinence and potency.

1. Coppen and Walk (1968) have reviewed the findings of seven separate studies (using the comparison of the "concordance," or coincidence of depression, in identical and fraternal twins) which, in combination, provide evidence, at a fantastically high level of statistical significance, of the role of genetic factors in this disorder. For a long time I attached no signification to the history of depression in my mother and some of her relatives and simply ignored the evidence which was accumulating from the empirical twin studies. However, the fact that I could still get depressed in 1966, despite the developments which I shall shortly describe, and the fact that I have responded favorably to the now available antidepressant drugs (Pertofrane and Vallium), forced me to recognize a constitutional factor in my own depressive tendencies and to take the trouble to read some of the now relatively voluminous literature on the genetic elements in depression and to discover that at least the first rudimentary steps have been taken in working out a rational biochemical (enzymic) explanation of mood disorders and their treatment (Mowrer, 1973b).

2. There is also considerable evidence that the loss of one or both of one's parents during childhood or early youth is conducive to later depressive trends (see, for example, Bowlby, 1970; Keeler, 1954). As previously reported, my own father died when I was just turned 13, at a time when I was very far from having

worked through my "ambivalence" regarding him. In the autobiography which appeared in 1966 I have said in this connection:

> My father's death had come after a very short illness and unsuccessful surgery. It was a great shock to all of us, for we had so little warning and virtually no opportunity to "prepare" for it. My mother went into a "decline" from which she never really recovered (although she lived on for some 27 years); and I was afflicted with a kind of numbness which reflected, on the one hand, my profound sense of loss (for years I dreamed my father was still alive), but also (I am ashamed to say) a sense of relief that he was now "out of the way" and I could more nearly do as I wished (p. 6).

The dream that my father had not really died (or had been "resurrected") would take the form of a report from someone that he had just seen him at such and such a place. I would feel extremely happy and would rush to the place indicated, only to wake up and find that I had been dreaming. Until recently I had never known of anyone else having had this type of dream following the death of a parent. But Keeler, in the chapter entitled "Children's Reaction to the Death of a Parent" which has already been cited, says:

> Reunion with dead parent was the second more common symptom, being present in eight [of 11] cases. . . . Reunion with the dead parent was effected through fantasy in six children, through dreams in five children and through visual and auditory hallucination in three children. These clearly served as a mechanism of defense and as a wish fulfillment (pp. 116-117).

I may add that I was unable to grieve at the time of my father's death, and it was years later that I became capable of more fully experiencing and expressing this emotion.

3. Earlier in this chapter I have alluded to the expectations which my family rather obviously had for me with respect to personal accomplishment, and which I willingly enough accepted and "introjected." Adler has frequently stressed the pathogenic nature of ambition or the striving for what he called "personality superiority" and the neglect of "social interest" (see Ansbacher and Ansbacher, 1964, pp. 240-241; also Mowrer, 1971a). Ayd, in his book *Recognizing the Depressed Patient* (1961), makes reference to the fact that depressives, during their nondepressed periods, are often very obsessional and "will push themselves to the breaking point in an effort to accomplish things in accordance with their standards" and as a result "often have strained interpersonal relations" (p. 5), that "the pre-illness personality" of the depressive is often "hypomanic" and that he has "a reputation for being a prodigious worker" (p. 81), that "most depressives have a good work record" (p. 125), and that "their obsessive personality makes them . . . dilligent and reliable workers" (p. 126). Rose Spiegel, in a recent article (1969), speaks of various ways in which

depression can be "masked," and refers to "driving overwork . . . as another escape" (p. 20). And Grosser (1966) refers to "the hypothesis offered by Mabel Cohen and her associates (1954) that upward mobility pressures or concerns are found in the history of manic-depressive patients" (p. 52).

"Failure" or "rejection" is obviously more catastrophic and more likely to create discouragement and self-castigation for the person who is primarily concerned with "going up" and "getting ahead" than for the person who has greater "social interest" and enjoys "reaching out" to other people. (Mowrer, 1971a).

4. Although the concept of repression, as Freud conceived it, is today stressed much less than it formerly was, one still hears reference to the phenomenon of "being out of touch with one's feelings" (and "insensitive" to other people); and much time is spent, particularly in certain forms of group therapy, in loosening up the capacity to experience feeling and to "interact" with others. My father, while a fair and in many ways kindly man, was however, a stern "disciplinarian" and would brook no "backtalk" or display of defiance or anger from his children (although given to violent outbursts of temper himself!). Following his death, I tended to accept his values in this area (although I had previously hated them); and during high school and also later, I adopted a severely depreciatory view of emotions and feelings generally. Perversely, I came to feel that ideas alone were the legitimate and worthy denizens of consciousness. Although in recent years I have made some progress in overcoming this crippling tendency, I cannot honestly say that my 700 or more hours of individual psychoanalysis (where the paramount objective is to "make the unconscious conscious") were very helpful in this connection. "Free association" (openness, honesty) in special groups and with Significant Others is, in my estimation, far more likely to be effective in this connection than any amount of individual psychoanalysis.

5. On an earlier page I have spoken of having had neither a rich nor a socially prominent family when I was a child, but I was nevertheless uniquely privileged (for details, see Mowrer, 1966a; see also Adler's common allusion to "pampering" as a precursor of "neurosis"). Once, a few years ago, when I was talking about my childhood experiences (and resulting "life style") with my friend Rudolf Dreikurs, he characterized me, in the context of my early family life and material circumstances, as "The Little Prince," which in a certain poetic and psychological sense I indeed was. But with the death of the King (my father), instead of succeeding him to the Throne, I suffered an enormous loss in status: instead of becoming King, I became, in my own eyes at least, a Nobody, Nothing! This kind of trauma is commonly seen in psychiatric practice as a prelude to depression; and it eminently qualifies as involving what Erikson (1968) has termed an "identity crisis." I have tried to deal with this aspect of my adolescent difficulties in the earlier autobiography as follows:

> Against this background, one did not have to be much of a prophet to
> see it was unlikely, following my father's death, that I would be able to

go to school, keep up my play activities, and take over his very considerable responsibilities. I certainly did not relish the thought of all the work that would thus be involved, but at the same time I was disconsolate at the thought of giving up our home. It was decided that my mother and I would stay on for a year on a trial basis, with such assistance as might come in the way of company if nothing else, by having our new minister and his small family live with us. For reasons I will explain later, I don't remember much about that year (my eighth grade in school); but it evidently didn't go well, for in the spring my mother decided to sell our home, go live in the country with my sister, and let me "board" in town with a family with whom we had long been friends so that in September I could enter high school.

That was a bad "fall" for me, if I may be permitted a poor pun. I had lost my father a year and a half earlier, then the home that had meant so much to me, and school itself was to bring some other bitter disappointments and failures. I "tried out" for football but was soon aware that the coach and even the other fellows felt I was simply occupying valuable time and space. I took the hint and "dropped out." There was a more serious problem. Latin and algebra were both difficult subjects for me. I could see no "point" to them, and to complicate matters still further I took a personal dislike to the woman who taught them. The upshot was that after a few weeks I dropped these two subjects, and I cannot now recall whether I substituted anything for them or proceeded with an incomplete program.

Suffice it to say that, all things considered, I was by now in a somewhat melancholic frame of mind, although nothing seemed to me in any way "abnormal." Then came a morning when I got up with a mysterious and quite disturbing feeling of unreality and "strangeness"— about my environment and, worst of all, even about myself. The nearest I had ever previously come to feeling this way was when I had been seriously ill with measles and somewhat delirious at the age of ten, and on one or two later occasions when I had slight concussions from falls. Now there was apparently no physical basis for such a state of mind, and I was totally mystified and frightened in a quite indescribable way. Although years later I was to learn that "depersonalization" (the feeling of strangeness or unfamiliarity with respect to oneself) and a sense of unreality with respect to the external world are common neurotic symptoms, I had at this time never known or heard of anyone else's ever having had such feelings; and much less did I know what one was supposed to do about them. Nothing I could think of myself seemed to help; and after a few days of this strange misery, I left school and walked the five miles to my sister's home in the country. There I told her, my mother, and other relatives about the strange experiences I was having. They were of course concerned, but seemed as baffled and helpless as I was (Mowrer, 1966a, pp. 6-7).

6. As already indicated, I grew up in a church where I often heard our ministers say that we Protestants did not confess our sins to other human beings

(James 5:16 notwithstanding); instead we took our misdeeds "directly to God in silent prayer." When, as an adolescent, I developed certain sexual conflicts and a crushing burden of guilt, it never once crossed my mind that I could usefully talk with anyone else about my problems. My only recourse was to pray—which did not prove, for me, very helpful.

I have already commented on the impetus for personal accomplishment which I received from my family. By the time I was in mid-adolescence, I had another, even more compelling reason for needing to "make something of myself": since my self-esteen was now extremely low in the moral area, it became all the more incumbent upon me to be good in terms of outward accomplishment. It has often been pointed out, not infrequently by Catholic writers themselves, that Protestants seem to be more ambitious, productive, and creative than Catholics. At the risk of oversimplification, I conjecture that this is due to the fact that in Protestant circles personal guilt is handled less adequately than in Catholicism (although much remains to be desired here, too) and that the "drive" associated with the Protestant Work Ethnic reflects, at least in part, an attempt to compensate, by means of achievement, for personal guilt which should be resolved in a very different way.

Thus, instead of having merely the proverbial "three strokes" against me as far as proneness to depression went, I had twice that number. However, Alfred Adler and his followers maintain that one's fate is not determined so much by what happens to a person as by the responses he makes to his life circumstances, what he does about them! I know I have made many grievous mistakes, but I seem also to have made some positive responses in the face of adversity. Perhaps Gandhi was right when he observed: "Anything of fundamental importance must be purchased with suffering."

INCEPTION AND FRUITION OF INTEREST IN INTERPERSONAL PSYCHOLOGY AND "GROUPS"

In this concluding part, I want to speak mainly of developments that have occurred during the decade, 1960-1970. But in order for this discussion to be fully meaningful, it will be necessary to drop back a quarter of a century, to the year, 1944-1945, the point at which I broke with Freudian psychoanalysis and had my first contact with Harry Stack Sullivan and his associates. This came about mainly as a result of my work in the Office of Strategic Services during World War II and in the seminar which I took with Sullivan, in the spring of 1945, at the Washington School of Psychiatry. Up to this point, under the sway of psychoanalysis, I had assumed that psychopathology consisted of personality "psychodynamics" and "complexes" which a person carried around inside his head, and that these could be constructively modified only in the transference relationship provided by the psychoanalytic situation. In contrast to all this, I soon discovered that Sullivan, himself an ex-Freudian, was suggesting that psychopathology "exists," so to say, in "interpersonal space," as a function of the nature and quality of the relationships which individuals have with the Significant Others in their lives. (I do not recall that Sullivan ever had much to say about the role of constitutional variables in psychopathology.)

In the context of Freudian treatment, there is very little one can do "on his own." The "work of the analysis" is done on the couch, in the presence of the analyst, where one free-associates, talks about his childhood memories and feelings, and reports dreams (which Freud called "the royal road to the unconscious"). Talking to other persons, outside the analysis, was actively discouraged on the grounds that it would weaken the transference; and no important life decisions or changes in life style were to be made until the analysis was completed and one's insight and judgment had improved. As a result of my contacts with Sullivan, peripheral though they were, it soon became evident to me that if what he was saying was true, the Freudian injunctions were countertherapeutic and that one ought to (1) start talking and relating to Significant Others in new and different ways as soon as it becomes evident that old ways are self-defeating; and (2) that the other changes in life style (new habits) likewise ought to be tried out immediately if they promise to be more useful than old ones.

After a few weeks in Sullivan's seminar, I put this reasoning into effect and took an action which none of my three Freudian analysts had ever so much as suggested—and which would, I am sure, have been strongly opposed by them (as well as by most Protestant ministers and Catholic priests): I shared with my wife, contritely but as gently and considerately as I could, the carefully guarded secrets of my adolescence—and some additional ones I had acquired after marriage. She was surprised, compassionate, in some ways angry, but, more than anything else I think, relieved and reassured; for here was a possible clue to the recurrent depressions which had caused both of us so much distress and an indication that I was repudiating certain forms of deviant (secretive, dishonest) behavior.

The disclosures which I made to my wife, in the spring of 1945, had, as I now see the situation, three major effects: (1) they improved my relationship with her (brought us closer together, made us more truly "of one spirit"); (2) they made me less disposed to depression (because of reduced guilt), and (3) they gave me a new "slant" on the whole problem of psychopathology. Having been trained as an experimental psychologist, when people had previously sought my assistance with "neurotic" problems, I had promptly "referred" them. But after my family and I returned to Cambridge in the fall of 1945, if someone in emotional difficulty came into my office, I would likely as not ask them to "pull up a chair" and tell me what was on their mind. At that time I was operating on two very simple, yet powerful premises: (1) that "neurotic" persons often have a lot of ongoing deception in their lives, and (2) that their conscience tries to get them to admit to this deception but is met with conscious (ego) resistance, with ensuing "repression" of conscience (superego) and compromise formations (symptoms) similar to those which Freud thought resulted when an individual repressed his instincts or impulse life (the id)(Mowrer, 1950, 1953).

If by this altered approach to the interpretation of symptoms we discovered secret guilt or if a person could directly admit to it, I then usually asked why he did not make a frontal attack upon the problem and simply acknowledge his guilty secrets to the person or persons to whom they had been most unfair or damaging. The almost invariable response was: "But the last psychiatrist [analyst, psychologist, clergyman, social worker] to whom I talked told me that whatever I did, I should never do that! It might hurt the other person terribly." I would then ask how the policy of continued duplicity, under the guise of loving consideration, had worked out. The fact that the person was now consulting me carried an implicit answer to this question. Sometimes important self-disclosures would then be forthcoming and, with a little encouragement, would be extended to others, either privately or in my office, often with dramatic relief and reconciliation.

But there were two classes of persons who were refractory to this approach: (1) those who, after many hours of both direct questioning and symptom interpretation, did not disclose any particularly grievous guilt, and (2) those who, although they yielded up their secrets to me, refused to do so to anyone else. Sometime in the mid-1950s (after coming to the University of Illinois), I quite by chance hit upon a device which is remarkably effective in overcoming the first of these difficulties: If the other person persisted in denying any secret guilt in his or her life, I would do what is today known as "modeling" (see, for example, Franks, 1969, Mowrer, 1966b; Yalom, 1970). That is, I would do what "the patient" was supposed to do—speak the truth about himself—except that I would do a better job of it than he or she had done. Time after time, this device of "sharing" breached the defenses of hitherto impregnable secrets, which, in due course, would be shared with family members, friends, and others.

Then, as I have indicated, there were those who would admit readily enough their inauthenticity but would steadfastly refuse to extend their openness to members of their family and intimate friends. But one day, as I was talking with a particular young man (we had already shared in considerable depth), I was struck by certain interesting parallels between his difficulties and those of another young man I was seeing. At the end of our appointment, I asked the first young man how he would feel about having another person with rather similar problems join us at the next meeting, with the idea that they would then talk mainly to each other rather than to me. The first young man readily assented, I contacted the second person, and he also agreed to the plan. This was my first "group," although I did not think of it in this way at the time. I simply noticed that each person now told his story to the other more freely than he had initially related it to me, and each was able to add significant details which had been either consciously withheld or not recalled during earlier interviews.

Encouraged by the favorable outcome of this "experiment," I began to enlarge our "group"; and we soon discovered that the practice thus afforded in talking intimately with carefully selected "strangers" gave individual members the courage (and encouragement) to make difficult disclosure to the hitherto shunned and estranged Significant Others. After such disclosures to persons outside the group—spouse, father or son, mother or daughter, or close friend— they might in turn be invited to join the group—and often responded favorably.

In the middle and late 1950s group therapy was certainly no novelty (Rosenbaum and Berger, 1963); and on more than one occasion I was asked: "But in your groups, what do you do that is any different from what most [psychoanalytic, client-centered, or "eclectic"] groups do?" Usually I pointed out that in our groups there was a systematic attempt to locate real rather than supposedly false or "imaginary" guilt in people's lives which had previously been kept carefully hidden, and that when this came out, instead of attempting to reassure the guilt-ridden person, something like this was usually said: "It's good that you've finally revealed these corrosive secrets; but now the question is: What are you going to do about them? In other words, how are you going to make restitution for the immediate advantage you gained by your deceptiveness and the long-term damage you have done, to yourself or others?" This was usually sufficient to convince questioners that there was a difference, but they also frequently concluded that our groups were very "moralistic" and could not possibly be either "scientific" or "therapeutic."

Thus we had elevated the principle of Honesty, Openness, or Transparency (Jourard, 1964) to a place of prime importance in our groups—honesty not just with a therapist, and not just with other group members, but also, whenever it was indicated, with persons with whom one was meaningfully associated in Ordinary Life (Schwab, 1971). To this we now gradually added a second principle, namely that of Responsibility, i.e., a willingness not only to confess but also to make restitution (which means, literally, to put something back where it should be, to set matters right).

In an era of permissive child rearing, psychoanalysis, client-centered "acceptance," and secret confession in the church, both Protestant and Catholic, it goes without saying that this approach was not acclaimed with much enthusiasm. In those days (the late 1950s and early 1960s), the simple fact was that we stood very much alone—and were highly suspect. Sullivan's interpersonal theory of psychiatry provided a natural framework for group therapy along these lines, but his followers were for some reason slow in pursuing this advantage (although it was later to provide the inspiration for what I like to call the Palo Alto School of Psychiatry, with its emphasis on communication—Watzlawick et al., 1967; Harris, 1967). And the prevailing supposition was still that individual treatment was the therapy of choice. However, I then began to gain some knowledge of Alcoholics Anonymous and to discover that their Twelve-Step Recovery Program (1939) also put much emphasis on Honesty ("admitting that we were . . .")

and Responsibility ("making amends"). I also made the personal acquaintance of Anton T. Boisen, who, almost single-handedly, had started the Pastoral Counseling Movement (1936, 1960); he was unreservedly supportive, even though the movement which he himself had started had by now largely abandoned him and joined the ranks of Freud and Rogers. About 1958, quite unexpectedly, I received a letter from Harold Duling, of the Lilly Endowment, expressing agreement with our theoretical position and approval of the thrust of our group work and intimating that financial support might be forthcoming if needed. After some preliminary negotiation, I made application in 1960 for and received (in 1961) a grant which permitted three theological seminary professors, chaplains, or pastoral counselors to be on our campus for an academic year, for a combined psychological-theological study of the problem of personal guilt. This program ran for five years; and although I was and am a secularist and these men were, for the most part, "committed Christians" of various faiths, I developed deep respect and enduring affection for them, and today they remain among my closest and most valued personal friends. (For examples of the publications which issued from this program, see Belgum, 1963, and Drakeford, 1967).

Then support began to appear from a different source: academic and professional circles. In rapid succession articles or books by other authors appeared which, although not entirely congruent with out developing position and practice, were expressing many of the same dissatisfactions with traditional approaches which we had voiced (Mowrer, 1973a). Also, we suddenly discovered that we had a great deal in common with the followers of Alfred Adler, notably Rudolf Dreikurs, Heinz and Rowena Ansbacher, and William L. Pew. Although as a graduate student I had tried to read Adler's writings, I could not get much out of them. But 40 years later, I regard Adler's work and that of many of his followers as extraordinarily perspicacious and far "in advance of the times." Adler's emphasis on "social interest" was sadly lacking in the work of most other psychiatric, psychological, and psychoanalytic writers during the first half of this century; and only today, when it is being realized that personal alienation is the plague of our times, are we beginning to have anything like a proper appreciation for what the Adlerians have long been saying in this connection (Mowrer, 1971a).

Further support for our emphasis on the "pathogenic secret" (Ellenberger, 1966) and the importance of confession and restitution came in the middle of the 1960s, from the remarkable rehabilitative work of Synanon Foundation (Yablonsky, 1965) and Daytop Village, Inc. (Shelly and Bassin, 1965), in special residential communities, with drug addicts. I was privileged to have some contact with both of these organizations (and, later, Gateway Houses Foundation, in Chicago); and I soon discovered that in addition to our principles of Honesty and Responsibility, the leaders of these residential communitues were also emphasizing a third principle, Emotional Involvement or Caring. As a result of his early contact with Synanon, the New York psychiatrist Daniel S. Casriel (1962) had developed, in his private practice, a type of group therapy in which special attention was given to the "release of feeling," both hostile and loving; and from these varied contacts, we began to introduce into our groups the third cardinal principle, that of Involvement. Although we did not go to the extremes of Esalen (at Big Sur in California) and even drew the line at some of the Casriel practices, we nevertheless began to "communicate" physically (e.g., by hand-holding or embracing) instead of by purely verbal means (see several articles on the phenomenon of "touching" in the 1969 fall issue of *Psychotherapy: Theory, Research, and Practice*). This added a powerful new dimension to our groups, change occurred more rapidly, and members began to regard Integrity Groups not just as a form of "treatment," but as a Way of Life. As the membership increased, the administrative procedures also became more democratic and responsibility more broadly shared.

Of necessity, many parts of the story of the development of Integrity Groups, especially during the last 10 years, have had to be omitted here. There are, however, four papers which ought to be specifically mentioned. In "Conflict, Contract, Conscience, and Confession" (1969), an empirical ethic is delineated which avoids both moral absolutism, on the one hand, and Fletcher's "situation" ethics, on the other hand. A monograph published in 1968 entitled "New Evidence Concerning the Nature of Psychopathology" reviews no less than a dozen empirical studies which consistently refute the Freudian supposition that the neurotic is an overly socialized, "too good" person; and a paper entitled "Belated Clinical Recognition of the 'Pathogenic Secret' " (1973a) presents both soft and hard evidence that, from the standpoint of mental health, honesty is the "best policy" and has real therapeutic power. Finally, attention should be called to a summary paper entitled "Integrity Groups: Their Principles and Objectives" (1972). We thus feel that Integrity Groups are now solidly grounded conceptually and that further empirical validation will continue to accumulate. (Since the foregoing was written, a letter has arrived from W. I. Penn, Research Associate at the Bexley Hospital, England, describing a study by Graham Foulds published in 1965, in which data collected by a quite novel procedure strikingly support the other findings described in the 1968 monograph cited above.)

For many years, my wife and I conducted what might be called a "private laboratory" in group procedures along the lines indicated above; but we hesitated to offer a formal course or seminar at the University in this approach. Those of us who have thus been associated with what we call the I.G. Thursday-Night Groups have long been convinced that the existence of paid leaders or "therapists" would cause a rapid disintegration of our whole enterprise, which is based on the principle of mutual rather than "professional" help (see Bixenstine, 1970; Hurvitz, 1970). Most graduate students are looking for a vocation, a way of "making a living" by rendering some sort of professional service, not an avocation in which they take part as unpaid members or co-equals. However, with the growing emphasis in recent years on community mental health, many salaried positions have become available for professionals whose main skill might be that of acting as catalysts for the "seeding" and nurturance of mutual-help and self-proliferating groups. Many such groups have come into being without professional help, and many more could develop if the encouragement of such groups was a major objective of formal community mental health programs.

Heartened by these considerations, in the fall of 1969 my wife and I offered an accredited seminar for the first time on "Integrity Groups—Theory and Practice," which involved a two-hour didactic session each week and three-hour practicums involving intensive group experience. The first semester we had 16 students (from psychology, education, social work, child development, and communications); the second semester the number doubled. Because of our long experience with groups, the practicum sessions worked out well, and many of the students have continued to "group" after the seminar formally ended. We were, however, less sure of our ground in the didactic part of the course, but we now feel more confident here too as the result of the experience gained this past year. Professor Anthony J. Vattano, of our Jane Addams Graduate School of Social Work, has joined us in this enterprise; and we have just completed the sixth semester of this seminar and are still growing—and learning.

It so happens that during 1969 virtually every large-circulation magazine in this country carried a feature article on the crescendo of interest in the small-groups movement (there have also been movies and TV programs on the subject). The reason for this rapidly growing interest is not difficult to understand. Our four primary social institutions—home, church, school, and neighborhood—are today all in varying stages of disarray and ineffectiveness. Great masses of people are not finding in them the sense of identity, the emotional warmth, and the cosmic meaning which they formerly found. It seems that in their resulting "identity crises" they are turning increasingly to improvised or "intentional" groups which, to varying degrees, are serving the needs which the older institutions are no longer able to meet. Whether these new groups will supplement and repair or perhaps, in some instances, replace the older institutions remains to be seen; in any case it now looks as if the Small-Groups Movement is here to stay and is no longer just a form of "therapy" but a much-needed, new social institution (Gendlin, 1970). Integrity Groups are just one small facet of this total movement, but we believe it is a sound and significant one.

My life has never been more meaningful or satisfying than it is at present. My family is devoted, harmonious, and loving. After years of professional neglect and rejection in many circles, I find our group approach, as I facitiously remarked to a friend recently, "both respectable and popular." Yet, like Paul of old, I have a "thorn in my flesh." As a result of extensive, often painful but change-producing experience in groups, I feel that I have largely overcome many of the characterological defects I had as a younger man and that I am today, at least in some ways, a better human being. But I have cited what is to me compelling evidence for believing that I am disposed to a type of depression that is largely constitutional, or "endogenous." Unlike reactive, neurotic, and involutional depressions, this type of depression seems to come and go, often without much rhyme or reason; and I have been subject to this periodic malady all my adult life. For a long time I tried to keep my depressions, along with a lot of other things, secret, feeling that if they were known it would stigmatize and disadvantage me professionally. But as I have learned the redemptive power of truth in other areas, I have become increasingly open about this aspect of my life also.

Fortunately, there are now forms of medication (the tricyclic antidepressants and the monoamine oxidase inhibitors used in combination with various tranquilizers) which often enable a person to continue to function during such a depression. He will not, to be sure, be entirely free from discomfort, "symptoms," or "side effects," but he need not be incapacitated, and that is a very great blessing, both to him and to those around him. (As noted earlier, I am personally most grateful for relief obtained from medication during my most recent—I dare not say "last"—depression.) Also, in instances where depression does not yield to medication, it is, for reasons which are still not fully understood (Rothman, 1970), often dramatically relieved by electroconvulsive shock treatment.

From one point of view it might seem that, within two or three generations, the congenital mood disorders could be virtually eliminated by an enlightened program of eugenics or "genetic counseling." Personally, I would like to see a widespread eugenic attack made on this and several similar problems; but there are many highly informed persons in this field who are against such a program (e.g., Karlsson, 1966), feeling that since the genetics of "mental illness" is very complex, it probably could not be banished in this way without also eliminating or impairing qualities which are essential to our full humanness. A book by David Rosenthal entitled *Genetic Theory and Abnormal Behavior* (1970) has just appeared which, in my estimation, provides the best overview presently available of this field. As Chief of the Laboratory of Psychology of the National Institute of Mental Health, Dr. Rosenthal can hardly be said to write with a "medical bias." He writes rather with an objectivity and scientific sophistication that are rarely found in either psychological or medical circles. In the Preface of his book, he says:

> For many years, I have been continually surprised to learn how little most mental health devotees know about the possible hereditary contributions to the phenomena they are studying and teaching. These include not only most clinical psychologists, but psychiatrists, psychiatric social workers, nurses, social scientists, counselors, physicians, and others who must deal with mentally disturbed persons (p. ix).

Then there is the old question of the relationship between "madness" and creativity or "genius." In his *History of Medical Psychology* (1941), Zilboory has this memorable sentence: "The whole question—what mental disease is, how it works in man, and how it makes man work—was knocking at the door of psychiatry [in the late nineteenth century]" (p. 464). This question is still knocking at our door. At the present time there seems to be very little inclination to try to solve it eugenically; but new forms of medication can at least blunt and lessen the duration of "attacks"; and the Small-Groups Movement which has just been described promises to reduce, for both genetically normal as well as "tainted" persons, other forms of suffering which come from modern man's ubiquitous interpersonal alienation and dehumanization. I am deeply grateful that the new psychotropic drugs have come in time for me to benefit from them personally as far as my emotional difficulties of a constitutional nature are concerned; and my growing awareness of the destructiveness of interpersonal isolation and anonymity and the opportunity afforded to have some small part in developing methods for overcoming problems in this area through special group procedures is something for which I shall also be forever thankful.

REFERENCES

Selected Publications by O. Hobart Mowrer

Preparatory set (expectancy)—a determinant in motivation and learning. *Psychol. Rev.*, 1938, *45*, 61-91.

A stimulus-response analysis of anxiety and its role as a reinforcing agent. *Psychol. Rev.*, 1939, *46*, 553-565. (a)

Animal studies in the genesis of personality. *Trans. New York Acad. Sci., Series II*, 1939, *3*, 1-4. (b)

On the dual nature of learning—A reinterpretation of "conditioning" and "problem-solving." *Harvard Educ. Rev.*, 1947, *17*, 102-148.

Learning theory and personality dynamics. New York: Ronald Press, 1950.

Psychotherapy: Theory and research. New York: Ronald Press, 1953.

Learning theory and behavior. New York: Wiley, 1960. (a)

Learning theory and the symbolic processes. New York: Wiley, 1960. (b)

Abnormal reactions or actions? In J. Vernon (Ed.), *Introduction to general psychology—a self-selection textbook*. Dubuque, Iowa: Wm. C. Brown Co., 1966. (a)

The behavior therapies, with special reference to modeling and imitation. *Amer. J. Psychother.*, 1966, *20*, 439-461. (b)

New evidence concerning the nature of psychopathology. In Marvin J. Feldman (Ed.), *Studies in psychotherapy and behavior change*, Buffalo, N.Y.: University of Buffalo Press, 1968. Pp. 111-193.

Conflict, contract, conscience, and confession. *Transactions* (Department of Psychiatry, Marquette School of Medicine), 1969, *1*, 7-19.

Adler's basic concepts: Neurotic ambition and social interest. In A. Nikelly (Ed.), *Techniques for behavior change: Applications of Adlerian theory.* Springfield, Ill.: C. C. Thomas, 1971. (a).

Integrity groups: principles and procedures. *The Counseling Psychologist*, 1972, *3*, 7-32.

Belated "clinical" recognition of the "pathogenic secret." In A. R. Mahrer (Ed.), *Creative developments in psychotherapy*, Vol. III, 1973. (a)

Stress, constitution, character, and integrity groups. *Psychother. Theory Res. Pract.*, 1973 (in press). (b)

(with Helen M. Jones) Extinction and behavior variability as functions of effortfulness of task. *J. Exp. Psychol.*, 1943, *33*, 369-386.

(with J. D. Keehn) How are intertrial "avoidance" responses reinforced? *Psychol. Rev.*, 1958, *65*, 209-221.

(with R. R. Lamoreaux) Fear as an intervening variable in avoidance conditioning. *J. Comp. Psychol.*, 1946, *39*, 29-50.

(with Willie Mae Mowrer) Enuresis—A method for its study and treatment. *Amer. J. Orthopsychiat.*, 1938, *8*, 436-459.

(with A. D. Ullman) Time as a determinant in integrative learning. *Psychol. Rev.*, 1945, *52*, 61-90.

(with P. Viek) An experimental analogue of fear from a sense of helplessness. *J. abnor. soc. Psychol.*, 1948, *83*, 193-200.

Other Publications Cited

Amsel, A. Hope comes to learning theory. *Contemp. Psychol.*, 1961, *6*, 33-36.

Anonymous. *Alcoholics anonymous.* New York: Alcoholics Anonymous World Service, Inc., 1939.

Ansbacher, H. L., and R. R. Ansbacher. *Superiority and social interest: A collection of Alfred Adler's later writings.* Evanston, Ill.: Northwestern Univ. Press, 1964.

Ayd, F. J. Recognizing the depressed patient. New York: Grune & Stratton, 1961.

Azrin, N. H., and W. C. Holtz. Punishment. In W. K. Honig (Ed.), *Operant behavior: Areas of research and application.* New York: Appleton-Century-Crofts, 1966.

Beck, R. C. Secondary reinforcement and shock-motivated discrimination. Unpublished Ph.D. thesis, Urbana: Univ. Illinois, 1957.

Beck R. C., and C. I. Brooks. Human judgments of stimuli associated with shock onset and termination. *Psychonom. Sci.*, 1967, *8*, 327-328.

Belgum, D. *Guilt: Where psychology and religion meet.* Englewood Cliffs, N.J.: Prentice-Hall, 1963.

Bixenstine, V. E. *Community House and its groups: A new approach to community mental health.* Kent, Ohio: Kent State University (mimeographed), 1970.

Boisen, A. R. *The exploration of the inner world.* New York: Harper & Row, 1936.

Boisen, A. R. *Out of the depths.* New York: Harper & Row, 1960.

Bowlby, J. *Attachment and loss.* New York: Basic Books, 1970.

Brogden, W. J., E. A. Lipman, and E. Culler. The role of incentive in conditioning and learning. *Amer. J. Psychol.*, 1938, *51*, 109-117.

Brown, J. S. Factors affecting self-punitive locomotor behavior. In B. A. Campbell and R. M. Church (Eds.), *Punishment and aversive behavior.* New York: Appleton-Century-Crofts, 1969.

Bugelski, B. R. *The psychology of learning applied to teaching.* Indianapolis: Bobbs-Merrill, 1964.

Casriel, D. *So fair a house: The story of Synanon.* Englewood Cliffs, N.J.: Prentice-Hall, 1962.

Cohen, Mabel B., Grace Barker, R. A. Cohen, Frieda Fromm-Reichmann, and Edith Weigert. Intensive study of twelve cases of manic-depressive psychosis. *Psychiatry,* 1954, *17,* 103-137.

Coppen, A., and A. Walk. *Recent developments in affective disorders: A symposium.* Ashford, Kent, England: Headley Brothers, Ltd., 1968.

D'Amato, M. R. *Experimental psychology: Methodology, psychophysics, and learning.* New York: McGraw-Hill, 1970.

Dollard, J., L. W. Doob, N. E. Miller, O. H. Mowrer, and R. R. Sears. *Frustration and aggression.* New Haven: Yale Univ. Press, 1939.

Dollard, J., and O. H. Mowrer. A method of measuring tension in written documents. *J. abnor. soc. Psychol.,* 1947, *42,* 3-32.

Drakeford, J. W. *Integrity therapy: A Christian evaluation of a new approach to mental health.* Nashville, Tenn.: Broadman Press, 1967.

Ellenberger, H. F. The pathogenic secret and its therapeutics. *J. Hist. Behav. Sci.,* 1966, *2,* 29-42.

Erickson, E. H. *Identity, youth and crisis.* New York: Norton, 1968.

Esper, E. A. *A history of psychology.* Philadelphia: Saunders, 1964.

Fischer, Gloria, W. Viney, J. Knight, and N. Johnson. Response recrement as a function of effort. *Quart. J. Exp. Psychol.,* 1968, *22,* 301-304.

Foulds, G. *Personality and personal illness.* London: Tavistock, 1965.

Franks, C. M. *Behavior therapy: Appraisal and status.* New York: McGraw-Hill, 1969.

Freud, S. *A general introduction to psychoanalysis.* New York: Liveright Publishing Co., 1920.

Gendlin, E. T. A short summary and some long predictions. In J. Hart and T. Tomlinson (Eds.), *New directions in client-centered therapy.* Boston: Houghton Mifflin, 1970.

Gibson, J. J., and O. H. Mowrer. Determinants of the perceived vertical and horizontal. *Psychol. Rev.,* 1938, *45,* 300-323.

Gray, J. *The psychology of stress and fear.* New York: McGraw-Hill, 1971.

Greenwald, A. G. Sensory feedback mechanisms in response selection, with special reference to the ideo-motor mechanism. Columbus, Ohio: Ohio State Univ. (mimeographed), 1968.

Grosser, G. H. Social and cultural considerations in the treatment of depression. In J. O. Cole and J. R. Wittenborn (Eds.), *Pharmacotherapy of depression.* Springfield, Ill.: C. C Thomas, 1966.

Harris, T. A. *I'm OK — You're OK.* New York: Harper & Row, 1967.

Herrnstein, R. J. Method and theory in the study of avoidance. *Psychol. Rev.,* 1969, *76,* 49-69.

Hull, C. L. *Principles of behavior.* New York: Appleton-Century-Crofts, 1943.

Hurvitz, N. Peer self-help psychotherapy groups and their implications for psychotherapy. *Psychother. Theory Res. Pract.,* 1970, 7, 41-49.

Ishihara, I. Comment on Prof. Mowrer's two-factor learning theory. *Psychologia,* 1962, *5,* 41-48.

Jeffrey, W. E. To complete Hobart Mowrer, *Contemp. Psychol.,* 1961, *6,* 358-361.

Jourard, S. M. *The transparent self.* New York: Van Nostrand Reinhold, 1964.

Kanfer, F. H., and Jeanne S. Phillips. *Learning foundations of behavior therapy.* New York: Wiley, 1970.

Karlsson, J. L. *The biological basis of schizophrenia.* Springfield, Ill.: C. C Thomas, 1966.

Keeler, W. R. Children's reaction to the death of a parent. In P. H. Hoch and J. Zubin (Eds.), *Depression.* New York: Grune & Stratton, 1954.

Konorski, J. *Conditioned reflexes and neuron organization.* (Trans. by Stephen Carry.) New York: Cambridge Univ. Press, 1948.

Konorski, J. Postscript to: On a particular form of conditioned reflex. *J. Exp. Anal. Behav.,* 1969, *12,* 187-189.

Konorski, J. The problem of the peripheral control of skilled movements. *Intern. J. Neurosci.,* 1970, *1,* 39-50.

Konorski, J., and S. Miller. On two types of conditioned reflex. *J. Genet. Psychol.,* 1937, *16,* 264-272.

McCall, R. B., and R. S. Hart. A reply to Ishihara's critique of Mowrer's learning theory. *Psychologia,* 1962, *5,* 210-216.

McMahon, Carol. Images as motives and motivators. *Amer. J. Psychol,* 1973 (Sept. issue).

Miller, S., and J. Konorski. On a particular form of conditioned reflex (with an introduction by B. F. Skinner and a postscript by Konorski). *J. Exp. Anal. Behav.,* 1969, *12,* 187-189.

Myers, C. R. Journal citations and scientific eminence in contemporary psychology. *Amer. Psychol.,* 1970, *25,* 1041-1048.

Pavlov, I. P. The reply of a physiologist to a psychologist. *Psychol. Rev.,* 1932, *39,* 91-127.

Renner, K. E. Coherent self-direction and values. *Annals of the New York Academy of Science,* 1972, *193,* 175-184.

—— Conflict resolution and the process of temporal integration. *Psychol. Rep.,* 1964, *15,* 423-438.

Rescorla, R. A., and R. L. Solomon. Two-process learning theory: Relationships between Pavlovian conditioning and instrumental learning. *Psychol. Rev.,* 1967, *71,*151-182.

Rosenbaum, M., and M. Berger. *Group psychotherapy and group function-- Selected readings.* New York: Basic Books, 1963.

Rosenthal, D. *Genetic theory and abnormal behavior.* New York: McGraw-Hill, 1970.

Rothman, T. *Changing patterns in psychiatric care.* New York: Crown Publishers, 1970.

Sahakian, W. S. *Psychology of learning: Systems, models, and theories.* Chicago: Markham, 1970.

Schwab, F. J. *The agony of honesty.* Jericho, N. Y.: Exposition Press, 1971.

Segundo, J. P., C. Galeano, J. A. Sommer-Smith, and J. A. Roig. Behavioral and EEG effects of tones "reinforced" by cessation of painful stimuli. In J. F. Delafresnage (Ed.), *Brain mechanisms and learning.* Oxford: Blackwell, 1961, pp. 265-291.

Seligman, M. E. P., S. F. Maier, and J. H. Geer. Alleviation of learned helplessness in the dog. *J. Abnorm. Psychol.,* 1968, *73,* 256-262.

Shaffer, L. F. *The psychology of adjustment*. Boston: Houghton Mifflin, 1930.

Sheehan, P. W. *The function of nature of imagery*. New York: Academic Press, 1972.

Shelly, J. A., and A. Bassin. Daytop Lodge—A new treatment approach for drug addicts. *Correct. Psychiat.*, 1965, *11*, 186-195.

Shields, J. Summary of genetic evidence. In D. Rosenthal and S. S. Kety (Eds.), *The transmission of schizophrenia*. Elmsford, N.Y.: Pergamon Press, 1968.

Skinner, B. F. *The behavior of organisms*. New York: Appleton-Century-Crofts, 1938.

Spiegel, Rose. The depressions. *Med. World News (Psychiat.)*, 1969, 18-21.

Sutterer, J. R., and R. C. Beck. Human responses to stimuli associated with shock onset and termination. Winston-Salem, N.C.: Wake Forest Univ. (manuscript), 1969.

Tolman, E. C. *Purposive behavior in animals and men*. New York: Appleton-Century-Crofts, 1932.

Ullmann, L. P., and L. Krasner. *A psychological approach to abnormal behavior*. Englewood Cliffs, N.J.: Prentice-Hall, 1969.

Watzlawick. P., Janet H. Beavin, and D. D. Jackson. *Pragmatics of human communications: A study of interactional patterns, pathologies, and paradoxes*. New York: Norton, 1967.

Wendt, G. R. Vestibular functions. In S. S. Stevens (Ed.), *Handbook of experimental psychology*. New York: Wiley, 1960.

Whiteis, U. E. Punishment's influence on fear and avoidance. *Harvard Educ. Rev.*, 1956, *26*, 360-373.

Woodworth, R. S. *Experimental psychology*. New York: Holt, Rinehart and Winston, 1938.

Yablonsky, L. *The tunnel back: Synanon*. New York: Macmillan, 1965.

Yalom, I. D. *The theory and practice of group psychotherapy*. New York: Basic Books, 1970.

Zilboorg, G. *A history of medical psychology*. New York: Norton, 1941.

Theodore M. Newcomb

Theodore M. Newcomb

I first drew breath on July 24, 1903, in the parsonage occupied by Ozro Robinson and Cora Mead Newcomb in Rock Creek, Ashtabula County, Ohio (population about 80 and elevation above sea level about 700, I believe). My father was a Congregational clergyman whose parishes were rural; during many of my childhood years there was no church for miles around, other than the one he served. My mother—unusually for her time—had earned a Master's degree before teaching in a Negro school in Tougaloo, Alabama. Our family included a grandmother whose parents brought Congregationalism with them by horseback from New England to the Western Reserve in Ohio in 1821. Ours was a family that put literacy next to godliness. If, as some of our relatives thought, we were longer on books than on bacon, we made up for it in family pride.

Such were the influences that inevitably sent my older brother and me (just turned 17) to Oberlin College—though not my younger sister, now Mrs. Constance Eck, who nevertheless survived to exert, especially through her high school teaching, an influence in public affairs and liberal causes. My brother Robinson, who earned his doctorate in economics, has held successively more responsible positions in Washington, D.C., and on international assignments. I might add that he and I, as youngsters, experienced the usual degree of same-sex sibling rivalry, given an age difference of two years. Due to some mixture of tempermental fit, later residential propinquity, and absence of early sibling rivalry, I have maintained a closer relationship with my sister than with my brother.

At Oberlin, by then loosed from its formal bonds with the Congregational Church, I soon found myself a Student Volunteer, as those of us who planned to be Christian missionaries overseas were called. During my years there I suppose I had few doubts that the life of the mind and that of (Protestant) Christian service were hardly distinguishable. I do remember, however, my first consternation when an admired professor (Charles Wager) seemed to be quoting with skepticism a line from Kingsley's poem: "Be good, sweet maid, and let who will be clever." It must have been about then that I began to realize that the two strands (the "spiritual" and the "intellectual") in the rope that bound me to parental influence could pull in opposite directions.

Not long after this minor jolt my father, in one of the very few of his sermons that I remember, took the theme that "a good heart" was not enough; one must also make ethical judgments, and be well enough informed to know what, in a given setting, constituted moral action. His illustrations dealt with some then-prominent public issues. Much of his own information, I suspect, came largely from *The Nation,* of which my parents were avid readers—and, as they assumed, the only ones in their community. At any rate, the concept of "informed social morality" was beginning to appeal to me more than that of "spirituality." Such early influence as I had in these directions came from home rather than from college, where I remember almost no generally recognized concern about public issues, on the part of either faculty or students.

The parental package that I took with me into my postcollege world thus included a not very well integrated set of religious-moral-intellectual components. The religious part of it was in no sense fundamentalist; my parents had by this time come to terms with Darwinian evolution together with its inevitable implications for the doctrine of the literal truth of the Bible, and so had most of the Oberlin faculty, including the theological professors. (Evolution was simply God's way of working, and the Old Testament was to be taken as general theological and moral rather than scientific truth.)

Of course the package also included some personal, psychodynamic ingredients. I was a second son of slight build and a conspicuous lack of athletic skills. I was the neighborhood "preacher's kid" in elementary school (my brother being in another school), and there were no playgrounds except at school; the occasional epithet of "Preach" was not particularly welcome. I don't remember any other kinds of self-perceived distinctiveness until my first year in a large high school in Cleveland, Ohio, to and from which I bicycled twenty-odd miles a day. At the end of the first month I was assigned to the rear seat in a science class (where, presumably, teacher monitoring was dispensable) because I had received the highest grades in the class. My initial incredulity was superseded by the usual level-of-aspiration phenomena; from that day on, no doubt, I was preordained to be the class valedictorian at graduation. (What I remember most clearly about that graduation ceremony was that I chose to speak about the recent injustice of the New York State Legislature in evicting two properly elected representatives, simply because they were Socialists. The fact that the high school principal neither approved nor forbade it gave me, I suspect, some additional satisfaction.) I also received a special medal (for city-wide excellence in French), and was thus ready to go to college as anything but a humble seeker after learning. To continue with that line of development, my priggishness was somewhat chastened by failing two courses in my sophomore year at Oberlin, after rejecting all advice not to take six courses, including two of the reputedly most difficult ones in the college. I paid for this indiscretion by having to console myself with a *summa cum laude* (in French) rather than a Phi Beta Kappa key.

My Protestant-ethic achievement motivation also took, briefly, another turn. At the end of my freshman year my precollege savings had been exhausted, and it had never been necessary to explain that there would be no financial help from my parents. So, in desperation, I accepted with profound misgivings a summer position of selling aluminum cooking ware to housewives. To my own surprise, I found that it could be done, and I finished the summer with the national sales record among all college students thus engaged that year. My take-home proceeds exceeded $1,000 (almost as much as my father's annual salary). Together with scholarships and loans, I made do with this bonanza for my next two years in college. Although I loathed the job, it gave me a kind of confidence, in the nonacademic arena, that doubtless alleviated my sense that I had nothing but academic skills to rely on—and even those were not of the best.

After a year of teaching high school French and English, and paying off my college loans, I became a student at Union Theological Seminary, in New York. This decision was a natural next step; the institution had a distinctive reputation for scholarship in both traditional and "liberal" ways; I could not have tolerated a fundamentalist environment. Moreover, several of my closest friends, mostly from Oberlin, were to be there. An additional consideration was the proximity of Columbia University and its Teachers College "right across Broadway." I was already set toward a teaching career; my missionary intentions were now wavering, and my "compromise" plan was to become a college teacher of religion somewhere—at home or abroad.

The ensuing four years turned out to be utterly decisive for me. I can hardly disentangle, at this distance, several sources of influence. First, perhaps, was my discovery that never before had I really wrestled with an intellectual problem. I watched with admiration as my professors (especially Old Testament Professor Julius Bewer) described and illustrated the processes of Biblical exegesis, which it seemed to me they carried out with uncompromising objectivity. At the same time I knew that I was not destined to become one of them—if for no other reason than that the barriers of Greek and Hebrew were both dull and formidable. Nevertheless my admiration for the Old Testament prophets has to this day not diminished; I still quote them, as my not-always appreciative children will attest.

A course in Comparative Religions also left a deep impression on me, I could not from my readings in the *Upanishads* or the *Analects* of Confucius, for example, derive, as did my professor, the conclusion that Christianity was superior to all other religions. I was indignant at his argument that Christianity obviously was superior to Hinduism, because in America we have no caste system. I went to endless lengths in digging up parallels between Christian and other scriptures—the Golden Rule, for example, appears in similar form in many of them. The only comment on my resulting paper that I recall was to the effect that "you can always find what you're looking for."

In an entirely different vein, Professor Harrison S. Elliott, through his own combination of Socratic and group-discussion procedures, demonstrated in his courses in religious education a kind of intellectual openness that I had never seen in any classroom. The sometimes unorthodox conclusions with which we emerged were never challenged as to "correctness," but considered only in respect to processes by which they had been reached. The effects on me of a course in Christian ethics, taught by Professor Harry Ward, indicate something about my own predispositions then as well as about Union Seminary. The "social gospel" was then, I believe, a fairly recent development in American Christianity, and Harry Ward was to many of us at Union its most devoted exponent. We heard, and most of us came to believe, that Christianity was empty without ethical behavior, which in turn was meaningless without social action. He cited yesterday's events and named names—especially those of "illiterate barons" of industry and press. Once, following a destructive raid on his office by Justice Department "thugs," his only reply to a request for comment was, "I only wish they had *read* some of those books they stole." I probably felt that he was a more sophisticated and more waspish version of my father.

Meanwhile, I had gradually been increasing the proportion of my course work "across the street" at Columbia. I began with a single course, in philosophy of education, under Professor William H. Kilpatrick ("There is no God but Dewey, and Kilpatrick is his prophet"). I found him provocative, and deeply concerned about the essentials as opposed to the bureaucratic trappings of the learning process—and he tried to practice what he preached.

My formal transfer to Teachers College (which was willing to accept many of my academic credits from Union Seminary) was "decided upon" at a single moment, during my second year in New York. Every Tuesday and Thursday at 9:00 I left Goodwin Watson's class in "Psychology of Character" for a required class in "New Testament Exegesis" at the Seminary. At the end of the latter class, on a certain Tuesday, the professor, who had just devoted the entire hour to lecturing on the Greek word for "straightway" (found almost uniquely in the Gospel of St. Mark), announced that he would need the full hour on Thursday, also, to lecture on that word. The contrast with the "Psychology of Character" (or was it the contrast with Watson?) was too much for me.

I "decided" at that moment that I would not complete the theological degree; I am not sure whether or not I ever returned to the New Testament class. At any rate Watson soon became, and remained, one of my two genuine mentors at Columbia. He was unfailingly provocative, learned, and helpful. I was, several years later, to have other kinds of close relationship with him. There was no one to whom I owed more, for some twenty years, and we still share interests and activities.

Edward Lee Thorndike and Robert S. Woodworth were of course the dominant figures in psychology at Columbia during the late 1920s, and at Teachers College Thorndike's shadow was the taller. I never knew him well, and never appreciated until later the full range of psychological problems that he illuminated during thirty-odd years of brilliant work. Nevertheless, his influence, direct or indirect, was among those that led me to want to be "an empiricist." An anecdote about him, apocryphal or not, was often repeated in those days. Turning to Irving Lorge, his then right-hand assistant, he is said to have remarked, "In ten minutes I have a class. Would the interests of science be better served if I prepared for it, or if I calculated another correlation? I think I'll do the correlation." Perhaps I remember the anecdote as a convenient rationalization for having sometimes chosen the same alternative, during the ensuing forty years.

My other principal mentor was Gardner Murphy. I elected his course in history of psychology because I had heard that it was the best way in the world to learn psychology. I was not disappointed, and it changed my life. He made even the most arcane problems seem important, and he followed each of them, developmentally. It was also awe-inspiring to discover that he apparently lectured without notes—mentioning names, dates, and places with the greatest of ease and with obvious knowledgeability. I saw him personally, too, and discovered that during this period—when he was also putting together the first edition of his *Historical Introduction to Modern Psychology* (1929)—an eye malady made it virtually impossible for him to read at all.

My profession and my personal relations with Gardner have long since become intertwined. I had met Lois Barclay, the future Mrs. Gardner Murphy, as a fellow student at Union Seminary before I met him. Particularly after 1934, when I went to Bennington College, our families, including children more or less of the same ages, intervisited in Bronxville or in Vermont or Holderness, New Hampshire, at least annually. These visits, I fear, were not fully appreciated by the children, who took a dim view of our perpetual discussions of "dull psychology." At any rate both my wife and I ended those visits feeling *au courant* with up-to-date developments in psychology. There has been hardly a year, since 1927, when one or both of us has not seen one or both of them.

My four predoctoral years were not as solitary as the preceding paragraphs might suggest. Almost every influence upon me, particularly while I lived in Union Seminary's dormitory, was relayed and reinforced, in the manner of social facilitation, by fellow students. Every exciting idea led to a sort of clan-gathering—especially ideas that stemmed from Messrs. Kilpatrick, Ward, Elliott, and Watson, as likely outside as in the classroom. Of the original five of us who were friends during undergraduate years and who influenced one another in coming to Union, I was to be the only one who moved into psychology. Fellow students whom I first met at or around the Seminary included Carl Rogers, Rensis Likert, and Ernest Hilgard. Here for the first time I experienced the exchange of intellectual stimulation closely related to what we were reading, or hearing in lectures, or hearing each other say in seminars. I am sure that these experiences had something to do with my present notions of what undergraduate education should be—and for me was not.

Whether by accident or not, this experiencing of intellectual excitement, though in a way dependent upon interchange with my peers, was accompanied by a personal sense of my own independence. My first year in New York I was deeply dependent upon peers, lonesome in the absence of my roommate, unhappy to eat alone, even choosing academic courses to be with my friends.

Three years later I lived alone and liked it, pursued an academic path that was all my own, and walked with a spring in my step.

Three years later I was also in psychoanalysis. I had sought it light-heartedly, at a time when a one-year analysis was not regarded as disreputable. I had the gall to explain to Dr. Frankwood Williams, one of the most eminent analysts in New York, that I was not so much seeking help as trying to make myself a better psychology teacher. He replied, in effect, "Young man, I suggest that you go home. Come back if and when you feel that you have some problems"—both of which I did, and he accepted me. My five hours a week for about eight months were often chastening, but I still remember some moments of blinding insight. I particularly appreciated his straight-forwardness and genuine helpfulness, as well as his freedom from orthodoxy. I also remember him for a skillful transference-dissolving act; some months after my departure he, as Editor of *Mental Hygiene,* wrote to me as a professional, asking me to review a book for that journal. (I can still recall almost every paragraph of that review.) My esteem for him increased further when, some months later, I first learned of his interest in societal change as an essential step toward preventing rather than merely treating psychological disturbances. I was eventually to become even less orthodox than he, psychoanalytically speaking, but my gratitude for his helpfulness has never declined.

And so, just before my twenty-sixth birthday, I had accepted both a Ph.D. degree and an assistant professorship in psychology at Lehigh University. I doubtless felt that I had earned the doctorate, but I had many questions about my new job, because I knew that my training in psychology had been neither long nor broad. I was proud to be teaching in a "secular" field, though I was hoping to teach a course in the psychology of religion. I had crossed the great divide. And if I had any regrets, they were primarily on my father's account; I remember trying to convince him that "going into psychology" was the equivalent, for me, of entering the ministry for him. I am not sure that either of us fully believed it.

In a sense, my professional life had begun as early as 1926, when I was one of several graduate students from Morningside Heights who served as counselors in a summer camp created on a shore of Lake Erie for the purpose of "studying" problem boys from the Child Guidance Clinic in Cleveland, Ohio, with a psychiatrist in residence. Though its financing was always precarious, Wilber Newstetter, then Dean of Western Reserve University's Graduate School of Applied Social Science, somehow raised the necessary funds for eight consecutive summers. I have often remarked, since then, that I owe nothing to that camp except my wife (née Mary Shipherd, whom I met at an adjoining camp), my doctoral dissertation, and my profession. I entered enthusiastically into the frequent clinical discussions, where all of us tried out our amateur psychiatric notions on a "case"; we used to say that we practiced psychiatry in the summer and read it in the winter. My dissertation (1929) was an attempt to test (on the basis of counselors' daily ratings and of some thousands of my own recorded observations of episodes of boy's behavior) the consistency with which each boy showed kinds of behavior that might be considered either extrovert or introvert. (I found very little of it.) Though the monograph was favorably reviewed in a couple of journals (doubtless because in those days all Teachers College dissertations were printed between hard covers), its influence upon the state of psychology was far less than its effects upon me: from that experience I learned about both the delights and the frustrations of processing and making sense of empirical data. A year or two later I found enormous satisfaction in demonstrating, from data also obtained at the camp, the testing of a hypothesis about the prevalence of "haloizing" tendencies on the part of raters (1931). I have never lost the sense of excitement in analyzing, sometimes endlessly, a batch of data of my own; I am sure that I have sometimes been overcompulsive about it.

In 1929 camp activities moved more definitely toward research rather than therapy, and Marc Feldstein and I initiated a two-pronged program. We began to gather what later came to be known as sociometric choices—we called it "the Personal Preference technique"—and our first report was printed in pamphlet form in 1930—though not in hard covers until 1938.

My particular responsibility later became that of devising scalable measures of observed behavior. The raw data were written reports of more than 10,000 minutes of observed behavioral exchanges between two or more boys, in ten-minute segments with a single boy as principal observee. After much trial and error, I hit upon the notion of scaling each discriminable incident (if relevant) in terms of degree of cordiality-antagonism. A list of verbs was selected, and judges sorted them into piles in Thurstone-like fashion. Then, after combining verbs that were judged as belonging close together and dropping those about which judges differed, a highly reliable nine-point sclae emerged. Unfortunately, from one point of view, I was so fully engrossed by the methodological problem that I never really used the technique for theoretical purposes before my interest turned in other directions (Newsetter, Feldstein, and Newcomb, 1938).

My camp experience later led to a part-time position (during the Depression, when moonlighting was almost necessary for subsistence) in the Cleveland Child Guidance Clinic, where, as a psychological examiner, I must have administered many hundreds of Stanford-Binet and other tests. At the same time, having left Lehigh University after one year, I was one of the three members of the Psychology Department at Western Reserve's downtown Cleveland College. There I taught what must have been one of the first courses in any American liberal arts college labeled "Psychoanalysis." Clearly, I was well on the road to becoming a clinical psychologist.

Meanwhile, I must have sensed, again, a craving for my own set of data, for in 1931, during my first year in Cleveland, I began a study that was to keep me engaged for some years. (I remember asking my dean—Dr. Caswell Ellis, a psychologist from Clark University in G. Stanley Hall's day—for funds to launch the study. Somehow he found $25.00. This was my first, and easiest, experience in grantsmanship.) The study (Newcomb and Svehla, 1937) had to do with parent-child resemblances in attitudes; it seemed to me that one could derive from Freud the expectation that sons and daughters would show different patterns of resemblance to like-sex and to opposite-sex parents. Besides, I was excited by L. L. Thurstone's new scaling devices for the measurement of attitudes, and wanted to try them out. With the tireless (though unpaid) aid of a student, George Svehla, responses to three attitude scales were obtained from members of several hundred families. The findings concerning like- and unlike-sex pairs of parents and children were less illuminating than an unexpected set of results. Several kinds of analysis of selected subpopulations made it clear that the common embeddedness of family members within the same religious or ethnic membership accounted not only for much of the intrafamily resemblances in single attitudes, but also for similar patternings of the several attitudes within each membership group that were distinctive for each group. Individual parent-to-child influence seemed to be "carried" via the larger group influence. This was not to be the last time that close scrutiny of my own data led me to see individual psychological processes within a matrix of group influences.

I had known about Bennington College even before its opening and so, when my friend and previous colleague at Western Reserve, Keith Sward, declined an invitation to go there and suggested my name, I accepted the ensuing offer with almost indecent alacrity. It was the first job that I had wanted before it was proffered. I suppose its attractiveness stemmed primarily from its "experimental" nature; after all, I had been nurtured in a hotbed of "progressive education" (thanks to Dewey, Kilpatrick, and Goodwin Watson), and I had been fascinated by Lois Murphy's accounts of Sarah Lawrence College, which had a sibling-like similarity to Bennington. As it turned out, my seven years there were anything but disappointing. It was there that I became convinced, through my own experience, of what I already more than half believed—that what students learn has no necessary relationship to professors' lectures. And it was there that I discovered that students could be motivated by the process of jointly planning and carrying out with them an experiment, the report of which was eventually published (1942).

I experienced there the deep satisfactions of family life in a lovely setting in the Green Mountains, of membership in a lively and congenial community, and of close acquaintance with several colleagues and students; I still keep in more or less close touch with several of the latter. Apart from these considerations, I soon found myself again engaged in two demanding enterprises. I had agreed, before leaving Cleveland, to take responsibility for revising about a third of Gardner and Lois Murphy's *Experimental Social Psychology* (1931). I was incredulous at receiving their invitation—who, me?—and pleased beyond measure. I spent my first three two-month winter periods (during which Bennington students took nonresident jobs) in the Columbia University library, and most of my summers and weekends writing at home. Never since, I suppose, have I felt so fully in command of the published literature in a particular field. My contributions—"Measurement of the Adult Personality" and "Social Attitudes and Their Measurement"—took up no less than 288 pages of the revised edition

(1937). Their importance for my own theoretical development can be fairly well indicated by the last sentence of the book: "The social psychology of attitudes is the sociology of attitudes illuminated by an understanding of the psychological factors which determine individual susceptibility to group influences." I had not started my work with the anticipation that I would end up with such a sentence, but it indicates where I felt that my perusal of the available studies had taken me. By now, at the age of 34, I was quite clear that social psychology was to be my specialty.

During my first year at Bennington I saw, or thought I saw, a remarkable kind of awakening, on the part of a student body many of whom had come there directly from rather secluded private schools for girls. I had just left a city that was peculiarly sensitive to the effects of the Great Depression, including the recent closing of all banks. I had been teaching in a downtown college, most of whose students knew, first-hand, the effects of unemployment. Like most of them, I had been somewhat radicalized (in 1932 I had voted for Norman Thomas rather than for Roosevelt, whose campaign had seemed to me rather bland, in view of three years of the Depression). I was therefore both surprised and pleased to find at Bennington a great deal of awareness of the "social revolution" that was occurring under the aegis of the New Deal. Many of the students, I discovered, were arguing vehemently with their parents. An early pretest of a sample of students convinced me that there was indeed a great deal of awareness of and even sympathy with the directions of contemporary social change, particularly on the part of older students. And so I determined to study the phenomenon, without further ado—even though I was deeply immersed in my chapters for *Experimental Social Psychology*. I spent the latter part of 1934-1935 developing an attitude scale, by processes of analyzing interitem correlations, beginning with items from a prepublication copy of a paper by Ross Stagner (1936), and adding various items of my own. I made similar use of items previously used by Rensis Likert (1932) on attitudes toward internationalism. Thus began my study eventually published as *Personality and Social Change* (1943).

This was my first "big study." It engaged me—and, at odd hours, my wife—very fully from 1935 to 1941. It was subsidized by two grants of no less than $750 each, from the Social Science Research Council. Its most important findings were not previsioned, at the outset, in the form of specific, theory-derived predictions. But the initial plan, according to which both cohorts and panels would be compared through the four college years, had the advantage that I could develop hypotheses as the study progressed. (It was Paul Lazarsfeld who first informed me, when I described the study to him in about 1941, that whether I knew it or not mine was a panel study, and the most systematic one that he had known about. It was he, also, who unbeknownst to me had the idea of publishing a review of this study when, long after it was out of print, it was reissued by the publisher in 1957.) Thus it came about that my best ideas were developed during the last two of the four years, following perusal of results already obtained. For example, I was able to obtain strong support for my informal observation that change in the nonconservative direction varied directly with the achievement of community respect and prestige, and with active participation in community life; and that the individual's perception of community norms was related in distinctive ways to her own history of change. Another kind of analysis that I found interesting was strictly *post hoc:* the tendency of individuals to make either extreme or nonextreme responses on a Likert-type item, or to agree or disagree, regardless of content. The idea stemmed in part from Thorndike. Such individual proclivities later came to be known as "response bias."

I suppose it was my several demonstrations of "normativeness" within the community, as social context within which attitude change typically occurred, that have particularly impressed most readers of this monograph. Years later I had some memorable conversations in Ann Arbor with Muzafer Sherif, whose experimental work on social norms (1935) is a well-known landmark. It was he who helped me to see that some of the Bennington findings could be fitted into the conceptual framework of normative reference groups, and who was thus indirectly responsible for my publication of a version of those findings in such terms (1952). Meanwhile, I had asked W. W. Charters, Jr., then a graduate student at Michigan, to work with me on an experiment in manipulating the salience of reference groups. These two contributions constituted the bulk of the section on reference groups in both the second and the third editions of *Readings in Social Psychology.*

The first of this series of readings (1947) was planned in the summer of 1945. Eugene Hartley and I took major responsibility for selecting and soliciting the 75-odd articles that it included. With only a single exception, I believe, both authors and publishers (not to mention the editors) waived royalties, and numerous people—Gordon Allport and Margaret Mead, for example—were helpful in many ways. The book proved an enormous "success," all royalties going to the Society for the Psychological Study of Social Issues, which had previously been a most impecunious organization. In its way, the book succeeded in its task, assigned by the Society, of helping to provide "more adequate teaching materials for students of social psychology."

I had been a charter member of SPSSI when it was formed at the annual convention of the APA at Dartmouth College in 1936. David Krech had laid the groundwork for the Society's formation, and served as its secretary-treasurer until 1941, when I succeeded him; Goodwin Watson was its first and Gardner Murphy its second president. I remained very active in it, in a number of capacities, for some fifteen years thereafter. I found it congenial as a focus for my interests in social psychology and in liberal social causes of many kinds.

The decade of the 1930s (roughly corresponding to my years in Cleveland and Bennington) was characterized by a good deal of "radicalization" in this country, and I was not immune to the prevalent influences. In Cleveland I had become, briefly, a member of the Socialist Party, and at Bennington I was active in the formation both of a Teachers Union and of a local of the Textile Workers Organization (the first CIO union in Vermont), and in developing a working liaison between the two. I was also very vocal in my support of the Loyalists in Spain. These "indiscretions" were later to raise repeated questions about my security status for government employment; as of 1970, I am still "cleared" for consultative services in some governmental agencies but not in others.

More important, from a professional point of view, is the question of the effects upon my studies of Bennington students of my status as something between a campus liberal and a campus radical. As of now, I have two comments. First, I frankly reported this possible "contamination effect" in *Personality and Social Change*. My own judgment, second, is that if my personal reputation had any effect upon students' responses, it served to exaggerate the differences between those students who tended to agree and those who tended to disagree with whatever attitudes they attributed to me. The evidence, behavioral as well as attitudinal, clearly shows a large preponderance of the former, from which I conclude not that my own influence affected responses but that possibly my own identification with certain causes, insofar as known to student respondents, may have led the majority of students in general agreement with me to exaggerate their own positions in that direction, while some of other students may have similarly exaggerated their positions in the opposite direction. Such, at least, are the questions that one has to face in studying natural settings of which one is a part.

Meanwhile (for I am running ahead of my chronology), I had been at the University of Michigan since 1941. My seven years at Bennington had been stimulating and almost invariably enjoyable, but life there had been a bit insular, and I missed male students, a larger number of whom than of women were likely to take a preprofessional interest in psychology; and in particular I wanted graduate students. My invitation, curiously enough, came from the Department of Sociology, which had developed a strong interest in social psychology during the long tenure of Charles Horton Cooley, whose work I had long admired. The Department of Psychology then had little interest in the subject, and I believe this was particularly true of Professor W. B. Pillsbury, its long-time chairman, who 31 years previously had been President of the American Psychological Association. I was warmly welcomed by my sociological colleagues, especially by their chairman, Robert Cooley Angell, for whom I soon developed strong admiration and fondness.

I was now not only at a major university but also the sole instructor (at my own rank of Associate Professor or at any other) whose only assignment was in social psychology. I dug in, I read and read—especially in sociology, with which I was dubiously familiar. And for me I thought it the best job in the world. But within weeks I had been pressed to accept a job in Washington, as had scores of other psychologists, as various Defense agencies were building up staffs against the inevitable day when war would come. I barely stayed to meet my last class at the end of January, and I was hardly to be in Ann Arbor again till nearly four years later. During most of that time I was in the Analysis Division of the Foreign Broadcast Intelligence Service, where our principal assignment was to report and interpret enemy radio broadcasts, based largely on content analysis by means of our own devising (we were generally known to the rest of Washington as propaganda analysts). The staff had been assembled and was astutely led by Goodwin Watson, until he was removed by an act of Congress to the effect that neither he nor Robert Morse Lovett nor William Dodd (specified by name) was to be employed by the U.S. Government (a bill of attainder, of course, which some years later was unanimously ruled unconstitutional by the Supreme Court). Thereafter I succeeded him. Our staff—including Otto Klineberg, Donald McGranahan, Alex George, Hans Speier, Bernard Berelson, and John Gardner, among others—developed a magnificent esprit de corps under Watson's leadership. We worked hard, acquired some special skills, and had some brilliant successes in the form of reading between the lines of Nazi broadcasts and divining both propaganda directives and unpublicized reasons for them, in ways that were sometimes neatly confirmed by documents found in Nazi files after the war.

My last eighteen months of this period were spent, successively, in the Program Surveys Division of the Bureau of Agricultural Economics, where, with Rensis Likert, Dorwin Cartwright, Angus Campbell, George Katona, and others (all of whom were later to join the Institute for Social Research at Michigan) I got my first lessons in survey research; in the office of Strategic Services, where Edward Tolman, Donald MacKinnon, James G. Miller, Urie Bronfenbrenner, Donald Fiske, and Ruth Tolman, inter alia, all worked night and day at the task of assessing, often in ingenious and sometimes in grueling ways, candidates for "special" (secret) service overseas; and, finally, in Rensis Likert's Morale Division of the U.S. Strategic Bombing Survey, where Daniel Katz, Eugene Hartley, Helen Peak, David Krech, Richard Crutchfield, among many others, worked (mainly in Bad Nauheim, Germany) on various aspects of civilian morale, especially as related to Allied bombing of Germany. We could not, in spite of using every mode of analysis that we could think of—based on captured documentary sources, hundreds of interviews held almost immediately after the cessation of hostilities, and other kinds of evidence—discover any important ways in which civilian morale had been disrupted as a consequence of bombing—at least not until everyone in Germany knew that they were soon to be totally defeated. Those of us who worked on this report have had little reason to believe that this finding has, subsequently, had much influence in councils of war.

My daily tasks in those years did not bring me very close to theoretical aspects of psychology, and I had little time for the books and journals that I would have been reading at home. Nevertheless, there were many social scientists in Washington, and I had memorable chats with several of them on theoretical matters. In particular, with my Bennington findings freshly on my mind, I was puzzled about systematic relationships between a person's attitudes toward persons and toward other entities, and began to lay the groundwork for what later became a subtheory of interpersonal balance. I also wrote a few memos to myself for future use, and laid more or less definite plans to write a textbook in social psychology.

As a matter of fact I tried to start work on that enterprise almost immediately after returning to Ann Arbor in late 1945. But there were too many new developments in the University. Foremost, for me, was the arrival of Donald Marquis as chairman of the Psychology Department. He had no need to be reminded of his charge to build up the department, which must have been one of the smallest in the country for a university of Michigan's size, nor was its staff conspicuous for fresh young blood. I believe my appointment to it was the first that Marquis recommended. At any rate I was soon a full professor in both departments, and found able graduate students from both of them in my seminars and other classes.

During 1946 and 1947 two interrelated sets of events were to determine my primary role at Michigan for years to come. First, a joint doctoral program in social psychology was created, supported by my two departments. Since I was then the only member of both of them, I became its chairman, holding the position until 1963. The second development was the university's decision to bring to Michigan nuclear staffs of Rensis Likert's Programs Survey Division (in Washington) and Kurt Lewin's Group Dynamics organization (at MIT). These two units were soon merged, administratively, into the Institute for Social Research, composed of Angus Campbell's Survey Research Center and the Research Center for Group Dynamics, initially headed by Cartwright. Relations between Program and Institute have been, from the first, effectively symbiotic: the Institute needed our students for help in research activities, and our students needed the Institute for research training. Many of our now well-known former students received an important part of their training there.

These matters attended to, and having more or less caught up on long-delayed reading, I returned to the writing of my textbook. I had convinced myself that social psychology has a kind of entity of its own, and above all I wanted to present a clear flow and development of successive themes. In what finally emerged (1950), "motive pattern" (better termed "motivated act," perhaps) was the first of my central concepts; the notion, adapted from K. Muenzinger (1942), referred to "a sequence of behaviors characterized by relative constancy of motivation." Attitudes, as learned predispositions to initiate motive patterns associated with discriminable objects (including the self and other persons), provide a basis for general stability of behavior over time. And many attitudes, in turn, are heavily influenced by persons' positions, with their attendant roles, in society and in subsets thereof. Since the manner of role-taking is influenced both by the individual's personal characteristics and by the role expectations that impinge upon him, the concept of role becomes focal in the sense of drawing upon both psychological and sociological determinants of behavior. If the book had any distinctive theme, it was this. Groups, I argued, were as real and ineluctable as intraindividual determinants of behavior—though the effects of the former are of course mediated via the latter. After all, psychology is the study of individual behavior not in a vacuum but in environmental settings; and one's position (in a society or a group) is simply a locus of selected social influences. And so, to understand behavior, we must also understand environments—in particular, those which exert influence by way of role prescriptions.

During most of the 1950s my heart lay in an ambitious research enterprise. Two interests—one old, one new—determined its nature. The developmental aspects of attitude formation had long fascinated me, but by now I had come to see interdependencies between an individual's interpersonal attitudes and certain of his other attitudes. I first formalized this position in *The Psychological Review* (1953), whose then editor, Carroll Pratt, managed to squeeze my article into the last issue before I was to succeed him as editor. I drew heavily upon Leon Festinger's predissonance "Informal Social Communication" (1950), and (with Schachter and Back, 1950) his "Social Pressures in Formal Groups." A single paper by Fritz Heider (1946) also provided the notion of balance, crucial to my formulation. Another source was Homan's proposition (1950) that frequency of interaction varies with liking, and vice versa. And, finally, my own analyses (not fully published) of my early study of Bennington College students had forced me to the conclusion that, in this setting at least, interpersonal attraction, our own attitudes, and attitudes attributed to others develop interdependently. Drawing upon all these sources, I ventured a theory according to which an imbalanced state among these three attitude variables leads to exchanges of information, as a consequence of which change toward balanced states is likely to occur.   •

The objectives of my "natural experiment," published as *The Acquaintance Process* (1961), were to test some propositions derived from this theory. Analysis of weekly responses by each member of two successive populations of total strangers who, beginning at a certain moment, lived closely together for several months, yielded significant support for the essential notions. There was one aspect of the study, however, that interested me more than it did most of the monograph's reviewers: I was able to trace the development not only of intraindividual balance (in terms of a subject's own attitudes and his attribution of attitudes to others), but also of interindividual balance (in terms solely of "own" attitudes of two or more individuals). The latter hypotheses were derived from the former as follows. If at least one of two or more persons, each of whom is characterized by a balanced state with regard to each other and some common object, incorrectly attributes attitudes to another (i.e., the dyad or larger group is "objectively" imbalanced), then, under conditions of continued communication, the error is likely to be discovered—with the probable consequence that one or more members will change toward psychological balance. It can readily be shown that such changes tend to result in "objective" balance. I suppose nothing is more characteristic of my recent concerns than that I like to search both inwardly and outwardly for the sources of both individual and group stability. This kind of concern is illustrated by the titles of two of my later papers: "Stabilities underlying changes . . ." (1963) and "Interpersonal constancies . . ." (1965).

Nearly 25 years after launching the original Bennington study, I began to plan for a follow-up. The first time around I had been able, post hoc, to point to some personal characteristics distinguishing individuals who did from those who did not change their attitudes. I had also shown that change was both broader and deeper at Bennington than on two "control" campuses, but I could only speculate as to college characteristics that distinguished the one from the other two. If, as I had reason to believe, both Bennington College and the prevalence of attitude change on the part of its students had considerably changed over a quarter-century, then I might be able to throw more light on the interaction effects between individual and community at the earlier time. Moreover, I was curious about the persistence of the attitude changes initially observed; after all, it would be reasonable to expect that most of the Bennington girls would have married and returned to communities like those from which they had originally come, with consequent regression toward their precollege attitudes. The question, of course, was not whether this had or had not happened to all of them, but rather what were the conditions under which regression did and did not occur. And I had some ideas about the matter that I wanted to test.

And so three tireless and imaginative students (Kathryn Koenig, Richard Flacks, and Donald Warwick) and I set to work. This time my grantsmanship was sorely tried; I had underestimated the cost, but eventually some $80,000 was raised from three sources. (My first grant had been for $25.00 in 1930; my second, in 1937, for $1,500.00—an increase of 40 times—while the second Bennington study, in 1960, represented another increase of more than 50 times.) At any rate we obtained interviews with nearly all our graduates from the classes of 1938, 1939, and 1940; questionnaire responses from large proportions of other alumnae and former students; and a wide range of data from the current Bennington students. This time punched cards and computers, instead of only pencils and desk calculators, were available.

It turned out (Newcomb et al., 1967) that persistence rather than regression was the rule. With regard to one particular issue, at least, it was clear that the fact of having attended Bennington a quarter-century ago was crucial: our subjects' sisters and sisters-in-law who had graduated from Bennington showed the same 90 percent preference for Johnson in the 1964 election as did our respondents themselves, while the comparable percentage for all other sisters and sisters-in-law was only 66 percent, closely resembling the total popular vote in that year. We also found substantial, though not conclusive, evidence that the large majority of persisters had in various ways found postcollege environments, including husbands, that supported their liberal attitudes, whereas the regressers typically had not.

As to the current Bennington students in 1960-1963, the striking difference was that even as prefreshmen they were strikingly liberal concerning public issues and showed little or no change during college years. We concluded that the very considerable changes found in the 1930s stemmed not just from college norms; rather it was an interaction effect between norms and the initial conservatism (input) of freshmen. At that time Bennington had no public image, or at least not an accurate one, so the contrast between expectations and the later experienced norms produced a conversion-like effect. Twenty-five years later a very different set of norms, fairly accurately anticipated by incoming freshmen, had the effect not of no change at all but of a consolidation and extension of preexisting attitudes. These considerations had much to do with my subsequent interest in the phenomena of accentuation.

Various forms of the general problem that had come to interest me were emerging in the 1950s and 1960s, most of which stemmed from Heider (1958, particularly), Festinger (1957, initially), and Osgood and Tannenbaum (1955). My own version, which I came to label "interpersonal balance" (1968), stemmed quite directly from Heider, whom I found congenial—doubtless because he too was concerned with interpersonal events. At any rate, I came to see a large class of human psychological problems as describable by the phrase "the triple confrontation"—i.e., the individual's need to cope, simultaneously, with three classes of demands posed by (1) objects and ideas in the outer world, by developing attitudes; (2) persons with whom one interacts and who are also coping with the same aspects of the same common world, by making attributions to them; and (3) one's own "inner" demands for "consistency" (see 1961, chap. 15). If, in a very inclusive sense, I have come to any general point of view with regard to social psychological problems, it is along the lines of this formulation.

In retrospect, virtually all my postdoctoral research has examined one or another aspect of this point of view. My early study of intrafamily relationships found attitude similarity to be associated with (presumably) generally favorable interpersonal attraction, mediated by common institutional influence. My original study of Bennington College students reported that attitude similarity was closely associated with sociometric choice—again closely associated with institutional influence, as reflected by community status. My reference-group studies indicated that (at least under specifiable conditions) attitude similarity was associated with the assumption of common identification with the same religious group, or the same college community. My Acquaintance study showed that, given the set of conditions of that study, dyads or larger sets of mutually attractive individuals tended to arise in such manner that members of the emerging cliques held similar attitudes. All these findings could have been predicted from interpersonal balance theory—though in fact only the last of them was so predicted.

Another aspect of my later theoretical position was not so clearly foreshadowed by my earlier work. In 1947, writing about "autistic hostility," I noted that, given an individual's state of strong dislike or hostility toward another person, a likely consequence is a cutting off of communication, so that the possibilities of obtaining further information about the offensive person are curtailed, and thus the hostile attitude is not likely to change. Much later (1968) I presented evidence that Heiderian balance (in triads composed of two persons and a common object of their attitudes) is less dependably found when interpersonal attitudes are negative than when they are positive. From the autistic hostility hypothesis alone this would not be predicted, since autism (uncorrected by renewed information) should give free sway to psychologically determined balance. The discrepancy, I assume, springs primarily from the fact that the available data include few interpersonal relationships characterized by extreme hostility and severed communication. I have, as yet, no data by which to test this assumption.

I suppose that I have spent about as many man-hours per year as most of my professional colleagues in the "scholarly" activities of teaching, reading, researching, and writing, and my professional self-image corresponds pretty closely to those activities. Nevertheless a great deal of my time, energy, and devotion has gone into two other activities that have been scholarly only in indirect ways.

The first of these, from 1947 to 1963, was, on a small scale, an administrative one: I was the Chairman of The University of Michigan's interdepartmental Doctoral Program in Social Psychology, as I have already noted. We were very serious about the jointness of the Program, even though the Graduate Faculty in psychology was always considerably larger than that in sociology. We were determined to avoid the then prevalent condition under which the two departments in most universities conducted separate if not somewhat antagonistic programs in each department—not surprisingly, since courses labeled "social psychology" had originated in both fields at about the same time, early in the century. During those sixteen years nearly 200 applicants were admitted to the Program, each of whom had already completed a year or more of graduate work, usually either in psychology or in sociology (whom we accepted in approximately equal numbers).

A score or so of my colleagues from both departments shared responsibilities for the Program, occasionally or continually, but none so fully as my twenty-year colleague and thirty-year friend, Daniel Katz. But I was of course closely identified with it, and doubtless regarded myself as its principal watchdog until my resignation—for reasons totally unrelated to subsequent developments—in 1963.

The Program boasted neither a budget nor the power of appointment—an arrangement which required close dependence on both departments. Given these close ties, there was little concern on either side about the Program's very considerable academic autonomy. There was, indeed, a good deal of pride in the unique arrangement. Naturally, those of us most closely associated with it felt that the pride was deserved. Within five years we were "producing" more Ph.D.'s a year than any department save four or five of the very large ones at the University. And, as later developments would show, not only were our students' postdoctoral publications to be cited in the social-psychological journals with disproportionate frequency, but also a considerable number of them were to achieve national recognition in the field.

The "structural" fact that far more psychologists than sociologists were available to man the Program had, from the beginning, been a source of potential threat to some members of the latter department. Psychology, having become a very large department, had adapted to the problem of size by creating what were, in effect, several subdepartments at the graduate level; each of them exercised a good deal of autonomy, so the social psychology program was deviant only in respect to its interdepartmental sponsorship. Sociology, on the other hand, increasingly preferred to "run a tight ship," in ways that at least one of its members felt should also apply to the interdepartmental program. Sociology preferred a more monolithic pattern, maintaining central supervision not only of committee appointments but also of curricular matters. Other members of the Program's policy committee, from both departments, felt that new restrictions were being proposed at a time when both students and teachers were feeling that the Program's development required more autonomy. A twenty-year period during which both the Program and the Department of Sociology had achieved considerable distinction was justification enough, they argued, for continuing the policy of rather wide autonomy. In spite of repeated attempts, lasting many months, to find a mutually acceptable solution, no compromise was found. In late 1967 it was agreed that the Program should be dissolved. In concurring (because I felt that no joint Program was better than one in a straightjacket), I helped to inter the enterprise that I had worked to create and for so many years to guide.

I am enough of a sociologist to seek "structural" interpretations rather than personal ones for such events. In this case, however, I agree with most of my colleagues, including those in sociology, that the crucial, irreversible steps were not explainable primarily in such terms. Individuals of strong determination, on both sides, moved toward irreconcilable positions on issues that had previously been negotiable. Each of them was regarded as personally offensive to some or even many of those in opposition. And so the immediate issues came to be polarized—first, I think, around persons each of whom invited strong loyalties from some quarters and strong repugnance in others, and then around grand policies and principles—about which, of course, compromise is unthinkable.

As for myself, I wish I could report that some important principle of organization or administration had been learned by some or all of us. What I have learned is no more, I'm afraid, than that a budgetless organization, serving to promote the overlapping interests of two strong parent organizations, cannot long survive beyond the time when those organizations' representatives, who must work together, have ceased to trust one another. And those behaviors that have to do with trusting and being trusted are rarely, I suspect, entirely a function of persons' positions in their organizations—though the consequences of "untrustworthiness" are likely to vary with position.

If I have dwelt too long on this chapter of my life, it is because the twenty-year story deals with events central to that life. I have often been asked, especially by former students, "How could it [the demise of the Program] have happened?" I can only answer in terms of classical tragedy: strong traits of character worked out to their inevitable ends. A fragile relationship among organizations cannot survive unless all those organizations are represented by persons who are not threatened by fragility itself.

My second deviation from the straight and narrow academic path was a venture in "applied social psychology," though it, too, came to include research activities which have more than practical and local implications. I had long been fascinated and puzzled by the phenomena sometimes described as pointing to "the power of groups over their members." I was pleased to have been able to document such effects in my early study of Bennington College, and came to see it in more systematic ways following my acquaintance with Kurt Lewin soon thereafter, and with his associates who came to The University of Michigan. My "applied" concern began to take shape in 1960-1961, when I faced the necessity of preparing two documents. One was a chapter on student peer groups (Newcomb and Wilson, 1966), sponsored by the Social Science Research Council; the other was a paper for inclusion in SPSSI's *The American College,* edited by Nevitt Sanford (1962). Each of them dealt, basically, with these questions: What reasons are there to expect that educational outcomes in American colleges are affected by peer-group influence? Under what conditions do these presumed effects enhance the intended effects of college experience? These concerns were to engage me rather fully during the decade of the 1960s, and in two quite different ways.

My first, rather primitive conclusions were paraphrased in the following figure: the social-psychological motors of student life in most American colleges are racing, but they are often (especially in large universities) disengaged from the wheels of intellectual growth. That is, there is plenty of evidence of peer-group effects, but there is no necessary connection between interests thus generated or supported and the intellectual objectives that colleges typically proclaim. With reference particularly to my own campus (presumably more or less typical in this respect) I came to describe this state of affairs as one of divorcement between peer-group life and academic or intellectual experience. The former is typically vital, spontaneous, and rewarding; the latter tends to be "extrinsically" geared toward courses, examinations, and grades in primarily individual ways that lack the shared excitement of the intellectual chase. This way of looking at the matter was not of course unrelated to my notions about interpersonal balance, according to which attitudes toward persons provide support for other attitudes (intellectual ones, for example), and vice versa.

If, as a result of existing arrangements in universities like my own, undergraduates' academic and intellectual concerns tend to be divorced from a major source of motivation and interpersonal support, then why not change those arrangements? I soon discovered that two of my colleagues (Dean, and later Academic Vice President Roger Heyns, and Professor Wilbert McKeachie) were thinking along similar lines. With their support, beginning in 1961, various proposals were prepared and officially considered, and within three years a plan was approved by the Faculty of Literature, Science and the Arts. Following three more years of detailed planning, what came to be known as the Residential College opened its doors to its first freshman class of 220 students. We had agreed to accept the parent College's objectives, but in our own, autonomous ways. We developed a core curriculum of our own, designed to provide "common intellectual experiences", expecially for freshmen and sophomores, with emphasis upon problem orientations rather than disciplinary ones, without fixed credit hours or letter grades. A governing body was devised, half of whose members were students, with final authority for all matters of community concern—not excluding the curricular. Our problems—especially including financing and the recruiting of a stable faculty—have been constant though never demoralizing, thanks to the talents of Dean James Robertson, the Director. But no one, I think, would challenge the statement that our students' interpersonal and intellectual lives do not suffer from divorcement. One of my deep satisfactions in this enterprise has been the opportunity of continuing my relationships with former students turned colleagues—including Alan Guskin, Patricia Gurin, and especially Robert Kahn with whom I have been associated in virtually every aspect of my work at Michigan.

I had insisted, from the beginning, that an enterprise so expensive in planning time and, as the planners believed, of such potential importance educationally, should include procedures for its own assessment. And so, while I continued to be involved in teaching, in committee work, and from time to time in community government, my official role became that of Associate Director for assessment and research. In close association with Donald Brown and several of his junior associates in the Center for Research on Learning and Teaching, the first of what I hope will be several research reports has already appeared (Newcomb et al., 1970). We were able, by comparing Residential College students with control populations in the parent college, to show increasing differences that could be accounted for primarily in terms of demonstrably different environments. I have also helped to plan and to conduct comparative studies in other universities that have recently launched small, residentially based colleges—including the campuses of the Universities of California at San Diego (where I spent two winter terms as Visiting Professor) and at Santa Cruz (where I participated in the planning of the first college in the summer of 1964).

I had become increasingly curious, meanwhile, about both theoretical and procedural aspects of measuring impacts of colleges upon their students. And so I was glad to accept an invitation from the Carnegie Corporation of New York to peruse the by-then considerable research literature relevant to the problem. Kenneth Feldman, a junior colleague and former student, spent nearly full time (far more than I) on a critical review of this literature, which eventually appeared in two volumes (Feldman and Newcomb, 1969). We were able—in spite of several procedural problems of great complexity and the shortcomings of most of the available studies—to make some sense of the interdependent effects of initial selection of students, of differential college environments, of extra-college influences, and of personal characteristics.

The aspect of this study that most fully engrossed me was a phenomenon that we labeled "accentuation"—a process by which students initially distinctive in some characteristic often, in contraregressive manner, became still more distinctive in that respect. Our far from adequate evidence suggested that the crucial event was the self-selection by students of some environment—perhaps a college, or a particular academic major—congenial to that characteristic, so that it became enhanced, and the initial differences between such students and others increased. There is, of course, nothing particularly surprising about such a process, which is almost certainly a very common one, by no means limited to college students. But the notion of accentuation did provide a useful paradigm for bringing together several of the sets of variables whose effects we had set out to study.

My life has of course consisted of more than being a psychologist, and yet I believe that the professional part of me has loomed large enough to reveal much about the rest of that life. At any rate, two strong imperatives have guided much of my professional life. First, beginning with my last predoctoral year, I wanted legitimacy as a psychologist. I was accorded the Ph.D. on the basis of work done in Union Seminary, in Teachers College, and in Columbia's Psychology Department—not a particularly good accreditation in the world into which I hoped to move. And, beginning long before that, I had at least a normal degree of wanting to be liked. Only belatedly did I come to recognize and to accept this latter ingredient—doubtless because it was interlocked with certain aspects of myself that I was not particularly proud of. These two motivational strands, inter-meshed with the earlier ones of intellectuality and concern for social causes, now seem to have tied together much if not most of my professional life.

On reviewing what I have written, I find what I have so often discovered in my own research data: consistencies (sometimes almost "too good to be true") as well as contradictions, surprises, and mysteries. Perhaps because, typically, I have spent years of living with each of a few major sets of data, I have always found more in them than could possibly have emerged from my own planning. Can the same be said of the "data" of my own life? Perhaps the possibilities are there, but I have neither the interest in reliving those data nor the talent to draw out major themes from them.

Nevertheless, I find a few of the mysteries intriguing. Why, for example, did a young man bent (as he thought) on legitimizing himself as a psychologist chuck a promising position in a large city to go to a small, unheard-of college for women in rural Vermont, where he would be the only psychologist? In retrospect, I suspect that it was the "cause" of progressive education (with which Bennington was then identified), and the prospects of community life there, that attracted me. I had no sense that I was putting my career in jeopardy, nor had I any thought of launching a major study there. Nevertheless, it was during those seven years that I "solved" my problem of professional identity—not with psychology as a whole, but with a subfield within psychology—as I then viewed it; I later came to view my own social-psychological problems as being sociological as well as psychological.

During those years I not only completed a major monograph but also five or six other publications, most of them heavily time-demanding. Except for the monograph, no one at Bennington knew that I was working on them, and I doubt if anyone there ever heard of any of them. What motivated me? I can only say that each task constituted a problem for me and, once intrigued, I could not leave it. I was doing what I wanted to do. The original research and the critical reviews were not what I had come to Bennington to do; I had indeed found the other satisfactions that I anticipated there—but they were not enough.

And why, during those years when I was carving out a kind of psychological niche for myself, had I engaged in several "radical" activities? Such "activist" participation, which I have already noted, was not actively appreciated by some colleagues and many townspeople. Somewhat naively, I simply took for granted the college President's support of my expressions of academic freedom—which indeed I had, though with less than adequate appreciation on my part of what it must have cost him. And, worse than any of these things from the point of a career orientation, I coedited a book for SPSSI on industrial conflict that was regarded by the contracting publisher as so offensive that our contract was canceled (Hartman and Newcomb, 1939), and which raised a minor tempest even within SPSSI. Such activities on the part of a presumably career-oriented academic still in his mid-thirties suggest that, among other things, he was a creature of those Depression years. But I like to think, in addition, that I was motivated by such simple considerations as a sense of justice, and that my personal metabolism was such that I preferred to get into the fray rather than remain on the sidelines.

I managed, without really trying, to gain a bit of a reputation as a radical during my early years at Michigan, but in less prominent ways. The major exception occurred in 1965, when I was one of the original planners of the first Vietnam Teach-In, and I still take a certain pride in that role. Perhaps I should regard it as another unsolved problem that my still rather considerable energies were increasingly spent in professional directions, rather than in social action, and increasingly on the national rather than the local scene. I certainly have no sense of having sought such responsibilities as the secretaryship and presidency of SPSSI, the editorship of the *Psychological Review* (which I first declined and never really wanted), membership for some ten years on the APA Board of Directors, and the APA presidency. As to this last honor, I suppose I should have felt that it fully legitimized my status as a psychologist, but I cannot honestly say that I so interpreted it. By 1954, when I became president-elect, I interpreted the outcome as meaning that some APA members wanted to see a social psychologist in that office, and at least some of them preferred one who had not only published books but who had been identified with social issues.

And so, in my life as in my research, there is more to be discerned than could have emerged from calculated planning. As to research, I have learned much from the "emergents"—and this in fact has been one of my justifications for preferring to work in natural settings rather than in laboratories. Can the same be said for the "unplanned" aspects of my career? I did not plan, initially, to become a psychologist or, later, a social psychologist. Nor, during or after the making of those decisions, did I plan a life of participation in "social causes"; indeed, a calculated planning of the two, together, would have been naive if not foolhardy. I did not plan to be an educational administrator, or an official in the apparatus of the American Psychological Association. Perhaps the situations which, nevertheless, led me to do these things may be regarded as a series of projective tests, revealing something of the person—precisely because they were not planned in advance. If so, that person must have been one who wanted both independence and social belongingness; who in certain areas was impelled by scientific curiosity and in others by overcertainty; and to whom both intellectual and moral values loomed large. He never learned, really, that each of these pairings included incompatibilities. In fact, he rarely stopped, as he so often had in the inspection of his research data, to search for serendipities in the array of his own life events. When he has noted some of them, as in the writing of this account, it has been with a certain wry ambivalence of feeling, dominated by the consoling thought that, after all, it has been a life of considerable zest.

REFERENCES

Selected Publications by Theodore M. Newcomb

The consistency of certain extrovert-introvert behavior patterns in 51 problem boys. *Contributions to education,* No. 385, New York: Teachers College, Columbia Univ., 1929, pp. 123.

An experiment designed to test the validity of a rating technique. *J. Educ. Psychol.,* 1931, *32,* 279-289.

(with G. Murphy and Lois B. Murphy) *Experimental social psychology.* New York: Harper & Row, 1937, pp. xi, 1121.

(with G. Svehla) Intra-family relations in attitude. *Sociometry,* 1937, *1,* Nos. 1-2, 180-205.

A technique for measuring some aspects of interaction through behavior observations. In W. I. Newstetter, M. J. Feldstein, and T. M. Newcomb, *Group adjustment: a study in experimental sociology.* Cleveland: Western Reserve Univ., 1938, pp. 66-92.

(edited with G. Hartmann) *Industrial conflict.* New York: Cordon, 1939, pp. xi, 583.

News and morale: a miniature experiment. In Goodwin Watson (Ed.), *Civilian morale.* Boston: Houghton Mifflin, 1942, pp. 175-185.

Personality and social change. New York: Holt, Rinehart and Winston, 1943, pp. 225. (Reissued in 1957.)

Autistic hostility and social reality. *J. Human Relations,* 1947, *I,* 68-86.

(edited with E. L. Hartley) *Readings in social psychology.* New York: Holt, Rinehart and Winston, 1947, pp. xiv, 688.

Social psychology. New York: Holt, Rinehart and Winston, 1950, pp. ix, 690.

Attitude development as a function of reference groups: the Bennington study. In G. E. Swanson, T. M. Newcomb, and E. L. Hartley (Eds.), *Readings in social psychology,* rev. ed. New York: Holt, Rinehart and Winston, 1952, pp. 420-430. Reprinted in 3rd ed., edited by E. E. Maccoby, T. M. Newcomb, and E. L. Hartley, 1958.

(with W. W. Charters, Jr.) Some attitudinal effects of experimentally increased salience of a membership group. In *Readings in social psychology.* New York: Holt, Rinehart and Winston, 1952, pp. 415-430.

An approach to the study of communicative acts. *Psychol. Rev.,* 1953, *60,* No. 6, 393-404.

The acquaintance process. New York: Holt, Rinehart and Winston, 1961, pp. v-xv, 1-303.

Student peer group influence. In N. Sanford (Ed.), *The American college.* New York: Wiley, 1962, pp. 463-488.

Stabilities underlying changes in interpersonal attraction. *J. abnorm. soc. Psychol., 66,* No. 4, 1963, 376-386.

Interpersonal constancies: psychological and sociological approaches. In Otto Klineberg and Richard Christie (Eds.), *Perspectives in social psychology.* New York: Holt, Rinehart and Winston, 1965, pp. 38-49.

(edited with E. K. Wilson) *College peer groups.* Chicago: Aldine-Atherton, 1966.

(with K. E. Koenig, R. Flacks, and D. Warwick) *Persistence and change: Bennington College and its students after 25 years.* New York: Wiley, 1967, pp. vii + 292.

Interpersonal balance. In R. P. Abelson et al. (Eds.), *Theories of cognitive consistency.* Skokie, Ill.: Rand McNally, 1968, pp. 28-51.

(with Kenneth Feldman) *Impact of college on students,* Vols. I and II. San Francisco: Jossey-Bass, 1969, pp. xi-474; 1-171.

(with D. R. Brown, J. A. Kulik, D. J. Reimer, and W. R. Revelle) Self-selection and change. In J. Gaff (Ed.), *The cluster college.* San Francisco: Jossey-Bass, 1970, pp. 137-160.

Other Publications Cited

Festinger, L. *A theory of cognitive dissonance.* New York: Harper & Row, 1957.

Festinger, L., K. Back, et al. *Theory and experiment in social communication.* Ann Arbor: Institute for Social Research, Univ. Michigan, 1950.

Festinger, L., S. Schachter, and K. Back. *Social pressures in informal groups.* New York: Harper & Row, 1950.

Homans, G. C. *The human group.* New York: Harcourt Brace Jovanovich, 1950.

Heider, F. *The psychology of interpersonal relations.* New York: Wiley, 1958.

Likert, R. A technique for the measurement of attitudes. *Arch. Psychol.,* 1932, No. 140.

Muenzinger, K. F. *Psychology: the science of behavior.* New York: Harper & Row, 1942.

Murphy, G. *Historical introduction to modern psychology.* New York: Harcourt Brace Jovanovich, 1929.

Murphy, G., and Lois B. Murphy. *Experimental social psychology.* New York: Harper & Row, 1931.

Osgood, C. E., and P. H. Tannenbaum. The principle of congruity in the prediction of attitude change. *Psychol. Rev.,* 1955, *62*, 42-55.

Stagner, R. Fascist attitudes: an exploratory study. *J. Soc. Psychol.,* 1936, 7, 303-319.

Paul Koby, Cambridge

393

S. S. Stevens

In 1929 my uncle sent me off to Stanford to study law, or so he thought. I wanted to be a writer or an artist, or so I thought. A writer writes and a painter paints, and if you have passed 23 with neither pen nor brush constantly in hand, you are neither writer nor artist. So what did I want to do? A romantic answer had popped out on a soft spring night when the moon lit the snowfields on the Wasatch peaks above the campus of the University of Utah. Two students were projecting their yearnings into the future, and I shocked the girl, my sweetheart since childhood, by opting for the role of spectator on the comedy of life. The girl, Phyllis, glowed with purpose, though. She knew what she wanted, and she went on to win accolades in the world of the theater and to have a New York playhouse named for her. Why, she asked, had I no ambitions?

So I was shipped off to Stanford for the junior year, only to indulge anew my predilection for courses that promised wide-roaming talk and conceptual excitement. Nothing in science, nothing in mathematics, nothing elementary. Only the windy subjects. The philosopher image seemed most congenial. But mainly, that first year at Stanford, I suffered the shock of severance. I knew no one, whereas the year before at Utah I had known almost everyone. Joining the debating team helped, but not much. We lost to some wits from Oxford, but we triumphed over St. Mary's in the hills behind Berkeley. The then-famous St. Mary's football team made up most of the audience.

Another transfer student, shipped west for some of the same reasons that may have motivated my own family, happened to land next door to me in a Palo Alto rooming house at 257 Byron Street. We were both intensely people-shy and succeeded in avoiding conversation until one day when we bobbed up at the same time on the edge of the swimming pool. That set off an intellectual sparring that grew into friendship. Dane Wilsey was wild, brilliant, and wealthy. His red convertible, and sometimes my green roadster, took him to San Francisco for most of his adventures, but the intellectual life of Stanford absorbed a share of his breathless energy. He bounded in one day and said, "I've got it, we can't waste our time on these philosophy courses. We should study medicine. The world needs us." So in our senior year we both registered for freshman physics, chemistry, and biology. In addition I registered for golf, because happiness, I was beginning to think, was an endless fairway. Fortunately, I got higher grades in science than in golf.

Wilsey could not spare the time for the laboratory toils. His adventures in San Francisco produced a wife (his second) and a job with a broker. But the market was tumbling, and one morning he got up from breakfast, walked into the bedroom, and took the exit by bullet, the exit that he and I had many times argued for and against as we bulled through the night at the rooming house.

The laboratory work was a bore, but I liked some parts of the exercises. Perhaps I was settling down now, because the rooming house days were past. During the spring vacation I had taken the train back to Salt Lake City and had returned, much to my own surprise, with a beautiful young wife named Maxine. No one was home at the rooming house, so we first had to scale the walnut tree to the roof of the back porch to find an open window. The landlady and her sloe-eyed daughter took a sour view of the marital proceedings and we soon moved to a duplex at 228 Kipling Street.

Adjustment to life at Stanford was impeded partly by age. I was three years older than most of my classmates. After finishing high school at 17 I had been sent on a 3-year mission for the Mormon Church. Both parents had died that same year, 1924, and I was carrying on my father's electrical equipment business, Stevens Sales Company, where I had always worked after school. The business was prospering and life was blithe and gay. My friends, Richard L. Evans chief among them, would assemble at closing time, and we would take off in my new 1924 Overland with its huge balloon tires that could ride high in the loose gravel on the dusty roads of the unpaved West. Gaiety subsided, however, on a seasick voyage from Montreal to Liverpool, and then from Harwich to Antwerp on the night boat. I reported in at the mission office in Liège, Belgium, knowing not a word of French, and was assigned a companion who was "counting the days" till his release. He was a musician and he tried to elevate my taste by a weekly exposure to opera, but I always slept through the second act.

Sometime near the end of the third month, that chattering, machine-gun language called French, which had been going by in a staccato blur, began to break up into words. A cloud was lifting. Soon I was taking my turn at the pulpit and taxing the ears of the faithful with fractured French in diphthonged accent. Two years later, though, my thinking and daydreaming had shifted over to French and I found myself translating back into English.

Every four months or so a missionary got a new companion, often accompanied by a change of scene. With a young Brother Nelson I was sent to open a branch in Charleroi, a sooty town noted for its mines and glass-blowing factories. We rented a small upstairs room with a gas heater and a water pitcher. You carried water up from ground level. The house was owned by two maiden sisters, angular and spare, somewhat on the design of gargoyles. They served us breakfast and cackled at our protests about its insufficiency. And when we discovered a back room with a bathtub, they refused to empty out the cans and bottles stored therein. You could buy a bath at the local hotel, they said, if you couldn't keep clean with rag and basin.

For a few weeks we knocked on doors, passing out brochures and a handbill announcing a coming *Conférence* in a hotel ballroom we had rented. The day of the *Conférence* dawned in a howling Belgian deluge, and all we had to preach to were the two landladies, a waiter, and a few missionaries from nearby towns. A miserable start, but I am told that many people have since joined the Mormon Church in Charleroi.

There was already a flourishing branch in Liège where earlier missionaries had leased a former beer hall complete with gas lights, stage, and balcony. Backstage there was a pistol target range and a boxing ring. Both saw action.

When two close friends were released early in 1927 I received a 3-month furlough to accompany them on a trip to Egypt and Palestine. The style and extent of the journey were dictated by the minimum fund of $362 saved up by one of them. Missionaries paid their own way, helped, of course, by family and friends; the Church paid only the passage home. By eating one meal a day, supplemented by bread, oranges, and chocolate, and by riding third class on the railroads and "deck" (without bed) on the ships, we got as far south as a day's camel ride to the Step Pyramid, and as far east as the Dead Sea. Swimming there was much like that in our own Great Salt Lake, where you float about like an empty bottle. Then from Tel Aviv by boat to Rumania on the Black Sea and back to Turkey, and then by train through the Balkans and on to Switzerland, where I reported in again and was placed in charge of the Swiss Conference of the French Mission. I was stationed in Lausanne, but my travel beat ranged from Besançon, France, to La Chaud de Fonds in the Jura Mountains, and my chief duty was to buck up the resident missionaries and visit the church members.

My own release came in time to enter the University of Utah in 1927 and begin a hind-end-to education, starting with advanced courses in philosophy, political science, Japanese sociology, history, and the like. It was rich fare, but it should have included some mathematics. As a matter of fact, I had registered for college algebra, but initiation into the Pi Kappa Alpha fraternity had set me so far behind in the exercises that I had to drop the course. Disaster! But how is a student to know what only a playback can reveal?

Money for mission and college came mainly from my father's insurance, about $15,000, supplemented by such jobs as teaching in the French phonetics laboratory. Summers I worked for the Idaho Power Company, starting as a grunt (hole digger and lineman's helper), living in a tent in a construction camp beside a mountain stream where you almost froze to death at night. I later worked up to summer utility man. That meant that I had a new job almost every two weeks as I replaced the man on vacation, whether meter reader, waterheater installer, or night troubleshooter. Forty years later, it becomes clear that my education for science took place more in the summers than in the winters.

Summer was for education in boyhood too. Released from the tyranny of inkwell and desk, I was transported by cinder-belching train from Salt Lake City to the paradise of Logan, Utah, where barn and corral and garden and river and irrigation ditches became the playground for three glorious months among cousins of all ages. My grandfather, Orson Smith, and his two remaining wives occupied houses on a major part of a town block, and some of his two dozen children had homes nearby. A polygamous household was a wonderful institution under a patriarchal mesomorph who had been born in a covered wagon and who had subdued his land by brains and energy. He educated himself and rose to the highest position in Cache Valley, but his vision often raced ahead of reality. Since markets sometimes plummet, it was almost inevitable that his elevator would be full of the valley's wheat crop when the panic of 1897 broke the price. Off he went to the Klondike to recoup in the gold rush, but again he overreached by trying to move in machinery while most others were panning the bright metal.

So there stood the great grain elevator tower for boys to climb and explore, forbidden and tightly locked, of course, but a boy could squeeze through a foundation vent if someone helped by pushing or pulling. And next door stood the "new house," waiting through the years, half finished, for lathe and plaster. We could climb up the studs from floor to floor and catch bats among the rafters. But all those boyhood castles held second place to the barn. We were not supposed to play in the hay, but no one kept watch as we burrowed and tunneled and contrived a slick chute down which we could plunge from ridge to stable—and frighten the chickens as we landed.

Best of all, though, was the running water. Whenever I was missing they knew exactly where to look: the wooden culvert that carried the irrigation stream across the road to plunge into a pool where toads sat fat on the bank and horses stretched their necks to drink. The clear swirling water was my first love, and the pool was my first point of call after the train ride from Salt Lake City. Other things could wait. The contriving of dams and water wheels delighted me and led the family to predict the career of hydraulic engineer.

Twice a week there were "water rights." During certain hours you could dam up the ditch and open the sluice gate to your own garden. Then barefoot with hoe you guided the precious water down the rows until the dusty earth would make mud curls through your toes. And you opened another weir and flooded the lawn, and the little kids ran splashing and rolling in four inches of sparkling water.

Then summer would end, as all things must, and my mother and I would take the branch line from Logan to Cache Junction to connect with the Oregon Short Line for Salt Lake City, and school would start and Phyllis would be there to stoke the tormenting fires of puppy love, as unfeeling adults presumed to call it. School was O.K., I guess, but they thought I would never learn to read. They had to give me a second try at conquering the first grade, but thereafter I seemed somehow to stand a little higher in class during each successive year. I was considered listless, as they phrased it, low in energy, and my round-shouldered posture had not responded to various braces and harnesses, except to provide a handle by which larger cousins could lift me to hang helpless off the ground.

My mother, who suffered a heart-valve leakage from girlhood rheumatic fever, worried much about me and about the gangs of boys that played and warred throughout the 8th East neighborhood, where the houses ranged from shacks to mansions. Some of us showed up now and then in juvenile court, but I can see now that even as boys we knew which of us were the bad guys and which went along for the fun. Three of the true delinquents later made it to the state penitentiary, one of them for a capital offense.

One day, when I was beginning the fourth grade, Mother asked me if I would like to go to live in Logan. What a question! My father's asthma was kicking up and his business was touch and go. We would be able to eat better in Logan, where we would stay with Aunt Maggie, my mother's oldest sister. Her husband, Will, was the genial chief clerk in the general store, a large endomorph, but a vigorous man, who pedaled a bicycle back and forth and brought home each night a big leather pouch full of coins to be counted. That Christmas two young cousins developed a theory, based on someone's offhand remark about a "windbag," that a pin would deflate Uncle Will. As he bent his great bulk over the coal scuttle they tested the hypothesis, and everyone thought Uncle Will had lost his wits as he cried out in shaking rage and grabbed one of the fleeing experimenters.

But the hardships of the adults were mostly lost on us children, even though the talk of the grownups in the evening circle around the potbellied stove told of trials—and of comedy. Whatever the childhood game in progress, you kept an ear cocked for a salty tale—and you appeared not to be listening. And when finally sent to bed you could undress by the warm stove in the kitchen where the bread was rising in its big pan under the dish towel, and you could poke in a finger and pull out a tangy swatch of dough to comfort your stomach and help ease the shock of the cold leap into bed.

Asthma, I was later to learn, was not the only thing troubling my father. There was another woman. My semi-invalid mother was walking out. Later on came a divorce, but it did not take. On many occasions Dad would be sitting by her bed when I came home at night and then one evening they told me they had married again. God, it made me happy. Mother's circulation grew worse and a couple of years later she suffered a stroke and died. Thereafter, Dad and I shared the cooking while I finished my last year at high school. We had always pulled well together, both at work and in our travels, and we continued to do so, always with very few words, for neither of us was a talker. Our silences never clamored to be broken.

One afternoon I returned to the school after a hard but exhilarating day at the finals of the state debating competition only to be told that they were looking for me. There had been an auto accident and Dad was dying. He was only 42, and everyone said "so young to die." I was 17 and I wondered that a parent could be anything but old.

Dad had been 18 when he lost his father, and he too had been sent on a mission—to Holland. He returned to start an electrical business in Ogden, Utah, the town where I was born in 1906 in a small wooden house on Stewart Lane, now called Ogden Avenue. The business failed and we moved to Salt Lake City, where Dad worked for Fairbanks-Morse until he could once again start his own business. His technical training came through correspondence schools, because the death of his father precluded college and ended his hope to study medicine.

Dad's father, Thomas J. Stevens, was born in Bristol, England, on the day gold was discovered in California. Soon thereafter his parents joined the Mormon Church, and at 16 he drove two yoke of oxen across the plains from the Missouri River to the mountains of Utah. Coming from a family of mechanics he had apprenticed the blacksmith trade, and he worked for the Union Pacific Railroad before he and his brothers started their own foundry and machine shop in Ogden. He later made a mark as treasurer of several institutions, and as Commissary General of the National Guard. And for 13 years he served the Mormon Church as Bishop of the Fifth Ward. A bishop is a kind of works manager, a chief of chores, the link pin in the chain between spiritual dispensation and temporal care. The bishop tithes, builds, counsels, buries, blesses, arbitrates, marries, christens, visits the sick, and carries food and fuel to the poor. My grandfather's journal records those daily acts of service.

For a time he filled in as head of the local Academy—now Weber State College. Like so many of those self-educated pioneers, he showed an exaggerated faith in formal education, despite being surrounded by examples of men whose achievements owed nothing to classroom or curriculum. Perhaps the generations produce little change, for here am I at Harvard teaching formal courses in subjects I was never taught, and seeming thereby to imply that the course is the only door to mastery.

I never knew Grandfather Stevens, but I remember his wife and the big house in Ogden, with its carriage barn behind. The house stood at 2575 Jefferson Avenue, across the street from the Eccles mansion—one of the grander places in the town. Grandma Stevens was one of 27 children fathered by Briant Stringham, pioneer and rancher, who built a house for each of his four wives, three of them Ashby sisters from Salem, Massachusetts. I was 6 when Grandma Stevens died, and her funeral was my first view of death, with Grandma lying serene and still in the parlor under the heavy overcast of odor from banks of flowers.

One of the questions we debated my senior year in high school was the mandate for compulsory education to age 16. We had to stand ready to debate either side of the question, and the background research led me to the new excitement concerning the intelligence test and the remarkable invariance of the IQ. That kind of library searching and reading struck a responsive resonance, I now think, but in those days I had no idea where I was going. "What do you want to be?" everybody kept asking. How could I tell them something I had never heard of? How could I answer, "I would like to become the world's first Professor of Psychophysics"?

It was in March 1929 in a philosophy class that I first became curious enough to ask Professor Ericksen what was meant by psychology. He said I could find out on the top floor. (Psychology was always relegated to the attic or the basement.) I climbed to the top floor and asked Dorothy Nyswander. She said I ought to take a course and find out. She was teaching comparative psychology and she challenged me to try to catch up with the reading and join the course. I accepted. Mostly I learned about the phyla, which is useful, and about rats running mazes, which is not. Dr. Nyswander despaired of making me appreciate animal training, as I called it. The text was a ponderous tome by J. B. Watson, but I gathered that he had written a more lively volume on *Behaviorism,* a volume that was supposed to have shaken psychology.

The next summer in Pocatello, Idaho, I discovered that Watson could also shake the parents' class in Sunday School, where I was conducting the lessons. Watson's blatant environmentalism went down hard with those anxious parents, some of whom had done everything they could to steer a wayward boy. Give him a dozen infants at birth, boasted Watson, and he could make each of them anything you named. Such rot made for a good sermon, and I believed it then, though the evidence leads me to wager that biology would have shattered Watson's myth if someone had supplied the infants he asked for. So much of our behavior style seems to be wired in at the start. Those parents, many from ranch and farm, had a sense of biology sounder than mine.

Teaching the parents' class seemed somehow to be my specialty, even after leaving the West for Harvard. In Boston in 1931 we met on Sunday mornings in an upstairs nightclub that featured green walls and a bilious odor. The group later moved to Cantabridgia Hall near Harvard Square, and now there are Mormon churches in many towns around. I finally gave up the parents' class after another upsetting issue had been aired: whether there is a conflict between science and religion. Mormon doctrine says no, and the lives of many distinguished scientists have demonstrated that churchgoing does not preclude first-rate research. But on method, I tried to argue, science and religion must stand opposed. Belief is what the ideal scientist, if there were such, would be totally free of. Only evidence would count for him, evidence viewed with dispassionate objectivity. But the suspension of intense belief comes hard. Few manage it at all. The young almost never do.

The parents' class churned with argument as I tried by Socratic induction to force the members to set the prophet's injunction to believe against the scientist's injunction to question. In that confrontation the teacher may have learned more than the students, for I was then trying to sort out from among my tangled intellectual inputs an explicit philosophy that I could live with. Many years later I would call it the schemapiric view, but in the early 1930s the quest for a congenial approach was leading me toward operationism, a topic on which I later wrote a series of articles.

But the problem of belief persisted, for believing, it seems, holds many attractions. Believing is easy—and lazy. And it fills people with a warm glow, so that when two or more believers are gathered together in common conviction about philosophy, politics, or divinity, they sense the cozy, comforting contagion of zeal. The zealot detects virtue in blind belief. The uncommitted mind regards such allegations of virtue with high skepticism. I was beginning to aspire to the suspension of belief.

My graduation from Stanford had been threatened by a failure to major in anything. I had never read the catalog, except to shop for courses, and beginning a premedical course in the senior year did not appear to fit the rules. It was then that my chemistry professor, who was also the registrar, dredged out of his memory a long-forgotten bit of legislation that prescribed a major for anyone who could offer at least one course in a half-dozen different areas of social science. I could do that with no trouble at all. But there was one penalty. Despite election to Phi Beta Kappa at the end of junior year, graduation with honors was ruled out because I was taking freshman courses in the senior year. Curricular rules take funny twists. I warn students not to let the curriculum interfere with their education.

Those freshman science courses in the senior year persuaded me that my previous studies were fitting me to talk about anything, but to do nothing. No skills acquired, no procedures mastered, no craft apprenticed. To be sure, I was by then getting my hands on something concrete in the laboratories, but in your twenty-fifth year you should be finishing, not starting. I was cheered a bit by comparative anatomy under Professor Stark, who liked to claim that his main mission in life was to keep the wrong people out of medical school. I hit one of his exams for 100, which he told the class had never before been done, and so I found myself admitted to Harvard Medical School, with two provisos: (1) that I send fifty dollars, and (2) that I take organic chemistry during the summer. Neither condition seemed attractive. When I vacillated, a student who had been turned down offered me $5000 to go in my place.

Decision never comes easy to me, and trying to decide to do something often tears me apart more than doing it. So I dallied and the deadline passed and I still had my $50 and there was no need for a four-year grind through medical school. What to do? Someone recommended the vocational interest test that E. K. Strong was developing. It told about interests, not abilities, and it told me that my interests correlated highly with those of the mathematician, the psychologist, and a few other academic types, and very poorly with the Y.M.C.A. secretary. Mathematics was out, of course, so I talked to C. P. Stone, who was known as a rat man, but who also taught abnormal psychology and who took the class on hospital excursions where we had exhibited to us dramatic examples of the classic psychotic syndromes. Stone advised me against psychiatry, which in those days meant tending a hospital, and he remarked that people trained in solid experimental psychology seemed best able to find jobs, which were then becoming scarce in the deepening Depression. Stone scorned my thought of going to Harvard, because Yale and its new Institute of Human Relations heralded the hope of the future. I promised to limit myself to one year at Harvard, which seemed to mollify the professor, and he then gave me some choice advice: "Wherever you go," he said, "ask the professor first off if there isn't some small problem you can work on for him."

The road to Harvard led first to Los Angeles for a combined summer school and marital vacation. I drove out to the new campus at UCLA, where gawky buildings rose lonely and comical from a treeless waste of hills and eroded gullies. Nothing much seemed to be stirring except rabbits. I wandered about and found the office of Knight Dunlap, a name I had heard of, but no one was home. So I drove back into town and signed up at USC, where things turned out to be bouncing. I found an old friend from Utah named Van Tanner, another college wanderer and bon vivant, who was in charge of student activities and who combatted boredom as a movie extra and stunt man. He led me through many novel exploits, a good supplement to courses in philosophy and psychology. I took statistics from H. E. Garrett and history from J. F. Dashiell, a pair of distinguished summer imports. For diversion one could sit in the old wooden house where Milton Metfessel had his laboratory and watch comedian Joe E. Brown making a movie with the USC football team.

Then back to Salt Lake City, where Maxine had been visiting her parents, and thence down the long dusty road "back east." Pavement began around Chicago and had become fairly continuous by Cleveland. There we visited some Stanford friends and were startled to find them a "first family" in a fabulous estate. We saw for the first time what great wealth and gracious living could be like.

We drove into Cambridge in a September drizzle, bought a newspaper, and telephoned a want-ad number that advertised rooms at 9 Sumner Road. It cost $10 per week for two small rooms separated by a curtain. One room served as bath and kitchen. Mrs. Clark, a Victorian-style Cambridge widow, was quite alarmed when we said we would move right in. Who were we, she wondered. Maybe we should come back tomorrow, she suggested. I pointed out that we would still be the same people tomorrow. Did we know someone she could call? No one in Cambridge. Gradually as the talk continued the alarm subsided, and we unloaded. The location turned out to be so wonderfully convenient to Harvard and Radcliffe that we were able to sell the faithful Hupmobile.

Having eschewed medical school I began to cast about for some other option. Always, it seems, I was looking for the easiest. While hunting around in the catalogue, which I had now decided was for reading, I turned up the interesting fact that tuition in the School of Education was only $300. We were borrowing money for Maxine's tuition at Radcliffe ($400), and so any bargain was appreciated. When I appeared at the office in old Lawrence Hall—the same building where in 1876 William James had set up a "laboratory for psychophysics"—the secretary assured me that I could not register because I had not applied for admission. "You don't just walk in," she admonished. My offer to go back and crawl in did not seem to amuse her. But officialdom finally bent and I was admitted.

There was only one course in education that looked interesting—advanced statistics under T. L. Kelley, who, like me, had just arrived from Stanford. About twenty of us registered for the course, but only two of us took the final exam. I had nothing to lose, and the other fellow was a Negro principal on leave who was required by his school board to take all exams. Kelley could not bring himself to flunk even half the class, but the questions made no more sense to either of us than the lectures had. Kelley was a bad teacher. Or was he? He pioneered in his field and he turned out distinguished students. Is there some surer mark of good teaching?

The $300 tuition purchased four courses, so for the other three I scanned the listings under Arts and Sciences. I wanted physiology, I thought, and I found W. J. Crozier in a vast new building that was then less than half full. Crozier gave me a room overlooking a pleasant quadrangle guarded by two great bronze rhinos, newly cast, whose cost seemed scandalous to him. "Think how much research that money would support!" Each time I pass those handsome bronze beasts I wonder whether they feel guilty.

The course started out with Crozier's blast at mentalism, followed by his display of the evidence that the tropism exhibited by young rats climbing a slope obeys the Mendelian laws. The rats inherit a climbing angle. Then Crozier disappeared and various other people showed up to tell about their research. Again a bad job of teaching. Or was it?

As the year ground on I found that Crozier had attracted an interesting array of talent into the south wing of the Biological Laboratories. On the first floor one day I walked in on a man who was busily plotting data. He said they were "eating curves" for rats and could be described by power functions. I told him I didn't know much math, and what was a power function? For the first time he turned and looked at me; then he waggled his head and dismissed me by saying, "The only way to get over an inferiority complex about mathematics is to learn some." That was my first and possibly my most profitable encounter with B. F. Skinner. Both his diagnosis and his prescription were just right, as it turned out.

Up in Emerson Hall I located E. G. Boring, Harvard's lone Professor of Psychology, the de facto chairman of a nonexistent department, for psychology was part of philosophy. Boring admitted me to the "systematic" course on perception, although he doubted its suitability for a student in the School of Education. Then I startled Boring by asking if I could work on some problem of his. Well, yes, perhaps. He had heard that when you mix red and green on a color wheel it looks gray only if you stand at the right distance. That seemed interesting, and up in the attic under the rafters I found a place where I could try it out. It worked all right, but so what? I tried various arrangements and noted that if I looked slightly away from the color wheel the gray turned greenish. Finally I got around to mixing a black and white to provide a gray that could be compared with the gray produced by red and green.

Then late one afternoon my scientific career began. There occurred that surge of elation, the *eureka!* that drives the investigator. I suddenly sensed that there was a law to be worked out. You could mix some green with the black and white and you could vary the amount in a way that would just cancel the effect of a change in distance. A function could be measured! Bursting with elation, I bounded down from the attic that evening and ran all the way back to Sumner Road.

Boring was right about students in the School of Education and their deficient background. During most of his lectures on perception that first semester I felt submerged under a strange, unstructured flow of esoteric words and concepts. Perception had no back, front, or sides. The final examination over, Boring wrote me one of his famous scrap-paper missives announcing my failure, but according me the courtesy of a passing grade because I was not a graduate student in psychology.

What do you do when the blast of your first failure shatters your prospects and your newly formed hope for a scientific career? I crawled up to my improvised desk in the attic and sat staring. The emotion of dismay was shot through from time to time by a surge of diffuse anger. Finally I went home and told Maxine that I had blown it.

Not long thereafter I asked one of the instructors in Crozier's physiology course how to go about getting a degree in biology. He said there were a lot of required courses, but that he had taken his degree in experimental psychology. There, he explained, you had only to pass the "prelims" and write a thesis. Why didn't I try that? Well, why not, even though I had already visited Yale and arranged to transfer there. It was then February, and exactly 100 days later the four 3-hour written examinations would begin. If I read and mastered 100 pages per day for 100 days, making 10,000 pages, that ought to tell whether experimental psychology was for me.

So the grind began. Boring agreed that I might be allowed to take the prelims, although he saw little prospect of success. Maxine, fortunately, had walked in on Radcliffe and been admitted despite initial assurances from everyone except the president that the college was full and that transferring from the University of Utah was out of the question. She later earned Phi Beta Kappa and was graduated with high honors in philosophy, so during the 100 days she was too busy herself to object to my 16-hour daily stint. Tension built up with the growing exhaustion, and spirits drooped as my conviction grew firmer that a Ph.D. lay far beyond reach. After all, I told myself, I was the first of either of my families to go to college, why should I aim so high? And then, when the examinations had been written and the cruel wait for the verdict began, I felt sure by the way Boring and Beebe-Center and other arbiters of my fate looked at me in the hallway—or didn't look at me—that I had blown it again.

Not at all! In fact, when the grades came out Boring seemed so pleased at my performance that one would have thought it was he who had passed. Now, said Boring, if I would transfer from the School of Education they would offer me the half-time Emerson Hall assistantship which paid $900. Imagine! You could earn money and go to school, too. No more thought of Yale, cancel the application to transfer. No more wondering whether we could make it through.

Instead, we packed up and sailed on the Bremen to Europe, for the round-trip fare was then at the all-time low of $120, third class, with all the food you could eat.

The International Congress of Psychology convened in Copenhagen that summer of 1932, so I had my first look at some of the people I had been reading about. I listened in on an animated discussion with Pavlov, his son serving as translator. The elder Cattell avoided the meetings but held court on the steps, smoking a big cigar. Warren had spent the summer in a German nudist camp and testified regarding the artificiality of clothes. Köhler sat handsome and serenely superior as chairman of one of the sessions. In the eyes of a graduate student it made a tremendous show.

Before leaving for Europe I had sent to a journal the manuscript describing the visual experiments with the color-mixing wheel. It would have seemed sensible to continue the visual studies, but there occurred one of those minor accidents that deflect careers. P. M. Zoll got himself admitted to Medical School. Zoll was the man using the oscillator—that wonderful new instrument out of which you could get an assortment of pure tones—and Boring suggested that I might take over Zoll's experiments on tonal volume. The field of audition, as it turned out, was then the scene of great ferment, generated by a new tool, the vacuum-tube amplifier. Audition was indeed the place to be. It was easy to make a thesis out of tonal volume, but my real excitement stemmed from other discoveries—that pure tones have the attribute of density, as well as pitch, loudness, and volume, and that intensity by itself can change the pitch of a tone. Those were new things.

By May 1933, I had three papers in press and a thesis defended before the full assemblage of all the philosophers and all the psychologists. I therefore applied for the Ph.D. No, said the administrative board, the year in Education plus the year at half-time in Arts and Sciences do not add up to the two-year residence requirement. But, I pointed out, the catalog says the Ph.D. is not predicted on the accumulation of courses. Besides, didn't I have a summer session at USC in 1931, and didn't I finish the A.B. requirements at Stanford one full quarter early? Should not that last quarter count as graduate work? Back and forth went the argument both written and oral. I can still see the Graduate Dean, staring ruefully at my record and muttering, "Graduate credit for freshman physics, freshman chemistry, freshman biology, and golf." He came down hard on the word *golf*.

They finally let me have the degree, though, because administrators would rather change their rules than look silly. No great advantage accrued, except relief from tuition, because there were no jobs to be had. I pleaded for another year as Emerson Hall assistant, because $900 would keep us eating. Boring said I had been the worst assistant they had ever had, and if they let me stay on would I do something besides my own research? I promised to clean up the laboratory.

One day I tackled the mess in the "battery room," where the upper reaches were ringed with shelves holding great crocks, each containing a human brain.

The collection was said to date back to William James. Anyhow, the James brains had to go, and so did the shelves of reagents and chemicals that no one ever used, among them a two-gallon bottle of ammonia.

Whenever you started a job like that, E. B. Newman was sure to poke his head in to see what was going on, and then start helping. We thought it would scare the janitor if he found brains in his barrels, so we decided to cut them up and flush them down the lone toilet in the laboratory. We set the crocks and the chemicals in the hallway and then arranged a fast system for chopping and flushing the brains. Toward the end, however, the chopping grew careless, and a thick slice of frontal lobe got stuck. No standard remedy by plunger seemed to work, so we unwound the fire hose and Newman jammed the nozzle tightly into the toilet. When I gave the signal, another helpful student, J. G. Needham, turned the valve. The water shot up out of the toilet like a geyser and the fire hose thrashed about like a stricken snake. The hose tipped over the ammonia bottle and the ammonia ran flooding down the hallway, and when Needham picked up the bottle and sniffed it, the fumes almost did him in.

Brute pressure was getting us nowhere, it seemed, so we decided to try chemical warfare. Sulfuric acid ought to dissolve a few brain cells, But pouring H_2SO_4 into water, as we knew, generates a lot of heat. "Pour slowly," I said. Newman dribbled it in, but not slowly enough. The water bubbled and steamed, and long before the brain gave way there was a loud bang and the bowl cracked open. We mopped up the mess, called the college plumber, and reported a toilet out of order.

One of the diversions that attenuated my effectiveness as a laboratory assistant was the brokerage business. From 10:00 A.M. to 3:00 P.M. the market tape in a Harvard Square office would go clacking by, displaying the rise and fall of prices. Dane Wilsey at Stanford had introduced me to the world of stocks and bonds, and in 1930 I had bought 10 shares of General Motors, which promptly rose to a profit. Making a living from the market looked like the easy way to support a would-be scientist. But action found itself stifled by scholarship, market scholarship, I mean. I subscribed to a course on stock chart reading, and I devoured all the broker's advisory manuals. Then I combed the library at the Harvard Business School and brought back a great stack of books. Since my growing erudition was occasionally consulted in the back room of the broker's office, I toyed for a time with the possibility of becoming a professional security analyst. My temperament ruled out stock trading, because in order to be successful you have to average two correct decisions on each trade. I am congenitally unsuited to the making of even one decision—correct or not.

Another demand on my time was electrophysiology at the Medical School. I had dropped in at Building C one day and asked Hallowell Davis if I could help with an experiment. Yes, I could keep protocol, meaning, write down everything that Davis or Derbyshire called out. It was a deadly job, but a first-rate apprenticeship, and after a time they allowed me to operate on the animals and run some of the experiments. The following year an NRC Fellowship enabled me to spend full time at the Medical School mapping the frequency response of the guinea pig's cochlea by damaging the hair cells at various positions along the organ of Corti and noting the change in the electrical response. The Medical School activities culminated in the book *Hearing* that Davis and I published in 1938.

Not long after I began work at the Medical School, Davis allowed me to give one of the colloquium lectures attended by the medical students. So there I was, a medical dropout, lecturing to some of the students whose class I would have joined had I sent along the $50. Davis also arranged for me to join the Neurological Supper Club, a lively, articulate group devoted to shop talk and new ideas. Lashley later joined the club, as did Norbert Wiener, and it was there that cybernetics was born—in arguments about the control of body movements through information and feedback. Years later, in 1948, Wiener recounted those origins in his book, *Cybernetics*.

When the NRC found itself out of funds, my request for the renewal of the Fellowship came to the attention of a part of the Rockefeller Foundation that wanted to foster interdisciplinary research by sponsoring training in a second science. They discussed my going back to school for a three-year retreading, this time in physics and chemistry. It sounded wonderful, despite their insistence that research was to be out for the duration (except perhaps during vacation), and also despite the offer of a job in psychology as instructor at $2,500. So I turned down the job and became a Research Fellow in Physics with an office in Lyman Laboratory, where I had already been auditing courses in physics and mathematics. But a man can absorb only so much schooling. There comes a stage of saturation when he drops it off at one end as fast as he takes it on at the other. Consequently, the following year, 1936, when the offer was raised to $2,750 I gave up physics to become a psychologist—until psychology later changed its central concern. I taught the laboratory course and four sections in Psychology 1. Later on I worked up an offering in mathematics for psychologists.

Psychology had the virtue of providing a haven for one who could never decide which star to steer by. Where else could a man be considered properly on the job even though he carried on research at the Medical School and dabbled in activities that ranged from electronic circuit design to philosophy? For extra money I sold various electronic devices to other laboratories and made hearing aids for a few customers who were willing to carry around an amplifier in a box.

But philosophy and the theory of measurement occupied many of my nonexperimental hours. The philosophers inhabited the first floor of Emerson Hall, and it was convenient to take a seat at their lectures. A. N. Whitehead was the chief luminary in the early 1930s, but toward the end of the decade there was an influx from Europe, particularly from the Vienna Circle, which produced an enormous ferment. Rudolf Carnap climbed up to my laboratory one day and proposed that we should form a shop club to discuss the Science of Science. I sent out the invitations, and on Halloween 1940 we inaugurated monthly meetings by listening to P. W. Bridgman defend his solipsistic brand of opera-tionism. Many notables followed. G. D. Birkhoff, called by one historian America's greatest mathematician, discoursed on the importance of invariance. The central problem in science, he insisted, is to locate the invariances.

My own central problem throughout the 1930s was measurement, because the quantification of the sensory attributes seemed impossible unless the nature of measurement could be properly understood. At a Congress for the Unity of Science in 1939, I had tried to describe the nature of measurement and to illustrate the different kinds of scales by examples from sensory psychophysics. It was a botch. Something was still missing, but I felt that I was groping in the right direction. In addition to the ordinal scale, I had distinguished between intensive and extensive scales and had tried to relate them to the determination of differences and ratios. In the aftermath of the debates that followed, most of them over semantic issues, I began to tabulate the various kinds of scales and the kinds of operations needed to create them. Then it became clear that each kind of scale permitted a different mathematical transformation, and suddenly one evening in Emerson Hall the picture snapped into focus—there exists a hierarchy of scales defined by the mathematical transformations that leave the scale form invariant.

The discovery of a simple principle generates two conflicting emotions: elation because of the new insight, and embarrassment because of the failure to see it sooner.

It remained to fix up the terminology by inventing new names, interval scale and ratio scale, names that I did not care for at first, but which have now become standard. When I called at Birkhoff's study in Widener Library to invite him to talk to us, I tried to interest him in the scale problem. My empirical orientation probably impeded communication, but he brightened up at the transformation feature, and spoke of the group structure of the scales. That was enough to send me to the mathematics library to learn more about mathematical groups.

At the next Congress for the Unity of Science in 1941, I was ready with a paper that outlined the theory of scales in a form that has since become rather widely accepted, so widely, in fact, that many authors feel no need to cite the origin.

Actually, my first presentation of the schema that defines measurement scales in terms of group invariance occurred in a symposium at the 1940 meeting of the Psychological Round Table, the PRT, a youth-fired rebellion organized in 1936. Five others—Graham, Hunt, Jacobsen, Marquis, and Newman—joined me in sponsoring the invitations. We called it initially the Society of Experimenting Psychologists, which was enough to incur the angry displeasure of my senior professor, and to draw blackballs against my name when I was later nominated for membership in the august Society of Experimental Psychologists. The PRT had no membership, but was run by a self-perpetuating band of six who issued invitations to an annual and thoroughly uninhibited meeting. One key rule was enforced: ejection at the age of 40. I am told that the PRT still carries on, and that its noisy good fellowship is still climaxed by a banquet that features the William A. Hunt Memorial Address, and the Address is still unprintable. But I wonder, does the spirit run as fierce and free as it did in the early years? Some of those who attended the first meeting will doubt it.

As it happened, I missed a part of that first meeting. In a tense face-off a few days earlier, Boring had insisted that no permission had been granted for me to be absent from my four Saturday sections in Psychology 1. I could either teach the sections or be cited for insubordination. I taught the sections. That retreat proved fortunate both for me and for the PRT. While I taught sophomores in Cambridge, the brethren gathered at a business meeting in New London, Connecticut, where they considered and rejected the set of rules that were supposed to govern the fraternal sodality. The business meeting dissolved after someone remarked that if six of us could organize such a splendid muster, who needed rules? So the PRT, like Harvard University, came to be governed by a small autocratic and self-perpetuating minority.

In 1936, shortly after our son Peter was born, a postpartum psychosis overwhelmed Maxine and devastated our lives. Maxine moved in and out of various hospitals as therapy by shock or insulin made dramatic but temporary changes in her state. During one of the brighter periods she returned to Utah to live with her parents, where she died some two decades later. My own reaction to the anguish of those wretched days was to plunge furiously into the job at hand. Work seemed the only road to relief. While Peter was small enough to be carried in a basket, I could take him with me to the laboratory, but he soon outgrew my ability to care for him alone. He then went to board with a warm-hearted, motherly woman in a nearby town. Peter is now an architect and father of three, and is here at Harvard this year on a Guggenheim Fellowship.

With nothing to do but work, it was easy to be productive, I could work all day and far into the night. Boring noted one year that my papers had produced more entries in the *Abstracts* than those of any other psychologist, and he cautioned that a reputation for superficiality might result. But research and writing could not be slowed, especially when they were going well. In one of my spurts, a 65-page manuscript called "Psychology and the Science of Science" got itself written between the APA meetings in early September and October 25. The editor never quite believed it.

And when not writing my own papers, I was sometimes writing for others. W. H. Sheldon showed up at Harvard with a staggering pile of photographs, data, and tables concerned with somatotypes and temperaments. The challenge appeared to me to lie in the measurement problem: can you really identify and scale the principal components of human physique?

I ran a test to see how well a person, given only brief instructions, could use 7-point scales to rate the three components of physique as exhibited in photographs of 50 men. Twenty people cooperated, and the correlations for all three components were high, 0.9, which was good enough to convince me.

Sheldon is by nature an observer, a naturalist, a systematizer of phenomena. He was once an ornithologist, and as a numismatist he is the author of a charming and definitive book on the early American cent—the large coppers—for which he devised a system that put an end to classificational chaos for the 327 known die varieties. I am by nature quite the opposite: more interested in abstract principle than in concrete fact. Together, however, we effected a fruitful collaboration, producing a pair of books, one on physique, the other on temperament. Sheldon taught me to look and to observe, or at least he tried. It has often impressed me that a principal difference between the psychologist and the biologist lies in the unwillingness of the psychologist to scrutinize the object of his study. Rather, he keeps his distance and permits no closer contact than a pencil-and-paper test, or a button to be pressed. Watching people the way a naturalist watches terns or foxes might instruct the psychologist concerning the limitations that nature has imposed on sociogenesis, the seductive myth that experience writes on an empty slate.

In 1937 Davis and I were making progress on our book on hearing. As I combed the literature in psychophysics it became clear that the experiments of a Hungarian physicist named Georg von Békésy would command much space in the book, provided we could trust his claims. His descriptions of procedure left much unsaid. Helped by funds from the American Otological Society, I went to Budapest in 1937 to see whether Békésy was a reality. Fortunately, E. B. Newman, who went with me, was fluent in German. At the end of the streetcar line we tramped down a dusty road and found Békésy in a large building belonging to the Hungarian post-telephone-telegraph. Békésy, who appeared to be the Bell Telephone Laboratories of Hungary, harbored a lively suspicion of time-wasting visitors, and it was not easy to convince him that we were serious. He showed us nothing, but he did not refuse our request to visit him the next day. On the second day we got to see some of Békésy's experiments and learned of his frustration at not having easy access to the superior amplifying devices made in America. As we warmed to one another, Békésy invited us to return the following morning, a Saturday, so that he could take us on a tour of the city. At dinner, in a great vaulted hall, Newman and I said we would like to try real goulash. Which one? We didn't know. So the waiter brought half a dozen different dishes on a Lazy Susan and we sampled them all. Then Békésy recommended a local specialty for dessert, which turned out to be corn on the cob.

Some 25 years later, after Békésy had become a member of our Psycho-Acoustic Laboratory, he won a Nobel Prize for his early work on the ear. Békésy was indeed a reality.

Although it did not get named until several months later, the Psycho-Acoustic Laboratory began its operation in 1940, more than a year before the Japanese attack on Pearl Harbor. My research has been supported by public funds continuously every since, which probably makes me the longest nonstop scientific dole in existence.

The process started when a Captain Dent of the Air Force called a meeting of some experts in acoustics to ask what could be done to quiet the intense noise in military aircraft, which was thought by some to cause pilot error in landings after long flights. The captain wanted some research done. A young physics instructor, L. L. Beranek, had prepared an estimate of the equipment he would need to study airplane quieting. He could borrow most of the instruments, but if he were to employ a part-time assistant, he would need at least a couple of thousand dollars. The captain asked how much faster it could be done with ten times that much money. Beranek gulped and said, a lot faster. "Speed is what we need," said the captain. He then turned to me and asked whether a project to determine the effects of noise would need to be at least as large. I allowed that it would. Two young scientists reeled out of that meeting, dazed and incredulous, for we had never conceived of so much money for research.

Next began a frantic hunt for a place to make a noise. Led by the chief of buildings and grounds, R. B. Johnson, I searched through attics and basements in every Harvard building that appeared at all likely to yield a laboratory, and even considered walling off a section under the stadium. We were growing thoroughly discouraged when Johnson hit upon it. "Let's look in Memorial Hall," he said. Harvard's flamboyant Gothic edifice had been built in 1875 in order, as William James said, to dispense honor to the dead and food to the living. Down among the reaches of abandoned kitchens we found a huge furnace room, unused since 1915 and black with soot. I said no, but Johnson argued that he could tear out the pipes, pave the floor, and produce a first-rate laboratory. He was right.

We put subjects in the furnace room and pummeled them with 7-hour noise exposures at 115 decibels. The subjects went from test to test through a battery of tasks designed to measure everything we could think of. We proved that the noise did nothing to performance, but it produced a temporary hearing loss. More important, when we tried to use the standard aircraft intercoms to communicate in the noise, the results were so bad that the design and testing of communication gear became the focus of our research. By the time Germany surrendered, all components of the intercoms had been redesigned. The tail gunner could now understand what the pilot was hollering about, even at high altitude. He was aided by an earphone cushion that was patented in my name and produced in vast quantity. For the patent rights, I was supposed to receive $1.00 from the government. I am still waiting.

As the Psycho-Acoustic Laboratory expanded to include some 50 people, more and more of the subterranean space under Memorial Hall—"intercellar space," it was called by Licklider—found itself partitioned and made usable. I hired a carpenter and we did much of the work with our own hands.

Then after the war the Provost, Paul Buck, allotted us $150,000 to finish the rest of the basement, plus the upstairs serving kitchens, in order to create room for the Psychological Laboratories, which could thereupon relinquish Emerson Hall to the new Department of Social Relations. The Provost exacted a promise that I would never ask for any more space. Two decades later a new president, Nathan Pusey, forced me to move out of that wonderful basement laboratory and into an office tower named for William James. Administrations, I have learned, have no memory.

Why did they create a new Department of Social Relations, or why, as a sociologist grumbled, did then move the disaffected professors into Sociology? There are many theories, but whatever the causes, a critical incident occurred, I think, when the Psychology Department voted to require mathematics as well as statistics in the examinations for the Ph.D. The chairman, G. W. Allport, our most eminent social psychologist, opposed the motion, but it was carried. Shortly thereafter we began to hear talk of secession.

Earlier in my career, one of the instructors had taken delight in issuing periodic warnings that I should move out of Harvard because the chairman would never promote me. The instructor was correct, in a sense. Allport opposed my promotion in a long letter that detailed my shortcomings, a chief one of which was my open disparagement of teaching. Another was the aversion shown me by some of the students.

Since the dean thought that insight might mend the defects, he discussed the letter with me. Allport was right, of course, for in neither temperament nor appearance am I the outgoing teacher. A constraining shyness, a longish face, and a low tolerance for prattle have too often defeated my efforts at affability. "Qu'il est sévère!" the Belgians used to say. A treasured need for solitude frequently overrides my need for people, and I have often sensed the bitter sweetness of melancholy. I told the dean, as I had already told Allport, that I would teach my courses faithfully, but to enjoy standing before classes was beyond my power.

Actually, two forms of teaching give me joy; the joint endeavor of laboratory apprenticeship, and editorial give and take with authors. In those two ways I seem always to be teaching. But deans count you at work only when you stand before a group with your mouth moving.

The promotion to a tenured position was made in 1944, without benefit of President Conant's famous procedure of first convening an extradepartmental *ad hoc* committee to consider all potential candidates. "Sometimes" said Conant, "we feel competent to make the judgment ourselves." That was good to hear, for Conant had assured me four years earlier that there was no opening and no possibility of my remaining at Harvard, despite Boring's exertions on my behalf. My assistant professorship was to be considered terminal. Pearl Harbor changed all that.

The war finally over, I got around to publishing the prewar work on the theory of scales of measurement, but then began seven lean years. Other people saw those seven years as rich and full of achievement. They could not sense the gnawing fear that the fire was spent, that science, the jealous mistress I had abandoned for war research, had now abandoned me, so that no new fruit would fall. There were honors, to be sure, and the Psycho-Acoustic Laboratory grew renowned for the eminence of its roster. Three different agencies vied to give us financial support, and since I served as chief mentor, I was later awarded a plaque and $1,000 by the Beltone Institute to signal my accomplishments as an educator! There was election to the National Academy of Sciences while still in my thirties, to be followed by the chairmanship of a division of the National Research Council. That meant commuting to Washington and sitting on numerous boards, committees, study sections, and panels. I was becoming a wheel in the bureaucratic busy work—the overhead of science. And when President Eisenhower invited a score of scientists to a State Dinner at the White House, I was among them, in white tie and tails. But somehow the road to Washington glittered less and less.

In my forty-second year I took up skiing—on a pair of elderly boards that someone had left in the laboratory. The imprudence led to Silver Lake, New Hampshire, and the purchase of an old farmhouse abandoned by a 75-year-old lady because nothing worked. Friends, students, and colleagues pitched in to renovate the place and turn it into a ski lodge with 18 beds, a pool table, and a practice ski slope out behind the barn. If happiness had once seemed an endless fairway, it now seemed an endless snowfield. But skis, I found, left much to be desired, and I began to experiment with them and to write articles for ski magazines. Since ski length was a principal variable, I cut some 18 pairs to various sizes, ranging from 2 feet upward, and determined that my standard skis had been twice too long. My new 40-inch skis have made the wonders of the high Alps into an alluring playground for a sexagenarian who skis in spite of the exercise.

I am really not a mesomorph, managing only a 4-4-4 in somatotype, an almost equal distribution among the three components of physique: fat, muscle, and lean. Sheldon says I am lucky, because with only a 4 in mesomorphy I have been spared the monkey trap of serious competition. I could never quite make the team. But it sometimes seems as though a balance among the three components puts you on a horse that tries to gallop off in three directions at once.

Three of the seven lean years were squandered on the *Handbook of Experimental Psychology*. The writing, editing, and rewriting of that million-word tome was a consuming chore—enlivened and lightened by the excellence of the contributors, 17 of whom have won election to the National Academy of Sciences. Most of the editing really fell to Geraldine Stone, who has ministered to the laboratory since its inception in 1940, and who became my wife in 1963. To celebrate that event our friends held a champagne reception on the snowfield near the summit of Mount Washington, and we then skied down Tuckerman's Ravine.

How do you break into research of your own when you have passed middle age and have grown rusty from directing others? In 1953 the barriers seemed firm. If I started to pick up a piece of apparatus, my shop assistants wanted to do it for me. How could I grasp my own soldering iron to fix a loose connection when my desk bloomed with important papers pressing for attention? Could I risk looking foolish on a piece of research that might flop, while at the same time my presence was wanted at the riskless tables of high council? If you insist on doing your own research, you have to perform the trivial and forsake the grand.

Actually, it was a former student who rescued me. W. R. Garner had conducted some very thorough experiments on the equisection and fractionation of loudness, two problems that had concerned me off and on for two decades. Could it be that equisection and fractionation gave results that differed as much as Garner seemed to find? What good is a scale of subjective loudness if intervals disagree with ratios? The problem troubled me so much that in the spring of 1953 I took over a small room, assembled some apparatus, and began to run subjects. Everyone who passed the door was hauled in and asked to make loudness judgments. Once again I was doing my own research!

One day during a coffee break Richard Held accused me of acting as though a person has a built-in loudness scale from which values can be read. That was an interesting idea. Why not try it? I presented a series of sound intensities in irregular order, and Held assigned numbers to them, apparently with no trouble at all. That method, magnitude estimation, which calls for the matching of numbers to perceived intensity, was soon to transform psychophysics. The procedure of matching subjective impressions is so simple, and yet so powerful. Why are the simplest things the hardest to discover?

R. J. Herrnstein hired on as assistant that decisive summer of 1953, and together we found ourselves working all day and half the night. To me it was like living again, thinking up new experiments and rushing to complete them. A curious effect (hysteresis) occurred in loudness bisections, and we wondered whether the effect would occur in visual brightness. We found a box—a rat shipping cage—cut a hole in one end, inserted some lamps, and before the day was done we had satisfied ourselves that hysteresis occurs also in vision. We rigged the laboratory projector so that subjects could make magnitude estimations of brightness, and we carried equipment upstairs to the lecture hall where a summer school class matched numbers to the brightness of a spot projected on a screen.

The summer over, Herrnstein went back to his pigeons, and I was left with sheets of data that seemed somehow to be trying to tell me something. There was contradiction and confusion in the evidence, but the main trend emerged strong enough to push the message through: in both vision and hearing the subjective magnitude of the sensation grows as a power function of the stimulus intensity. Not only that, but the two modalities, vision and hearing, seem to have the same exponent, namely, 1/3. I ventured to put that finding on record in *Science* (November 13, 1953) and to tell about it at the autumn meeting of the National Academy of Sciences.

No one seemed much impressed, as I recall, nor did it appear to me that anything especially startling had been discovered. Perhaps my power law would merely join the long parade of claims that psychophysicists had made since that day when Fechner lay abed on October 22, 1850, and conjectured a logarithmic law for the growth of sensation. Anyhow, it was good to be back at work.

So good, in fact, that I canceled a sabbatical leave for which arrangements had been made to spend a year at the Institute for Advanced Study at Princeton. When I explained the dilemma to the director, Robert Oppenheimer, he agreed that I should stay with the research. "You must lick that pot clean," he said. But he promised a raincheck.

I finally got around to a sabbatical leave in 1966, thirty years after I first became an instructor. Even then, my wife and I left the laboratory only for a 3-week tour of nine Alpine ski resorts in France, Italy, and Switzerland. Didi and I have introduced short skis to skeptical Europeans by skiing the slopes arm in arm.

By 1958 the measurement of sensation was going so well that the seven lean years had become only a cankered memory, but I still clung to some of the protective baggage of boards and committees, despite a growing distaste for paper shuffling. You can tell whether you are a scientist by noting what you do first each day: tend the experiment or read the mail. When my mail began to threaten a hopeless disarray, I wrote a batch of letters and resigned from all but one distraction. That distraction was the Space Science Board, which was trying to hold the space program together until Congress could set up NASA. Early in 1960 I resigned from the Space Science Board, too. That cleaned the slate, and by August of that year a nine-chapter monograph on visual brightness had been completed, with J. C. Stevens (no relation) as coauthor.

Research must feed on itself if it is to hold its excitement. One discovery must lead to another, with serendipity calling the turns. Over and over for 30 years I have had to stop and write a project proposal for the next year's funds—they ask you to predict what research will get done. Save for the first few years during World War II, I have chalked up a near perfect score: unless already half completed, the research fancied in the project proposal has never been performed. Something more exciting has always turned up when the time came to set to work—something no project proposal could have foreseen.

How could I have foreseen that every sense modality would respond according to a power law—what some of the textbooks now call Stevens' law? (It would, of course, delight any scientist to see his name become an eponym, if history so decided.) How could it have been foretold that a simple quantitative invariance would describe the operation of every sensory system that we have been able to stimulate? That basic invariance can be stated very simply: equal stimulus ratios produce equal subjective ratios. And the procedures that have served to confirm the invariance have also been used to scale many nonsensory variables, ranging from the prestige of occupations to the seriousness of crimes. That, too, lay beyond the reach of project-proposal prophecy.

In the 17 years since 1953, research in psychophysics has disclosed important but unsuspected human capacities. The normal sentient observer turns out to be a marvelous matching instrument. With surprising consistency he can assign numbers to any aspect of nature that appears to him to vary in degree, and he can make the numbers proportional to the strength of his subjective impressions. Already more than 40 perceptual continua have been scaled by simple number matching—magnitude estimation, it is called. Equally important, the human subject can match any variable to any other variable, such as apparent loudness to apparent brightness, or force of handgrip to warmth on the skin, or apparent duration to apparent area, and so on. The demonstrated success of such cross-modality matching means that the interrelations among all subjective variables can be quantified. Definitive descriptions of the operating characteristics of all the sensory systems are placed within reach. Much remains to be done. The prospect excites me.

EPILOGUE

I break off here, just as I begin my sixty-fifth year, in order to comment on the design of the foregoing career and to inquire what residues, if any, give promise of survival.

The career itself exhibits no plan or purpose, no overreaching strategy, only tactical maneuvers brought on when circumstance has confronted desire. A series of accidents, in fact. Any man's life builds on a succession of accidents. That explains only part of it, however, for among the chance encounters there are some that take effect, whereas against other exposures a person stands as though inoculated with some natural antibody, as though his ingrained nature has created immunity to alien rhetoric. One man's great teacher scores as another man's humbug.

Accidents of time and juncture seem to have determined the content of my career, including, of course, the languages spoken and the principles learned. You cannot study discoveries yet to be made. But a replay of all the circumstances with a different man on the scene would probably not have produced a professor of psychophysics. The students who fail to warm to the virtues of that subject are legion, which is good, for it averts the disaster of everybody's crowding in to toil at the same bench.

As an undergraduate I wallowed joyfully in the verbal compost of philosophy and the social sciences. Why did that exposure not produce a sociologist, or something similar? Why am I now put off by the chanting of a hypersyllabic idiom in which social scientists make nouns into modifiers, and correlation into causation? A man is a hunter, not for the food that our ancesters had to seek, but for the consonant path of life. Some men can sniff the agreeable trail first off, but others must keep on hunting decade after decade to locate the congenial calling.

As I write these lines on floor 9 in a tower named for William James, I look down on his house on Irving Street, where his grandson once presented me with a New Hampshire scene painted by William James, Jr., artist son of William. Think how William James struggled to locate his proper pursuit. He went through medical school, became instructor in physiology, and set up a laboratory of psychophysics. But then he drifted slowly into philosophy. His nature was coded by a template vastly different from mine, for my drift has been in the opposite direction. I started where James finished and finish where James began. Floor 9 is now called the Laboratory of Psychophysics. Had we been contemporaries at Harvard, our concerns might have coincided momentarily—perhaps where James shifted his interest from the physiology of emotion to the psychology of will.

Despite excursions here and there, my career has centered on the psychophysics of sensory function, which was once central to experimental psychology, but which may now stand so distant as to form a separate discipline. Students ask, why desert psychology? It is quite the other way: psychology has deserted psychophysics. There are now more than 30,000 psychologists who probably care nothing about sensory measurement, nor about how the sense-organ transducers operate to bring about the miracle of sensation. Psychology has moved so far toward social relevance, and has spilled so widely into media and marketplace, that those who man the old-fashioned experimental workshop must find a new label for their métier. My own choice was to become Professor of Psychophysics, a title exacted from the University in 1962 as the price for my resignation as Director of the Psychological Laboratories. I was being fired for trying to obstruct what was then called progress—the transplanting of the laboratory.

We moved. I have stuck it out. Békésy tried for a couple of years to sustain his research activities, spread vertically over four floors served by reluctant elevators, but he finally tendered his resignation.

Is there any residue from my career that will interest the future? Who knows? On an airplane flight from Washington, following the State Dinner at which Eisenhower honored the scientists, the wife of the President's Science Advisor said, "What's the matter with you scientists, why do you think you have to leave something permanent?" That is a good question. Especially when our great historian of science, George Sarton, observed that science is progressive and therefore ephemeral, whereas art is nonprogressive and therefore eternal. Unlike the artist, the scientist engages in the business of putting both himself and his colleagues out of business. New discoveries negate old notions, fashions in thought stir new enthusiasms, and only a few principles pass on to become gospel for future generations.

Many of my intellectual products of the past four decades promise to give way to better formulation and thereby demonstrate their ephemeral character. Some of them may ebb, perhaps to return on another tide. The operational outlook, which seeks to equate the meaning of a term with the concrete operations that underly it, seems currently to have lost its vogue. Its day will probably come again, however, even if under a different banner, for the issue remains too basic to disappear.

The outcome of experimental work can always be improved. My loudness scale has been standardized by an international body, but already I am proposing to change it slightly. And the standard procedure for calculating the loudness of noise, a procedure employed to assess noise pollution, has been renovated in a paper I am now preparing. Such matters undergo continual change, although a few sturdy principles may stay put. One such principle seems to me to concern the direct relation between the subjective scale of pitch, measured in mels, and the location in the inner ear where the different sound frequencies produce their excitation. But here again, the measurements of both pitch and place can be improved.

Then what about permanent residue? History likes to make comedy out of predictions, but predictions tell at least how it seemed at the time. With that in mind, in this year 1970 I venture to suggest that the remainders of long-term interest may prove to be the two principles of invariance that I have tried to formulate: one that applies to scales of measurement, and one that governs the ratio relation between stimulus and sensation—the "power law." Other than that, what has there been except the joy of search and solution in the contest to decipher nature's ways, and the great good fun of carrying on?

REFERENCES

Selected Publications by S. S. Stevens

The relation of saturation to the size of the retinal image. *Amer. J. Psychol.*, 1934, *46*, 70-79.

Tonal density. *J. exp. Psychol.*, 1934, *17*, 585-592.

The volume and intensity of tones. *Amer. J. Psychol.*, 1934, *46*, 397-408.

The operational basis of psychology. *Amer. J. Psychol.*, 1935, *47*, 323-330.

(with H. Davis and M. H. Lurie) The localization of pitch perception on the basilar membrane. *J. gen. Psychol.*, 1935, *13*, 297-315.

(with H. Davis) *Hearing: its psychology and physiology.* New York: Wiley, 1938.

Psychology and the science of science. *Psychol. Bull.*, 1939, *36*, 221-263.

(with J. Volkmann) The relation of pitch to frequency: a revised scale. *Amer. J. Psychol.*, 1940, *53*, 329-353.

(with C. T. Morgan and J. Volkmann) Theory of the neural quantum in the discrimination of loudness and pitch. *Amer. J. Psychol.*, 1941, *54*, 315-335.

(with W. H. Sheldon) *The varieties of temperament.* New York: Harper & Row, 1942.

On the theory of scales of measurement. *Science*, 1946, *103*, 677-680.

Mathematics, measurement, and psychophysics. In S. S. Stevens (Ed.), *Handbook of experimental psychology.* New York: Wiley, 1951, pp. 1-49.

On the brightness of lights and the loudness of sounds. *Science*, 1953, *118*, 576.

The measurement of loudness. *J. Acoust. Soc. Amer.*, 1955, *27*, 815-829.

Calculation of the loudness of complex noise. *J. Acoust. Soc. Amer.*, 1956, *28*, 807-832.

On the psychophysical law. *Psychol. Rev.*, 1957, *64*, 153-181.

(with E. H. Galanter) Ratio scales and category scales for a dozen perceptual continua. *J. exp. Psychol.*, 1957, *54*, 377-411.

Cross-modality validation of subjective scales for loudness, vibration, and electric shock. *J. exp. Psychol.*, 1959, *57*, 201-209.

(with J. C. Stevens and J. D. Mack) Growth of sensation on seven continua as measured by force of handgrip. *J. exp. Psychol.*, 1960, *59*, 60-67.

To honor Fechner and repeal his law. *Science*, 1961, *133*, 80-86.

Procedure for calculating loudness, Mark VI. *J. Acoust. Soc. Amer.*, 1961, *33*, 1577-1585.

The psychophysics of sensory function. In W. A. Rosenblith (Ed.), *Sensory communication*, Cambridge, Mass.: MIT Press, 1961, pp. 1-33.

The surprising simplicity of sensory metrics. *Amer. Psychologist*, 1962, *17*, 29-39.

(with J. C. Stevens) Brightness function: effects of adaptation. *J. Opt. Soc. Amer.*, 1963, *53*, 375-385.

(with M. Guirao and A. W. Slawson) Loudness, a product of volume times density. *J. exp. Psychol.*, 1965, *69*, 503-510.

(with F. Warshofsky and the Editors of Life) *Sound and hearing*, New York: Time Inc., 1965.

A metric for the social consensus. *Science*, 1966, *151*, 530-541.

Power-group transformations under glare, masking, and recruitment. *J. Acoust. Soc. Amer.*, 1966, *39*, 725-735.

(with H. Greenbaum) Regression effect in psychophysical judgment. *Percept. & Psychophys.*, 1966, *1*, 439-446.

Measurement, statistics, and the schemapiric view. *Science*, 1968, *161*, 849-856.

On predicting exponents for cross-modality matches. *Percp. & Psychophys.*, 1969, *6*, 251-256.

Neural events and the psychophysical law. *Science*, 1970, *170*, 1043-1050.

Issues in psychophysical measurement. *Psychol. Rev.*, 1971, *78*, 426-450.

A neural quantum in sensory discrimination. *Science*, 1972, *177*, 749-762.

Perceived level of noise by Mark VII and decibels (E). *J. Acoust. Soc. Amer.*, 1972, *51*, 575-601.

Psychophysics and social scaling. Morristown, N.J.: General Learning Press, 1972. 27 pp.

Psychophysics (being prepared for posthumous publication by G. Stevens).